Governing the Market

Governing the Market

ECONOMIC THEORY AND
THE ROLE OF GOVERNMENT
IN EAST ASIAN INDUSTRIALIZATION

Robert Wade

PRINCETON UNIVERSITY PRESS

PRINCETON, NEW JERSEY

Library of Congress Cataloging-in-Publication Data

Wade, Robert.
Governing the market : economic theory and the role of
government in East Asian industrialization / Robert Wade
p. cm.
Includes bibliographical references.
1. Industry and state—East Asia. 2. East Asia—Industries.
3. East Asia—Economic policy. I. Title.
HD3616.E183W33   1990   338.95—dc20   90-8236

ISBN 0-691-04242-X
ISBN 0-691-00397-1 (pbk.)

To Hunter Wade and Ronald Dore

Teachers of the art of trespassing.

CONTENTS

LIST OF FIGURES

LIST OF TABLES

ACKNOWLEDGMENTS

THIS VOLUME stems from a grant made by David Sainsbury of the Gatsby Charitable Trust to several researchers at the Institute of Development Studies (IDS), University of Sussex. The purpose was to finance fieldwork in China, South Korea, and Taiwan on the role of the state in economic development. Some of the results have already been published by Macmillan under the title *The Developmental State in East Asia*, edited by Gordon White (1988). I thank my IDS colleagues on the project, Jack Grey, Richard Leudde-Neurath, Mick Moore, and Gordon White for much enlightenment.

Prudence requires anonymity for the many Taiwan government officials who helped the inquiry, and some others in Taiwan would also prefer not to be publicly thanked. But I can record with pleasure my debt to: Jin-rong Julius Hong, Hen-shang Henry Wang, Julian Awdry, Tyler Biggs, Jui-meng Chang, Nora Lan-hung Chiang, Yun-han Chu, Hsin-huang Michael Hsiao, Men-fon Hung, James Klein, Joseph Kyle, Klaus Lorch, Livingston Merchant, Chien-kuo Pang, Barnaby Powell, Chi Schive, and Marnix Wells; also to Paul K. C. Liu, director of the Institute of Economics at the Academia Sinica, my base during four months of fieldwork in 1983, and to Tzong-shian Yu, vice-president of the Chung-hua Institution for Economic Research, base for two months in 1988. No finance came from Taiwan.

The book was mostly written during the weekends and holidays of a regular job at the World Bank. My supervisors, Hans Binswanger, Vinod Thomas, and Jaime de Melo, showed remarkable patience toward this rival for my attention, all the more so because the Bank does not recognize Taiwan and because my interpretation of East Asian economic success differs in many ways from the Bank's recipe for economic success.

The Woodrow Wilson International Center for Scholars awarded me a fellowship at a critical time, for which I thank Ronald Morse; as later did the Center for International Studies at Duke University, for which I thank Charles Bergquist. Elizabeth Crayford, Myriam Bailey, Ghislaine Bayard, and Felicitas Doroteo-Gomez helped to shepherd the manuscript through its revisions.

I would like to thank the following people for helping in one way or another to clarify parts of the argument: Alice Amsden, Colin Bradford, Teddy Brett, Fred Deyo, David Evans, Peter Evans, Martin Fransman, Alan Gelb, Gary Gereffi, Kitty Gillman, Julie Gorte, Stephan Haggard, Brian Hindley, Frank Holmes, Paul Isenman, Susan Joekes, Chalmers Johnson, Don Keesing, Anne Krueger, Deepak Lal, Danny Leipziger, Michael Lipton, Ashoka Mody, Elliott Morss, Elinor Ostrom, Gustav Ranis, Dorothy Robyn, Geoffrey Shepherd, Hans Singer, Paul Streeten, Frank Veneroso, and last only alphabetically, Larry Westphal. Manfred Bienefeld deserves special mention as the creator of an encompassing vision of the world economy from which I—and my long-distance phone company—have much profited. Would that I could also have talked to Dudley Seers and Andrew Shonfield, whose memory I salute. Hunter Wade and Ronald Dore, former New Zealand Ambassador to Japan and South Korea and renowned Japan expert, respectively, urged my attention to the shift in the world's economic center of gravity toward East Asia. They have shown me over many years how to follow big economic questions across the boundaries of social knowledge. I admire their juicy minds.

Finally, I wish to acknowledge my closest discussants, Imogen and Thomas Wade, who are also the youngest.

Princeton
November 1989

Governing the Market

_____

INTRODUCTION

NATURE, it is said, does not make jumps. But what has happened in capitalist East Asia during the postwar era is as close to a jump up the economic hierarchy of nations as nature ever makes. Japan leapt from the thirtieth richest country in per capita income in 1962 to eleventh in 1986; Taiwan from eighty-fifth to thirty-eighth; South Korea from ninety-ninth to forty-fourth.[1] By the early twenty-first century Japan, Taiwan, South Korea, and China will probably have as much weight in the world economy as North America or Europe. Taiwan and South Korea will be as rich as Great Britain and Italy.[2]

The West knows of this success primarily through trade. Japan was already the world's fourth biggest exporter of manufactures in 1965, and number two twenty years later. Over the same two decades Taiwan rose from twenty-eighth to tenth, Korea from thirty-third to thirteenth.[3] As suppliers of manufactured goods to the United States, Japan was number one in 1986, Taiwan was number four, and Korea was number five.

Behind these numbers lie some astonishing industrial achievements. Japan's need no mention, so much are they the staple of our daily press. Taiwan's and Korea's are less familiar. But their achievements are such that U.S., Japanese, and European multinational companies are beginning to seek out their firms not just as second-tier partners dependent on other people's technology but as equal partners in strategic alliances to develop new products. Both countries are mastering the microcircuit design and production which is at the heart of innovation in electronics and other electronics-dependent industries. In mid-1988 a Taiwan firm launched a "clone" of IBM's PS/2 personal computer, a machine introduced only the previous year and far harder to duplicate than any other personal computer. A public research institute has licensed its Chinese basic input-output system to IBM for use in its Asian personal computer, and has formed a joint venture with Hewlett-Packard to develop software for the Asian market. Some of Taiwan's many semiconductor design houses are close to the world leaders in application-specific integrated circuits. The Korean semiconductor industry is only nine to twelve months behind the leading Japanese and American firms in the technology for large-capacity memory chips, and is the world's third largest fabricator. Samsung, the most advanced of the Korean firms, agreed with IBM in 1989 to swap their semiconductor patent portfolios, the first time IBM has made a broad

---

[1] GNP per capita, *World Bank Atlas* data. The World Bank does not publish post-1980 data for Taiwan; the Taiwan rank for 1986 was calculated by a compatible method. See chapter 2.

[2] Klein 1986.

[3] See table 2.2.

semiconductor patent swap with a firm from outside Japan, North America, and Europe. This agreement signals Samsung's impending entry into the front ranks of the world semiconductor industry. In automobiles Korea may well become the first big new entrant into the world car industry since Japan in the early 1960s. In consumer electronics it is the second biggest producer after Japan of videocassette recorders and microwave ovens. Several other high value-added industries in both countries are very competitive internationally, including steel, machine tools, and petrochemicals. In short, Taiwan and Korea may be the first developing countries to join the dozen or so states in the world "club of innovators," whose membership has been remarkably stable during the twentieth century.

Anyone who claims to offer an explanation for the wealth of nations must be concerned to show how the East Asian capitalist cases fit the general theory, for if the fastest growers cannot be accommodated the theory itself is cast in doubt. There are those who hold that East Asian economic success is to be ascribed to economic openness and small government. With internal prices reflecting real scarcities and the state kept firmly in its place, resources flowed to their most efficient uses. The limitations of small domestic markets were overcome by exporting manufactured goods at competitive prices. Rapid export growth in turn generated a growth dynamic far greater than would otherwise have occurred. In contrast, countries which adopted more inward-looking strategies based on the domestic market have stagnated, partly because of small market size and partly because the regulations needed to support the strategy choked the initiative of private businesspeople, depriving them of the stimulus of competition and misdirecting their remaining energies into lobbying and other socially unproductive activities.

Other interpreters hold that government intervention was an important factor, but only insofar as it promoted exports and offset market failures. Government interventions "simulated" an ideal market, in their view. They would agree with proponents of the first approach that the East Asian experience confirms the truth of Charles Wolf's paradox: "If development is accorded dominant emphasis among national objectives and policy priorities, the recipes on which successful development seems to depend impose definite limits on the extent and character of government intervention" (1981:91).

These two "market-supremacy" interpretations of East Asian performance have occupied the mainstream of the economics profession over the 1970s and 1980s. Ranged against them, in varying degrees of opposition, are a number of other views. Some emphasize Confucian group-mindedness and frugal consumption preferences combined with a get-up-and-go entrepreneurialism. Others emphasize external demand generated by the rhythm of Western capital accumulation linked to Western defense against communism. Still others emphasize particular techniques of business management. But the most popular of the unorthodoxies stresses the importance in capitalist East Asia of a certain kind of government role in the economy, which makes for a new and more effective way of putting the institutions of capitalism together.

Some who make this "government leadership" argument say or imply that government intervention—most celebratedly by Japan's Ministry of International Trade and Industry (MITI)—was the *principal* factor behind East Asian success. A more tenable formulation is a synergistic connection between a public system and a mostly private market system, the outputs of each becoming inputs for the other, with the government setting rules and influencing decision-making in the private sector in line with its view of an appropriate industrial and trade profile for the economy. Through this mechanism the advantages of markets (decentralization, rivalry, diversity, and multiple experiments) have been combined with the advantages of partially insulating producers from the instabilities of free markets and of stimulating investment in certain industries selected by government as important for the economy's future growth. This combination has improved upon the results of free markets.

In the context of how poor countries can become less poor, the point at issue has far-reaching significance. Indeed, for many countries the current problem is not how to become less poor but how to stop becoming even poorer: two-thirds of middle-income countries had *declining* levels of investment in 1980–86.[4] The leading theorists of the International Monetary Fund and the World Bank, being among the more passionate supporters of the free market theory of rapid growth, have prescribed liberalization and privatization as the cure. As summed up by the *Economist*, "Increasingly, the two institutions have found themselves embroiled in the same set of policy issues: how can economies grow even when the international climate is unfavorable? The answer that the Fund and the Bank give can be summed up in four words: get the prices right" (1983, 24 Sept.:39). To have the most rapid development which their circumstances allow, developing countries must aim to integrate the domestic economy more completely into the international economy and reduce the extent of government "interference" in the market. If governments do not see reason voluntarily, the international agencies are justified in obliging them to do so in the best interest of their own citizens as well as the world economy as a whole.

Given their success, Taiwan and South Korea lend compelling support to this prescription—if the prescription fairly summarizes the mechanism of their success and if the conditions of the world economy in which the mechanism worked for them are sufficiently present today. But if the argument can be made that government steerage of the market has been an important factor in East Asia, then the general recipes for developing countries would need rethinking. For it could not then be said that more economic liberalization is always better; the desirability of integration into the international economy

[4] World Bank 1988, table 4, gross domestic investment.

becomes a matter of degree and circumstance, to be weighted against the desirability of improving existing arrangements for planning and controlling, and of relying more on growth in domestic demand than on export demand. The warranted limits on liberalization have to be specified with the same care as the arguments in favor and accommodated to the same body of rationalization. It could not be said that for reasons inherent in the nature of government, no government is able to expand the wealth of the nation faster than unguided entrepreneurs on their own. The capacity of governments to accelerate development by raising investment and promoting some activities ahead of others becomes a variable, not a constant.

The point at issue is also relevant to the citizens of the West. For the booming nations of East Asia are posing a competitive threat to their manufacturing industries. Indeed, when asked from where they saw the most serious competitive threat to U.S. manufacturing over the next five years, more than two-thirds of the 250 U.S. manufacturing executives questioned identified "the emerging countries such as Brazil, South Korea, and Taiwan." Only 29 percent picked Japan, and a dismissive 5 percent picked Europe (*Business Week*, 12 Jan. 1987). In the face of this competition there is a real possibility of decline in living standards for sections of the population who are displaced into lower-paying jobs or into no jobs at all. To think about strategies of response, it is essential to understand the mechanism of East Asian competitiveness. Is it based mainly on cheap labor and devotion to free markets? Or is it based on a different arrangement of the institutions of capitalism, with government helping to strengthen the competitiveness of selected industries? If the latter, it questions the viability of the philosophical aversion in the United States, especially, toward a government role in identifying and supporting specific industrial goals. It cautions against economic liberalization and less state intervention as the central thrust of the developed country response— unless we wish to follow the advice of the Goodyear vice-president who said, "Until we get real wage levels down much closer to those of the Brazils and Koreas we cannot pass along productivity gains to wages and still be competitive" (*Toronto Globe and Mail*, 19 June 1987).

Taiwan is one of the most successful cases of economic development on record. In less than a quarter of a century it has become a major trading nation and an industrialized economy. It has begun to show those twin characteristics of countries toward the top of the economic hierarchy: outflows of investment in search of cheaper labor, and inflows of illegal foreign workers in search of higher wages. This book is mainly about the institutions, structure, and operations of the Taiwan economy. Most of the literature on the "Taiwan miracle" portrays it as the result of nearly free markets. I shall argue that the role of government has gone well beyond the practice of Anglo-American economies and the principles of neoclassical economics, while at the same time resource allocation has occurred primarily through vigorously functioning markets. The same applies, as I shall show, to South Korea and Japan. All three countries have in common an intense and almost unequivocal commitment on the part of government to build up the international competitiveness of domestic industry—and thereby eventually to raise living standards. This commitment led all three governments to create rather similar policies and organizations for governing the market. Their outstanding economic success makes it plausible to suggest that they have created a more competitive form of capitalism, from which other countries would be wise to learn.

This book is intended for those interested in the uses of public power for accelerating economic growth and raising mass living standards. It assumes no prior knowledge of Taiwan or China, and most of the time only a nodding acquaintance with economics. For convenience I refer to Taiwan as a "country" or "nation," though it is not identified as such either by its own government, which claims to be the rightful government of all of China, or by the government of the People's Republic of China on the mainland. The government and people are referred to as Taiwanese rather than Chinese, and where necessary a distinction is made between "islanders" or "native Taiwanese" and "mainlanders" who came to the island from the mainland after 1945. Most references to Japan are to the period before 1973.

Chapter 1

STATES, MARKETS, AND INDUSTRIAL POLICY

> The economic role of the state has managed to hold the
> attention of scholars for over two centuries without
> arousing their curiosity. . . . The chief instrument of
> empirical demonstration on the economic competence of
> the state has been the telling anecdote.
> —George Stigler

THE PREDOMINANT approach to economic policy in the 1950s and 1960s assigned the state[1] a substantial role in repairing market failures. In the industrialized countries the experience of the Great Depression and wartime *dirigisme*[2] provided the impetus. The approach was also taken up by economists dealing with "underdeveloped countries" and made the basis of a newly emerging discipline of development economics. The early contributions to development economics concentrated on showing how the special circumstances of underdeveloped countries—low private saving, dependence on primary product exports, declining prices of exports in relation to imports, small internal markets, limited skills, few entrepreneurs adept at large-scale organization, and pervasive underemployment—required an even bigger role for the state than in the more developed countries.

These circumstances meant that underdeveloped countries could not expect to achieve full employment or earn enough foreign exchange to meet unrestrained demand in the context of an open economy, according to development economists. Almost regardless of the exchange rate and even with wages no higher than physical subsistence level, a shortage would remain of activities producing goods or services saleable on the international market. Reliance on the free market would perpetuate what was variously called dualism, marginalization, or the coexistence of precapitalist with capitalist forms of production. Hence the state should not only maintain macroeconomic balance and supply "public" goods and services, but it should also undertake direct re-

---

[1] I use "government" to mean the executive branch and "state" to mean the wider structure of governance institutions, but in practice the two words are often used interchangeably—less serious a confusion for Taiwan and Korea than for many other countries.

[2] *Dirigisme* in the French sense contains the idea of directional thrust, or orienting power, in the hands of government (*Petit Larousse* 1975). I use *dirigisme*, guided market and governed market more or less interchangeably, to mean strongly influenced rather than tightly controlled.

sponsibility both for augmenting the economy's investable resources and for establishing a mechanism to transfer those resources into productive investment. Capital formation, in this view, was the engine of development. By leaving significant amounts of an economy's resources underutilized, free markets in less developed country (LDC) conditions, would generate less investment than was socially desirable and allocate it in less than socially desirable ways. Development economics thus restored capital formation to prominence, which having been at the heart of economic theory from the eighteenth century to the First World War had then been displaced by issues of efficient resource allocation. But it combined capital formation with an activist view of the state in a way that classical economics had not.[3]

The late 1960s and early 1970s saw a downgrading of the role of the state in both developed and less developed countries. In the LDC context economists presented three main kinds of evidence:

1. the use of the state to promote import-substituting industrialization during the 1950s and the 1960s had resulted in inefficient industries requiring permanent subsidization, with little prospect of achieving international competitiveness

2. extensive government intervention tended to generate "rent-seeking" on a significant scale, that is, to divert the energies of economic agents away from production and into lobbying for increased allocations of government subsidies and protection

3. some of the most successful LDCs—including Taiwan, South Korea, Hong Kong, and Singapore—had achieved extraordinary industrial growth by using an outward-oriented model driven by market incentives and a strong private sector[4]

The generally favorable effects that followed the gradual liberalization of trade and capital flows among the developed countries during the 1960s pointed to the same conclusion. And immediate fiscal conditions necessitated smaller government; the 1973 energy price rise put acute pressure on state budgets in most oil-importing countries, so that public expenditures had to be curtailed.

Even where some form of government intervention could be justified by market failure the actual effects of such interventions are often perverse, it was said. Indeed, "government failure" is as pervasive and serious as market failure, if not more so. A small but lively band of economists developed gen-

---

[3] This approach was sometimes called "structuralism" because it emphasized the structural impediments to the working of markets seen, for example, in large differences between sectors in real product per worker. For the evolution of postwar thinking about the role of the state, I draw on Brett 1985; Bienefeld 1982; Lewis 1989. For early views which emphasize the employment problem and/or the foreign exchange gap in underdeveloped countries, see Nurkse 1953; Rosenstein-Rodan 1943; Lewis 1955; Myrdal 1957; Chenery 1959; Singer 1949; Streeten 1964.

[4] See in particular the seminal book by Little, Scitovsky, and Scott 1970; also Krueger 1974 on "rent-seeking."

10   CHAPTER 1

eral arguments to show why such failure is an inherent tendency of all governments.[5] Other economists working on developing countries said that the governments of these countries were even more likely to fail than those in developed countries, because, in Deepak Lal's words, "many developing countries are closer in their official workings to the rapacious and inefficient nation-states of 17th or 18th-century Europe, governed as much for the personal aggrandizement of their rulers as for the welfare of the ruled" (1983:108). In these circumstances, he continued, it is the height of folly to urge upon developing countries that "enlightened discrimination" toward foreign trade, transnational companies, technology, and the meeting of basic needs prescribed by traditional development economics; discrimination is seldom enlightened.

The upshot of these new circumstances and arguments was that by the second half of the 1970s, if not earlier, the mainstream of thinking about development policy (especially in the English-speaking academic community and international development agencies) had decisively shifted from the prescriptions of the 1950s and 1960s toward a "neoclassical" view of the appropriate roles of markets and governments. The need for a special economics of development was denied (Lal 1983).

In the neoclassical view, the engine of development is not so much capital formation as efficient allocation of resources. Once institutional arrangements are in place to generate an efficient allocation of resources investment can be left to take care of itself. Whatever investment is generated by these arrangements constitutes—with some small exceptions—the social optimum. The necessary institutional arrangements for generating efficient resource use are competitive markets, particularly domestic markets integrated with international markets. Hence government should leave private producers operating through market mechanisms to supply all but certain "public" goods. It should limit its own activities to improving the functioning of markets and to providing only those goods and services where the government has a clear comparative advantage relative to private agents. The resources so released can either be transferred to the private sector or used to improve the performance of the state's essential functions.

If prices reflect social opportunity costs, the underlying argument runs, profit incentives will drive the economy to its maximum production potential. So in a labor-abundant economy profit maximization by private producers will lead to the choice of labor-intensive production techniques. In the absence of trade distortions, exports of labor-intensive products will grow, generating beneficial second-round effects on the rate of aggregate growth. As labor demand increases faster than the supply, labor surpluses will be absorbed, leading to a rise in real wages and a change in comparative advantage guided by the changes in factor scarcities.

[5] For example, Wolf 1979; Buchanan and Tullock 1962.

The key development policy is therefore an outward-oriented trade regime, characterized by low or negligible impediments to imports, relatively uniform incentives for different production activities, and incentives for export sale equal to the incentives for domestic market sale. These conditions will maximize the economy's income and growth (in world prices) by concentrating resources on those activities in which the economy has a comparative advantage, leaving other forms of production to other nations. In addition, by expanding the proportion of the economy which is directly subject to international competitive pressures, the government's own ability to impose "political" prices is weakened; hence producers' uncertainty about government policy is reduced.

Other poorer nations also benefit. For as a country experiences increases in costs and improvements in technological capacity, so it exits light-manufactured exports—textiles, clothing, shoes, and simple consumer electronics— leaving them for the next tier, itself moving into more sophisticated products. As Bela Balassa describes the sequence, the newly industrializing countries (NICS) would "upgrade and . . . diversify their exports in line with their changing comparative advantage," leaving "countries at lower stages of industrial development to replace exports of unskilled-labor-intensive commodities from the newly-industrializing countries to industrial country markets" (1980:25–26).

THE PROPER ROLE OF GOVERNMENT

In the neoclassical view, the essential economic functions of government are to:

1. maintain macroeconomic stability
2. provide physical infrastructure, especially that which has high fixed costs in relation to variable costs, such as harbors, railways, irrigation canals, and sewers
3. supply "public goods," including defense and national security, education, basic research, market information, the legal system, and environmental protection
4. contribute to the development of institutions for improving the markets for labor, finance, technology, etc.
5. offset or eliminate price distortions which arise in cases of demonstrable market failure
6. redistribute income to the poorest in sufficient measure for them to meet basic needs

This list of functions is uncontroversial as far as it goes. The controversy comes at the step of recognizing market failures[6] in practice and deciding what to do about them.

---

[6] Market failure is defined as a situation in which the market system produces an allocation of resources which is not Pareto-efficient—it is possible to find ways of changing resource allocation

For example, many neoclassical economists would accept that markets for technology development, manpower training, and credit to small firms and exporters may fail seriously enough to warrant some offsetting government intervention.[7] With respect to technology development market failure may occur because knowledge leaks. If a firm invests in acquiring technological mastery over new processes it will have trouble keeping the benefits to itself. Other producers can ''reverse-engineer'' products. Employees can leave their firm and apply on the new job what they learned on the old. So while the firm bears the cost of the innovation it does not capture the full social benefit, and hence underinvests in technological effort. Also, some forms of technological development may require a minimum scale of effort, which a single firm acting on its own may not be able to mount. In cases where technology investments are suboptimal, tax incentives may be used to increase the implicit private rates of return on investment, while in cases where private scale is too small, government coordination of public and private technology development activities may be justified. The government also has a role in formulating and enforcing intellectual property rights, in the form of patents and copyrights.

With respect to manpower development market failure may occur if the benefits to society of having an educated population exceed the benefits which educated individuals can capture in the form of higher incomes. These benefits may include a healthier population, lower fertility, and a better informed citizenry. Education and training are generally difficult to finance privately because of the absence of nonfamily institutions that lend to individuals against uncertain and distant future income returns. Hence market forces generally lead to underinvestment in human capital, which a government may correct by a variety of subsidies.

With respect to credit allocation to small firms, market failure may occur if large firms have control over credit markets and apply bargaining power to obtain loans on privileged terms. Also, large firms may get privileged terms if they have an implicit government guarantee, in the sense that they are more likely to be rescued by government than small firms. These cases can provide a rationale for compensating government intervention to increase small firms' access to credit. Likewise, if action to remove exchange rate overvaluation and protection is ruled out, cheap export credit may be justified to offset higher private profitability of domestic market sales.

Such arguments can be used to provide a justification for a *functional* or horizontal industrial policy which is consistent with the principles of neoclas-

---

so as to make some consumer(s) better off and none worse off. Hence individual self-seeking behavior by consumers and firms will not achieve the highest level of welfare for society as a whole insofar as market failure is prevalent. It is predicted to occur in the presence of monopoly and oligopoly, externalities, public goods, and common property resources, in each of which individualistic behavior leads to suboptimal results. See Bannock, Baxter, and Rees 1978:287.

[7] See World Bank 1987b.

sical economics. It is difficult to use those principles to justify a *sectoral* or industry-specific industrial policy, however. A sectoral industrial policy aims to direct resources into selected industries so as to give producers in those industries a competitive advantage. It therefore aims to produce a different profile of industries compared to what would result from the decisions of unguided, unstimulated market agents on their own.

In the case of "sunrise" or "infant" industries such justification must rest, in economic terms, on positive side-effects between firms or on economies of scale. Positive interfirm side-effects, or "externalities," may take the form of benefits created by a firm, in the form of goods, services, or technological capacity, for which it is not fully compensated in market transactions. Or they may take the form of benefits from an investment activity carried out by one firm which are dependent upon complementary investments by other firms, in which case present market prices are unlikely adequately to signal the interdependence that exists among these investment decisions. Externalities may provide a prima facie case for intervention to offset suboptimal private investment through government coordination of investment decisions or incentives for additional investment. Economies of scale, as distinct from externalities, occur when costs per unit fall as output expands, generating an imperfectly competitive industrial structure as those with lower costs are able to drive others out of business. Here the prima facie case might call for government ownership, or price regulation, or measures to help firms travel down their declining cost curves. In "sunset" industries the justification has to rest on a demonstration that the pace or patterns of decline generated by the market are in some way socially inefficient or unacceptedly disruptive, for example, with respect to employment.

However, neoclassical economics teaches that market failure of a kind that could be improved upon by a sectoral industrial policy is rare. Indeed, some economists think that there are few inherent market failures and that existing market imperfections are often due to government actions which distort markets. They are pessimistic about politicians' willingness to resist the temptation to misuse economic powers, and still more pessimistic about the ability of governments to detect opportunities which private entrepreneurs have missed. Other neoclassical economists are more impressed by the infant industry case, but see the proper role of government as being confined to the provision of nondiscriminatory and nondiscretionary industrial promotion policies for the set of infant industries. All would agree with Assar Lindbeck that "in market-oriented economies, the role of government planning and public finance is largely to 'plan' the physical, social and psychological *environment* of private agents rather than to plan what these agents are supposed to do" (1986:8). In most LDCs application of this principle would mean a shrinkage in the size of government and a concentration of public attention on a much more limited set of tasks than at present. It would mean substantial economic liberalization and privatization.

What Does the Neoclassical Confidence Rest On?

Theory

The source of these policy prescriptions can be traced to the theory of comparative advantage. This theory shows that any one nation will be better off, in the sense of enjoying more output, if it concentrates on those activities in which its costs are relatively cheapest. Resources will be so allocated provided that international market forces are allowed to determine the relative prices of internationally tradable goods in the domestic economy. And that requirement, in turn, calls for free trade, or a close approximation to it, with low or no impediments to imports and with relative prices that give no more incentive to sell on the domestic market than to sell abroad.

However, the theory of comparative advantage covers only the effects of once-and-for-all changes in trade restrictions. It does not specify a casual mechanism linking realization of comparative advantage to higher growth. A leading proponent admits that "in its present state, trade theory provides little guidance as to the role of trade policy and trade strategy in promoting growth. . . . There is nothing in theory to indicate why a deviation from the optimum should affect the rate of economic growth" (Krueger 1980:288). Attempts to make the theory more dynamic, as in the stages of growth approach (Balassa 1981), show how changes in a country's educational and capital stocks produce changes in comparative advantage; but the changes in the stocks are taken as independent of the changes in the pattern of industrial specialization. Neoclassical economists instead rely on ad hoc factors to make the link between freer markets and higher growth. Some have suggested that opening the economy to international competitive pressures assists technical change, economies of scale, and indigenous entrepreneurship. Others say that a free trade regime is an important component of the task of confining government to its proper place, by making it more difficult for the government to go beyond the bounds of providing those public goods essential for civil life (Lal and Rajapatirana 1987; Krueger 1980). But these explanations shift the burden of argument well beyond the theory of comparative advantage to issues of government failure and technological change which have received little theoretical attention within the neoclassical framework (Fransman 1986).[8]

Some economists, indeed, have recently provided theoretical arguments which suggest that in certain conditions with real world analogues freer trade may not promote faster growth. In conditions of *increasing* returns to scale

---

[8] For a seminal attempt to theorize the connection between "dynamic comparative advantage" and growth from a non-neoclassical perspective, see Chenery 1961.

and imperfect world markets, a country's growth can be faster if it restricts trade to some degree. Paul Krugman concludes that "the new thinking about trade . . . makes one thing clear: the idealized theoretical model on which the classical case for free trade is based will not serve us anymore. The world is more complex than that, and there is no question that the complexities do open, in principle, the possibility of successful activist trade or industrial policy" (1986:15). One could still argue that the qualifications only apply in conditions not found in most developing countries, so that for them the classical case for free trade still holds. But to repeat, the classical case for free trade as a means to higher growth is shaky.

Evidence

Yet even if the causal mechanisms linking nearly free trade with higher growth are not well understood, neoclassical proponents claim that the record overwhelmingly supports such a connection. For example:

"The evidence is quite conclusive: countries applying outward-oriented development strategies had a superior performance in terms of exports, economic growth, and employment whereas countries with continued inward orientation encountered increasing economic difficulties." (Balassa 1981:16–17)

"Detailed and historical studies . . . have provided an impressive empirical validation of the theoretical case for the view that . . . free trade remains the best policy for developing (and developed) countries." (Lal 1983:27–28)

"It seems to be as firm a stylized fact as any in the economics of developing countries: a sustained movement to an outward-oriented trade regime leads to faster growth of both exports and income." (Lal and Rajapatirana 1987:208)

"The case for liberalizing financial and trade control systems and moving back to a nearly free trade regime is now incontrovertible." (Lal 1983:32)

"Experience has been that growth performance has been more satisfactory under export promotion strategies . . . than under import substitution strategies. . . . There is little doubt about the link between export performance and growth rates." (Krueger 1980:288–89)

Jagdish Bhagwati is probably correct to claim that belief in the superiority of what he terms the "export promotion" strategy over the "import substitution" strategy is all but universal among economists, "insofar as any kind of consensus can ever be found in our tribe" (1986:93). What Bhagwati calls export promotion, and others call outward orientation, is close to, though not identical with, free trade, a point to which we return.

The consensus among economists has become the standard recipe of the multilateral lending agencies, notably the International Monetary Fund (IMF) and the World Bank. In a recent survey of the world economy, the IMF said:

Another noteworthy element of policies in developing countries has been an increasing emphasis on a wide range of structural adjustment measures intended to
improve the allocation of resources and enhance growth prospects. For the most
part, these measures have involved restructuring prices and price-setting procedures towards a more market oriented approach. . . . These measures are already
leading to more robust development in some countries, and should bring further
benefits as their efforts become more widely felt.   (1985:66)

The World Bank, speaking of the same reforms, goes on to assure its clients
that, "however difficult the policy reforms may have been to adopt, in due
course they will create much easier conditions for developing countries than
would prevail if the reforms were diluted or abandoned" (1985:146). Both
statements express a ringing confidence in the force of the evidence.

Two kinds of evidence are involved. One is the cross-sectional study of the
relationship between "inward" and "outward" orientation, on the one hand,
and growth on the other, or some more disaggregated specification thereof.
The other kind is the in-depth study of one or more key cases, the key cases
being the East Asian NICs, including South Korea, Taiwan, Hong Kong, and
Singapore. These are judged to have been the most successful developing
countries of the postwar era, and therefore to show what policies and other
conditions make for superior development performance. Most of the rest of
this book relates to the second kind of evidence. Here I discuss the first. The
question is whether the cross-sectional evidence provides good grounds for
confidence in the neoclassical prescriptions. I do not attempt to appraise a vast
literature, but merely to indicate grounds for doubt.

Bela Balassa has carried out much research on trade regimes which all
seems to support the neoclassical position. But Colin Bradford has applied to
one of Balassa's studies a simple test (1987). Taking Balassa's eight inward-
oriented and six outward-oriented countries over the 1970s, Bradford found
their price distortion scores as calculated by the World Bank (1983). For the
overall price distortion index, as well as for the two most important components of the overall index (exchange rate distortion and interest rate distortion), he found virtually no difference between the averages for the outward-
and the inward-oriented countries. There are also virtually no differences in
savings rate and growth of gross domestic product (GDP). To compare averages for such a small sample is admittedly a crude test. But the failure of
Balassa's argument to pass it is reason to reject his own conclusion that "the
evidence is quite conclusive: countries applying outward-oriented development strategies had a superior performance in terms of exports, economic
growth, and employment whereas countries with continued inward orientation
encountered increasing economic difficulties" (1981:16–17).

Other studies have also found only a weak connection between export (or
outward) orientation and growth. Studies by Rostam Kavoussi (1985) and by

Hans Singer and Patricia Gray (1988) find export orientation to be positively correlated with growth performance only when world demand is growing fast (as in 1967–73). When world demand is growing slowly (as in 1973–77 and 1977–83) the correlation is slight, suggesting that in such conditions the gains from export orientation are offset by negative effects. In all conditions of world demand, the correlation is weaker for poorer countries than for richer countries.[9]

Howard Pack examines the connection between trade regimes and technical efficiency to see whether export-oriented trade regimes go with faster growth in technical efficiency, as some neoclassical economists have said. He concludes that, "there is no clear confirmation of the hypothesis that countries with an external orientation benefit from greater growth in technical efficiency in the component sectors of manufacturing" (1986:33). Even Jagdish Bhagwati, a long-time proponent of outward-orientation, has recently concluded that there is little systematic evidence to support an outward orientation (which he calls "export promotion") over import substitution on grounds of scale economies, innovation, savings, or technical efficiency (1988:38–40).

The World Bank's 1987 *World Development Report* makes a more ambitious attempt to demonstrate the virtues of outward orientation. Going beyond the dichotomy, it classifies forty-one developing countries into strongly outward-, moderately outward-, moderately inward-, and strongly inward-oriented categories for 1963–73 and 1973–85. It measures each category against six criteria of macroeconomic performance for both periods, or twelve indicators in all. The theory predicts an even progression in performance, the strongly inward doing worst, the strongly outward doing best.

The results show that the moderately inward-oriented countries do better than the moderately outward-oriented countries on six out of twelve indicators.[10] The moderately inward-oriented countries do better on inflation and savings in both periods, and better on the rate of growth of GDP and of gross

[9] See also Jung and Marshall 1985, who use a performance-based rather than incentive-based measure of "export led." They find that at the level of individual industries in thirty-seven countries output growth tends to cause export growth more frequently than the other way around, including in Taiwan, Korea, and Brazil. On the export growth link, see also Havrylshyn and Alikhani (1982:661): "the link between rapid growth of manufactured exports and rapid growth of income is by no means automatic"; and Michaely (1977:52): "growth is affected by export performance only once countries achieve some minimum level of development"—perhaps under "bad" import substitution policies. Presumably the effects of exports on overall growth in Taiwan, Korea, and Japan depended on their being manufactured exports, a point which is obscured when countries are asked to adopt an export orientation per se.

[10] The moderately outward-oriented countries include Brazil, Israel, Malaysia, Thailand, and others. The moderately inward-oriented countries include El Salvador, Honduras, Kenya, Mexico, Nicaragua, the Philippines, Senegal, Yugoslavia, and others. The strongly inward-oriented countries include Argentina, Bangladesh, the Dominican Republic, Ethiopia, Ghana, India, Peru, Sudan, Tanzania, Zambia, and others. The named countries are all those which appear in their category in both periods.

national product (GNP) per capita in the more recent period. They do worse on incremental capital output ratio and growth of manufactured exports in both periods. For the more recent period, 1979–85, the moderately inward-oriented do better on four indicators out of six, which is striking because the world economy over the next ten to fifteen years will probably be more like the 1973–85 period than the 1963–73 period in terms of instability and low growth of demand.

It is true that the averages for the strongly and moderately outward-oriented cases combined are substantially better than those for the combined inward-oriented categories. But the strongly outward-oriented cases include only Korea, Hong Kong, and Singapore. (Taiwan was not in the sample because the World Bank does not recognize Taiwan as a separate entity.) Since weighted averages are used and since the size of the Korean economy swamps the other two, the results from the strongly outward-oriented category are largely the results from one country (except for export growth). Only anthropologists are allowed to draw sweeping conclusions from a sample of less than two.

Besides which, it is striking that all the strongly outward-oriented cases happen to be East Asian. This raises the possibility that the causes of exceptional macroeconomic performance have more to do with East Asianness, or (absent Hong Kong) with industrial policies and managed trade, than with the attributes of strongly outward orientation.

The results do appear to support the neoclassical/World Bank position with respect to the strongly inward-oriented countries, which performed worse than the moderately inward-oriented countries on all twelve indicators. But as Hans Singer has shown, it cannot be concluded that they performed worse *because of* their strongly inward orientation (1988). They are much poorer than the moderately inward-oriented countries, with weighted average incomes little more than half. Indeed, over the whole sample per capita income is a better discriminator with respect to growth performance than trade regime. The results are consistent with the proposition that the poorer countries find it more difficult and less beneficial to maintain an outward orientation, especially because of the negative effect on growth of greater instability of exports and imports.

There is a further problem concerning the very meaning of the terms. Outward and inward orientation are taken to be near synonyms for free trade and controlled trade, respectively. The *World Development Report 1987* defines strongly outward-oriented countries as those where ''trade controls are either nonexistent or very low. . . . There is little or no use of direct controls and licensing arrangements. . . .'' Defining the moderately outward-oriented category the report adds another criterion, namely, that the range of effective protection rates to different sectors of the economy is low. By contrast, the moderately inward-oriented category is defined to include countries where ''the overall incentive structure distinctly favors production for the domestic market. The average rate of effective protection for home markets is relatively high and the range of effective protection rates relatively wide. The use of direct import controls and licensing is extensive . . ." (1987a:82). The definitions make a sharp distinction between moderately outward- and moderately inward-oriented cases, which makes the lack of difference in performance all the more striking.

Korea is the prime example of a strongly outward-oriented country. But does Korea really meet the criteria for a strongly outward-oriented case? Anticipating chapter 10, we can say here that several studies provide detailed evidence of selective trade controls in Korea. The rate of effective protection for manufacturing was 49 percent in both 1978 and 1982, according to Young (1984), which is by no means low. The locus classicus of the view that Korea has had a relatively free trade regime, the study by Larry Westphal and Kwang Suk Kim (1982), suffers from serious methodological problems and uses data from only one year, as long ago as 1968. And even if we take their findings at face value, it turns out that Korea had nearly as much variation in effective protection to different manufacturing sectors as Colombia, and more than Argentina; Korea had the second highest amount of interindustry dispersion in a six-country comparison (Balassa, et al.1982).[11] This would preclude Korea's classification as even a moderately outward-oriented country in the World Bank study, because even moderately outward-oriented countries are defined to have little variation in effective protection rates to different industries. Without Korea the strongly outward-oriented category contains only the Hong Kong and Singapore minnows.

Another source of cross-sectional evidence is the direct correlation between price distortions and economic growth. The neoclassical argument says that lower price distortions cause higher growth, while higher price distortions have an adverse effect on growth. This argument was given prominence in the World Bank's *World Development Report 1983*, which presents the results of a correlation between price distortion scores and growth rates for a sample of developing countries. The key finding is that "the average growth rate of those developing countries with low distortions in the 1970s was about 7 percent a year—2 percentage points higher than the overall average. Countries with high distortions averaged growth of about 3 percent a year, 2 percentage points lower than the overall average" (1983:61). This conclusion does not survive even casual scrutiny. By far the most influential component of the overall distortion index is the exchange rate. If exchange rate distortion is an important cause of poor growth performance, it should make its effect felt through lagging export volume. But there is no statistically significant relationship between the growth of export volume and the exchange rate distortion index.

[11] The Korean study shows much the same problems as the companion Taiwan study by Lee and Liang (1982), discussed in chapter 5. See also tables 3.2 and 3.3; and chapter 10.

The same holds for the relationship between agricultural growth and the measured distortion of agricultural prices. "It is difficult to argue that one is measuring one's distortions right if they fail to exert an influence where they are most relevant," Albert Fishlow observes. He concludes that "the widely publicized World Bank results are inadequately founded on a distortion index that has limited analytic content" (1985:140).

Indeed, some evidence suggests that deliberate "distortion" of some prices may *help* growth. Colin Bradford compares the price of investment goods relative to consumption and government goods in a number of countries, and finds that the newly industrialized countries are distinguished from other developing countries and from some of the poorer industrialized countries (such as Hungary, Italy, and Spain) by a relatively low price of investment goods. He concludes:

> These patterns suggest the possibility that NIC growth and export performance in manufactures have been accelerated by public policies that have lowered the cost of investment goods. These policies could have been in the form of domestic monetary policy affecting interest rates and credit allocations to industrial investors and borrowers or in the form of direct subsidies affecting the price of domestically produced investment goods. Such monetary and fiscal policies would have the effect of stimulating greater demand and supply of investment goods, which in turn spurs capital accumulation, industrialization and structural change.
>
> (1987:309)

What about the effects of trade liberalization, of a change in trade regime toward free trade? Recall the claim that this relationship—of a sustained change generating faster export and income growth—"seems to be as firm a stylized fact as any in the economics of developing countries" (Lal and Rajapatirana 1987:208). But the evidence in support of the claim conflates the effects of trade policy changes with the effects of commonly associated changes, such as macroeconomic stabilization. One study which attempts to identify the impact of trade liberalization alone concludes that "if truth-in-advertising were to apply to policy advice, each prescription for trade liberalization should be accompanied with a disclaimer: 'Warning! Trade Liberalization cannot be shown on theoretical grounds to enhance technical efficiency; nor has it been empirically demonstrated to do so' " (Rodrik 1988b:28).

Even where individual countries improve their performance after a trade liberalization (and certainly some do), this does not provide firm grounds for recommending trade liberalization as a general prescription. For one thing, the direction of causation is unclear. The liberalization of trade may itself be facilitated by the circumstances conducive to rapid growth, and even though under such conditions it helps to reinforce that growth, this beneficial consequence of freer trade cannot be considered universal. Indeed, when the conditions for rapid growth are no longer given, the social and political consequences of entering further liberalization could become destabilizing (Bienefeld 1982:34). In conditions of widespread unemployment, trade tends to become more adversarial than in full employment conditions. It becomes a means of allocating unemployment across countries, as well as the more familiar means to balance the commodity bundle in each economy (Drucker 1986).

There is also the fallacy of composition. Even the present very low levels of developing country penetration of industrial country markets for manufactured goods have triggered protectionist reactions. Presumably these reactions are part of the reason why the share of imports from developing countries in relation to total consumption of manufactured goods in industrial countries has remained roughly constant over the past decade, at just over 1.5 percent (*North-South* 1980:176; UNCTAD 1988:4; Cline 1982b). If many more countries increased their share of industrial country markets without displacing existing suppliers—which is the implication of a generalized export orientation strategy for developing countries—the protectionist reaction could be expected to be much stronger.

So the cross-country evidence relevant to neoclassical trade and industrial policy prescriptions is by no means unambiguous.[12] It supports instead a cautious assessment of what a free trade approach can be expected to achieve for a broad cross-section of developing countries. The state of the evidence is no better than that on the effects of IMF stabilization programs, about which a recent in-house survey concludes: "Little empirical evidence exists on the long-run effects of Fund programs, and *none at all* on the effects of various combinations of stabilization policies on economic development. . . . Even the informal evidence that is available is ambivalent on the relationship between financial stability and economic development" (Khan and Knight 1985:7, emphasis added)—this after nearly forty years of Fund stabilization programs. The paper was published by the IMF in the same year as the earlier-quoted IMF report on the world economy, which avowed that "these [market-oriented] measures are already leading to more robust development in some

---

[12] Rati Ram (1986), using a very large sample of 115 countries, finds that government size is positively correlated with growth in almost all cases; that the externality effect of government size is generally positive; that the positive effect of government size on growth may be stronger in lower-income contexts; and several more relationships which confute for the neoclassical argument. I do not give much weight to these results, however, because I cannot specify a mechanism by which such an aggregate variable as government size might have a positive impact on growth. One needs to specify government activity in line with a theoretical reason why the specified activity might be important for growth. The difficulties of trying to base policy generalizations on empirical evidence are seen in the fact that Ram (1986) and Landau (1986) published papers within a few months of each other with diametrically opposed econometric findings about the correlation between size of government in GNP and growth (Helleiner 1988). In formulating the argument set out in the text, I have benefited from discussions with Manfred Bienefeld (see Bienefeld 1988).

countries and should bring further benefits as their efforts become more widely felt.''

THE FREE MARKET (FM) THEORY OF EAST ASIAN SUCCESS

We turn now to the East Asian NICs. With some stretching of the category, pre-1970 Japan can be included as well. An abundant literature attributes the industrial success of the five NICs—Japan, Taiwan, Korea, Hong Kong, and Singapore—to their reliance on free markets. For example, Hugh Patrick declares himself to be ''of the school which interprets Japanese economic performance as due primarily to the actions and efforts of private individuals and enterprises responding to the opportunities provided in *quite free markets for commodities and labor*. While the government has been supportive and indeed has done much to create the environment of growth, its role has often been exaggerated'' (1977:239, emphasis added).[13] Referring to the five, Edward Chen asserts that ''*state intervention is largely absent. What the state provided is simply a suitable environment for the entrepreneurs to perform their functions*.'' Such practices as ''directing resources to the desired channels by state intervention'' are part of central planning and have no part in the development of the East Asian five (1979:41, emphasis added). Hence, according to Chen, the hypergrowth of the five demonstrates that ''the free market environment provides the necessary mechanism to gear the economies towards their optimal points on the production possibilities frontier'' (1979:185). Shifting into even higher rhetorical gear, David Aikman claims that Taiwan and Hong Kong ''demonstrate just how faithful, consciously or not, the rulers of these two countries have been to American conceptions of free enterprise'' (1986:116). Milton and Rose Friedman, in *Free to Choose*, make the same point on a still grander scale: ''Malaysia, Singapore, Korea, Taiwan, Hong Kong and Japan—relying extensively on private markets—are thriving. . . . By contrast, India, Indonesia, and Communist China, all relying heavily on central planning, have experienced economic stagnation'' (1980:57).

According to this ''free market'' (FM) theory, East Asia does better than other newly industrializing countries because the East Asian state interferes hardly at all in the working of the market. The other countries have been held back from the development they would have achieved in the ''normal'' course of events by excessive state intervention, especially in foreign trade. Or in a slightly different version of the argument, John Fei claims that ''the basic *causation of success* of the [East Asian] NICs on the policy front, can be traced to the *lessening of government interferences* in the market economy during the

[13] David Henderson (1983:114) claims that ''the real explanation for the Japanese economic miracle is the country's laissez-faire policies on taxes, antitrust, banking and labor,'' which prompts Chalmers Johnson to wonder whether Henderson understands French (1985:3). See also Hosomi and Okumura 1982:150.

E-O [Export-Oriented] phase. In Taiwan and Korea, interference with the market was considerably less as compared to other worse offenders in the near NICs and the Latin American countries . . . (1983:34, emphasis added).

THE SIMULATED FREE MARKET (SM) THEORY OF EAST ASIAN SUCCESS

Some neoclassical economists conclude that the governments of East Asia did more than just liberalize markets and lower distortions. In their view the governments also intervened more positively to offset other distortions, both those caused by other policies (e.g., import controls) and those remaining from government failure to change distortion-inducing institutions directly (e.g., segmented financial markets). Frederick Berger states the argument as follows: "I believe that the crux of the Korean example is that the *active interventionist attitude of the State has been aimed at applying moderate incentives which are very close to the relative prices of products and factors that would prevail in a situation of free trade*. . . . It is as though the government were 'simulating' a free market" (1979:64, emphasis added).

This is similar to Gary Saxonhouse's argument (1985) that Japan's peculiar institutional features are merely the functional equivalent of different arrangements in other countries. Its industrial policy, for example, is but a substitute for information which is provided by better-developed capital markets in the West.

Jagdish Bhagwati endorses a further type of government intervention in support of what he calls the "export promotion" (EP) strategy. An EP strategy is a set of policies which results in the average effective exchange rate for importables being approximately equal to that for exportables. The most important thing the government of an underdeveloped country can do to promote growth, he implies, is to maintain an EP strategy, and this requires government intervention. "The Far Eastern economies (with the exception of Hong Kong) and others that have come close to the EP strategy have been characterized by considerable government activity in the economic system. In my judgement, such intervention can be of great value, and almost certainly has been so, in making the EP strategy work successfully" (1988:33). However, Bhagwati's desirable interventions are restricted to those which increase producers' confidence in the government's commitment to the EP strategy. "By publicly supporting the outward-oriented strategy, by even bending in some cases towards ultra-export promotion, and by gearing the credit institutions to supporting export activities in an overt fashion, governments in these [Far Eastern] countries appear to have established the necessary confidence that their commitment to the EP strategy is serious, thus inducing firms to undertake costly investments and programs to take advantage of the EP strategy" (p. 34). He mentions in passing that the EP strategy does not preclude import substitution in selected sectors but gives no attention to this combination.

This "simulated free market" (SM) theory differs from the FM theory in terms of the distinction between a free (or liberal) trade regime and a neutral trade regime. The former is one with no or few impediments to imports; the latter is one where any incentive for domestic producers to sell on the domestic market rather than export, because of protection, is offset by export subsidies. This means that, overall, a U.S. dollar of exports fetches, in local currency, the same as a U.S. dollar of imports, when all export subsidies and tax credits and all import premia resulting from quantitative restrictions and tariffs are included. So a neutral trade regime may go with some government intervention, including protection of the domestic market. The important point, according to this theory, is that the incentive effect of such protection in biasing sales toward the domestic market should be offset, in aggregate, by export promotion measures. The Far Eastern countries have managed to do this, according to Bhagwati, which is a large part of the reason why they have been so successful compared to others which have not.

However, the proponents of the SM view have shown little interest in analyzing the nature of government intervention in East Asia, though they recognize its existence. And they also place primary causal weight on the character of the trade regime for explaining economic performance. For both reasons, the SM theory can be considered a variant of the core neoclassical theory, which links economic success to self-adjusting markets.

The Governed Market (GM) Theory of East Asian Success

Over the past decade or so, another stream of literature has emphasized the directive role of the state in East Asia. Parvez Hasan,[14] for example, writing of South Korea, draws attention to an "apparent paradox":

> [T]he Korean economy depends in large measure on private enterprise operating under highly centralized government guidance. In Korea the government's role is considerably more direct than that of merely setting the broad rules of the game and in influencing the economy indirectly through market forces. In fact, the government seems to be a participant and often the determining influence in nearly all business decisions.   (1976:29)

Edward Mason and associates come to a similar conclusion in their study of government-business relations:

> The rapid economic growth that began in South Korea in the early 1960s and has accelerated since then has been a government-directed development in which the principal engine has been private enterprise. The relationship between a government committed to a central direction of economic development and a highly dynamic private sector that confronts the planning machinery with a continually changing structure of economic activities presents a set of interconnections diffi-

[14] A World Bank staff member.

cult to penetrate and describe. Planning in South Korea, if it is interpreted to include not only policy formulation but also the techniques of policy implementation, is substantially more than "indicative." *The hand of government reaches down rather far into the activities of individual firms with its manipulation of incentives and disincentives.* At the same time, the situation can in no sense be described in terms of a command economy.   (1980:254, emphasis added)

Much the same has been said of Japan. According to this interpretation, the Japanese were the first to recognize that international competitive advantage could be deliberately created by government not just to nurture a few infant industries to supply the domestic market but to push broad sets of industries toward areas of growth and technological change in the world economy. In the words of a vice-minister of MITI (Ministry of International Trade and Industry):

> The MITI decided to establish in Japan industries which require intensive employment of capital and technology, industries that in consideration of comparative cost of production should be the most inappropriate for Japan, industries such as steel, oil-refining, industrial machinery of all sorts, and electronics. . . . From a short-run, static viewpoint, encouragement of such industries would seem to conflict with economic rationalism. But, from a long-range viewpoint, these are precisely the industries where *income elasticity of demand is high, technological progress is rapid, and labor productivity rises fast*. It was clear that without these industries it would be difficult to employ a population of 100 million and raise their standard of living to that of Europe and America with light industries; whether right or wrong, Japan had to have these heavy and chemical industries. . . . Fortunately, owing to good luck and wisdom spawned by necessity, Japan has been able to *concentrate its scant capital in strategic industries*.
>
> (OECD 1972:15, emphasis added)

Henry Rosovsky went so far as to say of Japan that it "must be the only capitalist country in the world in which the Government decides how many firms should be in a given industry and sets out to arrange the desired number" (1972:244).

Chalmers Johnson has sketched a model of the "capitalist developmental state," based on the institutional arrangements common to the high-growth East Asian capitalist countries (1981, 1982, 1983). These arrangements are characterized, he says, by the following features:[15]

1. The top priority of state action, consistently maintained, is economic development, defined for policy purposes in terms of growth, productivity, and competitiveness rather than in terms of welfare. The substance of growth/competitive-

[15] I have slightly revised the presentation of Johnson's model and have omitted one of his points, that the state supervises a heavy and consistent investment in education for all the people (which relates to investment allocation rather than to organizational arrangements).

ness goals is derived from comparisons with external reference economies which provide the state managers with models for emulation.

2. The state is committed to private property and the market and limits its interventions to conform with this commitment.

3. The state guides the market with instruments formulated by an elite economic bureaucracy, led by a pilot agency or "economic general staff."

4. The state is engaged in numerous institutions for consultation and coordination with the private sector, and these consultations are an essential part of the process of policy formulation and implementation.

5. While state bureaucrats "rule," politicians "reign." Their function is not to make policy but to create space for the bureaucracy to maneuver in while also acting as a "safety valve" by forcing the bureaucrats to respond to the needs of groups upon which the stability of the system rests: that is, to maintain the relative autonomy of the state while preserving political stability. This separation of "ruling" and "reigning" goes with a "soft authoritarianism" when it comes to maintaining the needs of economic development vis-à-vis other claims, and with a virtual monopoly of political power in a single political party or institution over a long period of time.

This picture of a centralized state interacting with the private sector from a position of preeminence so as to secure development objectives has been called the "developmental state" theory of East Asian industrial success (Johnson 1982; White 1988). It is not, however, much of a theory. Its specification of institutional arrangements is descriptive rather than comparative-analytic, so what the developmental state is contrasted with is not clear. It also says little about the nature of policies and their impact on industrial performance. Indeed, Johnson's institutional arrangements are for the most part as consistent with simulated free market policies as with more directive ones. I now propose a "governed market" theory which builds on both the idea of the developmental state and on the older development economics' understanding of the nature of the development problem.

The governed market (GM) theory says that the superiority of East Asian economic performance is due in large measure to a combination of: (1) very high levels of productive investment, making for fast transfer of newer techniques into actual production; (2) more investment in certain key industries than would have occurred in the absence of government intervention; and (3) exposure of many industries to international competition, in foreign markets if not at home. These are the proximate causes. At a second level of causation, they are themselves the result, in important degree, of a set of government economic policies. Using incentives, controls, and mechanisms to spread risk, these policies enabled the government to guide—or govern—market processes of resource allocation so as to produce different production and investment outcomes than would have occurred with either free market or simulated free market policies. At the third level of explanation, the policies have been permitted or supported by a certain kind of organization of the state and the private sector. Let us specify the policies and the organizational arrangements in more detail.

Johnson's picture of the developmental state can be recast to fit with concepts developed elsewhere in political science for comparing political regimes. The relevant distinctions are "democratic versus authoritarian" and "pluralist vs. corporatist." The first refers to the rules by which rulers are chosen. In democratic regimes the rulers are chosen by a process much influenced by popular preferences, while in authoritarian regimes they are selected by methods which give relatively little scope for the expression of popular sentiment. The second distinction refers to relations between interest groups and the state. In pluralist regimes, interest groups are voluntary associations, free to organize and gain influence over state policy corresponding to their economic or political resources. The process of government consists of the competition between interest groups, with government bureaucracies playing an important but not generally dominant role. In corporatist systems the state charters or creates a small number of interest groups, giving them a monopoly of representation of occupational interests in return for which it claims the right to monitor them in order to discourage the expression of "narrow," conflictful demands. The state is therefore able to shape the demands that are made upon it, and hence—in intention—maximize compliance and cooperation (Schmitter 1974; Stepan 1978; Zeigler 1988).

In these terms, the United States is the example par excellence of a pluralist democracy; Korea and Taiwan are examples of authoritarian corporatism; Austria and Switzerland illustrate democratic corporatism; and Japan illustrates corporatism combined with arrangements for selecting rulers which are intermediate between democratic and authoritarian, or what Johnson calls "soft authoritarian."

The corporatist and authoritarian political arrangements of East Asia have provided the basis for market guidance. Market guidance was effected by augmenting the supply of investible resources, spreading or "socializing" the risks attached to long-term investment, and steering the allocation of investment by methods which combine government and entrepreneurial preferences. In particular, the governments guided the market by: (1) redistributing agricultural land in the early postwar period; (2) controlling the financial system and making private financial capital subordinate to industrial capital; (3) maintaining stability in some of the main economic parameters that affect the viability of long-term investment, especially the exchange rate, the interest rate, and the general price level; (4) modulating the impact of foreign competition in the domestic economy and prioritizing the use of scarce foreign exchange; (5) promoting exports; (6) promoting technology acquisition from multinational companies and building a national technology system; and (7) assisting particular industries. (For Japan post-1970/73 we would also have to include industry-specific policies to ease decline. Throughout the reference is to Japan before this time.[16])

I am especially interested in the policies to assist particular industries. This is not because I think that industry-specific policies were causally more important than the others. But they were important enough, and yet have been almost completely ignored in most of the economics literature about the Taiwanese and Korean "economic miracles." Neglect of these policies matters particularly because it is in the histories of specific industries that one can most clearly see the government in action.

However, the existence of sectoral policies does not in itself mean that they produced significantly different outcomes from free market or simulated free market policies. They might merely put the government's seal of approval on some private sector projects by way of mild assistance for something that private firms would have done anyway in response to price signals alone. In that case we could dismiss sectoral policies as mere "hand-waving" or "window-dressing."

To clarify the issue, let us distinguish between leading the market and following the market. Sectoral policies lead the market when the government takes initiatives about what products or technologies should be encouraged, and puts public resources or public influence behind these initiatives. A clear case is where the government proposes a project to private firms, the private firms decline, and the government goes ahead through a public enterprise. On the other hand, sectoral policies follow the market when the government adopts the proposals of private firms about new products and new technologies. If private firms propose to make the quantum jump from fabrication of 16K to 64K DRAM chips and ask for government assistance, then government assistance follows the market.

Leading and following should be qualified by the degree of additionality. When government helps firms to do what they would have done anyway, this is—with apologies to the English language—"small followership." When government assists firms significantly to extend the margin of their investments, this is "big followership." We can use "big leadership" to refer to government initiatives on a large enough scale to make a real difference to investment and production patterns in an industry, and "small leadership" to refer to government initiatives which on their own carry too few resources or too little influence to make a difference.

The FM and SM theories of East Asian industrial success can accommodate the fact of sectoral policies by saying or implying that they constitute merely "small followership." The GM theory says that the governments' industry-

---

[16] By 1970–73 Japan's protection-promotion system began to be substantially dismantled. These years mark the end of an era—the end of catch-up, the beginning of large balance-of-payment surpluses, and a shift in industrial policy from growth, industrial investment, and export objectives, toward freer trade and social-overhead investment.

specific policies went beyond "small followership," to either or both "big leadership" and "big followership." Interventions of these types suggest that the production and investment outcomes were different from what would have occurred with free market or simulated free market policies, the difference being greater for big leadership than for big followership. The fact of a difference does not in itself imply that the difference helped or hindered development. Whether it helped or hindered has to be established independently.

Let us now summarize the main differences between the GM theory and the other two. The FM and SM theories emphasize efficient resource allocation as the principal general force for growth, and therefore interpret superior East Asian performance as the result of more efficient resource allocation than in other LDCs or NICs. This more efficient resource allocation comes from more freely functioning markets, including closer integration of domestic product markets into international markets. Hence these countries show the virtues of "getting the prices right," where "right" means domestic prices in line with international prices. The GM theory, on the other hand, emphasizes capital accumulation as the principal general force for growth, and interprets superior East Asian performance as the result of a level and composition of investment different from what FM or SM policies would have produced, and different, too, from what the "interventionist" economic policies pursued by many other LDCs would have produced. Government policies deliberately got some prices "wrong," so as to change the signals to which decentralized market agents responded, and also used nonprice means to alter the behavior of market agents. The resulting high level of investment generated fast turnover of machinery, and hence fast transfer of newer technology into actual production.

The FM and SM theories are silent on the political arrangements needed to support their policies. The GM theory emphasizes the developmental virtues of a hard or soft authoritarian state in corporatist relations with the private sector, able to confer enough autonomy on a centralized bureaucracy for it to influence resource allocation in line with a long-term national interest[17]—which sometimes conflicts with short-run profit maximizing. The state's steering of resource allocation is the economic counterpart to its political restrictions on "free trade" in interest groups.

THE QUESTION OF EVIDENCE

There is an unavoidable ideological loading in debate about the role of the state, for the issues lie uncomfortably close to the heart of the ideological

[17] Many writers in the tradition of political pluralism deny any meaning to the notion of the general good or the national interest, other than whatever happens to be the balance of demands between competing interest groups. I use "national economic objectives" or "the national interest" to refer to interests or objectives that are broadly rather than narrowly shared and enduring rather than short-term. Cf. Dahl and Lindblom 1963:501.

dispute in which the superpowers have clothed their global rivalry. There are also disciplinary interests at stake, as each discipline or subdiscipline tries to emphasize the importance of that factor—free markets, the state, culture, or something else—in which it can claim a comparative analytical advantage. But serious differences of opinion among scholars remain, which reflect the methodological difficulties with any theory which posits government steerage of the market as an independent variable. In part, the difficulties stem from the absence of an economic theory of sufficient credibility to provide a legitimate base from which technical economic analysis can act as a constraint on admissible arguments. In part, also, the difficulties stem from the same problem as with virtually all interesting social science questions: the absence of a counterfactual. The question of whether measures designed by a well-meaning bureaucracy can achieve results superior to those which a more liberal market system would produce is impossible to answer conclusively; what would have happened in the absence of the intervention is always unknown. Nonetheless, economists from Adam Smith onwards have not hesitated to make strong assertions, both positive and negative, about the effectiveness of government intervention without offering serious evidence to support their claims.

Serious direct evidence would have to separate out the impact of industrial policies from that of macroeconomic and other policies. Macroeconomic policies affect aggregate demand, but they also affect different industries differently although not intended to produce such differential effects. Industrial policies, on the other hand, are intended to affect production and investment decisions of decentralized producers. And industrial policies, as we have seen, come in two broad kinds—functional and sectoral—whose respective impacts also need to be distinguished. In addition to macroeconomic and industrial policies, there are also public goods policies, or what Adam Smith called the three "duties of the sovereign"—defense, law and order, and physical infrastructure. We should further distinguish policies aimed at changing income and asset distributions, whose results then affect the political feasibility of different macropolicies, especially ones for adjusting to economic austerity. The relationships among macroeconomic, industrial, public goods, and distributional policies is best thought of in terms of overlapping circles. The effects of one set are highly contingent upon the effects of the others. In particular, macroeconomic fiscal and monetary policies affect the general thrust of government economic actions toward growth and competitiveness vis-à-vis consumption and redistribution, and so have an important bearing on both the speed and composition of industrial growth.[18]

To assess the impact of industry-specific policies, one obvious method would be to take a number of industries and examine case by case the connection between promotion measures and subsequent growth. But the problems

[18] For example, Scott 1985.

include holding other things constant between high-assistance and low-assistance industries; commensurating different types of assistance (e.g., subsidies, protection, antitrust exemptions); and obtaining information on promotional measures which are not contained in financial disbursements or legal directives (such as the "announcement effect" of loans from the Japan Development Bank on the direction of commercial bank lending, which enables the Japan Development Bank to influence credit allocation with only a small amount of lending). Then there is the problem of interpretation: if industries which receive a lot of assistance grow more slowly than those which do not, does this indicate the failure of assistance or does it indicate targeting of industries that need assistance as a condition of subsequent fast growth? And always one needs to make an assumption about what would have happened in the absence of government help. Even for as nicely specific a policy as performance requirements on foreign direct investment (such as export ratios, local content conditions, requirements for ownership, and employment based on national origin) it has proved impossible to answer the question of how the requirements affect trade and investment. Assumptions have to be made about what other countries do when one country raises or lowers its performance requirements. The requirements may be redundant in that investors would meet them anyway or they may not be enforced.[19]

Again, take selective credit policies, used by many governments to steer resources into certain uses. In order to be effective, selective credit policies have to cause a net increase in credit to the priority use, and this net increase has to bring about a reallocation of real resources. To cause a net increase, the government or the central bank has either effectively to control and monitor the behavior of financial institutions or provide them with incentives to raise lending for the priority use. To bring about a change in resource allocation, the priority borrowers should not simply substitute cheap credit through the concessional scheme for more expensive credit which they would have obtained without the scheme, without altering their production plans. Finally, the effectiveness of selective credit needs to be weighed against the costs, in terms of the effects on other participants in financial markets of raising the extra revenue needed to pay for the subsidy. Obtaining information on these three sets of conditions for success is difficult, to put it mildly.[20]

Even if studies of selective intervention showed effectiveness at the industry level, they would still leave open the question of whether the population as a whole would have been better off in welfare terms developing industries other than those particular ones. There is a cost to selective promotion, which is the cost of diverting resources from currently profitable production (e.g., textiles) to production that *might* be profitable in the future (e.g., sophisticated elec-

[19] See Guisinger 1986:170.
[20] See Ghamen and Rajaram 1987, for Korea and Tunisia.

tronics). Industry optimality does not establish national optimality, and national optimality may be defined not only in terms of present or future consumption but also in terms of the competitive strength of national industries in relation to other countries. It is tempting to use aggregate production function analysis to estimate the extent of "national" optimality, with the size of the residuals indicating the maximum possible extent of the government's contribution. The problem is that the size of the residuals depends on how the production function is specified, which is a matter of very subjective judgment. The "national" issue can be got at another way, by comparing countries which in many important respects are similar but where the role of government has been significantly different (Japan and Italy in the postwar period, for example [Boltho 1981]). The hazards are obvious.

Faced with the manifold difficulties in determining the economic effects of government attempts to steer the market, we can use more indirect evidence to take the debate forward.

First, we can establish the extent to which the key neoclassical growth conditions have been present over time: to what extent trade has been free, the exchange rate in equilibrium, the labor market competitive, and interest rates high enough to reflect the real scarcity of capital. In other words, we can assess the degree of price "distortions" in different product and factor markets. The neoclassical (both FM and SM) presumption is that the lower these distortions, the faster the growth; so high-growth East Asia should show low distortions.

Second, we can get evidence of sectoral industrial policies by examining the histories of particular industries to see what kinds of activity the government was undertaking. We need to know how much control it exercised over investment decisions, and to what extent it was responsible for taking initiatives about products or production processes that private firms would not have undertaken at about the same time without assistance. The GM theory leads us to expect big followership or big leadership in some important industries.

Third, if the government is to exercise leadership it must have instruments for affecting investment decisions. The instruments might include trade controls, foreign exchange controls, export incentives, selective credit allocation, tax incentives, public enterprises, as well as other means of punishing firms that do not comply. Such instruments are needed for getting prices "wrong" and in other ways altering market behavior. If we do not find such instruments we can discount claims that the government has an important role. Of course it is not enough to establish that the instruments exist; they may exist on paper only, or they may dedicate only a trivial amount of resources, or they may entail too little change in costs and prices to have a resource-pulling effect. By looking at the "input" side we can get some sense of whether it is plausible to say that the policies have significant effects on the "output" side. The GM theory leads us to expect substantial variation between industries in the effects of government policies on relative prices, corresponding to the objectives of government promotional activity.

Fourth, we also have to be able to identify the institutional locus of the instruments—one or more central agencies vested with the powers to plan and coordinate within parts of the economy and with some responsibility for industrial success. Likewise we should find evidence of national goal-setting, going beyond the practice of Anglo-American economies and the principles of neoclassical economics, with goals relating substantively to industrial structure and international competitiveness as well as to macroeconomic balance, adequate market infrastructure, and "fair" competition.

Finally, the configuration of agencies, national goals, and industrial policy instruments is likely to be more effective where political power is relatively unified, and unified around groups of people who are committed to industrialization. This is what the GM theory predicts. If instead we find that political power is distributed in a pluralistic or fragmented way, with different constellations of domestic and foreign interest groups exerting pressure on different public policy issues, *or* if we find that political power is unified around groups of people whose interests are hostile to industrialization, then whatever the government claims to be the case we can discount the argument that its planning and coordination have helped industrialization. Relatedly, the evidence for the GM theory is stronger insofar as we can show why the "needs of political survival" are in line with the "needs of productive investment" rather than opposed—or why the political leaders do *not* adopt a Marcos- or Mobutu-like strategy of plundering the Treasury and pulverizing state-implementing agencies in disregard of the consequences for economic development. This involves the political calculations that shape industrial policies.

And that, roughly, is the sequence of chapters 3 to 9. Chapter 10 then brings information and argument from these earlier chapters together with material from Korea, Japan, and Hong Kong to address the question of how important governing the market has been in capitalist East Asia. Chapter 11 goes on to ask what lessons might be drawn from the East Asian experience for development strategy in other developing countries.

But before all this, we need to examine economic performance in East Asia, particularly Taiwan's. How good has it been?

Chapter 2

THE RISE OF EAST ASIA

THE RISE of East Asia is one of the biggest stories of the twentieth century. In the quarter-century that began in 1960 Japan grew just under 7 percent a year. The "little tigers" of Taiwan, Korea, Hong Kong, and Singapore grew at more than 8 percent. America and the European Economic Community (EEC) countries grew at 3 percent. Over the 1980s Japan slowed to 4 percent, but the little tigers rushed on at around 7 percent. Sustained for some time, such differences in growth rates make for huge changes in the relative position of nations. Between 1962 and 1986 Taiwan jumped from eighty-fifth to thirty-eighth in per capita GNP, while Korea jumped from ninety-ninth to forty-fourth, leapfrogging such other newly industrialized countries (NICs) as Mexico and Brazil (table 2.1). Hong Kong and Singapore have long been much richer than the other two, with per capita incomes two-and-a-half times Taiwan's in 1962 and twice as high today.

Of course, in terms of population and national income Hong Kong and Singapore are minuscule—gnats, not tigers. With eight million people they account for 0.17 percent of world population and 0.4 percent of world income. Even Taiwan and Korea, with 59 million people, account for only 1.28 percent of world population and 1.5 percent of world income (table 2.2).

But in terms of manufactured exports the four loom much larger—nearly 8 percent of world markets compared to Mexico's 0.4 percent, though Mexico is next door to the world's biggest market and East Asia is six thousand miles away. They produce over half of developing country manufactured exports. Taiwan, Korea, and Hong Kong each produce more manufactured exports than the whole of Latin America. Taiwan is now the tenth and Korea the thirteenth biggest exporter of manufactures in the world. Taiwan and Korea use 5.4 percent of world market economies' consumption of copper, a basic industrial ingredient—more than Brazil and Mexico combined. They are beginning to be a presence in world production of integrated circuits, the building blocks of the new electronics technology, accounting for 2.3 percent in 1987 and growing very fast, while Brazil and Mexico are insignificant (see table 2.2).

The East Asian five are much addicted to the American market. Japan sends one-third to two-fifths or more of its exports there, making it the United States' biggest supplier of manufactures (as of 1986). The four send roughly half of their exports there. Taiwan is its fourth biggest supplier of manufactures, Korea the fifth, Hong Kong ninth, and Singapore eleventh (table 2.3). On the

TABLE 2.1
GNP per Capita, Levels and Country Ranks (US$)

	1962		1986	
	Rank	Amount	Rank	Amount
Taiwan	Zaire 85 Congo, PR	$170	Greece 38 Malta	$3,580
Korea	Sudan 99 Mauritania	$110	Surinam 44 Argentina	$2,372
Hong Kong	Spain 40 Malta	$450	Saudi Arabia 28 Israel	$6,906
Singapore	Greece 38 Spain	$490	New Zealand 25 Bahamas	$7,411
Japan	French Polynesia 30 Argentina	$610	Sweden 11 Denmark	$12,838
China	Bangladesh 118 Burma	$60	Sudan 110 Zambia	$299
Mexico	Libya 51 Belize	$340	Uruguay 52 Malaysia	$1,839
Brazil	El Salvador 67 Iraq	$240	Fiji 55 South Africa	$1,811
United States	— 1 Canada	$3,095	Switzerland 2 Luxembourg	$17,475
Total number of countries with GNP per capita	129		135	

Source: World Bank Atlas data, except for Taiwan (the Bank does not publish any data on Taiwan). The Taiwan figures were obtained using a method consistent with the Atlas method.

Note: The countries in each cell are those above and below the given rank. The World Bank Atlas methodology is not always consistent from year to year. Figures for as early as 1962 carry an especially large margin of error.

TABLE 2.2

Population, GDP, Exports, Copper Consumption, and Integrated Circuit Production

| | 1982 Population[a] | | Gross Domestic Product (US$), Share[b] | | Manufactured Exports[c] | | | | Refined Copper Consumption, | Integrated Circuit Production | |
| | | | | | 1965 | | 1986 | | 1986, Share[d] | 1987, Share[e] | 1988/1987 (%)[f] |
	Absolute	Share	1965	1986	Rank	Share	Rank	Share			
Taiwan	18.7	0.41	0.2	0.7	28	0.2	10	2.6	2.52	0.52	43
Korea	40.0	0.87	0.2	0.8	33	0.1	13	2.3	2.86	1.89	62
Hong Kong	5.3	} 0.17	0.2	0.4	14	1.1	12	2.3	n.a.	n.a.	
Singapore	2.5				24	0.4	17	1.1	n.a.	n.a.	
Japan	119.3	2.60	5.3	15.4	4	8.2	2	14.9	16.53	40.82	34
Mexico	75.1	1.64	1.2	1.0	29	0.2	30	0.4	0.97	insigt.	n.a.
Brazil	129.7	2.83	1.1	1.6	30	0.1	20	0.7	3.30	insigt.	n.a.
United States	233.7	5.10	41.2	33.0	1	19.0	3	11.9	27.24	49.32	24

Sources: Col. 1, UN Statistical Yearbook 1982; Taiwan Statistical Data Book (TSDB) 1986; col. 2, World Bank, World Development Report 1988 (TSDB 1987); col. 3, World Bank, World Development Report 1988 (TSDB 1987); col. 4, World Bureau of Metal Statistics, World Metal Statistics 1988, Apr; col. 5, Integrated Circuit Engineering Corp., Mid-Term 1988.

a Absolute population in millions; share is of whole world.

b Excludes the Soviet Union and most other communist countries, but includes China. OECD figures in constant prices give somewhat different shares; see OECD 1988.

c See also GATT 1987; International Trade Report 86–87. China ranked fifteenth in 1986 with 1.5 percent.

d Excludes Soviet bloc and China.

e World market economies plus China; companies' production counted by country of headquarters. Taiwan foundry's production counted under Taiwan.

f Forecast mid-1988.

TABLE 2.3
Country Ranks in U.S. Market (United States as Importer), Manufactured Goods

	1962	1986
Taiwan	Portugal 21 South Africa	Germany 4 Korea
Korea	Bermuda 40 Egypt	Taiwan 5 Great Britain
Hong Kong	Switzerland 9 India	Italy 9 France
Singapore	Costa Rica 70 Indonesia	France 11 Sweden
Japan	Canada 2 Germany	— 1 Canada
China	New Caledonia 92 Qatar	Brazil 14 Switzerland
Mexico	Sweden 13 Philippines	Great Britain 7 Italy
Brazil	Argentina 29 Poland	Sweden 13 China

Source: UN Statistical Office, Commodity Trade Data File.

Note: The number of countries considered for this table is 201, including the Soviet Union.

other hand, their imports from America have been much lower, leading to chronic bilateral trade surpluses. They have bought more from Japan than Japan has bought from them, resulting in large deficits. Roughly speaking, the four import capital and intermediate goods from Japan to produce final goods for America. But the huge revaluation of the Japanese yen against the U.S. dollar which began in 1985 is making for fundamental changes in these flows. The four are exporting more to Japan, and Japan's trade surplus with the United States has finally started (in 1988) to decline. The United States continues to apply strong pressure on Taiwan and Korea to open their markets for U.S. goods and services, to some avail.

TAIWAN

Taiwan's 19 million people enjoyed an average income of US$3,600 in 1986, about the same as Greece.[1] Portugal, Brazil, Mexico, and Malaysia are much lower—all having been much higher in 1962. China's is one-tenth or less (see table 2.1).

Real gross national product (GNP) grew at an average of 8.8 percent between 1953 and 1986, population at 2.6 percent, and per capita GNP at 6.2 percent. If we assume that per capita GDP grows at 5 percent a year from 1980 to 2000, while Italy's grows at 1.9 percent and Great Britain's at 1.6 percent, Taiwan will have the same average income as Italy and Great Britain by the end of the century.[2]

Fast economic growth has been accompanied by unusually equal income distribution. Income distribution is more equal than in Japan, Korea, or the United States, and much more equal than in the typical developing country. Taiwan had by far the most equal income distribution in a sixteen-country comparison based on data from the late 1960s and early 1970s and using total disposable household income net of taxes. It was followed by Sri Lanka and Yugoslavia, with Korea fifth (Sen 1981:310).

Real earnings in manufacturing increased at 15 percent a year between 1960 and 1980. Unemployment dropped from around 4 percent throughout the 1950s and first half of the 1960s, to under 2 percent in practically all years from 1968 to 1982.[3] Almost all households in 1982 had electricity, televisions, refrigerators, and motorcycles, while two-thirds had piped water, telephones and washing machines.[4]

Trends in life expectancy, literacy, and population growth are equally striking. Between 1960 and 1977 Taiwan, together with Hong Kong, showed more improvement in both life expectancy and literacy than all other cases in a sample of one hundred developing countries, both capitalist and communist (Sen 1981). By 1982 life expectancy at birth was seventy-five years for women and seventy years for men. Virtually all primary-school-aged children went to school, almost all of them went on to junior high school, and 80 percent of

---

[1] More statistics on Taiwan's economy are available in Ho 1978; Kuznets 1979; Galli 1980; Hou 1987; Wheeler and Wood 1987; CEPD's *Taiwan Statistical Data Book* (TSDB); and DGBAS's *Statistical Yearbook of the Republic of China*. The latter two are the source of most of the figures in this chapter except where otherwise noted.

[2] Based on Klein 1986, who uses Summers and Heston (1984) for 1980 income figures. The starting points (in US$ at 1975 prices) are: Taiwan, $2,522; Italy, $4,661; Great Britain, $4,990. Korea's is $2,007, which would have to grow at 6.1 percent to catch up.

[3] These unemployment figures are based on the number who register as unemployed. Since registering brings few benefits, the figures are biased downwards. However, the evidence of one's eyes and reports from businesspeople are sufficient to show that real unemployment must be very low. Taipei has virtually no able-bodied beggars, in contrast to Washington, D.C.

[4] DGBAS, 1986, *Social Indicators of the Republic of China 1985*.

senior high school graduates went on to schools of higher education. Population growth dropped from 3.5 percent in 1953–62, to 2.9 percent in 1963–72, to 1.9 percent in 1973–82. By 1986 it was down to 1.2 percent.

One useful cross-country indicator of hardship is the number of hours it takes an unskilled male to earn enough to buy 100 kilograms of the staple food grain. In western Europe after A.D. 1400 unskilled male wages rarely fell so low as to cross the 200-hour line. Generalizing from western European experience Fernand Braudel says, "It is always serious when the 100-hours-for-one-quintal line is crossed; to cross the 200 is a danger signal; 300 is famine" (1981:134). In France, from the beginning of the twentieth century to 1920, the figure fell from about 65 to 40 hours. In Taiwan, the figure remained in the range of 150 to 200 hours for one quintal of rice during the 1950s and early 1960s; by 1970 it was down to 70 to 120 hours; by 1980, to 40 to 70 hours, or about the same as France in 1900–20 (table 2.4).The material conditions of life, even for the unskilled, have been transformed in a single generation.

This transformation in material living conditions rests on a transformation of the economy's relations with the rest of the world. Already by 1979 Taiwan was the biggest developing country exporter of manufactures to OECD (Organization for Economic Cooperation and Development). Between 1979 and 1984 its share rose from 17 to 21 percent, while Korea's fell from 16 to 15 percent (*OECD Observer* 1986).

These exports include not only textiles and clothes, but also radio and television sets, cassette recorders, electronic calculators, sewing machines, car parts, machine tools, and personal computers. Industrial products now make up 90 percent of total exports. Yet as late as 1955 exports were 85 percent agricultural or processed agricultural products, based mostly on rice and sugar. If trade dependence is measured by exports plus imports against GDP, Taiwan has become about the most trade dependent country in the world, excluding Hong Kong, Singapore, and some small petroleum exporters. The ratio has averaged 90 percent since 1980, up from 72 percent in 1972 and 32 percent in 1962.

Macroeconomic stability is remarkable, even astonishing. The transformation from a minor to a major trading nation, from an agricultural to an industrial economy, has occurred within twenty-five years without inflation, fiscal crises, periodic doses of stabilization programs, or high levels of foreign debt. The country has suffered no recession over the past thirty-five years, other than the oil-crisis-induced slumps of 1974–75 and 1981–82. Inflation has been modest, below 10 percent a year in all but eight years between 1953 and 1986, averaging 7.6 percent in 1953–62, 1.8 percent in 1963–72, and 6.7 percent in 1973–86. The current account of the balance of payments was unsurprisingly in deficit throughout the 1950s and 1960s, but turned positive in 1970 and remained positive every year since then up to 1988, with the exception, again, of 1973–74 and 1980. The debt service ratio has been a mere 5 percent or less.

TABLE 2.4
Hours to Earn Equivalent of 100 kg of Rice

Employees in	1952–54	1960–62	1970–72	1980–82
Textile mill, both sexes, wage earners, and others	174	211	119	66
Electricity, gas, and water, both sexes, wage earners only	150	152	73	39
Building construction, male wage earners	—	—	70[a]	57

Source: Rice price (retail, polished, Taipei city)—*Taiwan Food Statistics Book 1985*, Food Bureau, Taiwan Provincial Government: table 17. Average monthly earnings (including overtime)—*Yearbook of Labor Statistics, ROC, 1987*, DGBAS: tables 73, 75, 76; *Monthly Bulletin of Earnings and Productivity Statistics, Taiwan Area, ROC*, Dec. 1987, DGBAS: table 23. Average monthly hours of work—*Yearbook of Labor Statistics* (as above): tables 44, 51, 53, 54.

Notes:

1. The results are sensitive to the average monthly hours of work, on which the data is lacking, especially before 1976. Electricity, gas, and water employees are the only category with numbers going back to 1966. I simply guessed about hours of work before then. The sequence for the years covered by the table is: 200 hours for 1950–52, 210 for 1960–62, then for 1970 and beyond, 220, 228, 214, 210, 205, 200. For textile mill employees I used the manufacturing average for 1970–72 and guessed the rest, the sequence being: 1950–52, 215, 1960–62, 215, then for 1970 and beyond, 229, 227, 226, 220, 220, 217. For building construction workers average monthly working days are available but not hours of work. Based on trends in hours per day which can be calculated for 1966–76 for electricity, gas, and water workers, I assumed 9.5 hrs./day for 1976–78, and 9 hrs. for 1980–82, which works out to around 240 hours per month in the first period, 223 in the second.

2. Employees in electricity, gas, and water are public sector employees, and although the wage-earning employees are relatively unskilled they have been given some degree of protection from market fluctuations.

3. Braudel uses the wages of a plasterer's laborer as his denominator. The equivalent in Taiwan would probably be paid less than the averages used in the table. Only very rough comparisons between these figures and Braudel's can be made. The U. S. figure in the mid-1980s, using the legal minimum wage and the price of flour, is fifteen hours.

[a] For the years 1976–78.

While the developing world as a whole stagnated in the early 1980s following the second oil crisis, Taiwan's real GNP grew by 5.5 percent in 1981, 3.8 percent in 1982, and 7.1 percent in 1983. The year 1982 was the trough, when industrial production actually fell 1.8 percent, industrial capacity utilization declined to as low as 75 percent, and unemployment doubled to over 2 percent. But 1983 saw a strong recovery, with industrial production growing at 12.8 percent, wages at 10.4 percent, inflation at less than one percent, while the trade surplus hit US$5 billion. Even in the worst year, 1982, the balance of trade remained in surplus (see table 5.1). In the first half of the 1980s, while other newly industrialized countries struggled with debt and forced import cutbacks, the government of Taiwan worried about the country's excessively large foreign exchange reserves and a lack of demand for imports of higher-technology capital goods.

The government also worried about Taiwan's growing trade imbalance with Japan and the United States. From the beginning, Japan and the United States have been Taiwan's biggest trading partners by far, together supplying half or more of Taiwan's commodity imports and taking about half of exports. It has run large deficits in trade with Japan and large surpluses with the United States (table 2.5). As protectionist pressures have risen in the United States over the 1980s, the government of Taiwan has become concerned to find ways to reduce the trade surplus by exporting to other markets and switching from Japanese to U.S. sources of supply.

By the mid-1980s the onrush of Taiwanese wealth became still more hectic. With the fall in the price of oil and the rise of the Japanese yen, Taiwan became supercompetitive. Real GNP surged by almost 11 percent in 1986, and the volume of exports increased by almost a quarter. At the same time, investment collapsed, relatively speaking: gross domestic investment fell from 33 percent of GDP in 1980 to 18 percent in 1985 (less than the U.S.), signalling slower growth in the future. As Taiwan's foreign exchange reserves soared to become the second biggest in the world after Japan's by 1987,[5] pressures mounted to liberalize stringent foreign exchange controls that had been in place for almost four decades. Removal of most of the exchange controls in 1987 was a milestone in Taiwan's development. It signalled, long after the event, that Taiwan has moved so far from the normal condition of underdevelopment that it can generate sufficient export earnings to cover all expected demands for foreign exchange.

TABLE 2.5
Taiwan's Commodity Trade with Japan and the United States (%)

	Exports to			Imports from			Two-Way Trade		
	Japan	United States	Other	Japan	United States	Other	Japan	United States	Other
1960	38	12	50	35	38	27	36	29	35
1970	15	38	47	43	24	33	29	31	40
1980	11	34	55	27	24	49	19	29	52
1984	11	49	40	29	23	48	18	38	44

Source: TSDB 1985: table 10.10.

[5] The Economist, 27 June 1987. In US$billion, Japan had 63, Taiwan 60, West Germany 56, followed a long way back by France, 29. Taiwan's are by far the biggest per capita.

KOREA

South Korea's performance has also been impressive, though the country trails Taiwan in prosperity; per capita income in 1986 was US$2,400—two-thirds of Taiwan's US$3,600. If Taiwan suddenly stopped growing, it would take South Korea six to ten years to catch up. And while South Korean income distribution is about equal to the United States', Taiwan's is a good deal more equal—which is why Seoul seems to the Western eye more affluent than Taipei, Taiwan's capital, which still looks like a mix of shanty town and transit camp. Moreover, South Korea produces its lower level of per capita production with more effort: its manufacturing workers average fifty-nine hours a week, while their Taiwanese counterparts put in fifty-one hours.[6] (Nevertheless, anyone in Taiwan who works an average of less than forty-four hours a week is officially classed as a "part-time worker." One of the most vivid of all statistics about Taiwan is the one which shows rather few part-time workers, and the same applies, only more so, to Korea.) Korean life expectancy at birth is far below Taiwan's; in 1977, sixty-three years against Taiwan's seventy-two years (World Bank, *World Development Report 1979*). Korea's inflation rate has been higher than Taiwan's—15 percent a year between 1965 and 1981 against Taiwan's 8 percent. Taiwan's rate is about the same as the United States' and Japan's, while Korea's is higher than for any of the industrialized countries though lower than for Latin America. Figure 2.1 shows the rate of inflation in the two countries over time and the much more stable growth of real output in Taiwan.

INDUSTRIAL TRANSFORMATION

If Taiwan and Korea were plausibly called "export platforms" in the 1960s— importing capital and intermediate goods, adding further processing with cheap labor, then exporting—they have subsequently become highly integrated economies, moving speedily into high-wage, high-technology activities. Their industrialization has been extraordinarily "compressed." They achieved in fifteen years what took Japan twenty-five years and Great Britain over fifty years. And Korea followed Taiwan's path of structural transformation "with an eight-year lag explained entirely by the different income levels" (Kim and Roemer 1979, speaking of pre-1975).

Several indicators can be used to show the speed and timing of industrial transformation in Taiwan. Consider, first, the relationship between industry and agriculture:

> Gross industrial production (manufacturing, mining, construction, utilities) first exceeded agricultural production in 1963.

[6] Scitovsky 1986 is a valuable source for Taiwan–Korea comparisons.

FIGURE 2.1
Taiwan and South Korea: Consumer Price Inflation and
Growth of Real Output, 1951–83

(in percent)

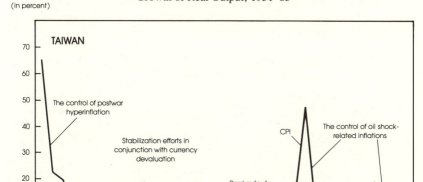

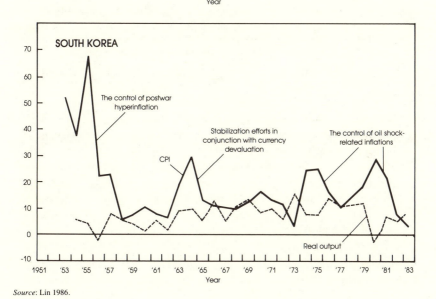

Source: Lin 1986.

Industrial exports first exceeded agricultural exports in 1966.

The absolute size of the agricultural labor force first declined in 1966.

The number of people employed in industry first exceeded the number in agriculture in 1973—which can therefore be taken as the end year in the transition to an industrial economy (Oshima 1986).[7]

Take next the share of manufacturing in GDP. In 1960 Taiwan was below average for the upper middle-income countries, at 22 percent. By 1985, it was well above average, at 29 percent (having been much higher again in the interim; see table 2.6).

The share of chemicals and machinery in total manufacturing is an indicator of industrial "depth" or "roundaboutness" in production. Table 2.7 traces this variable across time for Taiwan and Korea. In Taiwan the share of manufacturing production coming from these two sectors increased from 24 percent in 1961 to 50 percent only thirteen years later. Note for future reference that the share increased much faster in Taiwan than in Korea over the 1960s and early 1970s. Table 2.8 gives the aggregate share of "heavy" and "light" industry for both countries.

A more aggregate measure of industrial "depth" is given by the ratio of

TABLE 2.6
Share of Manufacturing in GDP

	Manufacturing as a Share of GDP (%)	
	1960	1983
Taiwan	22	29[a]
Korea	14	30
Japan	34	30[a]
Mexico	19	26
Brazil	26	28
United States	29	20
Average for upper middle- income countries	25	25
Average for industrialized market countries	30	23[a]

Source: World Bank, *World Development Report 1984, 1985, 1986*; TSDB 1986.
Note: Averages are weighted.
[a] 1985.

[7] The birth rate began to fall in about 1964, but not steadily.

TABLE 2.7

Industrial Deepening—Chemicals and Machinery in Total
Industrial Output, Taiwan and South Korea
(% of Value-added, Current Prices)

ISIC Code	Sectors	Country	1954	1961	1970	1974	1978	1982
35	Chemicals, petrochemicals, and rubber products	Taiwan	14.7	14.6	21.8	26.2	27.0	21.1
		Korea	9.7	10.4	18.1	20.2	19.6	20.8
38	Metal products, machinery, electrical machinery, transportation equipment	Taiwan	7.5	9.7	20.4	24.0	24.8	26.1
		Korea	9.8	12.4	14.4	18.8	14.9	19.6
35 + 38		Taiwan	22.2	24.3	42.2	50.2	51.8	47.2
		Korea	19.5	22.8	32.5	39.0	44.5	40.4

Source: Bank of Korea, National Income Accounts; Galli 1980: table 9; DGBAS, Statistical Yearbook of the Republic of China.

TABLE 2.8

Light and Heavy Industry, Share of Manufacturing in Taiwan
and Korea, 1965–84

	Country	1965	1971	1975	1981	1984
Light industry	Taiwan	51.2	50.7	46.7	43.4	41.5
	Korea	61.8	54.7	51.6	47.2	43.2
Heavy industry	Taiwan	49.8	49.3	53.3	56.6	58.5
	Korea	38.2	45.3	48.4	52.8	56.8

Source: Chi Schive 1986, based on Scitovsky 1986; TSDB, Major Statistics of Korean Economy.
Note: Light industry includes food, beverages and tobacco; textiles, clothing, and footwear; wood and wood products; printing, paper, and paper products; and miscellaneous. Heavy industry includes chemicals, petroleum, coal; nonmetallic mineral products; metals and metal products; and machinery, equipment, and fabricated metal products.

intermediate demand to total manufacturing output. Table 2.9 shows the rate of growth over ten-year periods in this ratio for Taiwan, Korea, Japan, and six other countries. Taiwan has by far the fastest rate of deepening, followed by Korea.

A related indicator is the change in the ratio of value added in light industry to value added in heavy industry (the Hoffman ratio). Taiwan and Korea moved from 4 to 1 in the space of about fifteen years, Taiwan reaching 1 around 1971, a few years ahead of Korea. Japan covered the same distance in twenty-five years (1910–35). Just to move from 2 to 1 took Great Britain, the

46 CHAPTER 2

TABLE 2.9
Industrial Deepening—Ratio of Intermediate Demand to Total
Manufacturing Output (% Rate of Change per Ten Years)

Taiwan	(1956–71)	10.0
Korea	(1955–73)	6.1
Colombia	(1953–70)	4.4
Japan	(1955–72)	4.2
Israel	(1958–72)	4.2
Yugoslavia	(1962–72)	3.1
Mexico	(1950–75)	2.8
Turkey	(1953–73)	2.0
Norway	(1953–69)	1.4

Source: Kubo, et al. 1986: table 7.1.

United States, and Germany between forty-five and fifty-five years (Watanabe 1985:98).

These changes in the mix of light and heavy industry have been accompanied by equally dramatic changes in the export mix. The composition of exports can be used to show how an economy is changing its "comparative advantage"—changing the industries in which it is most worthwhile to specialize in international trade. Machinery is a crucial sector for this purpose, for it typically develops quite late in a country's industrialization and is associated with relatively high-wage and high-technology production processes. In the decade from 1956–61 to 1966–71, the share of machinery (including electrical machinery and transport equipment) increased from about 4 percent of manufactured exports to 23 percent in Taiwan. Korea had a similar but smaller spurt, from 5 percent to 20 percent (de Melo 1985: fig. 9.2, Korea—1955–63 to 1970–73). Japan also had a machinery spurt, from 14 percent of manufactured exports in the early 1950s to 39 percent ten years later.

Indeed all the gang of four as well as Japan have been gaining world market share in the higher-technology industries, while losing share at the lower-technology end (table 2.10). This is just what the development process is supposed to entail. During the course of industrialization countries are supposed to abandon old products or processes and move on to new higher value-added activities, leaving production of the older products to move offshore to countries with cheaper wages. Those countries in turn are supposed to abandon their earlier leading products as the ones cast off from the more industrialized countries start up. But table 2.10 also suggests that the older industrial countries

TABLE 2.10
Gains in Export Market Share, East Asia Compared to
Old Industrialized Economies

	Sectors Ranked by Technology Intensity	
	Of top 20, number in which gained share	*Of bottom 20, number in which gained share*
Gang of Four	15	7
Japan	12	2
United States	5	13
Great Britain	7	13
Germany	4	14

Source: Based on Scott 1985a.

Note: Table reads: In a fifty-seven-sector ranking according to technology intensity (R&D spending as a proportion of U.S. sales in 1967–70), the East Asian gang of four (Taiwan, South Korea, Singapore, and Hong Kong) gained export market share between 1967 and 1981 in fifteen of the top twenty sectors, and gained in seven of the bottom twenty sectors. Note that export market share gives a misleading impression of U.S. performance, because the size of the U.S. economy makes exports less important for most U.S. producers. Share of world production would be more accurate.

are gaining market share more at the low end than at the high end. What happens to our understanding of the development process when the older industrialized countries are being beaten in the top end of the economy? What is it about Japan and the gang of four that allows them to reap the outcomes predicted by the theory while the Western industrialized countries do not? With respect to the gang of four, "the pattern is almost more striking than Japan's. . . . It is possible that in another decade a dramatic thrust toward higher technology exports and formidable competition from these newcomers will affect all the older industrial countries" (Scott 1985: 93).

Part of the answer—to anticipate—is that the four plus Japan have for a long time been investing much more of their national product than the mature industrialized countries. Taiwan averaged 28.4 percent of GNP between 1965 and 1980, Korea averaged 26.5 percent (Scitovsky 1986; and table 2.11). These are among the highest rates of capital formation in the world over such an extended period. Japan's were even higher.

DEVELOPMENT STYLES

Over the 1950s and 1960s Japan underwent the same kind of economic transformation as Taiwan and Korea during the 1960s and 1970s, accompanied by

TABLE 2.11
Gross Domestic Investment as a Share of Gross Domestic Product

	1960	1965	1970	1975	1980	1985
			(Percentage of GDP)			
Middle-income countries						
Taiwan	20	23	26	31	33	18
Korea	11	15	25	27	31	30
Hong Kong	18	36	24	24	29	21
Singapore	11	22	39	40	43	43
Malaysia	14	18	22	25	29	28
Mexico	20	22	21	22	28	21
Brazil	22	25	21	27	23	(16)
Industrial market economies						
Japan	33	32	39	33	32	28
United States	19	20	18	17	18	19
Germany	27	28	27	20	25	20
Austria	28	28	30	26	29	24
Great Britain	19	20	21	18	16	17

Source: World Bank, World Development Report, various issues; World Bank data files; Taiwan Statistical Data Book, 1986 (figure in parenthesis is for another year).

similarly high rates of GNP growth. In the first half of the 1950s nearly half of the Japanese labor force was engaged primarily on the land, another large part was in low-productivity tertiary activities, and manufacturing productivity barely reached 15 percent of the U.S. level (Boltho 1975:22). It had earlier, of course, been economically strong enough to support a formidable military machine, and even by 1950 it was the world's twentieth biggest exporter, far ahead of Taiwan and Korea in 1962. But the magnitude of its further transformation is suggested by its jump to third largest exporter by 1970, twenty years later. What is more, the "style" of Japan's development closely resembles Taiwan's and Korea's in contrast to the style of the United States and Latin America. This is suggested by the kites in figures 2.2 and 2.3. The kites measure development style along four dimensions: consumption pattern (indicated by density of passenger cars per thousand population in 1980); income equality (ratio of the income of the poorest 40 percent of the population to that of

FIGURE 2.2
Profiles: Japan and the United States

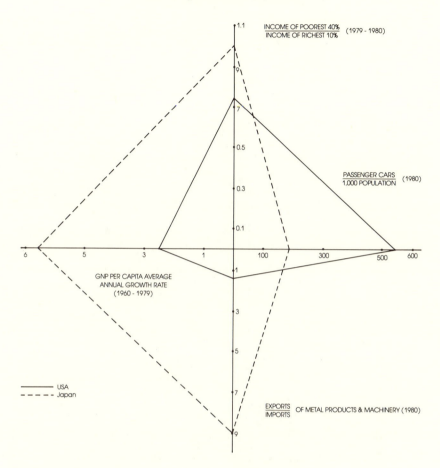

Source: Fajnzylber 1986.
Note: Metal Products & Machinery, ISIC 38.

the richest 10 percent between 1970 and 1980);[8] international competitiveness (ratio of exports to imports in the metal products and machinery sector, 1979–80); and long-term dynamism (average annual growth rate of GDP per capita between 1960 and 1979). The kites for Japan, Taiwan, and Korea are similar: all three show high dynamism, high international competitiveness, low ine-

[8] The income distribution figures must be taken as rough orders of magnitude only. They are based on disposable household income rather than individual income. If the latter had been used, Japan and the United States would be more equal. See World Bank, *World Development Report 1985*, technical notes.

FIGURE 2.3

Profiles: Taiwan, Korea, Mexico, and Argentina

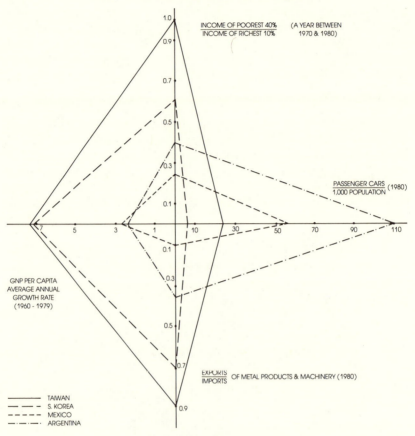

Source: Fajnzylber 1986; DGBAS 1985; Statistical Year Book, DGBAS, 1981; Report on the Survey of Personal Income Distribution.

quality, and relatively austere consumption. The United States and the two Latin American countries show lower dynamism, lower international competitiveness in manufacturing, higher inequality, and exuberant consumption. The causal connections between these indicators are not clear. The diagrams are intended only to suggest that there is indeed, as is often said, a family resemblance between the development style of Taiwan, Korea, and Japan, as well as one between the United States and Latin American countries.

A final word about methods and observation posts. People who write about the Productivity Miracle in East Asia normally dress in suit-and-tie and write from executive suites or university libraries. Reflecting a training in anthropology as well as politics and economics, I spent a lot of time over six months in conversation with government officials, businessmen, and scholars (but little with peasants and workers). Anthropology sanctions an immersion approach to the way that people habitually think and to the way their institutions work in practice. It says that to understand a trade regime you should talk at length to people who trade. The reply from economics is, "Don't take their word for it! Rely on what people do, not what they say—as revealed in the statistics." I tried to combine both approaches. Six months is too short by anthropological standards, especially for a non-Chinese speaker without research assistants. But it is long by the standards of those economists who have done most to define the mechanism of Taiwan's development, most of them foreigners, whose time is typically measured in weeks or days. One distinguished development economist who has written at length on how Taiwan grew rich through applying nearly free market principles, when asked why none of his three visits to Taiwan had exceeded one week, replied, "If I stayed longer I'd just get confused." Exactly so, but it would be a more sophisticated kind of confusion.

Chapter 3

THE NEOCLASSICAL EXPLANATION

VIRTUALLY ALL the economics literature about Taiwan comes from the neo-classical side of the debate.[1] Even non-neoclassicals who recognize that dirigisme was a factor in Korea's development are inclined to think that Taiwan fits the neoclassical prescriptions fairly well (Felix 1987). It is therefore widely agreed that the cause of Taiwan's industrial success is the coming to-gether around 1958–62 of four key conditions: a virtual free trade regime for exporters and a lowering of protection more generally; a free labor market; high interest rates; and conservative government budgeting. "There can be few such clear cases in economic history of cause and effect. . . . Apart from the creation of [these four conditions] . . . it is hard to find any good expla-nation of the sustained industrial boom of 1963–1973" (Little 1979:474, 480).

Throughout the 1950s until about 1958 the government operated an import substitution policy. Then, gradually over several years, it took a number of steps:

1. *Exchange rate*: Between 1958 and 1961 the multiple exchange rate system was dismantled and replaced with a sharply devalued unitary rate, giving a stronger incentive to export sale.
2. *Protection*: Tariffs were reduced and import controls eased.
3. *Export promotion*: In addition to (1) and (2), exports were further encouraged by allowing a rebate on customs duties paid for imported materials used for export production, tax incentives, cheap credit, direct subsidies, and government-spon-sored export promotion and marketing facilities.
4. *Foreign investment*: Foreign investors were granted 100 percent equity holdings, 100 percent remittance of profits, repatriation of initial capital at the rate of 15 percent a year (but no repatriation of capital gains), and equal access with do-mestic producers to investment and export incentives. Tax- and duty-free export-

---

[1] But see the pioneering paper by Amsden 1979. See also the excellent surveys of recent de-velopments in *Far Eastern Economic Review* 1988; and *Financial Times* 1988. Their accounts of recent drastic liberalizations serve to point up the nonliberalized character of the economy in the past. The former survey says, "Throughout [Taiwan's postwar development], the Taiwan Gov-ernment has played an enormous role in the economy—controlling through a combination of direct investment in strategic industries and regulation of exchange rates, business licenses, im-port duties and trade restrictions. The government invested heavily in industries which were too capital-intensive or too risky to attract private investment, such as heavy metals, petrochemicals and power generation. In addition, the underdeveloped financial sector made capital financing unavailable to all but the largest companies. As the major capitalist in Taiwan's economy, the government has thus guided policy by deciding which industries would be developed" (p. 53).

processing zones were established (the first in 1965, two more in 1969), especially to attract foreign investment.

In short, the years from 1958 to 1962 saw a decisive policy shift toward an "outward orientation." The new direction was maintained thereafter. Table 3.1 shows the acceleration in GNP and export growth.

These reforms affected GNP and exports chiefly through prices. In the new environment prices better reflected the real scarcities of tradables and nontradables, and in that sense were less distorted than before. In response, labor-intensive manufactured exports exploded. The home market also grew fast, not only because of exports but also because of the direct impact of the undistorted price environment. Fast export and home market growth created fast growth in employment and real wages, reducing income disparities and almost eliminating poverty. As demand pulled up labor costs, as labor-intensive exports encountered protectionist barriers abroad, and as savings grew, the economy's comparative advantage shifted toward more capital- and technology-intensive activities. Since then, the government's role has been confined largely to improving the infrastructure of the market system and to intensifying the liberalizing reforms began in 1958–62.

Far from being miraculous in terms of mechanism, Taiwan is shown by neoclassicals to be an economically "standard" case. It is standard in the sense that it fits the expectation that any country will experience big improvements in its economic performance if and when it follows the same principles. The many more cases which do not follow the same principles have to be explained in terms of politics or other noneconomic factors.

In what follows we summarize the evidence in support of this neoclassical interpretation,[2] starting with the above four policy elements and continuing with

TABLE 3.1
Annual Growth Rates before and after the Liberalizing Reforms (%)

	Real GNP	Total Exports	Industrial Exports
		(Current Prices, US$)	
1952–57	7.9	4.9	14.5
1957–58	6.6	5.0	17.1
1958–60	7.1	2.6	55.6
1960–63	8.0	26.5	37.0
1963–69	10.2	21.2	33.6

Source: TSDB 1985: tables 3.2b, 10.8.

[2] To talk of the "neoclassical account" of Taiwan is a simplification. Between the interpretations of Ian Little (1979) and Gustav Ranis (1979, 1981), for example, some daylight can be seen. Taiwan could not be mistaken for Hong Kong in Ranis's account. Yet for all the differences

...re that most economists would agree are important for rapid growth; ...eal effective exchange rate, high savings and investment, well-trained ...pply, competitive market structure, and stable government.

FREE TRADE REGIME FOR EXPORTS

If the producers of exports are to enjoy free trade conditions, two conditions must be met.[3] First, they should be able to import inputs into export production (raw materials, intermediates, and capital goods) without quantitative restrictions and tariffs. This allows them to purchase all internationally tradable goods and services at world market prices, or at the same prices as their competitors. If prices for domestically produced tradables exceed world market prices exporters will simply use cheaper imports instead. Second, the exchange rate facing exporters should be equal to the hypothetical free trade rate (that which would exist with all protection measures removed, and still produce the same balance-of-payment surplus or deficit).

After the trade reforms of 1958–62 Taiwan's producers were able to get exemptions or rebates on duties for that portion of their imports which went into goods sold abroad (but they had to pay import duties for that portion of imports used to produce goods sold on the domestic market). The ratio of total tariff exemptions and rebates to total government revenue was 16 percent in 1973 (compared to 1.9 percent in Thailand for the same year; see Sricharaychanya 1982). In the mid-1970s only about half of the total customs duties were being collected, the rest being exempted, rebated, or deferred. As we shall see in chapter 5, there are some qualifications to the proposition that imported inputs for export production did not pay tariffs and other charges, which are important if one's interest is in explaining industrial deepening rather than export growth. But we can agree that the first condition for a free trade regime for exports was largely met.

As for the second condition, the six-country comparison organized by Bela Balassa found that, based on 1969 data, Taiwan had the smallest difference between the official exchange rate and the hypothetical free trade exchange rate; the difference was 4.9 percent in Taiwan, 9.1 percent in Korea, and, at the other extreme, 40.0 percent in Argentina (Balassa, et al. 1982:15, 33).

The small difference between the official exchange rate and the hypothetical free trade exchange rate reflects low average protection. Low average protection means that only a small devaluation of the official exchange rate would be needed to compensate for the removal of all protection (and still have the

---

between individual authors, the family resemblance comes from the emphasis on the self-regulating market and the marginal attention given to government. For other examples, see Fei, Ranis, and Kuo 1979; Galenson 1982; Myers 1986; Myint 1982.

[3] I thank Alan Gelb, Graham Pyatt, and Larry Westphal for discussions on the following argument, though they must not be held responsible for the result.

same balance-of-payment surplus or deficit). Table 3.2 shows that Taiwan's average effective protection to manufacturing in 1969 was about the same as Korea's, and much less than Israel's, Colombia's, and Argentina's. Its protection to agriculture was negative, which is to say that agricultural exports were taxed. Negative protection for agriculture helped to make the economywide average protection even lower than for manufacturing. (In chapter 5, however, I point to serious problems in the method used to make these calculations, which suggest that the real rate of protection may have been substantially higher.)

Still another indicator of the second condition is the difference between the official exchange rate and the "unregulated" (or "curb") market exchange rate. The devaluations between 1958 and 1960—from about NT$25 to NT$40 per US$—brought the difference between the official rate and the unregulated market rate down to 6 or 7 percent. By 1965 that difference had been further reduced to around 4 percent. Subsequently it has rarely been much more than this (Lin 1973).[4]

In short, Taiwan's currency after about 1960 was not seriously overvalued, and exporters could obtain most of their inputs at close to world market prices. Both conditions together mean that exporters face a virtual free trade regime. They do not have to carry costs that would significantly disadvantage them in international competition.

But this condition is not sufficient to insure full "trade neutrality," in the sense of approximately equal incentives for export sale and domestic market sale. Even where exporters can get inputs at world market prices, they may still have a net incentive to sell on the protected domestic market. Table 3.3 shows the difference in incentives to export sale and domestic market sale in the same six countries as before. From row 1 we see that Taiwan's trade bias for manufacturing as a whole was very low in 1969, which is to say that the condition of full trade neutrality was met. Note, finally, that industry-agriculture bias was also small (table 3.2, rows 1 and 2).

Free Labor Market

The labor market in Taiwan is as close to a textbook model of a competitive labor market as one is likely to find. The price of labor has adjusted passively to market conditions of price and productivity.

Three kinds of indicators might be used. First, in terms of institutions: minimum wage legislation, public sector pay policy, multinational companies,

---

[4] The difference between the "unregulated" exchange rate and the official exchange rate is a convenient but imperfect indicator of exchange rate distortion. The exchange rate in the unregulated market is sensitive to such things as the amount of policing, the penalties for being caught, and the demand for the types of goods or services for which unregulated market foreign exchange is sought (likely to be untypical of consumption patterns as a whole).

TABLE 3.2
Incentives in Taiwan's Trade Regime,
Compared to Five Other Countries (%)

	Taiwan	Korea	Singapore	Israel	Colombia	Argentina
Effective protection						
Manufacturing	14	13	4	76	35	112
Agriculture	−4	18	—	48	−14	−13
Effective subsidy						
to manufactured						
exports	9	−14	−7	−17	7	−46
Intersectoral						
dispersion	8	36	2	25	71	38
Effective subsidy						
to manufactures						
for domestic						
market sale	10	14	1	16	28	45
Intersectoral						
dispersion	23	47	7	32	56	35

Source: Balassa 1982a: table 2.3, rows 1–2; rest derived from table 2.6.
Notes:

1. The data are for 1969 except for Korea (1968), Singapore (1967), and Israel (1968).

2. Effective protection measures the extent to which tariffs and quantitative trade restrictions increase the domestic value-added price over the world market value-added price. The figure of 14 percent for Taiwan manufacturing means that the combined effect of Taiwan's tariffs and quantitative restrictions in 1969 was to increase the domestic value-added price of manufactures by 14 percent, on average, above the world market value-added prices of the same items.

3. Effective subsidy is a more comprehensive measure than effective protection. It attempts to factor into the calculation of the domestic value-added price not only the effects of tariffs and quantitative restrictions, but also the effects of as many tax and subsidy schemes as can be measured, such as export credit.

4. The dispersion index refers to the standard deviation from the unweighted manufacturing mean of the seven manufacturing sectors (construction materials, intermediate products I [lower levels of fabrication], intermediates II [higher levels of fabrication], consumer nondurables, consumer durables, machinery, and transport equipment). The averages given in rows 1 and 2 are weighted and come straight from the source; those in rows 3 and 5 are unweighted and differ from those in the source. The problem of bias resulting from high effective subsidy rates for quantitatively insignificant sectors is reduced by the relatively large size of each subsector. Note that had the coefficient of variation rather than the standard deviation been used the results would have shown Taiwan's dispersion to be the same as Colombia's, Korea's as much greater. But the coefficient of variation is a misleading statistic when (as in this comparison) the denominators are not reasonably similar, and in particular gives absurd results as one of the denominators approaches zero. I thank Alan Gelb for making the dispersion calculations and for discussion of the results.

TABLE 3.3
Difference Between Effective Subsidy for Export Sale and for
Domestic Market Sale (%)

	Taiwan	Korea	Singapore	Israel	Colombia	Argentina
All manufacturing industries	4	7	−5	44	−22	−145
By trade orientation Export	12	31	0	−130	10	−91
Import-competing	−46	−61	−3	−88	−76	−190
Export and import-competing	−4	−46	−7	−65	−15	−164
Non-import-competing	21	16	3	−5	−4	−153

Source: Balassa 1982a:table 2.5.

Note: Export industries are those where more than 10 percent of domestic production is exported and less than 10 percent of total consumption is imported. Import-competing industries are those where less than 10 percent of domestic production is exported and more than 10 percent of domestic consumption is imported. Export and import-competing industries are those where more than 10 percent of domestic production is exported and more than 10 percent of domestic consumption is imported. Non-import-competing industries are those where less than 10 percent of domestic production is exported and less than 10 percent of domestic consumption is imported (Balassa 1982b:11–12).

employers' associations, and trade unions have not been intervening elements between the sellers and buyers of labor. Trade unions and other conventional methods of collective bargaining have been weak, partly because of government repression (Galenson 1979; Deyo 1987). Strikes are illegal under martial law, which has prevailed since 1949.

Second, the level of unemployment has been very low since the end of the period of "labor surplus" in 1968–70. The labor market has cleared.

Third, the share of labor in total manufacturing costs has been roughly constant over the period from the early 1960s to the early 1980s. More specifically, real wages have grown at about the same rate as, or slower than, the growth of labor productivity (output per person), except for short inflationary periods in the early and late 1970s. Which is to say, "wage push" has not been important in the level of wages (Lundberg 1979: table 4.11).[5]

These several points suggest a competitive labor market and an "undistorted" wage rate. The trends in labor costs and labor productivity help to explain the competitiveness of Taiwan's export industries and the relative stability of the price level. The flexibility in the labor market has also helped to

[5] The relationship between productivity growth and real wage increases may have changed in the 1980s. Real wages grew at 6.6 percent a year over 1979–84, and productivity at 4.8 percent. Real wage increases were greater than productivity growth over the same period in Korea and Singapore, but not in Hong Kong.

prevent prolonged overvaluation of the currency, and hence has helped to maintain near free trade conditions for exporters.

HIGH INTEREST RATES

Taiwan was one of the first, if not the first developing country, to adopt a high real interest rate policy. The real rate on bank savings deposits was 6 percent or more in virtually all years between 1955 and 1980, except for the high-inflation years of 1973–74 and 1979–80 when it turned negative. It averaged about 9 percent between 1955 and 1964, and about 8 percent between 1965 and 1972.

The high interest rate policy came in response to the hyperinflation of 1946–50, when prices rose by thousands of percent. In early 1950 the government, fearing for its very survival if inflation continued, ordered the banks to offer a rate on one-month deposits of 7 percent a month, or 125 percent a year. Allowing for inflation, this translated into a real rate of between 28 and 82 percent a year. Savings flooded into the banking system: time and savings deposits increased from 1.7 percent of the money supply (currency plus demand deposits) in March 1950 to 7 percent three months later. Price inflation came to a near halt. The government therefore cut the 7 percent monthly rate—which would be intolerable with stable prices—by more than half. Savings flooded in the opposite direction, as an alarmed public concluded that the government was breaking its word on interest rates. Inflation resumed at the rate of 65 percent in 6 months. So the interest rate was raised from a monthly rate of 3 percent to 4.2 percent, and savings returned to the banks. By late 1952 time and savings deposits amounted to 56 percent of the money supply. Prices stabilized (Lin 1973; Tsiang 1982).

With continued price stability, nominal interest rates were lowered over the 1950s. By 1958, the year of the start of the great reforms, nominal rates on time deposits had come down to 13.8 percent per year, giving a real rate of about 9 percent a year. At the same time, the nominal rate on unsecured loans in the "unregulated" money market was about 40 percent per year (Lin 1973: table 4.7).

Nominal interest rates continued to be lowered during the period of the reforms, and real rates came down with them; by 1963 nominal rates on time deposits were about 9 percent a year, and real rates, 5.5 percent, while the loan rates on the unregulated money market continued at around 30 percent a year. Nominal interest rates continued to be lowered slowly over the 1960s and early 1970s, until they were raised again in response to the 1973 oil price-induced inflation.

Nevertheless, both nominal and real rates remained high in Taiwan compared to other countries. In the mid-1960s the real cost of a secured bank loan in Taiwan was about 11 percent and the nominal cost around 14 percent, while the nominal cost in Japan was about 6 percent and, in the United States, about 5 percent. In Korea, the nominal rate was 26 percent and the real cost of "ordinary" or nonpriority loans was 17 percent, much higher than in Taiwan; but the real cost of "policy" or priority loans was very low or even negative, and such loans accounted for about half of total official loans (Korea Exchange Bank, *Monthly Review*, various issues).

Note, however, that bank interest rates in Taiwan have been set at levels well below market-clearing levels, as indicated by the large gap between bank rates and those on the unregulated money market. In 1981 the rate on a secured bank loan was about 15 percent, whereas a loan from the unregulated money market cost 35 percent. All the way through, any bank loan has been to some degree concessionary, and banks have had to ration their credit.

One cannot reach straightforward conclusions about the extent to which bank interest rates are in "disequilibrium" from the size of the discrepancy between the bank rate and the unregulated market rate, however: collateral requirements are more stringent for bank loans, increasing their real cost; compensating balances are often required for bank loans, again increasing the real cost; and the unregulated money market tends to be used for riskier investments, which would in itself make for an equilibrium discrepancy.

The price of credit in Taiwan has been kept higher than otherwise by preventing inflows of loanable funds from the rest of the world seeking to take advantage of the high rates. On the one hand, the high price of credit has helped exports, because exports are typically more labor-intensive than nonexports and costly credit confers an advantage on labor over capital. On the other hand, it has also meant that exporters might be disadvantaged by having to carry interest costs greater than those of their competitors. This is the significance of the government's export credit scheme, which from the late 1950s to the mid-1970s gave exporters substantial margins of preference for short-term loans compared to loans for nonexport production. As early as 1957, for example, the cost of an export loan in local currency was 11.9 percent compared to the cost of a nonexport secured bank loan of 19.8 percent. By 1977 the margin of preference had been reduced to 4 percent.

CONSERVATIVE GOVERNMENT BUDGETING

The proposition that Taiwan is a model of conservative government budgeting needs qualification, as we shall see in chapter 6. Our concern here being with evidence supportive of the neoclassical position, we can note that the government has indeed run budget surpluses in most years since the mid-1960s, which indicates public sector behavior rather different from that of most other countries. It is also true that direct taxes as a proportion of GNP are fairly low, so there is, as Ian Little says, plenty of incentive to make money (1979:478). Indirect taxes, on the other hand, are high; customs duties alone have accounted for a steady one-fifth to a quarter of total tax revenue since the early 1950s, and total indirect taxes (including customs duties) still accounted for almost 70 percent of total taxes in 1976–79 (Yu and Chen 1982).

On the revenue side, the budgetary surpluses have resulted from the success of the overall development policy, which enabled tax revenues to grow rapidly. Also, the tax reform of the late 1960s tightened collections, especially on professionals and public employees. Public enterprise prices have been set at levels so that in aggregate public enterprises are net contributors to the budget. On the expenditure side the surpluses result from a neglect of infrastructure investment until the 1970s, made possible by the fact that the Japanese left behind a relatively good infrastructure on their departure in 1945. Little has been spent on environmental protection or social welfare. Instead of transfer payments to the aged and the unemployed there is household income pooling and a dense network of wholesale and retail trade, as in Japan and Korea.

Government budget surpluses have helped to keep inflation in check, which in turn kept exports competitive and investment high (investment which might otherwise have been reduced if businesspeople worried that anti-inflationary policies would lead to recession or higher real interest rates). Also, the surpluses have left more room for the financial system to lend for nongovernmental uses, and prevented the displacement of savings out of the financial system into consumption or ''real'' stores of value (such as real estate or gold) which government deficits can cause.

Ian Little argues that the above four policy elements were in place in Taiwan by the early 1960s, and that they constitute almost sufficient conditions for the subsequent rapid growth. We can agree that they were present (with some qualifications to be discussed), while doubting that they were almost sufficient. Now let us consider five more conditions which most economists would also recognize as important for growth.

STABLE REAL EFFECTIVE EXCHANGE RATE

We saw earlier that Taiwan's real exchange rate has been relatively undistorted (prior to the mid-1980s), neither much overvalued or undervalued compared to the free play of supply and demand. A related but distinct point is that the real exchange rate has been remarkably stable over the whole period from 1956 to 1985; which is to say that the value of domestic currency has been kept stable in relation to the value of the currencies of principal trading partners. This of course is a great help to investors, who do not have to hedge against exchange rate fluctuations. Since the nominal exchange rate was fixed for most of the period, the stable real effective rate reflects Taiwan's low inflation rate in line with that of its main trading partners, the United States and Japan. The stability of the real effective exchange rate in Taiwan compared to other countries can be shown in terms of the standard deviation of the rates in the six countries shown in tables 3.2 and 3.3 for the period from 1978 to 1987: Taiwan, 6.4, Korea, 9.4, Singapore, 7.9, Israel, 6.4, Colombia, 17.2, and Argentina, 20.6.[6]

HIGH SAVINGS

Savings increased from about 5 percent of national income in the first half of the 1950s to over 30 percent in the late 1970s. By 1975 Taiwan's ratio of net savings to net national product had exceeded Japan's (25.3 percent against 22.7 percent). Since then Taiwan has had about the highest savings ratio in the world. Its 30.5 percent average between 1970 and 1979 may be compared with Korea's 17.5, Japan's 26.3, the Philippines' 18.1, and the United States' 7.6 percent (Sun and Liang 1982:404).

Because of this vast mass of savings, Taiwan's rapid growth has been accompanied by much less inflation and foreign borrowing than is common in developing countries, including Korea.

Surprisingly little has been written about the reasons for Taiwan's high and rising level of real savings. Two studies, one by Sun and Liang (1982), the other by Tibor Scitovsky (1986), go through the standard economic explanations for savings behavior, and find most of them unconvincing for Taiwan. It seems that the growth rate of income does not explain very much; nor does income distribution; nor interest rate changes; nor inflationary expectations. But these calculations are in terms of aggregative savings, and more can be learned by examining the components.

Savings occur in households, firms, and government (including public enterprises). The shares of each in Taiwan's total are shown in table 3.4. Note the large size of government savings. Over the period from 1970 to 1978 government savings averaged 38 percent of net savings, as against 35 percent in South Korea, 22 percent in the Philippines, 20 percent in Japan, and minus 14 percent in the United States.[7] High government savings have helped to keep inflation low.

But government savings may have partly substituted for private savings; had government savings been less private savings might have been higher. Even so, private savings have still been extraordinarily high, almost 20 percent of GNP over the 1970–79 period. If the rate of household saving is ex-

---

[6] The real effective exchange rate is calculated as the ratio of world prices converted into domestic currency, over domestic prices (using the consumer price index or the GDP deflator). The source for the figures is the IMF's exchange rate division. The year 1978 is the cut-off for readily available data comparable with subsequent years. See also table 5.1.

[7] International comparisons of government savings suffer from differences in definition as to what is included and what is excluded. In South Korea most public enterprises are included, but some are excluded for no obvious reason, their savings being put with corporate sector savings. I do not know whether there are similar problems for Taiwan.

TABLE 3.4
Sources of Net National Savings in Taiwan (%)

	Household & Nonprofit Institutions	Private Corporations	Government & Public Enterprises
1956–60	37.6	10.4	52.0
1966–70	57.5	9.6	32.8
1976–79	49.9	8.4	41.7

Source: Sun and Liang 1982:414.

pressed as a proportion of personal disposable income and the figure for Taiwan compared to that for Korea, the difference is tremendous: 17.6 percent for Taiwan between 1965 and 1980, 7.6 percent for Korea (Scitovsky 1986).

Why have household savings been so important in Taiwan? The underdeveloped state of the social security system is probably relevant. Savings are high because people save for old age or sickness. Only civil servants, soldiers, and teachers are entitled to a retirement pension, and then to only a small fraction of their full working income; most of them prefer to take the lump sum option. Firms are obliged to pay a lump sum on a worker's retirement (but the smaller companies tend to evade the obligation). Annual bonuses are usually paid, generally one or two months' full wage or salary, adjusted upward or downward according to the firm's profitability that year and perhaps the individual's work performance. The practice of annual and retirement bonuses helps savings because a worker who receives a lump sum payment rather than small installments is likely to save a larger proportion of it. A medical insurance scheme has wide coverage of the work force, but includes only the cost of treatment, not income foregone. For those without means of support there is a "poor law" safety net, but the size of the benefit is tiny and conditions of eligibility severe; a strong stigma is attached to being a recipient. So in the absence of more than rudimentary pension and social security arrangements, individuals must rely on family income pooling, or save. For house purchase a large downpayment is required (50 percent or more); and it goes without saying that, unlike the United States and Great Britain, mortgage repayments are not tax deductible. Little public housing is available. Only a few big companies help employees buy houses. Education is free for the first nine years, but at the university level private colleges have steep fees and few scholarships. (Half the universities are private colleges, which tend to be at the lower end of the prestige and quality scale, public colleges being at the upper end.) The hope that at least one child will go to college is remarkably widespread. It drives saving aimed at being able to support a child's college education, should he or she be among the one-third of applicants who get qualifying grades in a national examination.

So several features of social security, education, and housing help to explain the high level of household savings. But much the same features exist in South Korea, where household savings are much lower. Sun and Liang end their study of savings in Taiwan by suggesting that the frugality sanctioned by Chinese culture may be an important influence on savings behavior—which is probably true, but also shows why cultural explanations have a bad name.

Scitovsky, for his part, concludes that the much higher rate of household saving in Taiwan compared to Korea may be the cumulative result of several differences: the slightly faster growth of Taiwan's GNP; the slightly faster increase in the proportion of the labor force receiving part of its income in the form of bonuses (but in both countries, the annual bonuses amount to only one or two months' wages, so they are less important than in Japan); the greater proportion of the population saving to establish independent businesses (as indicated by the much faster expansion in the number of businesses, and their smaller average size); the greater proportion of the population saving to enlarge the more numerous already-established small businesses; a greater need to save for old age (if Taiwan's greater affluence has gone with a bigger shift from extended to nuclear households); and greater willingness to save in financial form because of higher real interest rates on deposits and, for the same reason, greater willingness to keep real savings within the country. All these explanations are plausible, Scitovsky concludes. He would be first to say that the subject needs more research.

Government policies have also directly helped savings, though neither Sun and Liang nor Scitovsky discuss their impact. Interest on time deposits is exempt from tax, and has been since 1971. (Dividend payments, on the other hand, received no tax exemption until 1981.) The use of savings for house purchase has been neither encouraged nor discouraged; but multiple house ownership has been discouraged by preventing the banks from lending for second house purchase and by taxing second houses more severely than ones occupied by the owner. A dense network of banking offices (one per ten thousand people in 1980) may also have helped to increase financial savings.

High and rising levels of financial savings are reflected in high and rising levels of monetization of the economy, as measured by the ratio of M2 to GNP. The higher this ratio, the more of an economy's productive activities are carried out through market transactions and the more savers hold financial rather than real assets—so the more likely savings will be moved through financial institutions into uses in which their real return is highest. Table 3.5 suggests that Taiwan has been well ahead of other developing countries in this respect since the early 1960s. Another indicator is the rise in M2 deflated by the wholesale price index, which represents the real lending capacity of the bank-

TABLE 3.5
Monetization of the Economy, Taiwan
Compared to Other Countries: M2/GNP (%)

Countries	1955	1965	1975	1980	1985
Taiwan	13	30	57	65	109
Korea	10	12	30	34	46
Japan	60	79	68	86	97
Philippines	19	25	17	21	21

Source: IMF, *International Financial Statistics*, various issues; *Taiwan Statistical Data Book*, various issues.

Note: M2 refers to currency plus bank deposits.

ing system. This grew 12 times between 1961 and 1970, making possible a huge expansion in the base from which bank credit expansion could proceed.

In the 1950s foreign savings accounted for 40 percent of total savings, mostly in the form of U.S. aid. Since the mid-1960s, however, foreign savings have been a very small part of the total. Domestic savings have exceeded even the exceptionally high state of investment in GNP, averaging 28.7 percent between 1965 and 1980 compared to an investment share of 28.4 percent. In Korea, only 70 percent of investment came from domestic savings, the rest mostly from aid and loans.

WELL-TRAINED LABOR SUPPLY

In 1960 Taiwan was not an especially literate country: with a 54 percent adult literacy rate it ranked twenty-sixth in a sample of seventy-seven developing countries. Literacy increased quickly, however, so that by 1977 Taiwan's rate of 82 percent put it seventeenth, the fourth best literacy improvement record in the sample (Sen 1981).

The first six years of school have been compulsory and free since before 1950, with enrollments always exceeding 95 percent of the relevant age group after 1956. The three more years of junior high school have been free since 1968. High school enrollment reached 80 percent of the age group in 1980. The tertiary ratio in much lower: 14 percent for men and 12 percent for women in 1985 (DGBAS 1986).

At the senior high school level and beyond there are both vocational and academic institutions. Since 1966 the government has been encouraging expansion of the vocational while restraining expansion of the academic institutions, so as to meet the growing demand for technically trained middle-level manpower in business. The number of students in vocational senior high schools has exceeded the number in academic ones since 1971, an exceptional state of affairs compared to other Asian countries (Lew 1978).

Engineering has been especially popular. Engineers are paid 20 percent more than arts graduates of the same age, on average, and 11 percent more than law graduates (National Youth Commission, 1983). In industry, an engineering qualification is considered such a fast track to management positions that worry has been expressed in government at the leaching of skills from the shopfloor.[8] The junior colleges have produced more than twenty thousand engineering diploma holders a year over the 1980s, the universities another ten thousand bachelor-level engineers a year (70 percent more than the United States in relation to population).[9] About one-quarter of all university graduates since 1960 have been engineers (law graduates, 1.2 percent). Science and engineering students together accounted for over one-third of post-high school (junior college plus university) graduates during the 1960s, more than 40 percent during the 1970s, half by 1980.

This fascination with engineering is not a recent phenomenon. Since the early twentieth century engineers in China have enjoyed high prestige and office. Of the Chinese students studying in the United States during the first half of the twentieth century, almost 30 percent took engineering as their main field of study (Wang 1966:511). Hence in 1971 Taiwan had more engineers per thousand people employed in manufacturing than any other of a sample of fourteen middle-income countries, with the exception of Singapore. The sample average was 4.6; Taiwan had 8 and Singapore had 10 (Zymelman 1980; Korea is not given). The presence in Taiwan of a large stock of engineers has helped to secure national control over technology imports and to acquire mastery over those technologies. Korea, with a population more than twice Taiwan's, has lately been graduating as many bachelor-level engineers in relation to population (over 20,000 a year in 1983 and 1984); but proportionately fewer junior college graduates (33,000 and 27,000 in those two years).[10]

[8] "Engineer" has no wider a definition in Taiwan than in English-speaking countries; so when one talks of the importance of engineers, it is not a reflection of a much wider definition. Celebration of engineers as leaders of national production is seen in the address by Minister of Economic Affairs Y. T. Chao to the Chinese Institute of Engineers: "The time has come for Chinese engineers to help shatter the long-held belief that imported goods are superior to domestic products. . . . The current mission of Chinese engineers is to accelerate industrial renovations, upgrade industrial structure, and sharpen the competitive edge of local products in the international market" (*China News*, 6 June 1983).

[9] *Education Statistics of the Republic of China 1986.* The United States graduated 73,000 bachelor-level engineers in 1983, Taiwan, 10,259. But many graduates in both countries leave the country after graduation. It is estimated that of the fifty thousand students (in all subjects) who left Taiwan for further education abroad between the early 1950s and 1978, less than six thousand returned (Chen 1981). Through the 1970s and 1980s Taiwanese constituted probably the single largest group of foreign students in the United States. The statistics show a sharp reduction in net brain drain since the late 1970s.

[10] Ministry of Science and Technology, *Science and Technology Annual 1984*, Seoul, p. 227.

Whether for reasons of incentives or socialization, Taiwan's workers work hard. A study of labor efficiency in nine Asian countries plus the United States found that in the early 1970s Taiwan had the third highest level after Japan and Hong Kong, higher than the United States (labor efficiency being measured by the time required to manufacture specific products; see Arthur D. Little, Inc. 1973, 4:55).

COMPETITIVE INDUSTRIAL STRUCTURE

Another important reason for Taiwan's success, according to many analysts, is the flexibility, low overheads, and lack of monopoly power of its business firms. The small family firm, it is said, has been at the heart of the country's manufacturing revolution. This is in contrast to Japan and Korea, where huge conglomerates dominate the economy. Taiwan is the "shrimp" to the Japanese and Korean "octopi." "Better the head of a chicken than the tail of an ox" is the proverb frequently invoked to explain this contrast—a cultural propensity to be one's own boss rather than work as a subordinate or member of a team.

Taiwan does, indeed, lack the large firms and huge business groups of Japan and Korea. In 1981 Korea had 10 firms in *Fortune's* 500 biggest industrial firms outside the United States, while Taiwan had only 2. Only 176 firms in Taiwan had more than 1,000 employees in 1976 (including public as well as private, foreign as well as domestic firms). Over 80 percent of firms had fewer than 20 employees (table 3.6).

Taiwan's business groups (clusters of interlinked firms with a social rather than legal identity) are much smaller in terms of sales and employment than their Korean and Japanese counterparts (see table 3.7). Hyundai, South Korea's largest private conglomerate, had annual sales of US$8 billion in 1983 and employed 137,000 people. Formosa Plastics Group, Taiwan's largest group, had annual sales of $1.6 billion and employed 31,200 people (Myers 1986:54). The groups are also less central in the economy. Only 40 percent of the 500 largest manufacturing firms belong to business groups, and most Taiwan enterprises remain single-unit operations. In contrast to Korea and Japan, Taiwan's business groups are associations of firms managed by the same set of people, usually close relatives. In place of a unified command or management structure for the group as a whole, the owners hold multiple managerial positions in several firms of the group. Only 40 percent of the groups have even one firm listed on the stock exchange. The groups are diversified across several industries rather than tightly coupled vertical structures (Hamilton, Orru, and Biggart 1987). So even in the organization of its business groups,

---

The 1983 figures for engineering bachelors and junior college graduates are 20,627 and 32,767, 27 percent and 45 percent of the respective totals. But the junior college figure is unusually high— the following year it was down to 27,046, 39 percent of the total.

TABLE 3.6
Size of Manufacturing Enterprises in Taiwan

| | | No. of Employees (%) | | | | | |
		1–19	*20–99*	*100–499*	*500–999*	*1,000+*	*Total*
1961	No.	←	99.2[a]	→	0.8[b]		
	Emp.		61.2		38.8	→	
	Prod.		35.5		64.5		
1966	No.	85.6	11.7	2.3	0.5[b]		27,709
	Emp.	21.4	21.4	22.5	34.8	→	589,660
	Prod.	19.3	15.2	19.9	45.6		85,085
1971	No.	81.9	13.5	3.8	0.8[b]		42,636
	Emp.	15.7	19.9	28.2	36.1	→	1,201,539
	Prod.	11.5	14.8	26.0	47.3		242,940
1976	No.	81.0	14.3	4.1	0.3	0.3	69,517
	Emp.	16.4	22.2	30.2	9.7	21.5	1,907,581
	Prod.	10.4	16.9	29.2	11.2	32.3	819,452
1981	No.	82.1	13.8	3.5	0.4	0.2	91,510
	Emp.	17.4	24.1	28.8	10.3	19.6	2,201,470
	Prod.	8.9	17.6	26.0	10.6	36.8	2,067,430

Sources: 1961—Hsing 1971: table 2.15. 1966—Third Census of Commerce and Industry: table 37. 1971—Fourth Census: table 38. 1976—Fifth Census: table 20. 1981—Provisional data from Sixth Census, Feb. 1984, DGBAS.

Note: Data refers to manufacturing enterprises. Number of plants is less than 2 percent larger than number of enterprises. The production totals are in millions of NT$ and refer to gross production, not value-added. Number of enterprises with more than 500 employees: 1966—131; 1971—321; 1976—445; more than 1,000 employees: 1976—176; 1981—167.

[a] For firms having 1–499 employees.

[b] For firms having 500+ employees.

Taiwan's industrial organization comes closer to the neoclassical ideal than the more patriarchal Korean or the more communitarian Japanese groups.

The contrast between Taiwan and Korea can be put another way. In Taiwan the number of manufacturing firms increased 250 percent between 1966 and 1976, while the number of employees per firm increased by only 29 percent. Korea shows a more familiar pattern: the number of manufacturing firms increased by a mere 10 percent, while the number of employees per firm doubled. The average size of manufacturing firms in Taiwan was twenty-seven employees in 1976, in Korea (for firms with more than four employees), sixty-nine. There are differences in the statistical definitions used to compile these figures, but they do not invalidate the broad and striking differences (Scitovsky 1985:223). Still another angle on the same contrast is the proportion of

TABLE 3.7
Characteristics of Business Groups in Taiwan, Korea, and Japan

	Taiwan	Korea	Japan
No. of groups	96	50	16
Total sales (in billions)	NT$634	W54,663	Y217,033
Equivalent US$ (in billions)	16.48	68.32	871.26
No. of firms	745	552	1,001
Firms/business group	7.8	11.0	62.6
Workers/firm	444	1,440	2,838
Percentage of total workforce	4.7	5.5	9.5

Source: Hamilton, et al. 1987: table 1.

Note: Data for Taiwan and Korea is from 1983; for Japan, 1982. Each country's biggest groups are included. Japan's sixteen groups include the six major enterprise groups and the ten largest industrial groups.

exports sold under the manufacturer's brandname. Although no figures are available, it is generally believed that a smaller part of Taiwan's exports—especially to the United States—are proprietary products and a larger part are made to order and sold under the buyer's brandnames (Sease 1987).

However, the small unit size of Taiwan's manufacturing sector can easily be exaggerated. Almost half of manufacturing production in both 1971 and 1981 came from firms with more than five hundred employees; only a quarter came from firms with less than one hundred employees. Eighty-two percent of firms with less than twenty employees in 1971 produced only 12 percent of production (though more of the production of small firms may escape statistical notice). Indeed, the share of manufacturing value-added held by firms with five hundred employees or more was unusually *high* by world standards as of the early 1970s. Firms of that size accounted for 57.9 percent of manufacturing value-added, compared to 52.7 percent in Korea, 48.7 percent in the United States, and under 40 percent in Japan, Hong Kong, Brazil, Peru, and many others.[11]

A further statistic suggests a dramatic concentration of industrial assets over the 1970s. If it is to be believed, the share of the top one hundred private (domestic) manufacturing firms in total private manufacturing assets increased from about 30 percent in 1972 to 44 percent in 1979 (T. Chen 1982). Another

[11] Biggs and Lorch, forthcoming; Amsden, forthcoming. The figure for Taiwan comes from the Fourth Census of Commerce and Industry, the others come from United Nations 1979.

study finds a surprisingly high degree of oligopoly in Taiwan's industry: in 32 percent of 134 sectors the top four companies accounted for 40 percent or more of sales in 1981 (T. Chen 1984). But for whatever reasons such a trend is not reflected in the census figures on share of production and employment by size of company. A third study suggests that in upstream, basic industries Taiwan has a more concentrated industrial structure than Korea, presumably because the market is smaller; though overall the Taiwan economy is much less concentrated (Biggs and Lorch forthcoming).

The census figures, it should be noted, understate the real degree of concentration in Taiwan industry by ignoring business groups. For census purposes each firm is treated as though it were entirely independent. The reason is that company law in effect prohibits holding companies. Furthermore, consolidated financial statements are not required for any purposes, while the interest of the tax authorities increases more than proportionately with size.

Nor is it the case that college and university graduates rush to become the "head of the chicken." A survey of 1984 graduates carried out two years after graduation found that only 6 percent had gone into their own or family businesses; and of Masters and PhD graduates, only 1.6 percent (National Youth Commission 1987). It may be that some of the vast majority who initially go to work as employees in large-scale organizations later leave to work in their own or their family's business; on this there is no data. But putting these several kinds of evidence together one concludes that the much cited proverb about the head of a chicken may be explaining the wrong facts.

At the top end of the scale, almost all the biggest fifty companies (using the census definition) have been established in the past thirty years. Some are still first-generation firms run by the founder, who typically lives by a code of hard work and no indulgence, which he preaches to others as the key to his success. At the very top there is remarkable stability in the relative position of firms. Of the fifteen biggest private industrial firms in 1971 (excluding foreign firms) twelve were still in the biggest fifteen in 1980. Nanya Plastics, flagship of the Formosa Plastics Group, was first in terms of sales every year from 1970 to 1980. Its 1980 sales put it as equivalent to the 441st U.S. industrial corporation. Lower down there has been more movement. Of the top fifty firms in 1971 only twenty-four were still there in 1980. The dropouts were mostly in textiles, food, and plywood. The newcomers were mostly in metals, machinery, chemicals, and food-processing (China Credit Information Service, 1972, 1981).

Amongst the many thousands of small- and medium-sized firms there is little sense of "belonging" to any one industry (Silin 1976). The owners are prepared to move, grasshopper-like, to wherever a chance of quick profit shows itself. The same person may be proprietor of several companies producing quite different products. One such person owns an air cargo agency, a travel agency, an apartment-leasing agency, a construction company, a company to manufacture video games, and another to make counterfeit personal computers. When the bottom dropped out of the video game market he was asked what he planned to do next. "Wait till I come back from the States," he replied. He returned with a bright new idea—to manufacture satellite receivers, perfect replicas of the one he had air freighted in. This he is now doing, along with everything else. Such characteristics must be important for Taiwan's industrial flexibility and high short-run supply elasticities.

In sum, Taiwan's industrial economy is dualistic, with a large sector of small-scale firms and another large sector of large-scale firms. The stereotyped image of Taiwan as an economy of mom-and-pop firms producing for the world market derives from too much emphasis on the former. Most of the small-scale firms have small, relatively labor-intensive plants making fairly standardized products which compete on the basis of price. But over the 1980s many small firms have sprung up in higher-technology sectors, such as computers, integrated circuit design, machine tools, high-quality sports goods, and expensive toys, where product differentiation and performance matter more and price matters a little less. Most of Taiwan's exports come from small- and medium-sized firms; in 1985 firms with less than three hundred employees accounted for 65 percent of manufactured exports, and a decade earlier, in 1976, the top five hundred domestically owned firms by sales accounted for only 27 percent of total exports (Biggs 1988). This is surprising against experience elsewhere. Typically exports come mostly from larger firms, which can better meet the transactions costs of participation in international markets. However, Taiwan's big firms are important indirect exporters in their role as input suppliers of petrochemicals, textiles, steel, and the like to the smaller direct exporting firms. Big firms are linked to smaller ones in other ways, too, as providers of credit, technical assistance, and trained personnel. So Taiwan's dualistic industrial structure is densely interconnected, and the export success of the smaller firms cannot be understood independently of the productive performance of the big firms. This being said, I should stress that the organization of firms—their size, the way they grow, their methods of doing business, and the relationships between them—is a major gap in the argument of this book. Any discussion of an economy's development should give a central place to the organization of firms and industries. But since little evidence is available on this subject for Taiwan, and since my primary interest is the uses of public power, I say little more about it.[12]

STABLE GOVERNMENT

Neoclassical theory pays scant attention to government organization as a growth variable, but most economists would agree that stable government is better for growth than unstable government. In terms of ethnic and class con-

[12] As this book was being completed Tyler Biggs and Klaus Lorch, of the Harvard Institute for International Development, were beginning to produce some interesting material on Taiwan's industrial organization.

flict, rioting and mob violence, military coups d'etat, and frequent changes of leadership, Taiwan has been among the most stable of societies since after the early years of the Japanese occupation in 1895.[13] Since the Second World War the island has been ruled as a one-party state by the Nationalist party (Kuomintang, or KMT). This party has provided the almost exclusive framework for the processes determining government policy and political leadership. The positions of president of the Republic, chairman of the party, and commander-in-chief of the armed forces have been held by only two individuals, Chiang Kai-shek up to 1975, and his son, Chiang Ching-kuo thereafter (to his death in 1988).[14] The legislature has been kept ineffectual by the powerful executive branch of government. All civil associations are controlled by the state or the party; labor unions, particularly, are kept inactive and dependent.

For all its unsavory aspects, Taiwan's exclusionary and authoritarian regime has allowed the country to avoid the political fate of many developing countries, of chronic fluctuation between fragile democratic experiments, incompetent authoritarianism, and demagogues. It has been able to give business-people the confidence that it will do what it says it will do. By contrast, businesspeople in Latin America are more hesitant to believe shifts in government policies and make adjustments in their own resource allocations; for they are often unsure whether the shift will be maintained or reversed. One study reports that its interviewees said they delayed taking action on government policies for periods ranging up to six months because they were uncertain whether the policy would be adhered to (Corbo, de Melo, and Tybout 1986:625). This is consistent with John Williamson's hypothesis that a major, even *the* major proximate cause of different macroeconomic performance between East Asia and Latin America is what he calls the "myopia" of Latin American political and business leaders as compared with their East Asian counterparts, or their "political reluctance to accept short-term costs in the expectation of longer run gains" (1985:568). He leaves myopia hanging, however. Perhaps it is a response to Latin America's much greater political instability. Perhaps the opposite in Taiwan, while achieved at high cost in civil and political rights, has encouraged farsightedness in the economic strategies of government and the bigger companies.

CAUSALITY

It is clear that many of the conditions prescribed by neoclassical development theory were present in Taiwan by the early 1960s. Since then, the real exchange rate has been kept relatively stable and undistorted, and incentives for producers to sell abroad or on the domestic market have been kept roughly equal (exports have not been discriminated against). Effective protection has

---

[13] But see qualifications in chapter 4.

[14] This is not literally true but the qualification need not concern us.

been low (taking the figures in table 3.2 at face value, although we shall later question them). Wages have been at market-clearing levels, bank interest rates have been kept relatively high, government has run budget surpluses, savings and investment have been very high, the labor force has been well trained, the industrial structure includes a sizable sector of small firms unable to exercise oligopoly power, and the domestic political environment has been stable.

Indeed, Taiwan seems splendidly consistent with Ram Agarwala's results for a sample of thirty-one developing countries (excluding Taiwan). He found a strong inverse correlation between price distortion and economic growth. Calculation of Taiwan's price distortion score by the same method gives the second lowest score in the sample, and Taiwan has the second highest growth rate (Evans and Alizadeh 1984).

In short, Taiwan seems to meet the neoclassical growth conditions unusually well. Yet other evidence shows that the government has been intervening for decades, often quite aggressively, to alter the trade and industrial profile of the economy in ways that it judges to be desirable. We then face a formidable identification problem. How can we decide to what extent Taiwan's exceptional economic performance is due to the presence of many of the neoclassical growth conditions and to what extent to the government's selective promotion policies? Ultimately I cannot resolve the issue. But for my purpose it is enough to demonstrate that the government has indeed been guiding the market on a scale much greater than is consistent with neoclassical prescriptions or with the practice of Anglo-American economies. For the fact of such guidance has been almost completely overlooked by neoclassical economists. Recall Ian Little's claim that "apart from the creation of [these neoclassical conditions] . . . it is hard to find any good explanation for the sustained industrial boom . . ." (1979:480). In twenty thousand-word essays on the mechanism of Taiwan's development, both Little and Gustav Ranis largely ignore the promotional role of government after the economic liberalization of 1958–62. Ranis does no more than devote a paragraph to listing some fiscal incentives, and claims they helped attract foreign direct investment. Little admits in passing that "if planning includes any promotion of industries that would not be likely to start in response to price signals, then there was considerable industrial planning in the 1950s, and again in the late 1960s and 1970s" (1979:489). He spends no time examining the instruments or effects of this planning, however, for the reason that whether it helped or not is, he says, a "futile question" in the absence of a counterfactual. Futile question or not, his own implied answer is that it was unimportant enough to ignore.

Chapter 4

STATE-LED INDUSTRIALIZATION, 1930s TO 1980s

THE STATE in Taiwan has been doing much more than the neoclassical accounts recognize to increase supply responsiveness and to steer the direction of industrial growth. State influence has been concentrated on, but not confined to, the relatively large-scale firms of the upstream industries, leaving the downstream smaller-scale firms much freer. I particularly emphasize sectoral promotion policies, these being less consistent with neoclassical prescriptions than functional promotion policies. The discussion is arranged chronologically: (1) the Japanese period, (2) the 1950s, and (3) the period of "outward orientation."

THE JAPANESE PERIOD, 1895 TO 1945

The development of Taiwan, as well as the two Koreas, has to be understood in the context of Japanese colonialism. For fifty years in Taiwan and for almost as long in Korea, they were Japan's principal colonies.

The Japanese took control of Taiwan, a peripheral part of the Chinese Empire, as a prize for defeating China in the war of 1895. After suppressing resistance to their rule they set about developing the resources of the island, but in a manner rather different from that of other colonialisms.

Drawing on Japan's own experience of "revolution from above," the Japanese administration undertook a major cadastral survey and land reform similar to the Meiji reform in Japan during the 1870s. Land rights were removed from a class of absentee landlords and transferred to the local landlords who had been managing the lands—who then became supporters of the Japanese regime. A good communications infrastructure was laid down, designed not with the narrow purpose of extracting some primary raw material but with the aim of increasing production of smallholder rice and sugar, both wanted in Japan. Under these policies, "expansion in irrigation and drainage, dissemination of improved or better seeds, and spread in the use of fertilizers and manures were all energetically attempted, sometimes even with the aid of the police force; the statistics indicate continuously rising trends" (Ishikawa 1967:102). Farmers were grouped into farmers cooperatives, irrigation associations, and landlord-tenant associations so as both to accelerate the spread of technical knowledge and keep them under control.

This promotion of an agriculture based on smallholder cultivation of the staple food crop differs from other colonial experiences. With respect to industrial development, too, Japanese colonialism differed from others by bringing the industry to the labor and raw materials rather than the other way around (Cumings 1984:12–13). During the 1930s, prompted by rising wages in Japan and by the government's plans for war, the administration began to develop in Taiwan such industries as food processing, textiles, plywood, pulp and paper, cement, chemical fertilizers, aluminum and copper refining, petroleum refining, and shipbuilding.

Manufacturing grew in real terms at 6 percent a year during the long period from 1912 to 1940, and by more than 7 percent a year in the 1930s (Lin 1973:21; Ho 1978:72). New research suggests that both Taiwan and Korea had higher rates of GDP growth than Japan between 1911 and 1938 (Japan 3.4 percent, Korea 3.6 percent, Taiwan 3.8 percent: Cumings 1984:2). Moreover, Taiwan was already by the end of the 1930s the biggest trader in the region, though most of the trade was with Japan. The annual per capita trade of Taiwan was $39, of Korea $26, of Japan $23, of the Philippines $18, of China $1 (Beal 1981). Already Taiwan was an intermediate link in a regional economy, importing raw materials from Southeast Asia and exporting processed products to Japan. But most of the industry was owned by Japanese firms headquartered in Japan.

Levels of welfare improved. Indeed, some evidence suggests that the welfare of the Taiwanese peasant in the first half of the twentieth century may have exceeded that of the Japanese peasant (Ouchi, in Amsden 1979:348). The death rate fell from forty per thousand in 1905 to twenty by 1936—a lower rate in 1936 than most of South Asia, Sub-Saharan Africa, and the poorest countries of Latin America had reached almost thirty years later, in 1965. The scope of primary education expanded so that by 1940 almost 60 percent of the relevant age group (males and females) were attending primary school (Lin 1973:227). As part of the agricultural development effort the Japanese instituted agriculturally oriented two-year secondary schools in the more populous parts of the country (one in each township). Nor were the Taiwanese as excluded from ''modern'' professions as is often suggested. By 1940 there were five times as many Taiwanese ''managers'' as there were Japanese, three times as many ''agricultural technicians'' and ''medical technicians,'' and the same number of ''professional workers,'' according to the census returns (Lin 1973:table A.35).

By the time of retrocession in 1945 Taiwan was probably the most agriculturally, commercially, and industrially advanced of all the provinces of China.[1]

[1] For good short summaries of the Japanese period, see Gold 1986; Cumings 1984; Amsden 1979; Ranis 1979; Lin 1973; Myers and Ching 1964. For longer treatments, see Ho 1978; Barclay 1954. There is sometimes an ideological undercurrent to discussions of the Japanese period. Those who are pro-Nationalist party and/or pro-neoclassical economics may be inclined to stress the adverse conditions of Taiwan in 1950, the better to highlight the contributions of the Nation-

Some Latin American countries also experienced substantial development during the first half of the twentieth century. What is unusual about Taiwan's experience (and Korea's) is that this process did not give rise to a high concentration of capital and leadership in the hands of a Taiwanese elite, because the Japanese kept almost complete control. This delayed the emergence of a dynamic Taiwanese capitalist class; but it also contributed to a more equal class and income distribution than in most other developing countries. The lack of existing local monopoly control made it much easier for the incoming Nationalist government to implement land reform and industrial policy.

THE INITIAL NATIONALIST PERIOD, 1945 TO 1960

With Japan's defeat in the Second World War Taiwan reverted to China—or more exactly, to the Republic of China. The Republic of China was the constitutional form of the Nationalist party (Kuomintang, or KMT), which was engaged in a long-running civil war with the Chinese Communist party and its army. In 1949 the Nationalist army was overwhelmed. With its leader, Chiang Kai-shek, it retreated to Taiwan, 150 kilometers off the Chinese mainland.

Between one and two million soldiers and civilians poured onto an island of six million people. They had virtually no knowledge of or ties to Taiwan. The islanders had no political movement or armed force to challenge their rule. Facing no internal opposition and having no social base within Taiwan, the Nationalist-mainlander government had unusually wide room for maneuvering. And it had an unusually dominant position in the economy, for it inherited all the productive assets and control mechanisms that the Japanese had built up over fifty years. The monopolies owned by the colonial administration, Japanese-owned shares in industrial enterprises, Japanese-owned lands—all passed to the incoming government.

---

alist government and the liberalizing reforms to the subsequent prosperity. Those who are opposed may do the opposite.

This is George Barclay's summary of the achievements of the Japanese administration: "The Japanese rationalized certain parts of Taiwan's agriculture, so that the island produced a substantial surplus of farm commodities each year. They established a strong and efficient government, the first that the island ever had. With a shrewd combination of police force and political guile, they imposed strict public order and penetrated every town and village with a structure of organized control. They constructed excellent facilities for transportation and communication where there had been none before, founded modern business institutions and commercial centres, promoted some industrial processing of the island's products, rebuilt the major cities, and stamped out the principal epidemic diseases. In short they transformed Taiwan from a 'backward' and neglected land into a thriving region that could regularly export a large share of its agricultural produce. This was a success that would satisfy most of the countries striving for modernization today" (1954:7). See also International Cooperation Administration: "The legacies of 50 years of development under Japanese rule include an economy more advanced than that of any other geographical region of China, excepting Manchuria, and a standard of living second only to Japan among Far Eastern countries" (1956:9).

Agricultural Development

Like its Japanese predecessor, the Nationalist government promptly instituted land reform. First it supervised a large-scale transfer of lands formerly held by Japanese owners to their tenants. Then, with American encouragement, it redistributed land above a ceiling of three rented-out hectares to the tenants. By noncommunist world standards the reform was significant, redistributing 37 percent of total cultivated area or 320,000 hectares (Ishikawa 1967:312).[2]

The economic effect was to make an agricultural sector able to produce a sizable volume of exports *and* generate linkages with other sectors; for of all forms of primary export production small-scale peasant production tends to have the most widespread effects. Some sugar exports came from large plantations; but the plantations were owned and managed by a public enterprise, not by privates. Over the 1950s heavy investment went into rural infrastructure and irrigation. Agricultural production grew at 4.4 percent a year between 1954 and 1967, faster than just about anywhere else in Asia. The surge of agricultural growth checked discontent with the Nationalist regime in the countryside, helping in turn to stabilize the industrial investment climate. By 1960 rice yields per crop reached three tons per hectare, the highest in Asia outside Japan (Ishikawa 1967:95). Agriculture could thus provide a generous investable surplus for the rest of the economy, and in the 1950s, for exports.

Overvaluation of domestic currency compared to the U.S. dollar provided a mechanism for extracting resources from the agricultural sector and transferring them to manufacturing. Exports, which were mostly agricultural, received less in domestic currency than they would have at an equilibrium exchange rate; so the overvalued rate acted as a kind of export tax. (Indeed rice and sugar exports faced an even more unfavorable rate than other exports under the system of multiple rates.) At the same time, the trade controls which accompanied the overvalued exchange rate increased the price of daily consumer goods, tending to lower agriculturalists' real income. On the other hand, industrialists benefited from the overvalued exchange rate in the form of lower costs of imported inputs, and benefited from the trade controls through higher prices for products sold on the domestic market. Also, the domestic terms of trade were biased against agriculture by means of land taxes and, more importantly, by means of both compulsory procurement of rice at below-market prices and the rice-fertilizer barter scheme. Under the latter, the government exchanged fertilizer, over which it had a monopoly, for rice at rates of exchange unfavorable to rice. The total tax burden on agriculture was significantly higher than for the nonagricultural sectors: for 1957–61 about 25

---

[2] But note the discrepancy between Ishikawa and Thorbecke (1979:173). The total area that changed hands would have been significantly greater than the amount redistributed by government because the reform induced private sales that would not have occurred without it.

percent of farm income went to taxes, against 19 percent of nonagricultural income (Chow, in Lundberg 1979:304). Contrary to popular prescriptions for agricultural development in the West, the government did not use high producer prices to stimulate agriculture; but relied on technology policies and heavily taxed the resulting surpluses for use in industrialization. This helped to keep the price of food down and therefore also the wage rate, allowing industry to have more internationally competitive costs than otherwise. After about 1964, as the rate of growth of agricultural income declined, the rate of growth of farm household income remained high as part-time work in industry expanded.

Industrialization

Given the country's lack of raw materials and a population then growing at over 3 percent a year, raising living standards required labor-intensive manufacturing. Recapturing the mainland—which remained a central preoccupation of the government through the 1950s—required the development of some upstream industries.

Over the 1950s the basis was laid for production of plastics, artificial fibers, cement, glass, fertilizer, plywood, and many other industries, but above all, textiles. By 1952–53 the prewar peak level of real output per head had been regained in industry as well as in agriculture. Manufacturing output doubled in the period from 1952 to 1958, an annual rate of about 12 percent. Gross capital formation held constant at 14 to 16 percent of GDP, which is high compared to other countries at similar levels of per capita income at the same time. (Ian Little mentions only its constancy—"investment was virtually stagnant from 1953 to 1957" [1979:474]—to underline the limitations of import substitution policies.) By the late 1950s a substantial industrial sector was in existence, with plants well beyond the cottage industry stage, backed by simple repair and maintenance enterprises and a small but fast-growing number of components suppliers. Manufacturing as a share of GDP reached 22 percent by 1960, the twelfth highest share among the fifty-five middle-income countries, putting it in the same league as Chile, Mexico, Brazil, and Israel.[3] Industrial production exceeded agricultural production for the first time in 1963.

Through the 1940s and 1950s trade and exchange rate policies were used to control external competition. Extensive quantitative restrictions on imports and fairly high tariffs were in force. The several official exchange rates were on average substantially overvalued. The black market rate of exchange with the U.S. dollar was of the order of 15 to 70 percent higher than the official rates (the range covers the least and most preferential of the official rates),

---

[3] See table 2.6; Reynolds 1983:472. Note that Taiwan's share of manufacturing equaled the weighted average for middle-income countries.

reflecting the lucrative windfalls that could be had from importing and import-substituting activities. Public sector importers had a more favorable rate than private sector importers. No free market in foreign exchange was permitted—all had to be surrendered to the central bank. Quotas were established for the allocation of foreign exchange by commodity categories. The authorities were besieged by import applications many times greater than the amount of foreign exchange on hand: during 1951–53, for example, they permitted only 20 percent of the requested amount (Lin 1973:43–47).

Export promotion efforts (for other than rice and sugar) began as early as the early 1950s. Twenty exports were singled out for government assistance in 1952, by allowing the exporter to claim a proportion of his foreign exchange earnings. But these were traditional, not new exports, and the reason for government encouragement was simply a domestic market glut. The scheme was abandoned after a couple of years, to be replaced by cash subsidies for exports, which in turn were stopped after a short time. Meanwhile, continuing through the mid-1950s, the government tried to make exporting more profitable by using export performance as an important criterion for judging import applications from private firms. And several times in the first half of the 1950s, the exchange rates facing non-rice-and-sugar exporters were devalued so as to increase their domestic currency return per unit of foreign currency. As early as 1955 rebates of duties paid on export inputs were allowed. In 1956 exporters were permitted to retain more foreign exchange for importing raw materials for their own use. In 1957 a concessional export credit scheme was introduced (Lin 1973; Scott 1979). Also, the high real interest rate policy gave an incentive to export sale insofar as exports were more labor-intensive than domestic market production.

Commonly the state established new upstream industries—often single factories—itself. Then it either handed the factories over to selected private entrepreneurs (in the case of glass, plastics, steel, and cement) or ran them as public enterprises. It acted as if following Arthur Lewis's dictum that "economic growth is bound to be slow unless there is an adequate supply of entrepreneurs looking out for new ideas, and willing to take the risk of introducing them. Thus a private enterprise economy will be retarded if it has not enough businessmen, or if its businessmen are reluctant to take risks" (1955:182).

Public enterprises dominated fuels, chemicals, mining and metal working, fertilizer and food processing, textiles, and utilities in the early 1950s. Throughout the 1950s they accounted for over half of industrial production. As new industries started the proportion fell, reaching 45 percent by 1963.

By 1957 the process of primary import substitution, begun in the 1930s, had been largely completed. The share of consumer goods in total imports had fallen to as low as 7 percent, and consumer goods imports supplied only 5 percent of domestic consumption (Ranis 1979:211).

TEXTILES

In the early 1950s the government gave particular attention to the textile industry, which was made the core of a loosely formulated plan for industrial development in 1951. The first textilers were mostly relocated mainlanders, who put their machines aboard ships as the Nationalist regime on the mainland crumbled and reestablished them on the other side of the straits. So the industry did not start de novo. Nevertheless, a whole battery of market-distorting and even market-replacing methods was used to establish the industry quickly. The market-distorting methods included tariffs and quantitative restrictions on imports of yarn and finished products, restrictions on the entry of new producers to prevent "excessive" competition, and controlled access to raw materials. From 1951 to 1953 a government agency, with help from the U.S. mission, replaced market allocation altogether. It supplied raw cotton directly to the spinning mills, advanced all working capital requirements, and bought up all production—and did basically the same at the weaving stage (Gold 1981).

The supply response was dramatic. Between 1951 and 1954 production of cotton yarn went up by over 200 percent, woolen yarn by over 400 percent. By mid-1953 Taiwan was more than self-sufficient in yarn and cloth. A U.S. advisor observed in 1952 that

> it seems as though everyone in Taiwan who has ever had a nodding acquaintance with a loom has jumped in and bought [some]. These people have gone ahead as a speculation, without any yarn allocation and without a supply of yarn in sight. . . . Some have managed to get their hands on yarn and some have been able to take on contract work for the Central Trust of China, but many of the added looms are still idle.   (Gold 1981:102)

The government response, in turn, was to end the system of comprehensive support and encourage vertical integration and economies of scale. Cheap credit was made available to existing firms for the purpose of expanding their equipment. (The Taipei office of J. G. White Engineering Corporation of New York—consultant to the government on industrial development issues—was responsible for evaluating each request.) The government also limited the entry of new firms or factories. Yet by the mid-1950s price-cutting wars were going on as competitors struggled for a share of a saturated domestic market. Many firms went bankrupt, while others began to export. Textile exports, which had been less than one percent of total exports in 1952, grew at a compound rate of 38 percent to 1958, when Taiwan became a net textile exporter for the first time. Vietnam and Hong Kong took over 90 percent of cotton textile exports in 1958. Between 1958 and 1959, following the first big change in the foreign exchange regulations in favor of exports, textile exports increased by almost 200 percent. For the next several years they grew at over 40 percent a year, mostly to the United States. In 1961 the United States imposed a textile quota on imports from Taiwan, as part of the Long Term Arrangement on Cotton Textiles, which imposed quotas on imports from the biggest exporting countries. The industry had come of age. In 1964 the United States took 34 percent of cotton textile exports, followed by Hong Kong with 17 percent and Thailand with 12 percent.[4] It is not clear what marketing help the government gave these early exports.

PLASTICS

The plastics industry was also established under state tutelage. As early as 1953 the J. G. White Engineering Corporation's prospectus on Taiwan's industrial development identified plastics as a suitable target. The government's chief economic planner, K. Y. Yin, supported the prospectus and searched for a suitable private investor in plastics. According to one version of the story, he used his access to information on bank deposits to identify Y. C. Wang as someone with enough entrepreneurial zest and enough savings to undertake the project, and then "told" him to do it. According to another version, Wang himself approached the Industrial Development Commission and asked for suggestions on investment opportunities. He accepted the suggestion of the plastics industry, having seen its potential during his several years in Japan (Gold 1981:118). In any case, the first plastics plant for polyvinyl chloride (PVC) was constructed under government supervision and handed to Wang in running order in 1957. Wang went on to become the country's leading businessman, head of the Formosa Plastics Group.

SYNTHETIC FIBERS

In the synthetic fiber industry, too, the government played the crucial initiating role. By 1954 Taiwan's chemical industry had developed to the point where it could provide most of the intermediate inputs needed to make rayon. The government then decided to oversee the creation of a rayon-making plant as part of a plan to diversify the textile industry away from cotton fiber. With much help from U.S. advisors it brought together an American synthetic fiber company[5] with several local textilers from both public and private firms, and oversaw negotiations on the terms of the joint venture. The U.S. company provided the planning, installation of equipment, and training of workers. The resulting corporation, China Man-Made Fiber Corporation, began production in 1957. It was the largest "private" firm on the island at the time—and the government retained a major influence over its operation (Gold 1981:105).

Many other industries received more indirect promotional attention through the 1950s. The instruments included import restrictions, sectoral allocation of foreign exchange, and concessional credit. With U.S. help and prodding, the

---

[4] Textile destination figures come from Wu Wen-tien 1975: table 15.

[5] The U.S. company was von Kohorn.

government established several organizations to assist industry: the China Productivity and Trade Center in 1955 (to give technical assistance), the Industrial Development and Investment Center in 1959 (to facilitate the entry of foreign investment), and the China Development Corporation in 1959 (to provide industrial finance). The government even took upon itself to penalize producers of low-quality goods. In one celebrated incident the chief economic planner ordered the destruction of twenty thousand light bulbs at a public demonstration in Taipei, and threatened to liberalize imports if quality did not improve. Quality improved and the threat did not have to be carried out (Scott 1979:315). In another case he ordered the confiscation of several tons of substandard monosodium glutamate, the food seasoning. These incidents suggest something of the stance of high public officials toward the business sector, and of the institutions which gave them the power to act as they did.

Planning

Like most developing countries of the 1950s Taiwan had multiyear development plans. The first plan, covering four years from the beginning of 1953 to the end of 1956, was called The Plan for Economic Rehabilitation. It was and remains a classified document, not publicly available. From what is known,[6] the plan assigned most of its resources to agriculture, fertilizers, and textiles. But it was little more than a collection of projects already underway or partially prepared for implementation. It gave no production targets for agriculture or manufacturing and attempted no modeling. The main thrust was to encourage government agencies through a three-pronged effort (import substitution, increasing traditional and new exports, and encouraging foreign capital from Overseas Chinese[7]) to lift the foreign exchange constraint. The complete failure of efforts to attract Overseas Chinese capital led to a number of policy changes in 1955, particularly an easing of foreign exchange controls for Overseas Chinese investors and guarantees against expropriation. The flow of Overseas Chinese investment began to increase the following year. The case of Overseas Chinese investment is an early example of the feedback from outcomes to policies.

The Second Four-Year Plan, from 1958 to 1961, was more sophisticated. It gave targets for the overall rate of growth of national income and investment, and for the share of investment going to the major sectors. It also specified the fiscal and monetary policies which were to improve the investment climate. The underlying assumption was that "capital shortage is the major difficulty in economic development," and hence, "*the Government should positively undertake to guide and help private investments so that they do not flow into*

---

[6] See Riegg 1978:72; Yin 1960:10; *Industry of Free China*, Oct. 1976:7–10.

[7] "Overseas Chinese" refers to all Chinese who reside outside of China, and in particular, in the 1950s investment context, to those who lived in Hong Kong.

enterprises which have a surplus productivity and a stagnant market'' (Executive Yuan 1957:26, in Riegg 1978:79, emphasis added). Fully half of gross capital formation in the 1958–61 period was carried out by government or public enterprises. Nevertheless, less investment went into agriculture and industry than planned (19 percent instead of 26 percent into agriculture, 42 percent instead of 52 percent into industry), while more went into transportation communications, commerce, and housing. This partly reflects the fact that in practice, the overall allocation of resources and the rate of economic growth were the results of pushing ahead as fast as possible in individual sectors rather than the starting point from which to begin planning in each sector.

The Role of the United States

What was the role of the United States in Taiwan's industrialization of the 1950s? The United States, which had heavily supported the Nationalist government on the mainland, concluded in 1949 that the government was beyond hope and ceased its assistance (Clough 1978). But with the outbreak of the Korean War a year later, Taiwan became a key post on the West's defense perimeter. Massive U.S. aid, both economic and military, resumed to help strengthen the Nationalist regime on Taiwan. In 1954 the United States undertook to assist Taiwan militarily against renewed communist aggression, and then used its aid leverage to dissuade the Nationalist leaders from embarking upon an assault on the mainland, into which U.S. troops would be drawn.

Over the 1950s economic aid equaled about 6 percent of GNP and nearly 40 percent of gross investment, and military aid was bigger still. The biggest share of economic aid, 38 percent, went to finance imports of intermediate goods (mainly cotton, yarn, ores, metals, and fertilizer); 30 percent went for consumer goods (mainly food); another 19 percent went for capital goods (machinery and tools). The United States supplied 35 to 45 percent of Taiwan's imports, and took 5 to 10 percent of its exports. U.S. economic and military advisors exercised considerable influence over the government's policies. In 1957, ten thousand Americans were present ''in an official capacity'' (Kerr 1965:417). ''As in Japan, the locals governed, but the Americans constituted enough of a shadow government to influence a wide range of political and economic decisions made by the Chinese'' (Gold 1986:58). Their influence declined in the early 1960s. Economic aid terminated in 1965, though military aid continued at least to the late 1970s.

''With that much aid who couldn't industrialize?'' it is sometimes said. Certainly U.S. aid was very important.

> By providing for the supply of food and rehabilitation investment goods at a desperately needed moment, it helped to stabilize the economy, the society, and the regime in the early 1950s.

Throughout the 1950s it gave local and foreign investors confidence that the regime would survive, because backed by the United States.

It helped to finance the land reform, including the cost of U.S. advisors.

It helped to dampen inflation and protect income distribution throughout the 1950s.

It was an important channel for technology transfer. This was true even for much of the military aid. Technical assistance to make better military uniforms helped the textile industry, and technical assistance on radars and avionics helped the electronics industry.

It strengthened the planning function within the state, first for land reform, and then for more general economic planning. Relatedly, aid helped to insulate the economic bureaucracy from party control (because of U.S. pressure).

It allowed Taiwan both to maintain a large military (of about half a million regulars, absorbing roughly 10 percent of GNP), while simultaneously growing quite fast.

Aid also helped to strengthen the role of the private sector. U.S. advisors used their aid leverage to check the hostility that Nationalist officials had shown toward private business on the mainland, and to exert pressure at the margin in favor of using aid for creating or helping private firms. U.S. officials themselves sought out private investors for new projects (as in plastics, rayon, and glass), and in several instances blocked attempts by the Nationalist government to put projects under public ownership. They also successfully thwarted plans to undertake several large-scale, capital-intensive projects, such as a steel mill, an airline, and a nuclear reactor. The first plastics plant in 1957 was a key battle; many hardliners in the Nationalist party fought to have it as a public enterprise, and their defeat marked a turning point in acceptance within large parts of government that new industries, even if in some sense strategic for the rest of the economy, did not have to be located in the public sector.

Aid leverage was used to reduce the discrimination in favor of mainlanders and against islanders in the allocation of government resources (such as the allocation of import licenses for cotton).

Aid helped to ease the transition to more liberal economic policies in the late 1950s and early 1960s. U.S. officials pressed for the adoption of a strategy for obtaining foreign exchange through increased exports and foreign investment, to substitute for the soon-to-be-terminated aid receipts. They helped to tip the balance of decision within the government in favor of a more outward-oriented development strategy.

For all this, aid can hardly be taken as a sufficient condition for Taiwan's superior economic performance. Several other countries have received similar or even larger amounts of aid per capita and have not used it as effectively (Jacoby 1966; Little 1979; Amsden 1984a; Ranis 1978). It was used effectively in Taiwan because the government—especially Chiang Kai-shek—realized the urgent need for reform, also because the United States wanted a strong and stable outpost on its western defenses, and both sides wanted a showcase of noncommunist development to contrast with communist development on the mainland. At the same time, the United States clearly did not "ride herd on the planning function," as Cumings claims (forthcoming); the gradualness of the economic liberalization and privatization is testimony to that, although it is also true that Western development principles of the 1950s were less suspicious of government guidance than they are today.[8]

As important as the direct U.S. governmental role may be the social ties which developed between Americans and Taiwanese, which facilitated the flow of commerce and ideas. Together with the legacy of familiarity with Japan, Taiwan was then in the unusual position of having good connections to both the largest and the fastest-growing markets in the world; whereas many other developing countries have close connections to only one of the less dynamic European ones. Indeed, the connections to the United States and to Japan have tended to be concentrated by ethnic group. In Liu's sample of leading businessmen with some foreign education, for example, 75 percent of the native Taiwanese businessmen received theirs in Japan and 23 percent in the U.S., while of the mainlander businessmen, 61 percent received theirs in the U.S. and 18 percent in Japan (1987:135).

The Role of Import Substitution

A study of the sources of growth in nine countries from the 1950s to the 1970s concludes that Taiwan and Korea stand out from the others in terms of the contribution of import substitution to the growth of manufactured output (de Melo 1985).[9] They are the only countries in the sample where import substitution contributed as much as one-third of manufactured growth in any subperiod. The subperiod in which import substitution contributed so much to total growth was 1955–60 in Taiwan and 1960–66 in Korea—the period prior to the very rapid growth of manufactured exports. The overall pattern of manufactured growth with strong import substitution preceding export expansion is observed in virtually all sectors in both countries. Furthermore, the study finds that from 1955 to 1971 in Taiwan and 1955 to 1973 in Korea, Taiwan did more import substitution than Korea in light industry, heavy industry, and machinery (de Melo 1985: table 9.4). Results from the sample are consistent with the proposition that countries which experience fast export-led growth have earlier had a period in which import substitution was a very important component in total growth. And the reason may be that, as Jaime de Melo suggests, "the experience gained from sales in the domestic market is a pre-

---

[8] See Riegg 1978 for an extended attempt to evaluate the impact of U.S. aid to Taiwan. See also Jacoby 1966.

[9] The other countries are Japan, Yugoslavia, Turkey, Israel, Norway, Mexico, and Colombia.

requisite for successful exports of manufacturers'' (1985:223). This is consistent with Thomas Gold's finding, that the entrepreneurs who emerged as Taiwan's industrial leaders in the protected environment of the 1950s remained as the industrial leaders after 1958–62, and continued to constitute the core of Taiwan's industrial establishment through the 1970s (1981:94). Neither point fits comfortably with blanket neoclassical criticism of import substitution policies.

Evidence of the contribution of import substitution to manufacturing growth in Taiwan before the trade reforms must qualify the argument of Ranis, amongst others, who stresses the "mildness" of import substitution in East Asia as compared to Latin America (1983:22). "Mildness" refers to relatively low price distortions. But note, first, that virtually no evidence is offered in support of the proposition that Taiwan had low price distortions in the 1950s compared with typical Latin American levels.[10] Second, "mild" can easily give the impression that the period of import substitution was not important in Taiwan and Korea's growth. Yet the evidence suggests that, overall, the policies of import substitution in the 1950s had a very important role in preparing the way for later export success. They did so both by channelling resources from agriculture to industry through the exchange rate and domestic terms of trade, and by more direct promotion of certain sectors.

Against all this evidence one sees how misleading are the neoclassical accounts that present Taiwan as a typical underdeveloped country in the 1940s and 1950s, "an agrarian backwater."[11] One also sees how misleading are accounts that assert that the initial stage of import substitution was a waste of time. Maurice Scott, for example, claims that protection was the reason for Taiwan's lack of industrial competitiveness in the 1950s, not a remedy for it. Hence, "the idea that a long period of protection for the domestic market is a

[10] It is quite plausible, however, that the exchange rate, wage rate, interest rate, and price of imports were less distorted than in many Latin American countries. Little, Scitovsky, and Scott (1970:163) give comparative figures for nominal tariff rates for manufactured goods in six developing countries (including Taiwan) for a year in the period from 1958 to 1966, which suggest that Taiwan had the second lowest average tariffs after Mexico (30 percent to Mexico's 22 percent, against Argentina's 141 percent). Note that Lee, et al. 1975 calculate the average nominal tariff for manufactures as over 60 percent in 1969, only three years later, which raises a question of the accuracy of Little, et al.'s figure.

[11] Lau 1986:3. For Walter Galenson, "Taiwan was a typical Asian country in 1952. Underemployment was widespread. There were open sewage canals in the cities; many cities were unpaved; much of the housing was ramshackle; pedicabs were still in use" (1982:86). Hla Myint says that "in the 1950s, Taiwan started out as a typical heavily populated underdeveloped country . . ." (1982:107). Little recognizes the advantage of Taiwan's social cohesion, value attached to hard work, stock of skilled manpower, and productive agriculture; but implies that they were neutralized by disadvantages such as lack of nonhuman resources, lack of good harbor sites, and high population density (1979:449). But compare Ranis (1979:211): "substantial industrialization and import substitution had begun in Taiwan well before 1953, when the curtain of analysis is usually opened."

necessary prelude to exporting is not borne out by Taiwan's experience''
(1979:380). Hla Myint agrees (1982:129). Neither offers evidence. The effect
of presenting Taiwan as a typical underdeveloped country in the 1950s, or of
viewing the period of import substitution as a waste of time, is to locate the
cause of Taiwan's success more firmly in liberal trade and price policies. The
evidence given here suggests a more complex story. The move toward more
liberal trade and price policies was at most a necessary condition for the high-
speed growth that was to follow (in the sense that growth would not have been
so fast without). It was not even remotely sufficient.

NEW EXPORT SECTORS AND IMPORT SUBSTITUTION, 1960 TO THE EARLY 1970S

In neoclassical accounts the state disappears from the stage once the liberalizing
reforms are in place. Only for the mid-1970s and after do the better neoclassical accounts recognize that the government attempts a promotional role.[12]
According to Samuel Ho,

> with protectionist sentiments rising in the developed countries, continued rapid
> expansion of the light manufactured exports on which Korea's and Taiwan's in-
> dustrial growth had been based appeared problematic. Rising wages in Korea and
> Taiwan also suggested that their comparative advantage was shifting away from
> the semi-skilled, labor-intensive industries that grew so rapidly in the 1960s. *To
> policy makers in both countries, these changes in external and internal conditions
> suggested a need to restructure the industrial sector.*

Accordingly,

> in both Korea and Taiwan, the economic plans that emerged in the mid-1970s
> (Taiwan's Seventh Plan for 1976–1981 . . .) reflected these concerns. Planners
> advocated a move away from the labor-intensive industries. . . . This new direc-
> tion of industrialization [toward heavy and chemical as well as skill-intensive in-
> dustries] was mapped out in the *mid 1970s*, shortly after the first oil crisis.
>
> (1981:1197, 1181, emphasis added).

Walter Galenson argues similarly that beginning around 1976

> the production of more capital-intensive goods began to accelerate—synthetic tex-
> tiles, paper, chemicals . . . tires, glass, steel products, machine tools, and heavy
> machinery. The supply of cheap labor was drying up, and Marshall's principle of
> substitution was operating.   (1982:78)

The point of dating the push into the new capital- and technology-intensive
industries in the mid-1970s is that it then appears to be a *response* to market

---

[12] Little (1979:489) implies that industrial promotion had either no effect or a bad effect.

forces, specifically to changes in costs, and not an *anticipation* of those changes. It is to that extent more consistent with the "self-regulating market" theory of Taiwan's success.

Export expansion has indeed constituted the major source of growth in Taiwan and Korea since the early 1960s. The earlier-mentioned study which found that Taiwan and Korea stood out from seven other countries in the relative importance of import substitution in their early growth, also found that they stand out in terms of the importance of export expansion in their later growth (de Melo 1985:223).

It is not true, however, that the state had no important directive role during the 1960s, or (closely related) that an accelerated move into heavy and skill-intensive industries began in the mid-1970s.

Plans

The new direction of industrialization was in fact mapped out long before the mid-1970s. The Third Plan (1961–64) already emphasized the need to accelerate the growth of heavy industry. "Heavy industry holds the key to industrialization as it produces capital goods. We must develop heavy industry so as to support the long-term steady growth of the economy" (Ministry of Economic Affairs 1961:34).[13] The Fourth Plan (1965–68) said:

> For further development, stress must be laid on basic heavy industries (such as chemical wood pulp, petrochemical intermediates, and large-scale integrated steel production) instead of end product manufacturing or processing. Industrial development in the long run must be centered on export products that have high income elasticity and low transportation cost. And around these products there should be development of both forward and backward industries, so that both specialization and complementarity may be achieved in the interest of Taiwan's economy.

Not only heavy and chemical industries were targeted. Planning documents from the early 1960s pick quite specific products in electrical appliances and electronics for promotion, including transistor radios, electronic components, watches, and clocks. These were thought to be of particular interest to foreign investors. By moving in these directions, the 1965–68 plan continued, "we shall then be able to meet the changing situation in the world market brought about by the rapid industrial progress of the emerging nations and the growing sophistication of the industries of the developed countries" (CIECD 1965:122, 124).

---

[13] The Third Plan also said that "while priority should be given to light industries requiring small capital but yielding quick returns in terms of income, employment, and foreign exchange benefits, heavy industries that serve to consolidate and broaden the foundation of the developing economy, as well as basic energy industries and natural resource development projects, should not be neglected despite heavy investments and slow returns" (1961:29).

These guidelines were approved by the political leadership in the early 1960s, several years before the end of labor surplus (conventionally put at 1968–70: Fei, Ranis, and Kuo 1979), still longer before protectionist barriers began to go up (except in textiles), and well over a decade before the plan to which Ho attributes the first expression of restructuring concerns.

At the same time as the state was reaffirming a leadership role, it also gave clearer signals than in the 1950s about the value of a large and vigorous private sector. Though it denationalized only a few small public enterprises after 1953, the public enterprise share of manufacturing production fell from 56 percent in 1952 to 44 percent in 1960 to 21 percent in 1970. The controversial granting of the first plastics factory to the private sector in 1957 was, as noted, a landmark in this change of signals. A year or so later, when the U.S. government decided that its foreign assistance programs should in the future place more emphasis on the private sector, the U.S. Mission on Taiwan made government enthusiasm for the private sector a condition of its help in attracting foreign investment, boosting exports, and obtaining loans from international lending institutions like the World Bank (Jacoby 1966:35). The 1961–64 plan said, "It is true that Taiwan is short of capital, but what is wanted most are entrepreneurs and their entrepreneurship" (1961:10), presumably a qualification to the previous plan's emphasis on capital shortage.

Production Trends

Taiwan experienced massive capital accumulation throughout the 1960s. Even in 1960, at the start of the export boom and not as a consequence of it, the rate of gross domestic investment to GDP stood at about 20 percent, which only developing countries with large natural resource investment and a few others including China then equaled (World Bank 1983:157). Though the bulk of this investment probably went into infrastructure and labor-intensive production, it is also true that even in the 1960s large amounts went into the development of new industries.

Between 1960 and 1977 manufacturing as a share of GDP rose from 22 percent to 37 percent, from a rank of twelfth among fifty-five middle-income countries to a rank of first equal with Argentina (see table 2.6). A large part of this increase occurred in the 1960s. Heavy and chemical industries increased from 49.8 percent of gross manufactured output in 1965, to 53.3 percent in 1975. Korea, by contrast, had a much smaller set of heavy and chemical industries by 1965, producing only 38.2 percent of gross manufactured output; but the share increased to 48.4 percent in 1975—still 5 percent less than Taiwan's (see table 2.8). Taiwan's growth in chemicals and machinery was especially striking, from 24 percent of manufacturing value added in 1961 to 50 percent by 1974. In the same period, Korea's chemical and machinery subsectors went from 23 percent to only 39 percent (see table 2.7). This all suggests that Taiwan laid down a relatively large set of heavy and chemical industries in the 1960s, at the same time as exports of light industries were growing at high speed.

But what of Galenson's earlier-mentioned statement that the production of capital-intensive goods began to accelerate around 1976? Table 4.1 shows the compound growth rate in Galenson's sectors for two periods prior to 1976 and two periods following 1976. With the single exception of basic metals, growth rates in both periods prior to 1976 were higher than subsequent growth rates. (In the case of basic metals, the average for both periods prior to 1976 is higher than the average for the two subsequent periods.) Galenson's statement is true only if one takes 1974 or 1975 as the starting point, years of slight decline in industrial production. This evidence is consistent with the argument that Taiwan's big push into these capital- and technology-intensive industries was state-led, not market-led, occurring in advance of the operation of Marshall's principle of substitution.

Trends in secondary import substitution and export substitution are consistent with this story. Secondary (as distinct from primary) import substitution refers to a decline in intermediate and capital good imports in relation to total

TABLE 4.1
Production in Selected Manfacturing Sectors,
Average Compound Rates, Pre-1976 and Post-1976

Sector	1965–69	1969–73	1976–80	1980–84
Textiles	31.1	26.4	8.3	4.4
Paper	17.8	20.2	13.6	4.0
Chemicals	25.1	26.8	18.4	12.2
Rubber products	35.6	26.2	7.6	11.6
Nonmetallic mineral products	15.1	13.4	7.8	4.3
Basic metals	12.1	18.0	16.3	15.7
Metal products	23.0	20.8	6.6	7.6
Machinery	17.6	16.2	9.0	6.3
Electrical machinery	52.6	43.5	17.6	21.5

Source: DGBAS, Statistical Yearbook, 1981, 1985.

Note: The production indices are based on 1976 = 100. Growth rates are calculated using a standard least-squares regression. The years 1974 and 1975 are dropped because in these years production untypically declined in the wake of the oil price rise. I thank Rao Katikineni for help with the computations.

supply of those goods, that is, to an increase of domestic production in total supply. Overall, the ratio of intermediate and capital good imports to total supply did not decline until the 1976–81 period. Earlier, exports grew so fast (27 percent a year in 1966–71, 21 percent in 1971–76) that domestic supply industries could not keep up. So there was no overall secondary import substitution until the second half of the 1970s. Since then, with greater domestic supply capacity and slightly lower export growth (17 percent a year in 1976–81) overall secondary import substitution has occurred (Schive forthcoming).

But secondary import substitution is discernible much earlier in individual sectors. At the heavy and chemical end of manufacturing domestic production as a proportion of total supply went up in eight out of twelve sectors between 1961 and 1969.[14] In eleven of those twelve, exports as a proportion of total domestic production also went up (Lin 1973:66). The subsectors where imports increased relative to supply were petroleum products, iron and steel, aluminum, and transport equipment, three of which process natural resources lacking in Taiwan, so that an increase in imports as the economy grows is hardly surprising. Synthetic fibers and electrical and electronic goods have shown strong import substitution from 1966 onwards, if not earlier.

In Korea, by contrast, overall secondary import substitution began earlier than in Taiwan (in the 1971–75 period); but this probably reflects the fact that Korea's degree of import replacement was much lower than Taiwan's in the 1960s, so that reduction of intermediate and capital good imports relative to supply was easier for Korea in the 1970s.

Sectoral Histories to the Early 1970s

Let us carry forward the sectoral histories begun earlier,[15] bearing in mind that the state barely appears in neoclassical accounts of the 1960s and early 1970s.

SYNTHETIC FIBERS

Synthetic fibers and plastics represent import substitution aimed at the upstream end of export industries. Synthetics, as we saw, began with rayon production by a publicly owned company in 1957. This particular joint venture between an American company and several domestic companies was important not just as the start of a new industry, but also because it set the pattern for foreign investment in many other sectors through the 1960s, with the government taking the lead in bringing together foreign companies and local producers to fill gaps in the production structure. The success of the arrangement

[14] Within ISIC 35, 37, and 38 the import share fell in rubber manufactures, chemical fertilizer, pharmaceuticals, plastics and products, other chemicals and chemical products, other metals and metal products, machinery, and communications equipment.

[15] Much of the material to follow comes from research by Gold 1981, 1986; Djang 1977; and for autos and electronics, Chu 1987a and b.

helped convince other potential foreign investors that the government could be relied on to keep agreements, allow repatriation of profits, and in general be helpful.

In 1962 this same state-sponsored rayon company, together with a state financing agency, created another company[16] to make nylon. It started production in 1964. Although initially using its own technology (it had tried but failed to reach a technical cooperation agreement with a Japanese firm), it shortly afterwards formed into a joint venture with another Japanese firm. Both of the first synthetic fiber companies, then, were largely the creation of the state. The original rayon company diversified into polyesters in 1967.

Private firms soon followed. Y. C. Wang, who had run the first plastics-making plant, started one to make rayon in 1964, and then another to make acrylics in 1967, the latter as a joint venture with a Japanese company. Many other businessmen moved to get a share of the market. By 1971 fifteen companies were making synthetic fibers; by 1977, twenty-eight. Most of the expansion has been carried out by wholly or largely privately owned firms; and the owners are mostly locals, not foreigners. Foreign technology has come less through joint ownership than through technology-licensing agreements. The government has remained active in overseeing the structural evolution of the industry, particularly by helping to find foreign companies willing to share technology, and helping to negotiate with them on the terms of the licensing agreement, which the government must approve. Taiwan by 1981 was the fourth biggest producer of synthetic fibers in the world (Tanzer 1981).

PLASTICS

In plastics as much as in fibers, Taiwan's firms had to use foreign technology, either in licensing agreements or joint ventures, and the state has had a still bigger role in steering the evolution of the sector. The starting point is the state-built PVC plant of 1957 handed over to Y. C. Wang to run as a private company. A state-owned enterprise began to make benzenes and xylene in 1959. In the same year, the state-owned Chinese Petroleum Corporation entered into a joint venture with two U.S. companies to produce fertilizer from newly discovered natural gas.

In the early 1960s the Chinese Petroleum Corporation and a U.S. company (Gulf) formed a joint venture to make lubricating oil. A further step occurred in 1964, when another U.S. company (National Distillers and Chemical Corporation) began negotiations with the government on a low-density polyethylene plant. The plant came on line in 1968, the first in East or Southeast Asia outside Japan. Meanwhile, the Chinese Petroleum Corporation had commis-

---

[16] This was called United Nylon Corporation. The state financing agency was the China Development Corporation.

sioned the first naptha cracker in 1965, which also came on line in 1968. Two-thirds of its production was guaranteed to the polyethylene plant.

In 1966 three more private firms started to make PVC. But all four PVC firms (including Wang's) made it by an inefficient method, which needed imported intermediates. At the same time, the Chinese Petroleum Corporation had excess supplies of ethylene, from which an intermediate suitable for processing into PVC could be obtained more cheaply than the imported ones. So *the government forced the four private producers of PVC to merge* in a joint venture with the Chinese Petroleum Corporation and another state-owned chemical company, in order to adopt a more efficient ethylene-using production method. The government guaranteed one-third of the naptha cracker's production to this joint venture.

By the end of the 1960s Taiwan's petrochemical industry was producing ethylene, polyethylene, polystyrene, PVC, PVAC, synthetic rubber, artificial fibers, and many other products. State-owned companies had a big role throughout the sector. In 1972 a high-density polyethylene plant came on line as a joint venture between the U.S. company which had earlier built the low-density plant, together with a large state-owned holding company and several private firms. Also in 1972 Arthur D. Little International, Inc., commissioned to advise the government on future industrialization, urged it to strengthen backwards integration in the petrochemical sector. In 1973 domestic and foreign shortages of intermediates resulted in panic buying, underlining Taiwan's vulnerability to supply cut-offs. The world oil price increase in late 1973 further demonstrated, in the government's mind, the desirability of expanding that portion of the supply located within Taiwan. The same point was made by the reemergence of the People's Republic of China (PRC) on the world stage in the mid-1970s, the consequence of which was seen to be possible PRC pressure on Taiwan's foreign suppliers to disrupt supplies. All these factors led to further expansion of petrochemical intermediates, generally in joint ventures with foreign (mostly U.S.) firms, under close government supervision and with much public ownership.

AUTOMOBILES

Automobiles represent a fairly standard case of import substitution of a durable consumer good, and here the government relied on private firms (Chu 1987a; Arnold 1989). Taiwan entered the industry by the familiar and relatively low-entry-barrier route of assembling semi-knocked-down kits under foreign license. The first automotive firm (Yue-Loong) was established in 1953. It began to assemble engines in 1956, helped by huge amounts of U.S. aid ($3.2 million between 1955 and 1956). The aid reflected the owner's close connections to the inner circle around the President. The first Taiwan-assembled passenger cars came on the market in 1960, from a joint venture with a Japanese firm (Nissan). In 1961 the government announced measures for the development of the automobile industry. These measures prohibited further investment in simple assembly and empowered the Ministry of Economic Affairs to impose whatever import restrictions and tariffs it deemed necessary to promote the domestic industry. A three-tier tariff was enacted, with 60 percent duty on finished passenger cars, 40 percent on commercial vehicles, and 15 percent on parts and components. In 1964 imports of commercial vehicles were banned to help the struggling domestic maker. A year later the tariff on parts and components was increased to 46 percent to help domestic producers (several of whom had licensing agreements with Japanese firms), while the tariff on finished cars went up to 65 percent. Also in 1965 the government added a 60 percent local content requirement, recognized to be unrealistically high but intended to give officials bargaining leverage with future makers. These infant industry arrangements were to be reviewed after another four years. In 1967 to 1969 four new firms were allowed to enter, each with Japanese participation (Lio-Ho with Toyota, three others with second-tier firms, plus the existing arrangement between Yue-Loong and Nissan). Here, in the early period, we see government attempting to promote the industry without using public enterprises or subsidized financial support, but instead relying on guiding private firms by entry requirements, import controls and tariffs, and domestic content requirements. But the overall market was tiny in relation to economies of scale, twenty thousand vehicles a year or less at the end of the 1960s, for a share of which five assemblers struggled.

ELECTRICAL AND ELECTRONIC GOODS

By 1968 the electrical and electronic goods industry was the second biggest exporter after textiles, and in 1984 it overtook textiles. Most of its production (80 percent in 1976) has been exported, chiefly to the United States. It is characterized by a few large foreign-invested assemblers, most from the U.S., and many locally and privately owned suppliers of components to them.

The origins of the industry go back to the late 1940s, when local radio sellers began to assemble radios from imported parts, and a number of firms transposed from the mainland began producing wire, light bulbs, transformers, and the like. In 1950 the government began to restrict the import of whole radios, to give an incentive to local assemblers. The first Four Year Plan (1953–56) indicated that protection and other incentives would be given for the production of radios, fans, meters, fluorescent lights, low-voltage transmitters, and cables. In 1953 a Taiwanese firm (Tatung) signed the first-ever technology agreement between a Taiwanese and a Japanese firm. The agreement was for producing the Japanese firm's electric watt-hour meters from locally made components. The Japanese firm agreed to take engineers from the Taiwan firm for training. The agreement was supported and even funded by USAID.[17]

---

[17] For convenience I use the more recent name of the U.S. economic aid agency. Earlier it was

By the late 1950s a number of Japanese firms began seeking local partners for electrical assembly, and seven joint ventures had been formed by 1963. Meanwhile, in 1961, the Stanford Research Institute, which had been asked by the government and USAID to help identify sectors and products of interest to foreign investors, urged that electricals should be one of seven priority industries. In 1962 the government formed a state-owned television broadcasting company, which began to assemble televisions from Japanese components. In the same year the government imposed local content requirements for the production of televisions, refrigerators, air conditioners, automobiles, diesel engines, and several other items. These requirements meant that an escalating percentage of total value had to be made up of locally produced parts. This represented the government's response to a calculation that much of the incoming Japanese investment gave low social returns, because it intended only to make items for sale on the domestic market with components shipped in from Japan (the tariff on assembled items being much higher than on components). At about the same time the government also revised the rules regarding foreign investment, to facilitate joint ventures and technical cooperation agreements with foreign firms. Several more technical agreements on production of electrical appliances and consumer electronics were signed between Taiwanese and Japanese firms in 1963.

At the start of the 1960s, U.S. electrical and electronics firms began to examine opportunities for relocating production to cheaper labor sites. Fairchild, the U.S. semiconductor group, established a factory in Hong Kong in 1961, and Philips of Holland opened one in Taiwan the same year. In both cases, the object was to cut costs by getting the labor-intensive part of semiconductor manufacturing—connecting the wire leads, and packaging—done more cheaply than was possible at home. The year 1961 thus represents a landmark in the history of East Asia. It is the beginning of the corporate strategy that came to be called global manufacturing, of manufacturing or purchasing around the world wherever components could be obtained at lowest cost. Of all regions of the world East Asia has benefited most from this strategy.

The government of Taiwan, with USAID's help, aggressively sought out U.S. companies. General Instruments was the first U.S. company to begin production in 1964. In the next two years twenty-four U.S. firms rushed to make production agreements. In 1965 the first export-processing zone opened, where foreign and domestic firms could enjoy unusually unfettered conditions in return for exporting all of their production. In 1966 the government published a plan to turn Taiwan into an "electronics industry center." The planning agency (Council for International Economic Cooperation and Develop-

called the Economic Cooperation Administration, later the International Cooperation Administration.

ment, CIECD) formed an electronics working group to assist in marketing, co-ordinating production with the demands of foreign buyers, procuring raw materials, training personnel, improving quality, and speeding up bureaucratic approval procedures. It also arranged two major exhibitions in 1967 and 1968 to bring foreign investors together with local producers. Earlier, in 1965, the publicly owned China Data Processing Center was established to push the use of computers in local industry. Electrical and electronics exports grew at 58 percent a year between 1966 and 1971.

OTHER SECTORS

In basic metals the government established a significant presence in steel production in 1962, when it took over a large, loss-making plant. Although the decision to build a large-scale integrated steel mill was not finally taken until 1970, the project was under active consideration from the mid-1950s onwards. Several feasibility studies were carried out by U.S., West German, and Japanese consultants and the project nearly went ahead in 1956 and again in 1961 (Djang 1977). Aluminum and copper smelting have also been carried out by state-owned enterprises. The government sponsored a big increase in production capacity in 1963. In shipbuilding a massive increase in capacity was made by the state-owned Taiwan Shipbuilding Corporation in 1962. At about the same time, two state-owned enterprises in the metal manufacturing sectors undertook large expansions.

A small pilot nuclear reactor was started in 1961. Construction of a full-scale commercial reactor by a public enterprise was begun in 1968 and completed in 1977, in time to help the country recover from the first oil shock and weather the second.

In the 1960s the government established several more research and service organizations to promote technological and managerial upgrading in industry, in addition to those established during the 1950s. Examples are the Metal Industries Development Center, started in 1963 to demonstrate improved production and quality control methods and to provide management training courses; and the earlier-mentioned China Data Processing Center, established in 1965 to promote the use of computers. Other government-sponsored and -guided research institutes were established for chemicals, mining, energy, glass, textiles, food processing, and, in 1955, an institute for nuclear science research (Fong 1968; Lumley 1981:86). The government also sponsored, in 1960, the formation of a joint public-private consulting service[18] to promote exports of machinery and whole production plants (Amsden 1984b:501).

This drive into heavy and electronics industries was not entirely innocent. The military wanted it, as well as the economic technocrats. The military ran its own production facilities, working closely with public enterprises or spe-

---

[18] This was called China Technical Consultants, Inc.

cial status private firms. By the early 1960s Taiwan's military-industrial complex was already capable of making much of the equipment and less sophisticated weaponry needed by the armed forces. By the end of the 1960s Taiwan
was producing machine guns, M-14 rifles, artillery, mortars, and the like. In
1969 a joint venture started for the production of military helicopters, and soon
afterwards, another for co-production of F5–E fighter planes (Amsden
1984a:52–53; Clough 1978). The Vietnam War was good for Taiwan's economy, as the Korean War had earlier helped Japan's economic growth at a
critical time. The United States bought large amounts of food and military
equipment from Taiwan, and the island developed the best military repair facilities in Asia outside of Japan. This war-induced demand helped to compensate for the termination of U.S. economic aid.

THE 1970s AND 1980s

By the early 1970s the economy was falling victim to its success. Its exports
began to face loud protectionist threats, especially in the United States; wages
were rising faster than competitors'; other newly industrializing countries
were moving into the same markets; and the physical infrastructure was over-
stretched. At the same time, world prices of nonoil commodities were rising,
and the effective devaluation of the Taiwan currency in 1971 and 1973 (it was
pegged to the U.S. dollar which was devalued in those years) raised the import
bill even more. Then in 1973 and 1974 came the quadrupling of oil prices.
Since imports equaled a third of GDP at this time, these changes in import
prices had a deep effect on the domestic economy. Real GNP grew at only one
percent in 1974, compared to an average 10 percent per year over the 1960s
and early 1970s. Inflation hit 40 percent, having been less than 2 percent a
year between 1961 and 1971. The trade deficit exceeded US$1,000 million.
At much the same time, Taiwan experienced a series of exogenous political
shocks. The United Nations derecognized Taiwan in 1971, Japan derecognized the country in 1972, and the U.S. government was making friendly
overtures to the People's Republic. In response, emigration and capital flight
to the United States increased, foreign trade and investment slowed, and university students began to voice dissent.

The government, in turn, asserted economic leadership and political control
even more strongly than before. The Sixth Fourth-Year Plan (1973–76) renewed the emphasis on export orientation, while also signalling state support
for advances in petrochemicals, electrical machinery, electronics, precision
machine tools, computer terminals and peripherals, and other such products.
Some subsectors were identified as suitable for development by local firms,
others as requiring joint ventures with foreign companies and public enterprises (especially petrochemicals), and still others as suitable for a mix of
foreign and local private firms (electronics). The plan also announced a big

increase in public sector investment for improving the physical infrastructure. The role of the public enterprise sector expanded over the 1970s, not only in infrastructure but also in heavy and chemical industries. Their share of gross fixed capital formation increased from around 28 percent in the 1960s to about 33 percent in the 1970s.

To handle the oil price increase the government adopted a high-risk—and in the event remarkably successful—macroeconomic strategy.[19] As inflation began to rise in 1973, interest rates through the banking system were gradually raised. Then as inflation accelerated in 1974, they were raised sharply, loan rates by a quarter to 16.5 percent for secured loans and deposit rates by one-third to 15 percent for long-term deposits. The prices of oil and other energy-related products were raised even more—gasoline by 85 percent and electricity by nearly 80 percent. Within a few months the rate of price increase started to fall, and in 1975 the Taiwan economy experienced a 5 percent decline in overall prices. In late 1974 the government reduced income taxes and tariffs to stimulate economic activity. In the same year huge public spending on a series of infrastructure projects began. Having been in the planning stage since before 1973, the projects started just in time to complement the fiscal stimulus. In the second half of the 1970s real growth returned to rates in excess of 10 percent a year and inflation fell to 3 percent. Fast export growth brought the balance of payments back into steady surplus.

The Sixth Four-Year Plan had to be scrapped in the wake of the 1973–74 disturbances, but much the same priorities were carried forward into the Six-Year Plan of 1976–81. The new plan, however, gave an even more prominent role to the state, for the experience of 1973 to 1975 had strengthened the government's determination to reduce Taiwan's vulnerability to fluctuations in the prices of key intermediates—which meant building even more capacity in heavy and chemical industries. The plan also called for an increase in state expenditure for education, especially vocational high school education.

The second round of oil price rises in 1979 and 1980 was milder in its impact on Taiwan than the first. Inflation reached 14 percent in 1979 and 22 percent in 1980, half as much as in 1973–74. Growth rates also fell, but only by half as much as the earlier fall. The trade account did not move into deficit, though the surplus almost vanished. In these circumstances the government chose to avoid the radical adjustments of the first round, and to rely instead on a gradual raising of interest rates, a gradual increase in oil and electricity prices, and a switch from a fixed rate foreign exchange system to a tightly managed "float."

The second round of oil price rises spurred a shift in the emphasis of industrial policies toward non-energy-intensive, nonpolluting, and technology-intensive activities like machine tools, semiconductors, computers, telecom-

---

[19] See International Policy Analysis 1985.

munications, robotics, and biotechnology; as also did accumulating evidence
that Korea was making faster strides in some of these sectors (Mody 1989).
The Ten-Year Plan of 1980–89 and the Four-Year Plan of 1982–86 reflected
this change of emphasis.

In fact, the government had made a priority of industrial technology from
the 1950s, when it promulgated the "National Guidelines for Long Range
Scientific Development" and formed the Council on Long Range Scientific
Development to implement the guidelines. Subsequently that council (since
renamed the National Science Council) has published a series of National Science and Technology Development plans. In line with these plans the government established and funded research and development (R&D) institutes in
strategic areas. It also started firms in industries it wished to develop, provided
incentives for investment in high-technology industries, provided other incentives for R&D activity, and offered financial aid for education and training.
The government's role reflects its belief that Taiwan's predominantly small-
scale firms would not undertake enough technology investment by themselves.
It complements the technology transfer that comes via knowledge and contacts
gained from the many researchers with foreign education or work experience,
90 percent of them in the United States.

Over the 1970s and 1980s the government intensified its efforts to deepen
an R&D capacity for the new growth sectors. A landmark is the Industrial
Technology Research Institute (ITRI), established in 1973. By 1987, ITRI had
a budget of US$215 million and a staff of over 4,500, organized into six insti-
tutes (electronics, machinery, chemical engineering, energy and mining, industrial materials, and standards and measurement).[20] These institutes are concerned only with civilian technologies; an ITRI-equivalent, with a staff of
twenty thousand, covers military technologies. Another landmark is the Hsinchu Science-based Industry Park opened in 1980 (but originally conceived in
1969), where foreign and domestic high-technology firms operate in close
proximity to ITRI laboratories and where the government is willing to take up
to 49 percent equity in each venture. The park caters especially to firms in

---

[20] The Ministry of Economic Affairs established ITRI in 1973 by putting three existing public
R&D organizations (for general industry, mining industry, and metallurgical industry) under one
organizational umbrella, and adding to them the newly created ERSO for electronics (*Central Daily
News*,19 Feb., 1983). ITRI's gross revenue for 1987 was NT$6.1 billion, of which $3.4 billion
came from government grants, endowment dividends and donations, and contract, fees, or proj-
ect-based grants. The staff of 4,236 in early 1987 included 114 doctorates, 904 masters, and 1,454
bachelors (ITRI *Annual Report 1987*). By November 1987 the staff had risen to 4,466. ERSO accounted for 46 percent of the total budget. I am grateful to Yun-han Chu for making this information available. There are also several other major research and service organizations outside
the ITRI umbrella, such as the Development Center for Biotechnology, founded in 1984 to seek
out suitable biotechnologies around the world, master them in-house, and transfer them to domestic firms. It also provides market research and assessment services for industry and government.

information, precision instruments, new materials, and biotechnology. Both projects reflect the aim of reducing Taiwan's dependence on technology transfer from abroad. Also in 1980 and as part of the same thrust, the government launched "national strategic programs" in eight fields—energy, automation, information, materials, biotechnology, electro-optics, hepatitis B control, and food processing—and established new institutional arrangements for steering these programs (chapters 7 and 9). With blossoming opportunities as a lure, it also redoubled efforts to repatriate more of the one in five of Taiwan's graduates in engineering, science, medicine, and agriculture who go abroad for further study, of whom only one in five returned during 1976–86. Related technology-upgrading measures include a government-sponsored program to diffuse labor-saving automation equipment, another to reach Japanese standards of quality control in certain industries, another to foster venture capital firms as a way of improving access to capital for high-tech enterprises, and another to give increased protection to intellectual property. Increasingly, the talk is of making Taiwan the Switzerland of Asia, emphasizing high quality in selected industries with relatively small-scale firms.

Cross-country indicators of R&D effort have to be taken with a grain of salt, for different countries use different definitions. By official figures, Taiwan spent 1.06 percent of GNP on nonmilitary R&D in 1985, compared to 2.51 percent in Japan, 2.01 percent in the United States, 1.87 percent in France, and 1.59 percent in Korea. Half of Taiwan's spending is classed as "public sector"; but this is a fudge, for it excludes government grants to certain nonprofit organizations. When the adjustment is made, the public share is about 60 percent, with private domestic and foreign firms accounting for the rest. In terms of number of researchers per ten thousand people (on a headcount rather than full-time equivalency basis), Taiwan has about fourteen, compared to thirty-three in Japan and the United States, eighteen in France, and eleven in Korea.[21]

In addition to these generic measures to upgrade industrial technology, the government also mounted some industry-specific policies during the 1970s and 1980s.

Steel

A large-scale integrated steel mill was given the go-ahead in 1970 and came on line in 1974. The mill is operated by a public enterprise (China Steel). It runs at a handsome profit, and although never intended to export a large part of its production it has been efficient enough to make Taiwan the second biggest steel exporter to Japan after Korea (Bruce 1983). Taiwan also has a large

[21] National Science Council (Taiwan), *Science and Technology Data Book 1988*; Ministry of Science and Technology (Korea), *Handbook 1987*; interviews with Science and Technology Advisory Group staff.

number of private mini steel mills, which at the start of the integrated mill project supplied about half of domestic demand, the higher-quality remainder being imported mostly from Japan. Many economists argued that Taiwan should continue to rely on imports, as they also said about petrochemicals. Most of the planners, on the other hand, wanted Taiwan to have its own capacity at the higher-quality end, partly because of worries about dependence on Japan and partly because of their understanding that such industries were needed for sustained growth and higher living standards. The mini steel mills still exist, concentrating on higher-quality specialty steels and alloys while China Steel concentrates on flat products and tubes. China Steel provides them with technical assistance.

Shipbuilding

The shipbuilding industry in Taiwan is structurally similar to the steel industry, in that a large public enterprise (China Shipbuilding) dominates the industry, producing virtually all ships of more than a few thousand tons, while many small private shipyards produce fishing boats and yachts. On the other hand, China Shipbuilding, unlike China Steel, has fairly consistently suffered losses. The company was formed in 1970 and its large shipyard came on line in 1974. But Taiwan remains a tiny shipbuilding country by world standards: its share of new world orders (measured in compensated gross tonnage) was only 0.7 percent in 1986, against second biggest Korea's 14.2 percent and first biggest Japan's 36.0 percent.

Machine Tools

Most of Taiwan's machine toolmakers are small in size and financial strength. However, the biggest firm (Leadwell), which makes half of all the numerically controlled machine tools, has about 2.5 percent of the world export market. But even it imports the most technologically advanced component—the numerical controller—from Japan. The development of the industry has been hindered by the government's refusal to contract defense manufacturing to civilian companies; all defense work goes to publicly owned defense-based firms. The main help given to the civilian machine toolmakers has taken the form of subsidized credit, training, and technology inputs.[22] State-sponsored technology institutes, notably one under the ITRI umbrella (Mechanical Industries Research Laboratory), make agreements with particular firms to help them design computer numerically controlled (CNC) machine tools and machining centers. Not only is the design help subsidized; the signing of a technology agreement with a state technology institute virtually guarantees a firm

[22] On Taiwan's machine tool industry, see Fransman 1986; Jacobsson 1984; Amsden 1977.

access to subsidized credit from the development bank. Training is also provided. Even without such an agreement, machine toolmakers are eligible for concessional credit for the production of stipulated items from the Strategic Industry Fund (chapter 6). Tariff protection has been unimportant, but imports of machine tools for which domestic substitutes exist are covered by agency and origin restrictions, such that they can be imported only by the end user and cannot be imported from certain countries—which happen to be the main competitors (chapter 5). In 1983 tariffs on about twenty items were increased to 20 percent. Machine toolmakers interviewed in 1983 ranked subsidized credit as the most important promotional measure, followed by subsidized technology assistance, protection, and export assistance, in that order (Fransman 1986). In 1983, at the time when the government increased the tariff, it also announced a plan to promote more specialization between existing producers. A holding company for the industry would be formed, with shares held by the development bank and a big multinational machine toolmaker, through which would come technology, marketing, and finance to local firms which agreed to specialize in line with the plan. The objective was to establish a stronger niche in high-precision machinery. Already by the early 1980s Taiwan was cost competitive and quality comparable with Japanese, German, and Swiss models at the less precise end of CNC machining centers.

Automobiles

Over the 1970s, as the Korean government embarked upon a plan to develop automobiles as a major exporter, Taiwan policy toward autos wobbled and drifted. The government's attention and resources were engaged elsewhere, in the development of petrochemicals, chemicals, plastics, steel, electronics, and in ten major infrastructure projects. Automobiles were squeezed out. The 1974 oil price crisis made matters worse by dampening expectations of rapid growth of demand. In addition, the government was split on how to develop the automobile industry. Some officials saw Taiwan becoming a major automobile exporter. Others doubted that domestic demand could ever be big enough to provide the base for an export drive, given Taiwan's small population (half of Korea's). They thought the emphasis should be on the development of a world-competitive parts and components industry. With no coherent government plan for the industry and no assistance beyond protection, the assemblers, six in number by 1979, produced some of the world's most deservedly obscure cars. Their average production was only 18,000 compacts, sedans, and light trucks a year (Arnold 1989; Chu 1987b).

In 1978, with some of the earlier preoccupations behind it and jolted by news of Korea's big push, the government announced a general proposal to establish a large-scale automobile plant with an annual capacity of two hundred thousand or more compact cars mainly for export. The strategy was to

induce a foreign carmaker of world repute to enter a joint venture with a domestic enterprise, through which would come technology not only for assembling but also for parts and components. The foreign joint venturer could not
hold more than 45 percent of the equity, however, and would have to export
50 percent of production. Later the government announced that the principal
local partner would be a public enterprise, China Steel. China Steel's chairman was made director of the "Big Auto Plant preparatory committee." With
this announcement the government demonstrated that it intended to keep tight
control of the project.

Several international carmakers expressed interest, with the final choice
coming down to Nissan and Toyota. In 1982 Toyota's bid was chosen. Seven
domestic firms (none in autos) were persuaded, some reluctantly, to split a 30
percent equity share between them.

Faced with this threat, the domestic assemblers began to show signs of life.
They issued export-oriented expansion plans, established a joint design center
to develop the island's first domestically designed model, and in the case of
the Ford joint venture, announced that the Taiwan subsidiary would henceforth
be integrated into its global supply network. Meanwhile the Toyota negotiations ran into trouble. The government insisted on an export ratio of 50 percent
and substantial technology transfer, despite Toyota's protestations that these
should be goals rather than targets; and the government added the further "request" of 90 percent domestic content. It planned to hold Toyota to a strict
timetable for achieving these conditions by refusing to allow it to take profits
from the venture if it failed to meet the timetable. Toyota feared that the conditions would be impossible to meet. On top of all this, Taiwan's cabinet was
reshuffled in 1984, bringing to the fore officials who had been more wary of
the Big Auto Plant than their predecessors. They wanted to concentrate on the
development of parts and components, leaving the existing assemblers in
peace; and not unrelatedly, the assemblers, led by the original assembler with
unusually close ties to the inner circle of the former and current presidents,
also wanted this option. The Toyota–China Steel joint venture was cancelled
in 1984, amid press cries of "the Big Auto Plant fiasco" (Arnold 1989). So
ended another episode in what is probably the Taiwan government's least successful industrial promotion effort.[23]

Meanwhile other Japanese makers began to show much interest in Taiwan.
Spurred by their interest, the government acted to make its policies more attractive. The new Automobile Industry Development Plan of 1984 reversed
several basic policies of the previous twenty-five years. It proposed to lower
tariffs and domestic content requirements on finished cars (limiting import

[23] Taiwan's economists like to take the automobile industry as the stock example of the evils of
protection. My view is that it is a case where protection has indeed had the predicted neoclassical
results, but it is an unusual case rather than the norm in Taiwan.

bans to small Japanese cars); it removed the earlier ceiling of 45 percent for-eign equity, allowing 100 percent foreign ownership in export-only car and components production; and it imposed export ratios and technology transfer requirements case by case. Hence the government gave up its earlier emphasis on domestic content and national control in order to maximize an export ori-entation. It encouraged the existing assemblers to merge or exit, but did not try to force a consolidation, unlike the Korean government. These measures can be seen as a compromise package between the two main positions: the existing assemblers would not be bypassed by a single government-controlled export-oriented car plant, but protection would be removed. The assemblers have responded by strengthening their links with Japanese companies. Nissan, Mitsubishi, and Toyota now have large equity stakes in some of the Taiwan firms. The existing joint venture with Ford continues. All are planning to make Taiwan an active offshore site for parts and components in the 1990s, and Toyota and Nissan are thinking of it for finished small car production as well. They may hope that Taiwan will become a fast track into the China market, ahead of Korea.

Electronics and Information

In consumer electronics Taiwan's firms (also Korea's) followed the strategy of moving into the price-elastic market left behind as the Japanese firms moved into more highly differentiated, more price-inelastic markets (Mody 1989). In the 1980s, with a good base of components, well-developed man-power, and producing and marketing experience at the simpler end, the firms began to differentiate their products and enter the advanced end of the range. However, while they have been able to reap technological economies of scale by virtue of the export market, their small size has limited their ability to reap organizational economies of scale compared to the Korean conglomerates (in the purchase of inputs, in international marketing, and in cross-subsidization of R&D). Therefore the role of the state has been especially important in build-ing technological competence in advanced electronics. All the more so be-cause the multinationals with subsidiaries in Taiwan had no interest in relo-cating high value-added production there until recently; they valued it mainly as a site for the more labor-intensive phases of production.

State officials made plans for Taiwan to acquire semiconductor design and production capability as early as 1972.[24] In 1974 they formed the publicly

[24] A semiconductor is a material that is neither a good insulator nor a good conductor of elec-tricity. Semiconductor chips are wafers, usually made of silicon, with embedded or etched cir-cuitry which directs or redirects electrical impulses which in turn store or retrieve data or perform functions or commands. Semiconductors are regarded as the building blocks for nearly all types of electronic equipment. Integrated circuits, transistors, and diodes are types of semiconductor devices. On Taiwan's information industry, see especially Chu 1987a; Li 1987; Schive and Hsueh

owned Electronic Research and Service Organization (ERSO) under ITRI's umbrella, with responsibility to recruit a foreign partner to help develop and commercialize the technology. In 1976 ERSO opened the country's first model shop for wafer fabrication, and a year later signed a technology transfer agreement with a U.S. firm (RCA) in integrated circuit design. By the late 1970s government officials had begun to envisage an integrated information industry for Taiwan, linking semiconductors, computers, computer software, and telecommunications. They gave it very high priority. A newly formed information industry task force headed by two senior cabinet ministers was made responsible directly to the premier. A comprehensive approach to the information industry was spelled out in the Information Industry Development Plan for 1980–89.

Leadership for the industry was vested in public research organizations and public enterprise offshoots from these organizations rather than with existing large private firms. In particular, ERSO was given responsibility for guiding the development of core technologies and new products, and for training microelectronics engineers, some of whom would then move to (private) industry. ERSO emphasized the need for Taiwan to build a capacity in custom-tailored chips (application-specific integrated circuits, or ASICS). An ASIC design capacity was essential, ERSO argued, because it provided a fount of innovation across the whole information industry from data processing to consumer electronics to telecommunications. It also differentiated Taiwan from Korea, which was then embarking on a quite different strategy of competing against U.S. and Japanese firms in high-volume products such as memory chips. Taiwan does not have the deep-pocketed firms needed to compete in this market. ERSO hoped that an ASIC capacity would allow Taiwan to keep a competitive edge over Korea by accelerating the number of new models of any one electronics-dependent product.

Commercialization of the advanced microelectronics technology developed in the public research labs has been undertaken primarily by United Microelectronics, a subsidiary of ERSO established in 1979 with a 45 percent equity share held by five private local firms. In 1982 United Microelectronics opened a state-of-the-art fabrication facility to make various kinds of ASICS. It also formed agreements with three Silicon Valley Chinese American firms relocated in Hsinchu Science Park, emphasizing advanced semiconductor design rather than production. By early 1985 a 256K CMOS DRAM[25] chip had been designed, and by 1986 a one-megabit chip. These projects were already quite advanced by world standards, indicating Taiwan's good infrastructure of design talent and its access to some outstanding designers.

1987; Mody 1989; *Financial Times* 1988:6; *Computer Products* 1987. I also draw on interviews with executives of AT&T and Micron Technology, Sept. 1988.

[25] DRAM, dynamic random access memory; CMOS, complementary metal oxide semiconductor.

But by 1986 no Taiwan firm yet had the capacity to make large-capacity (VLSI) chips in commercial quantities.[26] Fearing that the time for collecting technological rent would run out before a commercial-size fabrication facility was built, ERSO and its partners sold the production licenses for the 256K and one-megabit chips to one Korean and two Japanese firms—to the dismay of senior government officials.[27] This spurred the officials to redouble their efforts to find a multinational to make VLSI chips in Taiwan. Eventually, Philips reached an agreement to start a foundry-type VLSI factory in late 1986, with the government orchestrating the collaboration between Philips and several domestic public and private firms and contributing almost half the $135 million start-up cost. The new company is called Taiwan Semiconductor Manufacturing Corporation. The company has decided to concentrate on application-specific chips rather than confront the Japanese and Koreans in memories. And it will only make these chips to order rather than design and market its own, so as to reduce the risk to clients that it will steal proprietary knowledge embodied in the chip design. With access to Philips' state-of-the-art technology, the company claims that its technology as of mid-1988 is only nine months behind that of major U.S. firms like Texas Instruments and Intel (whom it includes among its nine U.S. customers). It is making ten thousand wafers a month, with a line width down to 1.5 microns and a yield of 1.5 to 2.5 defects per square inch, compared to a Japanese average of 0.8 to 1.5 defects per square inch. Its cost per wafer is estimated to be below the cost at the best U.S. facilities. A second $220-million plant is scheduled for completion by late 1989. By the early 1990s Taiwan Semiconductor Manufacturing Corporation will probably be a significant player in the world semiconductor industry, especially through the opportunities it gives for small start-up firms around the world to bring design innovations to market.[28]

[26] VLSI stands for very-large-scale integrated circuits, which are chips with one hundred thousand transistors or more, roughly equivalent to a 64K DRAM chip or bigger.

[27] To judge the design achievement constituted by the 256K and one-megabit designs one needs to know whether in production they gave a sufficiently high yield as to be economical. The Vitelic-United Microelectronics partnership sold the 256K design to Hyundai, Sony, and NMB Semiconductor, the one-megabit to Hyundai (source: Dataquest). I do not know what happened to the designs. A senior Micron Technology designer says (personal communication, Sept. 1988), that he has not heard of the Taiwan one-megabit design, which suggests that it has not had an important commercial impact, though this may reflect Hyundai's relatively poor performance as an integrated circuit producer rather than poor design. Note also that a national capability in integrated circuit design matters much less than capability in production, because of low entry barriers in the former and high entry barriers in the latter.

[28] Interview, TSMC executive, June 1988; interview, AT&T executive, Sept. 1988; *Electronics* 1988:169. TSMC makes semicustomized circuits such as gate arrays, specialized logic chips, and standard cell parts. Its defect figures and other indicators of yield suggest state-of-the-art facilities. (Yield data is a closely guarded secret. Mine come from a U.S. government source which cannot be further identified.) The second TSMC plant will have a capacity of thirty thousand six-inch wafers a month and an operating rule of down to 1.0 to 1.2 microns. An important and (for the

Meanwhile Taiwan has developed the biggest pool of chip design talent in Asia outside of Japan. Indeed, at least as impressive as the ability of some of its designers to work to a state-of-the-art design rule is the ability of Taiwan's semiconductor industry to both design and make large quantities of "yeoman" chips for consumer electronics products—chips of good quality, low price, and fast delivery. There are an astonishing fifty-eight design houses, compared to only 218 in the whole of Europe (though it is unclear what these figures mean, because a design house may contain anything from one to several hundred designers [*Financial Times* 1988:6]). Many of the design houses are staffed by former ERSO engineers. The country has also benefited from the movement of engineers and researchers back and forth between Taipei and California's Silicon Valley, where Chinese Americans are well represented among the design and computer firms. Some Taiwan firms are now beginning to make cheap, good-quality, though slow-performing, wire-bonding machines. They will soon be challenging Japanese and U.S. makers of other kinds of semiconductor equipment as well.

Nowhere else in Asia has the personal computer revolution spun off such a frenzy of activity. Taiwan has over one hundred computer manufacturers (compared with less than sixty in Korea). They do everything from "clone" making to add-on graphics and communication cards, Chinese-character computer systems, software packages, and the development of systems integration through multiuser workstations (*Financial Times* 1988:6). The imitation lag between introduction of a new personal computer product in the United States and the launching of a machine with similar functions by Taiwan's computer industry is now down to six to nine months or less for most products (Li 1987; IBM source). Acer, the leading firm, launched a clone of IBM's PS/2 30 model in mid-1988, followed by two more products from the top of IBM's PS/2 range but with superior operating characteristics. For these latter products, especially, a reputation for reliability is crucial for market success, because a malfunction in one unit can put a whole network of users down. Acer is currently shipping over 3 percent of the total world market for IBM-compatible personal computers, and about 6 percent of the market for the more powerful machines based on Intel's 386 microprocessor (*Far Eastern Economic Review* 1989b). This is just one of several achievements which place Acer only a few months to a year behind the state-of-the-art, or the most advanced technology commercially available. In 1987 it had 4,800 employees, 15 percent of whom were

first time) largely private initiative was announced in May 1989, when Texas Instruments and Acer formed a joint venture to make advanced memory chips. During the 1988 shortage of one-megabit chips Acer found itself unable to meet demand for its computers because of the shortage, while several of its main international competitors were less affected because they make their own chips. With a $250-million initial investment expected to come on line in 1991, this plant should greatly strenghten Taiwan's position in the world semiconductor industry (*Far Eastern Economic Review* 1989b).

dedicated to R&D, and spent US$10 million or 3 percent of revenues on R&D (industry source, personal communication). It plans to boost revenues from $550 million in 1988 to $1 billion in two years. It is diversifying rapidly into minicomputers, printers, telecommunication equipment, ASICs, and memory chips, and constructing a nearly worldwide distribution network (though a majority of its sales are still on an "original equipment manufacturer" basis rather than under its own logo). Acer and Mitac, the second main firm, signed agreements with IBM in 1988 to license IBM's personal computer patents on a running royalties basis. In return IBM receives an initial fee plus the right to license Acer and Mitac patents on the same basis. IBM has made such agreements with only three other developing country firms, all Korean. These five are the only developing country computer firms with sufficient mastery to be able to clone IBM's latest personal computers, in IBM's judgment.

Personal computers, peripherals, and add-ons are now a major component of Taiwan's exports (US$3.8 billion in 1987, 6.9 percent of exports, up from near zero in 1980; but about half of personal computer components are imported). Of the world market in computer add-ons, about one-third come from Taiwan.

The government has helped by identifying particular items on Taiwan's own production frontier and targeting them with fiscal investment incentives and concessional credit. In 1984 the government made a small response to the problem of integration between private firms and public research labs by establishing a fund with an annual budget of US$5 million to encourage joint development of new products between private firms and the public labs. It has not imposed domestic content requirements, nor has it granted protection.

Although almost all these computer firms are privately owned, ERSO continues to take a leading role. For example, it has provided the domestic makers of personal computer clones with an IBM compatible basic input-output system to strengthen their hand in warding off IBM lawsuits. Over the first half of the 1980s it dedicated major research projects to some twenty information products, including a microcomputer local area network system, a twenty-four-dot matrix printer, and even a thirty-two-bit microprocessor. Some of these projects have been undertaken in research consortia with a small number of domestic firms (often founded by ex-ERSO staff). Others are pushed to near commercialization point before ERSO, working with the government's Industrial Development Bureau, identifies firms willing to take the technology and run with it.

A public R&D organization is thus central to Taiwan's information industry. ERSO stands between the domestic electronics firms and the rest of the world for the purpose of facilitating the transfer and assimilation of advanced technologies. Commonly it licenses foreign technologies itself and then sublicenses to firms, thus eliminating price-raising competition between firms for the same technology. And normally it does not seek immediately to license a technology it wants; it buys items embodying the technology, reverse engineers them to see how they work, and then identifies precisely which technologies it needs to license and which it does not. By 1987 it had a staff of over 1,700 and a budget of about US$100 million.

In the software industry ERSO has been active too, but the lead has been taken by the publicly owned Information Industry Institute (established in 1979). The latter has evolved into a profit-making public enterprise, itself taking up nearly every major software project in the public sector instead of channeling demand to the private sector. Its competence is signalled by its agreements with top U.S. computer firms vying for the Asian market to commercialize many of its large-scale in-house projects. Two notable examples are a Chinese input-output system developed by the institute and licensed to IBM; and a joint venture with Hewlett-Packard to develop software for the Asian market (Chu 1987a:227). The Information Industry Institute also undertakes outreach programs to stimulate demand for computers within Taiwan. Again, however, much of the commercialization of the institute's results has been undertaken by a newly created subsidiary. With these advances in Taiwan's indigenous capability in electronics the country has remained attractive to multinationals—but now as a source of high-grade and relatively cheap skilled labor rather than, as in the past, a source of unskilled labor for assembly operations. By the 1980s virtually every major electronics multinational had a venture in Taiwan.[29]

CONCLUSIONS

Whatever a "typical" underdeveloped country is, Taiwan was clearly not one during the 1950s, contrary to most neoclassical accounts. It had a long experience of fast manufacturing growth, going back to the 1930s; an unusually productive smallholder agriculture; a more than averagely literate population; large amounts of U.S. aid and advice; unusual political stability; unusual leadership commitment to economic growth and military strength; fluid social stratification; and several other presumably progrowth conditions. Indeed, it was much more developed in terms of socioeconomic and political organization than its per capita income level would suggest. In Irma Adelman and Cynthia Morris's sample of seventy-four developing countries, Taiwan ranked forty-fourth in per capita income in 1961 and twelfth by their measure of "so-

---

[29] Taiwan sells 56 percent of its information industry exports from foreign subsidiaries, compared to 30 percent in Korea. It sells 28 percent on an original equipment manufacturer (OEM) basis, compared to 57 percent in Korea. It sells 16 percent under the domestic maker's brandname, compared to 13 percent in Korea. These contrasts hold for virtually all items (microprocessors, disc drives, printers, terminals, monitors, and peripherals). Taiwan's total exports of these items are $1,366 million, compared to Korea's $709 million. (Present tense refers to 1986; ERSO 1987.)

ciopolitical'' development (1967). In terms of what they call the "development potential'' indicator, Taiwan was fourth out of seventy-three around 1960 (1968). No other country but Korea showed such a discrepancy between high sociopolitical development and high development potential on the one hand, and low per capita income.[30]

There was good reason for economic policy to change in the late 1950s. The domestic market was by then saturated for many kinds of industrial consumer goods, price wars were going on, and more firms were going bankrupt than ever before. Yet industrial products accounted for only 19 percent of exports in 1957. Sugar and rice were still by far the biggest export commodities.

Given all this, it is hardly surprising that producers responded with alacrity to the opportunities opened up by the liberalizing reforms. These reforms encouraged goods already being produced for the domestic market to be sold abroad in order to overcome small market size. The producers of textiles, processed foods, plywood and wood products, chemicals, plastics, and metal products, soon began to think of exporting as a natural extension of what they had already been doing. But it is misleading to explain the rapid growth of manufactured exports largely in terms of market liberalization, in terms of the neutrality of incentives between export and domestic market sale. At the time of the liberalizing reforms Taiwan already had high growth potential, due in part to actions of the colonial state and the Nationalist state to create markets and market agents and shape their operations. In such conditions market supply response can be expected to be high, in line with neoclassical assumptions. A liberalizing shift in economic policy may therefore induce a much stronger growth response than the same policy change would elicit at a lower level of development. At most the liberalizing shift can be regarded as a necessary condition for the subsequent high growth rates. In the building of sufficient conditions the state had a critical role.

The neoclassical story of Taiwan also gives insufficient weight to the continued role of the state through the outward-oriented period. State control and leadership was focused on upstream industries such as synthetic fibers, plastics, basic metals, advanced electronics, and the like. The neoclassical story

---

[30] Adelman and Morris's sociopolitical score is based on factor analysis of such variables as size of traditional agricultural sector, extent of urbanization, importance of an indigenous middle class, extent of social mobility, extent of literacy, extent of mass communications, degree of cultural and ethnic homogeneity, crude fertility rate; and degree of national integration, degree of concentration of political power, strength of democratic institutions, degree of freedom of political opposition and the press, and extent of leadership commitment to development (1967). Their development potential score is based on four variables which together account for 97 percent of the discriminable variance between group means: degree of improvement in financial institutions, 1950–62, degree of improvement of physical overhead capital, 1950–62, modernization of outlook about 1960, and extent of leadership commitment to economic development, 1957–62 (1968). I assume that high sociopolitical development and low per capita income gives high potential for growth in per capita income. This could be tested.

occludes the existence of such industries, at least prior to the mid-1970s, as though the smaller-scale downstream industries were the only important part of the industrial economy. It is true that small and medium firms (under 300 employees) have accounted for a majority of direct manufactured exports (65 percent in 1985). And there is no doubt that export expansion generated high profits and that pressures of the export market forced producers—including upstream producers—to be competitive. But small and medium firms accounted for only 40 percent of manufactured output. And the translation of export profits into investment in further productive activity was not left entirely to the market. The state was the contrapuntal partner to the market system, helping to insure that resources went into industries important for future growth and military strength—including import substitutes for use in export production, such as synthetic fibers and plastics, and new export sectors such as electronics. Multinational companies became important players in these developments, but only *after* the state had a well-established presence and leadership position from which it could channel their activities rather than be made subordinate to a logic of global profits.

The several exogenous economic and political shocks of the early 1970s prompted the government to assert economic leadership more strongly than before. The management of the oil price rise shows the government carrying through a coherent shift in macrostrategy in response to changed economic circumstances. At the same time the government promoted intensified growth in heavy and chemical and in technology-intensive industries, so as to reduce dependence on imported intermediates and upgrade the export portfolio. The role of public enterprises expanded.

Evidence that in some (but not all) sectors the state led rather than simply followed the market comes from: (1) the trends in heavy and chemical industries during the 1960s and 1970s, which show fast growth *before* changes in comparative advantage (for example, before the end of labor surplus, in 1968–70); and (2) the history of state involvement in particular sectors, which suggests that the fast growth resulted from the state acting in *anticipation* of changes in comparative advantage.

In many sectors public enterprises have been used as the chosen instrument for a big push. This is true for the early years of fuels, chemicals, mining, metals, fertilizer, and food processing; but even in sectors where public enterprises did not dominate, such as textiles and plastics, the state aggressively led private producers in the early years. Later, during the late 1950s and 1960s, public enterprises accounted for a large part of total investment in synthetic fibers, metals, shipbuilding, and other industries. Even in automobiles, the state chose a public enterprise as the spearhead when it finally acted to restructure the industry at the end of the 1970s, bypassing the existing private makers—an effort which galvanized the existing makers into sufficient life that when the future of the public venture looked problematic the government reverted to applying pressure and incentives on the privates. In advanced electronics, public research organizations and public enterprise spinoffs have been used to acquire and commercialize new technology; and even in the software part of the industry a public enterprise has had a large presence over the 1980s.

To say that public enterprises have often played a central role in creating new capacities is not to say that private firms have been left alone. Incentives and pressure are brought to bear on them through such devices as import controls and tariffs, entry requirements, domestic content requirements, fiscal investment incentives, and concessional credit. Even in the case of machine tools, a small-scale industry relatively neglected until recently, the state nevertheless has provided subsidized design help, subsidized credit, and quantitative import restrictions. And large-scale private firms are often exposed to more discretionary government influence, taking the form of what in Japan is called "administrative guidance." (See chapter 9; figure 4.1 summarizes the role of the state in the industries described here.)

Functional (as distinct from sectoral) industrial policies have been vigorously pursued too, as in the several public sector industrial service organizations initiated in the 1950s or 1960s with the object of encouraging industrialists to improve products and production methods. The organization established in the mid-1960s to promote the use of computers in Taiwanese enterprises is a graphic example of the government trying to lengthen the time span of private decision-makers. By the mid-1980s, indeed, sector-specific

FIGURE 4.1
State Leadership Episodes in Taiwan's Industries

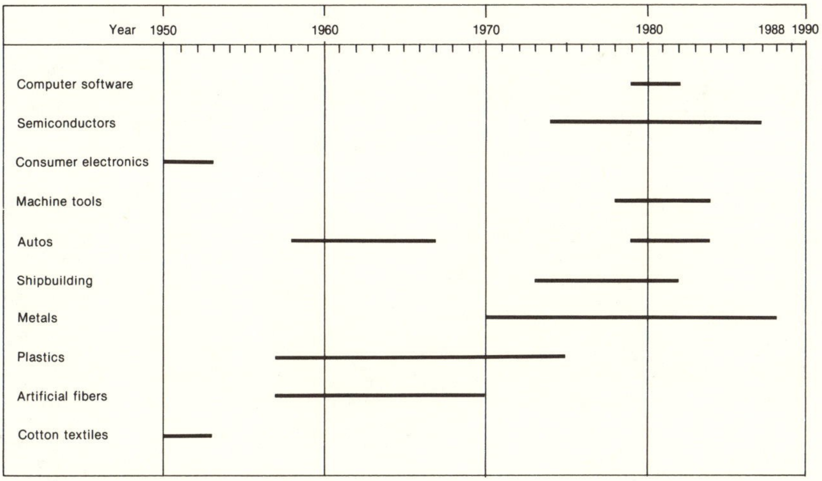

Note: The lines refer to big leadership. The dates should be taken as rough approximations. The diagram does not show all industries that have experienced big leadership, nor is it necessarily complete for the industries shown.

industrial policies have begun to give way to more functional policies, notably those to improve the communications infrastructure and those to build up Taiwan's research and development capabilities. The organizational design of Taiwan's national innovation system gives the government a continuing role in attaining international competitiveness in new industries, rather than simply sponsoring "basic" research.

All told, the material of this chapter creates a presumption that, contrary to the FM and SM theories, resource allocation in Taiwan has *not* been guided to a greater extent than in less successful countries by free markets and world prices. The material is more consistent with the GM theory's emphasis on *dirigisme* as a factor in the extraordinarily fast transformation of a predominantly private enterprise and market-based economy. This argument is strengthened by examining the array of policy instruments.

Chapter 5

MANAGEMENT OF FOREIGN TRADE AND
INVESTMENT

IT IS OFTEN SAID that an economy heavily exposed to the international market cannot be much affected by government attempts at directional thrust. Some economists even argue that the principal source of dynamic gains from free trade may be the confining effect of free trade on what the government can do. Free trade, they argue, makes it difficult for the government to commit more than small mistakes.[1] Taiwan is undoubtedly a very open economy—imports plus exports have been over half of GNP since 1970, and over 80 percent of GNP since 1976 (to 1986). The import content of exports rose fast, from 12.9 percent in 1961, to 19.7 percent in 1966, to 25.5 percent in 1971 (de Melo 1985: 235). And the economy is also outward-oriented in the sense that the average incentives to sell on the domestic market are about equal to the average incentives to sell on the export market (see table 3.3). Yet the government has undertaken more national economic goal-setting and exercised more surveillance and control over the economy in pursuit of those goals than is the practice of Anglo-American economies or than neoclassical economics can sanction.

The short answer to the paradox of national goal-setting in an economy heavily exposed to the international market is that Taiwan's openness and outward orientation have not been based on free trade. The government has intervened in trade so as to promote certain sectors, raise government revenue, reduce foreign exchange deficits (before 1971), and strengthen interstate alliances. Hence, the volume and composition of imports have not simply reflected domestic demand in relation to international prices. And exports have been promoted by both price and nonprice means. The trade regime has been dualistic, such that export-related production has enjoyed near free trade status (some industries, indeed, have had positive net incentives for export sale) while domestic market-related production has been protected.[2] It might be replied that Taiwan nevertheless has had freer trade than virtually all other developing countries, and that its success is related to this difference. I argue that Taiwan manages its trade differently from many other developing countries, but not less. It has offset the handicaps to export growth normally im-

---

[1] For example, Lal and Rajapatirana 1987.

[2] On the dualistic nature of the trade regime, see also Little (1979:475) and Scott (1979:330).

posed by import protection by using export incentives and other forms of assistance, in the context of macroeconomic stability.

The first section of this chapter discusses the problems of accepting the common view that Taiwan has had a relatively low level of protection—a neutral trade regime—compared to other developing countries. The second section describes the sequence of trade liberalization on both the export promotion and the import liberalization sides. Subsequent sections deal with the management of the economy's external involvements in the 1970s and 1980s. The topics include: tariffs, nontariff barriers, foreign exchange controls, the instruments of export promotion, and the management of foreign direct investment.

THE LEVEL OF PROTECTION

Consider tables 3.2 and 3.3. The figures describe levels of effective protection and effective subsidy (the latter being a more inclusive measure than the former) for six countries around 1968–69, including Taiwan.

In the nearly complete absence of other comparative data, these figures are the main evidence that Taiwan has had relatively low levels of protection. However, this conclusion is open to question on several counts. First, methodological weaknesses in the study introduce the possibility that either the real level of protection was much higher than the figures show or that the dispersion in protection levels to different industries was much higher. Second, if we take the 1969 figures at face value, we find that some important sectors of the economy had relatively high levels of protection even by this method. Third, some evidence for earlier and later years suggests higher levels of protection.

Methodological Problems

The figures in tables 3.2 and 3.3 come from a study organized by Bela Balassa, which employed the same method for calculating effective protection in six countries at about the same time. The method measures effective protection by price differentials between domestically produced and foreign-produced versions of the same items. The first problem of the Taiwan study (and the same holds for the Korean study) concerns the treatment of legal tariffs.[3] The authors, Lee and Liang, disregard them in almost all cases on the grounds of tariff redundancy. This procedure is crucial for the overall conclusion about low average protection because legal tariffs, they agree, were high by comparison with many other developing countries, averaging over 60 percent in 1969. But to ignore them on grounds of redundancy misses the point that the

---

[3] For a critique of the Balassa methodology as applied to Korea, see Luedde-Neurath 1986.

exemptions, rebates, and deferrals were targeted on *priority* activities. There was not much tariff exemption for producers who sold nonpriority products on the domestic market. For an importer of finished or semifinished goods for domestic market-related sale, the legal tariff was what he had to contend with.

The second problem relates to product specification and quality differences. The Taiwan study uses a comparison of 587 items in terms of their domestic and international prices, in order to measure the difference between domestic prices and what they would have been in a free trade regime. However, 39 percent of these items turn out to have negative price differentials, the domestic price being lower than the international price. How to treat these items? Lee and Liang include most of them (amounting to 25 percent of the whole sample) at zero protection. This procedure results in a lower average level of protection than would have resulted had they excluded the items with negative price differentials on the grounds that the two halves of the comparison are not really the same item because of quality differences. On the other hand, had they included the items at negative rates the average would have been still lower.

Moreover, the fact that so many items have negative differentials questions the validity of the price survey as a whole, or at least the level of disaggregation chosen. Korea was the only other case in the six-country study with a serious proportion of negative price differentials (45 percent). The same procedure—inclusion at zero rate of protection—was used. Since there is no compelling economic rationale for inclusion at zero rather than either exclusion or inclusion at negative rates, we cannot be confident that the averages shown in the tables for Taiwan and Korea are not biased strongly downwards or upwards relative to the averages for Israel, Colombia, and Argentina, whose price comparisons did not produce many cases of negative differentials.

Industry Bias

The low average effective protection to manufacturing in Taiwan shown in table 3.2 is generally interpreted to indicate low government intervention in trade. In particular, it is generally assumed that if overall protection is low, the dispersion between industries in levels of protection (or subsidy, to use the wider measure) will also be low; in other words, "industry bias," or the extent to which industries are differentially spurred on, will be low.[4] Table 3.3 shows further that for manufacturing as a whole the difference in effective subsidy for export sale and for domestic market sale is low, which is to say that "trade bias" is low, or "trade neutrality" prevails, or in still other terms, an "export promotion" (EP) strategy is being followed. As noted in chapter 3, this is just what neoclassical theory would expect to find in a successful grower.

However, the disaggregated figures force important qualifications. Table 3.2 also shows the dispersion of effective subsidy rates to seven manufacturing

---

[4] For example, World Bank 1987, chapter 5.

industries around the manufacturing average. The table distinguishes dispersion in subsidy rates for export sale and for domestic market sale, using standard deviation as the measure. Taiwan's standard deviation of 23 percent is
lower than for all countries shown except Singapore. However, it is not statistically significantly different from Israel's or Argentina's at the 5 percent
level.[5] A standard deviation of 23 percent still leaves plenty of room for big
intersectoral differences in effective subsidy rates. Indeed, in two important
sectors—consumer durables and intermediate products II (higher levels of fabrication)—Taiwan had the second highest subsidy levels in the six-country
study after Argentina.[6] Furthermore, had the 39 percent of the price comparison sample with negative price differentials been included at negative rates
rather than at zero, the interindustry dispersion would have been much greater.

The resource-pulling effect, or industry bias, of a given standard deviation
will probably be greater the lower the average. This is an intuitively rather
than rigorously derived proposition, which has the same plausibility as saying
that a change in tariffs from 30 to 10 percent has a bigger effect on resource
allocation than one from, say, 130 to 110 percent; or that an inflation rate
change from 10 to 20 percent is more significant than one from 110 to 120
percent (table 3.2, n. 4). Furthermore, when the dispersion is around a low
average it is more likely to result from intended differences between industries, whereas when it is around a high average it is more likely to result from
unintended, even quite accidental, causes, because all the numbers are large
and the dispersion is calculated as the difference between large numbers. If
so, Taiwan's standard deviation may have as much or more resource-pulling
effects than Israel's and Argentina's, and those effects are more likely to be
the intended result of policies. The same applies, only more so, to Korea.

Table 3.3 shows the relative strength of resource pulls toward export sale
and domestic market sale for each industry, rather than (as table 3.2) the relative degree to which industries are spurred on. We see that for Taiwan, resource pulls created by government policies have the net effect of favoring
export sale in the so-called "export industries" (row 2), while they have the
net effect of favoring domestic market sales in the import-competing industries (rows 3 and 4). Presumably, therefore, the export industries sold less on
the domestic market and more on the export market than otherwise, and the
import-competing industries sold more on the domestic market and less on the
export market than otherwise. (The "cost" of the policies is the domestic sales
lost by the export industries and the export sales lost by the import-competing
industries.) What is striking about the results for Taiwan (even more so for
Korea) is that (1) the export industries faced no antiexport bias, in contrast to

---

[5] But having only six degrees of freedom the calculation is of questionable worth. I am grateful
to Alan Gelb for making these calculations, and to both Gelb and Cristian Moran for discussion
of the results.

[6] Balassa, et al. 1982: table 2.6, D cols.

Israel, Argentina, and many other developing countries (but not Colombia); and (2) the import-competing industries enjoyed substantial net incentives to sell on the domestic market, because of protection and other devices, in line with the typical developing country pattern which economists normally deplore.

In short, there was a substantial amount of industry bias in Taiwan's trade and industrial policies in 1969. The government was trying to promote both exports and, in different industries, import substitution (and hence discriminate against exports in those industries). So government policies created different incentives for different industries. The picture of neutrality—both industry neutrality and trade neutrality—can be sustained only by limiting attention to the broad averages. Overall, we must be cautious about accepting the evidence from the Balassa-organized study that Taiwan had a low level of protection and a neutral trade and industrial policy regime in 1969.

Changes in Protection

There is remarkably little data on changes in protection over time. One study using 1966 figures found a rate of effective protection for consumer durables and nondurables sold on the domestic market of 126 percent, much higher than Mexico (22 percent), the Philippines (94 percent), and Japan (51 percent, in 1963) (Hsing 1971). Some indicators suggest that protection remained quite high to the mid-1980s. Average legal tariffs in 1981, for example, were 31 percent (Tsiang and Chen 1984), slightly less than the average import charge (tariffs plus other trade charges) of 34 percent for all developing countries in 1985 (Erzan, et al. 1988). Over half of Taiwan's imports by value were covered by nontariff barriers in 1984 (Tu and Wang 1988). But to get a better idea of what all these figures mean we need to embark on a more qualitative discussion of trade management procedures.

THE SEQUENCE OF TRADE LIBERALIZATION, 1958 TO EARLY 1970S

The 1969 figures are a snapshot of the trade regime roughly a decade after the onset of concerted trade reform. We now examine the sequence of these reforms over the period from 1958 to the early 1970s.

The initial big push came between 1958 and 1962, with reforms aimed at strengthening the existing incentives for exports, encouraging investment from the supply side, and encouraging more direct foreign investment. The United States had signalled that the large aid funds flowing in through the 1950s would be terminated in the foreseeable future, and the object was to create an economy which could replace aid receipts with its own foreign exchange earnings.

By the late 1950s real GNP had been increasing at over 6 percent a year for several years. Prices were relatively stable; the annual rate of increase had been less than 15 percent in each of the five years prior to 1958. Bank interest rates were relatively high and in that sense relatively undistorted, though set by the government. The government budget was in small surplus or small deficit in the four years before 1958 (on average in small surplus). The labor market was free, with no wage indexation. These were the conditions in which "liberalization" began.

Export Incentives

Most importantly, the multiple foreign exchange rates were collapsed by degrees into a devalued unitary rate. The magnitude of the devaluation is complicated by the fact of multiple rates, but roughly speaking it was from about NT$25 to NT$40 per US$, or about 60 percent in nominal terms, spread over the period from 1958 to 1961. According to Maurice Scott, this did not greatly increase the profitability of exporting, because inflation and rising money wages in 1960–61 eroded the nominal change, leaving little real change. The inflation was due not mainly to the devaluation but to natural calamities in 1960 and increased government expenditure for relief and reconstruction (1979:328).

Calculation of the real effective exchange rate suggests, however, that there was a real devaluation at this time, and that the improvement in competitiveness persisted until about 1964. From 1956–59 and 1960–64 the real effective exchange rate fell by around 9 percent (table 5.1). For a small and even then relatively open economy (the ratio of imports plus exports to GNP was 25 percent in 1959), this is a sizable, but not huge, shift in the ratio of domestic to world market prices. If we assume that, given Taiwan's trade ratio, about 20 percent of GNP had prices closely related to world prices, then a devaluation of 9 percent on average implies a decline in the prices of the remaining 80 percent of GNP of around 11 percent, which is quite a big drop. As a first approximation we can assume that exporters experienced an 11 percent fall in their domestic costs relative to their product prices, though this gain would have been offset to some degree by the effect of the devaluation in increasing the prices of their imported intermediates and raw materials. We can be fairly sure, contrary to Scott, that this netted out to a significant increase in export profitability. The other important point about the real exchange rate is its unusual stability over the whole period from 1955 to 1967 and beyond, compared to most other developing countries (see chapter 3; table 5.1).

Also in the late 1950s imports of raw materials and intermediates for export production were liberalized. The system of tax rebates—which allowed exports to be exempt from or claim rebates on all taxes (including tariffs) paid on imports used as export inputs—was amplified. Rebates of customs duty had in fact been allowed for all manufactured exports as early as 1954; but after 1958 other taxes were included in the scope of the scheme, the percentage of rebate in relation to duty actually paid was increased to nearly 100 percent, and the time for completing exports after importation was extended to twelve months (Lin 1973:101). Nontariff barriers were also reduced for export inputs. A price criterion was introduced in 1960 by which export producers could obtain an import license for raw materials and intermediates needed for their own production if no domestic substitutes were available or if the price of domestic substitutes was 10 percent above the c.i.f. (cost including insurance and freight) price of the corresponding import (Lin 1973:98). Since the price criterion was much more restrictive for imports for domestic market-related sales, the dual price criterion eased the disadvantages that exporters would otherwise have faced in comparison with competitors in other countries. Recall how quickly the import composition of exports rose, from 12.9 percent in 1961 to 25.5 percent in 1971. Finally, "harbor construction" charges were lifted on exports (but increased on imports from 2 to 3 percent of c.i.f. value).

In addition, several export promotion schemes were introduced or strengthened to give positive discrimination in favor of export sales. Exporters were entitled to retain a larger proportion of their foreign exchange (or more exactly, retain not the currency itself but an entitlement to get it from the central bank), and allowed to sell the foreign exchange entitlements to other firms. Concessional export credit, which had been limited in volume, was expanded. Fiscal incentives, such as a five-year tax holiday, were introduced for a wide range of industrial goods, even those already at high levels of import substitution or exporting, provided that exports equaled 50 percent or more of production. A small percentage of a firm's export earnings were made tax exempt (Lin 1973).

These measures resulted from a broadening of the focus of government concern from a preoccupation with import substitution toward a preoccupation with both import substitution and exporting. If the figures in table 3.3 can be believed, the net average effect of the measures was to make it as attractive for domestic producers to export as to sell on the protected domestic market, at least in 1969. Tibor Scitovsky estimates the value of all the readily quantifiable export incentives, expressed as a percentage of gross export receipts, at 10.7 percent over the period from 1962 to 1976 (1986:160). The implication is that substantial export incentives remained in effect over time.

Import Liberalization

Three stages of import control can be distinguished. During the 1950s import impediments included tariffs and nontariff barriers, especially direct foreign exchange budgeting. In 1961 direct foreign exchange budgeting was given up, leaving tariffs and other nontariff barriers. Between 1970 and 1974 nontariff

TABLE 5.1. Trade, Exchange Rate, and Macroeconomic Stability Indicators, 1958–85

	1958	1959	1960	1961	1962	1963	1964	1965	1966	1967	1968	1969	1970	1971
Export quantum[a]	125	93	98	103	114	124	132	114	120	116	123	128	132	136
Import quantum[a]	130	110	100	112	116	120	131	141	106	129	113	134	123	114
Balance on current account[b]	−25	−46	−42	−28	−51	7	40	−56	30	−58	n.a.	n.a.	1	171
Foreign exchange rate[c]	n.a.	n.a.	n.a.	40.0	40.0	40.0	40.0	40.0	40.0	40.0	40.0	40.0	40.0	40.0
Real effective exchange rate[d]	97.6	94.1	107.7	111.5	109.7	107.0	104.1	99.7	97.7	97.5	100.4	100.1	97.1	93.2
Relative price index[d]	137.2	125.2	108.6	104.1	105.9	108.6	111.6	116.6	118.9	119.1	115.7	116.0	119.7	122.6
Interest rates[e]	n.a.	n.a.	n.a.	16.2	15.8	14.0	14.0	14.0	14.0	13.3	13.3	13.3	12.6	12.0

TABLE 5.1. (continued)

	1972	1973	1974	1975	1976	1977	1978	1979	1980	1981	1982	1983	1984	1985
Export quantum[a]	134	123	96	100	150	108	124	107	111	110	103	119	116	105
Import quantum[a]	122	116	125	89	128	104	112	109	109	99	85	113	104	93
Balance on current account[b]	513	566	−1113	−589	290	933	1,639	165	−647	630	2,347	4,568	7,095	9,450
Foreign exchange rate[c]	40.0	37.9	38.0	38.0	38.0	38.0	36.0	36.0	36.0	37.8	39.2	40.2	39.4	39.8
Real effective exchange rate[d]	85.4	83.3	109.0	104.6	99.5	93.9	84.3	91.0	100.0	104.4	103.8	97.8	95.9	92.5
Relative price index[d]	123.7	124.8	100.0	105.1	110.5	110.8	110.5	107.8	100.0	92.3	93.4	94.4	97.4	100.2
Interest rates[e]	11.3	13.3	14.8	13.3	12.0	10.8	10.8	14.5	16.2	15.3	10.8	10.8	10.0	9.5

Sources: Taiwan Statistical Data Book 1986; Balance of Payments, Taiwan District, Republic of China, 1958–82; IMF's exchange rate division.

Note: The real effective exchange rate is defined by the IMF method, in terms of the value of the currency of trading partners in relation to the value of domestic currency. The figures here use 1977 imports as weights and include only Japan (55 percent) and the United States (45 percent) as trading partners. The relative price index relates Taiwan's consumer price index to Japan's and the United States'.

[a] Link index, last year = 100.
[b] In US$000,000.
[c] NT$ per US$, buying, end of year.
[d] 1980 = 100.
[e] Banks, secured loans, % per annum.

barriers were greatly reduced, leaving tariffs as the primary instrument thereafter. This, at least, is the official story, though much of the reduction in nontariff barriers may have been more apparent than real.

The tariff regime, both before and after 1961, was minutely differentiated
by product, ranging from zero to well over 100 percent. It was (and remained
until 1987) quite inconsistent with the two-tier structure often recommended
for developing countries, with a 10 to 15 percent uniform rate of effective
protection for all manufacturing activity other than the infant industries, which
should receive no more than double the normal rate (Balassa 1975). In the
1960s and 1970s it placed moderate duties (5 to 20 percent) on important agricultural and industrial raw materials, average duties (20 to 40 percent) on
semifinished or finished manufactures essential to health or education, high
duties (40 to 75 percent) on the vast mass of manufactured goods, and very
high duties on luxuries and on woolen and synthetic fabrics. However, the
percentage was calculated not on the c.i.f. price (which includes insurance
and freight) but on the c.i.f. price plus an ''uplift.'' The basic uplift was 20
percent before 1980, supplemented during the 1960s and 1970s by a few other
charges. Therefore a legal or published tariff of 60 percent translated into a
payment of 72 percent of c.i.f. value. And 60 percent was the average legal
tariff for manufactured goods in 1969, which is high by developing country
standards (Lee, et al. 1975). Table 5.2 suggests that average legal tariffs may
have increased somewhat between 1956 and 1960, decreased somewhat between 1960 and 1966, and increased between 1966 and the early 1970s.

Nontariff barriers include quantitative restrictions (such as quotas), as well
as limitations on the source of procurement or on the qualifications of the
import applicant, documents of approval from rival domestic producers,
variable levies or supplementary import charges, health and sanitary regulations, quality standards, domestic content requirements, and export restraints.
Taiwan has used many of these devices.

Quantitative restrictions have operated through the procedures of ''controlled'' and ''permissible'' imports. Controlled import items require special
case-by-case approval. Table 5.2 shows the proportion of controlled to permissible items over time.

Taken at face value, the figures suggest a mild reduction of quantitative
restrictions between 1956 and 1960, accompanied by a shift of items into
higher tariff brackets. No further reduction took place until 1970–74, many
years after exports began to boom and the balance of payments had ceased to
be a top preoccupation. However, we have no information on import items
weighted by value, so the significance of these changes is not clear. Perhaps
the 6 percent fall in the proportion of ''controlled'' items between 1956 and
1960 included the economy's most important imports, perhaps it included
only trivial ones. But at least we can be sure that the popular understanding—

TABLE 5.2
Evolution of Import Control, Tariff Rate,
and Tariff Burden, Selected Years 1956–81 (%)

	Share of Items Under Import Control	Share of Items with a Tariff Rate of			Ratio of Tariff Revenue to Total Imports
		0–30%	31–60%	61–165%	
1956	46.0	46.6	34.7	18.7	27.8
1960	40.5	39.5	45.0	15.5	16.8
1966	41.9	58.7	28.0	13.3	18.5
1970	41.0	—	—	—	16.1
1972	17.9	39.8	34.1	26.2	12.7
1974	2.3	—	—	—	11.5
1976	2.7	46.0	31.1	22.9	11.7
1980	2.5	58.1	25.8	16.1	9.6
1981	3.1	—	—	—	9.1

Source: Tsiang and Chen 1984.

Note: Items under control include those classed as "prohibited" and "controlled." The control is with reference to importing for domestic market use rather than for exporting. The share of controlled items in the 1970s *exclude* those whose imports are limited by the restrictions on permissibles described later. Figures for value-weighted shares are not available. See also Lee and Liang 1982:316; Scott 1979:331.

as in Galenson's statement that "beginning in 1958 quantitative restrictions on most imports were removed" (1982:77)—is wrong.

What about the criteria for inclusion of items on the controlled list? If these criteria became more stringent (perhaps by lowering the allowable price differential between a controlled item and the price of competing imports), this in itself could have constituted a means of bringing domestic prices closer to world market prices even without an increase in the amount of imports—provided that the domestic producers were able to meet the more stringent price criterion. Until 1960 any item which roughly equaled the quality of the import and whose production was enough to meet domestic demand could be put on the controlled list; no price judgment was made. In that year, two criteria were introduced, one for exporters and one for domestic market producers. Exporters, as noted, could obtain a license for importing "controlled" raw materials and intermediates for their own use if the price of domestic substitutes was more than 110 percent of the c.i.f. price. Domestic market producers could obtain an import license, however, only if (as a necessary but not sufficient condition) the price of the domestic substitute was more than 25 percent above the "import cost." But the import cost was raised much above the c.i.f. price by inclusion of tariffs, a defense surcharge (initially 20 percent of the tariff, increased in 1968), harbor charges, and even the importer's interest costs and his foreign exchange settlement fee; all these were added to the c.i.f. price as the base on which to calculate the allowable 25 percent extra, resulting in a permissible excess of the domestic over the international price of between 50 and 100 percent in many cases (Lin 1973:95).[7] Over the 1960s, some of the uplift charges were excluded and the allowable percentage was reduced to 10 percent in 1967—which still amounted to more than 10 percent above the c.i.f. price because the base still included tariffs, which were not much reduced. Despite the more stringent price criterion, the share of import items on the controlled list remained constant over the 1960s. The cost of importing was also reduced by a decline in the advanced deposit requirement (the amount that importers had to deposit in advance against the import cost, with no interest) from 100 percent between 1952 and 1967 to 50 percent thereafter. It was eliminated altogether in the 1970s.

We have considered what happened to tariffs and quantitative restrictions from the trade reforms of 1958–62 to the early 1970s. A word now about the foreign exchange budget, an important method of import control up to its abolition in 1961. The budget stipulated quotas of foreign exchange for various commodity classifications. By this means the government could prevent imports even of "permissible" items if the quota for that category was used up, thereby protecting imports of priority items. Priority items were, first, raw materials and capital goods, and second, "daily necessities." All other consumer goods were nonpriority. In terms of interindustry allocation, priority went to the industries designated in the first two plans, including textiles, cement, fertilizer, and ships. Little is known about how the system worked. But the effect was to place two hurdles, not just one, in the way of imports even for "permissibles." Elimination of the foreign exchange budget in 1961 meant that obtaining the import license was itself a sufficient condition for obtaining the foreign exchange.

However, neither tariffs nor quantitative restrictions seem to have fallen much during the 1960s. How then can the rapid increase in import quantities be explained (table 5.1)? The terms of trade improved sharply between the late 1950s and 1963, which is to say that import prices became cheaper relative to export prices, presumably reflecting the fall in world commodity prices at this time, especially the price of petroleum. These commodities were major items in resource-poor Taiwan's import bill. Presumably the cheapening of import

[7] A third necessary but not sufficient condition is that the cost of the imported raw material should not exceed 70 percent of the total production cost. See "Criteria Governing the Control of Imports," Foreign Exchange and Trade Control Commission 1960. Note also that a distinction is made between "controlled" and "prohibited" imports, which need not concern us.

prices through the terms of trade effect more than offset the increase in import prices through the devaluation effect. Also, as export quantities began to grow fast after 1960, so the demand for imported raw materials for processing into exports grew fast. Import quantities therefore grew because of both a price fall and a demand increase. The increasing imports were largely noncompeting imports, such as raw materials. Not being substitutes for domestically produced items, they did not expose domestic market producers directly to international competition. If by import liberalization we mean an increase in the extent to which domestic firms are faced with competitive imports, then Taiwan's rapid growth of total imports after 1960 does not necessarily signal an import liberalization.

Trends in secondary import substitution support the same conclusion. At the heavier end of manufacturing, imports declined as a share of total domestic supply between 1961 and 1969 in eight out of twelve industries. The four in which the import share increased were petroleum products, iron and steel, aluminum, and transportation equipment—the first three based on natural resources which Taiwan lacked, so an expanding import share in these sectors as the economy expanded is not surprising. The fact that the import share in the eight other industries declined does not necessarily mean that trade barriers remained constant or were raised, because a fall in import share in many industries is a normal part of industrialization, regardless of trade barriers. But if trade barriers had been substantially reduced, one would expect a considerable reallocation of activity between industries, even a sweeping away of some industries in the face of imports. This did not happen. Its absence strengthens the case that import barriers for domestic market production were not much reduced at this time.

All told, the evidence suggests that the 1958–62 reforms were not as thoroughgoing as they are popularly supposed to have been. They strengthened an already existing dualistic trade regime, such that import liberalization was limited mainly to export inputs.

Nevertheless, this made a fundamental difference to the effects of the protection system. As exports grew explosively more of the domestically produced import substitutes were used as inputs into export production even as the overall import content of exports rose. Domestic producers of intermediate goods still had a secure base of sales in the domestic market, but big expansion in their sales had to be in competition against imported inputs for export production; which meant that they had to bring their costs down to the point where they could sell to export producers at fairly close to world market prices. The protection system became geared toward promoting import substitution for export production. This is substantially different in its effects to the type of protection system associated with, say, Latin America, India, or pre-1985 New Zealand.

Although the protection system for nonexport production remained largely intact over the 1960s, competition on the domestic market was intense. It was accentuated by liberalizing administrative controls on factories and strengthening investment incentives, as well as by the indirect pressure exerted on domestic producers from the ability of exporters to buy most imported inputs at only a small mark-up on the c.i.f. price. Tight controls on the financial system also kept resources away from financial speculation and paper entrepreneurship, intensifying competition in goods markets. For these reasons, differentials between world market and domestic prices came down over the 1960s.

Between 1970 and 1974 many "controlled" import items were, finally, shifted to the "permissible" list (see table 5.2). By this time the balance of payments was no longer a concern (see table 5.1); exports and GNP were growing at high speed, while a wave of diplomatic derecognitions plus protectionist threats to exports made it urgent to tie other countries more closely to Taiwan on the imports side. Nevertheless, the tariff rate on many items was raised to substitute for protection lost by the reduction of quantitative controls, and for good measure a temporary 30 percent surcharge was incorporated into the tariff schedule.

IMPORT IMPEDIMENTS AFTER THE EARLY 1970S

During the period from the late 1950s to the early 1970s, export incentives were intensified while import protection for domestic market-related sales declined only gradually. I now show that substantial impediments to imports continued right up to the mid-1980s.

Trade control has had several objectives. One is revenue. In the 1950s about a quarter of total taxes came from tariffs and other trade charges, and this share—surprisingly—remained roughly constant up to the 1980s.[8] Trade charges constituted the biggest item of government revenue until 1981. A second objective has been to expand technological and supply capacity within Taiwan. A third has been to reduce the trade surpluses with the United States and the deficits with Japan, and, more generally, to lower the country's dependence on these two partners. Ever since the early 1960s about 30 percent of commodity trade has been with the United States alone. Trade with Japan accounted for another 30 percent in the 1960s, declining to 19 percent by 1980. So throughout the "outward-looking" period 50 to 60 percent of total trade has been with only two partners, whose trade with Taiwan is much less important for them than it is for Taiwan (see table 2.4). As surpluses with the United States soared, especially during the 1980s, the United States has put much pressure on Taiwan to reduce them, if necessary by impeding imports

---

[8] Taxes are here taken to include the revenues of the wine and tobacco monopoly. Table 6.2 excludes them.

from rival countries. Moreover, commodity concentration remains high: textiles and electrical goods have accounted for about half of total exports since the early 1970s. So the government has also sought to widen the product range of Taiwan's exports. Finally, trade has been used to substitute for diplomatic relations as the country has become diplomatically isolated by mainland China.

Tariffs

The government has been hesitant to lower tariffs. Between the mid-1960s and the mid-1970s, the trend was toward an increase despite booming exports (see table 5.2). In the mid-1970s almost half of the items in the tariff schedule still carried legal rates of more than 40 percent. Only after the dramatic fall in imports after the second oil price increase of 1979, together with U.S. pressure and governmental worry that firms were not upgrading their equipment fast enough, has a big fall in tariffs taken place. Still, average legal rates remained as high as 31 percent in 1984 (Tsiang and Chen 1984). When additional trade charges are added to the legal tariff, the average import charge would probably be higher, even in the mid-1980s, than the 34 percent average import charge for all developing countries (Erzan, et al. 1988).

There is substantial tariff redundancy, however. The average rate paid on all imports was only 11 percent in the mid-1970s. But about half of leviable tariffs were rebated, deferred, or exempted at that time, being for imports to produce exports or imports of machinery and equipment to make certain specified products. The average amount collected on the remaining imports was about 20 percent from 1969 to 1977 (compared to Korea's 14 percent in 1968). This constituted a large share—a fifth to a quarter—of total tax revenue. By 1988 the average effective tariff rate had fallen to 4 percent.

Let us consider the conditions in which tariffs are rebated, deferred, or exempted. The rule for raw materials and intermediates is simple: if they are used for export production they pay little or no duty (via rebate or exemption). The rules for imports of machinery and equipment are more complex. Imports of machinery and equipment to be used for production of certain specified items do not have to pay duty—provided that the machinery and equipment in question are "not yet domestically manufactured" (Statute for Encouragement of Investment," art. 21, Aug. 1982). To be duty-exempt the capital goods have to be used for the "sophisticated" industries in which Taiwan wants to expand its productive powers—iron and steel, electrical engineering, electronics, machinery, shipbuilding, chemicals, petrochemicals, and one or two others. Only those products which appear on a very detailed list are eligible, however. The list typically specifies items in terms of minimum performance or scale of production criteria as well as type of product. (In the electrical machinery industry, for example, only enterprises which have a certain minimum size of capital assets and which produce one or more of twelve items are eligible for duty-free capital goods imports. One of the twelve items is electric insulators with an insulating capacity of 24 kilovolts or more. In the electronics industry, cathode-ray tube production is eligible if annual production capacity is 1.5 million pieces or more.) Machinery and equipment imports for production of items which do not appear on the list do have to pay duty. And if the machinery in question is domestically manufactured, imports may still be allowed but the normal duty will have to be paid. The duty has typically been around 10 to 20 percent in the late 1970s which, with the various add-ons, works out to about 17 to 28 percent of the c.i.f. price.

Nontariff Barriers

The big increase in the proportion of "permissible" items in the import list after 1970 is generally taken to mean a big liberalization of trade. But in practice less liberalization occurred than the increase in permissible items suggests, because some of the permissibles are not really freely importable. In a good many of these cases, the reasons reflect the integration of trade policy with industrial policy.

It is well known that some of the permissibles have origin or agency restrictions (restrictions on where they can come from and on who can import them), but the significance of these restrictions for the principle of free trade is less familiar. Most garments, for example, are permissible, but only (until about 1980) from Europe or America, thus excluding the most competitive sources of such products. Yarns, artificial fibers, fabrics, some manufactured foodstuffs, chemicals, toilet preparations, machinery, and electrical apparatus were subject to such protective origin restrictions in the mid-1970s (Scott 1979:332). Many of the origin restrictions have been aimed at Japan, with the intention both of reducing the large bilateral trade deficit and reducing what the government sees as a dangerous dependence on Japan for new technology.[9]

Agency restrictions cover some of the biggest items in Taiwan's import bill. Crude oil, for example, which accounted for 14 percent of imports in 1976 and 17 percent in 1985, is classed as a permissible import—but can be imported only by Chinese Petroleum Corporation, the giant state-owned enter-

---

[9] In early 1982 the government announced a ban on the import of 1,500 consumer goods, trucks, and buses from Japan. The ban on trucks and buses was part of the agreement with General Motors (see below). The consumer goods ban was more symbolic than substantive because the 1,500 items accounted for only a small part of imports from Japan (King 1982c). The government wanted to show the Japanese government that it meant business in seeking ways to reduce its trade deficit with Japan, and hence to encourage the Japanese government to promote more imports from Taiwan. The ban was greeted with much fanfare in Taiwan and contemptuous silence in Japan. It was lifted (except for buses and trucks, vcrs, and a few other items) in less than a year.

prise. So it is not freely importable. When Y. C. Wang, the biggest private entrepreneur on the island, wanted to establish his own refining and supply facilities in the Middle East in the mid-1970s the government prevented him on the grounds that petroleum is a strategic resource which should be in the hands of the state. Prompted by Wang's initiative, Chinese Petroleum Corporation established an oil-refining and fertilizer plant in cooperation with the Saudi Arabian government.

Machinery items are classed as permissible, but many for which domestic substitutes exist have been subject to agency and origin restrictions. The agency restrictions say that only the end-user, not dealers or distributors, can import, while the origin restrictions say that imports are not allowed from a few countries—which just happen to be the only countries which pose a competitive threat to the local machinery builders, such as Korea and Japan (Amsden 1984b).

There are also restrictions on who is entitled to import goods for resale (as distinct from end-use). Private traders can get import licenses only if they have a certain minimum capital and if they exported more than a certain amount in the previous year (more than US$200,000 in 1983). This tying of import licenses to exports is designed in part to insure that those who get the windfalls (''rents'') from importing scarce commodities are at the same time contributing to the economic success of the country by exporting. Similarly, end-user restrictions which eliminate traders from the import trade in those items are designed to insure that windfalls go to the producers, on the presumption that they will use the windfalls more productively than the trader.

Origin and agency restrictions on permissibles are not the main point, however. The main point is that not all the permissible items are automatically approved for import even if the origin and agency restrictions are met. The controlled list is in fact bigger and more flexible than the official or publicly notified one.

When a would-be importer applies to a bank for a license to import an officially ''permissible'' item, the bank must check to see whether it is on the latest ''secret'' list which the Board of Foreign Trade periodically issues. If it is, the bank refers the request back to the Board of Foreign Trade, which generally passes it on to the Industrial Development Bureau. What happens next is difficult to determine. Industrial Development Bureau officials shrink from discussing the secret list system, yet they are the ones who are responsible for operating it.[10]

It seems, though, that a would-be importer of an item on the secret list will

[10] The list is secret in the sense that it and the system of import control to which it relates is little known except by those directly affected. But periodic updates are published in the monthly *Bulletin of the Ministry of Economic Affairs* (Chinese only). The existence of such a system was reported in Westphal 1978, a paper all the more remarkable for being based on only seven days of interviewing. See also Tsiang, Chen, and Hsieh 1985; Chen, Tu, and Wang 1987.

be asked to provide evidence that the domestic supplier(s) cannot meet his terms on price, quality, or delivery. He may be asked to furnish a letter from the relevant producers' association. Often he will not wait to be told; he will get the letter before applying. Or the officials may use their own information to make the judgment. This might be called the ''approval'' mechanism of import control, in the sense that reference must be made back to domestic producers of import substitutes to see how well they could meet the request.

The approval mechanism has probably been an important instrument of secondary import substitution in some sectors. Its function is to provide strong domestic demand for the products of the industries which the planners consider to be important, especially newly established industries. Maintaining their capacity at full utilization helps to spread overheads over larger output, allowing them to reap economies of scale.

Petrochemicals, chemicals, steel, other basic metals—sectors characterized by standardized basic products with high capital requirements—are covered by the approval mechanism. So also are some machinery and components, including some machine tools, forklift trucks, and bearings. At the least the mechanism serves the useful function of stimulating increased contact between purchasers and potential local suppliers, and of increasing market information (Westphal 1978). This would have to be balanced against the cost of delays, on which I have no information.

For machinery, the approval mechanism is probably not very restrictive. Computer-assisted devices permit higher-quality products and smaller—but still economical—production runs. So international competitiveness requires that producers have these devices. At the same time, the government gives very high priority to building up Taiwan's technical capacity in making such machinery, as a major skill-intensive industry of the present and future. Hence it adopts a flexible bargaining type of import control via the approval mechanism. Imports are generally allowed if the user insists upon a specification which cannot be matched in its particulars by a Taiwan supplier. There are stories of manufacturers poring over the catalogues of domestic suppliers, conveniently brought together in a government-sponsored library in Taipei, to determine what precise specifications cannot be made in Taiwan, so that they can say that such specifications are essential for their purpose and be allowed to import the latest West German model.

For more standardized capital-intensive products like chemicals, importing can be tougher once domestic capacity exists. In the case of nickel sulfide, for example, imports were unrestricted until a local producer started; since then requests for nickel sulfide imports have gone to him to see if he might meet the request. Similarly for styrene monomer (SM). When production began in 1976 local users were slow to switch from their overseas suppliers, although the local price was competitive. The government simply stopped granting import licenses, inventories dwindled, and customers turned to the local producer. The plant showed a profit in the second year of operation (Gold 1981:285).

Or take steel. Since the state-owned China Steel Corporation was formed in 1971 it has been difficult for steel of the types made by China Steel to be imported, although classified as "permissible." Right up to 1987 imports of most steel items have had to be approved by China Steel. For example, China Steel has allowed little import of steel to make ships. The shipbuilders, especially China Shipbuilding Corporation, also state-owned, have protested, to no avail. They complain, first, that China Steel produces only to order; which means that the shipbuilders either face long delays in supply or have to maintain costly inventories of their own. They complain, second, that China Steel prices steel plates for ships at the c.i.f. cost from Japan, plus 4 percent harbor dues; but since China Steel does not have to pay insurance, freight, or harbor dues, it should sell at the f.o.b. (free on board) price in Japan. Other steel users complain in even stronger terms, since the price they have to pay (except for steel for export products) is as much as 20 percent greater than the c.i.f. price from Japan. China Steel runs at a handsome profit. China Shipbuilding Corporation runs at a loss (though the price of steel is only one of several reasons).

These various forms of import control are minor if one considers the proportion of import items to which they apply. In 1984 over 80 percent of import items had no restrictions. (The corresponding developing country average was 60 percent in 1985: see Erzan, et al. 1988.) However, a recent study calculates, for the first time, the importance of the restrictions in relation to the value of the imports to which they apply, and reaches a different conclusion (Tu and Wang 1988). As of 1984 over half of imports faced restrictions. The most important kind is the "approval" mechanism. Twenty-nine percent of imports by value have to receive approval from a domestic agency, whether the producer of a domestic substitute (as in steel, cement, etc.), or from the Industrial Development Bureau, or from the Health Ministry or other ministries. Another 21 percent of imports are limited by who can import them, such as end-users or publicly owned trading companies. Origin restrictions now cover only 4 percent, though they would have been more important in the past (see table 5.3).

This system of import controls on "permissible" items has probably been in continuous existence since the 1950s. The official classification of "controlled" and "permissible" imports is cumbersome in the procedures needed to get items onto and off the controlled list (controlled items are reviewed only once every two years). These other forms of restriction are much more flexible. K. Y. Yin, the architect of Taiwan's industrial policies up to the early 1960s, argued in 1954 that "in the enforcement of the policy of protection, tariff and the control of imports are methods which should be both used at the same time. *A protection tariff itself lacks flexibility and cannot fully attain the*

TABLE 5.3
Share of Taiwan's Imports Subject to Nontariff Barriers (1984)

% imports	(1)	(2)	(3)	(4)	(5)	(6)
By items	0.03	1.76	3.86	1.24	8.00	81.27
By value	0.00	0.09	3.68	21.01	28.64	45.28

Source: Chen, Tu, and Wang 1987.

Notes:

1. Columns: (1) prohibited; (2) controlled; (3) limited by procurement area; (4) limited by applicants' qualifications (e.g., end-users, traders); (5) limited by approval document (from ministry, producers' association, etc.); (6) no restrictions.

2. Calculations are based on the eight-digit level of the BTN classification. They include a *small* degree of double counting, since items affected by more than one restriction are counted again.

objective for protection. The control of imports is more flexible in its operation because it can be readjusted from time to time in accordance with the actual requirement'' (in Scott 1979:379, emphasis added). It is likely that this argument is still current amongst many senior policy-makers, even though the government finds it necessary to publicly declare its intention to remove nontariff barriers as fast as possible, in response to U.S. pressure.

Commonly new producers in strategic and capital-intensive sectors (petrochemicals, for example) will be assured that provided prices move down toward international levels they will receive quantitative protection against imports for two to five years. The protection will then be removed, though they may still be buffeted against sudden falls in demand. For example, if the international price falls the government may—after negotiations between the producers and the users—agree to a temporary arrangement whereby the users must buy a certain proportion of their requirement domestically in return for being allowed to import the rest.[11]

In downstream sectors quantitative protection for new industries is likely to be still more conditional. In the case of videocassette recorders (VCRs), for example, the government granted an import ban in 1982 to help two of the

[11] An example: In the early 1980s China-American Petrochemical Company (25 percent Chinese Petroleum, 75 percent Standard Oil) planned an expansion of its PTA (purified terepthalic acid, feedstock for plastics and polyester fiber) capacity sufficient to meet the whole of domestic demand and more. The press then carried announcements by the Board of Foreign Trade (which would have been first approved by the Industrial Development Bureau) that domestic users "may" be required to buy locally 60 percent of their requirement, and may have to show evidence of doing so before being allowed to import (King 1982a). The use of "may"—the velvet glove on the iron fist—is typical, as is the use of the press to carry such announcements. Earlier there had been partial bans on PTA imports whenever inventory on the island built up. One problem created by such bans and local content requirements is that domestic users enter long-term contracts with foreign suppliers, and may then be put in a contradictory position once the partial ban is reimposed.

main domestic electronics companies to build their own production capacity. But a year later their prices were still substantially above those of Japanese VCRs. Warnings began to appear in the press that "if domestic manufacturers do not achieve international standards for technology and price within the period of guidance . . . then the government might consider bringing in foreign companies for joint investment ventures" (*Economic News*, 9 May 1983). Sure enough, eighteen months after the start of the import ban the government announced that it was allowing Sony to form a joint venture with a local firm (not one of the two which had already started), on condition that 50 percent of production was exported after three years. Here is a case where short-term protection has been granted and the protection has indeed remained temporary.

Operating the import control mechanism generates chronic disputes between firms and government about application of the rules. Especially in the case of exports, the officials have to weigh the need for exporters to get their inputs at c.i.f. prices against the need to protect domestic capacity utilization. But the "real" c.i.f. price may be contentious. The Customs Administration maintains its own "dutiable price list" for some two thousand import items (1986) based on previous import records and the prices of domestic substitutes, to which it resorts in cases of disagreement.[12] In the late 1970s, for example, exporters could buy domestically produced acrylonitrile (an important petrochemical) at between $0.53 and $0.54 per pound, which was said by the Customs Administration to equal the c.i.f. price from Japan. The exporters claimed that the c.i.f. price from the United States was $0.48, and petitioned to be able to import freely from the United States on grounds that the domestic producers could not match the real c.i.f. price. The Industrial Development Bureau refused. Instead it allowed them to purchase a smaller amount from the United States on condition that they brought a larger amount from the domestic producers (Westphal 1978:26). Or again, the dispute may be about how pure a domestic chemical is and whether a producer really needs a higher level of purity than can be domestically produced. A manufacturer who needs a purer caustic soda than available domestically may become so fed up with delays in his requests to import that he decides to help one or two local producers to upgrade to the point where he can buy his caustic soda from them— which is just what the government wants. This is a good illustration of how trade policy can be made to serve industrial policy.

Industrial policy objectives have also been served through the requirement that imports of equipment for a new plant receive prior approval. This requirement was dropped in the late 1970s, but approval is still required today if the producer wishes to obtain fiscal investment incentives. The authorities take into account the feasibility of the project, its priority in the national plan, and

---

[12] *Economic Magazine*, Sept. 1986 (Chinese).

whether the industry is already overcrowded. (But with some exceptions there has been no direct investment licensing of local industry since the early 1960s; control over imports for new plants is as far as central control goes.)

Import licensing can also be used to pursue diplomatic objectives. The maintenance of good relations with the United States is Taiwan's first diplomatic priority, which the growing bilateral trade surpluses increasingly threaten. The U.S. government has tried to persuade Taiwan to shift to an f.o.b. basis of import valuation for tariff purposes, because the present c.i.f. basis benefits suppliers closer at hand, notably the Japanese, whose shipping and insurance costs are lower. Otherwise any general liberalization would, it is feared, benefit the Japanese rather than the Americans. And still in the name of "free trade" the United States has pressed Taiwan to take more of its products even when more expensive and less well-serviced than competitors'. The Taiwanese have sensibly tried to limit imports of more expensive U.S. goods to those which will not much harm their international competitiveness—even including, as the trade surpluses have mounted, American-made ice cream, a fact which bemuses the old planners who struggled through the hard times of the 1950s. Indeed, they have even tried to choose products which are particularly important to the local economy of constituencies whose senators are pro-Taiwan.[13] The problem is that the government then has to find some pretext for reducing or excluding rival products from, say, Australia or South Africa (such as beef, citrus concentrate, and apples). All kinds of excuses may be used, especially ones to do with health. But ultimately, if the potential suppliers meet all the objections they will be told that the Taiwan government does not need to give a reason. The South African government has been particularly dismayed to find that even after it went to the trouble of joining the motley group of (mostly Central and South American) countries which recognize Taiwan rather than the People's Republic, Taiwan has taken little more of its exports. Which reflects the fact that many of its potential exports compete with American products and, as one local observer said, "The US has a knife at Taiwan's throat."[14] Even differential tariffs may be used. In beef, for

---

[13] The director of Taiwan's Board of Foreign Trade has stated that one of Taiwan's objectives in its buying missions to the United States is "to help our friends" by cultivating sister-city and sister-state ties as a means of influence. Youngnok Koo comments that "the Taiwan mission's long swing throughout most of the United States is considered a skillful public relations project and Congressmen are likely to appreciate such visits to their constituencies" (1985:15).

[14] Examples of the kind of action which the Taiwan authorities find worrying: In late 1982 the Footwear Industries of America filed an unfair trade complaint against Taiwan, on grounds that "Taiwan unfairly restricts imports of foreign shoes, sets abnormally high duties on shoe imports, and provides tax incentives for exports." An official of the Taiwan Footwear Manufacturers Association (on occasions like this the local association is generally used as the spokesman, not the government directly) replied that Taiwan's duties of 25 to 85 percent are in line with other LDCs' duties, that footwear had been removed from the "controlled" list a year before, and that tax incentives consisted only of the waiving of duty on the imports of high-technology shoe-making

example, a subcategory has recently been defined in terms of fat and hormone content so that it fits only U.S. beef, and is given no duty.[15]

Again, Taiwan is busy developing relations with several Latin American countries. Beef is one of the main things they would like to sell to Taiwan. But imports from outside the United States, Australia, and New Zealand are strictly prohibited on health grounds (mainly foot and mouth disease). Nev-

---

equipment, not subsidies (*Financial News*, 15 Nov. 1982). (The U.S. footwear industry has also been filing complaints against South Korea. Whatever the case for Taiwan, which runs large balance-of-payment surpluses, did it make sense for South Korea to spend very scarce pre-1985 foreign exchange on importing shoes?) In 1983 the U.S. Rice Miller's Association, complaining of illegal export subsidies on rice by Taiwan, compiled a list of Taiwan exports which could be retaliated against with tariffs or quotas, including fish, fruits, tires, screws, cotton shirts, and data processing equipment (*Financial Times*, 13 Jan. 1984:24).

The de facto American Ambassador made the following public criticism of Taiwan's trade practices (interview in *Economic News*, 4–10 July 1983). "US exports to Taiwan face a number of significant trade barriers, ranging from the indirect, such as excessive customs duties, to outright import bans. . . . Many items, covering the spectrum from general household goods to kitchenware to processed and packaged foods and even to orange juice concentrate, have as much as 70 percent added to their cost before they reach the market. . . . Equipment and goods which would be of great value to you in the commercial and manufacturing sectors also labor under excessive import duties. Word processing equipment has duties as high as 30 percent. Some computer peripherals as high as 25 percent. Kraft liner board and packing materials may be assessed as high as 44 percent. The list is long, and works to your disadvantage as well as ours. We would like to see Taiwan go to a free-on-board (FOB) system of calculating tariffs. We feel that this would be beneficial to both US and Taiwan interests over the long run. Another very serious problem is your use of de facto import bans to protect domestic industry. . . . Last year an import ban was placed on basic industrial use petrochemicals, such as PVC, LDPE, and HDPE in order to protect producers. It transpired that domestic producers were not able to meet market demand and petrochemicals were imported under an "orderly marketing" scheme. This, in effect, means that you allow imports when local producers and industries cry for help, and restrict them when there is a chance of foreign competition. Soda ash was banned for a period of time in 1982. Imports of frozen poultry, pears and peanuts are banned. In addition to outright bans, restrictions are put on imports. In fact just recently CAPD (Council for Agricultural Planning and Development) prepared a list of 148 agricultural products for which it wants to restrict imports or raise customs duties. Local content regulations requiring domestically produced parts to be used in manufacturing and mandatory exports for foreign investors are further barriers to free trade. We see this occurring now in the electronics industry, especially television sets. There are problems with health and safety standards for US pharmaceutical and health products because the Taiwan authorities do not consider US Food and Drug Administration certifications to be sufficient evidence of safety, even though they are accepted in most other parts of the world. US service industries, such as accounting, insurance and shipping, face restrictions here that do not apply to their Taiwan counterparts operating in the United States. I have just touched on a few of the import barriers which have contributed greatly to the trade imbalance between us. As you can see, these practices, this sort of trade restraint, cannot benefit anyone in the long run. They are certain to rebound adversely. It is precisely this sort of situation which fuels the growing protectionist sentiment in the US and which could seriously hurt your export industries. Liberalized trade is of paramount importance to both of us, and I sincerely hope that you will relax the restrictions that you place on US goods and services." See also Office of the U.S. Trade Representative, *Foreign Trade Barriers*.

[15] Interview with Board of Foreign Trade official, Jan. 1988.

ertheless, the government may secretly issue a license for a stipulated amount of beef imports from a Latin American country to one of the ''special status'' meat-importing firms (probably one staffed by ex-military), in return for some quid pro quo on the Latin American side.

Finally, the requirement that all exports (as well as all imports) be covered by licenses has been used to insure that whenever signs appear of an international or domestic shortage of important raw materials and intermediates, no exporting is allowed. This is a way to protect the capacity utilization of downstream users who need the petrochemicals, cement, and basic metals that would otherwise be sold abroad.

Protection and Industrial Policy

We have seen that different industries are given different incentives by Taiwan's trade and industrial policies. But can we go further and match the pattern of variation more directly to the government's industrial objectives? Larry Westphal, among many other critics, implies that the structure of protection is unrelated to industrial objectives: ''there is little, if any, economic rationale underlying the tariff structure; that is, effective tariffs rates are highly diverse and *bear no systematic relationship to the type of product or level of processing*. It is probably impossible to relate a highly differentiated tariff structure such as Taiwan's to industrial development objectives, which to be meaningful must be stated in broader terms'' (Westphal 1978:21–22, emphasis added).[16]

There is in fact precious little detailed evidence on the connection between protection and industrial objectives. But a recent study by Jui-meng Chang suggests that those who, like Westphal, assert the absence of an economic rationale are wrong.

Chang seeks to determine the correlates of the pattern of tariff and nontariff protection. With respect to tariffs (legal tariffs in 1981 and 1985) the following relationships hold (1987:142–48):

- Across industries, the higher the proportion of imports used as inputs for further production, the lower the tariff.
- The higher the proportion of output which goes for final demand, the higher the tariff.
- ''Strategic'' industries (in economic or security terms) are less likely to have tariffs reduced.

For nontariff barriers (NTBs), the findings are broadly in line with those for tariffs. Chang uses an index which brings together several such barriers into one number, and data from 1966, 1972, and 1984 (1987:164–70):

[16] ''The existing tariff system has no contemporary economic logic'' (Lee, et al. 1975:98).

The higher the proportion of imports used as inputs into further production, the lower the NTBS.

The higher the proportion of output which goes for final demand, the higher the NTBS.

"Strategic" sectors have higher NTBS.

Tariffs and NTBS were more closely correlated in 1966 than in 1984. Before the reduction in NTBS between 1970 and 1974 both NTBS and tariffs were used for cutting back the demand for foreign exchange. As the balance of payments moved into surplus in the early 1970s, this function declined in importance. Tariffs become relatively more oriented to raising government revenue, and NTBS became relatively more oriented to industrial promotion.

In short, Taiwan has a "cascading" structure of protection, as do most developing countries, with higher protection on final goods than on raw materials and intermediates. So the structure is clearly not random or chaotic, as Westphal implies. In standard trade theory, however, a cascading structure is thought to be less desirable economically than either free trade or an equal nominal tariff. Compared to these, it distorts the structure of domestic prices away from the relativities of world market prices, giving "too much" encouragement to final goods production compared to what would be in the economy's comparative advantage. Here, again, we find a discrepancy between the policies prescribed from standard economic theory and those adopted by one of the most economically successful of developing countries.

It should be emphasized that neither Chang nor anyone else provides evidence on an implied proposition, that if the industries classed as import-competing in 1969 (see table 3.3) included many of the ones the government was trying to promote, then the incentives to these industries must have changed (reversed) at a later stage to subsidize sales to exports or at least remove the antiexport bias. This postulated but undocumented reversal of incentives to infant industries is crucial to my argument. Note too that the unusually fast increase in the local content of final goods may reflect a variety of nontariff barriers on intermediate goods which escape Chang's index,[17] such as the "approval" mechanism described earlier or local content requirements.

Local Content Requirements

Local content requirements have been used to foster backwards linkages in a number of sectors, including autos, televisions, refrigerators, air conditioners, and diesel engines. They have been especially important in direct foreign investment agreements. The publicly notified requirements have often been set unrealistically high, and the failure of firms to attain such levels has been taken by some economists to indicate that local content requirements have had no

---

[17] Chang gives few details about the definition of his NTB index.

effect. The point of setting high public requirements is to give officials more bargaining leverage with the firms, both at the time of the agreement and subsequently; the conditions can be reduced case by case in return for some quid pro quo. In some cases local content requirements have been tied to the fiscal investment incentives, not having to be met if the investment incentives are foregone. Over the 1980s less weight has been placed on local content requirements. In particular the information industry has been free of them, including microcomputers and peripherals, unlike in Korea.[18]

Foreign Exchange Controls

Throughout the whole postwar period up to 1987 the basic principle of foreign exchange controls has been that only the central bank and designated commercial banks may hold foreign exchange, not citizens or firms. This gives the government a means to insure that foreign exchange is not used for purposes which it disapproves of, such as currency speculation, unproductive investments abroad, or import of restricted items. Prior to 1987 all foreign exchange transactions had to be backed by trade contracts or accounted for by evidence of invisible transactions (remittance of royalties, interest, etc.). Importers and exporters could not get goods through Customs without providing evidence of adherence to the foreign exchange procedures, which required them to show that they had entered an agreement with a foreign exchange bank to handle the foreign exchange relating to the transaction. They themselves could deal only in local currency. This was the principle, at least. In practice, such techniques as "transfer pricing"[19] allowed some escape from these controls (though the need to pay more customs duty on overvalued items checked the magnitude of overvaluation). Illegal businesses in foreign commodities and financial futures have also flourished, thanks to telephone links to Hong Kong and Tokyo brokers. The curb market and the jewelery trade can be used to whisk money overseas. Nevertheless, the foreign exchange controls have been a powerful instrument for insuring that trade follows the government's rules of trade management.

---

[18] Government procurement policies also help to steer demand to domestic producers. I have no details on their operation and significance.

[19] A local buyer may pay a foreign firm US$1 per unit, but on the invoice the price appears as $1.04. The local buyer pays the foreign firm $1.04, and the foreign firm deposits the difference in a bank account of the buyer's choice, generally in the United States or Canada, sometimes in Hong Kong. The amount of over-invoicing is often a matter of hard bargaining between local buyer and foreign firm. Foreign businessmen like to point out that some of the most outspokenly patriotic and moralistic public figures in Taiwan are themselves busy salting money away in overseas banks by such methods. Foreign firms operating in Taiwan themselves often overinvoice to a nominal head office in Hong Kong, which in reality may be little more than a post office box number. The Customs Administration collects extraordinarily detailed information on world market prices partly to check overinvoicing.

In 1986, under pressure from huge foreign exchange reserves, the government dropped the requirement that import and export transactions have prior approval from a foreign exchange bank. It announced an expanded list of reasons for approved nonbusiness use of foreign exchange, though individuals were still not allowed to hold foreign exchange themselves. In 1987, with the reserves still growing,[20] the president ordered his reluctant cabinet to accelerate the loosening of the controls. In mid-1987 individuals and companies were allowed to remit abroad up to US$5 million per year with no restrictions on the use to which it is put. However, individuals can bring into the country no more than US$50,000 a year, a restriction aimed at checking the inflow of money speculating on a revaluation of the Taiwan dollar. Normal trade-related currency movements are not affected by the restriction.

EXPORT PROMOTION

If parts of Taiwan's industry continued to be substantially protected during the 1970s to the mid-1980s, how then did manufactured exports grow so fast? A large part of the answer lies with export incentives. The export incentive schemes of the 1960s continued through the 1970s, but were slowly scaled back as foreign exchange reserves mounted. At the same time, the government gave more assistance to export marketing and quality control. We now consider several ways in which exports have been spurred on.

Export-Processing Zones

The most dramatic freeing of export production from protectionist constraints came in the form of export-processing zones (EPZs) and bonded factories (BFs), both initiated in 1965, when few other countries had them. Firms in the EPZs have to export all of their production in return for enjoying duty- and tax-free imported inputs, good infrastructure facilities, and simplified administrative procedures for trade and remittances. Bonded factories are like mini-EPZs, but are located outside the formal zones. EPZs have accounted for less than 10 percent of Taiwan's exports through the 1970s and 1980s, while BFs have accounted for 10 to 15 percent—which is to say that they have been quite, but not very, important in the economy's export production.[21] Over the 1980s little new investment has occurred in the EPZs, reflecting the improvement of infrastructure and duty-free procedures outside them.

[20] See chapter 2 n.5.

[21] The three EPZs have accounted for around 7 to 9 percent of exports. BFs numbered 27 in 1970, 169 in 1975, 264 in 1980, and 324 in 1985 (*Yearbook of Financial Statistics of the ROC 1986*). BFs produced 14 percent of exports in 1977, 14.3 percent in 1982, and 15.5 percent in 1986 (Inspectorate General of Customs 1987). In 1986 about half of the 356 BFs were in electronics.

Tariff Rebates

Most exports have had to obtain duty- and tax-free imported inputs by means of a rebate system. Since the 1950s when it was first introduced, the rebate system has grown to become a major part of the procedures of Taiwan's trade, affecting most exporters. In 1977, 477,990 applications for duty rebate were handled; in 1986, 551,080. Nearly 200 Customs Administration employees process the applications (out of a total Customs staff of almost 4,000: Inspectorate General of Customs 1987); and about 20 employees in the Industrial Development Bureau administer the calculation of the input coefficients on which the size of the rebate is based. The amount of money involved is very large: since 1970 (to the mid-1980s) total tariff collections have been reduced by approximately half through rebates, exemptions, and deferrals.[22]

However, the small exporting firms generally do not apply for rebates themselves, except perhaps for expensive inputs which they import directly. Normally they pass their export documents back to their domestic upstream input suppliers, from whom they buy at duty-free prices; and the big input suppliers, utilizing economies of scale in rebate application, apply directly. Nanya Plastics, one of the biggest companies in the country, had a department of forty people specializing in rebate applications in the early 1980s.

Calculation of the rebate is a complex matter which we need not go into here. Suffice it to note two points, which show how the rebate mechanism gives an incentive (albeit probably small) for exporters to buy their inputs from domestic rather than foreign suppliers. First, when the Industrial Development Bureau judges the domestic supply capacity of an intermediate good to be sufficient to meet domestic demand, it assumes that the intermediate was bought domestically rather than being imported when calculating the rebate due on a product which uses that intermediate, even though some may in fact be imported, the aim being to encourage exporters to buy domestically and thereby get back a higher percentage of the actual duty paid (since tariffs are lower for raw materials than at higher levels of fabrication). Second, except in the case of new products, the rebate formula for each item uses an average of the actual duties paid on imports of inputs for that item in the previous twelve-month period, which again gives an incentive for producers who use above average imports to switch to domestic suppliers in order to get back a higher proportion of the duty paid.[23]

Moreover, outside the EPZs and BFS, exporters do, in general, have to pay duty on imports of capital goods. Only producers of certain specified items are free of tariffs on machinery and equipment imports, regardless of whether they

---

[22] I use "rebates" as a shorthand for rebates, exemptions, and deferrals. The figure presumably includes the EPZs and BFS (*Annual Report of Customs*, various issues).

[23] For more on the rebate system, see Wade 1988c; Little 1979:475.

export or sell the items domestically, with the further proviso that the machinery and equipment is not domestically produced. Thus machinery and equipment for most exports cannot be imported at world market prices, because a duty, sometimes of 20 percent or more, has to be paid.

Nontariff Barriers

Exporters have not always been free to buy imported inputs in cases where domestic substitutes are available, whether intermediate or capital goods. As we noted, they have only been able to import items on the "controlled" list if the price of the domestic substitute is more than 10 percent higher than the c.i.f. price (Lin 1973:98). This constituted a significant restriction in the 1960s, when 40 percent or more of import items were on the controlled list, though it was a much less stringent criterion than that applied to nonexport production. During the 1970s and 1980s exporters have also been subject to the various restrictions on "permissible" imports we noted earlier, though less subject than producers for the domestic market. "If they give enough reason, if they have a special case, they can import a restricted item," one trade official explained. How exactly NTBs are eased for export inputs we do not know.

In the context of understanding how Taiwan has managed to build up its own intermediate and capital goods industries these are important qualifications to the idea that exporters enjoyed free trade conditions.[24] At the same time it remains true that exporters have been able to buy most inputs at close to world market prices because the authorities have used world market prices as a guide to what the prices of protected domestic items should be, using the threat of imports as a means to make sure their guidance is followed.

Export Tax Incentives

Export sales qualify for preferential tax treatment. They are exempt from business tax (total liability for which, not including reductions, amounted to almost 20 percent of total taxes in 1982). Exporting firms qualify for a tax-free reserve for foreign exchange losses equal to up to 7 percent of the outstanding amount of foreign currency loans, and for a tax-free reserve for losses arising from exporting not exceeding one percent of the previous year's export sales. Several other kinds of tax reductions are available for export sales.

Other methods of stimulating exports have included export credits, encouragement of export cartels, export quality control, provision of marketing information, export prizes, and export requirements in the fiscal investment incentive scheme. The last of these is discussed in the following chapter.

[24] On the positive link between certain types of protection (selective rather than across-the-board) and technological learning, see Westphal 1982.

Export Credit

Short-term export credit was a moderately important instrument up to the mid-1970s. It amounted to 6.3 percent of total loans through the banking system in 1972 (Kuo 1983:304). Under the export credit scheme a firm was entitled to concessional credit according to its previous year's export performance and its planned exports for the current year, or according to "letters of credit" in hand (showing export orders received). The problem was that firms often attempted to get credits through both channels simultaneously (from different banks, playing on poor communications between them). They could then lend the excess over their real requirement on the lucrative curb market—perhaps borrowing at around 9 percent and lending at 25 percent or more. This generated increases in money supply; and also, because the volume of exports was so large in relation to GNP (one-third or more over the 1970s), it tended to bring average domestic interest rates down toward the meant-to-be-preferential rate, blunting the intended effect of the government's high interest rates. Besides, by the mid-1970s Taiwan was generating sustained balance-of-trade surpluses. Accordingly the government cut back the volume of export credits and reduced the margin of preference. At the end of 1977, total export credit outstanding (whether preferential or not) amounted to only 2.9 percent of the previous twelve months' exports, while in South Korea at the same time the figure stood at 12.3 percent (Westphal 1978:28; Business International Asia/Pacific Ltd. 1976:150). The margin of preference was 4.0 percentage points, compared to a margin of no less than 7.0 points at the time in South Korea. (Indeed, for the entire period between 1966 and 1981, with one exception, the real rate of interest on export loans in South Korea was negative.) By 1981, export credit as a portion of total bank loans had fallen to 2.1 percent. As of 1983, general export loans were available at about one percent less than the normal short-term rate; and such loans generally required collateral, which is again a conservative banking practice not required in South Korea.

In practice, most export credit has probably come from nonbank sources. Large, upstream firms commonly provide credit to downstream manufacturers, including exporters. The former are able to get bank credit relatively easily and on-lend to their buyers, themselves becoming nonbank financial intermediates (see chapter 6). Japanese trading companies have been the second main source of nonbank credit. They routinely provide their suppliers in Taiwan with credit. Since they themselves get access to Japanese bank loans at cheap rates compared to bank rates in Taiwan, their credit has probably been as concessional as Taiwan's own official export credit. The significance of this point comes from the fact that they handled an estimated 30 to 50 percent of Taiwan's exports during the 1970s and 1980s. So it is misleading to focus only on banks as a source of credit for export production. Taiwan suggests that a well-developed mechanism for *bank* export finance need not be a prerequisite for export success, as World Bank documents tend to say (Rhee 1984). This being said, it is true that little is known about Taiwan's mechanism of trade finance.[25]

Export Cartels

Cut-throat competition in the domestic market during the 1950s led the government to encourage certain industries to form cartels to regulate output and stimulate exports. During the late 1950s and 1960s cartels were formed for paper, textiles, canned foodstuffs, steel products, rubber products, cement, and monosodium glutamate (Lin 1973:108). They subsidized exports by means of a levy on the domestic sales of each member, and set export quotas in proportion to each member's output (with a penalty if export sales fell short).

Subsequently the objective has shifted to restraining "excessive" competition in export markets. The rationale is spelled out by a government official as follows:

> Unorganized production and export often lead to excessive production and cut-throat competition in foreign markets, which inevitably cause a sharp decline in price, deterioration in quality, and finally a loss of the export market. To combat these shortcomings, the Government has encouraged unified and joint marketing of exports in foreign markets through limitation of production by means of export quotas, improvement of quality and unified quotation of export prices.

(Fong 1968:415)

---

[25] The government began supplying low-cost export credit as early as 1957, when the rate was 6 percent per annum payable in foreign exchange or 11.9 percent in local currency, compared to a nominal bank rate for a nonexport loan of 19.8 percent (secured) and 22.3 percent (unsecured) (Lin 1973). In 1975 the government expanded export credits to industries which had suffered a particularly big fall in export demand in the previous recessionary year. Other ingredients were a reduction in interest rates, reduction in import license fee, and a narrowing of the gap between the buying and selling price of foreign exchange (Hsu 1982). Subsequently the volume of export credit was cut back.

However, statements about the volume of export credit in Taiwan carry a high coefficient of ignorance. According to the chairman of one of the commercial banks (who is also an academic economist), the export loan totals given in the *Financial Statistics Monthly* are not all at concessional rates; and some of the nonexport ordinary loans may in fact be for export purposes and at a real cost equal to the cost of a concessional export loan (via adjustments in noninterest terms). These latter may be given to good customers who cannot get enough concessional export credit, to discourage them from shopping around at other banks. What is clear is that indirect exporters cannot get export credit as they can in Korea (Westphal 1978:27). It is also clear that the domestic letter of credit linked to an export letter of credit is not used to help indirect exporters get ordinary bank loans. Rather, the postdated check is the principal financial instrument between suppliers and buyers, and a postdated check from an exporter may be used as part of an indirect exporter's collateral in obtaining a bank loan. It would be worth investigating whether some public enterprises sold below cost to exporters in the past, as a disguised export subsidy.

Government-sponsored cartels continue to be established for these purposes today. Bench-top drilling equipment and telephones were two of the items coming under such arrangements in 1983.

Export Quality Inspection

The government has also interfered in relations between buyers and sellers to impose its influence on quality more directly. Until brandnames become established in the market, foreign buyers judge a product less by its manufacturer than by its country of origin. Hence the shoddy quality of a single product can penalize producers of other products from that country (a negative externality). Compulsory inspection of certain export items began in Taiwan in the 1950s to insure that they met Chinese national standards. Items made subject to inspection were those that attracted a disproportionate number of buyers' complaints. Soon, however, inspection acquired a momentum of its own and the number of items expanded rapidly over the 1960s and early 1970s independent of buyers' complaints, reaching a peak of about 60 percent of export value in 1976. However, the amount of work required to undertake commodity inspection on such a scale prompted a redesign of the scheme to allow a reduction of inspection intensity. The result was a combination of inspection of firms' quality control procedures with a lower intensity of inspection of their merchandise. Since the mid-1970s, factories producing items designated for export inspection within five broad sectors (textiles, electronics, electrical appliances, processed foods, specified miscellaneous) must apply for a grading of their quality control system if they wish to export. Factories which score below a minimum are not allowed to export. Factories above the minimum are put into three grades according to the adequacy of their quality control. Those in the top grade (mostly foreign-invested firms) can export without inspection of merchandise and with reinspection of their quality control system once a year. Those in the middle grade are reinspected for quality control twice a year and have a one in thirty chance of having each shipment inspected. Those in the bottom grade have a three or four times a year reinspection of their quality control and a one in fifteen chance of inspection of each shipment. Inspection fees are inversely related to grade. The merchandise inspections involve visual inspections for some products (e.g., toys, shoes), and lab testing for others. There is some flexibility in the thoroughness of testing to avoid delays in shipment; and if inspection delays build up to more than five days, the inspection agency must take samples and let the shipment go, the factory being downgraded for the next shipment if the samples fail. The government agency in charge of this scheme, the Bureau of Commodity Inspection and Quarantine, has 750 to 800 inspectors working on it from eighteen offices around the country. In addition, a number of sector-specific public testing agencies undertake inspection on behalf of the bureau for certain products (e.g., most electronics items by the Taiwan Electrical Testing Center, most plastics by the Taiwan Plastics Development Center). Some fifty separate laboratories are involved.[26]

Since the mid-1980s the number of export items for inspection has been drastically cut (to cover only 23 percent of exports by 1987), and the scheme has been reoriented toward inspection of imports and domestically made items for local sale. At the same time, several other schemes for improving quality in certain industries have been started. For example, a small number of the biggest producers in four industries—machine tools, heavy electrical machinery, umbrellas, and toys—have been brought together under government sponsorship into special quality-control associations. Each association has hired Japanese quality-control experts from the corresponding industry in Japan with the brief to get the Taiwan product up to Japanese quality.

Export Marketing

The government has also helped with export marketing, though it has often been criticized by the private sector for not doing enough. One expects that government marketing help could be especially valuable for the many small firms that produce a sizable share of Taiwan's direct exports. (Recall that in 1985 firms with under three hundred employees produced 65 percent of manufactured exports.[27]) But before 1970 the government did little. In that year it formed a parastatal market promotion agency, the China External Trade Development Council (CETRA). CETRA now has a staff of about five hundred employees and forty-two overseas offices (as of 1983, having grown from three hundred employees and sixteen overseas offices in 1977).[28] Its senior staff

[26] BCIQ 1981, 1984; interviews with senior officials, two long-time resident U.S. businessmen, and two forwarding agents. The merchandise inspection frequencies are those in force after 1984, before which they were somewhat higher. I have no idea how effective the scheme has been in improving quality compared to normal buyers' pressure. Do buyers know the quality control grades? BCIQ publishes the results in a large annual called *List of Quality Controlled and Graded Plants*, and some suppliers' catalogues give the grades. Both Japan and Korea have also had export commodity inspection schemes. My impression is that Taiwan copied Japan (adding the quality control inspection component in the mid-1970s at the suggestion of U.S. advisors), and Korea copied Taiwan's. Certainly the Koreans sent several groups of experts to Taiwan to study Taiwan's scheme in great detail in the late 1970s.

[27] Biggs 1988; Ministry of Economic Affairs 1985.

[28] Information on CETRA (formerly CETDC) comes from interviews in Feb. 1988; CETDC 1980; and Keesing 1988, the latter being based in turn on field work by Lawrence and Heidi Wortzel and on Scott 1984. Most of the overseas offices do not have Taiwan or China in their name for diplomatic reasons. The London office is called the Taiwan Products Company (the Board of Foreign Trade's London office is called the Majestic Trading Company). In the United States the CETRA offices go under the name of Far Eastern Trade Service, because the U.S. government declined to allow even the name "Taiwan" in the title. CETRA's work is also backed by private Taiwan trading companies operating in certain countries. For example, some of its information about New Zealand comes from a Taiwan family-run trading company long resident in the country.

tend to be ex-government officials (the secretary-general from 1970 to 1984, for example, was the former director of the Department of Commerce). Its council consists of a minority of government officials (appointed directly by the premier) and a majority of presidents of industrial and export associations. Its budget comes entirely from a small levy on exports (0.0625 percent), which gives exporters a modest interest in its effectiveness and provides it with more flexibility than condition-bound government grants. So Taiwan makes a clear separation between the organization for trade administration (the Board of Foreign Trade) and the organization for trade promotion (CETRA); they are, as CETRA officials like to say, two wings of the same bird.

CETRA's main functions are to provide information, organize participation in trade fairs, and carry out market research. It maintains a sophisticated computerized data bank on markets abroad, Taiwan suppliers, and domestic and foreign buyers. The data is kept up-to-date and relevant, and is readily accessible to domestic and foreign businesspeople for a small fee. Written trade inquiries run at an average of one to two hundred a day. CETRA also maintains a large library of suppliers' catalogues and other information in Taipei, and smaller ones in two other cities, providing a one-stop source of information about supply possibilities on the island. A foreign trade representative in Taipei described CETRA's information services as magnificent; and a visiting New Zealand customs official was impressed, not to say shocked, to see how much information was available on New Zealand, a very minor trading partner. New Zealand has no such central public data base for any trading partner, let alone one as unimportant as Taiwan.

Trade missions and trade fairs take up a big chunk of CETRA's resources. It organized the first trade delegation abroad in 1972, the first participation of Taiwan firms in international trade fairs in 1973–74, and the first trade fair in Taiwan in 1973 (for garments). In fiscal 1987–88 it organized participation in forty-one specialized international trade fairs in industrialized countries and four in developing countries plus participation in at least twelve broader trade shows.

About eighty professional staff in headquarters are devoted to market research and development, some organized by commodity, others by area. They advise exporters about foreign markets, including how to penetrate a particular market in a particular country, and they continually feed up-to-date information about their specialization into the CETRA data bank.

One of its most important overseas offices is in New York. The New York office, in addition to the usual functions of processing trade inquiries and organizing participation in trade shows, also carries out market research. For any sector it begins by studying the size and origin of U.S. imports by individual items. It then makes a first cut on which items Taiwan-made products could compete with. It studies their price and quality. When a particular item is identified as promising, the New York office asks firms in Taiwan to send samples and price lists. Representatives of the office then visit importers and wholesalers with the samples. If the buyers are interested, the office telexes back to the manufacturers. If the buyers are not interested, the office finds out why and sends the buyers' reasons back to the manufacturers also. Lawrence Wortzel's interview-based study comparing export promotion offices of five developing countries in New York City in 1980 found that the CETRA office came out a clear winner in effectiveness (ahead of Hong Kong's and Korea's).[29] This is related to, among other things, the large amount of information available to the government on the production range of specific firms.

But since the early 1980s, after most countries had derecognized the Republic of China on Taiwan in favor of the People's Republic, a growing share of CETRA's attention has been devoted to macroissues of economic relations with other countries, and relatively less to issues of individual buyers and sellers. In particular, CETRA has applied the idea of industrial targeting to the task of diversifying Taiwan's trading partners. It selects a small number of countries according to considerations of market growth, political stability, and strategic importance to Taiwan, and then concentrates its attention and resources on them (e.g., Kenya within Sub-Saharan Africa).

Finally, the government has also helped exports by requiring each producers' or exporters' association to maintain an up-to-date library and catalogue of its members' production interests. Firms' grades in the export quality control program are given in some catalogues. The government even arranged technical assistance to firms on how to design their catalogues. In the mid-1960s, for example, it paid for a U.S. expert to spend nearly two years traveling around the country on this task.[30]

Taiwan's own private sector trading companies remain small despite some government encouragement for the growth of large Korean- and Japanese-style trading companies. (The incentives have been meagre.) It is estimated that between 30 and 50 percent of Taiwan's export trade is handled by Japanese trading companies, which have a strong presence but low profile in the country.[31] They make little use of government marketing assistance. How they

[29] Personal communication. The countries were Taiwan, Korea, Hong Kong, Brazil, and Argentina.

[30] The *Taiwan Buyer's Guide*, published annually by the China Productivity Council, gives names, addresses, date of establishment, employment, and types of products for most of Taiwan's export firms (but not the quality-control grade). CETRA publishes annually the *Importers of the Republic of China*, which grades importing firms by volume of imports in the preceding year.

[31] Galli 1980:136 gives 30 percent for 1978, with another 10 percent in the hands of U.S. trading companies. The figure of 50 percent as the share of Japan's trading companies is commonly heard from foreign bankers and journalists and is cited by the economics editor of the *Economist*, Hugh Sandeman (1982b). Given the probably very important role of Japanese trading companies for Taiwan's small-scale export-oriented firms and the paucity of information about that role, one has to fall back on very rough indicators, such as the size of the trading companies' offices in Taiwan. The trouble is that while a big office indicates big business, a small office does

operate remains a mystery, as, indeed, does much else about the marketing side of Taiwan's export growth.

Export Awards

From the early 1960s, following Japanese practice, the government has offered annual export awards. Prizes are given to firms according to several criteria, chiefly the volume of exports and rate of growth of exports. The top prize winners get to walk on stage and receive a trophy from the premier, and their pictures appear in the newspapers. Lesser prize winners shake the hand of lesser dignitaries, while still others simply sit in the audience and get listed in a book of the top four thousand exporting firms. The awards are taken less seriously than the export prizes in Korea (Jones and Sakong 1980; Wade 1982a:95, 121). There is no panic as the cut-off day approaches, with firms trying to boost their export figures to win higher prizes. On the other hand, for smaller firms a prize is a sign of having ''made it.'' Even among the big firms who are prize winners year after year, the company president almost always turns up to collect the prize, and the prizes are prominently displayed at headquarters. In 1987 the criterion was changed from exports to exports plus imports.

Exchange Rate

One other point about export incentives. Over the 1980s, with the exchange rate fixed at close to NT$40 = US$1, the real exchange rate became increasingly undervalued, much as the Japanese yen had become increasingly undervalued in the late 1960s. One estimate puts the magnitude of undervaluation for Taiwan at around 25 percent in the mid-1980s (Hou 1987:12). This of course has given a powerful spur to exports, and only aggravated the problem of towering reserves. By December 1986 the rate had been appreciated to NT$35, and by December 1987 to NT$29.

MANAGEMENT OF FOREIGN DIRECT INVESTMENT

Domestic producers in selected sectors have been protected not only from import competition but also from foreign firms operating in the domestic market. The access of domestically based foreign firms to the domestic market has been controlled from the beginning. Fear of foreign domination of key sectors has been a major element in official thinking, as in Japan and Korea.

Foreign direct investment has been quite important in Taiwan's economy,

---

not imply small business because much business may be done by traveling representatives based at headquarters.

but not as important as is often thought. As a source of capital it accounted for only 3 to 10 percent of gross domestic capital formation over the 1970s, averaging 4 percent, and 8 percent of manufacturing investment. This is less than in the lower-saving Southeast Asian countries (Parry 1988) and in line with Brazil and Mexico. In terms of exports, about 20 to 25 percent of manufactured exports came from foreign firms over the 1970s (Lee and Liang 1982:332; Ranis and Schive 1985). Or in terms of "related party" trade (such as that between a subsidiary and a parent company), only a fifth of total exports to the United States in 1971 came through related party channels, much lower than for Brazil- and Mexico-U.S. trade (Helleiner 1981b: table 5.1). A calculation for 1981 shows that exports to the United States from U.S. affiliates amounted to only 9 percent of total manufactured exports to the United States (6 percent for Korea, 68 percent for Singapore, 11 percent for Hong Kong; Dahlman 1988: table 13, based on U.S. Commerce Department data). The role of U.S. affiliates in total exports has been even smaller: 6.2 percent in 1977, 3.9 percent in 1983. The figures for Korea are smaller again, at 1.4 percent and 1.3 percent, respectively, while the Latin American averages were much higher, at 9.8 percent and 13.4 percent: Blomstrom, Kravis, and Lipsey 1988). But in certain industries U.S. and other foreign firms have been much more important. Over half of foreign firms' exports during the 1970s were in electronics and electrical appliances, and foreign firms accounted for two-thirds or more of total exports from this industry. Most foreign investment has come from the United States, Japan, and Hong Kong.[32]

Technical cooperation agreements with foreign firms increased rapidly in the late 1950s for chemicals, basic metals, metal products, machinery, and especially electrical appliances. At the same time, the U.S. aid mission an-

[32] Electronic and electrical appliances accounted for about one-third of the total foreign direct investment up to 1974. Industries producing chemicals, machinery, basic metals, and metal products accounted for another 27 percent (Koo 1976: table 2). But note that these figures are based on approvals, not arrivals. It is estimated that in the early 1970s about two-thirds of firms in electric and electronic appliances operated with the participation of foreign capital (Koo 1976:136). See also chapter 4 n. 30. Gold (1983) presents an interesting argument about the differences in strategy between foreign enterprises of different nationality operating in Taiwan.

Foreign-owned companies (more than 50 percent equity held by foreigners) are surprisingly small; by no stretch of the imagination can they be said to dominate the economy. The following gives the rank order of foreign companies in terms of sales in fiscal year 1975/76 and then the rank order which that sales volume would give them in the top Taiwanese private corporations: (1) RCA Taiwan Ltd., 7, sales of NT$3.7 billion; (2) Texas Instruments Ltd., 18; (3) Zenith Taiwan, 32, NT$1.491 billion; (4) Admiral Overseas Corp., 33; (5) Capetronic (Taiwan), 34; (6) Philips Electronic Industries (Taiwan), 42, NT$1.201 billion; (7) China Gulf Oil, 59; (8) Sylvania-Philico Taiwan, 69; (9) Taipei Mitsumi, 79, NT$808 million; (10) General Instruments of Taiwan, 81; (11) Arvin (Taiwan), 115; (12) Trans World Electronics (Taiwan), 134, NT$544 million (China Credit Information Service 1977). Some of the big foreign companies have several registered firms in Taiwan (e.g., Philips); consolidation of their accounts would somewhat modify the picture suggested by these figures.

nounced that aid would soon terminate, and began to solicit private U.S. firms to step into the gap. Feeling wage pressure at home, both U.S. and Japanese firms were in any case beginning to search out areas of lower-cost labor where they might relocate some of their production. Taiwan offered political stability and cheap, skilled, disciplined labor. It was also linked to Japan by ties of sentiment and language from the colonial era, and to the United States by its strategic and symbolic importance as an anticommunist outpost. Most developing countries have close links with only one metropolitan country, usually a less dynamic Western European one.

The government, with USAID help, drew up a set of incentives to woo direct investment, just at the time when Latin American countries were beginning to feel worried about allowing too much in. Whereas Latin American countries compelled joint ventures and threatened expropriation, Taiwan offered 100 percent foreign ownership and management and guarantees against expropriation. Whereas they raised taxes on foreign investors, Taiwan offered a five-year tax holiday or accelerated depreciation; whereas they limited profit repatriation, Taiwan did not; whereas they had labor strikes and political instability, Taiwan had neither (Gold 1981:195). Japan, too, maintained direct foreign investment controls more stringent than Taiwan's; in particular, it prohibited remittance abroad of earnings or liquidation proceeds until 1963, and limited foreign firm share ownership in a joint venture to 50 percent or less (Weiss 1986).

Nor did the government wait passively for foreign firms to take the initiative. Often it sought out particular companies, sometimes paying them to visit with no obligation. Much effort went into making the firm feel welcome, one trick being to discover in advance some personal connection, however remote, between the firm and a senior in the Taiwan government. A senior executive of a U.S. firm, invited to meet a cabinet minister, was startled to learn that the minister's mother had been a classmate of the executive's wife's mother in college—startled because this suggested that the government had already investigated his company in some detail.

Taiwan has been less selective about foreign investment than Japan and South Korea, but it has become increasingly selective over the 1970s. Foreign investment proposals have been evaluated in terms of how much they open new markets, build new exports, transfer technology, intensify input-output links, make Taiwan more valuable to multinationals as a foreign investment site and as a source for important components, and enhance Taiwan's international political support.[33] Not much was rejected during the 1960s. But most

[33] Guidelines on foreign investment date from 1962 ("Explanatory notes" to 1954 Statute for Investment by Foreign Nationals and to 1955 Statute for Investment by Overseas Chinese). The guidelines limit foreign investment to industries which would introduce new products or direct their activities toward easing domestic shortages, exporting, increasing the quality of existing products, and lowering domestic product prices. Some sectors were made subject to local content

of the proposals were for export production, so that direct competition with domestic producers on the small domestic market was less of an issue.

Two landmark cases can be cited, both of which set a pattern for future agreements. In one, the government permitted the Singer Sewing Machine Company to set up a plant in 1963 over the objections of local assemblers and suppliers. The government argued that this would save foreign exchange and improve the quality of locally made parts. It imposed the condition that Singer procure locally 83 percent of required parts one year after start-up and assist local component producers to meet its specifications. Singer did not in fact meet such a stringent local content requirement after one year, but it did enough by way of transferring technology, upgrading the local industry, and boosting exports that local producers who initially opposed its entry soon admitted they were wrong (Gold 1986:85).

The second case concerns a low density polyethylene plant built by the National Distiller and Chemical Corporation, a U.S. firm. National Distiller began to look for overseas production opportunities in the early 1960s, selecting Taiwan as one possible site. The U.S. government encouraged its interest in Taiwan by offering guarantees against war and expropriation, and cheap credit for the purchase of U.S. equipment. The Taiwan government offered a five-year tax holiday, restrictions on imports of polyethylene for three years from start-up, guaranteed supplies of ethylene (the principal input) from Chinese Petroleum's new naptha cracker, and unlimited repatriation of profits. In return, the government required that five years after start-up National Distiller had to transfer shares to Chinese nationals, so as to convert a 100 percent foreign-owned subsidiary into a 50-50 joint venture; National Distiller would not establish production facilities in downstream sectors; and it should export any surpluses over domestic needs. A Japanese company which was also interested in supplying the polyethylene plant refused to make these concessions and withdrew from the negotiations. The National Distiller plant came on line in 1968 (Gold 1981:274).

Around 1970 the government decided on a concerted strategy to move the economy into a stronger position in the international market. With industrial deepening even more urgent than before, the involvement of both foreign firms and public enterprises increased. Foreign investments in labor-intensive production came to be discouraged or prevented.[34] Most foreign investors were faced with export requirements and/or local content requirements; and the government has been especially concerned to remove export restrictions

---

requirements, including refrigerators, air conditioners, transformers, televisions, radios, cars, motorcycles, tractors, and diesel engines (as from 1963 the local content requirements also applied to domestic firms operating in these sectors). Exemptions from local content requirements were often available for exported goods (Schive and Majumdar 1981).

[34] In 1973 about 13 percent of the total industrial workforce was employed in enterprises classed as ''foreign-owned'' (Koo 1976:142).

wanted by the technology supplier (to protect himself against the threat of future competition). The export requirements have generally remained in place through the 1980s, even as foreign exchange reserves ran into troublesome surplus.[35] Their function is now no longer to help earn foreign exchange; they now insure that the company brings to Taiwan a technology advanced enough for its products to compete in other (generally wealthy Western) markets, and second, to check the firm's access to the domestic market. Access to the domestic market has also been checked by such mechanisms as tough local content requirements for that part of production sold locally (but not always for that part sold abroad), and/or by requirements that investments oriented mainly to the domestic market take the form of joint ventures. The fact that foreign companies producing in Taiwan have occupied only small shares of the domestic market, except in chemicals and electric and electronic appliances, suggests that these restrictions may have been effective. Even in the case of chemicals and appliances, the volume of domestic sales from foreign companies has been less than that of domestic companies (table 5.4).

In some cases the government has also required foreign firms to undertake assistance to upgrade the capabilities of local suppliers as part of the approval process. And limits have been placed on the extent to which foreign firms can capitalize their technology; typically the technology can be valued at no more than 15 percent of the firm's equity contribution in the case of joint ventures, with the object of making the firm commit more equity to the project, thereby carrying more of the risk.

Much discretion is exercised case by case as to exactly what incentives and what obligations to impose on foreign investors—even if the discretion is probably less than in South Korea. Firms whose projects promise to open up new markets, bring in new technology, intensify input-output links within Taiwan, or enhance Taiwan's base of international political support will be given a lower export or local content requirement, special help in finding a suitable site, and/or help with feasibility studies than firms which can offer less. Import protection is important too, and here the subtlety of the approval mechanism is valuable. Firms which are highly sought-after may be told (according to an informant involved in these negotiations) that since Taiwan is a free-trading country it cannot offer sizable tariffs or import bans; but that the government will insure that the firm nevertheless gets an ample domestic market. What is being said, in effect, is that hidden protection via the approval mechanism will be given, while the outward appearance of little protection is maintained. In a late-1960 study of U.S. corporate investment in Taiwan Schrieber observes:

> Very important to these companies and *an inducement without which most would not have invested* is the diminution of risk through government assurance that it

[35] There was discussion in policy-making circles in 1983 about whether all foreign investment, without exception, should be required to export at least 50 percent of production.

TABLE 5.4
Sales of Domestic and Foreign Companies in the Export Market, 1976 and 1981 (%)

	1976				1981
	Taiwan Co. (% Exports)	Foreign Co. (% Exports)	Domestic Sales, Foreign Co./ Taiwan Co.	Total Sales, Foreign Co./ Taiwan Co.	Foreign Co. (% Exports)
Food	14	26	12	14	15
Garments and footwear	79	97	0.5	38	93
Textiles	28	85	0.4	20	74
Paper and pulp	14	13	14	13	10
Plastics and rubber	27	89	2	14	65
Chemicals	19	50	53	86	41
Nonmetallic minerals	n.a.	9	n.a.	37	15
Basic metals	17	58	n.a.	n.a.	53
Machinery equipment and instruments	n.a.	49	n.a.	n.a.	34
Electric and electronic	26	71	81	204	71
Exports as % of total sales	n.a.	61	—	—	54

Source: Gold 1981:95; Ministry of Economic Affairs, Investment Commission, 1982.

Note: Because of differences in categorization of domestic and export sales as between Taiwan companies and foreign companies the figures are to be taken only as orders of magnitude. Table reads (row 1): In 1976 domestically owned food-processing companies made 14 percent of their sales abroad (the rest domestically), while foreign-owned food companies made 26 percent of sales abroad. The domestic sales of foreign companies equaled only 12 percent of the domestic sales of domestic food companies, and total sales of foreign companies equaled only 14 percent of domestic companies' total sales. Column 5 is for the same variable as column 2, but for 1981.

will buy the entire output at a prescribed price. . . . These government assurances eliminate any fear that the companies will not be able to market their products profitably. In order to underwrite the assurance of sales, the privilege to produce a specific item is usually granted to one company only, and in essence constitutes a legal monopoly. The company in return has to construct a facility of sufficient scale to produce 100 percent of the island's needs for that product or an agreed-upon quantity.   (1970:66, emphasis added)

Of course if the firm then does not behave as expected the government can rapidly and without publicity remove its protection. A further negotiating variable is repatriation of capital; by law profits of foreign manufacturing enterprises can be remitted without restriction, but initial capital can be remitted only at 15 percent a year starting three years after the approved investment is completed (Business International 1976:158), and capital gains cannot be remitted at all. In practice these rules are flexible; a sought-after company will receive better terms than others.

The bargaining can be tough. Toyota found that in a proposed joint venture for cars the Taiwan government insisted upon stringent export, local content, and technology transfer requirements (50 percent of the cars to be exported after eight years, local content to rise to 90 percent). Toyota found these conditions unacceptable and withdrew in 1984. Moreover, foreign investors are sometimes dismayed to find that the government does not always regard a contract as fixed for a preagreed period once signed and sealed. Coming from an experience of Western law they are unfamiliar with the Chinese assumption that a contract is not much more than a basis for further negotiations; it is only a clarification of rights and obligations accepted by both parties as being reasonably balanced at the time, acceptance being made on the understanding that (at the time unforeseen) changes in circumstances may require changes in terms to strike a new ''fair'' balance.

How much selection and discretion is exercised in connection with foreign investment depends partly on Taiwan's diplomatic position at the time. The more threatened the government feels, the more big-name multinational companies are sought out. As Thomas Gold explains, ''the offices of [multinational companies] have taken the place of embassies in defining Taiwan's existence'' (1981:218). The worse the island's international diplomatic position, the more the government cites foreign investment figures to reassure itself and its citizens of its continued viability as a state.

Therefore, when the United States signalled its intention to derecognize Taiwan in favor of mainland China in the late 1970s, the government went out of its way to attract a big name U.S. multinational to build heavy trucks (Noble 1987). The objectives were to strengthen Taiwan's military-industrial capability so that Taiwan would not collapse if the United States cut off arms and military technology, and also to strengthen support for Taiwan's cause in the United States. In addition, it was argued that a heavy truck plant would help expand the auto parts industry, which was seen as having big growth potential. After discussions with the other two U.S. makers through 1978 and 1979, General Motor's proposal was accepted in 1980. GM was given extraordinarily generous, risk-free terms, under which it could pull out its entire investment plus interest at any time that the Taiwan government failed to give it ''adequate'' protection against imports. In effect, the government guaranteed protection indefinitely even if the joint venture never attained international competitiveness. Production started in 1982. The trucks were judged to be of good quality in engineering terms, but over 60 percent more expensive than trucks from Japan. In the meantime many features of the original situation had changed. By 1982 the growth rate had dropped; the Taiwan dollar had risen against the Japanese yen in line with the appreciation of the U.S. dollar (making imports of Japanese trucks still cheaper); GM no longer looked to be a world technology leader in automobiles; U.S. derecognition of Taiwan was not having the feared calamitous effects; and a new set of key actors had become involved in the heavy truck issue, notably a new minister of economic affairs who was much more concerned with economic efficiency and competitiveness than his predecessor. Negotiations were reopened, the government withdrew its promise of import protection, and General Motors decided to pull out with generous compensation for its trouble.

Another recent case illustrates the chronic conflicts of interest between foreign firms and the government, with the government seeking to modify the normal workings of the market in line with national objectives. Procter & Gamble (P&G), the big American maker of personal products, wanted to establish a plant in Taiwan. The government agreed provided it exported 50 percent of production, because the local market in Taiwan simply "isn't big enough for them to make money," in the words of an official (Specter and Tanzer 1983). P&G, taking the free market view, protested that it, not the government, should decide where the profit lay and how much to export, and threatened to urge the U.S. government to retaliate by cancelling Taiwan's preferential access to the U.S. market (under the Generalized System of Preferences, from which Taiwan gets more benefits than any other country). The government was in fact imposing no more stringent an obligation than it imposes on many multinationals, as we have seen. Its determination to stick to the export obligation despite Taiwan's overflowing foreign exchange reserves was strengthened by complaints from domestic producers of rival products that they would be out of business if P&G were allowed to sell without restriction on the domestic market. The government hopes that domestic producers will soon be able to compete internationally in these products—especially if they can get hold of modern technology from companies like P&G. The "national interest," as the government saw it, required the government to prevent P&G from doing something which, though privately profitable, would threaten too great a reduction of national control in the personal goods sector and reduce the chances that the nationally controlled part could later become internationally competitive. So the free market result was blocked—prices were not to be the determinant of how much P&G exported. But for most of the other major decisions (on product mix, organization of production, etc.) P&G was free to do what it wanted.

Finally, at the same time as the government has been attracting and constraining foreign firms, it has been active in reducing their enclave nature, especially those in the export-processing zones. Using detailed and quickly produced trade statistics (the government knows day-by-day how much is imported and exported from the country), it scrutinizes the flow of imports going to industries dominated by multinationals, sees what could feasibly be produced in Taiwan at roughly the same price, and takes the initiative to find local suppliers. It does the same with exports to see what could be further processed within Taiwan. One study of foreign investment by authors not predisposed to stress the wisdom of the government's interventions concludes that "most of the DFI [direct foreign investment]-concentrated industries had high linkage indices, indicating that the public authorities in Taiwan gave some consideration to potential linkages in directing foreign investment activities" (Schive and Majumdar 1981:19).

At the same time, the government has been trying to increase Taiwan's general attractiveness to firms in high-technology sectors. Taxes on technology imports were reduced in the early 1970s, and generous tax write-offs for research and development have been allowed. More importantly, Taiwan's science and technology infrastructure has been transformed by means of a dense network of government laboratories, industrial assistance organizations, technical education facilities, and special funds to buy foreign technology and develop domestic R&D. Another initiative is the Hsinchu Science-based Industry Park, which offers special inducements to high-tech firms, local or foreign. Suitable firms have been given a whole battery of incentives; but characteristically, the firms also have to meet some obligations, such as to establish a sizable research department and to train local personnel in advanced technology. Through these various measures, the government has taken on a more direct role in technology acquisition.

Incoming foreign portfolio investment—investment in local securities—has not been allowed, although Taiwan's high real interest rates would have attracted a substantial inflow. The government has feared the effects on interest rate policy and the possibility that sudden withdrawals could cause a financial crisis. Only in the early 1980s has serious consideration been given to allowing some investment of this kind—but only for indirect portfolio investment via a unit trust. The stock exchange is still out of bounds to foreigners.

All of Taiwan's small but rapidly growing direct investment abroad requires government approval, given only (before the mid-1980s) after stringent scrutiny. The government sought to control the export of capital as a way of preserving Taiwan capital for domestic use and insuring that exports of goods are emphasized over exports of capital. Hence overseas investment has been encouraged only insofar as it can be shown to contribute to the strength of the national economy (e.g., by facilitating market access or securing sources of supply). It grew at the rate of nearly 25 percent a year from the early 1970s to 1979. The first wave, from the early 1970s, was mostly to Southeast Asia (especially the Philippines and Indonesia) to secure raw material supplies. The second wave, from the late 1970s, was mostly to North America and the Caribbean to secure market access. In the mid-1980s the restraints on overseas foreign investment were sharply cut in response to higher domestic labor costs, currency appreciation, and troublesome foreign exchange reserves. With the average textile worker getting US$2.37 an hour in Taiwan compared with 58 cents in Thailand, a third wave of foreign investment toward cheaper labor sites began. By early 1989 some three hundred to four hundred projects were located in Thailand. Coastal provinces on the Chinese mainland are another favored site, with one hundred to two hundred projects mostly in shoes, textiles, and apparel. Investing in the mainland is supposed to be illegal, but can be arranged without difficulty through Hong Kong. Most overseas investment projects are small, in the US$1- to $2-million range. But some large ones have also been made, particularly in petrochemicals. Environmentalist protests have driven some new petrochemical projects abroad to the Philippines and the United States. The overall magnitude of outward investment is difficult to estimate, since much overseas investment goes out through unofficial channels to avoid taxation. Central bank estimates show actual overseas investment in 1988 to be between US$2.5 and $3.5 billion, or between 2 and 3 percent of GNP. If so, actual investment abroad exceeded incoming foreign investment for the first time. The tight domestic labor market means that little opposition to these outflows is likely to develop (*Far Eastern Economic Review* 1989; *Economist* 1988).

The direction and speed of the outward movement of investment has not been left entirely to unguided free market agents, any more than has diversification of the destination of Taiwan's exports. The Industrial Development and Investment Center ranks countries according to their priority as sites for Taiwan's foreign investment, using as criteria needed natural resources, opportunities for acquiring needed technology, marketing channels already in place, protective barriers which direct investment could jump, and lower production costs—in descending order of importance. The Ministry of Economic Affairs then modifies the ranking to factor in political considerations. Differential tax incentives are awarded to outward investment according to the overall rank of the country of destination.[36]

The other side of the trend toward outward-oriented direct foreign investment is a big increase in illegal foreign workers in Taiwan (estimated at between 12,000 and 30,000 as of early 1989), mainly from the Philippines, Thailand, and Malaysia. Both movements—of Taiwan capital to cheaper foreign labor and cheaper foreign labor to Taiwan—indicate the transformation of the economy and its role in the world.

Conclusions

The state has interfered in trade not less, but differently, than in many other developing countries. As gatekeeper for the national economy, it has scrutinized inflows and outflows and affected the terms of transactions in line with national objectives. It has balanced the need to bring international market pres-

---

[36] I am indebted to Klaus Lorch for this information.

sures to bear on domestic producers with the need to build up supply capacity in an increasing range of industries. It has accomplished this feat by avoiding both free trade and high, unselective, and unconditional protection, and by welcoming foreign investment while placing constraints on its role in the domestic economy.

If we accept at face value the figure on Taiwan's average effective protection to manufacturing shown in table 3.2, we might conclude that resource allocation in Taiwan has been governed by world prices to a greater extent than in less successful countries. This is what the neoclassical (FM and SM) theories predict. But as we have seen, the conclusion is unwarranted. First, the procedure for calculating effective protection ignores legal tariffs. But legal tariffs have been an accurate indicator of the extent of impediments to import of finished and semifinished goods for domestic market sale rather than export sale. And legal tariffs have not been low by LDC standards. Second, the low average effective protection results from a particular method of incorporating the large proportion of negative price differentials, alternative and apparently equally justifiable procedures for which would have given either a much higher or much lower average. Third, the interindustry dispersion around the average is quite high, which is not in line with FM/SM predictions. Fourth, the figure is for one year only, as long ago as 1969. Other bits and pieces from earlier and later years suggest that sizable protection existed. Fifth, the method of calculating effective protection by comparing domestic and international prices for the same item does not pick up important methods of protection. Zero price differentials could exist even with no competing imports being allowed across the national boundary. Finally, the government used many other methods of steering investment than those contained in the protection system. We now examine some of these other methods.

Chapter 6

MANAGEMENT OF DOMESTIC INVESTMENT

WITHIN THE DOMESTIC ECONOMY, the government has influenced the amount and composition of investment in many parts of the economy. It has done so by using the banks, the government budget, public enterprises, the fiscal investment incentive scheme, and direct investment controls.

THE FINANCIAL SYSTEM

Economists have been unimpressed by Taiwan's financial system. They commonly describe it as "rigid," unresponsive to market forces. They have generally refrained from trying to relate the rigidity of the financial system to the country's superior economic performance. Erik Lundberg, in a long essay on Taiwan's monetary and fiscal policies, has only this to say: "In spite of these shortcomings [rigidity, etc.] . . . the financial system as a whole *must have* contained enough resilience and elasticity to meet the most urgent needs of a rapidly growing economy in a great transformation process" (1979:280, emphasis added). It must have, indeed. Here I shall argue that some of the qualities which made Taiwan's financial system rigid also helped the government to implement its sectoral industrial policies, and according to the larger argument, thereby helped economic development.

Despite Taiwan's extraordinarily rapid rate of monetization (see table 3.4), the financial system has remained undiversified, dominated by the banks. Nonbank financial institutions, such as investment and trust companies, bill finance companies, insurance companies, and the like, accounted for only 5 percent of the assets of Taiwan's major financial institutions by 1980 (Liang and Skully 1982:174). Or in terms of financial claims outstanding at the end of 1979, nonbank financial institutions represented only 7 percent; government bonds, corporate bonds, and commercial paper outstanding represented another 6 percent; corporate stock, 13 percent; while claims on the banking system accounted for *75 percent* of the total (ibid.:189). The limited development of nonbank financial institutions could reflect a difficulty in competing against highly competitive commercial banks, just as a relatively large nonbank financial sector could reflect government-imposed handicaps on commercial banks. In Taiwan's case, however, the limited development of the nonbank sector reflects strict government controls over it, with the aim of preserving the dominant position of the not highly competitive banks. So in this case, the small size of the nonbank sector is a useful indicator of the "illiberal" nature of the financial system. Only since the mid-1970s has the government allowed an expansion in the nonbank sector—partly so that it could better control the nonbank financial institutions which were springing up anyway.

The significance of the banks can also be indicated by the percentage of private savings (including company savings) that are channeled through the banks. Since 1960 the figure has been around 45 to 50 percent—lower when company profits are higher (because profits are directly reinvested) and higher when profits are lower (because more savings comes from wages).

Taiwan's firms are typically highly leveraged in the sense that they depend more on borrowing than on equity capital. According to official figures, the ratio of corporate sector debt to equity was between 160 and 180 in most years between 1971 and 1980; which compares with figures of only 50 to 90 for Great Britain and the United States. But Taiwan's ratio is much lower than Korea's, whose corresponding figure was 310 to 380 (Scitovsky 1986: chart 1). However the "true" Korean figure is probably much lower than its official value, especially because of complications introduced by Korea's higher inflation rate and higher permitted rates of accelerated depreciation. One estimate puts the real Korean figure in the same order of magnitude as Taiwan's official figure (World Bank 1984:238 n.8). Japan's figure over the 1950s to the 1970s has been of the same order of magnitude as the Korean. We can safely say that in all three countries, financing choices have been weighted heavily in favor of debt rather than equity.[1]

There are two main sources of debt finance in Taiwan. One is through banks and the other is through the "curb" market. The curb market (as in street market) is an unregulated, semilegal credit market in which loan suppliers and demanders can transact freely at uncontrolled interest rates. The image of a street market is misleading, however, for much curb market finance consists of loans from supplying firms to buying firms in the form of "supplier's

[1] But Chiu (1982:431) talks of the "high equity position" of Taiwan's private manufacturing enterprises, referring to a debt/equity ratio over the 1970s of, according to his calculations, roughly 160 to 165. He has in mind the comparison with Japan, where he takes the ratio to be around 400. Bankers in Taiwan tend to take a debt/equity ratio of two to one as a rule of thumb. International comparisons of debt/equity ratios are plagued by differences in adjustment of asset values for inflation. The figures given in the text are not inflation-adjusted (except for the modified Korean figure). Also, the significance of a given debt/equity ratio depends on the size of the cash flow available to repay the debt, on the proportion of bank debt, and on the proportion of long-term debt. The macronumbers for Taiwan are roughly in line with the official figures of between 160 and 180 percent. If one takes industrial corporate assets as equal to 100 to 110 percent of GNP, as is common in middle-income countries, M2 as equal to 67 percent of GNP (see table 3.4), and M2 as roughly equal to corporate debt, this leaves 33 to 43 percent of GNP for equity. So a debt/equity ratio of 160 to 180 percent is not surprising, considering that part of M2 is not allocated to the corporate sector. (The same calculation for Korea would have to include its high foreign debt in relation to GDP, offsetting low M2/GDP).

credit.'' Between 1976 and 1981 it is estimated that private business borrowed about 60 percent from banks and most of the remainder from the curb market while public enterprises got 96 percent of borrowings from the banks (Shea 1983b:5). Small private businesses would have received less than 60 percent from the banks, large businesses more (Ho 1980).[2] In terms of capital formation, it is estimated that during the 1960s bank loans covered 30 to 35 percent of gross private capital formation, rising to over 80 percent in the 1970s (Riegg 1978:310).

The curb market has supplied some 30 percent of the total volume of loans processed through the financial system over the 1970s, at rates 50 to 100 percent higher than bank loan rates during the 1970s and three times higher during the 1950s (see pp. 58–59).[3] The curb market is important not only in providing financial flexibility, but also in supplying information. Since the early 1950s the central monetary authorities have conducted weekly curb market surveys. When curb market exchange rates shift, or interest rates rise, or when curb dealers experience a string of defaults, the central bank takes notice. When such changes are corroborated by other indicators, changes in monetary policy are likely to follow (Riegg 1978:253).

In short, large and medium-sized businesses depend heavily on banks for finance, while small businesses (less than, say, one hundred employees) depend more on the curb market. The banks are virtually all owned by the government. The four private banks had only 5 percent of deposits and branches of all the commercial banks in 1980, and the biggest of the four is only nominally private.[4] Government ownership goes with close government control, which the small number of banks makes that much easier. (Only seven banks accounted for almost 90 percent of total deposits of domestic banks in 1980.)

Senior staff are appointed by the government. Chairmen are mostly ex-Ministry of Finance or central bank officials rather than professional bankers and are appointed directly by the premier or the provincial governor, depending on whether the bank is owned by the central or the provincial government. The government sets salary scales of bank staff and regulates the annual staff bo-

---

[2] There are no good figures on the dependence of firms on bank loans by size of firm. However, in 1972 small and medium businesses (including manufacturing and commercial establishments of less than one hundred employees) took 23 percent of total domestic bank lending (in line with the share of manufacturing firms of this size in total manufacturing value added; see table 3.5). In 1980 small and medium businesses (by then redefined as businesses with less than three hundred employees) took 32 percent. Figures from Medium and Small Business Administration, compiled by Biggs (1988).

[3] Shea 1983a; Ho 1980; Sandeman 1982b. Presumably curb market rates vary greatly by size and reputation of company, a relationship on which I have no evidence.

[4] Liang and Skully 1982. The biggest of the four private banks was privatized in the wake of UN derecognition (1971), to enable Taiwan to have overseas branches of a domestic bank without running into the diplomatic problems posed by a ''government'' bank of a nonrecognized country. China Airlines is nominally private for the same reason.

nuses. It sets the structure of interest rates and imposes tight limits on how much can be lent to any one borrower and on the purchase of company stocks. These controls are reinforced by stringent reporting requirements. All banks must report all their transactions to the central bank weekly; all foreign exchange transactions must be reported daily.

Whereas South Korea denationalized most of its banks between 1980 and 1983, there was not even public discussion of such a move in Taiwan prior to 1985. So Hofheinz and Calder are wrong to say of South Korea that "no other non-Communist East Asian nation has such a substantial public presence in its financial system" (1982:129). Moreover, the Taiwan government has a major presence even in parts of the nonbank financial sector, owning or part-owning insurance and bill finance companies, while the Nationalist party is said to control the commission that runs the stock exchange.

Foreign banks have been kept on the margins. They were excluded altogether until 1958 when a Japanese bank was permitted—the only foreign bank in Taiwan until 1965. Even by 1972 only six more foreign banks had been permitted—one office each. So foreign banks operating in Taiwan had little role in the export boom. By the end of 1980, twenty-six foreign banks had been allowed to open one branch or representative office. Still today foreign banks are required to report all transactions daily to the central bank. They are allowed only very limited access to local deposits. They face a daily limit on foreign currency lending per bank and per customer. They are not allowed to take equity in Taiwanese companies. In effect, they are only allowed into those pockets of business which the locals cannot do well, in return for lending money to the country's international borrowers.

The principal instrument in this financial system is the postdated check.[5] When a borrower takes a loan he gives the lender a check drawn at some future date for an amount covering principal and interest. In a "normal" developed financial system, by contrast, checks are used as cash substitutes rather than as credit instruments, while promissory notes are used for credit and drafts for trade purposes. In Taiwan, however, the postdated check is used for all trade finance and is often used as extra security in all other kinds of financial transactions. Not only the curb market but also government banks rely on the postdated check. The basic reason is that the dishonoring of a check carries (since 1954) criminal, not just civil penalties, while the dishonoring of other instruments does not. That is, anyone who draws a check that is dishonored because of insufficient funds or line of credit is liable to criminal penalties, including jail. The merits of this arrangement for the lender are that it requires a specific person to be designated who can be nailed if the loan is not repaid, and that prosecution is automatically undertaken by the government rather than by the

---

[5] I draw on discussions with Jane Winn and Han-ming Su for this account of the postdated check.

complainant. These are considerable advantages, given that company accounts and financial statements, being notoriously unreliable, are no basis for sound lending decisions.

On the other hand, in terms of the financial system as a whole, there are several disadvantages which increase as the economy becomes more complex. First, the postdated check makes monetary control more difficult. Second, its availability as a credit instrument slows the evolution of a more impersonal and differentiated set of financial instruments and of better accounting practices. It means that loan decisions must continue to be based on a judgment of personal integrity, or on the borrower's susceptibility to criminal sanctions, or on collateral. This is no basis for a complex financial system, and especially not if Taiwan's is to become closely connected to the world financial system. Third, because the postdated check is the mainstay of the curb market and is sanctioned by the government, the government is in effect supporting the curb market, which makes it feel uncomfortable because of the semilegal status of the curb market. Fourth, the wrong people—those with no intention to defraud—frequently end up in jail while the crooks escape. A husband may conduct his business in his wife's name using her chop (name stamp); and when he fails to repay it is she who goes to jail, perhaps having to bring the children with her. From time to time the newspapers carry stories of men apprehended at the airport as they try to flee the country, leaving behind a string of bad checks and a tearful wife facing criminal prosecution.

As for collateral, Business International describes Taiwan as "the country where ultraconservative banking has turned collateral into an utter fetish" (1976:4). The banks are popularly known as "pawn shops." Their overriding concern is to protect the security of their lending, especially by means of immovable but readily saleable collateral such as real estate. They have not developed an analytical capacity for examining company balance sheets and making financial flow assessments, partly because of the unreliability of such company information. On the other hand, there is strangely little evidence on the degree of collateral (are most loans 50 percent collateralized, or 125 percent?), or on the quality of the security (how marketable and how stealable?), or on the extent to which projects which would have been funded in more "modern" banking systems have been turned down for lack of collateral. It may be that collateral is in fact less important than is generally alleged to be the case.

Bank loans tend to have short-term maturities. Between 1955 and 1975, 69 to 75 percent of bank loans had a maturity of one year or less. "These people are putting up factories on short-term credit!" exclaimed one American banker. From the lender's viewpoint, short-term loans reduce risk (an important consideration when most firms are too small or too young to have established reputations), and permit more flexibility between firms and sectors.

Banks have normally made big profits. This is the result of strong demand, limited competition, and government-mandated spreads between borrowing and lending rates. Profitability has declined in the 1980s, however, with the recession-induced fall in investment demand around 1982–83, the explosion of foreign exchange reserves, and the fall of the U.S. dollar in 1986.

Since the early l980s a series of moves has been made to liberalize the financial system. In particular, a committee of bankers is allowed to set actual loan and deposit rates month by month, within ceilings set by the central bank, restrictions on interest rates for certain financial instruments have been removed, and a market in bankers' acceptances is permitted. This in effect simply substitutes a banking cartel indirectly managed by the central bank for the old direct management by the central bank. But at least the central bank now has better price signals from the authorized money market than it did from the curb market to guide changes in the structure and level of bank interest rates. Other liberalizing moves include an offshore banking unit, a unit trust scheme for allowing foreign capital to take equity indirectly in Taiwan companies, a venture capital scheme, permission from the military to allow financial data to leave the country by high-speed computer transmission (this had long been resisted because it is difficult to monitor the content of what is sent by this method), and several other related schemes.

In 1982 the government made it a rule that postal savings must be passed on automatically to certain banks, which are obliged to lend them on medium or long term. Before this the use of postal savings for this purpose (following the Japanese model) had been constrained by the government's tendency not to pass on the postal savings to the banks whenever it wished to check the growth of money supply; and the savings were mostly lent short-term. Since postal savings amount to as much as 6 percent of the assets of all major financial institutions (1980) the new arrangements are beginning to permit a big increase in long-term lending. In 1983, the Ministry of Finance announced that foreign banks could accept time deposits for up to six months in local currency, on condition that the amount of deposits accepted not exceed 12.5 times the amount of capitalization already remitted into the country by the bank. ''The decision is seen as a milestone in liberalizing restrictions on foreign banks operating in the Republic of China,'' said a semiofficial newspaper.[6] In 1984 the executive arm of government began to prepare legislation to remove criminal penalties for the use of postdated checks (Winn 1986). Opposition from local banks, foreign bankers, and businesspeople stalled the effort, however, and only in mid-1986 did the legislature finally approve the legislation, which also introduces improved enforcement proceedings for promissory notes. This marks the end of the dominance of the postdated check as Taiwan's principal credit instrument. The intention behind this series of

[6] *China Post*, 27 Aug. 1983.

financial reforms is to make Taiwan the future financial center of East Asia outside Japan, once Hong Kong reverts to the mainland. As always the moves are being made gradually, so that a retreat can readily be made if the consequences of any particular change seem too costly.

During 1989 the legislature reviewed a long-awaited bank reform law intended to bring fresh competition to the banking sector. The bill would (1) allow new private commercial banks; (2) permit foreign banks into a somewhat broader though still limited range and scale of business; and (3) partially privatize the three main existing commercial banks. More than a dozen business groups have indicated their intention to establish their own banks under the new legislation. But the government, seeking to check the fusion of financial and industrial capital, has limited the share of a bank's equity held by a business group to no more than 15 percent. And only 51 percent of the existing commercial banks' stock will be sold to the public, the rest being held by the government. This will guarantee continued heavy involvement of the Ministry of Finance and the central bank. Many bankers regard the privatization as largely window dressing (Moore 1989).

However, the main point is that the banking system has been publicly owned and tightly controlled. The large curb market is a consequence, providing an important marginal source of finance for firms or households that are rationed out of bank credits. In any country where banks are not allowed to do certain kinds of lending, one expects such an unregulated market; and in particular one expects that big firms, which have ready access to bank loans, will become financial intermediaries for small firms. Such a system may lose some of the benefits of specialization that specialized financial institutions such as banks presumably bring. But it can gain by bringing the lenders and borrowers closer together and reducing the information and fiduciary problems of credit markets. At a certain stage of development, however, defined as being when firms have substantial retained profits, the continued existence of a large curb market may have bigger costs. Firms which could repay bank loans may instead borrow more and arbitrage for the higher returns of the curb market so that the cheaper bank funds go to those who do not need them at the expense of new projects which do. Here the solution is financial liberalization. Perhaps Taiwan's recent financial liberalization can be interpreted partly in these terms.

Guiding Financial Flows

In Japan and Korea, the channeling of high savings through government-controlled banking systems has been a key instrument of industrial coordination. In Taiwan this has been less important, but not much less important.

Note, first, that any bank loan in Taiwan is in a sense preferential, because the alternative is curb market credit at a price at least 50 percent higher. S. C.

Tsiang complains that while the function of the interest rate to attract savings into the banking system is well recognized in Taiwan,

> the function of the interest rate as a necessary criterion for efficient allocation of scarce investable funds seems not yet to have been recognized. To most planning authorities, the most efficient allocation is usually the one in accordance with their own discretion. They are generally interested in keeping the interest rate for loans as low as feasible so that they may have more options in allocating funds, even to projects which have relatively low yields but which might rank high in their own scale of priority.   (1980:341)

Erik Lundberg agrees:

> During the entire period [1950–70] the official interest rates, although relatively high, were below the natural rate that would clear the market. The credit market was functioning badly, with distortions from the point of view of an optimal allocation of available loan funds and savings. . . . The situation on the credit markets implied credit rationing by the banks.   (1979:293, 292)

The banks have transferred funds from actual or potential consumers to *investors*. Deposits from individuals have been at least four to six times the loans to individuals since the early 1950s (and most bank loans to individuals have in any case been for dwellings or farming, not for consumption). Government too has been a net depositor in the banking system. On the other hand, private and public enterprises have received bank loans each year at least three to four times greater than their deposits (Riegg 1978:317).

Since the 1960s the government has been slowly forging a more differentiated banking sector, with some banks specializing in particular types of lending. By 1980 there was a farmer's bank, a land bank, a small and medium enterprise bank, an export-import bank, and even a development bank (which retains its old name, the Bank of Communications). This is intended to be a way of targeting credit at certain sectors and of increasing the amount of medium- and long-term lending.

In addition to concessional credit for export production (described in the last chapter) the government has also indicated priority industries for bank lending (Riegg 1978:95–96). During the 1950s and early 1960s the banks received credit allocation targets for rather broadly defined sectors, supplemented by more detailed case-by-case instructions from the planners. By the mid-1960s the banks were receiving lists of six to twelve industries to which priority attention should be given. These lists were drawn up by the planning agency, with the Ministries of Finance and Economic Affairs and the central bank having opportunities to suggest modifications. During the 1970s the banks themselves began to participate more in drafting the lists. Each bank was required to select five or six areas it wished to focus upon for the coming year. With the increased participation of the banks came more open acknowledgment of the fact of credit targeting. For example, the 1973 *Annual Report* of the Bank of Communications says, "The government has directed the different banking institutions to provide special credit facilities for different industries" (1974:10). The 1974 *Annual Report* states, "The government has promoted a system of 'lead banking.' To comply with this policy the Bank has done its best to satisfy the credit demands of the 21 important firms that it has been made responsible for guiding" (1975:8). And the 1985 *Annual Report* is equally clear: "At present time when ROC industrial structure is undergoing a transformation, it calls for continuous government-supported low rate loans to the enterprises to stimulate their willingness in investment and to *guide the industries towards the development as government prescribed*" (1986:8–9, emphasis added).

Nicholas Riegg, writing in the late 1970s, evaluates the impact of loan preference lists as follows:

> The banks have taken pride in achieving a high degree of compliance with the lists. With up to 75 percent of loans flowing to the targetted industries it seems that the lists have been an effective means for guiding bank-financed development. Furthermore, as over 80 percent of bank lending goes to the private sector, the lists have obviously helped to guide private enterprise towards the goals of the development plans.   (1978:96)

In addition to bank loan lists, the government has created special-purpose funds. For example, in 1972 the government created a special facility for machinery imports, which over the following ten years lent US$600 million on concessional terms for new machinery in any sector (but with only a small margin of preference, of the order of one or two percentage points below the normal rate: Lee 1983:67). In 1979 the sense of national emergency created by U.S. derecognition prompted the government to establish a special fund of US$600 million to assist new machinery imports in selected industries—mainly textiles, electronics, and machinery. The terms were unusually generous, with an interest rate several points below the prevailing bank rate and a two-year grace and five-year repayment period, the collateral being only the machinery itself. By the end of 1982 about US$300 million had been lent under this scheme—equivalent to about 2.5 percent of total fixed capital formation in Taiwan in 1980.

From time to time the government has announced measures to help local machinery producers. The fund just mentioned made local machinery makers eligible for concessionary finance to import better machines to make machines. Earlier, in 1975, the government appropriated US$5 million to finance imports by the machinery industry of the latest technical know-how (Amsden 1977:233). Another effort also dating from the mid-1970s makes special financing available to buyers of domestically manufactured machinery. But it has had little effect because the terms are not competitive with foreign suppliers' credits—in particular because domestic interest rates in Taiwan have been kept well above international levels, so a large margin of preference is needed in special schemes to make domestic borrowing more attractive than foreign suppliers' credit, when it can be obtained.

A major new development in preferential investment financing is the so-called Strategic Industry Fund (or Preferential Loan Scheme for Strategic and Important Industries). Established in 1982 it initially amounted to US$250 million, and was doubled in 1983, its capitalization being maintained at this level up to 1989.[7] It is for the following uses:

1. Purchase of domestically produced machinery. The interest rate is set at two points less than the average of the minimum and maximum long-term interest rates (the average was 10 percent in 1983). Domestic machinery makers consider this is the first government promotional measure which brings them real benefit, for it equalizes the margins with foreign suppliers' credit.
2. Purchase of new machinery, from any source, by producers in the so-called "strategic" industries of machinery, automobile parts, electrical machinery, information, and electronics. As with the fiscal incentives (see below), there is a highly differentiated list of 135 "strategic" industry products which are eligible. Other products of these same industries are not eligible. The interest rate is two points less than the floor of the long-term lending spread.
3. Special cases to be decided by the planning agency, especially for the introduction of automation (labor-saving) equipment in any sector.

Established following the second oil crisis, the fund is to help diversify industry into less energy-intensive sectors. The terms are, by Taiwan standards, generous—not only the interest rate but also the pay-back period of eight years (maximum) with a two-year grace period. As with the other special funds, the collateral is the value of the machinery itself, a concession on normal practice.[8]

These various preferential financing funds are established by the government and administered by the banks, mainly (since the late 1970s) by the newly chartered development bank. The government sets the eligibility crite-

[7] At the 1983 exchange rate, US$250 million is the equivalent of NT$10 billion.

[8] Schive and Hsueh 1987 are sceptical about the effectiveness of the strategic industry policy (which includes not just concessional credit but also some fiscal investment incentives, discussed below, plus technical assistance in production improvements, and help with management). They point out that by March 1987, of the 199 "strategic and important" products, only seventy-two items had received technical assistance, forty-six had received management consultancy help, and eighty-two had received preferential loans. They also point out that by March 1987, out of total funds of US$1.25 billion only about 60 percent had been loaned out, 29 percent of which had gone to textiles (for textile machinery)—not everyone's idea of a "strategic and important" industry. These indicators of effectiveness are better than nothing, but they do not permit compelling conclusions.

ria but ultimately the decision on whether to grant a loan is made by the responsible bank, not by economic bureaucracy.

However, the planning agency (the Council for Economic Planning and Development [CEPD]) does have two funds under its direct control. It is worth describing what these funds are for and how they work, because their existence allows the planners more direct influence on resource allocation.

The first is the Sino-American Fund for Economic and Social Development. It was established in 1965 with U.S. aid money at the time when U.S. economic aid was brought to an end. It was intended to be used as a catalyst, as a net addition to existing efforts It was not to be used "for assistance to activities for which other finance is available on reasonable terms" and it was to be available "for research into, and stimulation of, innovations designed to increase productivity and trade" (Economic Planning Council 1965). About one-third of its disbursements has been in grants, two-thirds in loans. Eighty percent has gone to the public sector for "pioneer" tasks like family planning programs, pollution control, industrial park development, industrial technology research institutes, and loans to public enterprises especially when they wish to borrow abroad (a direct loan from the government helps to assure foreign lenders that the government is backing the project, making it easier to raise the loan). And a part has also gone for the creation of another special fund for small and medium businesses, a condition of loans from which is that the applicants attend a special course in business management. Disbursements amounted to about one-half of one percent of gross fixed capital formation in 1978.

The second fund is called, simply, the Development Fund. Whereas the first is entirely at the discretion of the planning agency, control over this one is shared with the Finance Ministry. It was established in 1973 with the object of making sole or joint investments (equity or loans) in "technology-intensive and important enterprises, as indicated in the economic plans" (Ministry of Finance 1982). The total lending or equity investment from 1973 to 1982 equaled about US$250 million; the 1978 figure amounted to about one-half of one percent of gross fixed capital formation in that year, much the same as the Sino-American Fund. About two-thirds has gone as loans, one-third as equity; 70 percent went to the private sector, 30 percent to the public sector. The maximum term is five years and the interest rate is decided case by case. It is often used to give more generous terms to high-priority private sector projects than the banks offer. In a recent case a cabinet minister concerned with technology promised a fifteen-year loan to an important U.S. electronics company wanting to open a factory on the island, only to be told by the development bank that fifteen-year loans were never given under any circumstances. So the minister (in dudgeon) got the Development Fund to make up the difference between what he had promised and what the development bank would offer.

Two more nonbank sources of preferential investment finance are disburse-

170   CHAPTER 6

ment from the government budget and access to foreign credit (which has been available on terms considerably softer than domestic credit). Both are under direct government control and have been used extensively by public enterprises. Indeed, the four major import-substituting and large lump projects of the 1970s—the integrated steel mill, the shipyard, the petrochemical complex, and the nuclear reactor—have been financed largely from these two sources (Westphal 1978:11).

Finally, the government has also sought to influence credit allocation by the loan guarantee. Small and medium businesses (and also "large mechanical enterprises selected by the Ministry of Economic Affairs") can apply for guarantees on their repayment of bank loans. The guarantee will secure them a bigger loan and/or better terms. Government planners (officials of the Industrial Development Bureau) scrutinize all applications above a certain size to see how they fit with investment priorities. The Guarantee Fund was established in 1974 and has grown rapidly since the late 1970s.[9]

It is difficult to arrive at a clear judgment about how important preferential financing has been as a way of encouraging resources to flow into certain activities. Less important than in South Korea, certainly (Jones and Sakong 1980). On the other hand it is known that between 1962 and 1974 "special" central bank rediscounted loans to banking institutions averaged almost one-half of total central bank loans to banking institutions (Lee 1983:63). The point of the "special" rediscounted loans was that the banks could on-lend them at lower than the normal rate. This in itself would suggest that preferential financing of some kind or other has been very important.

However, no figures are available on the uses of these loans. Nor indeed are figures available on the total amount of central bank "special" rediscounts after 1974, nor for the share of preferential export loans in total export loans,[10] nor on how the two special funds to promote machinery imports have been used. All this is classified information.

The secrecy which surrounds the use of preferential financing probably relates to two things. On the one hand the government is extremely anxious to eliminate any signs of policies which could be construed as "unfairly advantaging" export products, because such policies might give Taiwan's trading partners an excuse to raise protective barriers. Setting high nominal tax rates and then making selected exceptions is seen as less likely to arouse foreign suspicions than setting high interest rates and making selected exemptions. This helps to explain not only why preferential export credit really has been

[9] Between 1974 and 1983 the Small and Medium Business Credit Guarantee Fund handled 190,000 cases of loan guarantees, with an amount totaling nearly US$3 billion (Small and Medium Business Credit Guarantee Fund n.d. [1984]). The publicity for the fund says that amounts of under US$75,000 are automatically approved. According to a senior planner this is in fact not so; at least since 1980 the planners have scrutinized applications for smaller amounts.

[10] See chapter 5 n.25.

reduced, but also why little information is available on it. On the other hand, the dearth of information also reflects a habit of secrecy in bank affairs generally, as seen for example in the fact that bank balance sheets are not readily available in Taiwan. This in turn is related to the high level of profits historically earned by Taiwan banks. Publication of profit figures would provide regular irritation to businesspeople who say that banks should provide a public service, setting charges so as to break even—or at least charge them no more than their foreign rivals have to pay.

In conclusion, Taiwan is clearly not a good model of a competitive financial market. The financial system is based on credit rather than equity, and the credit institutions are tightly administered. This makes for rigidity, but also helps to reduce savers' risks and contributes to the extraordinarily high rate of financial savings. Equally, it gives the government the means for managing financial flows both at the border and internally.

Control at the border is a prerequisite for internal control. Tight foreign exchange controls have been in place from the early 1950s, based on the principle that residents are not allowed to hold foreign exchange. Internally, the credit institutions consist largely of banks which, being few in number and government-owned, are easily controlled. These features permit financial flows to be maneuvered toward national goals.

There is some evidence, cited earlier, that bank lending has corresponded fairly closely with government sectoral targets. Had the financial system been free of rigidities and compartmentalization, credit allocation techniques such as those practiced in Taiwan may not have been effective in increasing the supply of funds to designated sectors. As it is, "leakage" of bank loans into the curb market may have reduced the ability to target, though probably not by much because of the bank's monitoring of the use of loans. Taiwan's financial rigidities have therefore helped government-sponsored credit allocation to achieve its objectives. In turn, those objectives have been closely related to international competitiveness. Riegg reports that "the lists of industries that banks are to give priority attention to have basically been lists of those which have been identified by the planning agency as having strong export potential" (1978:382). Also, the central bank has shown preference for export bills when giving discounts to member banks, and a significant portion of total bank credit has been devoted to concessionary export loans (6 percent in 1972). Riegg undertakes an elaborate exercise to correlate the distribution of bank lending against various indicators of the development potential of different sectors. He finds that sectors with higher rates of reinvestible returns received relatively more bank loans, while sectors with low or unquantifiable returns, such as education, health, and public utilities, received very little (1978:360).[11]

---

[11] Riegg divided the economy into seventeen subsectors, of which nine were in manufacturing,

Riegg concludes, nevertheless, that government-owned banks have lent somewhat more to certain deserving sectors than purely private banks would have lent—to high-risk basic industries like shipping and to fledgling export industries like electronics, as well as to agriculture. But the discrepancy, if it could be measured, would not be large (1978:366).

All this being said, Taiwan's financial system is in need of research. The financial statistics are a problem, for although at first glance they seem solid, the closer they are examined the more they shimmer. In particular we need to know how the financial system was tied into the organization for coordinating investment and how the high real interest rates could work. After all, in many other countries where high real rates have been tried, they are said—not only by borrowers—to undermine export competitiveness, cause dangerously high debt/equity ratios, crowd out new borrowers, and fuel inflation. How did Taiwan avoid these effects? Why did the very high real interest rates on the curb market not give a bigger impetus to growth of the stock exchange, which before the mid-1980s remained very small, as a way of raising funds without incurring the obligation to repay such rates?

THE BUDGET

According to the neoclassical story, the government has shown significant restraint in its own expenditures, thereby allowing the private sector more room and reducing the scope for "political" prices. "Government expenditure *fell* from 19.6 percent of GNP in 1963 to 16 percent in 1973, whereas current revenue rose from 21 percent to 22.4 percent" (Little 1979:478, emphasis added)—which makes Taiwan a marvelous example of conservative budgeting. This restraint, in Little's view, is one of the three principal causes of the rapid rise in industrial investment (p.485). Walter Galenson agrees that "the government made a major contribution toward the facilitation of capital formation by keeping its expenditure down, despite a heavy defense burden. Taxes were maintained at a relatively low level, averaging about 14 to 15 percent of the GNP" (1982:80). Taiwan seems indeed to have had small, lean, minimal government, in line with neoclassical prescription.

Official statistics show, however, that government expenditure as a percentage of GNP (current prices) *increased* from 20.0 percent in 1963 to 23.0 percent in 1973 (CEPD 1982:table 8.4). The same statistics demonstrate that current revenue increased from 19.3 percent in 1963 to 25.8 percent in 1973. So the government sector was by 1973 substantially bigger than Little's figures suggest and the size of the budget surplus substantially smaller. (Little does not give the source of his figures, and it is not clear why the discrepancy has

---

and calculated their returns to capital, incremental capital output ratio, incremental capital employment ratio, incremental capital export ratio, and incremental capital to input demand ratio for the period 1966–75.

arisen.[12]) The share of government expenditure continued to rise after 1973, to 27 percent in 1980–81. According to Pathirane and Blades' careful comparison of seven developing countries Taiwan had over the 1967–78 period a bigger share of government consumption than all but one (1982:table 7).[13]

Adding government and public enterprise gross investment to government consumption we get a figure for "public sector final demand." Public sector final demand remained approximately constant between 1963 and 1973 at about 25 percent of GDP in current prices, then increased over the 1970s to about 33 percent by 1980 (CEPD 1982:tables. 3.8c, and 3.9a). In the period 1975–78 it stood at about 30 percent of GDP.[14] In the same period such putatively more socialist countries as India and Tanzania had a corresponding figure of 20 and 25 percent, respectively, Japan had 19 percent, the United States 21 percent, and Scandinavia 31 to 34 percent (Pathirane and Blades 1982:tables 1, 7).

So if public sector final demand is used as an overall measure of the size of the public sector it is simply not true that Taiwan has had an unusually small public sector. It has almost certainly been in the upper quintile of middle-income countries. In terms of public sector investment (government plus public enterprise), the share of the economy's total investment has been about half during the 1960s and 1970s, which is well above average for middle-income countries (World Bank 1983:48). In terms of employment the public sector as a whole (including public enterprises) employs 13 percent of the country's seven million workforce, or 4.71 government employees per 100 inhabitants (DGBAS 1983:11, 25). This is big by developing country standards. In a sample of twenty-one developing countries for which comparable figures are available, Taiwan's figure of 4.71 government employees per 100 inhabitants ranks number eight and well above average. The figure for South Korea is 3.65, for Japan 4.44.[15]

[12] Little explained in a personal communication that he had lost the notes which would have given the source (Nov. 1984). The official statistics suggest that government consumption (rather than expenditure) did fall as a share of GDP (constant prices) between 1963 and 1973, from 23.1 to 15.9 percent but declined little thereafter (CEPD 1982:table 3–8c). On the other hand, Pathirane and Blades' cross-country comparison suggests that Taiwan government consumption as a share of GDP did not fall between 1965 and 1978, oscillating between 15 and 18 percent (1982).

[13] Pathirane and Blades' sample includes Taiwan, Kenya (the exception), India, Panama, the Philippines, South Africa, and Tanzania. Their government consumption/GDP figures for Taiwan are: 1965—17 percent, 1970–74—16 percent, 1975–78—17 percent. In Reynolds' sample of forty-one nonminnow developing countries the median figure for 1980 is 15 percent, while six countries are in the 20 to 25 percent range (1983:971).

[14] Much "government investment" is for construction and communications projects, which Taiwan's difficult terrain makes unusually expensive.

[15] Heller and Tait 1984. Taiwan's figure for employment in "public administration" is, however, relatively low by the standards of Heller and Tait's sample. The absolute figures for Taiwan are (1981): government employees 855,000; public administration 275,000; workforce 6,835,000; inhabitants 18,136,000.

It is true, and important, that Taiwan has run budget surpluses in most years since the early 1960s—which indicates public sector behavior different from that of most other countries. It is also true that spending for welfare, social security, and public health has been small. All transfer payments, including welfare payments and grants to lower levels of government, have shown a very slow rate of growth in contrast to trends common in both developing and industrialized countries (Pluta 1979:30). The small size of transfer payments is good news for budget conservatives, but it also has another implication. It means that the share of government expenditure in GDP is a good measure of the share of total resources subject to state control. This is to make the contrast with OECD countries, whose government expenditure includes a large component of cash transfer payments (such as social security benefits), which do not constitute government spending on goods and services. When this adjustment is made, Great Britain's share of resources subject to state control is about 25 percent, much lower than the figure of 40 or 45 percent which is often heard, and about the same as Taiwan's.

Education took a rapidly rising share of current expenditure, from 11.6 percent in 1955–56 to 20.5 percent in 1970–71; since then its share has remained roughly constant. "Defense and diplomacy" accounted for around 75 percent of total central government expenditure in the late 1950s and early 1960s, falling to 60 percent by 1970 and 37 percent by 1987; of which over 90 percent has been for defense alone.[16] Military expenditures averaged about 10 percent of GNP from the 1950s to the late 1970s, compared to 5 to 6 percent in Korea in the 1970s (thanks to a bigger U.S. military presence) and 3 percent in other newly industrializing countries (Scitovsky 1986:143; Jacoby 1966:118; Lundberg 1979:302). But a sizable part of Taiwan's large defense budget has been covered by U.S. military aid, which continued to flow after the cut-off in economic aid in the mid-1960s.

As for Galenson's statement that taxes amounted to only about 14 to 15 percent of GNP, this was last true in 1967 (Galenson wrote in 1981). Taxes subsequently increased to 17 to 20 percent in 1980–85 (CEPD 1986:tables 8–9). Taxes have accounted for only about 70 percent of government revenue.[17] Government revenue increased from 22.7 percent of GDP in 1970 to 24.9 percent in 1980, falling to 24.4 percent in 1985.

Taiwan has relied heavily on indirect taxes (see table 6.1). Before 1980 only 10 percent of tax revenues came from levies on income. The largest share, one-fifth to one-quarter, came from customs duties alone—surprising in rela-

---

[16] The government's defense spending is secret. The figures are from Chang 1987:88, who uses a semiclassified source; and Wei 1987.

[17] Taxes include customs duties and monopoly revenues (mainly from the wine and tobacco monopoly). The main nontax source of revenue is the public enterprise operating surplus. In a sample of forty-seven developing countries, Taiwan had the fifteenth highest tax revenue to GNP ratio (17.8 percent) in 1969–71 and the eleventh highest (19.9 percent) in 1972–76 (Meier 1984:239).

TABLE 6.1
Tax Revenues by Type of Tax
(% of Total Tax and Monopoly Revenue)

	Income Tax	Customs Duty	Commodity Tax	Business Tax	Monopoly Revenue	Other
1960	10.4	18.4	10.2	5.7	21.4	33.9
1970	9.4	23.4	17.1	5.9	16.4	27.8
1980	17.2	21.8	16.0	7.9	9.3	27.8
1985	19.2	16.9	13.8	9.7	10.6	29.8

Source: CEPD 1986:table 8-6a.

Note: Monopoly revenue is from the Wine and Tobacco Monopoly. "Other" includes more than eleven kinds of taxes, such as land tax, house tax, labor dues, and license tax.

tion to the theory which says that by the time the tax burden is getting toward 20 percent of GNP revenues from foreign trade will be shrinking in relation to revenues from domestically oriented indirect taxes (Hinrichs 1968). Ministry of Finance officials, when pressed as to why tariffs remain so high, like to reply with a proverb: "Customs revenue is the keystone of government revenue, which is the bedrock of the nation" (Chang 1987:146).

The heavy reliance on indirect levies has been justified in terms of restraining consumption and protecting entrepreneurial incentives. As the demand for revenue has increased, the scope of goods and services covered by customs and commodity taxes has therefore been widened. The regressive effects on income distribution have been offset by such measures as land reform, education spending, and untrammeled access to small business ventures, notably in the retail trade.

Since 1960 the government has tried to harness the tax system for savings and investment objectives as well as revenue ones. Consumption has been restrained by providing incentives for personal savings (see chapter 3), by maintaining government expenditures below government revenues, and by selective taxes on luxury goods and amusement services. Production has been encouraged by property taxes which provide a disincentive to leave assets idle, by taxes on the incremental value of land and on rental buildings, and (until 1970) by allowing firms to exempt up to 25 percent of taxable income provided it was reinvested. An investible surplus was transferred from agriculture to higher-return industry by means of land taxes, the rice-fertilizer barter scheme, and tenants' payments for land-reform land.

PUBLIC ENTERPRISES

Neoclassical accounts say little about Taiwan's public enterprises other than to note their declining share of output. Ian Little reports that "public ownership of the means of production is limited'' and that ''public industry has until recently been of rapidly declining quantitative importance'' (1979:467, 468).[18] The 1982–85 plan points to the fall in the share of public enterprises in total industrial value added from 18.8 percent to 18.2 percent between 1975 and 1980 (0.6 percent decline in five years), and to the fall in their share of industrial fixed capital formation from 59 to 52 percent over the same period (7 percent in five years), in order to demonstrate the proposition that ''production by the private sector has played an increasingly important role in overall economic activity'' (CEPD 1983:11). To emphasize the limited and declining role of public enterprises is to remain consistent with the argument that market liberalization is the primary cause of Taiwan's success.

In fact, public enterprises have had a major role in the economy all through the period of outward-looking growth, as chapter 4 shows. From the early 1950s onward Taiwan has had one of the biggest public enterprise sectors outside the communist bloc and Sub-Saharan Africa. Short (1983) compares the importance of public enterprises internationally in terms of the percentage share of public enterprise output in GDP at factor cost and the percentage share in gross fixed capital formation. Taiwan had 13 to 14 percent, and 30 to 35 percent, respectively, over the 1970s. By both measures the country is in the top decile of non-African developing countries. In Asia only India and Burma are of the same order of magnitude; in Latin America only Bolivia. Some illustrative comparisons are shown in table 6.2. Note that Taiwan's public enterprise sector is much bigger than Korea's, about whose public enterprise sector Jones and Sakong remark, ''a minor paradox of Korean development is that an ostensibly private-enterprise economy has utilized the intervention mechanism of public ownership to an extent which parallels that of many countries advocating a socialist pattern of society'' (1980:141). Is it not then misleading to say with Ian Little that ''public ownership of the means of production is limited'' and to emphasize only its diminishing quantitative significance?[19]

[18] Little is referring in the first quote to all four East Asian NICs, in the second to Taiwan only. After using the declining share of public enterprises in industrial output to demonstrate the point that ''public industry has until recently been of rapidly declining quantitative significance,'' he goes on to note that ''public industry's share in fixed capital formation shows, in contrast, no such marked trend.'' He mentions that the share in fixed capital formation increased from 21 to 31 percent between 1965 and 1974, and suggests that ''it is likely to go on rising with the development of steel, petrochemicals and some new big infrastructure projects. But nothing has been nationalized'' (1979:468). These remarks are made by way of *obiter dictum*, the thrust of his argument being to show public enterprises as marginal. Ramon Myers, contrasting Taiwan with China, says that ''on Taiwan the Nationalist party adopted a minimalist course of intervention with policies to encourage private enterepreneurs to become more productive. . . . The private sector not only responded to those groups with investment capital and efficient management but also grew more rapidly and efficiently than the state-owned, protected manufacturing sector'' (1983:539). Ranis 1979:259–60 has a less tilted discussion.

[19] More size indicators: Public enterprises owned 35 percent of industrial assets in 1980–83 (Central Bank, Economic Research Department, various issues). In Reynolds' sample of 41 LDCs

TABLE 6.2
Output and Investment Shares of Public Enterprises

		Percentage Share of GDP at Factor Cost	Percentage Share in Gross Fixed Capital Formation
Taiwan	1951–53	11.9	31.4
	1954–57	11.7	34.3
	1958–61	13.5	38.1
	1962–65	14.1	27.7
	1966–69	13.6	28.0
	1970–73	13.3	30.5
	1974–77	13.6	35.0
	1978–80	13.5	32.4
Korea	1963–64	5.5	31.2
	1965–69	—	24.2
	1970–73	7.0	21.7
	1974–77	6.4	25.1
	1978–80	—	22.8
Japan	1966–69	—	12.7
	1970–73	—	9.9
	1974–77	—	11.6
	1978–80	—	11.4
India	1960–61	5.3	34.7
	1962–65	6.1	36.8
	1966–69	6.5	29.6
	1970–73	7.3	29.0
	1974–77	9.8	33.8
Asia (average)	1974–77	8.0	27.7
Tanzania	1964–65	—	9.2
	1966–69	9.3	22.7
	1970–73	12.7	48.2
	1974–77	12.3	30.3
Argentina	1968–69	—	15.4
	1978–80	4.6	19.6
Brazil	1968	—	14.0
	1980	—	22.8
Great Britain	1962–65	10.3	19.8
	1978–81	10.9	17.0
France	1962–65	12.8	20.6
	1970–73	12.2	15.4
Europe (average)	1974–77	6.6	23.4
United States	1960	—	4.0
	1978	—	4.4

Source: Short 1983.

Individual public enterprises are typically among the largest firms in their sectors. In 1980 the six biggest industrial public enterprises had sales equal to the fifty biggest private industrial concerns.[20] Of the ten largest industrial enterprises seven are public enterprises; of the largest fifty, nineteen are public enterprises (1981). Korea's structure is similar: twelve of the sixteen biggest industrial enterprises were public enterprises in 1972 and twenty of the biggest fifty (Jones and Mason 1982:38).[21]

Though covering a wide range of sectors, the public enterprises are concentrated on the commanding heights to which European socialists wistfully as-

---

the public sector share of manufacturing is "often," he says, in the 20 to 25% range (1983:973). Taiwan's figure was in this range during 1968–70 (before it was higher, since then it has been lower). Given the ideological significance of figures on the relative size of the public and private sectors, one would like to know more about the statistical basis on which they are calculated. Massaging cannot be ruled out. In terms of control over decision-making, the effective public enterprise sector is bigger than the statistics suggest. The statistics are based on the 50 percent equity criterion. The government, not wishing to be seen to be increasing the size of the public enterprise sector, has sometimes used devices to retain control while not meeting the equity criterion (see chapter 9). On the other hand some of the big public enterprises are popularly called "independent kingdoms." The point is that the public/private distinction is very unclear, as it is in Japan and South Korea.

[20] This statement excludes the wine and tobacco monopoly. If included, the sales of the top five industrial public enterprises would substantially exceed the sales of the biggest fifty private enterprises. But in all such comparisons it must be remembered that Taiwan's figures on "firms" are misleading because they do not recognize business "groups" (see chapter 3).

In 1980 the Ministry of Economic Affairs owned fourteen public enterprises (PEs) in the following sectors: power, petroleum, mining, aluminum, phosphates, alkali, sugar, chemicals, fertilizer, petrochemicals, steel, shipbuilding, engineering, and machinery. The Ministry of Finance owned four banks and eight insurance companies. The provincial government owned six industrial PEs in iron, fertilizer, pulp and paper, food processing, textiles, and wine and tobacco. It also owned five banks. One bank was owned by the city of Taipei.

Disaggregated data on public enterprises in Taiwan are scarce. One of the few sources is the annual publication by China Credit Information Service Ltd., a private organization, called latterly, *Top 500: The Largest Industrial Corporations in the Republic of China*. This gives information on sales of individual PEs for some years since 1970, and on employees for 1971. But the lists of PEs vary from year to year, making comparison difficult. For example, the 1971 list, the last to give PE employees, omits the wine and tobacco monopoly, which in 1976 is listed as the third biggest PE in terms of sales. According to this source, the seventeen industrial PEs in 1971 employed 76,100 people; the biggest twenty-nine private industrial firms, about the same (and the top fifty privates, 90,700). The 1971 sales of the seventeen PEs amounted to NT$32 million; of the top fifty privates, NT$35 million. In 1980 the six biggest industrial PEs (Chinese Petroleum Corp., Taipower, Taiwan Sugar, China Steel, China Shipbuilding, BES Engineering) had sales of NT$270.105 billion, the fifty biggest private industrial firms, NT$272.016 billion. The eighteen industrial PEs for which 1980 data is available had sales of NT$307.412 billion. But these exclude two very large PEs, as well as two smaller ones. The two large ones are the Ret-Ser Engineering Agency (third largest PE in sales in 1981) and the wine and tobacco monopoly. If included, total sales of the top twenty industrial PEs would substantially exceed NT$350 billion. Important nonindustrial PEs include the Central Trust of China (the main government purchasing agent); the first and third biggest insurance companies in Taiwan; and virtually all the domestic banks.

[21] But the Korean figures are in terms of value added, the Taiwanese in terms of sales (a less satisfactory measure).

pire: petroleum refining, petrochemicals, steel and other basic metals, ship-building, heavy machinery, transport equipment, fertilizer—in addition to the standard electricity, gas, water, railway, and telephone utilities. They are important, that is, in sectors where the efficient scale of production is capital-intensive and large relative to both product markets and factor markets, and where linkages to downstream industries are high. These are just the characteristics which, Jones and Mason suggest, give a relatively high benefit/cost ratio of public ownership in mixed-economy developing countries (1982:41). Public enterprises also dominate the banking sector and have a substantial presence in insurance.

The reasons for a large public enterprise sector are not simply a matter of economic costs and benefits, however. Many public enterprises have from the beginning been closely linked to the military. They form a vertically integrated, closed production system which is the basis of Taiwan's own defense industry.

The public enterprise sector is also used, whether for military or civilian production, as a substitute for attempts to induce private firms to enter new fields with high entry barriers. The main import-substituting projects of the 1970s—petroleum and petrochemicals, steel and other basic metals, ship-building, and nuclear power—were carried out by public enterprises; and major expansion projects in heavy machinery, heavy electrical machinery, trucks, and integrated circuit production have been undertaken by public enterprises (Industrial Development Bureau 1982).

It is possible, though I know of no evidence, that the use of public enterprises as joint venture partners with foreign companies has helped to keep down the level of protection given to the project. In Japan, which has not had public enterprises able to play the same role, relatively high levels of protection were necessary to induce private firms into sectors with high entry costs. Taiwan's public enterprises, by contrast, could be given political instructions as to which activities they entered. Public ownership might be seen here, unconventionally, in a trade-off with protection.

Moreover, the fact that the public enterprises are concentrated in upstream sectors gives the government indirect influence over the downstream sectors. It can use public enterprise price policy to adjust raw material prices throughout the economy, for example. After the first oil price hike in 1973 the government, via Chinese Petroleum Corporation, immediately raised the price of ethylene in line with the increase in the petroleum price, as part of a strategy of adjusting to the new price of energy and the decline in real income which it represented by means of a short, sharp economic squeeze. After the 1979 oil price rise, on the other hand, it tried to keep Taiwanese industry competitive without devaluing by suppressing the prices charged by public corporations in basic industries.[22]

---

[22] Hofheinz and Calder 1982:57. By May 1980 the price of fuel oil in Taiwan was 66 percent

The point about government influence over downstream producers goes beyond prices. For the major concentrations of private productive capital are mostly in sectors which depend heavily upon upstream public enterprises. Through Chinese Petroleum Corporation, for example, the government has indirect leverage on synthetic fiber and textile producers, who include the island's biggest private industrial groups.

But it is not just a matter of public enterprises giving government leverage over private capital. Public enterprises are strongly represented in sectors which one would otherwise expect to be dominated by multinational corporations. As it is, multinationals are important in many of the sectors dominated by public enterprises. Indeed, multinationals, especially in petrochemicals, have sometimes preferred to have a public enterprise rather than a private firm as a joint venture partner, because this gives stronger assurance of the government's own commitment to the project. The government for its part has been determined not to allow foreign firms to dominate these sectors, and has structured the alliance so that the state holds its own, keeping control over key sectors within Taiwan (Amsden 1979, 1984; Gold 1981, 1986).

Overall, public enterprise prices have more than covered costs of production. Over the 1970s their surpluses contributed an average of 10 percent of the government's net revenue, which makes Taiwan an exception to the familiar thesis that government-owned corporations tend to deplete rather than add to government revenues. Moreover their profit rate (operating surplus/ capital + net worth) has generally been positive (negative in only two years between 1952 and 1974; Pluta 1979: table 10).

However, public enterprises have also received preferential investment financing in various forms. These include direct disbursement from the government budget, loans or grants from the two special development funds under the planners' control, foreign loans (all access to which is controlled by the government), and preferential access to long-term finance through the banking system. They have been able to borrow at concessional rates, but never more than a few percentage points less than the normal rate for secured loans; and when credit is tight the government may—secretly—instruct the banks to make money available for public enterprises before private ones.[23] Some public enterprises have also been in a monopoly position. These are the ones which tend to make big profits, such as Chinese Petroleum Corporation, Taipower, China Steel, and the wine and tobacco monopoly. Many of those which face private sector competition tend to suffer losses. In some cases those losses may reflect pricing policies designed to provide concealed subsidies in the form of extra-cheap inputs.

Economists have been highly critical of the public enterprise sector, urging

---

that in Japan and 72 percent that in Korea (Ho 1981:1194). Domestic energy prices have been a topic of heated debate in policy-making circles.

[23] Interviews 1983; Tanzer 1982; Silin 1976; Shea 1983a.

privatization.[24] A recent study compared the performance of twelve public manufacturing enterprises with that of the three hundred top private firms in terms of financial indicators such as rate of return on sales and assets over the 1976–84 period. By all indicators the public enterprises' average performance was worse. The study went on to compare the performance of the four public enterprises which face the most competition from private firms against that of their competitors. The result was the same. But there are many problems with the data and method of analysis, so the findings are hardly conclusive. The authors do not address the question of whether performance would be enhanced if the firms were privatized. And they ignore performance criteria other than efficiency, notably national control.[25]

The government has frequently repeated its intention to sell public enterprises to the private sector, as in its declaration in 1960 that "the government will continue to transfer enterprises to private ownership and will no longer make investment in enterprises other than public utilities and innovative or demonstrative projects."[26] But although four public enterprises were divested as part of the 1953 land reform, only a few small ones (in fishing, textiles, and chemicals) have been divested since.[27] Over the 1970s, indeed, the scope of state enterprises has expanded, often in competition with the private sector.

---

[24] Sun Chen, one of the senior-most economists in government and a senior academic as well, calculates that public enterprises used 30 to 35 percent of cumulative capital formation in the period 1965–79 and produced only 12 percent of Net Domestic Product, while privates used 45 to 50 percent of cumulative capital formation to produce as much as 75 percent of NDP. He concludes straightforwardly that the productivity of capital would be increased by comprehensive denationalization (1981:10). Since public enterprises are disproportionately concentrated in capital-intensive sectors, this evidence permits no presumption that denationalization will improve the productivity of capital in those sectors.

[25] Yen and Chang 1985. They paint a relentlessly bleak picture. The situation is, they say, "appalling." "We were surprised to learn that most SMEs [state manufacturing enterprises] rely primarily on static or historic information whenever a prediction of market demand is called for." Because of clumsy hiring procedures and lower wages than private competitors, SMEs face a manpower shortage, which makes them "notoriously lacking in innovative activities." SMEs lack managerial expertise at the top, the evidence for which is that of the twelve central government-owned SMEs five had board chairmen from military, political, or high government official circles in 1980. SMEs' profit-making incentive is blunted by the requirement that they turn over their profits to the Treasury. Top managers face no risk of dismissal or even demotion if the company performs badly—and so on, in the same one-eyed fashion. Their argument suffers from no serious comparison with private sector firms (e.g., on prediction of market demand), except with respect to the financial criteria mentioned in the text. And that comparison suffers because: (1) they give no data on the similarity of the SMEs and the private sector comparators, in terms of size, financial structure, markets, etc. (China Steel and a small private specialty steel firm would be a poor pairing); (2) they make no assessment of the reliability of the data, especially for private firms; (3) the comparisons involving all twelve SMEs include several that have no close local counterparts; (4) the authors do not address the question of whether performance would be improved by privatization, except by assertion.

[26] From the Financial and Economic Reform Program, quoted in Li 1976:364.

[27] They were divested in the late 1960s. In 1983 a loss-making public smelter was sold to private capital (Humphrey 1983).

China Steel and China Shipbuilding, both created in the 1970s, are almost entirely state-owned, although one of the original plans stipulated that they should be largely private. A state-owned automobile company was formed to be the instrument of a big push in automobiles in the early 1980s, despite the presence of six private companies already in the field. Taiwan Sugar Corporation started a sugar cane pulp paper plant in direct competition with a plant run by a private company. Tang Eng Iron and Steel Company was taken into public ownership after suffering chronic losses under private management. The state took over the previously private Taiwan Salt Works in 1982. Still, senior politicians continue to reiterate the government's determination to privatize, as in Economic Affairs Minister Chao's statement that "No matter where you are . . . state enterprises are never so efficient as private enterprises. . . . I want to reduce their activities to the minimum to provide more resources for the private sector. Only a free economy can be a sound economy" (Tanzer 1982:49). Such statements are intended to assure people at home and abroad that the government is committed to the private sector and therefore deserving of support from the private sector and from the Free World.

The urge to downplay the significance of public enterprise is especially evident in Jacoby's important study of the impact of U.S. aid. "By far the most important consequence of US influence [he argues] was the creation in Taiwan of a booming private enterprise system" (1966:138). He says virtually nothing about public enterprises except to note their rapidly decreasing share of industrial production. He does not draw attention to the fact that in 1962–64, just before the study was written, public enterprises still accounted for 45 percent of industrial value-added. Nor does he remark on the fact that two-thirds of U.S. aid was allocated to public enterprises or public agencies (1966:51).

FISCAL INVESTMENT INCENTIVES

The Statute for the Encouragement of Investment, first promulgated in 1960, is one of the principal tools for steering private investment decisions. It spells out specific tax incentives, while criteria for eligible products and firms are listed in implementing rules. These criteria are frequently updated in response to changing conditions (eleven times between 1960 and 1982). Taiwan was one of the first developing countries to adopt such a scheme, drawing on the experience of Puerto Rico in the 1950s.[28]

The scheme combines two approaches to industrial promotion. One is to make incentives available to many industries but stipulate sufficiently high performance standards (economies of scale, domestic content, upgrading pro-

---

[28] The transfer of experience was made by the Arthur D. Little Company, consultants to both governments.

duction technology, exporting) that only a few firms will be eligible in each industry. The other is to target the incentives on a narrow range of "strategic" industries (those with rapid growth and export potential) and make them available to many firms within these industries (United States International Trade Commission 1985:243).

The incentives include the familiar devices of the tax holiday (five years for new projects, four for subsequent increases in productive capacity), accelerated depreciation, investment tax credit, duty-free import of capital goods, and reduced rate of business tax. They are equally available to private and public, domestic and foreign firms.

Some, as we saw in the last chapter, are specific to export sales. Others are product- rather than sales-specific. Initially, the eligible products included important export categories like textiles and footwear, and many categories carried explicit export requirements (a certain percentage of production had to be exported for the incentive to be given, typically 50 percent or more). During the 1970s the items given fiscal investment incentives have increasingly been concentrated on intermediate and capital goods currently being imported or on new export sectors, while export requirements have in most cases been dropped. Spinning and weaving ceased to be eligible for fiscal incentives in 1971. None of today's major export items is eligible. Moreover, the products which receive tax incentives also tend to receive encouragement through import controls, concessional credit, and other government promotion.

Three separate lists are distinguished. The first and most inclusive is of products eligible to receive the tax holiday or accelerated depreciation. The second, a subset of the first, is of items eligible to receive the investment tax credit plus duty-free import of capital goods. The third, a subset of the second, is of items eligible to receive a maximum business income tax rate of 22 instead of 25 percent.[29] The industries which get not only the tax holiday but also one or more of the other incentives are basic metals, petrochemicals, machinery, shipbuilding, and electronics—the secondary import-substituting sectors plus the new export sectors.

It is often suggested that tax incentives make more sense at early stages of the industrialization process. "The more industry a country has, the more the revenue gains will be offset by the loss of tax revenue on existing industries which have to be granted exemption to avoid inequities and on new industries which would be established even in the absence of an exemption system" (Bryce 1965:213). Also, the more industry a country has the greater the pres-

---

[29] The lists are titled, respectively, Categories and Criteria of Productive Enterprises Eligible for Encouragement, The Criteria for Encouragement of Establishment or Expansion of Industrial and Mining Enterprises, and Categories and Criteria for Special Encouragement of Important Productive Enterprises. The strategic industry list, referred to later, is called Applicable Scope of the Strategic Industry. The lists are published by the Industrial Development and Investment Center, 7 Roosevelt Rd., Sec. 1, Taipei.

sures to make temporary exemptions permanent and to broaden the area of exemption, so much that large revenue losses occur. However, Taiwan has responded to these problems by making its tax incentive scheme increasingly elaborate over time. It has resisted economists' appeals to make the scheme broad and unselective so that the government will have no influence over which products are produced. The lists of eligible items have become more and more precisely defined. Minimum scales of production are commonly specified for chemical and petrochemical products and for metal manufacturing; minimum levels of performance are commonly specified for machinery and electrical machinery; local content requirements have to be met for some electronic products and most transport equipment (especially cars and car parts). These side conditions further increase the differentiation of the lists. Over time many items have been dropped and many of those that remain have had their performance requirements raised as more producers became eligible. (Before 1976 circuit breakers had to have a capacity of 11kv to get the reduction in business income tax; in that year the requirement was raised to 24kv.) Regular updating of the lists overcomes one of the disadvantages of detailed rather than broadly specified categories, that it quickly becomes out-of-date. Business has little direct role in influencing these updates, and there is no requirement that applications for inclusion in tax-exempt status be published with provision for objections to be received.

Excerpts from two of the lists, one for 1970, the other for 1982, are given in appendix A. Reading the items one has the distinct impression that the Taiwan planners know where they wish to see the economy go and do not intend to let the market determine the direction entirely unaided. The compilation of the lists of products eligible for fiscal incentives involves them in making detailed judgments about which products should be promoted at any given point in time.

Little research has been done on the scheme. We know that total taxes foregone under the statute equaled 11 percent of total tax collected in 1980–82 and about 14 percent over the 1970s. We also know that total tax foregone as a percentage of gross domestic fixed investment by private and public firms was 5.5 percent in 1980–82 (Ministry of Finance data). Whether the incentives have been effective in increasing investment, especially in "frontier" products, is another question. All that can be said is that the incentives do make a pronounced difference in user cost of capital between sectors. The coefficient of variation (with the economy divided into thirty-four sectors) was 0.42 in 1966, 0.61 in 1976, and 0.45 in 1984 (Chou 1987:69). These results suggest that especially in the 1970s the fiscal investment scheme could well have exerted resource pulls between sectors.

Since 1984 the preceding measures have been supplemented by other tax incentives for particular industries and for research and development spending. Research and development spending is encouraged by a 20 percent tax credit for firms with yearly R&D spending above their maximum in the previous five years, provided their spending is above a certain minimum (which varies by industry and size of firm). Large firms which fail to meet the minimum have to pay the balance into a government R&D fund. In addition, firms in certain high-tech industries, which also meet the R&D minimum, can defer income taxes and face a maximum total income and surtax rate of 20 percent of annual taxable income. They can retain profits of up to two times their paid-in capital (two to four times more than non-high-tech firms), they are eligible for up to 50 percent government funding for their R&D expenses, and are also eligible for government purchase of equity. And firms specifically in electronics and machinery are eligible for special low interest loans for equipment (at 2.75 points less than the prime rate) and for government cost-sharing of up to 50 percent for putting in approved manufacturing or financial systems. To encourage technology transfer from abroad the government allows technical know-how or patent rights to be supplied as part of an equity share (up to 25 percent), and exempts foreign enterprises from taxes or income gained through furnishing approved patent rights. All told, this looks to be an impressive array of additional tax incentives in favor of technology-intensive industries. I have no information on what they have amounted to in practice.

CONTROL OF ENTRY TO AN INDUSTRY

Control of entry to certain industries has been used to prevent overexpansion or entry of firms poorly equipped, financially or otherwise, to make the grade, as well as to insure that too much industrial control does not become concentrated in the wrong hands. Industrial licensing of new plants was stopped in the late 1950s. But approval for plant and equipment imports for new plants was required up to the late 1970s, and is still required today if the owner wishes to apply for fiscal investment incentives. Moreover, all technology import agreements must still be approved by the government. So potentially powerful levers affecting the ability of private (or indeed public) firms to enter new sectors are still in place.

These controls have been used mainly where the minimum efficient scale of production is large. Synthetic fibers, polyethylene, and other petrochemical derivates are obvious cases in point, where entry of firms has been staggered so as to keep all producers at close to efficient levels of production, much as in Japan (Ozawa 1980; Weiss 1986). In some cases, however, controls have been applied more in the interests of preventing undesirable concentrations of private capital than of insuring efficient production, as in the government's refusal to allow Y. C. Wang to build his own petrochemical refinery in Saudi Arabia, or its refusal to allow private producers to integrate backwards into naptha cracking, or the condition on National Distiller that it not expand from its low-density polyethylene plant into downstream sectors. In most parts of the economy, on the other hand, entry controls have not been applied—the growth in the total number of firms over the past twenty years is phenomenal (see table 3.5).

INDUSTRIAL REORGANIZATION

Industrial reorganization programs—to promote mergers, encourage greater specialization between firms in the same industry, and promote modernization of equipment—have been attempted only selectively. Most of the time the government has encouraged and supported an industry's own efforts at greater specialization and modernization, but has not tried to compel them; and it has been distinctly ambivalent about promoting mergers. Modernization of equipment and expansion of plant size has been given explicit encouragement by means of fiscal and credit incentives, a special loan fund to reduce the risks of innovation, and technical advice from a kind of industrial extension service (the Automation Task Force, described later). The same methods are used to encourage greater specialization, as in the Automation Task Force's efforts to get the automobile firms to rationalize parts production.

Occasionally, however, the government has taken the initiative in promoting mergers when vital sectors of the economy are in trouble.[30] In one such case the government virtually ordered the four polyvinyl chloride (PVC) producers to merge. By the mid-1960s Taiwan had four PVC producers all using an inferior imported feedstock, while Chinese Petroleum Corporation had surplus supplies of ethylene, which was a superior feedstock for PVC. Moreover, the government felt uncomfortable with PVC production entirely in private firms. It instructed the four privates to form a joint venture with Chinese Pe-

---

[30] "Picking losers," identifying the industries currently or soon to become uncompetitive internationally, and giving them help to make an adjustment—which has been an important theme of Japanese industrial policies over the 1970s and 1980s (Dore 1986)—has not been important in Taiwan. Hardly any industries (defined at the four-digit level) have experienced absolute declines. In terms of employment between 1974 and 1981, the major declines were in canned food (labor force declined from 31,665 to 21,604), tea products (11,878 to 2,591), and knitted products (90,636 to 81,449). Total labor force in manufacturing increased from 1,444,902 to 1,855,982 over the period (DGBAS 1979:table 22; 1982:table 22). The main area where the government has been active in organizing a reduction in surplus capacity has been in copper and aluminum smelting in the early 1980s. With Taiwan's power derived mostly from imported oil or nuclear fuel, and with little or no copper or aluminum ores of its own, the rise of energy prices over the 1970s made it uneconomic to continue with any sizable smelting capacity in Taiwan. Because these activities were done by public enterprises the government moved only slowly to reduce their capacity, partly because it feared the criticism which would be made in the legislature that it was throwing people out of work at a time when their chances of getting new work in range of their existing homes was not good. Unusually, it gave the impression of being in a quandary about what to do. By mid-1983 one of Taiwan Metal Mining's two copper smelters had been shut down, while production from the other continued; aluminum smelting also continued, but at much reduced volume. By 1986 the remaining smelters had been shut down.

troleum Corporation and another public enterprise, which would use ethylene as the raw material. This led to better PVC, reduced imports, and greater state control in the upstream part of the petrochemical chain.

Another example is the merger of five of Taiwan's major synthetic fiber producers in 1977. They had been running steady losses since the 1973–74 oil crisis, reflecting their insufficient scale and intense competition from Korea. At first, the government's response was to help the firms individually with low interest loans, delayed payment of taxes and customs duties, restrictions on imported substitutes, and joint export arrangements. But with the firms still limping several years later the government pressed for a merger, a strong action in line with the government's heightened sense of responsibility to restructure the economy that emerged at this time. In return for the merger the government converted the companies' bank debt into shares and took representation on the new board (Gold 1981).

In general, though, mergers in Taiwan have come about at the initiative of the companies concerned, with the government providing general encouragement. It has rarely tried to force mergers on unwilling partners. Instead, the Industrial Development Bureau has initiated a program to encourage the formation of long-term and multipurpose relations between buyers and sellers in industries with a dense interdependence of supply. Called the Program for Promoting Center-Satellite Factory Systems, it was established in the early 1980s as a way to provide subsidized technical assistance to firms wishing to enter long-term contracting relations. The center-satellite systems are of two main types: a final assembly factory and its parts and components suppliers; and a major material supplier and its downstream buyers who convert the materials into final goods. By 1987 forty-two such systems had been formed, involving forty-two central factories and 874 satellites, mostly in electronics, automobiles, chemicals, bicycles, and motorcycles. The government helps train the central factories how to "intensify their guidance capability given to satellite factories" (IDB 1987:6) in management techniques, production layout, quality control, and standardization of parts; and gives them longer-term credit at cheaper rates than normal. But with long-term subcontracting relations being unfamiliar in Taiwan, the results so far have been meager.

INVESTMENT CHOICE

Taiwan's industrial policy-makers have not had much training in economics, as we shall see. How then have they made investment choices? Clearly they have not made much use of the standard optimizing techniques, such as social cost/benefit analysis, domestic resource cost calculations, and the like, especially prior to the mid-1970s. Yet somehow they have chosen certain sectors as deserving high priority for expansion. Beyond saying that they have used relatively simple heuristic rules to do so, not much is known. Indeed, the way that sectoral investment choices are made in practice, as distinct from how they *should* be made, has received little analysis anywhere. As Nathaniel Leff observes: "Scholars have devoted relatively little research to the question of how individual sectors are selected for high-priority treatment in particular countries and times. Consequently, the process of inter-sectoral preference formation is not yet well understood" (1985:346).

But a little more can be said. Sun Yat-sen's economic philosophy laid out broad guidelines for the use of public power, which are discussed in chapter 9. Partly for reasons to do with the curious basis for legitimacy of Nationalist party rule, also discussed later, the political leadership has treated these guidelines very seriously. Other sources of ideas at senior levels were Arthur Lewis's *Theory of Economic Growth* (1955) and Walt Rostow's *Stages of Economic Growth* (1960). The latter shaped the argument of a book by K. Y. Yin, hailed as the architect of Taiwan's industrial policies up to his death in 1963, called *Economic Development in Taiwan: 1950–1960*. The book argued that by 1960 Taiwan had just reached the take-off stage. Hence more investment should be poured into manufacturing and specifically into a small number of leading sectors, which to become leading sectors should be export-oriented. The book was important not just for its notion of strategy, but also because of its rousing mobilizing quality, its conviction that Taiwan was going to make it.

To identify promising industries government officials used a combination of criteria. They studied trends in income demand elasticities and technological change for particular items in Western markets, identifying subsets of products which ranked high by one or both criteria. They probably also employed some other diagnostic criteria which Japan's MITI was then using for the same purpose (described in chapter 10). In the 1950s, much weight was given to engineering feasibility and foreign exchange saving, on the grounds that almost any project which met both criteria had to be worth doing. Even subsequently, investment choice has been influenced by essentially engineering concepts of take-off, linkages, gaps, substitutions, and incremental extensions—conceived in the first instance in physical rather than value terms. This reflects the importance of engineers in the planning process. For example, when the government decided to build a stainless steel plant in the early 1980s (through a joint venture between three U.S. steel companies and a public enterprise), the justification was "to fill a gap in Taiwan's infrastructure" (King 1982b). Developments in electronics are being promoted with the aid of an input-output map which highlights gaps in the production structure within Taiwan. Conversely, the composition of imports is examined to identify items in demand which are within reachable distance up the product ladder—a process which the extremely detailed and up-to-date import statistics make easier. Again, considerations of economies of scale have been important in deciding which products to promote. Planners have sometimes set higher levels of protection for mechanical components than for finished products, in contrast to economic principles, to encourage domestic producers to reap the economies of scale which are thought to be particularly important in the manufacture of some components. In some sectors there is a military factor: the government has found that the U.S. government tends to be unwilling to supply many kinds of advanced military and intelligence technology until Taiwan is about to acquire the capacity to make the items domestically, at which point the U.S. will supply. This consideration lies behind the choice of some of the items for encouragement.

The fact that Taiwan has not been near any world technology frontier until very recently makes the selection of "winners" easier than for more advanced countries. There are examples to follow, Japan above all. It is commonly assumed that Taiwan is, in the Japanese metaphor, descending the same stretch of the river Japan descended some fifteen to twenty-five years before. The underlying assumption is spelled out in a report by an American consultant on how to develop certain key sectors. Japan, it said,

> is a somewhat more developed economy which has many of the same aspirations, resources, and resource deficiencies found in Taiwan. Therefore, it is an economy most likely to contain a mix of products within each BIG (Broad Industry Group) that most closely resembles the mix to be aimed for in Taiwan, presently or in the near future. Furthermore, the production functions should not be too dissimilar as a result of the similarities in the types of resources available. The fact that Japan's economy is further advanced than that of Taiwan makes the process even more appropriate in that the structure of Japan's industry can then be considered the type that Taiwan might (or even should) develop. (Arthur D. Little Inc. 1973:10)

The same assumption is implied in Djang's remark that "the present stage of development of the petrochemical industries [in 1976] is not dissimilar to that which Japan passed through between 1961 and 1966" (1977:87). I have even heard a Taiwan planning official suggest that Taiwan is gaining five years on Japan in every ten, so that if Taiwan in 1975 took the Japan of 1955 as the model it now (1985) looks to the Japan of 1970. Of course, application of the principle of tracking Japan is shaped by the fact that in some sectors technology has changed too much for the comparison to be relevant, and present-day Japan, as well as present-day Korea and the United States, are looked to for ideas on what Taiwan should be doing next.

But the use of engineering concepts and Japan as a model is constrained by the emphasis on export performance. Export performance is used as a principal source of feedback information as investment choices are unfolding, and the choices may be altered in response to the feedback. Moreover, businesspeople have come to understand that export performance is one of the main standards by which government responds to them, one of the principal criteria by which unexpected contingencies are resolved. In this sense the government has created an "export culture," with exporting becoming a focal point of government-business relations.

MANPOWER PLANNING

Finally, we need to consider how the government has steered investment in education. The educational system has changed greatly since the early 1960s in at least three ways. First, post-junior high school enrollments in vocational institutions expanded much faster than enrollments in academic institutions, raising the proportion from 40:60 in 1963 to 69:31 in 1986. At the tertiary level, 55 percent of students are now in vocational colleges, 45 percent in more academically oriented universities. Second, the proportion of tertiary students in engineering expanded from 24.6 percent in 1955–56 to 32.8 percent in 1985–86, while the proportion in humanities and fine arts fell from 15.8 percent to 9.1 percent in the same years. Finally, the proportion of senior high, college, and university students in private institutions rose from 22 percent in 1960 to 58 percent in 1985 (Ministry of Education 1987). While the expansion of engineering can be understood partly as a response to demand (engineers tend to be paid more than graduates of other subjects), this change and still more so the other two are the result of deliberate manpower planning. From 1966 onwards, a series of Manpower Development Plans have guided educational expansion. The actual results, in terms of expansion of enrollments in different subjects, balance between private and public schooling, overall rate of expansion, and proportion of GNP for education, have corresponded fairly closely to the targets (Woo 1988). Moreover, except for the expansion of engineering the targets have tended to run against social demand. For example, the expansion of private schooling had nothing to do with allowing more scope for private or local preferences, for the private schools are tightly controlled in terms of curriculum, pedagogy, and fees. The object, rather, was to shift more of the cost onto the beneficiaries. The expansion of vocational institutions and the slowdown of academic institutions also went against demand, for academic high schools are the main route to universities, and university degrees (including in engineering) confer higher rates of return and prestige. Again, the government lowered the allowable rate of expansion of places in tertiary institutions from 5 percent a year in the fourth Manpower Development Plan (1972–76) to 3 percent in the fifth (1977–81), so as to avoid an expected problem of graduate unemployment. This target, too, was met, while demand for scientists and engineers was greater than expected, resulting in a current shortage.

The government has also organized programs of overseas study to complement Taiwan's own educational system. In 1975 there were 2,301 students studying abroad under government auspices; in 1986, 7,016 (over 90 percent of them in the United States). Before 1983 the government offered a variety of incentives to those who wished to return, but a majority of those who went abroad stayed abroad. In 1983 the government launched an aggressive program to induce more to return. Instead of waiting to be contacted, it set about contacting all likely candidates. A government agency (the National Science Council) used its four offices in the United States to build up a list of ten thousand Chinese students and employees in high-technology fields whose skills would be of interest to Taiwan. It then contacted every name on the list to explain the incentives to return. It keeps in touch with potential recruits and regularly reminds them of the opportunities. It also administers a related program to entice Taiwanese and other Chinese engineers and scientists to return for short-term assignments. Some 3,200 people came under this scheme between 1970 and 1980 (Woo 1988). By these means, what was perceived as a "brain drain" comes to be seen as a "brain bank."

CONCLUSIONS

From this review of industrial policy instruments several points stand out. First, the government has the means to mediate the involvements of domestically based firms in the international economy by way of import controls, export controls, foreign exchange controls, and direct foreign investment controls. Modulation of the impact of external volatility on the domestic economy has helped to encourage long-run investments.

Second, within this context of enhanced stability, the government has attempted to target industries for intensified growth by using several kinds of instruments. This is to make the contrast with, say, the United States, or post-Allende Chile, or Zambia, where instruments comparable to those described here for Taiwan are mostly lacking. Whether the government's attempts to target have been effective is a separate and difficult-to-answer question, to which we return. But at least we can say that the instruments have controlled enough resources to make it plausible that they affected output significantly. This is immediately obvious in the case of public enterprises, which together account for an unusually large share of industrial investment compared to other noncommunist countries. As for other instruments, we saw that the dispersion in effective protection given to different manufacturing sectors is big enough to matter, especially since the dispersion is around a low average. We saw that the tariff rebate scheme makes a huge difference in the amount of tariff collected. We also saw that the fiscal investment incentives significantly affect the user cost of capital between sectors. Almost certainly domestic content requirements and entry restrictions to certain industries affected resource use in a significant way in the 1960s and 1970s, if not later. What is less clear is the importance of targeted and concessional credit. The amount of concessional credit has been less than in Korea (as seen in Taiwan's much lower export credit in relation to export value, for example). But Korea made exceptional use of concessional credit as a steerage instrument. Perhaps Taiwan's fiscal investment scheme along with its public enterprises helped to compensate for less concessional and targeted credit by giving the banks clear signals as to which sectors deserved preferential treatment in the government's view.

Third, some of the instruments require government officials to be selective about the products to be encouraged; and some—notably the quantitative import controls, direct foreign investment screening, public enterprises, and control of entry to certain industries—require them to exercise discretion case by case. The operation of quantitative trade restrictions, for example, often calls for them to weigh up the claims by users that a certain imported item is of distinctly better quality than the domestic substitutes (so they must be allowed to import it), against claims by the domestic producers that their quality is as good as the import. On the other hand, the fiscal incentives involve little use of case-by-case discretion. Anyone who produces the specified items is entitled to them (though the categories of eligible products have discretionary edges). In this respect Taiwan's fiscal incentives differ fundamentally from the French scheme of "fiscal contracts," in which enterprises in important sectors individually negotiate the broad lines of their production, location, and employment with a planning commission or Ministry of Finance official, against a lower tax bill (Wiles 1977; Zysman 1983). Compared to fiscal incentives, the various mechanisms of concessional credit involve less use of rule-bound selectivity between activities and somewhat more use of discretionary judgment by officials or bank loan officers.

Fourth, the instruments use a mixture of controls and incentives. Controls affect the behavior of economic agents by threatening a penalty if the prescription is not followed; incentives affect behavior by offering a reward if certain things are done. The control instruments include quantitative import restrictions and export licensing, foreign investment screening (incoming and outgoing), approval for capital goods imports for new plants (until about 1980), no nongovernmental borrowing of foreign funds, and restrictions on entry to certain sectors. The incentive side includes tariff rebates, tax incentives, and concessionary credit. In-between are industrial reorganization policies and the practice of "administrative guidance" made famous or notorious by Japan, a kind of governmental persuasion able to utilize both sorts of measures to affect firms' behavior in line with policy goals. Table 6.3 classifies the main instruments in terms of their reliance on controls or incentives, and in terms of whether their use requires discretionary judgment by officials.

Finally, Taiwan's industrial policies affect firms in the small-scale sector very little, at least until those firms wish to deal with the international economy; and even then the potential for discretionary intervention is by no means generally used. For large parts of the economy, the policy strategy has been to structure the incentive environment in such a way that autonomous profit-seeking will lead firms to behave in ways that aggregate up to national goals—

TABLE 6.3
Taiwan's Selective Industrial Policies

| | *Discretionary Judgment* | |
	No	Yes
Incentives	Tariffs	
	Tariff rebates	Credit
	Fiscal investment incentives	
		Industrial reorganization policies
		Administrative guidance
		NTBS
Controls		Approval for capital goods imports for new plant
		FDI controls
		Public enterprises
		Controls on entry to an industry
		Local content requirements

or at least not aggregate to something inconsistent with national goals. Firms in the large-scale sector, however, have been much more affected by the policies, both those which regulate their international involvements and those which regulate or encourage their domestic behavior. But even here, the government has not attempted to exercise anything like comprehensive influence. Nor has it, in general, tried to set prices much below market-clearing levels. If it had tried to do either to any significant degree it would have required a much larger administration and more political power, for discretionary controls tend to breed further controls which in turn need to be administered and sanctioned. Its authority would have been more continually applied and therefore more continually at risk. Instead, the government's use of nondiscretionary levers for guiding the behavior of most private domestic firms (excepting the "approval" mechanism of import control), and its restriction of discretionary techniques to a small number of specific parameters (excepting the bigger foreign investors, the big lump projects, and new projects on the technology frontier) means that it saves scarce administrative talent. By so doing, it allows the decisions about which products to pick, what tax incentives and credit concessions to offer, and what export ratios to insist upon to be concentrated in the hands of a small number of able people who have the resources and skills to exercise foresight in a way which the ordinary businessman could not afford to cultivate.

In terms of the neoclassical and GM theories, the discussion of the last two chapters has shown that the government has been able to use a large array of instruments for modifying a market-determined allocation of investment in line with government preferences. This fits the GM theory. We now look at the organization for forming and wielding those instruments.

Chapter 7

THE ECONOMIC BUREAUCRACY

GOVERNING THE MARKET requires a small number of powerful policy-making agencies able to maintain the priorities expressed in the routine accumulation of particular negotiations and policies in line with a notion of the national interest. It also requires ways of preventing formal centralization from becoming informal incapacitation. And it requires that the agencies be able to recruit from amongst the more gifted members of their generation. In Chalmers Johnson's account of the developmental state, a pilot agency or economic general staff is one of the core features. The pilot agency performs think tank functions, charts the route for economic development, decides which industries ought to exist and which industries are no longer needed in order to promote the industrial structure which enhances the nation's international competitiveness, obtains a consensus for its plans from the private sector, acts as gatekeeper for contacts with foreign markets and investors, and provides positive government supports for private economic initiative. Japan's Ministry of International Trade and Industry (MITI) is the classic example. The pilot agency is the elite of the economic bureaucracy, staffed by the best managerial talent available in the system. But the wider economic bureaucracy is itself an elite body, occupying a position of preeminence in the society. How well does this picture fit Taiwan?

THE ECONOMIC BUREAUCRACY

The Nationalist government on the mainland before 1949 had attempted to operate a strong central state apparatus, but internal factions and the wars against the communists and the Japanese led to fragmentation and lack of discipline in the later period. When it came to Taiwan it took over the preexisting centralized structure built by the Japanese and reinforced it. From the beginning powers of policy formation and social control were vested in a well-trained bureaucratic cadre, within which authority was concentrated at the top. Still today economic policy-making is intensely centripetal; it is carried out entirely in Taipei and almost entirely within the executive branch, with some input from the top of the party. The process is dominated by little more than a dozen individuals. They range from the president, to a number of relevant cabinet ministers, to senior people in several government ministries or commissions, to managers of the largest public enterprises, to a few private businessmen who are well connected to the party (Tedstrom 1986). The president and premier have much more control over the policy-making apparatus than, say, their Japanese counterparts (Pempel 1987; van Wolferen 1986–87).

At the top is the president, currently Chiang Ching-kuo. (The present tense refers to the mid-1980s, except where otherwise stated. Chiang died in early 1988.) Chiang is head of state, commander-in-chief of the armed forces, and chairman of the Nationalist party. Directly under the president are the five yuans, or branches of government. The ministries and commissions responsible for economic policy-making are within the executive yuan. There are approximately two dozen major ministries, councils, and commissions within the executive branch, of which the most important for industrial and trade policy are the cabinet, the Council for Economic Planning and Development, and the Industrial Development Bureau of the Ministry of Economic Affairs.

The head of the executive yuan is the premier, who chairs the cabinet and acts as liaison between the executive branch and the president's office. The cabinet, including the premier, is appointed by the president from outside the legislature. For economic issues, an informal inner group within the cabinet has decisive influence. Its members include the minister of economic affairs, the governor of the central bank, the minister of finance, the director-general of budget, accounts and statistics, one or two ministers without portfolio, and one or two others. Known as the Economic and Financial Special Group, it meets fortnightly with the president.[1] To this group the most difficult economic issues are referred. The president has no economic staff of his own, relying instead on this group for advice.

Three agencies together perform functions of an "economic general staff." They are the Council for Economic Planning and Development, the Industrial Development Bureau, and for agriculture, the Council for Agricultural Planning and Development (the former Joint Commission for Rural Reconstruction).[2] We consider the first two.

Council for Economic Planning and Development

The Council for Economic Planning and Development (CEPD) is an advisory body to the cabinet, and all but one of its twelve councillors are cabinet mem-

---

[1] It did not meet regularly with the president in 1982 because of his poor health; meetings resumed in 1983. Formally the inner group is treated as a part of the presidential office. It does not include the head of cabinet, the premier. The activities of the Economic and Financial Special Group are shrouded in secrecy. Before 1978, when Chiang Ching-kuo was premier, the special group reported to the premier; when he became president it reported to the president.

[2] The Joint Commission on Rural Reconstruction (JCRR) was responsible for the formulation of the land reform and other agricultural development programs. It was headed by a council of three Chinese and two Americans, with a small but highly competent staff. The staff never exceeded 260. Like CUSA, CIECD, EPC, and CEPD, it was an autonomous agency outside the civil service, answerable to the premier. The staff were paid salaries double or more those paid to mainline civil servants of equivalent rank.

bers.[3] K. H. Yu, governor of the central bank and undoubtedly the most powerful figure in financial policy-making, has been its chairman since 1978.[4] The council meets on Wednesday afternoons, following the meeting of the Nationalist party's standing committee on Wednesday mornings and preceding the cabinet meeting on Thursday mornings. At present four of the twelve members of CEPD's council are involved in all three meetings.

CEPD has a staff of over three hundred professionals and nonprofessionals. Of the 250 with university qualifications, 20 percent are engineers, 40 percent are economists, and most of the rest are graduates in finance, accounting, or statistics. It constitutes by far the biggest concentration of economists in government service. The staff is divided into seven departments—overall planning, sectoral planning, economic research, urban development, performance evaluation, financial administration, personnel administration, plus a subdepartment of manpower planning.[5] Their responsibilities cover the formulation of the one-, four-, and ten-year macroeconomic development plans; analysis of the current situation of the economy; and evaluation of large-scale public enterprise projects.[6] They are also used to arbitrate disputes between ministries (perhaps over big issues like revision of investment incentives, or over small issues like whether fluorescent lights should be classified as electrical appliances and thus be eligible for fiscal incentives, as the Ministry of Economic Affairs says, or as home appliances and thus ineligible, as the Ministry of

[3] The councillors include the governor of the central bank of China, the ministers of economic affairs, finance, and communications, the director-general of budget, accounts, and statistics, four ministers without portfolio (all of whom have held one or more of these portfolios in the past), the secretary-general of the president's office and his counterpart in the Premier's office, and one of the council's vice-chairmen.

[4] K. H. Yu was made premier in 1984.

[5] The economic research department has about fifty professionals, each of whom monitors one subsector in addition to other duties. The sectoral planning department has a staff of forty-four, of whom twenty-four are divided into three "task forces" on electronics, petrochemicals, and machinery. Relations between the two departments are not always the most cordial. The organizational division corresponds with the distinction between economists and engineers.

[6] A Commission for Nationalized Enterprises, part of the Ministry of Economic Affairs, is responsible for coordinating the activities of the various public enterprises. It does not, however, have an in-house capacity for economic analysis. The requirement that CEPD approve major public enterprise investment projects was introduced in the late 1970s. Before then the budget of each public enterprise received scrutiny in the annual budgetary process, as part of which the cabinet might refer particular projects to CEPD on an ad hoc basis. It was felt, especially in CEPD, that this procedure was not strict enough to prevent public enterprises from making wasteful investments in the mid-1970s—hence, the new control requirement. The management board for each public enterprise is appointed by the ministry to which the enterprise is affiliated; in the major public enterprises, the senior positions are appointed directly by the president or premier. (The government, assigning extreme importance to control over appointments, makes decisions about personnel at strikingly high levels of the political structure.) Board members tend to be ex-ministers, ex-senior officials, or ex-military officers rather than private industrialists or academics. I found no one who had more than a casual knowledge of how public enterprises are controlled.

Finance says). But CEPD has no executive authority of its own; the staff advises the council and the council advises the cabinet, where authority lies. Normally, the cabinet rubber-stamps the council's decisions, since the council is a subset of its own members.[7]

As an advisory body to the cabinet, CEPD is outside the ordinary machinery of government. This has the substantial advantage of allowing it to pay higher than normal civil service salaries and to recruit people without making them take the usual civil service examination. In this way the council can attract higher-quality talent. On the other hand, it also means that CEPD's plans and suggestions carry little more than moral authority. One indicator of the weakness of their authority is that on a project-by-project basis the opinion of CEPD staff is not normally sought by the banks or by enterprises. Indeed the staff have little contact with individual firms, except some of the public enterprises (whose big projects they have to approve). Clearly, then, CEPD is not the equivalent of the French Planning Commission or Japan's MITI, both of which had, in the past, more powerful tools of market guidance at their direct disposal. In Japanese terms it is somewhere between MITI and the Economic Planning Agency, except that being the main source of advice to the cabinet on proposals coming from the economic ministries, it is more centrally placed in economic decision-making. And we should recall that it does have direct control over a development fund which disperses an amount equal to about one-half of one percent of gross fixed capital formation in recent years, and shares control of another fund with the Finance Ministry which lent or bought equity in about the same amount—significant at the margins. Given the importance of public enterprise investment in total investment (over half of total fixed industrial investment in 1975–80), the requirement that CEPD must approve all public enterprise projects above a certain size is another significant tool for influencing the direction of expansion.

CEPD has been primarily a reactive rather than an initiating organization in economic policy-making. The majority of its work consists of reviewing policy proposals or investigating policy issues generated in other ministries or in the cabinet itself. But a not unimportant part of its work consists of staff-generated ideas for review by the council, which in turn decides whether to take the proposal on to the appropriate ministry or the cabinet. Self-initiated policies have become more important in the 1980s than before.

CEPD's role as advisor to the cabinet limits its public profile. It publishes statistical abstracts, summaries of international trends, an annual economic report, and a journal (*Industry of Free China*). It publishes little by way of commentary; its constituent divisions can publish almost nothing on their own initiative; and any article by a staff member has to be approved at high levels before being shown to an outside audience. The economic plans are published,

---

[7] Weak or absent factions in the cabinet is an almost necessary condition for this to follow.

but with surprisingly little bally-hoo; a declamatory, incentive-creating effect is neither intended nor achieved.

The authority and scope of CEPD has varied over time. What is now called the Council for Economic Planning and Development began as the Council on United States Aid (CUSA) in 1948, the Chinese counterpart of the U.S. aid mission.[8] The council, chaired by the premier, included top-level representatives from ten other ministries or boards. It was the peak economic coordinating body between the various parts of the government on Taiwan and the U.S. Mission. It was also responsible for programming the use of U.S. aid funds (a responsibility shared with another body, the Economic Stabilization Board, up to 1958). Because U.S. aid constituted a large part of the economy's investment, CUSA was in effect a central planning agency. (It had much help from the U.S. Mission, with an average total staff of about 350.[9]) However in 1958 much of the detailed planning was decentralized out of CUSA to the Ministry of Economic Affairs, the Ministry of Communications, and the Joint Commission for Rural Reconstruction. They were asked to prepare plans covering their sectors, and CUSA was to integrate their plans to form the Third Four-Year Plan.[10]

In 1963, with the termination of U.S. aid in sight and with the United States pressing for less government direction of the economy, CUSA was reorganized. Its name was changed to the Council for International Economic Cooperation and Development (CIECD). But CIECD continued to act, like CUSA, as a superministry, coordinating especially the Ministry of Economic Affairs and the Ministry of Finance. It retained a wide range of responsibility, a semiautonomous status within the government, and a highly talented staff with experience gained over many years. Even more important for its influence was the power of the person in charge. Its first chairman was the premier (Chen Cheng), who was succeeded by the man who would later become vice-president and then president following the death of Chiang Kai-shek (C. Y. Yen). From 1967 to 1973 it was chaired by Chiang Ching-kuo, son of President Chiang Kai-shek, who was made vice-premier in 1969, premier in 1972, and president in 1978. He used the office to learn about economic decision-making and to woo key

[8] CUSA was one of the first institutions created under the Marshall Plan principle requiring a host country counterpart to the USAID Mission. The figures on personnel which follow are from interviews with ex-CUSA staff; Jacoby 1966; Gold 1986:68.

[9] The U.S. economic aid staff alone was 138 at the end of 1955, including contractors such as the J. G. White Corporation (International Cooperation Administration 1956:13).

[10] Another important locus of coordination at this time was the Foreign Exchange and Trade Control Commission, another interministerial council drawing top-level representation from the same agencies as CUSA and also chaired by the premier. It was responsible for allocating foreign exchange and for formulating and implementing nontariff barriers. It was abolished in 1968, having seen a decline in its powers after 1961 when direct foreign exchange allocation by use was abolished. Thereafter the central bank had more power over foreign exchange matters and the Ministries of Economic Affairs and Finance had more power over trade policy.

economic officials. His emergence as one of two contenders for his father's positions had been opposed by many civilian officials but supported by the military. When the premature death of the other contender assured his succession a wave of gloom swept the more liberal parts of the economic bureaucracy. It was feared that he would institute a more comprehensively controlled economic regime and become generally more repressive. Instead, he went out of his way to receive the most intensive teaching about economic matters from the key economic officials, of which his chairmanship of CIECD was just one part.

When he left the council in 1973 CIECD was down-graded to vice-ministerial rank, a change signalled by a more mundane title, the Economic Planning Council. At the same time, however, the key economic ministers who had been on the council continued to meet regularly, but informally, almost surreptitiously, with no agenda and no minutes; they became known jokingly as "the gang of five." This was the origin of the Economic and Financial Special Group referred to earlier. The group met weekly to discuss coordination of policies affecting industry, agriculture, and finance, and reported directly to the premier.

The decline in the planning council's status after 1973 was related to a decision to give the ministries more power to formulate their own plans and implement them—and especially to give more power to the Ministry of Economic Affairs. This in turn was partly related to a conviction that a planning capability should not be concentrated in one place, but dispersed throughout the implementing agencies. And it was partly related to the appointment of a very powerful figure as minister of economic affairs (later to become premier). It served his own interests to have a relatively weak council while he was in charge of economic affairs.

But in 1978, upon his appointment as premier, the council was upgraded to ministerial rank again, and another very powerful figure, the governor of the central bank, was put in charge. Relatedly, the premier's successor as minister of economic affairs was weak. A strong council and weak economic affairs minister now better served the premier's interest in being able to coordinate economic policy himself. Also, the change was a response to the South Korean challenge. During the mid-1970s many commentators and policymakers in Taiwan began to worry that Korea would soon outcompete Taiwan in industrial development. They asserted that Taiwan needed an economic planning agency with more power than the Economic Planning Council, similar to Korea's Economic Planning Board. A mission visited Korea in 1977 to report on the Economic Planning Board, and recommended a substantial increase in the power of Taiwan's planning agency. The upgrading in 1978 was signalled by another change of name to the present Council for Economic Planning and Development.

However, CEPD has never regained the status of a superministry. The senior members of the council and notably Chairman Yu himself are anxious that the council in its planning work should follow the maxim "Respect the other ministries' planning capacity; make indirect suggestions only." The rule of plan presentation is, in the words of a senior official, "Don't be too explicit, but do not be so general as to be propagandistic. CEPD must not be seen to be above the other ministries, nor must it be seen to be merely following them." So the published plan documents are full of empty-sounding guidance phrases like, "continue to tighten inspection standards for export goods," "strengthen the role of large trading firms," and "further import liberalization." Care is taken to insure that none of it will offend anybody. The draft annual plan for 1984 said steps should be taken to "stimulate exports," which was changed in the final version to "maintain export growth."

The plans are basically statements of public sector investment intentions, coupled with econometric estimates for the rest of the economy. Plan preparation begins with a top-down view, in which basic targets like rate of GNP growth and exports are chosen first and then the sectoral implications calculated. At the same time, consultations are started with the various ministries. The ministries are asked to send in statements of their own expectations of the growth of their sectors, their intentions, and a report on progress in the previous year. Once this information is in, the staff of the overall planning department examines it, checks its consistency, compares it against overall objectives, and then meets with senior representatives of each ministry or bureau. This may be the only occasion in the year when people from a range of ministries have sustained communication with each other. The plan goes into effect at the start of the calendar year. Halfway through the year a review of the previous year's plan performance is undertaken by the performance evaluation department of CEPD. These are the procedures used for the one-year plans. The four-year plans are prepared in much the same way. The flexibility in the four-year plans comes through the one-year plans; the four-year plans themselves are prepared only once in four years, not on a rolling basis.

Industrial Development Bureau

The key agency for industrial development policy is the Industrial Development Bureau (IDB), one of several bureaus of the gigantic Ministry of Economic Affairs.[11] Its functions are to turn CEPD's broad guidance plans into

[11] In addition to a number of departments (mining, commerce, international cooperation, etc.) and some commissions, the Ministry of Economic Affairs has four large bureaus: the Industrial Development Bureau, the Board of Foreign Trade, the Bureau of Commodity Inspection and Quarantine, and the National Bureau of Standards. These report to the ministry, which consists of the minister plus three vice-ministers. Coordination meetings are held once or twice a week (generally over breakfast) between the vice-ministers and the heads of the four bureaus, with the minister often present.

detailed sectoral working plans; to draw up the lists of items to be given fiscal incentives and the lists of tariffs and import controls; to decide case-by-case requests for importing items on the "approval" list, and more generally to encourage firms to make purchasing agreements with domestic suppliers; to organize the calculation of input-output coefficients for the duty draw-back scheme; to help establish orderly export marketing arrangements in industries where cut-throat competition is resulting in buyers' complaints; to oversee price negotiations in sensitive sectors like petrochemicals; to grade the production facilities of firms in key industries; to approve applications for loans from various special loan schemes and for loan guarantees; to provide administrative guidance to firms; and still more. One American manager described IDB as "the spear throwers, the shock troops, the main point of contact between foreign companies and the bureaucracy."

The parentage of IDB goes back to the Industrial Development Commission originally set up under the Economic Stabilization Board in the early 1950s, and then transferred to the Council on U.S. Aid when the Economic Stabilization Board was abolished in 1958. The Industrial Development Commission planned the work of creating an expanding industrial structure; or in the words of a contemporary publication of the U.S. Mission, "the commission assists in the establishment or redevelopment of promising industries, some principal examples of which are plastics, rayon, cement, glass and fertilizer plants" (International Cooperation Administration 1956:14). In the first half of the 1950s, K. Y. Yin (described as the architect of Taiwan's industrialization) had his base there; and two of the cabinet ministers influential in shaping economic policy over the past two decades (K. T. Li and Walter Fei) each headed one of its main divisions (General Industry and Process Industries, respectively). It had a staff of about seventy professionals, mostly engineers, with one or two economists.

The Industrial Development Commission had the same anomalous position with respect to the "line" ministries as did CUSA, the Economic Stabilization Board, and CEPD today. It was outside any ministry, being responsible directly to CUSA, which was in turn responsible directly to the cabinet. When CUSA was transformed into the Council for International Economic Cooperation and Development in 1963, the Industrial Development Commission went with it to form the sectoral planning component of CIECD. As the 1960s progressed, criticism began to be made of the concentration of planning capability at one point in the state machinery. The downgrading of CIECD in 1973 was preceded by a move of some thirty-five engineers, mostly from the sectoral planning department, into the Ministry of Economic Affairs. There, in 1970, they formed the Industrial Development Bureau (IDB).

For a while all sectoral planning within the industrial sector was done by this body. Over time, however, IDB acquired more administrative/regulatory functions, while the business of planning Taiwan's industry got neglected despite a rapid increase in staff. In 1978, as part of the reupgrading of the planning agency, a group of engineers moved from IDB to CEPD to set up the sectoral planning department of CEPD, responsible for drawing up sectoral plans to guide the detailed work of IDB. (But IDB people claim that CEPD people are too divorced from the world of business to make sensible plans, so they put CEPD plans straight in the show window while they get on with devising their own.)

During the several years before 1983 IDB had a professional staff of about 180, of whom 130 were engineers and another thirty were financial or marketing experts. (It had no economists before 1981, then for a short time it employed six, and subsequently has made do with three.) The staff were divided into four vertical divisions—metal machinery, electric-electronic, chemical, and daily necessities—which formulated programs and solved problems at the industrial sector level. Three more divisions—industrial estates (including export-processing zones), industrial regulations, and research (corral of the economists)—formulated and coordinated policy across industries.

IDB has faced a continuing problem: the tendency for tedious regulatory work to distract its attention from policy formulation. Since the early 1980s more routine work (form filling, licensing, and the like) has been passed on to administrative agencies, including industrial associations; and more of the procedures have been computerized. In 1983 the staff was expanded and changes were made in the scope of the divisions. The new vertical divisions are: the steel system (steel, machinery, vehicles, forklifts, etc.), electronics and information, petrochemicals and chemicals, and consumer goods. The new horizontal divisions include one for land use, another for planning and coordination with banks, customs, and taxation, and a third for industrial organization, industrial law, and pollution. There are also administrative subdivisions and a computer center.

Two features are important for understanding how IDB operates. One is the interplay between horizontal and vertical divisions within the same hierarchy, which facilitates coherence in policy. The second is its responsibility for trade and foreign investment policy as well as domestic industrial policy, which gives it much more power than it would have if trade policy were the responsibility of a separate agency. The Board of Foreign Trade is principally an administrative body, taking its instructions from IDB on industrial matters. By threatening to restrict or liberalize imports of a particular item IDB can exert powerful bargaining pressure on domestic producers.[12]

---

[12] What about the organization for promoting exports? The China External Trade Development Council, formed in 1970, was discussed in chapter 5. But CETRA is a parastatal agency, not part of the core government apparatus, and its council does not include the political leaders. Japan and Korea both constituted regular high-level coordination councils to oversee the export drive— Japan's Supreme Export Council, formed in 1954, and Korea's monthly national export meetings, started in 1965. Both were elite bodies bringing together senior officials, ministers, and business

The advantages of having the same organization handle both trade issues and the more domestic parts of industrial policy were particularly clear in the early 1980s, during difficult negotiations between upstream and downstream producers in the petrochemical sector. When the world oil price went up at the end of 1979, Chinese Petroleum Corporation, the giant state enterprise, raised its price of ethylene (the basic feedstock for the petrochemical industry, made by cracking petroleum). At the higher price, the cost of production of intermediate products exceeded the landed price from North America and Mexico, where intermediates could be produced more cheaply from natural gas. So the intermediate producers in Taiwan wanted to pass their higher costs of production on to the downstream users (to those who took the plastics, artificial fibers, and synthetic rubber and turned them into final products). The latter, naturally, wanted to import the intermediates from abroad, arguing that if they were prevented from doing so they could not compete in export markets. It was IDB's job to handle these extremely sensitive negotiations, which brought together many of the biggest enterprises in Taiwan and implicated a third or more of Taiwan's exports. (Relatedly, the then-head of IDB, a civil engineer, was replaced in 1981 by a petrochemical engineer.) IDB used the threat of blocking, or allowing, imports as the means to effect a compromise between downstreamers wanting imports regardless of the consequence for upstreamers' capacity utilization and profits, and upstreamers wanting no imports regardless of the effects on downstreamers' export competitiveness.

IDB has been one of the main sources of pressure for protection within the government, while CEPD has been the main source of opposition—a split which mirrors the one between engineers and economists.[13] It is a matter of degree, of course, because IDB engineers are well aware that the domestic market is small and cannot achieve large economies of scale even with high protection. But IDB has a greater role in industrial policy formulation than CEPD and this helps to explain why, rhetoric apart, Taiwan has moved only gradually to liberalize imports in sectors it wishes to encourage.

Consider the procedures for revising industrial tariffs. Formal authority for

---

leaders to discuss export progress. Japan's was chaired by the premier, Korea's by the president himself (JETRO 1983; Rhee 1984). Taiwan has not had a close equivalent. Through the 1960s export progress was monitored on a regular and systematic basis within CIECD—but by officials only. This function was shifted to the Board of Foreign Trade after its inception in 1969. It seems that there has been no forum in which several of the senior-most leaders of the government have themselves been regularly involved in assessing and spurring on the export drive. See further Wade 1988b.

[13] Many other parts of the government are sympathetic to protection. In 1983 the Board of Foreign Trade, acting under cabinet instruction, compiled a huge list of several thousand import items, and sent the list to forty-nine government agencies to see if those agencies still wanted protection for the imports that were their particular concern. Of the forty-nine only nineteen had replied some months later, of which only one agreed to any relaxation (*China Post*, 29 Aug. 1983).

tariffs rests with the Ministry of Finance because of the importance of tariffs for government revenue. But IDB is responsible for drawing up the preliminary list of revisions. This may often require hard bargaining intramurally between, say, engineers of the Daily Necessities Division, who cover textiles, and those of the Metal-Machinery Division, who cover textile machinery, the former wanting lower tariffs on textile machinery, the latter wanting higher ones. Once the preliminary list is drawn up within IDB, it goes to a special tariff commission comprised of high-level officials of other affected ministries plus CEPD, chaired by a vice-minister of finance. In general, the Ministry of Finance is cautious about lowering tariffs in order to protect government revenue. CEPD tends to tolerate higher tariffs on unessential consumer goods because they do not affect the country's competitive edge, while urging low tariffs on everything else. IDB tends to be more inclined to protect capital goods, especially to achieve economies of scale and learning. The list which emerges from the negotiations of this commission goes to the cabinet, which passes it to CEPD for final scrutiny.

The procedures for fiscal investment incentives are roughly similar, and again IDB has the first and preponderant voice. The ''approval'' mechanism of import control is almost entirely the responsibility of IDB. And in the discussions of the Investment Commission, to which all foreign investment proposals go, IDB again has the predominant say.

It is worth giving some details on Taiwan's bifurcated approach to foreign investment proposals. Two organizations, the Industrial Development and Investment Center and the Joint Industrial Investment Service Center, attract foreign investment, while the Investment Commission screens all proposals. The commission also screens proposals for outgoing foreign investment by Taiwan's own entrepreneurs. The commission is part of the Ministry of Economic Affairs, responsible to one of the vice-ministers. Its members are representatives of the concerned ministries, with IDB, CEPD, and the Ministry of Finance providing the core, and other representatives brought in according to the proposals being considered. For example, China Petroleum Corporation is always represented when a petrochemical project is being considered, or the chairperson of an export-processing zone attends to examine proposals relevant to that zone. The commission has only a handful of administrative staff of its own. Most of the paperwork relating to submissions is prepared with the help of the two attracting organizations, and much of the evaluation work is done in IDB. The commission has the authority to bargain with the investor to determine what is needed to attract a desired project, to weigh the total package of incentives and performance requirements, and to commit other government agencies to the agreement. It usually meets once a fortnight.

Still another of IDB's functions is to organize export cartels when competition between exporters begins to get out of hand. In the case of cordless telephones, for example (whose export volume rose by 250 percent in the first seven months of 1983), IDB noticed a swelling chorus of foreign buyers' complaints. Its inquiries showed that competition had become especially intense after a large number of low-overhead "underground" factories began production, cutting prices and quality to gain market share. IDB called a meeting of the largest producers and urged them to form a joint export company. It reminded them during the course of the meeting of the importance of exports for the welfare of the nation; it hinted that the tax authorities might take a close look at their accounts if action on the joint export company was not forthcoming; and it offered some assistance in setting up the company and in preventing the underground factories from exporting (by requiring the Board of Foreign Trade to be especially vigilant against exports from such factories). The joint export company may in reality consist of no more than a man and a telephone undertaking mostly brokerage functions. Its significance is that it constitutes a government-orchestrated limitation on competition.

IDB has an important role in screening applications for loans from the various concessional credit funds described in chapter 6—notably, since 1982, the Strategic Industry Fund. The Bank of Communications (the development bank in charge of the Strategic Industry Fund) normally passes applications to IDB for its judgment, though there is no requirement that IDB must approve a loan. IDB also screens applications for loan guarantees from the Small and Medium Business Guarantee Fund, and as this fund became quite important in the late 1970s, IDB used its power of approval to encourage investment in priority fields. However, IDB has almost no financial resources under its own control. Only in 1982 did it get a small fund of its own for supporting product or machinery innovations. If IDB or its consultants recommends that a manufacturer buy a certain kind of machine which is available in Taiwan, the fund pays for him to see the machine in action; if it is not available in Taiwan the fund initially pays for the import, the manufacturer paying only if he decides to keep the machine. Likewise, a manufacturer can get a loan for developing a new product on preferred terms—no collateral, lower interest, and repayment partly as a share of royalties. IDB officials also undertake informal brokerage between firms and banks to help favored firms get loans. But this is done surreptitiously, as though it should not be done. Overall it is probably true that IDB officials (also those of CEPD) exercise less influence over bankwide credit policies and over specific loans than officials of Korea's main industrial promotion agencies.

The IDB staff do not do all of this screening and judging work themselves. When an application for a loan from the Strategic Industry Fund comes in, for example, the IDB division covering the concerned industry may ask one of the government-sponsored research institutes to examine it. If the loan request is sizable a small team of people will normally visit the firm to examine its financial, technical, managerial, and marketing position as well as the economics of the specific project. The team members may be from IDB or from the relevant research institute.

Whatever the purpose, IDB officials typically spend several days a month visiting firms. These visits help the agency acquire a working knowledge of the production capabilities of individual firms in priority sectors. Hence it is often well placed (allowing for the notorious unreliability of companies' accounts) to judge which firms are equipped to undertake the next step up the product cycle in a particular industry.

Although little is known about "administrative guidance" to firms in Taiwan, there seems to be a lot of it within the industries IDB is trying to promote. In computer printers, for example, officials of the electrical-electronics division, working with staff of the Electronics Research and Service Organization (ERSO), concluded that Taiwan should develop more sophisticated dot matrix printers. While ERSO was mastering the technology, IDB and ERSO people initiated talks with a small number of qualified private firms. They encouraged them to seek joint venture partners, and indicated the help that the government and ERSO could provide. Similarly with packaging equipment. The IDB official responsible for the industry segment that includes packaging equipment noticed that Taiwan imported all its sophisticated multipurpose packaging equipment. After investigating the possibilities, he and his division chief concluded that Taiwan should start to upgrade its own production. IDB issued a press notice and had the packaging equipment industry association do the same, to the effect that Taiwan should develop its own multipurpose packaging machines. In the meantime, IDB had already been making efforts to find local producers willing to undertake the project.

Of course, things do not always go smoothly, especially when the local company or companies fail to meet the agreed performance standards. The recent case of videocassette recorders (VCRs) considered briefly in chapter 5 illustrates IDB's modes of industry guidance. IDB was keen to build up VCR production in Taiwan, and two Taiwanese companies had the capability and willingness to do so. IDB agreed to give them a complete ban on all VCRs from Japan (the only competitive source of imports) for a limited period of eighteen months from the start of production, and then to review the position. But it also limited the number of sets they could each produce until the companies met a stipulated local content rate. The companies went ahead with production, but because of their limited scale of allowable production (they said) their prices were much higher than the prices of Japanese imports. Toward the end of the period of the import ban, IDB began to let it be known in the press that "if domestic manufacturers do not achieve international standards for technology and price within the period of guidance [note that Japanese word "guidance"] . . . then the government might consider bringing in foreign companies for joint investment ventures. . . . [F]oreign companies that invest in VCR production in Taiwan must promise to expand their exports in ratio to the percentage of shares they hold in the companies. The goal in this is to promote the development of VCR production technology in Taiwan and to establish an independent local industry" (*Economic News*, 9 May 1983). The government then decided to allow Japan's Sony to invest on condition that 50 percent of the joint venture company's production be exported and that local content initially reach 35 percent. Despite the objections of the two local companies the government stuck to its position and lifted the import ban. The two local companies began to search for rival Japanese joint venture partners to compete against the one led by Sony (*China Post*, 18 Aug. 1983).

Legacy of the National Resources Commission

The form of organization represented by IDB and CEPD owes much to the National Resources Commission on the mainland before 1949 (Kirby 1986, forthcoming). From its inception in 1932 to its abolition in 1952, the National Resources Commission was a technocratic civil service, relatively insulated from the rest of government and responsible for both long-term planning and managing the public enterprises. It began as a secret "brains trust" of fifty technical experts working directly with Chiang Kai-shek, responsible for planning basic industries and preparing for economic mobilization in the event of war with Japan. From these small beginnings it grew to an enormous size by 1947, with nearly 33,000 staff and 230,000 workers, most of them in its public enterprises. Yet it retained a reputation for technical competence, nonpartisan integrity, and relative honesty. Most of its staff, including many of its top leaders, remained on the mainland to continue their work under the new communist government. However, a sufficient number came to Taiwan to constitute the core of industrial planning and public enterprise management there. After NRC's abolition in 1952, its planning staff went into the Council on U.S. Aid and the Industrial Development Commission, bringing ideas about industrial strategy and organizational arrangements formed over many years on the mainland. Its alumni have included eight of the fourteen ministers of economic affairs from 1949 to 1985, one premier, plus many vice-ministers, bureau directors, and public enterprise managers (Kirby 1986).

The Central Bank

Among the other constituents of the economic bureaucracy which affect industrial policy formulation is the powerful and autonomous central bank of China. Monetary and foreign exchange policies emerge largely from the central bank, with the Ministry of Finance serving as more of an implementing agency. The governor of the bank, K. H. Yu, we have already met as chairman of CEPD. He has been the architect of Taiwan's monetary and foreign exchange policies since 1969, when he was made governor. His great influence derives in large part from his almost unrivaled access to the president. He is reported to be in charge of the president's personal finances (so is sometimes disparagingly referred to in private as the president's "housekeeper"). Earlier he was Chiang Kai-shek's personal assistant for many years, based on his father's close friendship with Chiang.

But there is a more important reason for the central bank's power. Any government which is serious about inflation has to insulate the money supply from manipulation by the protagonists in the competitive struggle, and thus has to find an institutional mechanism which puts the central bank beyond the control of groups interested in the outcome of what it tries to regulate. The government of Taiwan has been extremely serious about limiting inflation. Having learned a bitter lesson on the mainland, it has given the central bank great power and autonomy, much more than Korea's central bank enjoys. Until 1980 the central bank was not even legally accountable to anyone other than the president, including the cabinet and legislature. The change in 1980 altered the rule but not the substance. Even so S. C. Tsiang and other monetarists consider that change a grave mistake because, as Tsiang says, "There is clearly a danger that from now on monetary and foreign exchange policies will be determined largely by popular clamor rather than by expert opinion" (1982:268). At the same time, the central bank is integrated into the wider economic policy-making process. The governor has always been on the council of the planning agency (and indeed K. H. Yu has been its chairman since 1978), and has always been in the cabinet and in the Economic and Financial Special Group.

The Ministry of Finance

The Ministry of Finance (MOF) is responsible for monetary and fiscal policies and for tax collection. In addition, any aspect of industrial policy which has implications for government revenue requires its approval. That includes, in particular, tariff and fiscal investment incentives.[14] It is not responsible for budgeting; that task belongs to DGBAS (below). Hence, MOF has a good deal less power than its counterparts in other countries which oversee both revenue and expenditure. Furthermore, while MOF is formally responsible for control of the banks, this is in practice carried out mainly by the central bank. And at least since K. H. Yu has been governor of the central bank, the appointment of the finance minister has been, in effect, his decision.

---

[14] The MOF includes four departments: Taxation, National Treasury, Monetary Affairs, and Customs. It also includes the Inspectorate General of Customs, the National Tax Administration of Taipei, and the Securities and Exchange Commission. There is also a small research institute, the Taxation and Tariff Commission.

Directorate-General of Budget, Accounts, and Statistics

The matching of funds to priorities across the whole economy is done by a budget process administered by the directorate-general of budget, accounts, and statistics (DGBAS). It begins in October with a two-year forecast of the overall rate of growth of national income, the price level, government expenditure, and government revenue, made by DGBAS's own forecasting group. MOF has to be consulted about the forecast for government revenue, on which it has its own set of forecasts. When DGBAS and MOF reach agreement on the revenue forecast, the whole set of forecasts is turned over to CEPD for assessment of the macroeconomic implications of different scenarios. The agreed guideline figures (if agreement cannot be reached at this level the matter is settled by the cabinet-level Economic and Financial Special Group) are then sent to all the ministries and other public spending agencies to guide their budgets. Normally budget formulation is done by altering the previous year's budget at the margins. Then all the budgets are gathered together at DGBAS to be allocated to one of several special cabinet subcommittees. One such subcommittee may deal with the Ministry of Finance and its enterprises, another with science and technology, another with defense, and so on. Each subcommittee is headed by one of the ministers without portfolio (who by that fact is assumed to be more impartial than a minister in charge of a department). Its members include people from DGBAS and MOF, and perhaps one or two other review agencies directly responsible to the cabinet (such as the Research, Development, and Evaluation Commission). DGBAS staff provide the administrative back-up and write the agendas and the minutes. The subcommittee may call for changes in the budget in light of past trends or special projects. Then the revised budgets are looked at as a package by the four ministers without portfolio. Each agency gets its revised budget back in January or February; in March the whole package goes to the legislature, where a special committee scrutinizes each budget in turn (and may call spokespeople from the concerned agency to answer questions). Examination by the legislature normally takes two months. At the end, the legislature votes on the budget package but can only approve or reject it in total, not line by line. The approved budget package goes into effect at the start of June. (The formal "plans," on the other hand, are based on the calendar year.)

DGBAS is largely an administrative agency.[15] Its main task is to make sure the correct budgetary procedures have been followed by the ministries, and that they have stayed within the rules on such things as personnel numbers,

---

[15] At least this is what is generally said. However, the head of DGBAS is always in the cabinet, a minister in all but name. The current head is a very powerful person, concurrently chairman of the Nationalist party's finance department and one of six persons with a direct telephone line to the president. Security checks at the DGBAS building were as tight as any I came across in Taipei. Perhaps the DGBAS is more important in policy or security matters than is generally acknowledged.

cars, and so on. When budgetary claims exceed the allowable total, the usual procedure is to reduce all budgets by a pro rata amount. When a judgment of priority between ministries or other spending agencies is required, it is made by the four ministers without portfolio meeting as a group.

CONSULTANTS AND TASK FORCE

Policy is not formed entirely within the government. Taiwan has a large establishment of universities, research institutes, and consulting firms heavily involved in policy formation, and foreign consultants have also been much used. Until the end of U.S. aid in 1965 hundreds of U.S. consultants were involved in industrial planning and project design work. The U.S. Mission had a staff of some 350 people, including consultants and contractors. Much of the industrial screening work was done by the J. G. White Engineering Corporation of New York, which kept an office in Taipei with twenty-five to thirty-five American staff members over the 1950s. Although U.S. consultants were important during the 1950s and 1960s they did not necessarily make the decisions. A senior U.S. official in Taiwan in the early 1960s recalls how impressed he was by the ability of Taiwan officials to listen respectfully to all consultants, treat them all with hospitality, give them all the impression that their advice was invaluable—and then to be very selective in deciding which advice to accept and which to reject.[16] Indeed there is said to have been a chronic state of tension between K. Y. Yin and the U.S. Mission in the last several years of his life.

In the early 1960s the U.S. Mission paid the Stanford Research Institute to prepare detailed advice on the next steps in industrialization. Through the 1970s and 1980s the government has employed Arthur D. Little International Inc. for the same purpose. The company makes very specific recommendations about which products should be encouraged in each of the industries it examines—petrochemicals, machinery, electrical machinery, and electronics. Over the same period Taiwanese consultants have also been employed, many of them in government-sponsored research institutes but some in private consulting firms. When IDB decides it is time to revise the list of fiscal incentives, for example, it may contract out the work of preliminary revision to research institutes in the relevant fields—such as the Machinery Industry Development Center, the Mechanical Industries Research Laboratory, or the Electronics Research and Service Organization (all of which are parastatal agencies). When an IDB official needs to decide whether to impose quantitative import restrictions on a certain petrochemical product in response to requests from the domestic producers, he may ask Chinese Petroleum Corporation to tell him whether the local product matches the quality requirements of the currently

---

[16] Howard Parsons (personal communication, 1984).

importing end-users or not, and he will check with the users too. Innovations such as venture capital firms, or foreign investment in the stock exchange via a unit trust, or offshore banking units, may be proposed to the Ministry of Finance (MOF) by private consulting firms, which may be contracted to design the scheme in toto for MOF approval. MOF may then circulate the proposals to interested parties under its own name, sometimes with acknowledgment of the consulting firm, sometimes not.

Foreign advisors remain very important in the Science and Technology Advisory Group, established to oversee implementation of the National Science and Technology Program. The group is the responsibility of Minister Without Portfolio K. T. Li, since the 1950s a leading figure in Taiwan's industrialization strategy. The advisory group has a Chinese staff to undertake coordination across dozens of agencies. But the advisors are all foreign—Americans or American-based Chinese with the exception of one European, all combining specific expertise with experience in science and technology policy (some have business experience as well). They include, for example, a former French minister for science and technology, and a former chief executive officer of Texas Instruments. Li has explained why it is important to bring in nonlocal judgment:

> To promote science and technology in a small economy has many inherent difficulties. One of these is the difficulty in establishing a viable, independent and effective peer review system for R&D planning and evaluation. In a small, tightly knit R&D community, where everyone knows nearly everyone else in his own field, it is almost impossible to ensure that personal bias is kept out of review opinions. (1981:202)

This group of seven to ten advisors meets twice a year, once in Taiwan and once in the United States, for a week at a time. It scrutinizes the soundness of proposals for new initiatives in Taiwan (should Taiwan go into production of large-capacity memory chips, what types of robots should be made?), and also scrutinizes what is happening in industrial R&D elsewhere in the world for its relevance to Taiwan.

The task force, an ad hoc assemblage of people brought together to accomplish a delimited task, is a common feature of large-scale Chinese organizations, perhaps because, so it is often said, horizontal coordination between hierarchies is especially difficult in Chinese society. Certainly they are common in each of the statutory bodies we have been considering, and ministers may have several task forces reporting directly to them. They are used not only for purposes of horizontal coordination, but also to provide competition with established statutory bodies. Statutory bodies with regular budgets are always in danger of going to sleep, and the task force can be a way of either waking them up or passing them by. But the result can be a terrible organizational tangle, at least on paper; and the resulting flat hierarchies produce a constant danger of overload at the top.[17]

In 1981 a new deputy director-general came to the Industrial Development Bureau. He had been deputy director of the Economic Research Division of CEPD. Earlier he had spent ten years as a student in Japan studying Japanese industrial policy, and was midway through writing a book comparing industrial policy in Japan and Taiwan. Convinced that urgent government action was required if Taiwan was to keep moving up the product ladder (his phrase), he set about changing the definition of IDB's role, transferring much administrative and regulatory activity to other agencies. Together with the Science and Technology Advisory Group, he also created a number of new task forces outside IDB.

There are now task forces for each of the following: industrial automation (promoting production rationalization and use of labor-saving equipment), energy conservation, textiles, plastics, machinery, raw materials, and exports.[18] Sizable numbers of people are involved: the automation task force has a staff of ninety professionals, energy conservation has seventy, machinery twenty-five. The staff are recruited mostly from outside the civil service (including some from private industry); this flexibility in recruitment is said to be essential for attracting up-to-date experts, including PhDs returning from overseas. The task forces are less constrained by civil service regulations even than CEPD, which is less constrained than the line departments (including IDB).

The task forces have no core budget. Their funding comes project by project, and IDB has the right to approve or veto their projects. This budgetary control is said to be the key to keeping them effective.

[17] For example, the following special commissions and councils are directly responsible to the cabinet: the Overseas Chinese Affairs Commission, Mongolian and Tibetan Affairs Commission, DGBAS, Government Information Office, Central Personnel Administration, Council for Agricultural Planning and Development (formerly the Joint Commission for Rural Reconstruction), CEPD, the Research, Development and Evaluation Commission, Council for Cultural Planning and Development, Science and Technology Advisory Group, National Science Council, Atomic Energy Council, Vocational Assistance Commission for Retired Servicemen, National Youth Commission, Committee of International Technical Cooperation, Central Election Commission, Department of Health, the Food and Drug Bureau of the National Health Administration, Central Weather Bureau, and the Taipei Observatory (*Directory of Taiwan* 1983).

[18] Of these the least successful is said to be the one concerned with exports. It was placed outside the Board of Foreign Trade (instead made directly responsible to the Minister of Economic Affairs), so the BOFT saw it as a threat and dragged its heels on everything the task force wanted to do. The energy task force is said to have been less successful than the one for automation, partly because it is more difficult to identify from short factory visits just where and how energy can be saved and at what cost.

In July 1984 a new task force was formed to run the central-satellite factory program (see chapter 6). By 1987 it had seventy staff members, mostly engineers apart from twenty assistants or administrators, ten with master's or doctor's degrees, forty with bachelor's. Only four are IDB staff, while most of the others come from outside the government. It works closely with the China Productivity Center.

The intention of creating the task forces is, according to the public version, to allow IDB to take more of a planning and coordinating role, while the details of policy for each sector are left to the real experts—to the people who really know about industrial automation, energy conservation, and the like, now brought into the task forces. This may well be true. But it is also the case that the new deputy director-general saw that parts of IDB itself had gone to sleep, and used the task forces to get results without having to take the impossible step of sacking people. Let us consider the biggest task force, the one for factory automation.

The National Science and Technology program placed particular emphasis on the need for Taiwan to introduce more automation into its industry. The question was how. One of the leading advocates of automation for Taiwan was Caspar Shih, a Taiwan-born engineer working for General Electric in Canada. He was concerned that by not moving quickly enough away from labor-intensive production processes, Taiwan risked being outcompeted either by highly automated production in the advanced countries or by countries with cheaper labor. On visits to Taiwan in the early 1980s he lectured on the need for automation and proposed a task force to help firms automate. He was persuaded to take leave from his job in order to initiate the task force himself. He is now directly responsible to the Minister of Economic Affairs, and great importance is attached to his ready access to the minister. But officially the task force is within the ambit of the Industrial Technology Research Institute, a parastatal organization, which means that its staff are recruited on conditions applicable to government scientists, considerably better than those of line civil servants. From a professional staff of five at the start of 1983, numbers grew to ninety by early 1984, and are expected to go to near 150. All but two are engineers. It represents a major new concentration of engineering talent within the government, in a position to exercise influence across a wide range of sectors.

Its core work is to promote the introduction of automative technology by individual firms. One method is by lectures: in 1983 some nine thousand business executives attended automation task force lectures. The more important method is the factory visit. Six hundred and fifty factories were visited in 1983, most of them more than once. The visiting teams found, however, that the first priority in most cases was not process automation; simple "rationalization" of production was the first priority in 35 percent of the cases, which involved rearrangements on the production line without adding capital or replacing labor. In other cases the visiting teams recommended computerization of management information, packaging equipment improvements, and the like. Where they recommend capital investment in a machine not made in Taiwan, they can use IDB's special innovation fund to cover the cost of importing it. And any applications for loans from the Strategic Industry Fund for the purposes of automation have to be approved by the task force.

The automation task force has been used by IDB to concentrate attention on the automobile industry and on machine tools. These sectors are identified by IDB and CEPD as high priority, but IDB's own staff in charge of them were not especially capable and it was difficult to bring in people from outside with the requisite expertise and dynamism to replace them. Hence the task force.

It became glaringly apparent during the negotiations with foreign carmakers over the Big Auto Plant that IDB's automotive staff were deficient in information and skills. The details of Taiwan's auto policy in practice emerged under the pressure of the negotiations, with the result that the detailed requirements for technology transfer, local content, and exports changed en route. Not until the automation task force and an ITRI laboratory made a detailed study of Taiwan's auto components industry in 1982–83, long after the start of the negotiations, did the planners have a thorough knowledge of the capacity of the components makers. This study then helped to inform the Automobile Industry Development Plan of 1984 (Arnold 1989).

In machine tools, there is concern that if Taiwan does not undertake more vigorous government promotion its industry will be eclipsed by South Korea (Amsden 1977; Jacobsson 1984). The issue came to a head in 1983 when CEPD pressed the premier to agree to a reduction in tariffs on machine tools from about 10 percent to 5 percent. The premier asked the head of the automation task force for his views. The head of the task force said to him, "Do you want a machine tool industry in Taiwan or do you not? If you do, you must have a higher duty." The premier asked him how high the duty should be. "Forty percent," he replied. The premier pointed out that even the machine tool industry association was only asking for 20 percent. So the head of the task force agreed to 20 percent. Shortly afterward, the duty on some machine tools went up to 20 percent (on about twenty locally produced items—including lathes and drilling machines of various types). With higher protection in place, members of the task force went off to Japan to see for themselves what Japanese machine tool makers were doing and what the government was doing for them. On their return they began to formulate plans for greater specialization between existing producers, so as to eliminate the present levels of capacity underutilization and reap economies of scale. They had good intelligence about the production and managerial competence of firms to go on, derived from their own factory visits and those by IDB (made to assess concessional credit or loan guarantee applications), and visits by the Bureau of Commodity Inspection to assess the export quality control system. The plan was to form a holding company for the industry, with shares held by the development bank and a big name non-Japanese machine tool maker. The foreign partner would supply the latest technology and marketing. Financing would come from the government. The local firms who agreed to specialize in line with the plan would get access to the technology, marketing network, and finance, as well as design and managerial help. The firms who did not agree to specialize in this way would not get these things, though they would not be prevented from going their own way. The head of the task force said that his objective was to create an environment in which the owner of each machine tool company says to himself, "If I cooperate I'll be sure of profit."[19]

The task force is one way the government can maintain the vigor of its guiding, pushing, and prodding activities, taking effective power from dead parts of the bureaucracy and/or rousing those parts to new life. Other techniques are also used. The China Productivity Center, started in 1955, was intended to run management training courses, and did so with some effectiveness for twenty years. Over the 1970s it sank into torpor, with little new recruitment and an increasingly aged staff. Being a parastatal agency, none of the staff could be made to leave. So IDB pressed the Minister of Economic Affairs to cut off all additions to its regular budget, which will now decline in real terms with inflation. IDB also began to foster a number of private management consultancy firms to undertake substitute training courses. Faced with this threat to its existence, the China Productivity Center began to show renewed signs of life. Indeed the automation task force in 1985 was absorbed into it—or more accurately, took it over.

The Industrial Development and Investment Center, started in 1959 to encourage foreign investors, is another parastatal which fell into decline over the 1970s. The solution in this case has been to create a whole new organization parallel to it. The Joint Industrial Investment Service Center, established in 1982, is on another floor of the same building, with the same functions but carried out by a younger and enthusiastic staff, whose name badges carry mottoes like, "I'm here to say Yes!" When the senior-most figures of the old Industrial Development and Investment Center finally retire the two organizations will be merged, with the by-then experienced but younger cadres of the new organization put on top.

Moreover, the Nationalist party provides an organization parallel to the bureaucracy, containing offices to monitor the performances of specific bureaus. This is another source of pressure for bureaucratic compliance and responsiveness.

Any government that seeks to accelerate the pace of advance in predetermined directions must be alert to inertia. Organizations must either be prevented from going to sleep or bypassed. Ways must be found to bring up-to-date expertise to bear on priority problems. Taiwan has used several techniques for doing these things, but has used the task force above all. What is interesting is the ability of people near the top to spot organizations short of expertise or vigor and then to initiate various kinds of responses, so that the bureaucracy continues to push and shove the industrial structure in certain directions even though the organization chart is a mess and even though parts

---

[19] This was one of the first attempts to form a central-satellite factory system, which then led into the bigger program described in chapter 6.

of the bureaucracy may do very little. The parallel party organization may help to do this spotting.

PERSONNEL

As noted, economic policy-making in Taiwan is dominated by scarcely more than a dozen people. Many of them have been at or near the top for years. (This reflects the youth of Taiwan's economic planners in the 1950s—the forty whose birth dates are known had an average age in 1952 of thirty-eight [Lin 1987:51]). Indeed, from the early 1960s to the mid-1980s, just five men had a preponderant voice in economic policy, including monetary, fiscal, industrial, and trade policy.[20] (The central bank had only two governors between 1960 and 1984.) Extending the boundaries to include people such as vice-ministers and bureau chairmen, we find that they have typically worked their way up through a variety of posts in government and public enterprises, gaining important political and technocratic experience and developing long-standing working relationships with their colleagues. Most have graduated from the same two or three elite universities, lead by Taiwan National University in Taipei.[21] Almost all belong to the Nationalist party,[22] and many hold concurrent party posts; but they hold the latter because of their positions in the economic hierarchy rather than the other way around. The combination of party ties, common educational background, and most importantly, long-standing working relationships with colleagues make for an uncommon amount of personal and professional empathy among top officials (Tedstrom 1986:25). This in turn helps to create a broad consensus among them on the general goals of Taiwan's economic policies. Indeed, in the 1950s and 1960s many senior officials and public enterprise managers shared an esprit de corps based on their common membership in the prestigious National Resources Commission on the mainland. There is little inflow of people from private business, nor much movement in the opposite direction, even at retirement. But many of the senior economic decision-makers have had business experience in public enterprises.

Most recruitment to the economic bureaucracy is by way of a keenly com-

[20] C. Y. Yen, K. T. Li, and P. Y. Hsu for most of the 1960s (after K. Y. Yin's death in 1963); and K. T. Li, K. H. Yu, and Y. S. Sun from 1969 onwards. Sun became premier in 1978, K. T. Li having declined on (genuine) health grounds. In 1984 Sun suffered a stroke, and Yu took over as premier. Pang 1988 presents useful biographies of the leaders.

[21] Zeigler's examination of personnel records suggests that at the "lowest" ranks (not further defined) of the Ministry of Economic Affairs about 40 percent are graduates of Taiwan National (1988:179). About 80 percent of Japan's higher-level civil service in the 1960s graduated from Tokyo University (Zeigler 1988:172).

[22] Zeigler's results are puzzling in this regard. He gives two tables with data on the characteristics of Ministry of Economic Affairs officials. One shows that at the top two ranks (number of people not given) 100 percent are KMT members (table 7.1). The other shows that at the top two ranks only 41 percent of Taiwanese and 58 percent of mainlanders are KMT members (table 7.2).

petitive examination. Just to pass it confers prestige. Surveys of where university graduates find employment show that a sizable proportion join the government or public enterprises. More masters and doctoral graduates of the mid-1970s went into government service than the private sector, though only half as many of their 1984 counterparts entered government service as the private sector (see table 7.1). (But even the 1984 graduates joined the public sector—including both government and public enterprises—in as large numbers as those going into the private sector.) Government service attracts a substantially higher proportion of university graduates than college graduates, which in an intensely meritocratic educational system like Taiwan's probably means a higher proportion of the more able students. But these are very aggregate figures, and the more relevant question is whether the key economic agencies of the central government are able to recruit from amongst the "best and brightest." On this there is no serious evidence. Interviews with Industrial Development Bureau staff suggest, however, that the bureau has been able to recruit graduates from the top 20 to 25 percent of their classes (except recently in electronics). Discussions with younger staff suggest that they joined the bureau partly for the familiar motives of security of employment, regular working hours, and the benefits of getting experience in many industries rather than just one. But they also talked of the respect which accrues to them as officials of the central government and of their satisfaction in serving others.

TABLE 7.1
Employment of Graduates in the Public and Private Sectors (%)

		Government	Public Enterprises	Education and Research	Private Business	Other	Total
Graduates 1974–77 (in 1979)	Masters and Doctoral	19.3	12.1	43.2	18.5	6.9	1,359
Graduates 1984 (in 1986)	Masters and Doctoral	11.7	13.8	43.7	23.2	7.6	1,019
	Bachelors	8.3	10.0	19.8	54.0	7.9	18,172
	College	5.2	8.8	14.1	72.0	.0	26,085
Returnees 1978–83 (in 1984)	Masters and Doctoral	14.4	8.9	46.5	23.8	6.4	1,672

Sources: Publications of National Youth Commission, Executive Yuan, Taipei: "An Analysis of the Employment Situation of Graduate Students in the ROC," 1979; "Report on the Employment of University and College Graduates, 1984 and 1985," 1987; "Analysis of the Employment Situation of Returned Scholars and Students," 1984.

Note: Returnees are those who returned to Taiwan with a foreign degree. I am grateful to Chien-kuo Pang for drawing this data to my attention and translating relevant portions.

"If you have a relative who works for the Industry Bureau you will be proud of him"; "My father and mother are very proud that their daughter is a [central] government official"; "You can be of service to many people"; "I want to make a good environment for my child, and so I want to make a good environment for my country"—these are typical replies.

Salary differentials are large—commonly 30 to 50 percent lower in the government than in the large-scale private sector.[23] For example, a thirty-seven-year-old deputy division chief, in a division of about twenty people, with thirteen years' experience in IDB, gets NT$30,000 a month plus an extra month's bonus, before tax. Private firms have offered her twice as much for starters. Her boss, forty-three years old, makes NT$33,000, and could also easily double his salary in the private sector. Yet they stay, and fairly happily.

None of this is consistent with Lucian Pye's point that Taiwan is the first and only society of Chinese political culture—including mainland China, Korea, and Vietnam—to have downgraded political authority and indeed all of government to a point where it has reversed the traditional status order between government and business. He claims that in Taiwan from the 1970s onward, "working for the government not only brought no prestige but was taken as a sign that one could not make it in the 'real' world" (1985:234). But the claim comes out of thin air. My data, though not conclusive, contradict Pye's central point. However, it may well be true that Taiwanese value and honor the public service somewhat less than the Japanese and Koreans, especially because public service tends to be seen as dominated by mainlanders, and therefore its evaluation is caught up in the mainlander-native Taiwanese tension.

Most ministers and senior officials with responsibility for economic affairs graduated in engineering or science. Eleven out of fourteen past ministers of economic affairs have had such qualifications, plus five out of fourteen ministers of finance or chairmen of the central bank.[24] K. Y. Yin, chief industrial planner in the 1950s and early 1960s, had a degree in electrical engineering. Of his two chief assistants, one was a physicist, the other a civil engineer. The premier in the early 1980s was trained as an electrical engineer, the minister of economic affairs as a mechanical engineer. IDB is dominated by engineers,

[23] This is based on interviews with several officials in IDB and BCIQ rather than on a systematic survey. However, Liu and Liu (1988) find that, in a recent government survey of 58,000 people, public sector incomes (only wage or salary, not bonuses or other components) are higher than private sector incomes for all of seven categories (professionals, managerial, clerk, etc.). Public sector professionals average 16 percent more than their private sector counterparts, public sector managers, 19 percent more. All the evidence I have, however, suggests this is not true in the central economic agencies of government.

[24] Compiled from Pang's biographies (1988). Six men are listed as having been both minister of economic affairs and of finance (successively), of whom four had engineering or science degrees. Five out of fourteen ministers of finance had qualifications in economics, finance, or business administration. See also Liu 1987: chapter 3.

as are the new task forces. It is true that engineers are now outnumbered in
CEPD by economists (the degree-level staff are 40 percent economists, 20 percent engineers). But in the influential sectoral planning department, the staff
are almost all engineers. And economists have only outnumbered engineers in
the organization as a whole since the mid-1970s. Before that, CIECD and CUSA,
ancestors of the present CEPD, were staffed mostly by engineers.

Familiarity with engineering concepts even at the top levels of industrial
policy-making has made for an easy translation from the broad choices to what
exactly must be done to get specific projects off the ground. It encourages a
"can-do" attitude, which blends into the conviction that the government
should guide private firms. "Because of the small size of companies [in Tai-
wan], they are not as well informed as government in deciding what is best for
them," said a vice-chairman of CEPD recently, himself an engineer (*Financial
Times* 1988:5). At the same time Taiwan's engineers are confident of their
abilities in economics. K. Y. Yin even said that to be an engineer one must
have a scientist's spirit of searching for truth and the practical methodology of
an economist. "An engineer is a scientist who is knowledgeable about economics," he said (Liu 1987: 60–61). K. T. Li described economic modernization as a "huge engineering system that requires extremely careful and elaborate planning" (ibid.:61). Both Yin and Li studied the Japanese experience
carefully, visiting Japan to see what was being done to develop particular industries (ibid.). In Japan's MITI, too, engineers had an important influence.
According to Allen (1981), MITI's engineers "were the last people to allow
themselves to be guided by the half-light of economic theory. Their instinct
was to find a solution for Japan's post-war difficulties on the supply side, in
enhanced technical efficiency and innovations in production. They thought in
dynamic terms."

Taiwan's economists fall into two unfriendly camps. On the one side are
the so-called "editorialists" or "local" economists; on the other, the "academics," also known as the "monetarists" or the "foreign" economists.
Members of the first group tend to be in journalism or business, with some in
government. They tend to be educated in China, Taiwan, or Japan. Members
of the second group dominate in universities, in government-sponsored economic research institutes, and in CEPD. They have typically been to universities in the United States (certainly not in Japan). They charge the first group
with being theoretically and quantitatively primitive. The first group replies
that the second knows little about the real world, and in particular, little about
Taiwan.

The economics profession within Taiwan is dominated by the "academics." They tend to be critical of government intervention, assessing it against
the standard of a smoothly functioning competitive market. They present
themselves as champions of consumers and small producers against greedy
entrepreneurs who want more subsidies, concessions, and protection. To take

a different view is to invite excommunication by the economic divines. Institutional inquiry and economic history are neglected, even scorned. In these respects Taiwan's academic economists are little different from their Japanese counterparts. Shinohara reports that MITI's industrial policy was "looked on unfavorably by the vast body of Japanese economists. . . . These scholars seem to have thought that saying anything favorable about MITI would hurt them professionally" (1982:45–46).

The prevailing belief within the academic circle is that Taiwan's success is due to the liberalization of the economy from government control. In the words of another vice-chairman of CEPD, one of the senior-most economists in government, "I think we should reduce the policy-oriented sector as much as possible. I believe Taiwan's success is due to the reduction of government intervention, to the release of market forces" (interview, Aug. 1983).[25] He is the person to whom visiting economists are taken for a briefing on Taiwan's economy.[26] (Real power is held by the other vice-chairman, an engineer.) Or in the words of another ranking economist: "Most essential to its success were the spirit of free enterprise espoused by Adam Smith and, of course, the Confucian emphasis on education, saving and hard work. Thus Confucius and Adam Smith were the true creators of Taiwan's economic miracle" (Hou 1987:18). Having control of university funding and good international connections, this group organizes international conferences on Taiwan's economy to which like-minded Western economists are invited. In this way the argument is propagated that Taiwan has been successful because of the release of market forces.[27]

[25] Or take the comment of another leader of this group, a professor at a distinguished American university. He was looking at the list of products eligible for the five-year tax holiday (see appendix A).

Economist (shaking head): "Could you draw up a list like this? Could you implement it?"

RW: "They seem to do it in Japan and Korea."

Economist: "Oh, come on, it's common sense! Are there equivalents in the U.S.?"

RW: "What about Japan and Korea?"

Economist: "I heard the President of Korea Development Institute say recently that they were going to give up all these controls and subsidies, because they don't work."

The economist went on to reveal that he had refused to help draw up the list of items to be eligible for assistance from the Strategic Industry Fund. "It's impossible to do it sensibly. We're trying to get the government to give up intervening, to remove all these regulations and let things be decided by the market, by the entrepreneurs themselves."

[26] Visiting economists can be delighted to find that at several important economic agencies (notably the central bank and CEPD) they have ready access to a senior official who is himself or herself a prominent academic. It is common for an academic economist with a reputation in the English-speaking economics profession to be appointed to a senior position in such agencies. This person has an important public relations function—especially to assure the visitor that the government is doing its best to liberalize even further—but tends to have less influence than others of his or her rank.

[27] The record of the 1967 conference gives testimony to the long-term stability of the interests and beliefs of certain leading economists. "Professor Fei mentioned the necessity of considering

In the early 1950s reaction against the kind of economics then being taught in the universities and advocated in government was overdue. Economics was either antiempirical and macroscopic, or it was accountancy, and whichever way had not much to say about the urgent practical problems facing the country. The younger generation of economists returning from postgraduate training in the United States battled to remove the "old fashioned" economists from their jobs and influence. Initially they carried great prestige at the highest levels of government for their ability to do input-output analysis and the like, and so talk to engineers and American advisors on their own terms. But their determination to keep the economics of the free market at the center of economic discussion tended to marginalize them in the policy-making process.[28]

Disillusionment began early, when at the start of the 1950s some of these new-generation economists argued that Taiwan should import fabric rather than yarn or raw cotton, on the grounds that cotton fabrics could be imported more cheaply from Japan than they could be domestically produced with imported yarn. It was not in Taiwan's comparative advantage to make cotton fabric. K. Y. Yin rejected this view. Taiwan, he thought, simply had to acquire the capacity to turn cotton into yarn and yarn into fabric. So he established the comprehensive nurturing program described earlier (chapter 4). A similar pattern, with the "academic" economists offering advice and criticism based on simple notions of efficiency and comparative advantage and the government taking limited notice, was to be repeated often over the following thirty years.

K. Y. Yin's own chief economist, Wang Tso-jung, received degrees in economics from a Chinese university on the mainland and from two U.S. universities. His dissertations were on theories of planned economies and on the experience of Japan and Russia. His early belief in the Soviet type of central

---

the economic development process as independent from policies" (Academia Sinica 1967:56). Professor Chenery, unable to attend, tabled a question as to how Taiwan has "managed to develop a large export industry rather than confine itself to import substitution as is the case with most other developing economies" (p.54). Robert Dorfman disturbed the unanimity of the occasion by emphasizing "the role which the Chinese government has played in development and the evolution of the government's policies over time"; and even proposed that "liberalization such as occurred in Taiwan around 1960 is best seen not as a retreat from mistakes, but as a move from an old to a new phase of economic development" (pp.194–95). Ranis and Tsiang leapt to correct him: "There appeared to be a 'wistful look backwards' to the time when planners rather than the market controlled distribution [said Ranis of Dorfman's remarks]. Although admitting that the market mechanism is imperfect, he stated his belief that government cannot make more rational allocations over an extended period of time" (p.108). Tsiang likewise "took exception to the view [attributed to Dorfman] that government should continue policies of control" (p.108).

[28] The most prestigious economists have been T. C. Liu, S. C. Tsiang, Y. C. Koo, Gregory C. Chow, and John Fei. They have all been associated with the Institute of Economics at Academia Sinica. They were invited by Chiang Kai-shek to advise on economic policy, especially tax reform and monetary reform. They were probably most influential in monetary policy. But they complain that the government has been slow to take their advice even there (e.g., Tsiang 1982).

planning later gave way to belief in the merits of the Japanese combination of government planning and markets. "The Japanese way is the way of Taiwan," he wrote (in Liu 1987: 62). After Yin's death in 1963 he was ousted from government service. He has been able to retain a teaching post at the prestigious Taiwan National University—in the less prestigious faculty of agricultural economics. He remains, however, the venerable leader of the "editorialists."[29]

The "editorialists" have better access to the local press than the "academics." They use this platform to urge more government support for business, frequently criticizing the government for not doing as much as the South Koreans and the Japanese. They argue in terms of national vulnerability, economies of scale, external economies, and the like, ideas which feature little in the arguments of the "academics." They tend to support the engineers in wanting to target incentives and disincentives quite precisely, in wanting managed rather than free trade in priority sectors.[30] (Interestingly, bankers also tend to want precisely targeted incentives, so that they know who is entitled to what.)

But the image of "economist" has been appropriated by the "academics." Of economists defined in this way, one senior industrial policy-maker, himself an engineer, remarked, "We really don't have much respect for economists. Most of them are just teachers and don't know anything about the real world. So we don't listen to them too seriously." He said this in 1983. Subsequently, academic economists have at last ridden into the center of the economic policy debate, capturing some of the power formerly held by engineers. They are the experts on issues of economic liberalization, which by the mid-1980s have risen to near the top of the policy agenda. But the younger generation of engineers is also changing views about the appropriate role of government. Compare the earlier quoted remark by the older-generation engineer who is one of CEPD's vice-chairmen with the opinion of the new young director-general of IDB, an electronics engineer, appointed in 1987. The former said that because Taiwan's firms are small the government is better informed than they are about

[29] He spent 1948 at the University of Washington in Seattle, 1957–58 at Vanderbilt University. Not only in the United States but also before and afterward in Taiwan, he spent much time studying the history of Japanese and Russian industrialization. In the famous television debate on interest rates (see chapter 9), he was one of the main speakers against the government's line.

[30] Chien-kuo Pang suggests I have overdrawn the contrast between the "academics" and the "editorialists." He writes: "Many of the editorialists are actually the friends or students of the academics and have different views from Wang Tso-Yung. Therefore there are different groups in the editorialists. For example, the editorial writers of the *Economic Daily News* [a branch of the *United News*] often hold different opinions against the editorial writers of the *Commercial Times* [a branch of the *China Times*, headed by Wang Tso-Yung]" (personal communication, July 1987). In the mid-1980s Wang's views have moved closer to those of the academic economists. He now urges removal of protection and most government controls as a condition of Taiwan's graduation to a higher technological stage.

what is best for them. The latter, referring to the list of "strategic industry products" eligible for subsidized loans (chapter 6), said, "According to my personal idea we don't need that list. In the future our incentive program should be redirected away from incentives for specific products or sectors and towards a more general upgrading of industry" (*Financial Times* 1988:5). Notice that he refers to the future. He too agrees that selective promotion was needed in the past.[31]

Organizational Advantages

By way of conclusion let us review the ways in which the intragovernmental organization of policy-making contributes to good use of industrial policy instruments. First, the agencies mainly concerned with industrial policy-making—the Industrial Development Bureau and CEPD—are located in the heartland of government and wield much power. Hence industrial concerns receive greater consideration in the formulation of macroeconomic and monetary policies than where responsibility for industrial policy is located in a distinct and politically marginal agency, and where the most powerful economic agency is concerned only with macroeconomic balance and the budget (as in Great Britain). Furthermore, because the industrial policy agencies both have planning responsibilities, they constitute a lobby within the heartland of government for the long view. Second, the scope of the Industrial Development Bureau allows responsibility to be matched with authority, because it includes both planning and implementation of industrial policy. And the inclusion of both trade policy and domestic industrial policy gives it great power, because in an economy so dependent on international transactions, influence over trade policy allows much leverage over the domestic economy as well. In addition, the vesting of trade policy and industrial policy in the same agency allows for a better integration of the two, since bargaining over trade-offs can take place intramurally where there is more give and take. The bureau's staff of 180 professionals is reinforced by the forty-four professionals of the sectoral planning department of CEPD and the more than two hundred in the various task forces established in the early 1980s.

Other parts of the organization for economic guidance also show good sense. In the case of direct foreign investment, for example, there is a clear separation between the agencies for attracting foreign investment and the agency charged with negotiating the terms of entry. Such separation is desir-

---

[31] Interview, Feb. 1988. The economist mentioned earlier who had been deputy director-general of IDB since 1981 (Wu Hui-jan) hoped to become director-general on the retirement of the incumbent in 1987. But K. T. Li felt Wu was too devoted to heavy and chemical industries (and besides, he was an economist). Li used his influence to secure the appointment of a young electronics engineer from CEPD, Yang Shih-chien, partly to strengthen IDB's role in electronics. Wu left to become head of the National Bureau of Standards.

able because of the difficulty of having a single organization do both functions effectively. Where a single organization has been tried one or other of the functions comes to dominate (Encarnation and Wells 1986). Taiwan's screening organization is centralized enough to negotiate on behalf of all the concerned ministries but not so centralized as to "disenfranchise" agencies that have an interest in the outcome of negotiations, since the organization is made up of representatives of these agencies who are senior enough to commit their agency to the decision. This arrangement of foreign investment screening permits a range of technical expertise to be drawn into each negotiation, and at the same time encourages the whole package to be assessed in terms of a national rather than a ministry-specific interest and in terms of the precedents it will create. By permitting quicker negotiations than would a more decentralized approach, the arrangement also reduces the costs of negotiations for the foreign investor.

Third, in terms of personnel, the top decision-makers in industrial policy generally reach their positions only after long experience in several agencies and public enterprises, during which they build close working relationships with a stable core of colleagues. These ties later help to overcome the difficulties of horizontal communication across ministries, and provide a basis for consensus about the broad strategies of industrialization. The device of overlapping and sequential memberships—for example, between the cabinet and other key economic agencies within the state—reinforces this basis for coordination.[32] The central economic agencies are able to recruit from the top quarter of university graduates in a country where only one-third of university applicants are accepted. Task forces are a way of bringing in new talent on a more flexible basis than civil service recruitment would permit,[33] and of providing competition with formal agencies of government. Industrial policymaking and implementation have been done largely by people trained in engineering, and, at senior levels, with close knowledge of Japan's industrial policies. Until recent years economists have been held at a distance so that

[32] Particular care has been paid to having an overlapping membership at the top of the monetary and industrial policy arms of government. The most spectacular example is K. Y. Yin, who held the following posts concurrently or in close sequence: permanent member, then deputy head, Taiwan Production Board; general manager of Central Trust of China; member and then secretary general of Economic Stabilization Board; convenor of the Industrial Development Commission; minister of economic affairs; head of the Foreign Exchange and Trade Control Commission; vice-chair of CUSA; chair of the Bank of Taiwan. His concurrent memberships in the Bank of Taiwan, CUSA, and the Foreign Exchange and Trade Control Commission were especially important for policy coherence (Gold 1986:68).

[33] Even IDB is able to evade some of the conditions of ordinary government employment; it can recruit by more flexible procedures (it has a relatively high proportion of "black officials," as they are sometimes called, including the new director-general), and can offer somewhat better employment conditions.

their preoccupation with efficiency criteria would not subvert the process of identifying industries and products for intensified growth.

Fourth, the high degree of centralization of decision-making within each economic hierarchy helps coherence. But it also makes for overload at the top and long delays in getting decisions out. (Robert Silin has found that reports from subordinates to superiors in Japanese firms tend to provide only the information that substantiates the action suggested by the subordinate, whereas Taiwanese reports tend to be wider in scope and contain more data. Japanese submit plans for approval from seniors, Taiwanese submit alternative courses of action for decision by higher authority: 1976:141–42.) Yet it seems that the bureaucracy has learned—somehow—to be good at filtering out the issues or demands that really matter and giving them prompt attention. Which things really matter vary over time, but generally include: (1) sizable exports, especially to new markets, (2) major foreign investments (more than US$2–$3 million in the early 1980s), (3) new technology which the government wants Taiwan to acquire, or (4) the risk of serious social disorder. Where one or more of these attributes apply, the matter will be treated as urgent; it will be sent up quickly to the top decision-maker(s), it will be drawn to their attention ahead of all the other less important things that are also sent up, and their decision will be acted upon quickly once made. Here, leadership by fiat rather than consensus (which is one way of stating the difference between Taiwan and Japan) can be an advantage in gaining speed. If, however, the decision is made to delay action, then the matter can be made to disappear into the bureaucratic labyrinth while the foreigner is given to understand that the delay is due to bureaucratic inefficiency and red tape which the minister deeply regrets but over which he unfortunately has no control. (Which is not to say that all bureaucratic delay and inefficiency is tactical.) Many other things the bureaucracy has to deal with but which do not count as really important are carried out in the manner of a paper-shuffling state. In short, the bureaucracy in Taiwan is an effective filtering mechanism; as it is selective in its interventions in the market, so it is selective in those things it deals with quickly and those it does not.[34]

One final point. It would be helpful to know more about how differences of interest and opinion between the main economic agencies of government are managed, and especially to know more about the power of CEPD and the Ministry of Economic Affairs compared to other agencies. My guess is that they are less preeminent than, say, MITI or Korea's Ministry of Trade and Industry. This would partly reflect their smaller direct influence over bank credit than that of their Japanese and Korean counterparts, in turn reflecting the greater autonomy of the central bank and the higher priority at the top levels of gov-

[34] We need a study of the operation of the economic policy-making parts of government to match Johnson's study of MITI (1982).

ernment given to low inflation. But even the nonfinancial ministries may be able to avoid cooperating with the Ministry of Economic Affairs when they feel such cooperation would threaten their own interests.

In the recent case of telecommunications, for example, the Ministry of Economic Affairs wanted to use public procurement of telecommunications as a lure for U.S. telecommunications companies to transfer advanced semiconductor technology, as the Koreans were doing. But the Telecommunications Authority, under the Ministry of Communications, was lukewarm, even hostile to the Ministry of Economic Affairs' plans. Only after explicit instructions from the cabinet did it agree, reluctantly, to cooperate (*Commonwealth*, Dec. 1983:34, in Chu 1987a:224). This is one reason why Taiwan negotiated a less satisfactory agreement with a U.S. multinational than the Korean government was able to get (see chapter 10).

Nevertheless, the review of industrial policy instruments in chapters 5 and 6 and the discussion here of CEPD's and IDB's activities show that the government as a whole holds ample power resources for modulating the volatility of market processes and for pursuing selective industrial promotion. Prior to 1973, when the superministry Council for International Economic Cooperation and Development gave way to the more modest Economic Planning Council, the agencies responsible for industrial success had even more power than they have today.

Chapter 8

THE POLITICAL SYSTEM

TAIWAN'S ECONOMIC BUREAUCRACY fits into a wider set of political arrangements of an "authoritarian-corporatist" kind. The rules for selecting the rulers give little scope for the expression of popular preferences, and specifically, do not allow competition between political parties (prior to 1987). Interest groups are not voluntary associations, but are chartered or even created by the government. They function more as dependent auxiliaries of government than as autonomous aggregators of members' interests. This type of political system enables the political leaders to articulate a public philosophy and broker political demands within the framework of that philosophy. In particular, it enables them to exercise much influence over public investment decisions and policy choices.

A more complex picture for Taiwan should recognize three sets of power-creating institutions in the state: one for development, one for legitimation, and one for security (Winckler 1984:485). The development set, run by the premier, includes: economics, planning, finance, banking, transport, public corporations, and on the margins the big private corporations, as well as such mass extensions as industrial associations and labor unions. The legitimation sector, presided over by the party chairman, includes the ruling party, elected representative bodies, the media, education, culture, and such mass extensions as the youth corps and women's associations. The security sector, commanded by the president, includes foreign policy, external and internal security, and such mass extensions as the political warfare department and the retired servicemen's association. The analytical task is to characterize the interplay between these power-creating institutions in ways relevant to political stability and industrial strategy.

The present state of knowledge, however, does not permit more than the first steps in this direction. Ironically, much more is known about the Chinese Communist party than about the Nationalist party. And if little is known about the Nationalist party, even less is known about the military and security services (Winckler 1981; 1984).[1] This chapter concentrates on the legitimation

[1] Edwin Winckler, who knows as much about Taiwan's political system as anyone writing in English, laments that, "the basic nature of the political system remains undefined. If the island has been a military and political client of the United States, we know little about the international and interbureaucratic workings of the relationship. . . . If the island has been a dictatorship ruled by Chiang Kai-shek and his son Chiang Ching-kuo, we do not have political biographies of either for their Taiwanese periods. . . . If the island has been a police state dominated by military inter-

sector, specifically on the Nationalist party. If we want to know the source of state power and autonomy—why Taiwan is a relatively strong state, with substantial definitional autonomy and implementing capability for industrial policy—we have to understand the organization of the Nationalist party and its strategy of rule.

FORMATION OF A ONE-PARTY STATE ON THE MAINLAND

The strength of the Nationalist party is related to events before 1949. The events and choices of the mainland period have had political consequences for the whole period of Taiwan's postwar industrialization, as the party system established on the mainland took on a life of its own.

Several circumstances favored the emergence of a one-party state on the mainland. First, one-party states tend to be found in societies in the early-to-middle stages of development. Before this any formal large-scale organization is likely to be weak and prone to break up; in later stages, too, many other organizations are likely to be strong enough to oppose the concentration of power in a single dominant party. China in the late nineteenth and early twentieth centuries meets this early-middle condition. Second, the Nationalist party was born to fight wars. Its parental organizations had organized the overthrow of the dynasty that had ruled China for 250 years. It was formed out of them in 1912 to fight the local warlords and consolidate a national state in China. From the beginning, then, it faced an enemy and a clear goal. Third, the struggle to consolidate power was long and intense. War was a dominant feature of the party's history right up to 1949. From 1926 to 1949 the party and its army held control over a fluctuating part of China, war being constantly fought on the boundaries—first against the warlords, then against the communists, then against the Japanese, then against the communists. In these circumstances the party came to be dominated by the military and power came to be concentrated in the hands of the person who held the highest military command. Finally, the party reflected the bifurcation of society into a small Westernized, urbanized elite on the one hand, and the mass of peasantry on the other. It was a party of and for the former, systematically excluding the peasantry—a fundamental weakness on which the Communist party was later to capitalize.

These are the sort of "situational" conditions which can be expected to give rise to a strong one party regime (Huntington 1970). Some important cultural and ideological conditions also pushed in the same direction. The cultural definition of leadership emphasized (and continues today to emphasize) the di-

---

ests, we lack institutional descriptions and political histories of its internal and external security agencies. . . . If the island has been successful in managing its economic development, we do not have a political account of the persons, agencies, and interests involved. If the island has been ruled by the Kuomintang, we know little more about the party's politics and administration than its own glossy brochures tell us." (1981:17)

dactic and initiatory role of the leader, who is assumed to lead because of his superior knowledge. This reflects a characteristic pattern in the history of China, of a leaning toward a central organization and a central authority figure who sets the legal and moral pattern. For centuries one man, the emperor, was seen as the source of all political authority. In Japan, by contrast, the primary function of leaders is not to initiate actions on the basis of superior knowledge, but to represent the collectivity to the outside and coordinate interpersonal relations inside (Silin 1976:133). China's Confucian culture has been more consummatory than the Confucian variant which evolved in Japan, in the sense that intermediate and ultimate ends have been seen as more closely connected, with the emperor given a pivotal position in the definition of ultimate ends (Huntington 1984:208). One of the consequences is that China's Confucianism has generally been more hostile to social bodies independent of the state.

These cultural dispositions toward a single source of authority and a restriction of interest group pluralism were powerfully elaborated in the ideology of Sun Yat-sen. The early leaders of the Nationalist party on the mainland agreed that, whatever form of government might "ultimately" be suitable for the Chinese people, a powerful tutelage by government was necessary "for the time being." It was necessary because the overwhelmingly important task was to throw off the yoke of foreign powers and restore China to her former greatness in the ranks of nations. This could only be done by government direction, all the more so because nationalism had become so weak under the impact of foreign control that, as Sun Yat-sen said, the four hundred million Chinese had become like a wash of sand. Weak nationalism had to be compensated by a leviathan state, one of whose primary duties was to generate the missing nationalism. Some argued for tutelage under an enlightened despot (not a term of abuse), while others preferred a dictatorship by a vanguard party. Sun Yat-sen was the leading proponent of the latter, and as leader of the party as well as its chief theoretician, his view prevailed. The ideology of the Nationalist party thus had the idea of a vanguard party and the imperative of nationalism at its center from the beginning.

This ideology demanded agreement among party members not just on procedural rules but also on the content of behavior and belief; it provided a single imperative perspective. While it was less transcendental than the Marxism-Leninism of the Chinese Communist party and lacked a sense of class struggle as the great engine of history, it did posit a form of society—a blend of private and public property, of market and government guidance—which, it said, the advanced countries were themselves moving toward. In this way it showed believers that history was on their side, giving them a higher purpose which served to erode commitment to lesser goals, as Marxism-Leninism did.

The factional nature of Chinese politics also pushed the leadership to think in terms of a strong one-party state. With the removal of the dynasty in 1911 the skein of hierarchical relations that had characterized the old Chinese bureaucracy unraveled into warring, disintegrative factions (Nathan 1976). Within the Nationalist party itself, the leadership found that the party's effectiveness was being seriously weakened by politicians seeking their own political fortunes. Its response reinforced the effects of war in producing a political order capped by a supreme figure gripping the financial, military, personnel, and intelligence reins of power and buttressed by a legitimating ideology that stressed the nation and the person of the leader. In the early 1920s Sun Yat-sen brought in Russian advisors to reshape the party along Leninist lines, the better to control the factions within and the enemy without. A Leninist vanguard party, Sun thought, would better allow the concentration and expansion of state power which the tasks of nation building and war-winning required (Bedeski 1981).

In fact, however, the political and military turmoil constantly eroded the party's attempts to operate like a Leninist vanguard. On the other hand, the attempt to personalize the power of the leader, to foster a cult of personality, was far more successful. After Sun Yat-sen died in 1925, Chiang Kai-shek, coming from the military wing of the party, held all three top positions right up to his death in Taiwan in 1975. He was not only chairman of the party but also commander of the armed forces and president of the republic. He and a substantial number of his followers came to believe that party policies and national interests were identical with his personal convictions, and that dedication to his personal convictions was a sign of dedication to the interests of the nation and the cause of the party. He made an important exception, however, in the realm of economic and especially industrial policy. The pattern was later to be repeated under Mao Tse-tung, except that in the latter part of his rule he did not make any exceptions.

FORMATION OF A STRONG ONE-PARTY STATE ON TAIWAN

When the party retreated to Taiwan in 1949 situational, ideological, and organizational factors all became more favorable for the formation of an effective one-party state.

Situation

The new situation helped in several ways. The Japanese had imposed a strong colonial state on Taiwan for fifty years, standing above and apart from a weakly organized civil society. The situation in Taiwan was even more extreme than in Korea, for unlike Korea, Taiwan had never been an independent state with its own indigenous bureaucratic and landed elite. The Japanese had no preexisting cohesive and legitimate organ of state power to deal with, which therefore gave them an unusual need and an open opportunity for establishing their own structure of control and guidance. They established an administrative structure which penetrated right down to villages. The whole population (2.5 million around the turn of the century) was divided into units of ten households in turn grouped into units of ten, their elected Taiwanese leaders closely supervised by Japanese police. The colonial government insured that the natives developed no formal organizations beyond locally based kinship or residential groups. They prevented the establishment of large-scale religious institutions, such as Christian churches. They prevented any significant concentrations of wealth in Taiwanese hands. They also kept Taiwanese out of senior managerial positions in large-scale commercial and governmental organizations. So by 1945 the populace had much experience of an alien military and police presence intruding into many areas of social life, while it lacked experience of managing large-scale organizations and self-rule.

The Japanese pullout at the end of the war thus left a leadership and managerial vacuum. The Nationalist party on the mainland sent over some administrators to fill the gap, but until the party realized it might have to retreat to Taiwan it viewed the island as a minor responsibility. The administrators sent to Taiwan acted as plunderers, and made use of a civil disturbance in 1947 as a pretext to wage war on the island's intellectual and social elite, such as it was. Estimates of the numbers killed in this onslaught range from ten thousand to twenty thousand (Kerr 1965:310). Then came the influx of one million to two million military and civilian refugees, including the defeated core of the government that claimed to rule China. Their arrival supplied missing skills. (Israel is probably the only comparable case in modern history of such ''walk-aboard'' skills.) But by swelling the island's population by about 25 percent it caused further disorganization (Gold 1986).

The arrival of the mainlanders also created an ethnic conflict. The six million islanders, though originally from the mainland two to three centuries before, had not had any significant contact with the mainland during the fifty years of Japanese occupation. The Japanese prevented such contact, actively discouraging a sense of ''Chineseness'' amongst the natives. By 1949 few of the islanders could speak the national language of China, Mandarin, while a large proportion could speak some Japanese.[2] On the other hand, virtually none of the incoming mainlanders had any connection with Taiwan or could speak the language. They had rapidly to be provided with jobs and housing

[2] The Japanese in Taiwan comprised at most, toward the end of the period, 5 percent of the population. Migration from the mainland was halted by the Japanese so that by the 1920 population census less than half of one percent of the population was born on the mainland—if the data is to be believed (Barclay 1954: table.1:11). People of recent mainland origin were marked out with care by the Japanese, who felt it necessary to control their activities to forestall the development of close ties between the islanders and the mainland (1954:17). ''[T]he literacy rate among Taiwanese rose from 1 percent in 1905 to 12 percent in 1930 to 27 percent in 1940'' (Ho 1978:33)—literacy defined as the ability to read and/or write in Japanese.

because their loyalty was vital to the regime's survival. Soon the native-born found themselves elbowed aside in government appointments, business, and housing, despite their three or four to one majority.

Managing this tension has remained one of the party's central preoccupations. That there has been remarkably little violence perhaps reflects a general political quiescence among the islanders in response to seeing their embryonic elite wiped out not once but twice in the space of sixty years, first by the incoming Japanese colonialists at the end of the nineteenth century and then by the incoming Nationalists in 1947.[3] But the tension between the two groups has persisted. Mainlanders (those who came after 1946 and their dependents) account for 12 to 15 percent of the population. Personal identity and social interaction are still shaped by the "mainlander" and "native Taiwanese" distinction. A 1970 survey found that 97 percent of the three best friends reported by native Taiwanese respondents were also native Taiwanese while, more surprisingly in view of their small numbers, 87 percent of the three best friends reported by mainlanders were mainlanders. The incidence of intermarriage remained very low (Appleton 1976). A survey in the mid-1980s found that only 25 percent of respondents had close kin married across the native Taiwanese/mainlander line (including respondent, parents, siblings, and children: Wei 1987:70). Distinct cooking styles remain important as affirmations of identity—not only between mainlanders and native Taiwanese, but also by province of origin within the mainlander group.

Again, the government's basis of legitimacy was quite distinct from that of most other governments. The only "legal" basis for its rule of Taiwan was—and remains today—the claim that it is the rightful government of all China, of which Taiwan province is only a small part. The dilemma is clear. As long as it claims to be the rightful government of all China it cannot allow the government to be dominated by people from one small province. So the Taiwanese majority had to be excluded from taking a share of real power remotely resembling their share of the population, and therefore the government's claim to speak for them was constantly open to question. Besides, the party had to get its own supporters into secure positions in order to protect their loyalty, and in that sense it had to operate as the instrument of the mainlanders often

---

[3] The main postwar incidents have been the 28 Feb. 1947 uprising, and the Kaohsiung incident of Dec. 1979. The former erupted out of the rising resentment on the part of the native Taiwanese at the "carpetbagging" behavior of the first group of Nationalist officials sent to the island. The government suppressed it with extreme brutality (Kerr 1965). In the Kaohsiung incident, demonstrators commemorating World Human Rights Day clashed violently with members of the security forces. Over sixty participants, including most of Taiwan's political opposition leaders, were arrested, and the eight major defendants received long prison sentences in judicial judgments which accepted the government's indictments virtually completely, ignoring the courtroom debate (Jacobs 1981).

against the islander majority. On the other hand, exclusion raised the danger of mass unrest, which might easily be exploited from across the straits.

Finally, the confrontation with its communist neighbor provided the state with a permanent excuse for repression. The looming threat from 150 kilometers away allowed any domestic opposition to be construed as sedition. It justified a condition of hypermilitarization of society and the maintenance of an extensive police system.

In short, the Nationalist party came to power in Taiwan much as a foreign power occupies an unfriendly region. The party responded by enforcing strict authoritarian controls. It faced little temptation to bargain with established powerful groups for support over crucial issues, a strategy which would probably have diluted the priority given to goals of economic development and mainland recovery. Such a temptation was lacking for the reason that existing organizations and elites were weak. Clearly the situation of the Nationalist party in Taiwan is exceptional in the annals of development experience.

Ideology

The Nationalist party came to Taiwan with an already well worked out ideology about the appropriate relations between party, state, and society. The ideology of the party defined the ideology of the state, and the ideology of the state defined the identity of the nation. Hence the Nationalist party defined the Republic of China as being based upon Sun Yat-sen's Three Principles and Chinese nationalism. As a consequence, opposition to the party (which would be legitimate under democratic rules) was seen as opposition to the state, and therefore treasonous.

The ideology specified that the state, under party guidance, should take a tutelage role in the economy. It should consider economic issues in a comprehensive framework of interdependence, not in a "muddling through" incremental way (Lindblom 1959; Jowitt 1971:8). It should minimize commitments to existing social groups so as not to constrain the future options of the vanguard party. In these ways Nationalist ideology was informed by a Leninist orientation to socioeconomic problems, in particular by its comprehensive perspective, vanguard consciousness, and sense of urgency. But it also sanctioned primary reliance on markets and private property, which set constraints on state actions.

The ideology was more nationalistic than the Chinese Communists—less transcendental and less infused with an internationalist mystique. The problem facing "nationalistic" regimes when they come to power is, as Kenneth Jowitt observes (1971:63), a fundamental conflict of goals: the goal of citizenship, of community, of reconciliation, of preservation of "traditional" (precolonial) ways, may substitute for the goal of rapid socioeconomic development. This conflict the Nationalists on Taiwan avoided, for the reason that their nationalism related essentially to the whole of China. It deliberately could not grip the island of Taiwan as the unit of sentiment. The only way that the whole of China could be regained was through the creation on Taiwan of a powerful military and a strong economy. So although the ideology of the Nationalists was in a sense more nationalistic than that of the communists, this did not lead them into the bargaining for support, the attempt at reconciliation, and the dilution of development goals which often go with nationalism.

Organization

The party came to Taiwan with a history of nearly forty years behind it, in contrast to many other one-party states where the party is created more or less at the same time the leaders take over (Castro's Cuba, Nasser's Egypt). And it achieved power because it possessed an army, in a situation in which the party and the army were the only large-scale organizations with a distinctive identity and trained, reliable personnel.

The party had tried but failed on the mainland to operate like a Leninist vanguard. In the smaller and more manageable circumstances of Taiwan it was more successful. Being convinced that one of the main reasons for defeat in the civil war was "party indiscipline" (abusing positions of power thereby bringing the party into discredit, rather than plotting against the leader), the leadership undertook a comprehensive party reform in 1950–52 to purge the party of "indisciplined" elements and tighten party organization (Jacobs 1978; Durdin 1975). Right down to the present the party continues to be organized on "democratic centralist" principles, though this phrase from the Leninist lexicon is not actually used. The party's constitution (1976 revision) says:

> The organizational principles of this party are: party members, as the most important part of the party, and cadres, as the backbone of the organization, combine with the broad masses to form the party's base. In organizational life the individual obeys the organization and the minority obeys the majority. There is free discussion before a decision is made, but, as soon as a decision is made, all must obey in order to implement organizational democracy and disciplined freedom.
>
> (quoted in Jacobs 1978:241)

The corresponding passage from the constitution of the Chinese Communist party reads:

> The party has been organized according to the system of democratic centralism. The entire party must obey the discipline of the democratic-centralist system: the individual must obey the organization, the minority must obey the majority, lower levels must obey higher levels, and the entire party must obey the Center.
>
> (1977 version, in Jacobs 1978:241)

The structure of the party is similar to Leninist parties, with the same split between large, honorary bodies (like the national party congresses and the central committees), and small, policy making bodies (the Nationalist party's standing committee, the political bureaus of the Leninist parties). Up to the early 1970s the Nationalist party was as restrictive, as elite in its membership as the typical ruling Communist party: of the sixteen ruling Communist parties in 1970–71, only eight had *lower* rates of membership in the total population than the Nationalist party's 6.9 percent (Jacobs 1978:242). The party's prescribed role in the political system is also similar to that of Leninist parties. Party members are to exert leadership and control throughout the society, and especially within the government. The party's constitution states:

> This party's relationships with government are: to formulate policy according to the ideology [of Sun Yat-sen's Three Principles of the People], to choose personnel according to policy, and to *utilize the organization to control party members working in the government*. Party members working in the government must be charged with the responsibility of completely implementing party decisions.
>
> (in Jacobs 1978:242, emphasis added)

The appropriate role of the Chinese Communist party has been described by senior party figures in very similar terms.

The party's organization stretches from the standing committee at the top to cells in schools, universities, factories, and neighborhoods. At the higher levels it has a structure of offices to watch over the rest of the society, and in particular to watch the various arms of public authority. Within the military (about half a million regulars and over a million reservists) it operates a Soviet-type commissar or "political warfare" system, with a hierarchy of political officers running parallel to the ordinary military hierarchy. Almost all senior civilian officials and military officers are also party members, and many hold high party offices as well. In consequence there is a constant blurring of the distinction between party and state at the top. The party also has many industrial and commercial enterprises under its more or less direct control, through which comes much of its finance.

In short, for situational, ideological, and organizational reasons the Nationalist party leaders created on Taiwan a single, elite, disciplined party and gave it a position of preeminence in the social system.

STRATEGIES OF RULE

Any one-party state is vulnerable to a questioning of its exclusive claim to power. The Nationalist party on Taiwan has tried to mute such questioning by a combination of measures, some aimed at preventing it from being heard, others, from being acted on, and still others at checking the desire to question.

Excluding Native Taiwanese from Top Positions

For most of the postwar period the native Taiwanese, in an 80 percent or more majority, have held few top positions in the state or party. The cabinet during the 1950s and 1960s included hardly any; over the 1970s and 1980s the number increased gradually to reach ten out of thirty-one in 1987. Of posts of vice-ministerial rank and above, however, only 14 percent were held by native Taiwanese in 1987. Their exclusion from the top levels of the military and the police is even more complete: they hold only 4 percent of generals' rank and above, and 7 percent of police bureau chief rank and above. They have done a little better in the party's central standing committee: they had no members in the 1950s, two members (out of seventeen to twenty) in the 1960s, five out of twenty-three in 1975, twelve out of thirty-one in 1985, and fourteen out of thirty-one in 1987. Their share of seats in the legislative yuan rose to 22 percent by the 1980s (Kau 1988).

Limiting Civil and Political Rights

The government emphasized, and continues to emphasize, the many freedoms available to the citizens of the Republic of China, by contrast with the People's Republic. But those freedoms cannot be of one's own choosing. They must be ordered, permitted, scrutinized, and accepted according to a set of government prerogatives.

Raymond Gastil has attempted to compare countries according to their civil and political rights. Civil rights are the rights of the individual against the state, of free expression and fair trial; political rights are legal rights to take part in determining who governs and what the laws of the nation shall be (1973:5). In 1972 Taiwan came about halfway down a ranking of middle-income countries, with a score of 11 out of 14, the same as South Korea, Spain, Portugal, Tunisia, Iran, and Rhodesia. China and North Korea both scored 14 out of 14, the worst possible score.[4]

Since 1949 Taiwan has been ruled on the basis that the country is still at war with the People's Republic. All constitutional guarantees of civil liberty have been abrogated by the state of siege promulgated in May 1949. Taiwan has had the longest-running martial law in the world. (The present tense refers to the mid-1980s. Martial law was lifted in 1987.)

Taiwan's martial law proscribes public meetings, strikes, demonstrations, petitions, and "spreading of rumors by letter, slogan or other means." The

[4] Middle-income countries are those so classed in the World Bank's *World Development Report 1978*. Gastil gives scores for fifty-five of these countries in 1972. Twenty-nine countries had lower scores (wider freedoms) than Taiwan and Korea in 1972. Note that Taiwan did much worse by Bollen's index of democracy (1980), based on 1965 data. It was number forty-eight out of fifty-six middle-income countries. Korea was twenty-sixth, surprisingly high.

police can still arrest without a warrant and call in suspects or witnesses for interrogation without a formal summons. The independence of the judiciary is in serious doubt. In political trials, the confession extracted from the prisoner is usually the main or sole evidence used for conviction. Political trials are generally held *in camera* by military courts. Mass arrests took place in the early 1950s, but have not been repeated. Estimates of the number of political prisoners in 1980 range from about four hundred, according to sources close to the government, to several thousand, according to opposition leaders. Most are students, businessmen, or local politicians; arrests of workers for political reasons are rare (Amnesty International 1980).

The daily press, the radio, and the television stations are all owned by the government, the military, the party, or people very close to the party. (The "private" owners of the two main newspaper groups are both on the standing committee of the Nationalist party, as is the editor of the party's own mass circulation daily.) It is illegal to establish a daily newspaper without government permission. When one of the big newspaper groups was in financial trouble some years ago, Y. C. Wang, the biggest entrepreneur on the island, wanted to invest some money in it—a wish which the party covertly blocked though the group is "private." The main organization responsible for internal security (Taiwan Garrison Command) has powers to seize or ban any publications that "confuse public opinion and affect the morale of the public and the armed forces," in the words of the government order (Chang 1983:43; Jacobs 1976). Censorship comes less by prepublication scrutiny than by punishment after the event. The contents of papers and magazines are monitored by—Orwellian irony—the Government Information Office. Although dissident views can be expressed more readily in weeklies or monthlies, few if any have circulations of more than fifteen thousand, compared to the two main dailies' circulations of nearly a million each. Nevertheless, one or more issues of nearly a dozen political journals were banned during 1982 and three suspended for one year. One noted opposition publisher calculates that it is economic for him to keep two journals going at once but has three registered on the assumption that at any one time one of them will always be banned. The three television networks are owned by the party, the military, and the government, respectively.

The provisions of the state of siege sharply restrict freedom of association. Any gathering of more than two people is illegal unless registered first with the police. (Interpretation has been kept sufficiently lax so as not to inconvenience restaurant diners.) In line with the general principle of limited freedom to associate, the government has attempted to eliminate or control all groups with potential for independent interest articulation in order to make sure that no opposition force can coalesce around these groups.

> A citizen of the Republic of China [says an official directive] may organize a civil
> group by applying to the pertinent government authority for its permission; there-

after, this civic organization receives the *guidance and supervision* of the authorities concerned in its operations. At present, the Government is furnishing *positive
leadership* to civic organizations at all levels.

(Research, Development and Evaluation Commission of the
Executive Yuan, n.d. [1981]:166, emphasis added)

Indeed, as in other authoritarian-corporatist regimes, if the political leadership
senses demands for organizations in the populace it may move to create them
in order to control them from the start. Communications flow downwards from
the party to the officially recognized groups, in contrast to the upward flow
from groups to political leadership said to characterize democratic regimes.[5]

However, it must be remembered that the limits to state control and repression are also narrower than in communist regimes, as Gastil's scores suggest,
and this has been true from the beginning. Neither on the mainland nor in
Taiwan did the party try to abolish private property, which was sanctioned in
the ideology of Sun Yat-sen. So the regime attempted much less internal transformation than in the communist cases. Apart from that, the weakness of existing elites and organizations meant that to establish its preeminence the regime did not have to use such violence against potential counterelites as in
many of the communist cases. Also, the fact that the regime did not proclaim
itself as revolutionary, and indeed had lost a civil war to "communism," assured it of U.S. support; whereas the hostility of the West toward the Soviet
Union was one of the factors pushing the Soviet regime to retain tight control
over the peasantry and industrialization.

Controlling Students and Teachers

Universities are problematic institutions for political regimes of any kind, but
especially for authoritarian ones. There is a constant danger that faculty and
students will voice basic criticisms of the exclusionary political order, a danger compounded in cultures such as China's where scholars carry high prestige
in the society at large. The Nationalist party from the beginning gave careful
attention to preventing Taiwan's many universities from becoming centers of
dissent.

The result is a brilliant control system full of redundancy lest any part

---

[5] Associations have to be registered with the relevant ministry. If there is already an association
in broadly the same area the government is likely to refuse permission to register—and the informal penalties, rather than legal penalties, will insure that the association will not be formed if
permission is refused. In 1982 a group of mainly university-based biologists and ecologists proposed to establish a National Parks Association. There was no such organization in existence. The
group did its paperwork carefully, and thought the chances of getting permission were good. The
proposal went to the Ministry of the Interior, from where after months of delay came the reply
that the forestry department of the provincial government was thinking of establishing a similar
organization, and so the applying group should join that association when it came into existence
(under close government control).

should fail. First, the university president is chosen at very high levels of government, the faculty having virtually no say. For the several most prestigious universities, the president of the republic himself has selected the appointee, and the premier has a large say in all the others. Second, the faculty have no tenure; they are on two- or three-year contracts, and the fact that the contracts are virtually always renewed does not remove an individual's knowledge that if he expresses dissent on such issues as the role of the party or the government's claim to be the legitimate ruler of China his contract may not be renewed. Third, faculty promotions are decided within the Education Ministry, on recommendation from the university. Fourth, the faculty in the more potentially troublesome departments like political science, sociology, and law have been mostly mainlanders, who are unlikely to make serious criticisms of the regime.

Fifth, each campus contains many professional military officers who serve as "military tutors." The one or two assigned to every department teach the two-hours-a-week course on military matters which is compulsory for first- and second-year male students (nursing for women). They also act as "master" of each student dormitory. Whether in the department or the dormitory they are concerned to keep abreast of what the students are doing and advise them on extracurricular activities. They expect to be notified in advance of meetings the students plan to hold. Sixth, students are under a tight disciplinary system, such that if they get more than a certain number of graded penalties they can be expelled. Taking part in political activities on behalf of non-party political candidates is grounds for such discipline. The penalties are entered on the students' university record given to prospective employers. Seventh, the student council is elected by an elaborately tiered method of indirect representation, which can be readily manipulated to insure pliability. Eighth, the party has fairly active branches among students and faculty, and is generally assumed to have an extensive network of informers.

Given all this, it is no surprise that university faculty who are critical of the status quo will rarely speak out at public meetings or even in private meetings with students. They save all but "technocratic" criticism for trusted colleagues. Students are under family pressure to refrain from political activity, especially because of the risk of expulsion. In 1987, when television began to show pictures of demonstrators outside the legislative assembly, it was not uncommon for parents to ring up their children to check that they were not present. "You endanger not only yourself but also your family," they warn.

But the groundwork for this system of control has already been well prepared in the schools. Quite apart from the content of what school students are taught about discipline and obedience, the sheer amount of formal instruction keeps them in line. The school day is from 8 a.m. to 4:30 p.m. on weekdays and 8 a.m. to noon on Saturdays, for eight months a year, in classes of forty-five or more. However, by the age of twelve or thirteen those whose parents or teachers aspire for them to do more than the minimum will be having extra lessons. The objective is to score well enough in the high school entrance examination to enter a good high school, which is marked out by its ability to get its students through the intensely competitive national university entrance examination into the best universities. So it is that by age thirteen, children who are bright and/or have parents of means and ambition will be taking over sixty hours a week of formal instruction. Take, for example, the eighth-year class (twelve to thirteen year olds) of a school in a certain medium-sized city. About one-third of the four hundred pupils follow this timetable: Monday–Friday, arrive at school at 7 A.M. for one hour of supervised preparation for the day's schoolwork; leave school at 5:30–6:00 P.M. after additional lessons. Saturday, arrive at 7 A.M.; leave about 8:30 P.M., after an afternoon of extra science and an evening of extra English. Sunday morning, two to three hours of additional mathematics. In the wealthier suburbs of Taipei the hours are even longer, because the extra weekday lessons run into the evening. It goes without saying that the four months of holidays are also filled with private lessons—except when the children are on cheap summer holidays in the great outdoors organized by the party's Youth Corps. Parents normally pay for the extra lessons on Saturday, Sunday, and holidays, and teachers with good examination records can easily double their salaries.

On top of all this, most young men in Taiwan have had to take between two and three years of full-time military training. (University graduates get by with a little less because of their compulsory first- and second-year military training courses.) With so much of their formative years spent in the closely controlled institutions of schools, summer camps, universities, and the military, Taiwan's young people have not had time for casual fun, crime, drugs, or dissident political thoughts.

Building Support—Participation and Ideology

From the beginning the Nationalist party on Taiwan realized that preventing dissent alone was not a viable strategy of rule. It attempted to win more active support by assimilating the islander population to the regime.

One of the first steps was land reform. The more than three hundred thousand hectares that changed hands constitutes one of the biggest (noncommunist) land reforms on record. The reform gave land to people who might have fed a revolt, thereby giving the bulk of rural dwellers a stake in the new regime—all the more important when the Chinese Communist party was carrying out a land reform on the mainland, knowledge of which could incite landless Taiwanese cultivators against the Nationalists. It also removed the existing concentrations of wealth in the countryside, which though small in scale might have constituted the focal point for counterelite organization. Since the land reform no landlord group has existed to exercise power, maintain social stability, and supply the cities with food. With little class differentiation there have been no clear oppositions which could drive those who see themselves as more privileged to identify with the state as protector of their privileges, and to act in some sense as the state's local agents. Hence the state has had to undertake the task of control more directly. At the same time, opportunities for doing so are not limited by having to share power with local landlords. The state accordingly followed up the land reform by organizing farmers into farmers associations and irrigation associations (or more exactly, by reactivating the associations that the Japanese had established). The party dominated the associations—and their functions were too important for islander farmers to remain uninvolved. Within the associations limited scope has been allowed for elected councils. Rural people have met the party not only through the farmers and irrigation associations, but also through public service centers. Public service centers, one for each township, are staffed by full-time party officials whose job it is to advance party interests and maintain surveillance over the associations and the local government administration.

In addition the party took the unusual step of allowing elections to local and provincial government bodies. ("Provincial" government existed as a separate level, because of the fiction that the central government was the government of all China, and so needed a separate government for Taiwan province.) Nonparty candidates could and did stand against party candidates in these elections, and win. The electoral competitions between party and nonparty candidates have frequently been very lively. The majority of voters were islanders, and voter turnout has been consistently high (rarely less than 70 percent). The party has been forced to adopt islander candidates in order to have a chance of winning, and so has been forced to assimilate islanders into the party membership. Local factional considerations have often predominated over the requirements of the party apparatus in the choice of candidates. Since nominees with their own vote banks are partly independent, the need to win local elections has tended to erode the power of the party organization at the base.

However, while these elections have increased the participation of islanders in the political system, no significant resources have been at stake at these levels. The party took great care to keep the rewards mainly symbolic. Real power continued to lie at central levels, where mainlanders predominated. The synapse is most visible in the provincial government, where the provincial assembly is elected but the provincial executive is appointed by the central government (Jacobs 1978:244). The national legislature, which purports to represent all of China, is still composed largely of mainlanders elected on the mainland before 1949, but is also without significant power.[6] ("It is like an

[6] On the recently increasing power of the legislature, see chapter 9. As of Feb. 1988, the legislative yuan had 312 members. Of these 216 were "old" members elected on the mainland (average age eighty-one), ninety-six were "supplemental" members elected on Taiwan since 1949. Of the supplemental members, seventy were native Taiwanese. Of the total of 312, all but

eyebrow,'' says one of its younger members. "It does nothing useful, but shave it off and you'd look silly": Sandeman 1982a.) In short, to quote Edwin Winckler, "Elections have functioned largely as control devices for co-opting local elites" (1984:482).

The land reform, the reestablishment of farmers' associations, and the introduction of local and provincial elections took place in the early 1950s and represented the party's first attempt to win popular support from the islanders.

Subsequently, the party has laid great stress on the development of mass organizations that incorporate particular social groups into the body politic—not only to prevent the emergence of alternative organizations but also to represent their interests. Winckler summarizes the pattern:

> In the legitimation sector the party has a mass role. It approves values, supervises education and monitors the media. It orchestrates the election and meeting of representative institutions, and performs ombudsman and welfare roles at the local level. It runs such mass organizations as the Youth Corps and Women's Association. Similarly, the security sector does not just repress mass participation, but also incorporates significant public groups. The political warfare system has a pervasive network of agents and clients, including many politicians whose careers it has aided. Police, particularly the ordinary civil police, constitute another important channel for offering services and mobilizing votes. (1984:492)

The mass organizations of the legitimation and security sectors plus the industrial associations of the developmental sector therefore

> give the ordinary citizen numerous alternative channels of access to the state through which he can pursue his private concerns. In addition, most people have numerous contacts within the political-economic establishment deriving from their personal networks, quite apart from organizational memberships. Both elite and ordinary individuals on Taiwan remain more likely to pursue individual interests through private contacting for individual favors than through collective lobbying to achieve legislative change. (Winckler 1984:493)

Complementing the mass cooptation strategy, the party launched an intensive campaign to win support by ideological molding. Sun Yat-sen had been well aware of the importance of shaping people's beliefs and desires as a technique of directive rule; for the more completely their beliefs and desires are molded, the more completely the government can cause them to act in a particular fashion without them seeing themselves as forced to act against their own will. One would expect in the general case that the state ideology would be more elaborated, its promulgation more vigorous, the greater the perceived

thirty-three were Nationalist party members. Of the thirty-three, thirteen were members of the newly formed Democratic Progressive party, eleven were members of the old and strictly nominal opposition parties, and nine were independents. The eleven members of the old opposition parties should more accurately be included as Nationalist party members (*China Times*, 4 Feb. 1988).

threat to sovereignty from powerful neighbors and the more dangerous the internal cleavages are seen to be. In extreme cases, one finds a cult of the leader, mass mobilization, and a blending of the metaphors of nation and family such that the state is considered an extension of the family. Maoist China, Kim Il Sung's North Korea, Ceausescu's Romania, and Japan between the two World Wars are clear examples. President Park of South Korea was the subject of an ever growing personality cult until his abrupt demise in 1979 (Cumings forthcoming).

In Taiwan the nation, the family, and obedience to authority have been constant themes, rallied around the symbols of Sun Yat-sen, Chiang Kai-shek, the national flag, and the Three Principles of the People.[7] Sun is officially described as "one of history's greatest and most successful revolutionaries," "the father of the people," "founder of the Republic." His Three Principles of the People—nationalism, democracy, and livelihood, which define the appropriate role of central control and individual freedom, of government and markets—are presented as the superior catechism to communism. Chiang Kai-shek, on the other hand, is portrayed as a military man ("from boyhood his dream was to be a warrior"), as the "savior" of the nation rather than the teacher, and the myths that school children are taught about him highlight his self discipline, frugality, and determination to succeed at all costs. He is "one of history's great men of all times." When he died in 1975 a competition was held for a memorial design befitting his stature. From many entries, his son (now president) chose a design with a strong resemblance to the palace at Peking where the emperor went once a year to worship the heavens and ask for their blessings.

School children begin their day with a flag-raising and anthem-singing ceremony, and end the day with a simpler ceremony to lower the flag. Even toddlers in nursery school, before they can sing the anthem, undertake flag rituals. Youth Corps camps in the summer begin the day with a solemn flag ceremony accompanied by the anthem and a reading from Sun Yat-sen. On national holidays—the anniversary of the 1911 Revolution, the birthdays of Sun Yat-sen and Chiang Kai-shek—all houses are expected to display the national flag, and most do; if not they will be reminded by their friendly neighborhood policeman. Cinema audiences solemnly rise to their feet at the start to hear the national anthem and witness an uplifting documentary on the life of Sun Yat-sen, Chiang Kai-shek, Chiang Ching-kuo, and the many economic achievements of the Republic of China. All important gatherings sponsored by a public authority—down to the level of the annual meeting of the members of an industrial association (though not the monthly directors' meetings), or a faculty meeting at the teachers' training university (which is more party-influ-

---

[7] The quotations which follow are from *Republic of China, A Reference Book*, Government Information Office, 1983.

enced than most other universities)—commence with the congregation rising to its feet to sing the national anthem. The chairman then recites the last testament of Sun Yat-sen in semiliturgical tones, the congregation bows three times to the portrait of Sun, and sits down. Photos of Sun and Chiang abound in places such as school assembly rooms or meeting rooms in state agencies and public enterprises. Larger-than-life statues of both Sun and Chiang are to be found in front of the town railway station, in the entrance to a public enterprise headquarters, in botanical gardens, and in every school. Statuary is a common idiom in China, and on Taiwan many other people are commemorated in this way, but Sun and Chiang win hands down in terms of numbers and size.

Intensive teaching of the Three Principles of the People continues today. High school students study it throughout their career for two hours a week. One of the six compulsory papers for university entrance is on the political thought of Sun Yat-sen, the significance being that competition to get into university—any university—is intense, only 30 percent of applicants being accepted. At the university they continue to study the political thought of Sun Yat-sen for two hours a week over one year, as a compulsory course (in addition to military instruction). During the two to three years of military service for young men, Sun Yat-sen-ism is again heavily impressed.

Both inside and outside the formal teaching of Sun's thought, the underlying theme is put across that the student's first duty is loyalty to the country—and "country" means *both* the whole of China *and* the government on Taiwan—the latter then being symbolically equated, during his lifetime, with the person of Chiang Kai-shek. China is big and rich in potential, they are taught; Taiwan is small and poor. The separation from the rest of China is unnatural. The communists have "stolen" the government of China. Hence the Chinese-language press always refers to the mainland government leaders as "bandits" (Deng Chou-ping becomes Deng Bandit Chou-ping); and the government collectively is always referred to as the "false Chinese government." If *Time* magazine publishes a photo of a PRC leader, the distributor must stamp each copy with the work "bandit" before sale; if a popular Hong Kong magazine shows a PRC soldier, the distributor must ink out the star on the soldier's cap.[8] In school, the geography syllabus gives as much space to mainland China as to Taiwan and the rest of the world. And it is the geography of pre-1949 China, taught as though it were the present. A child who refers to a province which did not exist before 1949 (perhaps because she has heard of it from her grandparents recently returned from a visit) will be marked wrong.

The three state-owned television networks are even blander than the news-

---

[8] This does not always apply at English language bookshops frequented by foreigners. I have seen shopgirls wearily working their way down a towering pile of magazines, opening each one to a set page, banging the ink stamp onto the smiling face of a PRC leader, closing it, transferring it to a growing pile on the other side, and beginning again with the next one.

papers, celebrating Confucian family relationships and the martial arts, with American fun-and-dance shows for variety. State-sponsored slapstick humor has been used to hammer home social lessons: that children should respect their parents, husbands should not gamble away the family's income, businessmen should not cheat their customers.

The main aim of this ideological effort is to create a sense of common Chineseness amongst the whole population, islanders and mainlanders alike, to make them all part of the "chosen" political force against the regime on the mainland under the direction of the Nationalist party; while at the same time preserving structural arrangements which give the Nationalist party an almost exclusive power and prevent islanders from enjoying more than a sprinkling of top leadership positions.

Building Support—Economic Development

In the early postwar period the development-oriented technocrats were overshadowed by the military. The military gave top priority to the reconquest of the mainland, in the interests of which it wanted continued state control of the Taiwan economy for purposes of defense and social stability. Only gradually, by the late 1950s, was economic development given top priority. By this time it was clear that the communist regime on the mainland was firmly consolidated, making an assault from Taiwan unlikely to succeed. The U.S. government threatened a cut-off in aid if such an assault were attempted. The party elders came to see that economic development could be a better guarantee of the party's survival—it would soften the islanders' resentment of their exclusion from real power, and would allow the mainlanders to prosper on Taiwan without having to reclaim their position and assets on the mainland. For these reasons the military began to lose influence in the state as a whole, while the economic technocrats gained (Amsden 1984a). As rapid economic development occurred, repression, controlled participation, and ideological molding became adjuncts to the central basis of legitimacy: the claim to be able to govern so as to generate mass prosperity, as the People's Republic could not, and hence to win a moral if not a military victory. Conversely, the repossession of China, which had begun "as a fierce resolve . . . became an aspiration, then a myth, then a liturgy" (Crozier 1976:351).

This shift in the top priority of state action went with a decline in the influence of the military and the party over economic decision-making, restoring the power of the technocrats. The National Resources Commission on the mainland in the 1930s and 1940s enjoyed a considerable autonomy from party and military, as we noted earlier. It is worth describing how this autonomy came to be established, in order to deepen understanding of how the industrial policy-makers on Taiwan were able to be free of politics for most of the postwar period, the Leninist character of the party notwithstanding.[9] The technocrats of the Nationalist government during the 1920s had clear aims for industrial development in China, but were defeated by the structure of government. Responsibility for industrial policy was so diffused that no less than five ministries claimed to be in charge of China's industrial policy for much of the 1920s and early 1930s. And politics, not proficiency, determined appointments to leading economic policy positions, resulting in the estrangement from the government of some of China's most talented scientists, engineers, and planners. However, the shock of Japan's seizure of Manchuria in 1931 and the resulting sense of external threat finally convinced the political leadership that, like it or not, it had to rely on "scientific" government planners organized in a highly educated and nonpolitical (but patriotic) bureaucracy. In particular, Chiang Kai-shek, who dominated the political leadership from his military position, came to accept this view. With his support, a decisive change was affected in higher education, from an emphasis on liberal studies to an emphasis on "utilitarian" subjects like engineering. And in 1932 the National Planning Defense Commission was formed, working directly with Chiang Kai-shek to formulate a long-term plan and prepare for war mobilization. In 1935 it changed its name to the National Resources Commission. Over the next fifteen years it retained a large measure of autonomy from the party and the military, even as it expanded rapidly in size. Being seen as the agency running the "national defense enterprises" at a time of national emergency gave legitimacy to its technocratic orientation. Chiang Kai-shek recognized that a large cadre of experts in production and planning were needed for the very survival of his regime. He appointed senior officials who themselves strongly believed in keeping the organization free of political interference. One of them summarized his philosophy roughly as follows: "governments and political forms are transitory, the problems facing a nation are not." Hence the commission recruited its employees largely on the basis of technical expertise. Ideologues in the party criticized the commission for its stance; but in the disputes between "experts and pinks," the experts won, unlike the outcome when the dispute reemerged under Mao in the 1960s.

So by 1949 the technocrats had already won a large measure of independence from party and military control. They lost some of it for a time in the 1950s, but regained it toward the end of the decade. They regained it not only because the goal changed from military reconquest, but also because many of the party ideologues did not come to Taiwan. U.S. advisors strongly helped the technocrats, and Chiang Kai-shek reasserted his support. Bureaucratic autonomy expanded again in the mid-1970s, as Chiang Ching-kuo gained effective control. He was less preoccupied than his father with loyalty to his per-

---

[9] The following account of the NRC comes from an excellent paper by Kirby 1986. For further details, see Kirby (forthcoming).

sonal convictions, and still more concerned to recruit the central economic decision-makers according to demonstrated technical abilities.

THE RESPONSE TO POLITICAL DISCONTENT

Economic development proved to be, not surprisingly, double edged. As economic opportunities expanded, the islanders absorbed themselves in business and local government elections. After fifty years of passivity under the Japanese, their political consciousness was not high. But as they became more educated, urbanized, and secure, many began to feel their exclusion from real power. ("I have just produced the future vice president," said an islander in 1983 to announce the birth of his son. "Why *vice*-president?" asked a foreigner. "Because my son and I, we are [native] Taiwanese.")[10] Even within the mainlander group, the legitimacy of ethnic exclusion and Nationalist party monopoly came to be questioned. Periodically, resentment at the Nationalist party's monopoly of real power has resulted in stunning electoral defeats. In 1964, for example, nonparty candidates were elected as mayors in three of Taiwan's five major cities, contrary to Nationalist party intentions. Again in 1977 Nationalist party nominees suffered an unprecedented number of defeats at the hands of nonparty candidates, including twelve out of sixty-nine nominees for the Taiwan provincial assembly (Jacobs 1979). These successes encouraged still more non Nationalist politicians to enter politics, and emboldened Nationalist politicians to consider the alternative of an independent candidacy.

The government has responded in several ways. One is repression, to control disunity within the elite and prevent manifestation of mass dissatisfaction. The apparatus of security services, police, and informers has been strengthened. Escalations on both sides after the 1977 election surprises and the sense of national crisis as the United States moved toward derecognition led to the suspension of the December 1978 elections and the arrest or exile of the more extreme opposition leaders.

A second step has been to transform the party from an elite vanguard to more of a party of mass incorporation. By 1976–77 the rate of membership to total population was greater than in all but two of the sixteen ruling Communist parties (10.4 percent), having been more restrictive than half of the communist cases in 1970–71 (Jacobs 1978:242). Now membership is put at about two million in a population of eighteen million, and islanders are said to comprise about two-thirds of the total membership (but 85 percent or more of the total population). At powerful levels of the party, too, the proportion of native Taiwanese has increased: in the 1984 standing committee of the party islanders

[10] In 1988 Lee Tang-hui, a native Taiwanese, was made president on the death of Chiang Ching-kuo.

account for over a third of the membership, and the 1984 cabinet is two-fifths islanders.

A third measure has been to allow more opposition; for example, by permitting an increase in the number of nonparty candidates—with the vital proviso that the nonparty candidates do not come together to form an organized opposition. Before late 1986 the articulation of organized opposition was allowed only within the framework of the single party, a situation paralleled in many communist countries.[11] When the suspended central elections of 1978 finally occurred in 1980, the nonparty candidates received 30 percent of the vote and 2 percent of the seats (Winckler 1984:494). By accepting this result the government demonstrated that it could live with a more substantial opposition than hitherto. At the same time, the Nationalist party began to concentrate huge amounts of expertise on planning election strategies (many of Taiwan's best political scientists now devote themselves to this task). In the 1983 elections, the Nationalist party did somewhat better, the nonparty opposition somewhat worse than in 1980. This was less because of shifts in public opinion or social structure than because of the Nationalists' growing sophistication in electoral strategy and the inability of the loosely organized opposition movement to discipline itself (Winckler 1984:495–96).

There has also been a gradual liberalization in the content of politics. Even in the 1950s and 1960s, it is important to remember, politics was not totalitarian: outside the schools and army the regime did not insist that people should say or write the required things in the approved form; it only insisted that they not say certain things of which it disapproved (especially criticism of the president, praise of the People's Republic, or support for an independent state run by the native Taiwanese majority). There were always limits to the development of a fully-blown cult of the leader and a mobilizatory politics. One never found, for example, that works on economics and politics had to be spliced with quotations from Sun Yat-sen nor even affixed with an obligatory frontpiece quotation. The massed politics of the street, so important in fascist Germany and Italy, have been absent. The only attempt to get a massed rally together has been on the anniversary of the founding of the Republic, October 10, when attendance is obligatory for school children, civil servants, officials of industry associations, and the like. But most people, even on this occasion, stay at home or go walking in the mountains, as everyone does on the two saints' birthdays. It has always been uncommon for photos of the leaders to be displayed in private homes. Above all, the metaphorical overlaying of nation and family has been weak. The family is given great importance as the unit of primary obligation, and so too is the nation, but the nation is not presented as an extension of the family. The leader's family is not held up as a

[11] The government acquiesced in the decision of the nonparty candidates to form an organized opposition party (Democratic Progressive party) to fight the Dec. 1986 election.

model of virtue for the rest of the citizenry to emulate, neither in the case of Sun Yat-sen, nor Chiang Kai-shek, nor Chiang Ching-kuo.[12] In this sense Taiwan has always been less totalitarian than Japan between the two World Wars or South Korea during much of the Park era.

Nontotalitarian elements have become much more pronounced since the mid-1970s. Chiang Kai-shek's son, who became president in 1978, has tried to establish a less autocratic, more populist image for himself. "President Chiang Ching-kuo is a man of the people. He seeks his inspiration and sustenance from them in frequent trips to the countryside. . . . An accessible President, he is famous for his street chats with residents of the island . . . [with whom he enjoys] personal bonds . . . approximating a familiar relationship," says the official government account. "He stepped into some of Asia's biggest shoes and they fitted him perfectly." Chiang Ching-kuo presents himself on these occasions not as guide and instructor, but as a kindly uncle taking an interest in how his charges are getting on (Durdin 1975). His birthday is not a national holiday, though the papers, radio, and television carry lengthy eulogies.

This change in the president's image has been accompanied by a general softening of the militaristic, mobilizing qualities of the regime. The exhortatory slogans—"Protecting national secrets is the responsibility of all of us," "Guard against the bandits" (mainland spies), "Unite to retake the mainland," and the like—have been removed from public buildings, universities, and schools. On the large bare spaces thus revealed many schools display attractive designs with no political content whatsoever. (But the slogans are still there on post boxes and on shopping receipts, the latter also providing a telephone number in case you find a spy.) Till the late 1970s it would be common for someone coming to a new post in a public office or in the educational system to be given a ceremonial plate or cup with a portrait of Chiang Kai-shek on it; but not today. Till then, anyone going abroad would be warned against having contact with mainlanders; now, if anything, people may be

---

[12] Chiang Ching-kuo lived for twelve years in the Soviet Union, has a Russian wife, and is popularly believed to have at least two illegitimate sons. His father, also Moscow-trained, had three wives. It is said on insider authority that the president retains a secret link with the Soviet Communist party, on the "your enemy's enemy is your friend" principle, his anticommunist rhetoric notwithstanding. See Durdin 1975 on the president's twelve years in the Soviet Union. "In Moscow he was a bright, quick learner at Sun Yat-sen University, a training center the Russians had set up . . . for Chinese revolutionary cadres. Impressed by the frugality and discipline shown by Chinese communist students at the university in contrast to the loose behavior of some Kuomintang [Nationalist] enrollees he joined the Communist Youth Corps. . . . [Later] he became the leader of a secret Trotskyite student underground among the Chinese . . ." (pp. 96–97). Then he joined the Soviet army, became an alternate member of the Russian Communist party, and rapidly climbed the promotion ladder, becoming chief of staff at a division at his military academy. He wrote a major thesis on tactics of guerrilla warfare. Later, he was forced to labor on a collective farm and then in a Siberian gold mine. He managed to return to China in 1937.

encouraged to take with them glossy publications on the achievements of Taiwan in order to show them to mainlanders, amongst others. The intensive training of students and teachers in the Three Principles, at frequent intervals, has been much diminished. High school mathematics teachers, for example, in a two-week refresher course at university, used to have two full days set aside for political teaching; since 1981, no longer. Nowadays, ideological appeals are increasingly limited to schools and barrack rooms, television, and to Western governments, firms, and journalists who need reminding of Taiwan's anticommunist, procapitalist, free-market stance.

As the government has softened its use of ideological appeals since the mid-1970s, so it has become less jittery about criticism. There is now a two-week "no holds barred" period in the run-up to elections at which candidates can say almost anything at public meetings, as long as the meetings are not televised. It has even been possible in the 1980s for a candidate to declare from a public platform that Chiang Ching-kuo is the source of all corruption in the land and not be thrown into jail—despite an electoral law which expressly forbids any criticism of the head of state. (A candidate who in 1975 said more or less the same thing is still incarcerated.) In the face of opposition criticism of the continued imposition of martial law a cabinet minister recently argued that it had been lifted in all but name. "It only takes away three percent of your freedoms," he said, a remark which led opposition journals to speculate disrespectfully on where he got the 3 percent from, and yet they were not penalized.[13]

Along with these other changes, there has been, finally, a marked change in the party's definition of its role, from a source of initiative to a source of coherence and order. In economic affairs its functions have been increasingly concentrated on: (1) providing a channel through which the views of important socioeconomic groups can be heard, without reducing the semi-insulation of the economic bureaucrats; and (2) putting pressure on the economic ministries to give more weight to workers' welfare. The party's department of social affairs is concerned to keep watch over important industries, among other ways by arranging meetings of representatives of these industries. Not much dialogue of this sort takes place even within the party; but what the party does is nevertheless important because of the dearth of other forums within which

[13] The minister was Minister of the Interior Lin. One account of the origin of the 3 percent appeared in an opposition monthly under the title "Where Minister Lin Got His Three Percent From." An (unidentified) man visiting the whorehouse was asked to wear a condom. He protested. "But why should you object?" she asked. "It only covers three percent of your body." The journal was not censored. Native Taiwanese recognize that Lin is one of the few islanders in a senior political position; that the top-most people in government, themselves mainlanders, are not wholly averse to fun being made of prominent native Taiwanese because it lends support to their protestations: "We keep trying to bring you (native Taiwanese) on, but look how silly you are."

dialogue might take place. The party has insisted upon some of the price "distortions" much disliked by economists, such as subsidies to farmers and subsidies on items of essential consumption, and has kept pressing the relevant government ministries to give serious attention to a labor pension and insurance scheme. Following the 1973 oil price rise, the party insisted that the price of diesel fuel be increased by less than the price of gasoline (50 percent, against an 85 percent increase in gasoline). This was especially to soften the cost increases on public transportation and on fishermen (a strategic group in the government's eyes, because of their ability to traffic undetected with the mainland). As one free marketeer complained, "The President is not an economist—he came up through the military. He thinks the government should use its political power to take care of poor people. So the rice price is subsidized to keep poor people happy, and diesel oil is subsidized to keep the people who use the buses happy. It has taken us years of fighting to convince the government that this is not the thing to do—it should let those things run in a business-like fashion. But the government always tries to please the people." Indeed, many businessmen and officials privately criticize the Nationalist party's "little fellow" philosophy, by which, they say, the judgment always goes in favor of the one who is less well off. On labor-management arbitration boards (to which a worker might appeal if given an unfairly small retirement bonus, for example) the obligatory Nationalist party official always leans over backwards in favor of the worker, or so employers grumble.

The change in the party's role took place much earlier in the economic sphere than elsewhere. But as suggested earlier, the same general trend is apparent, with a lag of ten years or so, in other contexts, so that since the mid- to late 1970s the party has become primarily concerned with integration and order. One indicator of this change is the rapid expansion in membership in the 1970s, reducing the party's vanguard character. Nevertheless, the top party bodies still have the right to approve or veto important policies, including in the military, foreign affairs, and even the economic jurisdictions.

Finally, in 1987 the government lifted martial law for the first time since 1949, and at the end of 1986, acquiesced when election candidates opposing the Nationalist party formed an opposition party (the Democratic Progressive party). The aged and ailing President Chiang Ching-kuo determined to leave his mark on history as the man who transformed Taiwan from a one-party state reigned by partisans elected forty years ago on the mainland to something closer to a liberal democracy in the Japanese style. China's emerging economic virtues in 1985, President Marcos's ouster from the Philippines in 1986, and South Korean students' protests at President Chun's attempts to rig the nomination of his successor in 1987, may have helped to force his hand. Allowing the opposition party breaks new ground in Chinese history—it is the first time a Chinese government has recognized legitimate opposition, and it constitutes a profound modification of the founding myth of the Republic of China, that the identity of the state is defined by the ideology of the party.

CONCLUSIONS

The state in Taiwan is both authoritarian and corporatist. Very limited scope for popular preferences in the selection of rulers goes with tight restrictions on interest groups. Indeed, the state sanctions a small number of interest groups and gives them a monopoly of representation. Austria, Norway, Sweden, and Switzerland are among the other countries which fit the criteria of corporatism (Schmitter 1981; Zeigler 1988). But those countries choose their rulers by democratic rather than authoritarian means. Partly as a consequence, their interest groups have more power in relations with the state than do interest groups in Taiwan.

How well does Taiwan fit Johnson's model of the political institutions of the developmental state? It clearly meets the condition of "a virtual monopoly of political power in a single party or institution for a long period of time." It clearly has a panoply of "reigning-not-ruling" institutions. On the other hand, "politicians," in the sense of office holders in these "reigning" bodies, are less important than in Johnson's model, because the "holding off" and "safety valve" functions are less necessary. They are less necessary because civil society is kept weakly organized to limit groups within it from exerting autonomous demands on the state. "Politicians" in the sense of members of the political executive, however, are more important than in Johnson's model, in relation to both the legislature and the bureaucracy.

Recruitment to the political executive is determined by the party, whose criteria do not depend mainly on wealth. This type of arrangement blocks the transformation of business profits into real political power, but allows transformation of profits into largely symbolic power at more parochial levels of the system. In Johnson's model the same blockage of wealth into real power is attained by removal of real power from the political executive.

Johnson's account also leaves out the military. Yet Taiwan, like Korea, is not merely a militarized regime; it is a militarized society. The military has veto power over the selection of the top-most political leaders; and beyond this, it inculcates military notions of discipline, authority, and vigilance throughout the society.

Civil society is kept weakly organized by measures that go well beyond Johnson's soft authoritarianism. Indeed, even today the state shows resemblances to a Leninist party-state. It lacks the element of class struggle, and it explicitly sanctions private property and markets; but it shares with Leninist states a need to limit commitments to existing groups, a sense of urgency to develop, a comprehensive perspective on the development problem, and a tutelary notion of government.

These conditions have helped to produce Taiwan's exceptional political stability—an absence of insurgencies, military coups, mass demonstrations common in other poor countries, and sharp swings in the direction of policies.

The 1970s have seen a softening of the authoritarian qualities of the regime, a greater tolerance for criticism, a blunting of martial law, and an emergence of multiple centers of power. These moderating trends reflect growing mass affluence coupled with the sheer "historical givenness" of the system, which together provide a powerful basis of legitimacy independent of ideology. Furthermore, the external threat from the mainland has become much less pressing, while the durability of the communist regime eroded any serious intention of toppling it by invasion. As old memories go, and several generations of islander children learn nothing but Mandarin in school, so the split between mainlanders and native Taiwanese becomes less important in daily life (though it remains important in terms of politics and recruitment to the top levels of the state).[14] We can agree with Winckler's assessment of the future: "Taiwan's political leadership will continue to substitute soft sell for hard measures at approximately the rate that new political strategies are necessary to achieve the old political outcome—Nationalist dominance" (1984:499). The Nationalist party's political strategists have been paying the closest attention to how Japan's Liberal Democratic party has managed for thirty years to avoid any serious danger of being removed from office in free elections.

Yet what is striking, I think, is how late this softening comes—long after the regime was well formalized and institutionalized, long after the threat from the mainland receded, long after the period of economic breakthrough, long after living standards began to rise for everyone. In terms of Gastil's measures of political and civil rights, the liberalizing trends of the 1970s were sufficient only to move Taiwan from eleven out of fourteen in 1972 to ten out of fourteen in 1983 (the lower the score the better the record), a change which simply maintained its position about halfway down a ranking of middle-income countries.[15] Perhaps no regime with a tight control apparatus lets up until the volume of disaffection generated by the controls begins to exceed the probable volume of disaffection which the controls suppress. Perhaps the delivery of a

[14] Says Bruce Jacobs, an authority on Taiwanese politics, "the Taiwanese/Mainlander split has become less important. There has been more intermarriage and an increase in Mandarin speaking among (native) Taiwanese of Taipei. Several of my 'opposition' friends who are in jail now for supposedly Taiwanese Independence 'crimes' have children who only speak Mandarin!" (personal communication, Sept. 1984)

[15] Thirty-one out of fifty-eight middle-income countries had lower scores (wider or better protected freedoms) than Taiwan in 1983. Taiwan's score put it with Tunisia, Egypt, Sudan, Liberia, Ivory Coast, Paraguay, and the Philippines. Korea stayed at eleven out of fourteen in 1983, falling to the bottom third of the ranking (Gastil 1984). Korea, a close U.S. ally and beneficiary of forty thousand U.S. troops stationed there to defend it from communist attack, ranked the same as Nicaragua in 1983, whose Sandinista government's curtailment of civil and political rights has been highlighted by supporters of the Reagan administration's attempts indirectly to overthrow it.

continuously rising living standard, plus the fact that singing daily hymns to the regime is considered normal and not an irksome infringement of an individual's time or musical taste or right to withhold applause for the powers-that-be, prevented disaffection with the controls from rising to that point. In any case, the regime has continued to be deeply preoccupied with the legitimacy question, with insuring its survival in power. Its industrial policy has been much affected by this preoccupation, as also by the content of its ideology.

Chapter 9

POLITICS OF INVESTMENT AND INDUSTRIAL POLICY

TAIWAN'S AUTHORITARIAN and corporatist politics give power firmly to the state. But what are the economic goals to which the power of the state is directed? And how are those goals translated into policies, with what role for which interest groups? It is well to remember that Mexico, hardly a model of economic success, also has authoritarian and corporatist political arrangements, but directed at different goals and with different interest groups.

In Chalmers Johnson's picture of the developmental state, the bureaucracy directing economic development is protected from all but the most powerful interest groups so that it can set and achieve long-range industrial policies. On the other hand, all the East Asian developmental states, according to Johnson, depend to a high degree on public/private cooperation between the managers of the state and the managers of private enterprise. "This cooperation is achieved through innumerable, continuously operating forums for coordinating views and investment plans, sharing international commercial intelligence, making adjustments to conform to the business cycle or other changes in the economic environment, deciding on the new industries needed in order to maintain international competitive ability" (1981a:13). The resulting conservative coalition between the state and big business provides the social foundation for industrial policy.

This picture, however, takes too much for granted. It assumes that the wider configuration of classes in society is such as to encourage industrial investment. It assumes that the institutions of policy-making are used to promote a strategic policy choice in favor of industrialization. And it assumes that the main producers are private rather than public enterprises. Absent these conditions, the same institutional structure of Johnson's developmental state might be used for different objectives (macroeconomic stability plus income redistribution, for example), or might use different means of coordination between central officials and producers (through ownership control, for example). I shall argue that while Taiwan fits Johnson's "bureaucratic autonomy" condition, it does not fit his "public/private cooperation" condition.[1]

---

[1] Johnson does not examine the tension between the "autonomy" and "cooperation" conditions. Since I argue that the second condition hardly applies to Taiwan, I do not examine it either.

STRATEGIC CHOICES

Why have the state leaders placed so high a priority on economic growth and industrialization? Why have they created and maintained a structure of investment which restricts the use of wealth for unproductive purposes? And why have they exercised a leadership role in parts of the economy, especially by using public enterprises?

Recall the circumstances of the Nationalist party's arrival in Taiwan. The existing structure of state-society relations, shaped by Japanese colonial government during fifty years, placed a strong, production-oriented state over and apart from a weakly organized civil society. The incoming Nationalists had no existing ties and commitments in Taiwan. A sizable part of an administration and army designed to rule several hundred million people was squeezed onto an island of six million, causing massive social dislocation. The resident population was economically homogeneous, because the Japanese had kept it that way and because war-time damage and inflation made it still more so. The population had no experience of self-rule and lacked organization with which to resist. U.S. aid, amounting to 6 percent of GNP through the 1950s, provided the state with the necessary resources to exercise great leverage over the economy. The island's small economic size and lack of natural resources meant that the range of options about the broad direction of economic policy was narrow. Agriculture was already well developed by the end of the Japanese era.

These circumstances—above all, a weakly organized society facing a strongly organized state—facilitated the emphasis on industrialization and state leadership in the economy. But circumstances do not make choices. The response might have been different. To understand what happened, we need to know about the broad concerns which helped to guide the leaders' response. These concerns of the leaders on Taiwan reflected debates and experience on the mainland before 1949. In particular, they derived from the economic philosophy of Sun Yat-sen, from the experience of the National Resources Commission, and from the leaders' diagnosis of the causes of the mainland defeat.

Sun's Economic Philosophy

Chinese culture has always emphasized the didactic and initiatory role of the leader, who is assumed to lead because of superior knowledge. Sun Yat-sen's philosophy made this general idea the basis for a forceful endorsement of government leadership in the economy. The pivotal issue for Sun, as for all Chinese leaders since the country's ignominious defeat in the Opium Wars of the mid-nineteenth century, was how to make the country rich and strong again, how to restore it to the epicenter of the world. Suspicious of capitalists and especially Chinese capitalists, he advocated market socialism, looking first to Bismark's Germany and then to Meiji Japan and Russia's New Economic Policy for guidance on ''the method to develop by government action the natural resources of China.'' From the examples of these countries he concluded that state ownership of the means of production in key sectors was a ''practical and reliable system,'' and on this premise drafted an ambitious industrial plan for China (quoted in Wang 1966:152–53). The International Development of China Plan emphasized industrial development over other sectors and a synthesis of central state planning, public enterprises, and foreign capital as the means to carry out industrial development. With respect to land, Sun proposed to retain private ownership but abolish landlordism through a land-to-the-tiller land reform, and to limit private capital gains from urban land by a land tax or public purchase. With respect to capital, he stressed the need for the development of ''national capital'' and the limitation of private enterprise. By national capital he meant ''state operation of industries, state control of capital, and state ownership of profits.'' The industries to be under state control would include all major transportation, mining, and manufacturing enterprises. ''When . . . [these industries] are all developed, profits from them each year will be immense; and under the system of state control, they will be shared by all the people. In this way capital will be a source of blessing to the people in the country, not a source of misery as in some foreign countries, where capital is concentrated in private hands'' (Tai 1970:411). But small enterprises in competitive markets should be left in private hands. This complex of ideas he described as the Principle of the People's Livelihood, which together with the Principle of Nationalism and the Principle of Democracy made up the catechism called the Three Principles of the People.

The National Resources Commission

Sun's philosophy and industrial priorities were followed after his death in 1925 by his Nationalist party successors, who stressed to an even greater degree the priority of industry over other sectors and the necessity of foreign technology transfer to state-owned enterprises (see Kirby 1986; Kirby forthcoming). The formation of the National Defense Planning Commission in 1932, shortly thereafter renamed the National Resources Commission, marked the beginning of coherent industrial planning in practice as well as on paper. The planning was based on the premise that the survival of the Nationalist government depended on the creation of nationally controlled, import-substituting heavy and chemical industries, by means of programs of technology transfer from advanced Western—mostly European—nations. Through the more than one hundred large public enterprises that it came to manage, the National Resources Commission created a pattern of central government control over industrial and technological development in concert with foreign firms. The participation of private domestic capitalists in these ventures was not allowed; the National Resources Commission remained, like Sun, anticapitalist. The commission also created a pattern of technocrats being chosen on the basis of expertise rather than politics, even while much of the rest of the Nationalist state suffered from political appointees. And the commission established an organizational integration of trade policy with industrial policy. To circumvent the constraint of limited state funds for industrial development the commission itself marketed the coal, iron ore, tungsten, antimony, and tin produced by its enterprises, using the proceeds to import whole plant facilities and other forms of technology. In all these ways, the commission prefigured what was subsequently to be done in Taiwan.

The outbreak of the Sino-Japanese War in 1937 forced the planners to give up their broader industrialization plans and redirect foreign exchange to the purchase of munitions. Nevertheless, the war, which continued up to Japan's World War II defeat in 1945, provided the impetus for a huge growth in the commission, which was given power to nationalize preexisting industrial, mining, and electrical enterprises, to assume direct control of enterprises producing "daily necessities," and to regulate the production, pricing, and export of specific products. By 1944 it had a staff of over 12,000 and 160,000 workers, and owned over 100 enterprises. Its enterprises accounted for three-quarters of the total paid-up capital of public enterprises in China, which accounted for 70 percent of the total paid-up capital of both public and private enterprises.

Planning for the postwar era began during the war. The planners were in broad agreement on the direction of postwar economic strategy: it should be based on state-run heavy and chemical industries. Detailed schedules were prepared for policies in key industrial sectors—iron and steel, chemicals, machinery, electrical machinery, mining, electric power, textiles, and autos. The planners knew this would require massive foreign help, which only the United States would be in a position to provide. So began a wholesale redirection of technology transfer efforts from Europe to the United States. By 1945, thirty U.S. industrial consulting firms were engaged in a series of industry-by-industry, site-by-site surveys of Chinese industries and mines.

In fact, however, much less U.S. assistance was forthcoming than had been anticipated, due in large part to U.S. misgivings about the pro-state, anti–private enterprise direction of the commission's development plans. The United States pressed for an open and free market in China, following its conviction that only an open global economy could prevent the trading blocks and high tariffs that contributed to the Depression. This pressure ran against the Chinese view that although U.S. firms were welcomed they had to be regulated by the needs of Chinese plans and should also receive endorsement from the U.S. government. Given the heavy dependence of the Nationalist government on the United States for imports and exports as well as for advice, it is remarkable that the commission refused to bow to U.S. pressure on the question of how Chinese industry was to be organized. Most of the staff, and even most of the top leaders of the commission, stayed on under the communist government rather than move to Taiwan. But in relation to the size of Taiwan, a large number did go (some of them between 1945 and 1949 to run the industries taken over from the Japanese). There they were in a powerful position to put the commission's strategies into practice in a more tractable setting.

Causes of the Mainland Defeat

What the Nationalist government did on Taiwan also reflected the leadership's diagnosis of the causes of defeat on the mainland. The diagnosis pointed to five main reasons: (1) agricultural tenants rebelled against exploitation by landlords, while the Nationalists continued to be identified with the landlords; (2) the labor unions ran out of control; (3) bankers and financiers also broke loose, fueling a catastrophic inflation; (4) the government became beholden to "vested interests"; and (5) party discipline collapsed. The leadership was collectively determined to insure that these causes did not repeat themselves on Taiwan. The leadership's determination to carry through was all the stronger because of the urge to avenge the humiliation of their defeat and overcome the sense of estrangement which is the state of exile.

Claim to Legitimacy on Taiwan

An important part of the Nationalist party's claim to rule Taiwan is that it is the institutional custodian of the philosophy of Sun Yat-sen, founder of the Republic of China. Like it or not, it has to claim to be following his principles—so as to justify its right to rule not only in the eyes of others but also to itself. The Constitution states that

> National economy shall be based on the principle of the People's Livelihood and shall seek to effect *equalization of land ownership* and *restriction of private capital* in order to attain a well-balanced sufficiency in national wealth and people's livelihood. . . .

> With respect to private wealth and privately operated enterprises, the State shall restrict them by law if they are deemed detrimental to a balanced development of national wealth and people's livelihood. . . . *Private citizens' productive enterprises and foreign trade shall receive encouragement, guidance and protection from the State.*   (arts. 142, 145, emphasis added)

Note the similarity between the last principle and the one governing formation of civic organizations (p. 239).

The Fourth Four-Year Plan (1965) reaffirmed an important role for the state in setting the limits of private enterprise. Under the principles of Sun Yat-sen, it said,

> the main characteristic of private enterprise—the profit incentive—will be preserved, and the weakness of private enterprise—concentration of wealth—can be avoided, thus solving at once the problem of production and income distribution. For private enterprise will be protected and assisted; reasonable personal income will be protected and the freedom of economic enterprise will be respected. However, personal economic interest, manipulation of society's economic lifeline in the hands of a few and over concentration of wealth will not be allowed. Under this system the government must take positive measures to ensure that economic resources are used to the best advantage and that personal economic returns will be commensurate with one's economic contribution and effort. Consequently, the *government must take part in all economic activities and such participation cannot be opposed on the ground of any free economy theory.* But the government will never adopt a state controlled economy or even centralized planning.
>
> (CIECD 1965:1, emphasis added)

Any group which wants a reduction of the government's economic role must show how such a reduction would remain consistent with the economic principles of Sun Yat-sen. Any group which wants extensive denationalization must counter those who say that public enterprises in the commanding heights are essential to those principles. This helps to explain why even today the public enterprise sector remains unusually large and diversified compared to other middle-income countries; indeed, public enterprises tended to widen their scope over the 1970s in ways that brought them into competition with the private sector—this despite repeated government declarations that the sector would be curtailed, that public enterprises would not be allowed to enter new fields, that the government would not allow them to encroach upon already established private sector markets. Similarly for banks. One reason why Taiwan has not followed Korea in denationalizing the banks during the 1980s is that Sun Yat-sen's philosophy regards banks as prime candidates for tight public control, because they have elements of natural monopoly and provide services vital to the people's livelihood.

Fortunately, Sun Yat-sen's writings are sufficiently multifaceted, or confused, also to carry an interpretation which sanctions a progressive widening of the sphere of free markets. At the least it can be said that Sun was referring to the need for aggressive state direction in the early stages of China's industrialization, which Taiwan has superseded. But at the level of general ideological principle, the appropriate balance between government and markets remains more steadily tilted toward the former than it is in countries where economic liberalism has a strong institutional base.

War Economy

Quite apart from the above, the leadership on Taiwan faced the imperative of getting the economy moving quickly so as to provide livelihoods for the new-comers and an economic base for a large military force. Industrial develop-ment was essential for both. Throughout the 1950s the economy operated on a war footing, with all foreign transactions subject to extensive regulation and the state running all of the infrastructure and much of the industry inherited from the Japanese. Economic austerity took precedence over economic wel-fare, political security dominated political participation.

Ethnic Conflict

Right up to the 1980s the leadership remained fearful of the potential for native Taiwanese economic power to be translated into political power. Given the relative numbers, it could not prevent native Taiwanese from controlling many of the biggest companies (amongst the three hundred biggest private domestic firms in 1976, 70 percent were owned by islanders).[2] But the ethnic distinc-tion, the sense of being outsiders, and the lingering perception that they were the estranged rulers of all of China, helped the leadership to remain aloof from the local economy and its small-town businessmen. The continuing autonomy of the state owes much to these impulses.

The circumstances facing the Nationalist party in Taiwan, the goals em-braced by the leadership, and its diagnosis of the reasons for the mainland defeat, all made it want to restrict the autonomy of economic groups outside the state and curtail the channels of unproductive investment. And this it did, with a vengeance.

CLASS STRUCTURE OF INVESTMENT

For the better part of a century the state in Taiwan—first the Japanese colonial state, then the Nationalist state—has acted to restrict the opportunities for ac-cumulating wealth through unproductive investment and to restrict the influ-ence of domestic groups outside the state on economic policies. Unproductive as distinct from productive investment relates to a familiar distinction in eco-nomic analysis between "privately profitable" and "socially profitable." In-vestment which is privately but not socially profitable is "unproductive." Any investment which redistributes income upwards rather than generating it is unproductive in this sense. Beyond a certain point wealth accumulation through buying up land to live on the rents is unproductive; as also is wealth

[2] Little 1979:479. White 1980:57 reports the results of a 1975 survey of the biggest 132 firms by sales, which show that 52 percent were owned by native Taiwanese.

accumulation through money-lending, and through use of military or civilian office to redistribute scarcity premia.[3] This line of argument invites formulation of a serious socioeconomic theory of investment. For present purposes, however, it is enough that the distinction between productive and unproductive investment is accepted (though better seen as a continuum rather than either/or), as also the idea that some classes are based on a high proportion of productive, or unproductive, wealth-earning activities. What is striking about Taiwan is that many of the steps the leadership took to bolster its political position also had the effect of limiting the use of investment resources for unproductive purposes.

Landlords and Farmers

While the Nationalist party had been identified with the landlords against the peasants on the mainland, it was not so identified on Taiwan. Its landlord supporters who fled with it to Taiwan left their assets behind. It was not beholden to Taiwan's own modest class of landlords. And partly as a preemptive strike in case they should act as foci of opposition, the party moved decisively in the early 1950s to expropriate their tenanted-out land above a low ceiling. A low ceiling on agricultural land ownership has remained in force ever since, ruling out—or at least greatly restricting—investment in land as a means of accumulating wealth.

The associations into which the beneficiaries were grouped (such as farmers associations and irrigation associations) bound them to the regime by making them dependent on the party-dominated associations for inputs and marketing. State control of key inputs and much of the marketing allowed it to determine the transfer of resources from agriculture to industry. It maintained a careful balance between giving farmers incentives to produce and remain politically quiescent, on the one hand, and squeezing out enough resources to support the urban population, especially the army, school teachers, and civil servants, who received entitlements to subsidized food and who were disproportionately mainlanders.

Financial Capitalists and Money-lenders

The Nationalist party also acted decisively to control financiers. The aim was to prevent inflationary outbreaks and prevent the private holders of money from exercising power over industry. So the formal banking system still remains almost wholly state-owned, and only slowly has the government allowed the growth of a formal secondary money market. "Disrupting the money market" is one of ten offenses punishable by death under martial law—

[3] See Hamilton 1983.

a graphic indicator of the government's fear of inflation and unfettered financial power.

Bank chairmen are ex-Ministry of Finance or central bank officials, appointed directly by the premier or provincial governor. The regulations governing bank employees are basically the same as those for civil servants. Bank boards have little autonomy to set charges or even to decide on such matters as the speed of automation. All transactions have to be reported once a week to the central bank, and all foreign exchange transactions have to be reported daily.

The banks have not been encouraged to take an interest in the well-being of their borrowers. There has been no development of "industrial banking" in the French, German, or Japanese style—yet. Banks are prohibited by law from taking shares in the companies to which they lend, or from having representatives on the boards of big borrowers. Even the development bank, chartered in 1979, only began to take equity positions in 1982. Banks have not developed a capacity to analyze company finances, industry structure, or the commercial feasibility of projects.[4]

The government's overriding concern to prevent a merger of financial and industrial power helps to explain why it has made no move to denationalize the banks following the Korean example of 1980–83. The government does not want companies to have their own sources of financing or to build conglomerates around banks. Hence company law prohibits holding companies, and prohibits private nonbank financial institutions such as insurance companies from owning industrial firms. The government has also tried to restrict the growth of an "official" money market (in discounted bills, promissory notes, etc.). In the mid-1970s it relaxed some of the restrictions on the official money market and on financial-industrial conglomeration. The results were as feared: financial speculation, real estate speculation, and the failure of some respected business groups.

The unimportance of private financial interests is symbolized in the newspapers that Taiwan's businesspeople read: the *Economic Daily News* and the *Business and Industry Times*. The weekly is *Business Week*. In Japan, where financial interests have also been less important than industrial interests, the main business daily is the *Economic Times*, followed by the *Manufacturing Times*, the *Industrial Times*, the *Industrial and Economic Times*, and one other. The contrast, of course, is Great Britain, with its *Financial Times*, and the United States, with its *Wall Street Journal* (Dore 1986:118).

Professional money-lenders account for a sizable portion of "curb" market loans. But they have to operate with care, for they exist in a grey area of the law under government sufferance. Their activities are fairly carefully monitored by the central bank, which in return for information turns its eye from

---

[4] For parallels with "modern" banks on the mainland before 1949, see Wang 1966:486.

minor infractions. Since the bigger the money-lending operation the more scrutiny it receives, this sets a ceiling on wealth accumulation through money-lending. The stock market, too, is rather small (as of the mid-1980s) and seen as very risky, so fortunes are not made or invested there.

Urban Real Estate Owners

Multiple house ownership has been discouraged by preventing banks from lending for second house purchase and by taxing second houses more severely than ones occupied by the owner. However, to accommodate both the merging of house property within extended families and the difficulties of scrutinizing the large number of extended families with more than one house, the tax authorities, so it is generally believed, concentrate their attention on those with four houses or more, or the equivalent in office space. Because the marginal rate of the highest tax bracket is high (60 percent) and because capital gains tax on the sale of real estate is very high, most people with the wealth potential to own more than three houses prefer not to do so in order to avoid the tax collector's attention. This places a limit on wealth accumulation via urban real estate. And as far as is generally known, few affluent families derive a large part of their income from urban rentals.

The Military

With a standing force of close to half a million throughout most of the postwar period, the military wielded great influence in the security and legitimation complexes of the state. The bureaucrats from the mainland who took over most government administrative positions needed the military to assure them of their position in an alien land. Several of the most senior political leaders of the 1950s were ex-military, and a majority of the Nationalist party's standing committee during the 1950s and 1960s were either current or past military officers (Chang 1987:86).

However, the military did cede control of the development complex to the technocrats, especially from the late 1950s onwards. We considered some of the reasons earlier. In addition, the big change in economic policy around 1958–62 was sponsored by one of the military's own, the then premier and former general, Chen Chang. Subsequently, the generals continued to refrain from exercising control, partly because they have been bought off. They have been generously provided for in terms of public funds—with U.S. military aid up to the late 1970s and perhaps beyond, and with a sizable share of the state budget. Defense accounted for around 70 percent of total central government expenditure in the late 1950s and early 1960s, falling to 35 percent by 1987.[5]

---

[5] See chapter 6 n.16.

The generals have also enjoyed their own relatively closed production systems based on public enterprises and special status "private" firms, and have had first call on foreign exchange for military equipment.

Any government, but especially one with a military of this size, has to insure that those who do not rise up the hierarchy find secure jobs on reentry to civilian life, lest their disgruntlement prompt them to seize the levers of state power. Little is known about how this reentry transition is managed in Taiwan, but a few points are clear. Senior military personnel are commonly offered posts on the boards of public enterprises when they retire. Others are given help through the many special status private firms run by ex-military. For example, the Vocational Assistance Commission for Retired Servicemen (VACRS) is in part a huge holding company, probably the biggest conglomerate on the island (one estimate put the employees in its firms at well over one hundred thousand in the mid-1970s). VACRS provides equity capital and management. It runs a multiplicity of businesses including dairy and trucking farms, orchards, restaurants, trucking companies, and construction firms that have built dams and highways in Taiwan, roads and runways in Vietnam and other Southeast Asian countries, and miscellaneous construction projects in countries as far east as Saudi Arabia. It even operates a Royal Crown bottling company. Its business empire keeps expanding, and it has begun to recruit non-veterans (Lee 1975:73).

Outwardly there may be nothing to identify the firms as part of VACRS; they appear to be ordinary private businesses. But the VACRS connection gives them a variety of privileges in matters such as tendering for public contracts, marketing, importing, and so on. Its engineering company need not put in tenders for public work contracts; it can negotiate the deal directly with the agency concerned—and may then simply subcontract to a fully private firm, taking its 10 percent commission. (The same applies to the two properly public enterprise engineering companies.) Its importing companies can get imports from places where no one else is allowed to get them from (e.g., from Australia, secretly, during a foot-and-mouth-disease embargo on all Australian meat imports in 1983).[6]

But there is more to the military's restraint than the fact it has been well provisioned. One needs to distinguish at least two kinds of militaries, one whose ethos leans toward swashbuckling and corruption, the other whose ethos emphasizes military engineering and strategic planning (with corruption as a sideline). The Nationalist army on the mainland had plenty of officers inclined toward the former. But most of them either did not come to Taiwan or left within a few years for richer pickings in Hong Kong or the United States. Those who remained tended toward the second type, being more in-

[6] Interview with meat trader, 1983.

clined to apply their professionalism to security and legitimacy tasks than to run the economy or enrich themselves with tribute, Indonesian-style.

Legislators

There has been some, but not much, opportunity for transforming wealth into political office and using the powers of office to accumulate more wealth. Most such opportunities lie at the local rather than the central level, and are limited to the rather restricted opportunities available within the range of activities handled by local governments (especially public works projects and land zoning). At the central level, as we saw, the legislature has been composed mostly of members elected on the mainland before 1949, frozen into office by the fiction that the government of the Republic of China is the rightful government of China. In Taiwan they have not had to cultivate a constituency. In return for preserving their livelihoods and their function as legislators, they have echoed back the executive's policies. Within the party hierarchy wealth has not been a prerequisite for rank, which partly reflects the fact that the party has alternative means of financing its activities, especially through its business enterprises.

Industrial Workers

Labor unions are tightly circumscribed. Most are based on the company rather than the occupational category, with the exception of some countywide unions for specialized workers such as welders. Unions' financial resources are restricted by law, and the head of the union is paid by the company for which he works. The right to strike is prohibited by martial law. All unions within a county are grouped into a county federation, tightly controlled by the party. There are also several inactive provincial associations of county federations, staffed by life-long party-appointed officials with no contact with the rank and file.[7] The availability of private safety-nets, such as the retail trade and family income-pooling, together with the long-standing shortage of many kinds of skills, have further reinforced the powerlessness of labor unions.

Private Industrialists

The upshot of this social structure of investment is that for most of the postwar period the routes to wealth accumulation in Taiwan have been principally three (ignoring investment abroad via capital flight). One is through household investment in children's education, which can yield a direct return through income-pooling as well as several kinds of indirect returns. A second is through

[7] I am indebted to Yun-han Chu for discussions on labor unions in Taiwan.

savings accounts in banks, whose interest rates have been high while interest income has been tax free up to a ceiling roughly equal to the annual after-tax salary of a mid-thirties central governmental official. Especially for those approaching retirement this is an attractive option. (Commonly a household will also put part of its savings into the more lucrative but much riskier curb market.) Bank lending goes, in turn, mainly to industry. Direct investment in industry or trade is the third main route. Since most industrial production, for all the earlier qualifications, faces a fairly high degree of competition, industrial investment tends to have to be productive rather than redistributive.

The government has encouraged the widest possible accumulation of industrial capital and untrammeled use of that capital, provided it remains small and until the point where its transactions involve the external world. This is the industrial equivalent of the land reform strategy. Indeed, the land reform, coupled with what some contemporary critics called overinvestment in rural electricity supply, directly helped small-scale industrial investment. The low and enforced ceiling on land ownership prevented reinvestment in land assets as a household expanded in size or wealth, thereby encouraging it to look to industrial or service activity for additional income, the establishment of which was aided by abundant electricity.[8] Permitting untrammeled use of small-scale property avoided resentment from those who would have found the restrictions irksome, and freed the government to concentrate on preventing big business from organizing in ways that threatened the regime; but has given rise to serious pollution problems, chaotic land use, and labor conditions whose only check is competition between firms for workers.

The government's relaxed attitude toward counterfeiting is part of the same calculation. One source suggests that 60 percent of the world's pirated manufactured goods come from Taiwan (*Business Week*, 16 Dec. 1985). In a late 1970s case, several factories were found to be manufacturing circuit fuse breakers with forged Westinghouse and Mitsubishi labels. When Mitsubishi complained to the authorities, the firms were fined all of US$600. The government publicly denied that this was a serious case, while privately saying that "political factors" made it impossible to take tough action (Simon 1988b:216). Those political factors were the adamant opposition of most Taiwan firms and industry associations to any signs of tough enforcement, since they saw themselves as handsome beneficiaries of nonenforcement. And the government itself tended to view counterfeiting as a shortcut to industrial success. As recently as 1983 an unattributed government document entitled "Intellectual Property Rights Protection, a Republic of China Perspective," said with remarkable candor, "The R.O.C. government has viewed imitation as a necessary process in the evolution of human civilization and believed that commerical counterfeiting is an inevitable phenomenon in most developing

---

[8] I owe this point to Richard Barnett, personal communication.

countries. Local officials were cognizant of the negative aspects of counterfeiting although they made little effort to accommodate overseas interests or enhance domestic enforcement efforts when such aspects were seen to be outweighed by the positive development of the industrial base'' (cited in Gadbaw and Richards 1988:349). Only in the mid-1980s has the government finally acknowledged the severity of the counterfeiting problem and taken serious steps to crack down.

Likewise the government exercises strikingly little vigilance over company accounts and the accountancy profession. The law says that if a firm's records are inadequate for the Ministry of Finance to determine the appropriate tax rate, the firm will be assessed at the average rate for that sector. This is to accommodate the fact that many small firms do not keep adequate records. But it has the consequence that if a larger firm, which does keep adequate records, prepares a false set of books for tax or credit purposes and destroys all relevant documents, it suffers no penalties and is levied at the average rate. Accountants are not legally liable for any consequences which follow from having certified financial statements which turn out to be grossly inaccurate (Winn 1987).

Not surprisingly, the profession of certified professional accountant (CPA) is notoriously venal. Some 80 percent of CPAs are ex-government employees or ex-military officers rewarded—after passing an easy examination—with profitable CPA credentials upon retirement or discharge from government service (Shiao 1983). The other 20 percent is made up mostly of young persons who have passed an extremely rigorous examination, with an average pass rate of about one percent in recent years. But even in principle, accounting and auditing standards are only very broadly and incompletely specified. The accounting standards issued by the National Federation of CPA Associations of the Republic of China total thirty-four pages, compared to the thousands of pages issued by its U.S. counterpart. The auditing standards total sixteen pages, compared to the two thousand pages issued by the U.S. counterpart. The unreliability of company accounts is one reason why the banks insist on collateral and/or postdated checks, and also why the stock market has been slow to develop.[9]

The government's relaxed attitude to counterfeiting, the loose entry restrictions to the CPA profession, lack of CPA procedures, banks' insistence on collateral, and few lawyers are part of a wider pattern. The institutions which help to generate impersonal trust and allow trust-requiring business between people not already embedded in personal relations[10] are only weakly devel-

---

[9] The number of pages and the pass rate come from an unpublished anonymous paper, ''American Bankers' Comments on Accounting and Auditing Standards in Taiwan,'' presented to ROC-US/US-ROC joint economic council meeting, 1983.

[10] Trust-requiring business is business in which one party must commit resources before knowing that the other will carry through his agreed part.

oped. The comparison is not only with the West but also—impressionisti-cally—with other societies of roughly the same per capita income. Taiwan businessmen emphasize how important it is, in doing business with a stranger, to start with minor transactions in which little trust is required because little risk is involved and then move toward major transactions, personal trust grow-ing from the process of exchange itself.[11] However, the huge increase in the volume of business transactions over the past several decades could not plau-sibly have been limited to relations of personal trust. Perhaps the existence of a financial instrument which *is* heavily defended by impersonal penalties—the postdated check backed by criminal penalties—has been crucial to overcom-ing the trust problem. Most firms are linked to suppliers and buyers in a dense network of commercial credit based on the postdated check. It would be inter-esting to know how businesses have adjusted since mid-1987 when criminal penalties were removed from the postdated check. What alternative devices are developing for generating impersonal trust and discouraging malfea-sance?[12]

Although government has exercised little vigilance over the small-scale sec-tor, it has been much concerned to prevent large-scale capital from acquiring enough autonomy to shape the regime. The ability to control raw material imports and bank credit gives the government powerful and selective instru-ments of control, should it wish to use them. Restrictions on entry to an in-dustry have also sometimes been used to prevent individuals not closely con-nected to the regime from acquiring excessive power, as in the case of Y. C. Wang's attempts to integrate backwards into naphtha production, and subse-quently to establish a petroleum refinery in Saudi Arabia. The party is said to control the stock exchange through its de facto control of the Securities and Exchange Commission, which must approve all share issues. The commission has great discretion about how carefully it checks a company's balance sheet before allowing the company to proceed with a share issue (the more assets a company claims to own the better the share issue is likely to be). Many busi-nessmen avoid the stock exchange because to issue shares on it exposes them

[11] My informants sounded as if they had studied Peter Blau (1968:454). Blau's argument, which he states in universalistic terms, may apply better in Taiwan than in the West where the institutions for generating impersonal trust are better developed.

[12] The duty rebate scheme (chapter 5) may have helped to strengthen relations between sup-pliers and buyers based on the postdated check; if so, the gradual dismantling of the scheme since the mid-1980s, with fewer items entitled to rebate as the general level of tariffs is brought down, may be another factor altering supplier-buyer relations and calling for alternative devices. Ex-porting firms usually write two postdated checks to a supplier—one for the duty-free amount of the purchase (including the supplier's profit), the other for an amount covering the duty paid if the goods are used as export inputs—because it gives the exporter a strong incentive to pass back his export documents to the supplier so that, in return for the export documents, the supplier will give him back the second check. If the exporter fails to pass back the export documents, the supplier simply cashes the check.

not only to possible loss of control of their own companies, but also to Nationalist party arm-twisting. Control of the stock exchange is useful for the party not just as a means of discretionary influence on particular firms, but also because the stock exchange can be made to boom around the date of the national anniversaries which are symbolically important in the party's history and thus made to show the solid business support for the regime.

Foreign firms have been regulated to prevent them from occupying the most profitable niches in the domestic market. They are used to get access to new technology and markets and to win political sympathy at high levels of the U.S. government. Had they been allowed unrestricted access to the domestic market, the government would have been vulnerable to criticism particularly damaging to political legitimacy because of the preoccupation of China's leaders since the Opium Wars with how to escape the yoke of foreign domination. The same applies, only more so, to foreign banks. They have been kept on a tight leash so that the profitable parts of the banking business remain in local hands, and so that they cannot be used as instruments for easy foreign takeover of Taiwan's highly leveraged firms.

Domestic industry is, nonetheless, intensely organized into industrial associations. Any sector with more than five firms must form an association according to law. And the associations really are formed. There is a Taipei Commercial Sculpture Association, a Taiwan Feather Exporters Association, a Taiwan Match Association. Textiles boast eighteen associations, including the big ones like Cotton Spinners, Man-Made Fibers, and Apparel, down to the Towel Makers Association, Hosiery Association, and Fishing Net Association.

It is not legal to form an association without government approval, and all associations must be registered with the relevant ministry. The government and behind it the party appoints the secretary of all the important associations, while the board of directors is, nominally at least, elected by the member firms from amongst themselves. ("Yes, we are sent the ballot papers," said a member of one association covering an important sector, "but do you think we ever see the election returns, do you think the elections are ever audited? They appoint who they want.") The party's social affairs department watches over the associations, the current head of which is said to be one of the most powerful people in the land. The secretaries—who run the associations by virtue of being, unlike the chairmen, full-time—tend to be ex-military, security, or government officers, whose loyalty is unquestioned. Their incentives are to respond to suggestions and instructions from above, not, whenever there is a conflict, to act as spokesmen for the interests of their members. Until 1972 the formal rules governing associations used the phrase "petition a superior" to describe the form of an association's correspondence with the government, and the word "orders" to describe the government's correspondence with the association. Since then the phrasing has been changed to "letters" (Jacobs

1978:243), but a decidedly hierarchical relationship persists. To the extent that the associations are active, it is primarily at the behest of the government, and in particular of the Industrial Development Bureau.

The two national business federations, the Chinese National Federation of Industries and the Chinese National Association of Industry and Commerce, do very little. One of them has been run since 1961 by C. F. Koo, a prominent co-opted native Taiwanese who owns Taiwan Cement Corporation and has been a member of the Nationalist party's standing committee for many years. From 1981 to 1987 Koo was chairman of the other federation as well, before relinquishing the position to a friend and member of the legislative assembly who is equally close to the party. One of President Chang's sons has been director-general of this second organization for many years. Neither organization comes close to the function carried out by, for example, Japan's *Keidanren*, which is an organization of the private sector able to represent its interests to the bureaucracy. Koo, indeed, believes that such an organization is unnecessary in Taiwan. To a foreign visitor he explained that

> the economic interest groups in Taiwan are not so well organized and do not do as much lobbying as those in the United States and other Western countries. This is probably because the national policies of the Republic of China are guided by the three people's principles as upheld by Dr. Sun Yat-sen. On the economic side, the principle of the people's livelihood contains a well-designed model to balance the different interests of different economic groups while the economy is developed under the market system. There is, therefore, no need for a special interest group to lobby to urge the government to take action in its favor.
>
> (In Zeigler 1988:182–83)

A remarkable statement from the man best placed to be industry's spokesman to government.

Public Enterprises and Semipublic Enterprises

Public enterprises account for a larger proportion of total investment in Taiwan than in 80 to 90 percent of other noncommunist countries (see table 6.2). Being concentrated in the upstream, capital-intensive, and oligopolized sectors, they account for a much larger share of total investment in these sectors. Their continued role owes much to the importance attached to public enterprises by Sun Yat-sen, coupled with the Nationalist government's need to present itself as the institutional custodian of Sun Yat-sen's thought. But the continuity with the mainland period is still more striking. Taiwan's public enterprises are concentrated in the same sectors as the National Resources Commission's enterprises before 1949, especially in petroleum, steel, shipbuilding, heavy machinery, and engineering. The National Resources Commission staff who came to Taiwan constituted a powerful cadre of technocrats during the subsequent decades—providing eight out of fourteen ministers of economic affairs, one premier, and many vice-ministers and directors of public enterprises. Its members pursued on Taiwan a modified version of the earlier strategy of state-led heavy and chemical industries linked to multinational firms, the other side of which was a wariness of large private Chinese capitalists. The anti-big capitalist bias of most of Taiwan's senior industrial policy-makers helps to explain the weakness of the policy network with private firms. So does the ethnic tension between the mainlander government and the native Taiwanese businesspeople. But even if no such tension had existed, the same attempt to maintain a balance of power in favor of the government and against private firms would have been made, as on the mainland before 1949.

It is misleading to consider only the legally public enterprises, those that meet the criterion of 50 percent or more of equity owned by the state. Many other firms are much influenced by parts of the state without being included in the public enterprise sector. The airline and one of the larger banks are private so as to allow them to operate in countries which do not recognize Taiwan; but their private status is only nominal. Also, in order to bolster the image of economic liberalization, the government may take a minority share in an important firm and make up the balance through the party's holding company (Central Investments Holding Company). This method has been used to keep multinationals under scrutiny: the government persuades or cajoles the multinational to accept the party's holding company as a joint venture partner, in return for which the holding company appoints a few senior managers who act as the eyes and ears of the government within the company. The technique has been much used in petrochemicals.

Apart from these, there are many special status "private" firms linked to the party, the military, government agencies, or senior individuals of these organizations. The large holding company belonging to the military, VACRS, was mentioned earlier. Outwardly there may be nothing to identify a firm as part of the VACRS empire, but its firms may obtain a variety of advantages over non-VACRS competitors. The party too owns a range of manufacturing and service enterprises. During the 1970s, for example, the party's finance department directly owned six companies and through these seven more: in textiles, paper and printing, cement, pharmaceuticals, fiber and glass, electronics, electrical construction, insurance, and the investment and trust business. Over the 1980s several firms were sold or merged, and the finance department added a securities and brokerage house (*Independent*, 12 Feb. 1988). In addition, the cultural affairs department owns several profitable businesses, including a television network, a radio network, and a daily newspaper (*Central Daily News*). Altogether the party owns about fifty firms. One of the big advantages of party enterprises to society-at-large is that the party does not need to use organizations such as industrial associations, farmers' associations, or the government bureaucracy itself to raise revenue on its behalf, corrupting performance as a result.[13]

Then there are ostensibly private firms established by a particular ministry. The Ministry of Communications, for example, has its "own" private engineering company, as does the Ministry of Economic Affairs; neither company has to put in tenders for projects awarded by its ministry. These and other similar special status firms are used by government agencies to avoid the restrictions placed on public enterprises, as well as to provide reliable retirement schemes for senior officials. Personal special status firms also exist in abundance. Whenever a government agency is in the position of buyer there is a chance that the middle-man enterprise to whom it contracts the buying will be run by a relative or a senior official of that agency (as was said to be the case for a time with China Shipbuilding). Similarly with financial policy formulation contracted out to private consulting firms, which happens on a considerable scale (e.g., for design of a venture capital scheme). It is commonly alleged that the real rather than the putative owners of these private consulting firms are officials of the allocating agency or their relatives. The main point, however, is simply that public and semipublic enterprises have a large place in the social structure of investment.

So the Taiwan government has restricted wealth accumulation through land ownership, financial dealings, urban real estate, military office, and legislative office and has thereby helped to channel investment into productive rather than unproductive activities. Second, by limiting these opportunities as well as the organizations of workers and private industrialists, and by privileging public and semipublic enterprises, the government has insured that it has ample power resources compared to those outside the state. Combined with features of the political regime which block the translation of wealth into power over the direction of national economic policy, the result is that political dominance does not lie with groups whose interests are hostile to fast industrial growth, in contrast to the Philippines, Indonesia, and many other developing coun-

---

[13] Compare India, Wade 1985. One should note, too, the private firms owned by close relatives of senior people in the party. There was some cynical laughter in the business community when the government began to promote the wearing of motorcycle helmets by its own employees, threatening to dock their pay if they did not comply. It is common knowledge that the monopoly supplier of the material from which helmets are made is the son of a most prominent political figure. (In fact, the government was unable to enforce the rule, and the monopoly supplier is said to have lost a lot of money.) Often the connections only come to light when something goes wrong. When a foreign company took a local company to court over a trade dispute, the foreign company's lawyers were convinced they had a copper-bottomed case. Just before the case was due to be heard, however, it became known that the real owners of the local company, as distinct from the putative owners, were so well connected with the party hierarchy that they also owned the building which houses the Board of Foreign Trade. The board's evidence was crucial to the plaintiff's case. When it was learned who the real defendant was, the Board of Foreign Trade refused to testify and the case was quickly dropped.

tries, nor even in a coalition where priority to industrialization is diluted by bargaining with nonindustrial groups. This in itself is a good part of the explanation for Taiwan's superior economic performance. But it is in turn the result, in part, of government actions to shape the class structure of investment, which stems from the motives and interests of the political leadership. The creation of such a structure was not attended by nearly as much conflict as one would expect from other societies, because of a difference in sequencing. The basic structure of a strong state was established in Taiwan before the emergence of a substantial business class and industrial labor force, and before the arrival of foreign firms and banks (Deyo 1987). The state has been able to check the autonomy of these groups as they have subsequently grown, and thereby found it easier to maintain its own autonomy. It has exercised much influence over the formation and operation of economic interest groups and over which interest groups can gain what type of access to the state. The Latin American contrast is sharp.

INDUSTRIAL POLICY-MAKING AND THE PUBLIC SECTOR

Industrial policy-making in Taiwan takes place within a narrow coalition which includes, at the core, the technocrats and ministers of the central economic bureaucracy plus the senior managers of public enterprises and public research organizations, with Nationalist party leaders and military leaders having veto power. At the edge are selected managers of large foreign and domestic firms. Small businesspeople, workers, and peasants are excluded.

Relations between central economic officials and public enterprise officials tend to be close. Many senior officials in economics agencies have worked for a time in public enterprises. And most ministers of economic affairs have had management positions in public enterprises, such experience being considered an important step in the career ladder for someone aspiring to ministerial office in economic matters. Some senior officials and political executives may reenter public enterprises as board members on retirement.[14]

Whenever this policy coalition has wanted to give a big push to a particular industrial sector it has tended to look to public enterprises to lead the way, sometimes with and sometimes without the participation of private domestic firms (see chapter 4). In the information industry the Electronics Research and Service Organization (ERSO) and the Information Industry Institute are good examples. Not only have they, as public enterprises, been assigned a leadership role in research and development; they have both often relied on their own subsidiaries to commercialize their results rather than transfer the technology to existing private firms. Similarly in biotechnology, a big public lab-

---

[14] This is a very inadequate account of the relations between central officials and the managers of public enterprises. I was able to discover little information about them.

oratory established in 1984 to bridge universities and industry has created its own wholly owned subsidiary to bring its results to market. And in automobiles, the government also turned to a public enterprise to be Toyota's Taiwan partner in an export car plant, though in the end the project failed and the government reverted to encouraging the existing private firms.

Public enterprises or public research organizations are also used as sources of advice on particular policies. And they are routinely called upon to provide officials with advice on technical disputes which arise in the course of policy implementation—such as whether Monsanto's imported polyester sheeting really is superior in quality to that made by local producers, as Monsanto says, or whether it is not much different, as the local producers seeking an import ban say.

Industrial Policy-Making and the Private Sector

Compared to Japan and Korea, one sees in Taiwan more of a cleavage between the government and the private sector, relations between which are often described as "cool" and "distant." What one sees is not the whole story, but an important part of the story. Both business and government—especially government—resist being seen in a collective huddle. A few businessmen, it is true, are well known spokesmen for "business-in-general"; but they are co-opted as individuals, not through any formal position of representation. The civil service has a career system which is nearly closed to inflow of middle- and senior-rank people from the private sector; and ministerial-level appointments virtually never involve someone from a private sector background. Senior officials rarely enter private business, even on retirement. There is no tradition of the "descent from heaven," Japanese-style, whereby senior officials, when they fail to move further up the increasingly pyramidal ladder, leave to join firms or associations anxious to have their governmental expertise and contacts. Normally, in Taiwan, those who in Japan would leave stay on, but are pushed sideways into "advisory" positions with the same rank but no power, or join a public enterprise.

To see the cleavage, consider the composition of the three most authoritative bodies involved in industrial policy-making. The cabinet did not include someone with a background in private industry until 1981. CEPD's twelve councillors are all government officials (no business representatives); and the ten-man advisory council to the CEPD council is made up entirely of academics. The standing committee of the Nationalist party had only two private industrialists out of twenty-seven members in 1983[15] (but the owner/editors of the three main newspaper groups are members).

[15] To be exact, only one out of twenty-seven was on the 1983 standing committee primarily as an industrialist (Koo of Taiwan Cement). Lin of Tatung joined primarily as occupier of a senior

CEPD officials have little contact with the private sector and show no great inclination to do so. Private industrialists for their part have no need to come to CEPD, for it can offer little help in getting finance or other concessions. CEPD has more contact with public enterprises because of its role in scrutinizing and coordinating public enterprise investment projects.

It is true that during the period from 1978 to 1980 a series of meetings was arranged at the council between K. H. Yu, the newly appointed chairman, and leaders of various industries. But these were for the purpose of informing him about the situation in their industry. (His previous experience was only in banking, which in Taiwan does not call for detailed knowledge of industry.) Observers at the meetings have remarked how Yu himself said virtually nothing; he listened—whereas the normal stance of a senior government official toward private industrialists is to instruct. Equally, however, the meetings did not amount to "an exchange of views." Once the range of major industries had been covered the series stopped, and no further "consultations" have been held.

The national plans (one-, four-, and ten-year) prepared by CEPD are basically public sector plans plus estimates of macroaggregates derived from econometric models of the whole economy; their preparation requires little knowledge of the intentions of the private sector, not even investment intentions.

The budget is prepared, in great secrecy, by the process described in chapter 7, and its publication occasions very little public discussion. For one thing, over half of public expenditure for most of the postwar period has been classified as secret because it is related to defense. The legislature has had to approve the budget but is given little time or expertise with which to debate it.

Only one televised debate on economic policy has ever been held, which took place in 1982. The issue was whether interest rates should be higher or lower than the government-set rate then prevailing. The government did not represent itself directly. It hired to face the assembled ranks of industrialists two distinguished Chinese-American academic economists. The debate became so heated, the cleavage so sharp, that two of the most prominent industrialists on the island—who wanted lower rates—stormed out of the meeting in what is by Chinese standards an extraordinary display of emotion. (This was cut from the televised version.) The experiment will not be repeated in a hurry.

The National Science and Technology Program, amongst the handful of top priorities of the government's whole development strategy, emerged from two major science and technology conferences, one in 1978, the second in 1982. Some four hundred invitees attended the conference of 1982. They were di-

position in the state—speaker of the Taipei assembly. The importance of membership in the standing committee should not be exaggerated—influence is not always closely tied to organizational position. One of several other important criteria of influence is who has one of the six telephones which connect directly to the president.

vided into eight working groups to discuss specific topics over a week-long period. It is striking that only 15 percent of the participants at the conference were from private industry. The particular industry leaders to be invited were chosen by the chairmen of the eight working groups, co-opted as knowledgeable individuals, not as representatives. A senior official defended this procedure on the grounds that, "We have worked with industry for more than 30 years, *so we know who is able to represent each industry.*"[16]

Take again the formulation of the details of the fiscal investment incentives and the tariff rates. As we have seen, there is no industry representation on the committees which decide these matters, and not even institutionalized ways of getting the views of industrialists. Tariffs and fiscal incentives are handled in high secrecy by a small set of officials entirely within government, mostly from the Ministry of Finance and the Ministry of Economic Affairs. Formal approval of the legislature is necessary, but it comes after secret discussion in the Finance and Economics Committee rather than open debate.

However, the process of formulating nontariff barriers (NTBs) has always been more open to interest group pressure. As the description of the process in chapter 5 implies, individual producers or industrial associations can apply for NTB protection to government agencies such as the Industrial Development Bureau, the Board of Foreign Trade, or the Council for Agricultural Planning and Development. These agencies then forward the applications with their opinions to a central coordinating committee (the International Trade Commission, formed in 1968 as successor to the Foreign Exchange and Trade Committee) where final decisions are made, generally with little change in the recommendations of the forwarding agencies.[17]

The arrangements for the Strategic Industries Program show an interesting new development. The program, started in 1982, gives soft loans for making specific products of the "strategic" industries (machinery and information). The new development is that representatives from the relevant industry associations have been present on the committee to select the items for encouragement. (The preliminary list of products was drawn up by the Industrial Development Bureau and the development bank, starting with a similar list prepared earlier in Japan.) The reason industry representatives could be invited to the strategic industry committee and not to the committees for fiscal incentives and tariffs was that inclusion in the strategic industry lists did not confer automatic entitlement to the assistance. The development bank still had to evaluate each project separately, and the list was left open-ended for other items deemed important to be included if approved by CEPD. Inclusion in the fiscal incentive or tariff lists, by contrast, was itself determining of the taxes or tar-

[16] Interview, Aug. 1983, emphasis added.

[17] The International Trade Commission was formed as the successor to the Foreign Exchange and Trade Control Commission, abolished in 1968. It was dissolved in 1985, and its functions placed with the Board of Foreign Trade and the International Development Bureau.

iffs to be paid—so "vested" interests would be stronger in the shaping of these lists than in the strategic industry list. So the vested interests had to be excluded.

Chang's findings on the correlates of Taiwan's tariff and nontariff barriers are consistent with the difference in openness to interest group pressure. He finds that the tariff structure is hardly affected by interest groups: it is *not* related to degree of concentration in an industry, special political connections between industry leaders and senior political figures, importance of foreign investment, or importance of public enterprises. What is more, it is negatively related to the degree of labor intensity in an industry (1987:135–48). We noted in chapter 5 that the tariff structure is correlated with a number of "national policy" variables—for example, the higher the proportion of imports used as inputs for further production the lower the tariff; the higher the proportion of output which goes for final demand the higher the tariff. These results, in short, give no support to an interest group model of tariff policy formation and substantial support for a national policy model, as the governed market interpretation of Taiwan would expect.

The interest group model does a little better in the case of NTBS. NTBS are related positively to importance of public enterprise, primary as distinct from secondary or tertiary sector, and special political connections. However, such other interest group variables as import penetration and importance of foreign capital are unrelated, while NTBS are negatively related to concentration of firms (1987:164–70). Even in the case of NTBS most of the explanation comes from a national policy rather than an interest group model.

As the final example of public/private cleavage, consider the research and service organizations. The government has sponsored a forest of research and service organizations to serve industry (chapter 4). The research and service organizations were intended to get much of their budget from the private sector. In fact, only a small part of their revenue has come from private domestic firms. For one thing, private firms have not been inclined to ask them. This is the reason stressed by government officials and by the staff of the research and service organizations. The director-general of the Industrial Technology Research Institute (ITRI) said in an interview that one of ITRI's biggest problems has been "in transferring our technologies and research results. This is because industries must reach certain technical levels before being able to receive *what we give them*. They must also digest what we give them to make it applicable for commercial production" (*Economic News*, 13–19 June 1983, emphasis added). Not the distinctly top-down view of the transfer process.[18]

On the other hand, it is also the case that the staff of these organizations

---

[18] Director-general Fang said in the same interview, "I think the deepest regret I have on this score [to do with technology transfer] is that the state-run enterprises, which are supposed to emphasize R&D and promote it among private businesses, are proving very reluctant to do either."

have not been anxious to go out and persuade private firms that they could be helpful, and especially to listen to the private firms before setting their research priorities.[19] So the twenty major information industry products on which ERSO has been working over the 1980s were picked by ERSO staff, who also (with Industrial Development Bureau help) chose firms to commercialize the products, sometimes ERSO's own subsidiaries or joint venture partners. In general, the government has been less pressing in its invitation to private domestic firms to join forces in R&D compared to Korea and Japan; and the private sector has been less responsive to those invitations the government has made. ITRI gets less income from contract research and royalties and more from government grants than its Korean counterpart, the Korea Advanced Institute of Science and Technology (KAIST). In the late 1970s over half of total R&D spending in Taiwan was undertaken by the government, only 30 percent by the private domestic sector.

In practice the main incentive for ITRI to keep its work relevant to commercial applications is the opportunity for its staff to spin off their own companies to commericalize products they have developed. This is explicitly encouraged, and the opportunities for doing so (backed by public assistance) are used to lure back Chinese scientists and engineers from U.S. companies. But individual research managers are not always keen to see their stars leave the team or go half-time. Indeed, as of late 1988 great alarm is being expressed about "destructive attrition" at ITRI, especially at ERSO, as key professionals leave to reap lucrative returns in industry. (Stock options and deferred bonus plans are being considered as means of retention.)

The method just mentioned is one way to close the gap between research and the shop floor. But apart from its disruption of government-funded advanced technology programs, it also has the big disadvantage of largely bypassing established private firms. The task forces described earlier are intended, in part, to counteract the neglect of existing firms. They are to be a kind of industrial extension service, parallel in function to the agricultural extension service. They are to take the initiative in putting factories in touch with research organizations, or to provide scientifically based advice themselves. The rapid acceleration of military R&D in the late 1970s in response to improving U.S.-Chinese relations has also helped; the military has even approached private firms to participate (Simon 1988b).

INDUSTRIAL ASSOCIATIONS AND THE PRESS

Many industrial associations are active as the arms and legs of the government. They may be used to collect data on the production capabilities of mem-

---

[19] There may be a cultural attitude toward business involved here. Silin quotes a university professor saying "Teachers (i.e., academics and researchers) feel that people in industry have not made their money honestly and are not happy about being associated with them" (1967:29–30).

bers, so that IDB knows where to get the information when needed. They may draw IDB's attention to a gap, a "weak link" in the production structure of their industry, and help IDB find firms willing to invest in the gap. This is what the Taiwan Textile Federation is doing with respect to dyeing and finishing facilities on the island. Again, the associations may be asked by IDB to carry out negotiations between would-be importers and local suppliers to see if agreement can be reached on local purchase in place of imports. For example, when one Taiwanese firm expanded its capacity to make a particular type of glass, IDB instructed the Taiwan Electrical Appliance Manufacturers Association to begin negotiations between the two suppliers of this specialized glass and the three buyers on the island with a view to insuring that all the additional capacity was taken up. One of the three buyers strongly objected to being made to buy from the local supplier. But despite being one of the biggest and longest established foreign firms on the island, it was not allowed to deal with IDB directly on the matter. All the discussions had to go either through the association or directly to the minister of economic affairs himself, with IDB monitoring closely in the background.[20]

In textiles, on the several occasions when parts of the industry have faced excess capacity IDB has prodded the relevant industry association to negotiate a pro-rata moth-balling and arrange inspectors to police the agreement. Without IDB prodding the chances of making and sustaining such arrangements are not good. Again, in petrochemicals the regular (generally four-monthly) negotiations between the various upstream firms and their downstream buyers typically involve the industry association of the downstream firms facing the monopoly producer of a particular upstream product. In PTA production, for example, a joint venture between Chinese Petroleum Corporation and the U.S. company AMOCO faces the Man-Made Fibers Association. Ostensibly IDB is not involved unless the negotiations reach an impasse. In fact, however, according to a participant, IDB is constantly engaged in nudging and prodding behind the scenes, but it wishes the decision to emerge from the negotiators themselves. The government's style, said this participant, is to do things quietly, by telephone or over lunch, as though behind a screen. An impasse was reached during the oil crisis of 1980–82, however, and here IDB took a more overt role than usual. Not only then but also in normal times, the umbrella Petroleum Industry Association was simply bypassed.

The industry associations may well attempt to lobby IDB and other agencies for import protection. And given that as of 1984 some 29 percent of Taiwan's imports by value could only be imported after approval by a stipulated party (see table 5.3), of which a sizable (but unknown) portion requires approval from the association of competing producers, these efforts sometimes bear fruit. My guess, however, is that Taiwan's industry associations have much

---

[20] Interview with senior manager, June 1983.

less scope, on the whole, for determining the level and type of imports than their Korean counterparts (Luedde-Neurath 1986). One reason for the share of imports in machine tool investment being much higher in Taiwan than Korea is that the decision to allow imports is in the hands of IDB in Taiwan and in the hands of the machine tool industry association in Korea (Jacobsson 1984). The Taiwanese locus seems the more sensible in terms of national interest.

So the Taiwanese industrial associations, or many of them, have plenty to do as the government's hand-maidens, and much of what they do is useful. Some are active in supplying their members with regular information about developments in their industry—though of the eighteen textile associations, only one produces a weekly or monthly newspaper for members, which is a poor record compared to their Japanese counterparts (Dore 1983). Some provide training courses and even scholarships for advanced study overseas. Some help members to participate in trade fairs. And so on.

But they do not provide significant inputs into policy-making, they have too little independence to constrain the actions of government, and in few cases do they have much power to regulate the behavior of members.[21] Hardly ever are they even invited to present their views on policy issues. Only since a speech by the premier in 1981 calling on industrial associations to play a more active role has any consideration been given to the matter. The association of the seven automobile makers (Taiwan Transportation Vehicles Manufacturers Association) was never asked to participate in the formation of Taiwan's auto policy, even after the collapse of the Big Auto Plant project left them as the instruments of the government's automobile plans. Even an association like the Taiwan Shipbuilders Association—covering an industry which is extremely important for an island economy dependent on trade and under threat of blockade—has never been asked to give its views on what appropriate policies for the industry should be. The apex bodies, like the Chinese National Federation of Industries, have at most a weak voice.

Ironically, the American Chamber of Commerce probably has more of a consultative role than its Chinese counterpart, which reflects the diplomatic as well as the economic importance of foreign investors. It is often consulted on proposed policies and may even take part in their design. For example, the initial proposals for a major expansion of the export quality control program in the mid-1970s were made by two U.S. quality-control experts, then worked

[21] The Taiwan Footwear Manufacturers Association established and funded the Shoe Designers Association in 1982 to train young shoe designers. The training consists of six months in class and six months in the factory, with free tuition and guaranteed jobs upon graduation. University graduates who join get a two-year scholarship to study shoe design and manufacturing in West Germany (*Footwear News*, 26 July 1982). An exception to the generalization that associations do not have much power to discipline their members is the Taiwan Fishing Boat Owners Association, which uses its monopoly of shore-to-sea communication facilities to make sure that each owner follows the rules (e.g., about not taking on a crewman who is indebted to another owner).

over by the Bureau of Commodity Inspection, and then presented to the American Chamber of Commerce. The government hoped that if the big foreign firms were willing to participate then the local firms, many of whom were known to be hostile to the scheme's expansion, would fall into line. The American Chamber, in the words of a participant, "vomited the proposals onto the table on grounds of complete unworkability." The Chamber put together a team from its member companies to draw up a feasible scheme, and the scheme put into operation bore a close resemblance to the one drawn up by the Chamber.

The main exception to this picture is the Taiwan Textile Federation, established in 1976 as an umbrella for the eighteen separate textile industry associations. It now has a staff of two hundred and has become a significant source of policy ideas for the textile sector. But this policy function has developed only since the 1981 recession (being added to the existing functions of handling the complex business of quota allocation—in the formal role of "advisor" to the Board of Foreign Trade—and of collecting data on the industry for government use). Another exception is the Man-Made Fibers Association, whose power, though, comes less from the association as such and more from the fact that its membership is small and includes the most powerful industrialists on the island. The government cannot afford to ignore what it says.[22]

In this situation, with the obvious institutional channel for communication between specific industries and the government being controlled by the government, businessmen may resort to the press. One procedure is for a group of aggrieved businessmen to present their case in a paid advertisement. Or they may take out a normal advertisement for their products, in return for which the paper grants them free space in the news section for which the businessmen supply the story. The story then appears as though it were written by one of the paper's own "disinterested" reporters. Or they may simply pay a reporter to write what they want to say; the illicit payment of journalists in return for favorable stories, especially economic journalists, is common practice. Of course there are limits to venality; the papers are all owned by senior party members, which insures that the papers will not carry a story which implicates the Nationalist party (as distinct from the government bureaucracy). Some of the newspapers, too, are known as probusiness, and make it their job to articulate a business interest. One of the big dailies organizes a weekly discussion forum between three or four invited guests, who might include businessmen, academics, and sometimes a senior government official; the newspaper selects the theme for discussion and then carries an edited tran-

---

[22] Mention should be made of the monthly working breakfasts arranged by the secretary-general of the president's office in conjunction with the president of the Small and Medium Business Association, to which selected industrialists are invited. This is only one of several ways by which the party orchestrates contact between public or party officials and businessmen; indeed, the party is more active in this role than the government.

script. Strong criticism of the government is accepted. But whether at the behest of businessmen or because that is what the reporters and editorial writers believe, the criticism comes from outside government. Use of the press to air interministerial or interagency disputes in public is rare.

The government is extremely sensitive to what is carried in the newspapers, and an agency which receives unfavorable attention will normally act quickly to counter the accusations or promise wholehearted reform. The role of the press is similar to the "safety valve" function of politicians in Johnson's model: the guardians of what the press does or does not carry are senior party figures, and officials are very sensitive to press criticism.

Officials may be sensitive to press criticism not just because of the connection between the press and the party. In addition, they may calculate, pragmatically, that the principal criterion for finding fault with their work is that they failed to anticipate negative consequences of a decision which other persons (press commentators, for example) did anticipate. If so, they will pay careful attention to what rival commentators outside the state are saying, even though they are not subject to democratic accountability or lobbying. To the extent that they are also concerned with the attainment of wider national goals, their attention to outside information centers will be even greater. Whatever the explanation, Taiwan's combination of centralized information production within public administration together with a more decentralized information system appears to have promoted, within a nondemocratic government, a high degree of sensitivity to problems in the wider society.

COVERT RELATIONS BETWEEN GOVERNMENT AND PRIVATE BUSINESS

Although formal mechanisms to solicit private sector views on economic policy are almost nonexistent, informal contact is frequent. Many IDB officials spend several days a month visiting firms for one reason or another. But senior officials would still feel uncomfortable to be seen at lunch or on the golf course with businessmen. Most of the contact is with businessmen representing themselves or a small group of firms rather than a larger aggregation of interests. As Tai put it, "In case of businessmen, they prefer to channel their influence through individual contacts with government officials rather than through their associations" (1970:423; see also Tedstrom 1986:31). Almost by definition the operation and effects of these informal connections are slippery to analyze; there is little evidence to go on. Here the intention is only to give an indication of the kinds of covert connections that are common.

Taiwan's industrial officials are engaged with the bigger industrial firms in relations that would be called "administrative guidance" in Japan. They make suggestions as to suitable products or technologies, in line with a wider conception of where the industry should be going. The author of the only study in English of Taiwanese enterprise management, writing at the end of the 1960s, observed that "large firms receive unofficial and semi-official suggestions as to the direction of expansion. In some cases, allegedly, particular product lines are specified" (Silin 1976:18). Each side in government-firm bargaining knows that it depends on the other. The Industrial Development Bureau may decide that the existing state of electronics technology on the island could be stretched to include production of sophisticated computer printers. The concerned officials know that only a few Taiwan firms have the capacity to undertake the project. They approach the firms—domestically owned ones first—to discuss the prospects, offering them help (protection, fiscal incentives, credit, finding of joint venture partners, design help via one of the parastatal research organizations, etc.). The firms know that the project is considered important and that only a few could carry it through, which gives them a strong bargaining hand. On the other hand, the firms know that the government has a variety of more or less subtle ways to make life awkward if they do not respond. The government side may hint that an unusually careful look may have to be taken at their tax returns; or that import licenses may be held up; or that land-zoning laws may have to be enforced (in the common case where a firm has a factory outside the zoning); or that capacity expansion plans may not be eligible for fiscal investment incentives. "The Ministry [of Economic Affairs] can make life agony if it wishes to," reports Harmon Zeigler (1988:180).

The process can be frustrating for firms affected by but not party to the dealmaking, especially because of its opaqueness. Consider again the case of specialized glass, mentioned earlier. There are two local suppliers and three local buyers. One of the local suppliers recently expanded its capacity in response to increased demand from its tied (local) buyer, but for technological reasons the increase in capacity was much greater than needed to meet the extra tied demand. It pressed IDB to declare an import ban on such glass, on the grounds that local production capacity could now meet all needs. IDB instructed the Electrical Appliances Industries Association to negotiate an agreement between the parties. One of the two other buyers was a big-name multinational. It had previously been getting its supplies from the other of the two local suppliers (its own subsidiary), and from its own factory in Japan. It had great difficulty finding out how much the move to ban all imports was aimed mainly at imports from Japan (as part of a general attempt to reduce Taiwan's trade deficit with Japan); and how much it applied to imports from anywhere. If the former, it could still import from South Korea, where it owned another factory producing acceptable glass; if the latter, even that was out. It did not want to buy from the first local supplier for reasons of price and quantity, and also because if forced to switch to this supplier it would have to get its glass-using products recertified by all the international standards' bureaus, which could take up to a year. Yet the firm felt frustrated that it could not get a clear picture of what the government was trying to do. It suspected that IDB was giving special consideration to the request of the first local supplier because it was a nationally owned firm and that the third buyer, also a nationally owned firm, had made a secret deal with this firm to buy glass at a cheaper price than it, the big multinational, was going to have to pay, and hence the third buyer was lukewarm about resisting the import ban. This is a world where, in the eyes of this multinational (one of the longest established in Taiwan) relations between government and nationally owned businesses are close and thick and very secret.

Senior officials exercise much discretion in their dealings with firms and industries. Those near the top of bureaucratic hierarchies are assumed to have reached their position by their superior knowledge and strength of moral character, which frees them from the constraints of formal law. The contrast with conventional Western notions can be made in terms of a sporting analogy. The Western mode allows anyone to enter the field and play the game provided all agree to follow the rules and respect the referee. The Chinese mode shuts off the entire field, screens those who wish to play, and then allows those who pass the test of moral character and superior knowledge to do whatever they wish without interference from referees or regulations—up to a limit.[23] The imperial scholar-official tradition taught officials to feel superior to their businessmen clients and to exercise leverage with them. Today's officials are descendants of that tradition.

In these conditions, businesspeople are preoccupied with building up contacts in the government and party. To do so they may use the obligations of kinship, schoolmateship, military service in the same unit, or same county origin. Big companies generally employ several people who are specialists in government and party connections. They may be called "public relations managers." They are always mainlanders, and in native Taiwanese firms the people of this title may be the only mainlanders in the whole firm. Allan Cole's observation from the mid-1960s remains largely true today: "Especially in head offices in Taipei, some [native] Taiwanese enterprises retain a few mainland staff members because of their contacts with national officials through whom they can seek state contracts and expedite action on various kinds of applications" (1967:646).

Personal connections may be sweetened with money. Salary differentials between central office holders and their private sector equivalents are large, as noted in chapter 7—commonly 30 to 50 percent lower for a mid-level official. Taiwan businesspeople know the techniques of negotiating bribe money with officialdom as a fine art. They listen for what the official says about the cost of living, what he says about his hobbies. They may bring him a cookie box full of money, present it to him as a gift for his children, and wait to see if he returns the box and contents. Or they may simply leave him with a "red en-

---

[23] The analogy comes from Paul Hsu, cited in Winn 1987.

velope,'' as it is called, full of "gift" money. Such special persuasion is concentrated in the expected places: in offices of public works, taxes, urban planning, customs, duty rebates, and traffic police. As Cole explained, "when mainlander officials observe the prosperity of enterprisers, especially the Taiwanese, they feel that it is equitable to exact their slice as application forms come over desks requiring their chops [official seals]'' (1967:649).

It would be generally agreed that the prevalence of corruption has much diminished since the 1960s. Cole already observed a change in the mid-1960s:

> There is some evidence . . . that the tide may be turning: Until the early 'sixties, officials from the mainland generally had the upper hand in regulating and exacting. But national and provincial governments and their administrators are becoming more aware of how dependent they are on the cooperation of major enterprisers. And the latter are becoming more aware of the increased leverage afforded them by the emphasis on economic planning and accelerated growth. (1967:649)

The change was particularly marked after Chiang Ching-kuo came into effective power in the 1970s. Soon after his father's death he had forty-five government officials arrested for customs violations, including members of the feared military intelligence branch. Another twenty officials, plus his own personal secretary, went to prison for bribery (Zeigler 1988:175). The aim was to establish an image of incorruptibility in government. This was important to establish especially because Chiang Ching-kuo saw more clearly than his father the need to bring native Taiwanese into senior positions within the state. But he was also aware of the danger that this would lead to a swamping of the state by concealed patron-client and kinship solidarities—previously kept in check by the ethnic cleavage between mainlanders and islanders. So in his appointments he placed great weight on "cleanness" of reputation, and induced a fear throughout the central bureaucracy not just of taking bribes but also of being seen in bars, dance halls, and expensive restaurants.[24]

Since then, little scandal has surrounded top figures, despite a weekly and monthly press which would certainly have broadcast it.[25] Having few positions in the central legislative body open to election helps to reduce the pressures

[24] President Lee, who succeeded Chiang Ching-Kuo after his death in Jan. 1988, is one of the clearest beneficiaries of the weight placed on cleanness of reputation in the promotion of native Taiwanese. From the time when he was singled out by Chiang Ching-kuo in the early 1970s and groomed for high office, Lee has been said to be absolutely clean; not even "pink" information exists about him (allegations of involvements with other women), something which cannot be said about all current holders of the top offices of the state.

[25] "Little" is an impressionistic comparison with other countries. But see the remarks about the Cathay scandal later. Many of the rumors of corruption in high places concern "self-dealing" (use of public office to allocate contracts to self or relatives). In a recent case a senior minister is alleged to have used his earlier position as head of Chinese Petroleum Corporation to insist on unusual contract specifications that could be met by only one firm, which happened to be closely linked to his wife. I have no idea of the truth of the allegations.

for using the power of office to raise money for fighting elections. The fact that the party has its own revenue base helps in the same way. And there are well-established techniques for quietly moving aside officials who are strongly suspected to be corrupt; such as moving them to one of the many "dumping grounds" within the bureaucracy, where they have plush offices, outsized name plates, secretaries, and everything they need to save face—but no power to influence events. The clearest example is the complete set of government ministries for the mainland, perpetuated to prepare for the reestablishment of Nationalist rule. But even parts of the "mainline" bureaucracy may be parcelled out for the same purpose. It may be that a role of task forces is sometimes to provide a reconcentration of decision-making on key issues to compensate for parcellization within the mainline bureaucracy (as well as to provide established bureaus with competition and to bring new skills to bear on policy formulation). In any case, businesspeople who deal with central government bureaus today, such as the Industrial Development Bureau or the Bureau of Commodity Inspection, report very few cases where an official has taken money or some other substantial favor, despite those large salary differentials.

Most rumored or reported corruption takes place at the local and provincial government levels where nothing major for the national development effort is at stake. At the central level, that which comes to light occurs primarily among politicians and much less among bureaucrats. Even where large and lucrative, it is generally money corruption of the common garden-variety—greed spiced with the cynicism about the public interest that comes in handy in the presence of an open honey pot. This is different from the corrupt exercise of power which "gangrenes" the sinews of the state. Corruption is also fairly regular in terms of price: the standard kick-back on a normal sized public works project is around 10 percent plus or minus two; customs officers normally take one carton of meat in one hundred, one bottle of whiskey in twelve or twenty-four, and so on. Within the customs, the levy is on imports rather than exports and is concentrated on import items that are not crucial for economic development. So while imports of electronic components and industrial chemicals do not pay bribes, imports of foodstuffs routinely do.[26] Customs officers, too, act in

---

[26] Customs officials can extort by threatening to impound goods because of a typing error on the bill of lading. They can threaten to send back to the country of origin the balance between what is stated on the bill of lading and what actually arrives—until some payment is made. They have power to open containers without the importers being present, and can "arrange" to have some of the contents be missing. One importer I know was having particular trouble of this sort with tennis racquet strings.

Consider further the following story, which illustrates the bureaucracy, politicians, and the press at work. The duty on milk powder is 25 percent. However, if it is more than six months old it is disallowed for human consumption, and as an animal feedstock has to pay only 5 percent duty. Routinely over-the-limit material is imported as animal feed and then sold as human food, in return for a small consideration to the authorities. Recently the importing firm which had the franchise to import from countries A and B lost its franchise to another firm. To get revenge it

line with a common understanding of what things are really important and what are not. In all these ways corruption in Taiwan contrasts with corruption in many other countries of South and Southeast Asia. Corruption on public works projects, for example, occurs in Taiwan (also Korea) mainly through overcharging for correctly built structures. In India it occurs mainly by substandard construction of correctly priced structures, which are that much more likely to wash out in the next monsoon. Taiwan's mode is probably less damaging to economic development than India's.[27]

FRAGMENTATION AND RECONSOLIDATION IN THE MID-1980s

This system of politics and policy-making began to undergo rapid change in the early to mid-1980s, so much so that from the perspective of 1988 we might refer to it as the "1950 to 1985" system. Many of the changes stem directly from its successes. First, economic development, urbanization, and the growth of industry have created a "new middle mass"[28] whose wealth is secure enough for worries about the quality of life, especially the environment, medical care, and consumer protection, to become pressing. Second, new individuals and groups began trying to win public support by articulating these worries. In the early 1980s environmental protests occurred; an environmental movement and a consumer movement took root. These new individuals and groups are sometimes within the party but more often outside. Third, elections for the legislative yuan became more common as the old nonelected legislators died; and voters faced a diversification of options, which culminated in the formation in late 1986 of the first opposition party, the Democratic Progressive

---

wrote an article for a local newspaper describing how Customs and the Board of Foreign Trade (BOFT) were turning a blind eye. There ensued a predictable and partly orchestrated chorus of protest about the government's laxity. BOFT promised publicly to stop the practice forthwith. All aged material would be specially treated so that it could not be used by humans. The importer who had acquired the A and B franchise and governments A and B were very worried. To treat the powder in this way was not only expensive, but the treatment could only be done in Singapore before being sent on to Taiwan. The importer thus devised a two-pronged strategy. First, he got the issue out of the press by taking out some expensive advertising in the papers which were carrying the story; which prompted the papers not to publish things damaging to the interest of a new and promising client. Second, his agent paid off whom he thought were the relevant officials. However, two customs officials of one of the main ports, organized by a legislator of the provincial assembly, let the importer know that they had not received their share of the payment. They could not allow nontreated aged powder through their port unless the importer agreed to an initial payment plus an open-ended commitment to entertain them once a week for dinner. Fortunately the importer himself was not required to attend these dinners. He sent his agent to the provincial center where the three lived, and the agent arranged each week for the dinner and entertainment. After seven weeks the importer decided to test the water. He sent the agent off on an overseas assignment, informed the three diners, and awaited their response. None came, the importer concluded that he had satisfactorily paid his dues, and the nontreated material continued to enter this port at the low rate of duty.

[27] See Wade 1982b, 1982c, 1985; Hamilton 1983.

[28] A term used by Marakami for Japan; cited in Pempel 1987:279.

party. Fourth, the United States was no longer willing to pliably absorb Taiwan's exports, and the foreign exchange reserves began to reach embarrassing levels in the early 1980s, continuing to grow through 1988. The United States also made a rapprochement with China, upsetting Taiwan's earlier lock-step compliance with U.S. foreign policy. Fifth, generational change occurred, so that many second- and third-rank policy-makers, and a few at the top, had no direct experience of the mainland before 1949 and were much more influenced by their education in the United States. The changes are very similar to those which occurred in Japan in the late 1960s and early 1970s, some fifteen years earlier, which also led to basic changes in politics and policy-making (Pempel 1987).

The change might be described as a shift from "state corporatism" in the direction of "social corporatism" (Zeigler 1988). The corporatist structure continues, with the state regulating interest groups. But the balance of influence between the state and interest groups is shifting from being overwhelmingly in favor of the state toward more of an equality. In other words, the preferences of the political leadership and bureaucrats are becoming less determinative of policy decisions. Senior officials find themselves into a strange wind, forced to respond for the first time to social movements, agitational politics, and a rival political party. When the Bureau of Commodity Inspection announced in early 1987, in response to an Industrial Development Bureau request, that the makers of packaging for electrical appliances would be subject to compulsory export commodity inspection (on grounds that poor packaging was spoiling the market) the director-general suddenly had to face an angry delegation of forty packaging makers protesting the decision. This was the first time such resistance to the inclusion of an item on the list for export inspection had been seen. The two members of the legislative yuan leading the delegation threatened to bring a crowd of three thousand demonstrators in front of the legislative yuan if the decision was not reversed. The outcome is to be noted: The director-general spoke to them to explain the background of the decision and then proposed a compromise. The packaging would be inspected for a trial period of six months only, and the inspection would not begin for another six months to allow firms time to adjust (though the second condition is in any case normal procedure). Firms which were given a low grade would not have to pay the higher fee which normally went with that grade; but buyers of the packaging equipment would still have an incentive to switch to firms which got a good grade because they would face less risk of delays and other hassles on account of the more intensive inspection of products from lower-grade firms. On hearing this proposal the two legislators urged the delegation to accept, which it did. The shift toward pluralist politics has begun but it has not yet got very far.[29]

---

[29] In Aug. 1983 the Ministry of Economic Affairs arranged a two-day public hearing on the

The legislature has been acquiring a louder voice over the 1980s as the number of younger, elected members increases.[30] It has begun to use its power to call government ministers to answer questions and to delay its approval of the budget until the main items have been discussed. When it approved the ending of almost four decades of stringent foreign exchange controls in 1987, it also denied the executive the right to reimpose controls without its consent— a dramatic example of a new assertiveness. A Consumer's Foundation was established in 1980 alongside the official, party-sanctioned—and inactive— Consumer's Association, playing on the rivalries within the government. It has published some damaging reports on consumer items, including products of big-name U.S. multinationals whom the government does not wish to offend. Attempts to squash it have failed. The press has carried its reports with glee, making them available to a mass audience.[31] At the same time, a growing grassroots environmental movement has forced the government to awaken to the need to come to grips with the pollution problem. In one area, groups of ten to twenty local residents have kept a rotating vigil outside a refinery of Chinese Petroleum Corporation in protest at the firm's plans to build Taiwan's fifth naptha cracker there—a vigil which by February 1988 had lasted for seven months. Spurred into action, CPC announced it will spend over US$400

---

proposed trade law. According to press accounts, the main point made by industrial and commercial leaders, and specifically by the Chinese Federation of Industries, was that

> the screening of applications for imports and exports be participated in by scholars and the private industrial and commercial sectors. [The Chinese Federation of Industries] also suggested representatives of trade and industry associations and manufacturers to be invited to take part in the deciding of goods classifications, and restrictions on foreign trade. Some attendees contended that the administrative authorities were granted too much power [in the new law] while manufacturers and businessmen have few rights, interests or assistance designed for them in the preliminary draft.'' (*China Post*, 21 Aug. 1983)

[30] See chapter 8 n.6.

[31] The group of intellectuals behind the Consumer Foundation prepared a careful strategy for getting the new organization authorized. Because the Consumer Association was registered with the Ministry of the Interior they proposed to register the foundation with the Ministry of Education, in order to exploit the rivalry between the two ministries. They also proposed to call it a foundation, not an association, to make it sound like something different. The consequence was that they had to rely for finance not on subscriptions but on the sale of their journal. The foundation has been controversial from the beginning because of its willingness to criticize (on the basis of studies commissioned from scientific organizations) the products of big companies. For example, it accused Johnson & Johnson of selling inferior baby powder in Taiwan as though the powder were identical with what the company sold in the United States. Such boldness has caused consternation in the government, and the vice-minister of education who allowed the foundation to be formed came under internal criticism. In late 1983 the head of the foundation was asked by the president of his university to choose between his university post and his job with the foundation (it was said, apparently with some justification, that he was neglecting his teaching). The rest of the foundation's board waited anxiously to see if the party would try to wrest control or close it. In fact, the university president backed down and the head of the foundation did not have to choose. The thirteen-member board is self-selecting and none is close to the party.

million during the next three years on environmental protection improvements. In January 1988 the Consumer Foundation sponsored the formation of
a new association, the New Environment Foundation, to support environmental organizations (Moore 1988).[32] The government has responded to the envi-
ronmentalist pressure by hugely increased spending on environmental clean-
up; the budget of the environmental protection agency is not far short of its
U.S. counterpart's.

In other contexts, the government is being forced to modify its laws and
regulations as the economy shifts beneath them. In the late 1970s and early
1980s, increasing economic complexity together with mushrooming money
supply and foreign exchange reserves led to a proliferation of financial services on the grey-to-black side of the government's restrictive financial regulations. The growth of these services challenged the government's long-standing concern to separate financial power from productive power and to limit
stock and real estate speculation. Investment and trust companies, for example, had been authorized under a statute of 1970 to invest trust funds derived
from assets such as pensions and estates, and to return to the depositor a share
of the dividends. They were not to establish branches, or issue credit cards, or
accept checking, demand, or savings deposits (so they were not to compete
with banks). On the other hand, they were allowed wide discretion in making
investments, except for tight restrictions on how much equity in other companies they could own (no more than 30 percent of the trust company's own
capital, excluding its customer trust funds). However, the imbalance between
their legally limited access to funds and their wide investment discretion has
made for much instability and evasion of the law (Winn 1987). In order to
expand their lending base, they began to offer guaranteed dividends (interest
in all but name); to offer credit card facilities, which the banks were not per-

---

[32] In late 1983 some of the leading industrialists were locked in a bitter dispute over market
share in the cement industry. The side which stood to lose market share appealed for environmentalists' support. The site was Toroko Gorge, one of the finest scenic spots in Taiwan. Wang of
Formosa Plastics wanted to build a cement plant near the gorge, because of the existence of
potentially the best limestone on the island. He had not previously produced cement. The existing
producers included some politically powerful men. They did not want Wang to upset their cozy
marketing arrangements, which included the requirement that buyers pay for cement at the time
of ordering. Since the order may not be filled for some time, the makers have a tidy pile of money
in hand which can be put to other uses. They joined with environmentalists to oppose Wang. The
son-in-law of the leading cement producer became head of the special environmental group
formed for the purpose. Economic Affairs Minister Chao announced that he opposed the Wang
plant—and he and Wang ceased their much commented-upon monthly game of golf. The minister
of internal affairs (like Wang a native Taiwanese) announced in favor of the plant.

Farmers associations have acquired more autonomy from government since the late 1970s,
though penetration by the party has not declined. Irrigation associations, however, have remained
more tightly controlled by the government. Their elective councils were suspended from 1975 to
1982 as part of a reassertion of control from above. The reasons seem to have been a mixture of
poor managerial performance by the staff, leading to farmer complaints and refusal to pay water
charges, and capture of some IA councils by people unsympathetic to the regime.

mitted to do; to open branches; and to invest heavily in real estate speculation and company takeovers, breaking the rules about equity holdings in other companies. They began to operate like banks and holding companies rolled into one.

The government has clearly been split on what to do about them. After internal disputes, it has changed the rules to legalize the situation on the ground, permitting branch offices and credit card facilities. But it has resolved to enforce the original limits on equity holdings in other companies and to prevent the trust companies from accepting checking accounts, and has stiffened restrictions on lending to "related persons." Nothwithstanding, a series of financial scandals shook the Cathay group in 1985 (once Taiwan's biggest investment and trust company), implicating people high up in the political executive and questioning the adequacy of the government's entire financial regulatory system. Cathay's owners had been channelling money by illegal means out of an affiliated savings and loan institution into real estate speculation and worse, perhaps protecting themselves by bribing Nationalist party legislators. They had opened an exclusive club conveniently close to the legislative yuan in downtown Taipei, granting free membership to legislators and senior officials while businessmen paid small fortunes to join. The secretary-general of the party was forced to resign, as well as the finance minister, the economic affairs minister, and some officials in the Ministry of Finance. In the wake of the scandal the government again attempted to tighten financial control over the companies. By 1988 at least ten firms were under investigation for banking law violations and possible fraud (Moore 1988). They are suspected of operating large-scale pyramid arrangements in which long-standing investors are paid with deposits from new investors. Observers say that the investigations are intended to prepare the ground for a full-scale revision of financial regulations, to legalize and liberalize a much wider range of activities than in the past. Still, many senior officials worry that by being seen to act under pressure, the government is being made to look an ass.

One of the government's responses to this groundswell of change is to strengthen the policy network, so as to expand and institutionalize decision-making inputs from industrialists, financiers, and others. For example, the Ministry of Economic Affairs has been making an effort since the early 1980s to seek comment from private sector groups on draft legislation before submitting it to the cabinet. In 1982 the director of the Board of Foreign Trade pressed his agency to seek information and feedback from the private sector in a way that his predecessors had not. The following year the social affairs department of the party held a series of meetings with industry associations to discuss why nothing had happened since the premier's 1981 speech calling for the associations to be more active. An important new development is contained in the procedures for formulating the strategic industry list, initiated in 1982. As noted, representatives of the concerned industry associations are now formally involved in the deliberations. The procedures for revising tariffs have also been changed in a small but significant way: since 1982 proposed tariff changes have been made public before being sent to the legislature, and reporters are now allowed to attend the previously secret meetings of the Finance and Economics Committee which discusses the proposals on behalf of the legislature.

The almost complete overhaul of the laws of intellectual property which occurred in 1985–87 resulted from a confluence of support from both private domestic firms and government officials. Foreign firms operating in Taiwan, and the U.S. government, had long pressed for these changes, to no avail, but several developments occurred in the mid-1980s to tip the balance in favor of action. One was a new get-tough policy of the U.S. government to levy trade sanctions (under both the GSP [Generalized System of Preferences] program and Section 301 of the Trade Act) unless the changes were made. Another was the government's growing commitment to high-technology industries, and its belief that better protection of intellectual property rights would stimulate more domestic R&D spending. Third, many of the larger exporting firms found that Taiwan's ability to export legitimate products was being hampered by the country's reputation as a counterfeiter, especially as they shifted into highter value-added exports. A newly established National Anti-Counterfeiting Committee of the Chinese National Federation of Industries voiced its support for new laws. The Consumer Foundation joined in. With input from these groups and from the American Chamber of Commerce, the existing laws of patents, copyright, and trademarks were substantially tightened. However, many firms consider the changes have gone too far, and the government, wary of exciting unnecessary opposition, has been cautious on enforcement. The tightening is being done gradually, with inconsistencies and reversals along the way (Gadbaw and Richards 1988, chapter 10).

This is true more generally. The policy network involving private economic interest groups and the legislature is being strengthened, but by Japanese and Korean standards it remains weak. Several times since 1982 the executive, acting under intense U.S. pressure, has unilaterally reduced tariffs without waiting for approval from the legislature (Chang 1987:125–27). When the young, sophisticated, mostly U.S.-educated staff of the Science and Technology Advisory Group decided to hold a series of meetings in 1983 to hear the voice of industry, it called meetings of industry association representatives at two days' notice with no agenda, and spent the time exhorting the representatives to adopt the latest technology rather than listening to what they had to say. Listening to the citizenry is a habit not easily acquired.

Conclusions

If economic corporatism means that only those economic interest groups sanctioned by the state get access to the state, then Taiwan is an extreme example of the genre. The central bureaucracy is unusually well protected, because the many state-licensed interest groups have very little autonomy. As one observer notes, "The government sanctions or represses organizations and supplies them with officers" (Zeigler 1988:180). This makes for an important difference between Taiwan's type of corporatism and the European variety as found in Austria and Sweden, for example. The differences are in the freedom to organize, the balance of influence between the state and its incorporated economic interest groups, and the inclusion or exclusion of labor. The European cases grant much greater freedom to organize interest groups, even though they restrict access to the state. The balance of influence is more equal, with formal mechanisms of consultation and exchange. And labor is clearly incorporated into the arrangements. The European form can be called "social corporatism" to distinguish it from Taiwan's "state corporatism," the principal criterion being the balance of power between the state and interest groups. Even Mexico, which like Taiwan is both authoritarian and corporatist, is closer to the "social corporatist" form than Taiwan.

In terms of Chalmers Johnson's model of the developmental state, Taiwan meets the "bureaucratic autonomy" condition but fails to meet the "public-private cooperation" condition. The policy network between government and private firms is, in general, only thinly developed. The government is able to get quite a lot of information about the production capability of individual firms (though much less about finance) through such means as the export quality-control scheme, the loan guarantee scheme, and the external marketing agency (CETRA). And central officials do undertake quite a lot of administrative guidance of large private firms, even though less than is common in Korea and pre-1970 Japan. But the guidance mostly takes place in bilateral negotiations between government officials and individual firms rather than with aggregations of firms. Private sector representatives are little involved in policy formation. Harry Oshima's claim that "in Taiwan, despite an authoritarian central government, economic policy decisions are made with proper consultation with relevant groups" (1982:96) is simply wrong.

On the other hand, a little understood but apparently vigorous policy network links the central economic bureaus with public enterprises, public banks, public research and service organizations, universities, foreign multinationals with operations in Taiwan, private consulting firms, and some "special status" private manufacturing companies connected to the party, the military, or the economic ministries. This calls for further qualification to the popular idea that Taiwan, like the other East Asian countries, has a "lean" government in contrast to the bloated bureaucracies of the West (Hofheinz and Calder 1982:33).

The "state corporatist" power structure has facilitated the government's efforts to pursue a "leadership" role in important industries, rather than simply a "followership" role. But the structure in itself did not dictate such a choice, nor did it dictate an overriding commitment to economic growth and industrialization. Strategic choice is a partly independent variable from the structure of power. The difference between Taiwan and Mexico, for example, is less in the structure of power as in the choices made by the political leadership.

Taiwan's political structure not being securely legitimated, the government has felt under much pressure to deliver an "economic miracle" in order to win acceptance of its right to rule Taiwan. But driven by an anti-big capitalist conviction reinforced by fear of the political potential of native Taiwanese economic power, the government has only weakly developed a policy network linking the central economic bureaus with the private sector, relying more on public enterprises and other public agencies. This has made long-term strategic bargaining with important private economic groups difficult (though not impossible). Without a framework for bargaining, the government has given particularly high priority to economic stabilization, even at the cost of very rapid industrial restructuring, because economic instability could easily aggravate underlying tensions to jeopardize political stability and the Nationalist party's position. The high priority to economic stabilization reinforced the position of the monetary authorities vis-à-vis the industrial authorities, limiting the use of selective credit as a primary instrument for steering the behavior of private firms as compared to Korea. Hence the government's reliance on public enterprises, trade controls, and tax incentives.

The organization of public power is in flux as of the mid-1980s, as a stronger policy network with the private sector is constructed in response to increasing social mobilization and demand politics. The interesting question is how the more open political system will handle the pressures from rising labor costs, ballooning financial assets, Taiwanese investment abroad, and reactions from trading partners. We return to the implications of these developments after considering the evidence for the governed market theory in capitalist East Asia more generally.

Chapter 10

CONCLUSIONS (1): GOVERNING THE MARKET
IN EAST ASIA

WE BEGAN by considering two broad approaches to cross-country differences in industrial performance. One is the neoclassical approach, which sees efficiency in resource use as the principal general force for economic growth. It says in essence that East Asian countries did better than others because their markets worked better, with fewer price distortions, producing a more efficient allocation of resources. We distinguished two variants of this market supremacy interpretation. The free market (FM) theory says that markets for goods and factors of production were freer than in other countries. The simulated free market (SM) theory recognizes the existence of market distortions and industrial policies in East Asia, but says that industrial policies merely offset existing market distortions, creating overall neutrality in resource allocation. Neither variant pays much attention to political arrangements.

The political economy approach treats capital accumulation as the principal general force for economic growth. It interprets East Asian success as the result of a higher level and different composition of investment than in less successful countries. The difference in investment is due, in important if difficult to quantify part, to government actions to constrain and accelerate the competitive process. These actions were carried out by a relatively authoritarian and corporatist state. We called this the governed market (GM) theory of East Asian economic success.

GM policies have aimed to channel resources into industry based within the national territory, and thereby raise the domestic demand for labor. By means of politically determined constraints and rigged prices, they have steered the competitive process into higher-wage, higher-technology alternatives and away from short-term speculative or labor cost-reducing alternatives within or beyond the national territory. The policies include: maintenance of a post–land reform ceiling on agricultural land ownership, so as to limit wealth accumulation in land and intensify agricultural productivity; control of domestic and crossborder sources of credit, so that finance remains subordinate to industry and amenable to government direction; stabilization of the main macroeconomic parameters of investment choice; modulation of international competitive pressure in parts of the domestic economy; export promotion; investment in technological capacity; and assistance to specific industries. Under all these headings the governments have gone well beyond the limits of what would be

sanctioned by FM or SM approaches, or what pluralist and democratic governments practice.

Corporatist political arrangements have contributed to East Asia's fast
growth both directly and indirectly. Compared to more pluralist regimes they
help to limit conflict between major economic interest groups and promote
continuity of institutional forms, both of which help sustain high levels of
investment. They also contribute through the power they give to the state to
govern the market, especially by protecting the central bureaucracy from all
but the most powerful of interest groups.

Further discussion of the rationale of these policies is saved for the next
chapter. Here we need to take up one particular issue, which concerns the
effects of the industry-specific or targeted policies. The existence of targeted
policies does not by itself mean that they made any difference. A neoclassical
economist might want to argue that they merely put the government's seal of
approval on the investment intentions of some private firms. In that sense they
merely followed rather than led the market, making little difference to what
would have happened anyway. Those who believe that the policies made a
difference are like Glendower in Shakespeare's *Henry IV, Part 1*, who claims,
''I can call spirits from the vasty deep''; to which Hotspur replies, ''Why, so
can I, or so can any man; But will they come when you do call for them?''

A possible rationale for this interpretation might run as follows. East Asian
governments need to appear to be responsible for industrial success because,
more than most others, they have based their claim to popular support on their
ability to sponsor economic prosperity. They can appear to be responsible,
without actually being so, if they can buy into an association with private
sector industrial projects which will be successful. The government consults
with business in order to find out what the private sector thinks are good bets
(rather than to exercise leadership). The government then puts some of its own
resources behind some of those bets, in the form of fiscal incentives, concessionary credit, tariffs, and so on. But the amount of resources is typically
small, for the purpose is less to modify private sector decisions as to obtain an
association with decisions which the private sector would have made anyway.
The fact that the private sector would do the projects whether assisted or not
is some assurance that the projects will be successful; and if they are not, both
the private sector and the government have a joint interest in blaming failure
on external events beyond anyone's control. So the government can distance
itself from failures, while associating itself with successes.[1] In this way the
government not only bolsters its popular support, but also induces assisted
capitalists to see that their interests lie in the longevity of the regime and its
rules. A second and complementary rationale could run in terms of the relative

---

[1] I am indebted to Brian Hindley for suggesting this line of argument. See his spirited attack on
industrial policy in Western Europe and Japan (1984).

power of government and business. Private business is strong enough to shut out the government from a more directive role even if the government were to want such a role, it might be argued. The underwriting of some private sector bets is the outcome of negotiations between government agencies and firms in which firms can invite government help but can prevent government from making them do things they do not want to do.

We could call this the "government followership" theory of East Asian industrial policy—provided we remember that followership here means "small followership" in terms of the distinction introduced in chapter 1. Assistance constitutes small followership when firms would have done the project anyway. Assistance constitutes big followership when firms would not have done the project without assistance. Big followership is more consistent with the GM theory of East Asian success, because it makes for a difference between actual outcomes and free or simulated free market outcomes.

The government followership theory fits the universal motivation of bureaucrats as understood in neoclassical economics. Bureaucrats are highly risk-averse, and do not want to expose themselves by being connected with failures. If no private firm could be persuaded to enter an activity without government help, the officials who went ahead and gave the help would be in an exposed position. They are unlikely to do so.

The argument also provides a way of accommodating the fact of Hong Kong. Hong Kong's industrial success is very important for those who say that government—other than as provider of the essential neoclassical functions—is unimportant in explaining East Asian success. If Hong Kong did as well as the other apparently more *dirigiste* countries, this shows that industrial policies must have been unimportant in the development of the others because Hong Kong is as near to a free market economy as it is possible to get.

So a neoclassical perspective can accommodate the coincidence of East Asian success with East Asian industrial policies in two ways: (1) by suggesting that those policies were primarily functional rather than sectoral, which simply offset what were in any case small market distortions; and (2) by suggesting that insofar as industrial policies aimed to promote specific industries, they merely followed the initiatives of some decentralized private producers, marginally assisting them to do what they would have done anyway.[2]

[2] Since my concern is to highlight the role of leadership, I tend to treat followership as a residual. In a more complete formulation one would have to make a distinction between industrial assistance which helps firms do whatever they want to do, even at the cost of lower efficiency and flexibility (Wade 1982b), and assistance which helps firms to do things within the set of actions consistent with competitive principles. One might bring in here the distinction between assistance given in dyadic relations between government and firms, and assistance given to help groups of firms overcome collective action difficulties (Noble 1988).

Followership interpretations are elaborated in Samuels (1987), about the role of the Japanese state in the energy industries, and in Bhagwati (1986). Says Bhagwati of Japan: "the Japanese MITI is not the omnipotent and omniscient agency that industrial policy proponents in the United

TAIWAN—REPRISE

To test these theories, we need to establish to what extent their postulated causes have been present in East Asia. For Taiwan, we have seen much evidence consistent with the FM or SM variants (chapter 3). For example, export producers have enjoyed near (but not complete) free trade conditions, thanks to the duty drawback scheme and an accompanying easing of nontariff barriers. The labor market is free, being little affected by trade unions, minimum wage legislation, public sector pay policy, multinational companies, or employers' associations. The unregulated or "curb" market for finance also fits the FM theory, and it is quite substantial, accounting for roughly 30 percent of loans processed through the whole financial system over the 1970s. The myriad small firms also operate in fairly free domestic market conditions, untrammeled by government controls and little affected by government incentive schemes—until their transactions involve the international economy. Recall, however, that the 96 percent of firms with under one hundred employees produce only about a quarter of manufacturing output and value-added. Finally, one should include here the government's provision of a range of public goods. These include macroeconomic stability (as seen in low inflation and a stable real effective exchange rate), and heavy investment in education and infrastructure.

The simulated free market (SM) theory also receives support from several policy areas. Figures from 1969 suggest that in that year export subsidies offset the incentive bias of protection, resulting in no overall discrimination in favor of importables and against exports. So in that year and quite possibly in subsequent years too, the trade regime was on average neutral, or in Bhagwati's terminology, export-promoting. Also, overall incentives toward agriculture and industry were in the same year approximately neutral between them. (But as we have seen and will see again, methodological weaknesses lower our confidence in the picture of overall neutrality derived from the 1969 figures.) The market for bank credit fits the SM theory insofar as interest rates, though set by government, have been high compared to other countries (notably Korea and Japan), though still well below the curb market rate. The government's functional industrial policies—to subsidize vocational education, improve the access of small and medium businesses to credit, and subsidize industrial research and development—could be taken to support the SM theory. Although government expenditure to GNP has not been low in relation to other countries at roughly the same income level, the government budget

---

States would like to believe. I believe instead that the correct way to analyze its role is precisely to see it as an agency that plays this assurance-providing role. While Mitsubishi, Sanyo, et al. really make the decisions, MITI is giving them the assurance that stems from a symbiotic relationship between the capitalists and the government'' (1986:94). In my terms, MITI is merely following the decisions made in the private sector. Bhagwati cites Gary Saxonhouse as his authority.

has been in overall surplus in most years, providing a cap on the government's interventions in the market and specifically on its ability to "distort" prices by tax-subsidy measures. The large public enterprise sector has been a net contributor to government revenues (though some individual public enterprises consistently suffer losses).

Finally, whether as the result of free markets or simulated free market policies, Taiwan had a very low overall distortion score during the 1970s, as measured by Agarwala's price distortion index (see chapter 3). Its rapid growth is just what neoclassical theory would predict for a low-distortion country. But serious scholars have dismissed Agarwala's index as having "limited analytic content" (Fishlow 1985). And in any case it is based on very broad categories which do not pick up "distortions" within the boundaries of each category.

However, the main point is that plenty of evidence from Taiwan fits the FM and SM theories. The issue is how to weigh it against that which better fits the GM theory. There are two central questions: (1) To what extent have the government's interventions changed the pattern of investment from what free market prices would have generated, so as to carry out a planned pattern of sectoral growth? (2) To what extent have the government's interventions made for faster economic growth than otherwise? Or to put the questions another way, how much economic liberalization has occurred, and how important was that degree of liberalization to the result?

How nice to be able to construct a megalomaniacal multisectoral model of the economy with all macro- and industrial policies represented. One would calculate second- and third-round effects, and then draw conclusions about both the net bias of incentives between industries and the effects of those incentives on output and investment. A neoclassical economist would hope to find that assistance given to one industry is cancelled out by assistance given to others, so that the result of all those industry-specific efforts is, in the end, neutrality. The conclusion would probably be drawn that the entire array of industry measures could be withdrawn at a stroke, leaving relative prices and resource allocations unchanged. For it is commonly assumed in neoclassical analysis that the allocation of resources in an economy where neutrality is being contrived by policy measures is much the same as where there is no government intervention.

But the assumption rests on faith. My argument for Taiwan is more modest. I accept that much investment has been undertaken in response to relatively uninhibited price formation. From that point on I make a whole series of qualifications. First, the process of relatively uninhibited price formation reflects the underlying "social structure of investment." The government has acted to alter this structure profoundly, making it more conducive to industrial investment. The land reform is a clear example, which removed the possibility of future wealth accumulation in the form of large land holdings, Filipino-style.

The financial system controls are another clear example, which limited the possibility of future wealth accumulation through money-lending. In short, by preventing nonindustrial classes from acquiring wealth and political power the government helped to form a class of industrial capitalists and assure that its interests dominated those of the private owners of land, real estate, and financial assets. These government efforts to shape the social structure of investment indirectly affected the pattern of even the freely formed prices.

Second, the government has affected relative prices in such a way as to enhance industrialists' profits and thereby encourage more investment. It fixed low agricultural prices in the 1950s and 1960s (compensating farmers by low input costs and by socializing risks), which allowed industrial wages to be lower and industrial profits and investment to be higher. It insured that labor costs were not driven up by union power. It has protected some domestic industries, allowing higher prices. It used fiscal investment incentives and concessional credit to lower costs of production and thereby drive investment first in heavy and chemical industries, more recently in electronics and machinery. It lowered the costs of export production by subsidies, duty-drawbacks, and the like.

Third, the government has used a number of more direct methods to shape the investment pattern. This is clearest in the case of the public enterprise sector, one of the biggest in the noncommunist world. Controls on incoming and outgoing direct foreign investment are another case in point. Also, the government has exerted a direct influence over the sectoral distribution of investment funds by means of its ownership of the banking system and its control of foreign exchange.

Almost certainly some of Taiwan's industries and some of its exports would not have been initially profitable without state encouragement. That they were profitable after the event reflects the use of the price mechanism to validate investment decisions taken on grounds other than current efficiency. The government pushed and pulled the structure of relative prices to secure a pattern of growth which it mapped out in advance in rolling plans.

Admittedly there is not much "hard" quantitative evidence for this interpretation, any more than there is for the FM and SM theories. But ironically, some supporting quantitative evidence comes from the same data as others use to say that Taiwan has a neutral trade regime. We saw that this conclusion is questionable on methodological grounds. The methodological difficulties aside, we find, taking the figures at face value, that different manufacturing industries have different policy-induced incentives. The dispersion of effective subsidy rates with respect to domestic market sale in 1969 was not far short of Argentina's (see table 3.2); and for two important manufacturing sectors, consumer durables and intermediate goods of higher levels of fabrication, Taiwan had the second highest effective subsidy levels in the six-country study. Since the dispersion is around a low average, it is likely that the differential resource pulling effect is greater than the same dispersion around the high Latin American averages. And it is also likely that the dispersion results from intended differences between industries rather than from accidental causes. Furthermore, government policies make for much variation between manufacturing sectors in their incentives to sell abroad or on the domestic market (see table 3.3). There is an "incentives twist" between export-oriented industries and import-competing industries, the former having net incentives to sell abroad and the latter having net incentives to sell domestically. By contrast, policy incentives in developing countries commonly give net disincentives even to export-oriented industries (by comprehensive protection and perhaps by export taxes). In this respect Taiwan is on the side of neoclassical virtue. But its antiexport bias for the import-competing industries (achieved in large part through protection) is against neoclassical precepts. Recall, however, that these figures, being for one year only, do not allow us to test a crucial proposition of the GM argument, that the incentives for industries classified at one point in time as import-competing subsequently are reversed so as to remove the earlier antiexport (pro-domestic market) bias. Finally, it must be remembered that surprisingly little information is available on how the level of protection in Taiwan compares with other countries'.

Still another kind of evidence refers to the timing of events. The period 1968–70 marked the end of "surplus labor" and can therefore be taken as a rough indicator of a basic change in Taiwan's comparative advantage. If investments in heavy and chemical industries were determined as a response to changes in comparative advantage—a response to changes in market signals—one would expect to find high investment and rates of growth following the end of labor surplus. But if government was the principal influence on investment in heavy and chemical industries and if it acted to anticipate changes in comparative advantage, one would expect to find high investment and rates of growth prior to the end of labor surplus. This, in fact, is what we find (see table 4.1).

This evidence suggests that the government "led" rather than "followed" the preferences of private market agents in the heavy and chemical industries during the 1950s and 1960s. Our examination of sectoral histories provides more evidence of leadership. Cotton textiles, synthetic fibers, plastics, other petrochemicals, basic metals, shipbuilding, machine tools, automobiles, and industrial electronics show that the government has frequently initiated new capacities in important industries, often using public enterprises linked to multinational corporations. Broadly speaking, government intervention of a leadership kind has focused on industries or projects which are capital-intensive (e.g., steel, petrochemicals), or which use technology that must be imported from a small number of potential suppliers (e.g., semiconductors), and also industries with an intimate relationship to national security (e.g., shipping). Leadership is concentrated on industries that are expected to become internationally competitive but have not yet become so, and on industries which, though losing competitiveness, the government considers important for the economy's future growth. It is absent in industries or projects without these various characteristics (e.g., wigs, wallets, and most nondurable consumer goods). Within "high-intervention" industries, leadership episodes are concentrated at the stage of creating distinctly new capacities (whether in new or existing industries), especially when such creation faces large indivisibilities or other entry barriers. So in any one industry, and in the industrial sector as a whole, we can distinguish episodes of leadership, followership, and laissez-faire. Sometimes the episodes begin with leadership and then move to followership (as in some of the heavy and chemical industries); sometimes they begin with laissez-faire or followership and then move to leadership (as in machine tools, where the government saw that without more assistance most of Taiwan's machine tool makers would not succeed in making the jump to computer-controlled machine tools).

As well as the sectoral histories, we examined policy instruments directly, and found that the government has a powerful enough register of instruments to exercise market leadership (chapters 5–6). For example, the apparatus of trade management could be used to give the government powerful leverage, because of the importance of trade for the whole economy. Public enterprises could be used to undertake big pushes in important industries. They tend to be concentrated in upstream sectors, from where they can create incentives and pressures for growth in downstream industries. And they tend to be strong in industries that would otherwise be dominated by multinational companies. The rules governing entry of direct foreign investment—as to industry, technology transfer, local content, and exports—enable the government to use direct foreign investment as another way, in addition to public enterprises, of creating incentives and pressures for further growth of domestic firms and industries the government wishes to encourage. Evidence shows the government to have been fairly successful in directing foreign investment into industries with high potential linkages (Schive and Majumdar 1981).

The organizational arrangements for formulating and implementing industrial policies are such as to make plausible the claim that the government led the market in a coherent rather than ad hoc way. This is the conclusion of chapters 7–9, which cover the goals and motivations of the state elite, the organization and resources of the economic bureaucracy, relations between bureaucracy, banks, and firms, and the place of the state in society at large. Until recently the policy network hardly included representatives of private business, and the government retained a striking degree of autonomy in setting the directions and details of policy. This reflects the leaders' suspicion of big Chinese capitalists, a suspicion formed during the mainland period and nurtured within the National Resources Commission, where many of those who formed Taiwan's industrial policies were trained. But a few policy instruments do grant private producers some influence. Nontariff barriers, for example, are set through procedures which give private actors somewhat more influence than is the case for tariffs and fiscal investment incentives. And as we saw, interest group variables do in fact yield a little more quantitative explanation of nontariff barriers than of tariffs—though even nontariff barriers are explained mostly by national policy variables (chapters 5, 9).

However, most businesspeople would scoff at the idea that government led the market in a coherent way. They are quick to voice an ineradicable gloom about the government's ability to do anything right. They treat agencies like the Industrial Development Bureau and CETRA as a joke—for which they pay with their taxes. The case of CETRA is telling. Although businesspeople often claim it is useless, a study of the trade promotion offices of five developing countries in New York showed the CETRA office to be the most effective. Computer firms which complain about the incompetence of ERSO, the national R&D laboratory for electronics, nevertheless join ERSO's R&D consortia not once, but several times over (Noble 1988). The reason why many Taiwan businesspeople deny that government helps business has to do with basic political facts. Most businesspeople are native Taiwanese, facing a government that they still tend to identify as mainlander-dominated and therefore different, if not still alien. And many senior industrial policy-makers have not altogether concealed their distaste for private businesspeople, in deeds if not in words. These two factors help to explain the "culture of pessimism" about the government to be found in native Taiwanese business circles.[3]

In short, several kinds of evidence suggest that the Taiwan government has exercised a significant amount of big leadership in some industries some of the time, meaning government initiatives on a large enough scale to make a sizable difference in investment and production patterns in the industry. We can also be fairly sure it has exercised a significant amount of big followership, even though it is difficult to judge case by case whether firms would have undertaken the investment without the assistance. In terms of the confrontation with the FM or SM theories, what matters is that the Taiwan government has gone well beyond small followership in its sectoral industrial policies, while small followership is the only interpretation of East Asian sectoral industrial policies which those theories can comfortably accommodate.

The fact of big leadership or big followership does not mean that government intervention has been effective in promoting economic growth; it only means that government intervention cannot be dismissed as having made a negligible difference to outcomes. But the balance of presumption must be that government industrial policies, including sectoral ones, helped more than

---

[3] See Metzger 1987 for a related argument. I remain puzzled by the propensity of many Taiwanese to express a hyperbolic cynicism about the government and to deny Taiwan's prosperity or attribute it to luck. See Pye's section on Taiwan (1985) as an example of undue credence.

they hindered. To argue otherwise is to suggest that economic performance would have been still more exceptional with less intervention, which is simply less plausible than the converse. Beyond presumption, we can be sure that the nonprice and distorted-price squeeze on agriculture in the 1950s and 1960s helped overall growth; for Taiwan was already near the productivity ceiling for rice-based agriculture, which was much below the possibilities in industry. For particular industries, all we can be sure of is that vigorous assistance has not impeded their international competitiveness (e.g., in steel, petrochemical, large-capacity chips).

Yet to repeat, plenty of evidence from Taiwan is consistent with the FM/SM theories. In a sense, the Taiwan economy can be thought of as containing both the Hong Kong paradigm and the Korean or Japanese paradigm. Those who say that Taiwan's success is due to free markets tend to assume that the small-scale segment constitutes the whole economy. Those who emphasize the developmental state or governed market aspects may overlook the extent to which most firms, in terms of numbers, have had relatively untrammeled freedoms. However, while the government's direct role in the small-scale sector resembles the Hong Kong approach, the sector works rather differently from Hong Kong's. The large-scale sector provides an envelope for its activities through interdependence on both the demand and the supply sides. Large amounts of credit, technical assistance, and skilled labor come to small firms directly from large firms. By setting directions for the large-scale sector, the government influences the configuration of risks and profit opportunities for small-scale firms. Indirectly, through its effect on investment within the large-scale sector, the government influences broad trends within the small-scale sector as well.

KOREA

The same argument I have made for Taiwan can also be made for Korea. Its political institutions, too, are authoritarian rather than democratic, and state-corporatist rather than social-corporatist or pluralist (Cumings 1984; Wade 1982a). Compared to Taiwan, it got a ten- to fifteen-year late start in creating a strong economic bureaucracy and a financial system able to mobilize savings and channel them to favored borrowers, and it began from a much lower per capita income.

Korea's state institutions have supported much the same mix of FM/SM and GM policies as in Taiwan. In terms of the FM/SM approach, one indicator will suffice. Korea's fast growth went with low price distortions as measured by Agarwala's index. Of the sample of thirty-one developing countries (not including Taiwan), Korea had the fastest growth of GDP over the 1970s and the third lowest price distortion score (a rank shared with four others). Taiwan had a somewhat lower distortion score and somewhat slower growth.

In terms of the GM approach, the Korean government also undertook a fundamental reshaping of the investment structure through land reform and a publicly owned banking system; created an enclave of relative stability for long-term investment decisions through its control of key parameters (foreign exchange rates, interest rates, and aggregate demand); modulated the economy's exposure to international competitive pressures in the domestic market; restricted the activities of foreign companies in Korea so as to keep control in Korean hands; aggressively pushed exports; and exercised leadership in selected industries (Hamilton 1986). The banks, publicly owned until 1980–83, were a central tool of market guidance, more important in this respect than in Taiwan (Jones and Sakong 1980). Even after denationalization they have continued to be under close government control and are still used for industrial targeting.

Three quantitative indicators can be used to show the similarity with Taiwan. First, Korea was no more "typical" an underdeveloped country in the 1950s than Taiwan, and still less a "basket case" as some contemporary observers claimed. It ranked fifteenth out of seventy-four countries by Adelman and Morris's sociopolitical development score as of the late 1950s and early 1960s, a little below Taiwan in twelfth place. But it ranked sixtieth in 1961 per capita income, far below Taiwan in forty-fourth place. (Mexico, by contrast, was fourteenth in per capita income and twenty-first by sociopolitical score.) No other country showed such a big discrepancy between low average income and high sociopolitical development. As in Taiwan, Korea's high sociopolitical rank reflects the development actions of the Japanese colonial government. And as in Taiwan, the alacrity of firms' response to the trade liberalization that began around the mid-1960s is due in part to government actions over the previous several decades.

Second, Korea has sustained almost equally high levels of investment as Taiwan, averaging 26.5 percent of GDP between 1965 and 1980, compared to Taiwan's 28.4 percent.

Third, a study of effective protection in Korea in 1968, using the same method as in the companion Taiwan study, found that Korea had the same level of effective protection to manufacturing as Taiwan in 1969 (14 percent for Taiwan, 13 percent for Korea: table 3.2). It also showed that Korea's intersectoral dispersion in effective subsidy rates to different manufacturing industries was greater than Taiwan's and not significantly different from Argentina's or Colombia's (see table 3.2; chapter 5). Since this was around a lower average, like Taiwan's, we can presume that in Korea's case too the dispersion had a greater and more intended effect on resource allocation than in the Latin American cases. This suggests that by the late 1960s and probably earlier, the Korean government was pursuing vigorous sectoral industrial policies, going beyond SM limits, the significance being that in the conventional chronology the onset of sectoral industrial policy occurs at the start of the heavy and chemical industry drive around 1973. (If we pool the data for Taiwan–Korea and for Argentina–Colombia to get a better statistical base—though still with only thirteen degrees of freedom—we find no significant difference at the 5 percent level in the degree of dispersion between "East Asia" and "Latin America." The thesis that East Asia has more neutral industry incentives than Latin America is rejected.)

However, the Korean study is open to the same methodological problems as its Taiwan companion, which means that it may understate the true average level of effective protection in Korea in 1968. An even higher proportion of the items in the Korean price comparison sample had negative price differentials between international and domestic prices than in the Taiwan sample (45 percent in the Korean case, 39 percent in the Taiwan case). Most of these were included at zero rate of protection rather than excluded on the grounds of quality differences. High average legal tariffs (54 percent for all items, compared to 60 percent in Taiwan) were ignored, as was the dense array of quantitative restrictions on Korean imports. Indeed, 74 percent of the items in the Korean price comparison were either subject to quantitative restrictions or to legal tariffs of 60 percent or more or both. This suggests that we ought to be wary of accepting the study's conclusion that "protection in the domestic market has generally been quite low by international standards" (Westphal and Kim 1982:270; Luedde-Neurath 1986: chapter 2). Other studies for the same period—late 1960s and early 1970s—show much higher average effective protection rates, roughly double that of the first one, including an estimated 67 percent for consumer durables, 106 percent for transport, and 67 percent for machinery (Kim 1982). The principal study using data for more recent years finds that the effective rate of protection for manufacturing averaged 49 percent in both 1978 and 1982 (Young 1984). This suggests, and most observers would agree, that protection in Korea increased substantially over the 1970s, to levels that were on the *high* side by developing country standards. However, protection was administered, as in Taiwan but in contrast to most other countries, in a conditional way; it was not equivalent to absolute protection and did not contain outlandish, Latin American-style tariff levels. In 1978, for example, at the height of the selectively protectionist phase, imports classified as restricted accounted for 75 percent of all manufactured imports by value (the biggest items being raw materials and machinery). Imports of these restricted items were scrutinized and controlled by the government, but were certainly allowed when they met a national interest test (World Bank 1987b). In 1983 the government announced a tariff reduction package intended to bring average rates down to those of the industrialized countries by 1988. And the average (nontrade-weighted) tariff rate has in fact fallen from 23.7 percent in 1983 to 12.7 percent in 1989. Most formal quantitative restrictions on industrial imports have been removed, though agriculture remains heavily protected, while customs practices, government procurement rules, and domestic content requirements continue to give informal or indirect protection to some domestic industries (Office of the United States Trade Representative 1989:115–23). Again, Korea's late but genuine import liberalization mirrors Taiwan's experience.

One basic difference between Korea and Taiwan is the size of firms (see table 3.7). During the 1970s the Korean government promoted the growth of giant conglomerates (*chaebol*) in imitation of Japan's *keiretsu*. The rationale was to concentrate resources on entrepreneurs with proven track records, and to encourage technological and organizational economies of scale. By 1984 the combined sales of the top ten *chaebol* equaled two-thirds of Korea's GNP, up from one-third five years before (Amsden 1989:116). Hyundai group, the largest, has thirty different companies spread over many industries, with 1983 sales of US$8 billion, five times the sales of Taiwan's largest group. Samsung, the second biggest, has twenty-nine companies.

More has been written about Korea's industrial policies than about Taiwan's, and the argument that the Korean government has exercised industrial leadership is less novel. Yusuf and Peters (1984), for example, test two models of investment behavior on Korean data, one based on planners' preferences and the other a standard neoclassical model explaining investment as a lagged function of changes in output or profitability. They find that the former gives better overall results than the latter, and better for heavy industry than for light industry. This is just what the GM theory would expect. However, the government's methods of leadership differ in emphasis from Taiwan's. To illustrate the point that there is more than one way to govern the market in pursuit of international competitiveness, let us consider the automobile, electronics, and petrochemical industries, following from the account in chapter 4 of these industries in Taiwan.

Automobiles

From the start the Korean government exerted a stronger hand in shaping the automobile industry than Taiwan.[4] In 1962, four years behind Taiwan's, a public enterprise established the first assembly plant (also in cooperation with Nissan). At the time the plant went into production the government instituted tight import controls on finished vehicles, duty-free import of components, and tax exemptions for the producer. In 1965 the government transferred the hitherto publicly owned assembler to a private firm and approved a new technology agreement with Toyota. A domestic content requirement of 50 percent in five years was also instituted and, unlike in Taiwan, rigorously enforced (through loss of preferential allocation of foreign exchange). With heavy protection

[4] On Korea's auto industry, I draw on: Chu 1987a, b; *Financial Times* 1988; *Business Korea*, various issues in 1985, 1986, and 1987; *Automotive News*, various issues; Korea Exchange Bank 1983.

plus domestic content requirements in place and with domestic components production growing fast, three more private firms were allowed to enter between 1965 and 1969 to fight for a market of less than twenty thousand units a year. So by 1970 the structure of the automobile industry in Korea resembled Taiwan's.

Subsequently Korea's industry forged ahead with government leadership of private firms, while Taiwan's languished. Autos were identified as one of the priority industries in the Heavy and Chemical Industry Plan of 1973. In 1974 an industry-specific plan for automobiles was published covering the next ten years. The objectives were to achieve a 90 percent domestic content for small passenger cars by the end of the 1970s and to turn the industry into a major exporter by the early 1980s. The government stipulated the three primary producers (Hyundai, Kia, and GM Korea—later called Saehan and then Daewoo), each a part of one of the big conglomerates. The government further stipulated the minimum size of each producer and the maximum size of car engines; and it had to approve their plans. Also in 1974 the government launched a complementary promotion plan for the parts and components industry. The plan required the three primary producers to meet a domestic contents schedule; it required them to cooperate in the production of standardized parts and components (which the Taiwan government tried but failed to get its producers to do); and it empowered the Ministry of Trade and Industry serially to select certain items and their assigned producers for special promotion, with a complete import ban once the item met the government's price and quality standards. Later the three producers were required to set export targets (consecutively in Southeast Asia, Latin America and the Middle East, then Canada, all by way of preparation for a big push into the U.S. market); they were encouraged to set their export price below cost of production; they received heavy direct and indirect export subsidies (especially credit); and they were allowed to import a limited number of top-of-the-line models in kit form for lucrative domestic elite sale, the number tied to their export performance. In these circumstances the Korean producers invested heavily in anticipation of the export drive (unlike their Taiwan counterparts). And they really did set export prices below cost of production, with domestic sales subsidizing exports. The Hyundai Pony cost US$3,700 in 1979, sold domestically for $5,000, and sold abroad for $2,200 (Chu 1987:205). The practice continues today (*Automotive News* 1988).

In 1980, following the second oil crisis and the rapid deterioration of domestic and world economic conditions, the government undertook a comprehensive rationalization of heavy and chemical sectors, including autos. It forced one of the three makers to exit from passenger car production in return for a monopoly in light trucks, a decision not reversed until 1987. It informed the other two that their rivalry in cars and power equipment was counterproductive, and asked them to choose one each. The Hyundai group got cars. The government also reduced the excise tax on cars to stimulate domestic demand, halved the export targets, and greatly increased the volume of concessional credit. The investment drive resumed in 1982 as the economy recovered. Hyundai Motor's debt to equity ratio soared to 5:1. By 1986 the Hyundai Excel became by far the best-selling new car import in U.S. history, following its earlier success in Canada. (But note that the Excel is a near-clone of the Mitsubishi Mirage, including Mitsubishi-made engine and transmission. Mitsubishi has owned 10 to 15 percent of Hyundai since 1982.) In 1988 Hyundai produced 650,000 automobiles, half as many as Fiat and Renault, of which 63 percent were exported. The industry as a whole produced 1.1 million units, of which 52 percent were exported.

In response to this ample evidence of Korea's automobile manufacturing capability, Ford and Chrysler rushed to establish joint ventures with Korean partners in order to catch up with GM's already existing joint venture with Daewoo. Ford tried to line up with Hyundai, which declined; then reached agreement with the second biggest, Kia, with the help of its Japanese equity partner, Mazda, which had a small equity stake in Kia. Chrysler lined up with Samsung, but Samsung failed to get government permission to start an export-oriented joint production plant.

Meanwhile, the government works to keep control in Korean hands and to reconcile the objectives of international competitiveness and high domestic content. (The Taiwan government, by contrast, has given up on national control and high domestic content in the interests of doing everything possible to enhance exports.) Korea's domestic market continues to be highly protected and the government prevents new domestic entrants. In response to intense U.S. pressure for trade liberalization, the government announced an automobile liberalization schedule in 1985, which permits small car imports to begin in 1988 for the first time in over twenty-five years, but with a duty of 200 percent to be lowered to 100 percent after two years, with additional restrictions on small cars from Japan. Imports of cars above 2,000cc were liberalized in mid-1987 but at least up until early 1988 none had actually made it through the maze of import procedures.

One of the most important reasons why the Korean auto industry may succeed in becoming a major world producer is the government's ability to restrict entry of new producers, and thereby protect economies of scale. Not only the Taiwan government but also those of other would-be car exporters like Brazil, Mexico, and Argentina have been much less successful in restricting entry. Whether one or more of the Korean makers will succeed in becoming major players depends on such factors as whether the Korean won continues to appreciate; whether real wages continue to rise at their recent level of 20 percent a year; whether the makers can improve their relatively low product quality ranking; whether the domestic market for cars grows to substantially more than its present 450,000 units a year; whether imports can compete in the domestic market; how quickly Hyundai and the other producers move their final assembly and parts operations to locations within the market of sale (Hyundai is building several plants in Canada); and whether Korea succeeds in building close automotive ties with the Chinese market. Much also depends on whether they can develop their own design capability and make their own engines and transmissions (at present mostly imported), and hence become technologically fully independent rather than remain as semi-independent technological subsidiaries of the big Japanese and U.S. makers. According to James Womack and Daniel Roos, "the intent of the Korean producers and their likely success is perhaps the greatest topic of debate in the world motor vehicle industry today" (1988:40).[5] For a country which at the start of its automobile push in the early 1970s had a per capita income of under US$600 this is a remarkable achievement in only fifteen years.

Electronics

Within electronics, we can concentrate on semiconductors, telecommunications, and computers, beginning the story with semiconductors.[6] Korean government policy toward the semiconductor industry has moved through three main stages, roughly corresponding to decades (Park 1987). In the 1960s the government encouraged foreign direct investment in semiconductors and other electronics at the same time as it adopted a very restrictive posture regarding foreign direct investment in general. In the 1970s the government established an infrastructural base for Korea to acquire its own technological capability in semiconductors. In the 1980s the emphasis has shifted toward strong government support for firms' initiatives. It is often said that Korea's semiconductor success owes little to government assistance. C. H. Yoon, professor of economics at Korea University, says, "Unlike in Japan, the governmental role in the development of the Korean semiconductor industry was not important at all" (1988:1). This is unpersuasive.

In the 1960s the government encouraged foreign direct investment in semiconductors (mostly from U.S. companies such as Fairchild and Motorola) primarily to increase Korea's exports rather than to obtain technology for Korean firms. And in fact little technology diffusion occurred, because U.S. compa-

---

[5] Hyundai's Excel sales faltered in the United States in late 1988 and 1989 (*Business Week*, 25 Dec. 1988; *Automotive News*, 3 July 1989; *New York Times*, 31 Oct. 1989). Out of 37 name plates, Hyundai ranked 22nd in terms of number of problems reported per 100 cars in 1989. Its sales of 150,000 cars in the United States in the first three quarters of 1989 were 30 percent down from the same period in 1988.

[6] On Korea's information industry, I draw on Chu 1987; Park 1987; Mody forthcoming; World Bank 1987; Bae 1987; *Financial Times* 1988. I also draw on interviews with executives of IBM, AT&T, and Micron Technology. For my general interpretation of the Korean government's role in development, see Wade 1982a: chapters 1, 8.

nies located only the labor-intensive and peripheral stages of production in Korea (as also in Taiwan).

In the early 1970s the government decided to make a big push for an indigenous technological capacity in electronics and informatics. The electronics industry was selected as one of the six industries to be promoted under the Heavy and Chemical Industry Plan of 1973, despite being neither heavy nor chemical. The Eight-Year Electronics Industry Development Plan, published in 1974, identified three main thrusts. The first was to create mission-oriented research institutes, both public and private. The second was to expand advanced training capacity in electronics. The third was to encourage technology imports via licensing and consultants rather than by foreign direct investment. Over the 1970s and 1980s the government targeted concessional credit at the industry, gave it protection (as of 1984 over a third of the 450 electronics products listed in the tariff schedule were subject to quantitative import controls), imposed domestic content requirements, and used public procurement rules to steer demand toward Korean-made products. It also helped many companies to negotiate technology transfer deals with multinationals. The importance attached to electronics was affirmed by the "The Year 2000" study (Ministry of Science and Technology 1986b), which shows a high percentage of industrial output coming from the industry.

To enhance Korea's own technological capacity the government established in 1976 a new public research institution, the Korea Institute of Electronics Technology (KIET). Its charter gave it responsibility for planning and coordinating semiconductor R&D, importing, assimilating, and disseminating foreign technologies, providing technical assistance to Korean firms, and undertaking market research (Park 1987). However, it was to operate in close consultation with private firms, and its governance arrangements were designed accordingly. The board of directors included four from government ministries, one from KIET, one from universities, one from the Electronics Industry Association, and five from firms. Responsible to the board of directors were three working groups: one for equipment, one for the work program, and one for the training program, each of which included representatives from industry as well as from government and KIET.

Internally, KIET was divided into three functional divisions (semiconductor design, processes, and systems), each headed by a Korean with both academic training and industry experience in the United States. In addition, a project development division processed information on marketing opportunities and kept abreast of foreign technologies.

The function of keeping abreast of foreign technologies was also central to the work of another important component, KIET's liaison office in Silicon Valley, center of the U.S. semiconductor industry. Established in 1978, the liaison office helped KIET obtain equipment and technology licenses, build contacts with U.S. semiconductor firms, and, crucially, create a network among

Korean researchers working in U.S. semiconductor companies. Through the network, KIET was able to help Korean firms identify particular individuals with skills or access which they needed, and either enlist their help while remaining in situ or repatriate them to work in Korea. KIET also mounted training programs for Korean firms, and administered a program to send Korean engineers and scientists abroad for experience in research institutes or firms. It took an active part in all technology transfer negotiations between Korean firms and foreign firms, and here its Silicon Valley outpost and project development division were especially important. KIET opened Korea's first pilot wafer fabrication facility in 1978, two years after Taiwan's, in a joint venture with a leading U.S. semiconductor firm (VLSI Technology). A year later it began to build Korea's first full-scale commercial wafer fabrication facility, intended initially to produce 16K DRAMS.

However, by the late 1970s most of the semiconductor industry in Korea was still concentrated at the assembly, packaging, and testing stages, with little spillover into core processes. Only a few local firms had established fabrication facilities, and these were dedicated to semiconductors at the bottom end of the market (for watches, telephones, etc.) The existing local firms were clearly much too small to undertake the huge investments needed to make large-capacity chips or to establish their own R&D capability. On the other hand, some of Korea's already huge *chaebol*, those with a major presence in consumer electronics, were keen to invest in advanced semiconductor production, especially because of their big in-house demand for semiconductors and their sense of vulnerability to manipulation by foreign semiconductor suppliers. The question for the firms and the government was how to overcome the huge entry barriers.

Two of the *chaebol* took over existing local semiconductor firms in the late 1970s to provide their entry point into semiconductor fabrication. A third entered with completely new investments. Then the government began to restructure the whole information industry so as to facilitate their success, as laid out in the Basic Plan for Promotion of the Electronics Industry, published in 1981. The aim was to integrate upstream and downstream segments (maximizing economies of scale and technological spillovers), in conscious imitation of Japan's structure of semiconductor companies being divisions of larger electronics companies, themselves part of giant conglomerates.

One of the key steps was to use the government's tight control of telecommunications to aid the big Korean firms' entry into advanced semiconductors. The telecommunications industry was overhauled, with some private firms being forced out and others assigned government-selected monopoly segments, and with all technology agreements with foreign telecommunications firms being subject to renegotiation. This was partly to align the champions in semiconductors (Samsung, Goldstar, Daewoo) with profitable segments of protected telecommunications. At the same time the government announced a multibillion-dollar expansion and modernization of telecommunications infra-structure, most of which would be guaranteed to the semiconductor champi-ons. They were then able to enter joint ventures with multinational firms (ITT, AT&T, Northern Telecom) by offering lucrative and risk-free business in tele-communications in return for transferring specified telecommunications and semiconductor technology; and were also able to cross-subsidize their own efforts in semiconductors from the profits of telecommunications.

In 1982 the government published the Long-term Semiconductor Industry Promotion Plan for 1982–86. It targeted a wide range of fiscal investment incentives on the four main semiconductor firms (by this time Hyundai had been allowed to enter the race), plus a large amount of cheap credit (US$350 million over 1984–86), at the same time as the government was cutting back on targeted credit in general. With government help two of the firms suc-ceeded in going from green-field sites to operating plants for 64K DRAM chips in only eight months in 1984, half the time it took in the United States and two-thirds of the time it took in Japan (*Forbes* 1985). The scale of the South Korean investment is huge. The four champions committed more than US$1.2 billion to semiconductors over 1983–86, ten times more than the combined investment of Taiwan's three semiconductor projects over 1984–87/88 (ex-cluding the new Philips VLSI foundry).

KIET, having pioneered the mastery of medium-scale semiconductor tech-nology, found that by about 1984 the *chaebol* had much superior fabrication facilities and were rapidly expanding their in-house R&D capacity. So its man-date was changed. Rather than lead the way into the next stage—fabrication of the 64K DRAM—it left this to the firms. It sold most of its fabrication facil-ities to one of the *chaebol*, changed its name to the Electronics and Telecom-munications Research Institute (ETRI, the new name signalling the bridge be-tween semiconductors and telecommunications), and initiated parallel basic research efforts in semiconductors, computers, and telecommunications. These efforts are focused on technology frontiers farther from commerciali-zation than KIET's work had been; for research close to commercialization could now be left to the *chaebol* on their own.

With the entry of the *chaebol* into advanced semiconductors, the govern-ment planning mechanism changed to give a still bigger role than in the past to the firms in setting the content of government policy. The government re-alized that in a field changing as rapidly as semiconductors it could not keep abreast of markets and technologies and could not even be confident of the effect of its policies on firms. So firms had to be more integrally involved in policy-making. Hence an even more elaborate consultative system was estab-lished than in the past, drawing in experts from firms, universities, national R&D laboratories, as well as government officials. ''The answers to the ques-tions of where the government should intervene, and how it should do so, were to a significant extent sought from the appropriate sections of local industry''

(Park 1987:102). In short, the leadership or vanguard role of government in semiconductors lasted for about a decade, from around 1974 to 1984.

By the time the 64K DRAM chips were produced, they had already passed the time of high scarcity premia. Moreover just at that time demand for semiconductors slumped worldwide, and the aggressive pricing strategy of Japanese makers lowered the price still further. Korea's several VLSI facilities operated in 1985–87 at only 30 percent of capacity or less much of the time, with the price well below cost of production. Yet the government did not pour in fresh money. It was reluctant to commit itself to assisting another high-risk, capital-intensive industry in difficulty, having just finished the restructuring of the heavy and chemical industries which it had so directly promoted in the 1970s. The popular impression that Korean firms have made it up to the world frontier in semiconductor production without government help probably owes much to the government's refusal to help the firms in trouble at this time, as well as to the government's and the firms' anxious concern to conceal assistance for fear of retaliation from Japan and the United States on grounds of "unfair" competition.

By 1986, the government decided to get more involved again. In conjunction with ETRI it tried to induce the leading firms to form a Japanese-style R&D consortium to develop the four-megabit chip, promising $175 million in grants and low-interest loans.[7] Urgency came in part from concern over Korea's excessive dependence on foreign design technology, which puts the country's firms at a disadvantage as the rate of innovation accelerates. The government was also concerned about the amounts that Korean firms had to pay out in royalties. Moreover, the government is building a national computer network costing several hundred million dollars for which most contracts are being steered to Korean companies. Joint development of the most advanced chip will be a giant step in that direction, especially because large capacity memory chips are considered to be the "technology driver" for several kinds of advanced semiconductor technologies.[8] However, agreement between the companies on complementary research programs proved impossible, and the area of cooperation extended only to agreement on standards and specifications. The companies each developed a prototype independently, under an agreement that those whose prototype met ETRI standards would not have to repay the government loans. One of the four companies had to repay.

---

[7] Reference is sometimes made to a government attempt to organize a consortium for the one-megabit chip, as well as for the four-megabit. I have no details. The source for the $175-million figure is Report on Korean Economy, No. 440, 1–15 June 1986, Chinese Embassy, Seoul, cited in Chu 1987:240. See also Korea Industrial Research Institute 1986.

[8] Manufacture of large capacity DRAMS provides lots of learning experience which can be applied to other kinds of chips and later generations of the same chip, especially in fine-line lithography and clean-room technology. It does not drive all semiconductor technology, however (such as computer-aided design).

Unexpectedly, the world price of memory chips started to rise in 1988, and the conglomerates, which had been prepared to wait until the 1990s, have already begun to earn big profits on semiconductors. Korea is now the world's third biggest fabricator of large-capacity memory chips, after Japan and the United States.

Samsung, the clear technological leader, was shipping 1.5 million one-megabit DRAMs a month in late 1988, from zero a year before, to customers who include several big American computer makers anxious to reduce dependence on Japanese suppliers. It produced more one-megabit chips in 1989 than all the U.S. merchant producers together. It introduced engineering sample four-megabit DRAMs in late 1988, only six months behind Toshiba, the world leader, and began shipping commercially in late 1989. The colossal investment needed for this achievement, and the attendant risk, is reflected in the debt/equity ratio of the firm that manages Samsung Group's semiconductor interests—nearly 7:1 in mid-1987. Since much of the debt is in the form of bank loans, and since the government still controls the banking system, we can be sure from this figure alone that the government has been heavily involved in facilitating Samsung's four-megabit strategy. The terms of financing are extraordinarily generous, with virtually no interest and a multiyear grace period before repayment of principal. Moreover, Samsung has massively cross-subsidized from other profitable parts of the group, whose profits are much aided by the government's protectionist trade policies. In 1985 Samsung Semiconductor contributed only 2.5 percent to the group's sales and made a third of the group's investment. R&D is receiving high priority. Samsung Semiconductor's R&D institute had more than six hundred researchers and a budget of over US$40 million in 1986, and its Silicon Valley outpost had a staff of 213 full-time employees. Goldstar is deploying R&D resources on an almost comparable scale. However, ETRI has not been eclipsed. Its staff numbered 1,200 in 1985, with a budget of $40 million (Ministry of Science and Technology 1986a).

But the high point of Korea's semiconductor story to date must be the thirteen-year cross-licensing agreement between Samsung and IBM signed in early 1989 (*Electronic Engineering Times*, 3 Apr. 1989; senior IBM source). In return for a substantial one-off fee from Samsung to IBM, each company now has free access to the other's entire portfolio of patents relating to the design and manufacture of semiconductors. This implies that IBM considers Samsung as an important and independent developer of advanced semiconductor technology. IBM has broad semiconductor patent-swapping agreements with less than twenty non-U.S. firms, Samsung being the only one from a "developing country." Indeed, Samsung is now (early 1989) one of very few firms in the world with a synchrotron in operation or under construction. A synchrotron generates the X rays needed (in the view of many but not all experts) for the next big step up in semiconductor technology. Because of huge investment costs, IBM is the only U.S. firm with one under construction. When Samsung's comes on line, it may place Samsung with only a handful of other firms at the leading edge of semiconductor technology.

As for computers, local firms began producing personal computers at the start of the 1980s, helped first by obligatory public procurement of Korean-made machines and then by a complete import ban (removed in 1988). Also at this time, a group of science and technology advisors at the Blue House (the president's office) began to formulate a plan to create a national computer network, on the assumption that Korea's whole future depended on its ability to accelerate its information-processing capabilities. This called for much more assistance to the local computer industry. Working with the Ministry of Communications, this elite group formulated the Computer Industry Promotion Master Plan of 1984. The plan sponsored the creation of a subsidiary of the Korea Telecommunications Agency to buy and develop the technology for the architecture of the new computer network. It also greatly expanded ETRI's capability in computers. ETRI then seconded staff from the four *chaebol* to work on joint projects. The plan also provided low-interest loans to software firms of up to 90 percent of their R&D spending. The public sector undertook to expand its use of microcomputers and to target its demand on domestic suppliers according to their levels of domestic content. In 1986 the government announced domestic content guidelines for all microcomputers and peripherals whether they are sold to the state or not. Domestic content rules are being used to substitute for more familiar forms of protection. Meanwhile the major Korean companies are trying to diversify their output from relatively cheap clones by forming technology alliances with foreign firms (such as AT&T, Honeywell, Hitachi, and IBM), with much backing from research organizations in the public sector. At the same time as the Samsung–IBM patent swap in semiconductors, Samsung agreed to pay IBM an undisclosed amount for access to IBM's personal computer patents on a running royalty basis, with IBM getting access to Samsung's personal computer patents in return. This is less of an accolade for Samsung than the semiconductor swap, but it is an accolade nonetheless, for it signifies IBM's recognition that Samsung is able to reverse engineer its most advanced personal computer products (*Electronic Engineering Times*, 3 Apr. 1989). The only other "developing country" firms with which IBM has made similar personal computer agreements are Hyundai, Daewoo, Mitac, and Acer—the first two Korean, the second two Taiwanese.

In short, during the 1960s government assistance followed the entry of foreign companies to make electronics products in Korea. Then for an extended period during the 1970s and 1980s, the Korean government led rather than simply followed the entry of Korean firms into semiconductors, telecommunications, and computers. It took major initiatives in the area of products and technologies, put sizable amounts of resources behind those initiatives, and got different results than had firms received no such guidance. During the

1980s, however, the government has been moving toward more of a follow-ership mode, but now following the major *Korean* companies as they show themselves to be capable of casting global shadows. It has been concentrating more on basic R&D, leaving commercialization and marketing to the firms and setting its R&D agenda in consultation with them.

Petrochemicals and Other Heavy and Chemical Industries

In petrochemicals John Enos (1984) has carefully documented the government's leadership role. He compares adoption of the same petrochemical technology from the same U.S. suppplier by three countries (Korea, Hong Kong, and Chile), and finds that Korea's lead on a number of adoption indices can be related to specific government actions. The government persisted in playing the lead role not only in planning and negotiating with foreign firms for the technology, but also in the later stages of organizing construction and implementing the design, even though the project was being undertaken on the Korean side by a wholly "private" firm.

However, many economists claim that Korea's promotion of petrochemicals and other heavy and chemical industries (HCIs) is a classic illustration of the follies of trying to lead the market. They say the HCI drive of the mid-1970s to early 1980s, which included government promotion of steel, nonferrous metals, petrochemicals, machinery, automobiles, shipbuilding, and electronics, yielded meager returns in relation to costs. There are several answers to this criticism. First, from the perspective of the mid-1980s and beyond the results do not look nearly as bad as in 1978–80, when many of the negative evaluations were made. By 1984 60 percent of Korea's exports came from HCIs (in line with the target set in 1973, at which time the figure was 24 percent). Even by 1980 the value-added structure of the economy had shifted decisively toward HCIs, from 7.2 percent in 1970 to 14.5 percent in 1980. By 1984 there was no significant difference in the cost of capital between HCIs and light industries or in the return on capital, HCIs having been lower in both respects through the 1970s (World Bank 1987, II:103). Industry-by-industry analysis shows some striking achievements. We have considered automobiles and semiconductors at length. In steel, POSCO, the state-owned enterprise, is described by the World Bank as "arguably the world's most efficient producer of steel" (1987, I:45)—a fine irony, for the Bank turned down a loan request in the early 1970s on the grounds that Korea had no comparative advantage in steel. In 1987 POSCO began to provide technical assistance to steel plants in the United States. It is an especially clear example of state leadership, because initially the government tried to induce private producers to undertake the project. Even shipbuilding sharply raised its share of world markets and operated profitably during the boom of the late 1970s, though subsequently far-ing as badly as shipbuilding everywhere else. The weakest results of the HCI drive has been in fertilizer and heavy machinery.

So one answer to the criticism is that the medium-term results are much better than the short-term results. The World Bank itself concludes that "in a comprehensive, dynamic perspective it is difficult to demonstrate that an alternative policy would have worked better" (1987, I:45). The second answer is that, to the extent the results are not as good as they should be, they reflect not the inherent inability of governments to pick winners but an unusual departure from the government's normal practice of using international competitiveness as a criterion of continued promotion. The feedback mechanism from export performance to selective interventions was blocked (in some industries only), because, unusually, military and national security objectives dominated economic ones.

Some evidence suggests that Korea's manufactured exports now tend to be of higher quality, category by category, than Taiwan's. Using as an index of quality the value per item or per unit weight, and taking exports to the U.S. market at the four-digit level (about one thousand items), Biggs and Yoon find that whereas Korea's mean-weighted unit value index was 10 percent lower than Taiwan's in 1978, it was 4 percent above Taiwan's in 1987 (1989; see also Rodrik 1988; Mody forthcoming). This is not what one expects from general notions of comparative advantage, which would give the edge to Taiwan. Taiwan's advantage, rather, is in the *speed* of entry to new markets. The difference may reflect differences in industrial organization (Korea's much larger firms), or the role of government (Korea's greater *dirigisme*), or both.[9]

LEADERSHIP DIFFERENCES BETWEEN KOREA AND TAIWAN

In short, in automobiles, semiconductors, telecommunications, petrochemicals, and many more industries the Korean government has from time to time aggressively orchestrated the activities of "private" firms. Sometimes it has

[9] Surprisingly, Taiwan residents apply for (and get) five times as many patents in the United States as Korean residents (3,350 in 1985–87, against 627). Taiwan is the tenth biggest country in these terms, Korea the eighteenth. The same sort of discrepancy is found in trademarks (Department of Commerce 1988). Does this mean that Taiwan is more innovative than Korea? Probably not. Taiwan's lead in trademarks reflects the smaller size and greater number of firms, each of which has much smaller production volumes of each item and hence more trademarks. As for patents, the discrepancy probably reflects: (1) Taiwan's smaller firms, which, other things being equal, tend to have more patents per unit of sales than bigger firms; (2) Taiwan's larger number of firms, which makes for more independent desires to patent; (3) Taiwan's huge trade surpluses, which lower the opportunity cost of filing many patents; and (4) Taiwan's exports tend to be in more patent-intensive industries, such as auto parts, chemicals, and mechanical widgets, while Korea's are in less patent-intensive industries such as automobiles and semiconductors. One should weigh the number of patents against the quality of patents, as measured perhaps by the number of citations per patent. My guess is that Korean patents tend to be of higher quality. I thank Frederic Scherer for thoughts on this question.

directly ordered them to do certain things and not do others. At the same time, its policies strengthened some of those firms, helping the emergence of very large conglomerates whose strength subsequently reduced both the government's leadership potential as well as the economic advantages of government leadership. In addition, partial liberalization of the financial system in the early to mid-1980s made it more difficult for the government to use targeted credit as a steerage instrument; and import liberalization similarly reduced the government's bargaining leverage with the big firms.

In contrast to Korea, the Taiwan government has relied more on arm's-length incentives to steer private firms, and often used public enterprises or public laboratories to undertake big pushes in new fields, as in semiconductors, computer software, automobiles, and biotechnology, to take only recent examples. Over 70 percent of R&D spending in the information industry in 1985 was by public organizations, compared to only 45 percent in Korea (Chu 1987:232). The difference in use of public enterprises should not be exaggerated, however, for compared to many other countries public enterprises have been important in Korea too—Jones and Sakong note as "a minor paradox of Korean development" that "an ostensibly private-enterprise economy has utilized the intervention mechanism of public ownership to an extent which parallels that of many countries advocating a socialist pattern of society" (1980:141).

The difference in overall style is seen in the differences between Taiwan's ERSO and Korea's KIET (or ETRI). Both have played leadership roles in their country's mastery of semiconductor and computer technologies, and both are publicly owned. But ERSO is bigger in terms of staff and budget per employee, gets more of its revenue from government grants and less from industry contracts, and lacks KIET's elaborate consultative arrangements with industry. While ETRI switched to a big followership role in the early to mid-1980s, ERSO remains in a big leadership role.

In part these differences in the style and tools of assistance reflect mundane economic differences. The Korean savings rate has always been much lower than Taiwan's, which means both that Korea borrowed much more abroad and that it squeezed nonpriority sectors harder in order to channel funds to priority sectors. (Four-fifths of total manufacturing investment went into heavy and chemical industries between 1977 and 1979.) Unlike Taiwan's, Korea's macroeconomic management has always tended to generate excess demand, which meant that greater incentives were needed to pull resources into designated sectors. To some extent Korea's sectoral industrial policies have been designed to protect important industries from the adverse impacts of excess aggregate demand. Timing is important, too: Korea's push into heavy and chemical industries began much later than Taiwan's. Taiwan, influenced by the heavy and chemical industries' orientation of the National Resources Commission officials who came from the mainland, and not having the luxury of nearly as many U.S. troops to defend it, began to build up heavy and chemical industries in the 1950s, acquiring at a relatively sedate pace a bigger heavy and chemical industries complex than Korea's by the early 1970s. At this time, partly in response to the U.S. rapprochement with China and the threat of a U.S. troop withdrawal, the Koreans began a crash course, doubly squeezing other sectors.

After these and other such factors are taken into account, a large residual remains. There are also political reasons why Korea relied mainly on private firms as the agents of a big push, intervening to make some of them big enough and to orchestrate their activities, while sacrificing some macroeconomic stability in the interests of industrial transformation. Its technocrats were not steeped in an anti-big-capitalist philosophy, as were Taiwan's for much of the postwar period. And they faced no ethnic tensions between themselves as outsiders and native businesspeople. Indeed, the sense of wounded ethnic pride induced by forty-five years of Japanese colonialism in a previously unified kingdom with unchanged boundaries for one thousand years helped to foster a powerful Korean nationalism able to support the notion of the whole (South) Korean people as a team against the rest of the world.

The perception of an underlying fusion of interests between government and large private firms helps to sustain a relatively well-developed policy network between the economic bureaucracy and those firms. In this context long-term exchange relationships can develop, in which the government makes help available in return for specified performance on the firms' part. It is particularly through such reciprocity that the conglomerates emerged as Korea's national champions.[10] The fact that they acquired enormous economic power is not seen as a threat to the regime as it would be in Taiwan. Once in existence, the conglomerates have been better able to undertake activities with high entry costs, partly by cross-subsidizing from currently profitable ones. As they have grown in size and diversity, they have also become better able to resist government directions; and so the government has sometimes resorted to more aggressive ways of obtaining compliance on certain issues, while also reducing the number of issues on which it seeks their compliance. The availability of massive government assistance encouraged them to adopt the high-risk strategy of competing head-on with U.S. and Japanese firms under their own brandnames, in contrast to the more risk-averse, niche-seeking Taiwanese firms.

The Korean policy network has in turn strengthened the hand of the industrial development agencies within the state. The Economic Planning Board and the Ministry of Trade and Industry have more power than their Taiwan counterparts, especially through their greater responsibility for the budget and

[10] For an argument which emphasizes the importance of reciprocity in Korean government-business relations, see Amsden 1989.

their greater influence over monetary policy. The central bank (Bank of Korea) is subordinate to the Ministry of Finance (unlike in Taiwan), and the Ministry of Finance is itself more *dirigiste* in outlook than its Taiwan equivalent. Especially through being able to influence both the broad rules of lending and the details of particular loans, industrial development officials have at their disposal—or had until the early to mid-1980s[11]—a range of detailed instruments able to discriminate between individual firms. Their Taiwan counterparts, lacking as much concessional credit and not having very large private firms, rely relatively more on public enterprises for initiatives in high entry barrier sectors. Both bureaucracies are highly centralized, but the Korean one more so because the Ministry of Trade and Industry is able to exercise more leverage over other ministries than Taiwan's Ministry of Economic Affairs.

Telecommunications shows the differences. The Taiwan government attempted, like the Korean government, to forge a close integration between telecommunications and semiconductors, but with less success. Taiwan's telecommunications industry was largely in the hands of joint ventures which linked two major U.S. multinationals (ITT and GTE) with local minority partners unusually closely connected to high levels of the Nationalist party. For reasons relating to Taiwan's more dependent relations with the United States and to the local firms' party ties, the government was anxious not to offend these companies by renegotiating the agreements. The Ministry of Economic Affairs decided to bypass them by negotiating directly with AT&T for advanced telecommunications and related integrated circuit technology using the lure of public sector procurement. But given the existing agreements not so much business could be assured to AT&T, and in any case the Ministry of Communications was lukewarm about the AT&T deal, having closer relations with ITT and GTE. In the face of the Ministry of Communications' foot-dragging the Ministry of Economic Affairs was able to negotiate a less beneficial deal than the Koreans in terms of equity participation and technology transfer.[12] This reflects the lesser preeminence of Taiwan's Ministry of Economic Affairs in relation to other parts of the nondefense bureaucracy than its Korean counterpart, the Ministry of Trade and Industry.

In short, the Korean government has a more centralized management structure, which assigns preeminence in industrial policy to the Ministry of Trade

---

[11] On Korea's economic liberalization over the 1980s, see World Bank 1987; Luedde-Neurath 1986.

[12] For example, AT&T got a 70 percent equity stake in Taiwan, a 45 percent equity stake in Korea. The agreement with Taiwan called for technology transfer in eight rather general areas within which AT&T had much choice, while the one with Korea called for transfer of stipulated technologies. An industry source says, "The Koreans are far more aggressive at forcing localization of production (that is, at enforcing a commitment to buy a high percentage of local parts and components). The Taiwanese are serious about it too, but they are more serious about getting the technology at the lowest price. The Koreans are prepared to pay more for the technology in return for more localization" (personal communication; see also Chu 1987).

and Industry and the Economic Planning Board. Top officials of these agencies can exercise broad control from a single position, acting through command hierarchies and relating to business groups as leaders rather than equals. The Taiwan government, on the other hand, is less centralized, with power over industrial policy issues dispersed amongst more ministries and agencies. Officials have a narrower scope for the exercise of their authority, and use it more circumspectly in their dealings with private firms. At the top of the government, coherence may be achieved by the same person occupying top positions in several different organizations, wielding influence that attaches more to his person than to the positions themselves.

Interestingly, these differences are congruent with the differences in the organization of conglomerates or business groups, as described by Gary Hamilton and his collaborators (1987). Korea's *chaebol* groups occupy a central position in the economy (see table 3.7). They are highly centralized, most being owned and controlled by the founding patriarch and his heirs through a central holding company. A single person in a single position at the top exercises authority through all the firms in the group. Different groups tend to specialize in a vertically integrated set of economic activities. Taiwan's business groups, on the other hand, are much less central in the economy. Internally they are only loosely integrated in terms of capital transfers or shareholdings, and are typically spread across industries rather than vertically integrated. Most of them lack a unified management structure. Instead, the same set of people, normally the founder and his close relatives, occupy the principal managerial posts in several firms of the group. Control is exercised more through face-to-face relations than through chains of command. Hamilton and his collaborators describe the principle of Taiwan's business groups as "patrilineal networks," in contrast to Korea's "corporate patriarchy."

The same contrast in seen in government-business relations and relations between government agencies. The common denominator is that Taiwan supports weaker or more bounded authority structures than Korea, such that face-to-face relations are more necessary for exercising control. This further helps to explain why the Taiwan government has relied so heavily on public enterprises and public research and service organizations to make big pushes into high entry-barrier activities. The ownership tie strengthens relations of control in a society where relations of authority are weaker than in Korea.

Through this mass of publicly owned assets and organizations, the Taiwan government has been able to guide the market no less than the Korean government, but differently. It has relied less on direct steerage of private investment decisions and more on public investments to induce a downstream response. It has also made the cost of entry for small businesses very low. But the difference with Korea is one of degree rather than kind. The Taiwan government, too, has used credit, taxes, domestic content requirements, trade policy, and direct foreign investment controls to steer private investment decisions, though less forcibly overall and with less reliance on selective credit.

The difference in strategy is due in large part to the "political" factors we have been discussing. But these same factors help to explain the contrast in size of firms and concentration of industry, which in turn becomes an important reason for the difference in government strategy. Taiwan's small and nimble firms were quite responsive to profit opportunities opened by the public investments; while Korea's concentrated structure allowed the government to target its industry-specific policies at a small number of firms each capable of a substantial response. Moreover, Korea's big firms, undertaking more head-on challenges to multinationals in high-volume, low-profit markets, needed direct assistance to surmount the high entry barriers. Taiwan's niche-seeking firms needed less firm-specific help (which would in any case have been more expensive to deliver, because of numbers), but had relatively more need for stable prices and real exchange rates, being more vulnerable in export markets to price and exchange rate instability than the risk-spreading Korean business groups.[13]

The discussion suggests a conclusion about chronologies. The standard chronologies show Taiwan and Korea beginning with a period of primary import substitution (lasting until about 1960 in Taiwan and about 1963/65 in Korea), followed by a phase of export promotion or outward orientation (until the early to mid-1970s), followed by a period of secondary import substitution (lasting until the late 1970s/early 1980s), followed by a period of "course correction" or liberalization. Each import substitution period is associated with more government intervention, each export promotion period with less government intervention. It is remarkable how these chronologies are repeated with so little examination of their analytical underpinnings. If one thinks of intervention in terms of leadership and control, one will *not* find a close connection between amount of intervention and the periods of import substitution and export promotion. In both Taiwan and Korea, there is no sharp fall in government leadership at the time of the first economic liberalization episodes around 1960–65. So the familiar neoclassical assumption that an increase in outward orientation goes with a reduction in "government intervention" is not supported by these cases.

JAPAN

Japan has invested even more heavily than Taiwan and Korea. As a percentage of GNP, investment rose from 27 percent in the early 1950s to 32 percent in the latter part of the decade, and averaged 33.6 percent in 1955–63 (Kuznets

---

[13] See the interesting discussion of these contrasts in Biggs and Levy 1988. I draw on conversations with Tyler Biggs in framing my argument.

1968:411; also table 2.3 above). Since Japan was the "textbook" for Taiwan and Korea, it is no surprise that it shows the same array of governed market elements: redistributivist land reform, postreform ownership ceilings, restrictions on financial institutions, a bank-based financial system able to sustain high debt/equity ratios, exchange rate controls, protection, direct foreign investment controls, export promotion, and selective government leadership in investment and technology.

The issue of government's industrial leadership role was the subject of an intense debate in the early postwar period. Economists in the Bank of Japan and the Ministry of Finance who subscribed to free-trade doctrines wanted a long-term development strategy based on the traditional theory of comparative advantage (Shinohara 1982). They called this the "natural" path of industrial development, reflecting Japan's relatively low labor costs and comparative advantage in labor-intensive industries such as textiles. MITI argued that this path would perpetuate low productivity and low incomes. Public policies should be designed, it said, not merely to make the most efficient use of existing resources, in the static sense of conventional theory, but to furnish the directional thrust and raise the finance for a set of heavy and chemical industries that had to be created. In particular, Japan should take special steps to encourage the automobile industry. From that time onward MITI saw as one of its key functions to encourage the introduction of new technologies through new investment. In this respect MITI differed from analogous ministries in Western Europe and North America, which did not see themselves as responsible for long-term technology policies until much later (in the 1970s and 1980s) and even then were guided by very different conceptions of comparative advantage (Freeman 1987). But MITI was the model for its counterparts in both Taiwan and Korea to accept the same responsibility for promoting new industries and advanced technologies.

The greater emphasis on consensus in state-society relations in Japan, however, makes it particularly difficult to establish the fact of government leadership. The government usually does not act until there is enough agreement between it and the concerned firms for a consensus to be declared, whatever the relative influence of government and business in reaching the agreement. The government's acting is the symbolization that consensus exists.[14] This

[14] As this book was going to press, I read Richard Samuels' book on how the Japanese state has attempted to structure and transform domestic markets (1987). It is an impressive argument, rich in empirical details from the energy industries. But he fails to make a good case that the pervasive interventions of the Japanese state have constituted followership with very little if any leadership, in my terms. Part of the problem is his narrow empirical base (the energy industries); he makes no attempt to address evidence from other industries (e.g., Magaziner and Hout 1980; Johnson 1982). But the primary weakness is the concepts themselves. His principal indicator of "market-displacing" interventions is the use of public enterprises. His secondary indicator is strong government influence over credit allocation. Most other interventions are put in the residual category of "market conforming," regardless of how much they affect relative prices or how

emphasis on consensus through frequent and often informal consultations is congruent with the internal organization of Japanese business groups, in contrast to Korea's and Taiwan's. Hamilton and his collaborators (1987) describe the organizing principle as "a community of firms." Affiliated firms are highly connected to each other through frequent meetings of the presidents, mutual shareholding, interlocking directorates, shared trademarks, joint public relations, and, of course, a sense of distinctive identity and mutual benefit. But central control of either the Korean or Taiwanese kind is weak. The differences in business group organization between Japan, Taiwan, and Korea, and the similarities within each country between business group organization and government-business relations, speaks of distinct kinds of authority relations. Among other things, this serves to qualify an argument which attributes the "distance" between government and private business in Taiwan solely to the mainlander/native Taiwanese tension. I shall not speculate on what the underlying differences in authority relations may be due to except to note that Japan's prewar *zaibatsu* groups were organized as centrally and with as much emphasis on command as Korea's groups today, and their move to consensual decision-making reflects both their greater age and the role of the occupation government in making holding companies illegal.

In terms of state structure Japan differs from both Taiwan and Korea. It is a democracy, and its style of corporatism is closer to European-style social corporatism by virtue of the greater equality in relations between the bureaucracy and interest groups. But both its democracy and its corporatism are unusual. Under democratic rules one party has enjoyed a virtual monopoly on legislative power since the party's formation in 1955. Likewise before World War II: between 1892 and 1937 the party in power was never replaced by election (Scalapino 1968:283). The legislature from the beginning until the present has had less influence in the major decisions that affect national welfare than in any other industrial democracy, while meritocratically selected technocrats have more. Its corporatism largely excludes labor, like Taiwan's and Korea's

much they constitute state initiatives about products or technologies to be encouraged. We know that Japan makes little use of public enterprises. Samuels dismisses in one short paragraph the argument that the government has strongly influenced credit allocation in some sectors (1986: 277). The conclusion appears to follow that the government's interventions in the market have been overwhelmingly market-conforming, which is implicitly taken to mean that they have made little difference to the pattern of investment and growth. This is simply unconvincing. Nevertheless, Samuels makes a good case for analysts who begin with state structures and public policies to pay more attention to the negotiation of policies and implementation with private actors. My own concern to counter the neoclassical emphasis on nearly free markets and neutral policy incentives may have led me to underestimate the extent of private sector influence on the formation and implementation of policies, even in Taiwan, though the enormous difficulty in getting evidence about government decision-making is another basic reason. On the other hand, Samuels pays too little attention to differences between countries in the broad balance of power between the state and interest groups, so concerned is he to counter the statists' emphasis on state power.

(see Aoki 1988:262). Even today interest group leaders are often former public officials; while in the late nineteenth and early twentieth centuries "almost all of the important interest groups were approved . . . or established . . . by law. The conduct of their activities was very often governed by a need to help spread and develop the policies of the government" (Ishida 1968:302). This description would apply well to Taiwan today.

These features have given the Japanese state an unusually high degree of autonomy compared to its counterparts in other industrialized capitalist countries. Yet officials from the central economic bureaucracies are in frequent contact with businesspeople in both official and recreational contexts. How do they stay unbought? There are several reasons. On the supply-of-corruption side, much of the contact is with industry associations, whereas corruption tends to be for the benefit of individual firms. The industry associations act as a policeman on the practices of their own members. On the demand side, the relative prestige of officials and businesspeople gives officials an internalized sanction against accepting bribes. Vulgar money bribes are for politicians, not for civil servants. Civil servants are, however, much interested in jobs after retirement (the civil service has a relatively young compulsory retirement age). Getting a good job upon retirement is a considerable source of satisfaction, which can be promoted by corrupt use of discretionary powers. But so too is remaining pure a considerable source of satisfaction. The balance does tend to tip toward the former as one approaches retirement—which is to say that at senior levels "getting a good job" may be stronger than "remaining pure," while at junior levels the position is reversed. But the tradition of group work within the bureaucracy makes it difficult for a boss to behave corruptly without his juniors finding out, which serves as a powerful deterrent.

Many analysts claim that when the Japanese government tried to lead particular industries its efforts either had no effect or hindered what would have been still better national performance. How good is their evidence?

Effectiveness of Leadership in Japan

Richard Caves and Masu Uekusa's study of Japanese industrial organization is often cited in support of the anti-industrial policy position. The study admits that "only scant evidence is available on the effects of MITI's custodial efforts on economic welfare" (1976:152). It also concedes that "the favorable and unfavorable possibilities arising from ministerial guidance are strong enough to leave the net evaluation in doubt" (p. 152). Of the unfavorable possibilities it says that "there is *no doubt* that the ministry's policies have engineered some allocative inefficiency by strengthening collusion and some technical inefficiency by distorting incentives for additions to capacity and diverting rivalry into non-price channels" (1976:152, emphasis added). But even taken on its own static-equilibrium, exogenous technical change terms, the evidence presented to document these inefficiencies is, by my reading, weak. Indeed, in the text of the book as distinct from the conclusions, the authors themselves are more cautious. On the effects of collusive practices they acknowledge that "the effects of cartels and other collusive practices on technical efficiency are equally hard to identify, and indeed have almost never been documented in statistical investigations" (1976:57)—including their own. In the text of the book they are prepared to say no more than that "the abundant evidence in Japan of tacit or formal price collusion and the luxuriant growth of these forms of non-price competition suggest that these efficiency costs *might* be significant" (1967:57, emphasis added).

Philip Trezise, one of the more vigorous proponents of the view that Japan's industrial policy has had at most a marginal effect, stresses that "in Japan public funds have not been directed *in any sizable amounts*, relative to total investment requirements, to the private industries or economic sectors with high growth potential" (1983:16, emphasis added). At issue, however, is not the absolute amounts of public funds but whether they had an important signalling effect on private bank lending or on company management. The close correlation between the sectoral composition of industrial loans from public financial institutions and the same for private financial institutions suggests a strong signalling effect. The correlation coefficients are 0.90, 0.94, and 0.98, respectively, for the periods 1960–65, 1966–70, and 1971–72 (Ueno 1980).[15]

Take also the work by Gary Saxonhouse on Japan. In a paper entitled "What Is All This about 'Industrial Targetting' in Japan?" (1983b), he refutes the argument that direct policy instruments have been used to benefit Japan's high-technology sectors. It is sufficient to note here that the argument is only about the 1970s and 1980s, and cannot touch the proposition that industrial policy was important in restructuring the economy in the 1950s and 1960s— the more important proposition for my purpose. Saxonhouse has also carried out econometric work which comes to the conclusion that over the longer period, "if Japanese experience is properly normalized for Japan's capital stock, labor force, geographical position and natural-resource endowment, there is little left to be explained by an industrial policy which is more than a substitute for market processes or, for that matter, by trade barriers" (1983a:271). It is all a matter of *what* is to be explained. Saxonhouse tries to account for the fact that Japan's imports include only a small share of manufactured goods compared to other industrialized countries. His econometrics has been criticized as unable to support his argument.[16] But that aside, Saxonhouse does not even

[15] Neither Ueno nor Borrus and Zysman, who cite Ueno as demonstrating the connection between public and private lending (1985:147), calculate the correlation coefficients—a microcosm of the neglect of quantitative evidence by those who emphasize the role of the state. The coefficients given in the text are based on eleven sectors and three time periods, with public industrial loans as the independent variable and private industrial loans as the dependent variable.

[16] See Takeuchi 1988, which takes issue with Saxonhouse's assumptions.

try to explain what is really unusual about the Japanese trade pattern, which is that Japan imports few manufactured goods in those sectors in which it exports.[17] All other industrialized countries, by contrast, show a pattern of dense *intra*industry trade. The difference may reflect denser relations of diffuse reciprocity between Japanese firms and more vertical integration causing low import demand elasticity (Dore 1987). But it presumably also results from the Japanese strategy of closing the domestic market to imports in the case of industries to be encouraged, so that the domestic producers have a stable base of demand on which to move down the scale and learning curves until unit costs are low enough for the product to be internationally competitive (Magaziner and Hout 1980; Lawless and Shaheen 1987). At this point one of two things may happen. The import barriers may be reduced—but few imports appear because the domestic producers are by then internationally competitive and the other factors just mentioned tend to tip the decisions of domestic buyers in favor of local products. Or the import barriers are retained, allowing domestic producers to act as discriminating oligopolists, selling their products at high prices on the protected domestic market and using the resulting profits to help export sales at lower prices. So even if Saxonhouse is right as far as he goes, his argument does not mean that industrial policy—including trade policy—is irrelevant for explaining what is really distinctive about Japan's trade pattern. Note, in particular, that the absence of barriers to the Japanese market in a particular industry at a given time is quite consistent with the proposition that such barriers had an important role at an earlier time in allowing the industry to capture economies of scale and learning. Only disaggregated studies over time could pick up the real effects of protection on trade patterns and industrial growth, and such studies have not, to my knowledge, been made.

A favorite example of the ineffectiveness of Japanese industrial policy is the case of automobiles in the 1960s (Schultze 1983). Thinking there were too many makers, MITI tried to consolidate them in order to reap economies of scale. The makers declined, and went on to achieve world supremacy without consolidation. Hence, it is said, MITI's intervention was a mistake. This argument overlooks several points. It ignores the long history of government leadership of the automobile industry before the 1960s (Taizo 1984); it ignores government intervention to restructure the auto components industry in the 1950s and 1960s, the success of which helped the unconsolidated assemblers to be internationally competitive (Magaziner and Hout 1980: 58); it ignores the fact that the "mistake" never occurred, because MITI backed off in face of the firms' resistance; and it ignores the effect of the "mistake" on the unconsolidated firms' investment and export strategy, which was to redouble their efforts to prove MITI wrong and themselves right because they knew that if

---

[17] See Scott 1985:61; Borrus and Zysman 1985.

they were not successful MITI would be back with a new consolidation plan at a later date (Thurow 1985:244).

HONG KONG—EXCEPTION OR CONFIRMATION?

Hong Kong has long been wealthier than Taiwan or Korea, with a per capita income two-and-a-half times Taiwan's in the early 1960s and twice as high today (see table 2.1). If Hong Kong has done as well or better than the other apparently more *dirigiste* East Asian countries, does this not suggest that public management of industrial restructuring and external transactions is a minor element in the superior economic performance of all the East Asian capitalist economies? Has not Hong Kong been as close to a free market economy as it is possible to get?

There are several arguments against this view. One is that Hong Kong is too special to be put alongside the others as an equivalent unit (Ranis 1979). Hong Kong's population is small (five million in 1980, against Taiwan's eighteen million). It has no significant—and productivity-depressing—agricultural sector. It did not face the same temptation to establish heavy and chemical industries. It benefited from an organizational and marketing capacity which was already in place prior to industrialization, built up over decades by British-linked trading companies, in a way that Taiwan and Korea did not. And its economic growth is a function of its service role in a wider regional economy, as entrepot trader, regional headquarters for multinational companies, and refuge for nervous money. Finally, its small size means that even with industrial and financial capital operating from a strictly *international* perspective, full employment and wide diffusion of the benefits of growth within the population can occur.

A second argument presents Hong Kong as a variant of the corporatist state. Hong Kong's peak private economic organizations, notably the major banks and trading companies, are closely linked to the lifetime expatriates who largely run the government. (Just one bank, the Hong Kong and Shanghai Banking Corporation, holds assets worth well over twice the colony's annual GNP.) This coalition, and in particular the association of large banks, provides a point of concentration of power at which negotiations in line with an implicit development strategy can be conducted. Both the generation and implementation of policy is insulated from the demands of small business, organized labor, and other nonestablishment groups by the exclusionary and authoritarian colonial state (Deyo 1987). Ironically, the Chinese government has helped to check the disruptiveness of left-wing unions over the 1970s and 1980s, as its direct interest in the colony's prosperity grew.

It is true that the formal institutions of government perform mainly custodial functions and that Hong Kong has no controls over imports, foreign exchange, foreign investment, and wages and prices. Tax revenues to GNP are very low, at 13.7 percent in 1977, compared to Taiwan's 24.2 percent (Hofheinz and Calder 1982:34). But to conclude from this that Hong Kong is close to a free market economy is misleading.

Not only is the economy managed from outside the formal institutions of government by the informal coalition of peak private economic organizations, but the government itself also has available some unusual instruments for influencing industrial activity. It owns all the land, which it sells on leasehold to raise revenue instead of relying on taxes. It controls rents in part of the private housing market and supplies subsidized public housing to roughly half the population, thereby helping to keep down the cost of labor. And its ability to increase or decrease the flow of immigrants from China also gives it a way of affecting labor costs. All told, the Hong Kong economy works very differently from the textbook picture of a free market economy or from economies of the Anglo-American kind (as does Singapore's: Lim 1983).

A third argument questions whether Hong Kong has done as well as the other more *dirigiste* countries. Its investment ratio has been well below the others', its rate of industrial restructuring over the 1970s and 1980s has been much slower, and its export composition has remained stuck at the relatively low end, with labor-intensive and low-technology goods continuing to make up by far the largest share (see tables 2.3, 10.1). Most exports are still textiles, toys, consumer electronics, or watches and clocks. From the mid-1970s to the

TABLE 10.1
Industrial Restructuring in Hong Kong, Taiwan, and Korea

(a) Export Composition, 1975 (%)				
	Clothing & Footwear	Other Clearcut Consumer Goods	Standardized Intermediates excl. Textiles	Capital Goods
Hong Kong	46	20	1	3
Taiwan	28	15	9	10
Korea	32	12	15	7

(b) Composition of Electronics Production, early 1980s (%)		
	Consumer Appliances	Industrial Appliances	Components
Hong Kong	68	2	30
Taiwan	45	6	49
Korea	40	10	50

Sources: Joekes 1986: table 7, based on background paper for World Bank's *World Development Report 1978*; Joekes 1986: table 14, based on H. Coote 1983.

mid-1980s its rate of growth of export value-added has been slower than in Korea, Taiwan, or Singapore (*Far Eastern Economic Review*, 26 Sept. 1985). Indeed, concern that Hong Kong's industries are slipping behind Taiwan's and Korea's pushed the Hong Kong authorities in 1987 into what officials call a "radical" departure. The government is entering the business of what it calls "development support." To help companies with training and technology transfer in areas where it believes the Hong Kong electronics industry should be focusing, it is setting up a digital communications laboratory, a surface mount technology laboratory, and a customized integrated circuit design center. The government also plans to employ consultants to study promising new technologies with industrial applications, and to see whether support services should be provided for them. These departures have echoes of a late conversion to a "help to make the winners" policy (*Financial Times* 1988:5).

Hong Kong's restructuring success has been in finance rather than in industry, led by the major banks. This difference in performance is consistent with the governed market argument for institutional consolidation, which has been stronger for finance capital than for industrial capital in Hong Kong (Deyo 1987; Haggard 1986).

So whether we take Hong Kong as a special case or as a less successful variant of the authoritarian-corporatist state, we can at least reject the argument that since Hong Kong is a free market economy, and since the causes of successful performance must be something Taiwan, Korea, and Japan share with Hong Kong, therefore industrial policy must have been unimportant.

Government Failure in East Asia

If we have at least three East Asian cases, not just one, where outstanding industrial performance is associated with governed market policies, this strengthens the conclusion that those policies helped produce the superior performance. We can also turn the argument around, to ask what limited the extent of government failure (the counterpart of market failure). After all, governed market policies require the government to exercise much discretion and discrimination. Economics presumes that such power in the hands of government bureaucrats and politicians is bound to yield worse results than the nearly free market. The question is: What keeps the use of state power in line with a national interest in East Asia?

Government failure has been the subject of much assertion but little comparative analysis (Wolf 1979; Lal 1983). We can distinguish two kinds. One is failure of attempts to "pick winners." The other is failure resulting from frailty or abuse of public power—from incompetence, corruption, goal displacement (the tendency of nonmarket organizations, dependent for income on grants rather than sales, to develop de facto goals only distantly related to their ostensible public purpose), or from the disproportionate commitment of public resources to satisfy small pressure groups. The first kind of failure may occur because of the second, but may also occur in the absence of the second.

Making Winners

It is often said that many governments—including Western European ones—have tried to pick winners, with disastrous results. Why were East Asian governments able to succeed where others failed? This, however, misstates the issue. "Picking winners" implies that the potentially competitive industries are out there waiting to be discovered, as though the problem is to find those that most closely correspond with the economy's given comparative advantage. The governments of Taiwan, Korea, and Japan have not so much *picked* winners as *made* them. They have made them by creating a larger environment conducive to the viability of new industries—especially by shaping the social structure of investment so as to encourage productive investment and discourage unproductive investment, and by controlling key parameters on investment decisions so as to make for greater predictability. The instruments included protection to modulate international competition, restrictions on capital outflow so as to intensify reinvestment within the national territory and drive the export of goods rather than capital, and controls on domestic financial institutions. In this environment lumpy and long-term investment projects were undertaken which would probably not have been undertaken in an economy with free trade and capital movements, because they would not have been consistent with short-term profit maximization.

Within these "outer wheels," particular industries were chosen for special attention by looking to outside reference economies. Japan looked to the United States and Europe. Taiwan and Korea look more to Japan, with the perception that they are descending the same stretch of the river (in the Japanese metaphor) as Japan did fifteen to twenty-five years ago. Shifting the national technology frontier and industrial structure toward Japan's is much easier than relying on abstract planning techniques to get a sense of direction. Japan has been their textbook. Taiwan and Korea also keep a close watch on each other. They watch not only obvious things such as which markets the other is being successful in (Taiwan went into Eastern Europe after observing Korea's earlier success); they also copy policies in meticulous detail. Korea sent teams to spend months in Taiwan examining the duty drawback scheme and the export inspection scheme, for example, and Taiwan took Japan's programs for promoting the machinery and information industries as a starting point for formulating its own. Indonesia and the Philippines, by contrast, do not have such obvious models. Nor do officials of many other countries have the same willingness to play the pupil with respect to other countries—always on the assumption that the diligent pupil can eventually do better than the master.

Surprisingly little is known about the techniques by which government officials selected industries for special attention, but a few points can be made about how Japan's MITI did it. First, MITI officials studied income elasticities of demand for various items in the main markets of the world, especially the United States. Second, they examined trends in technological change in various industries. Third, they checked industries with high income elasticities and high potential for technological change against Japan's specialization index, or the share of each industry in Japan's industrial exports over the share of that industry in world trade. So if chemicals accounted for 5 percent of Japan's exports and 10 percent of world trade, Japan's specialization index was 0.5. If world demand was growing especially fast for some particular item, the planners would get worried if Japan's specialization index for that item was not going up too. On the other hand, if Japan's specialization index was already high for an item whose world demand was not rising, they would not worry if its exports did not keep up. Fourth, they checked the trends against another index called the "export and industrial estrangement coefficient." This measured the relationship between an item's importance in Japan's total industrial output against its importance in exports. If machinery accounted for 15 percent of industrial output but only 10 percent of industrial exports, the export and industrial estrangement coefficient would be 0.66. With these measures, the government could identify sectors where measures for encouraging greater output and exports should be stepped up (*Economist* 1963:50–53).

It is likely that both Taiwan and Korea used similar methods to help select industries for promotion, supplemented by study of import composition, demand- and supply-linkages, and Japan's industrial structure. Like Japan before the mid- to late 1970s, they have both been some way off the world technology frontier, which means they have plenty of other examples to follow. This is important because some evidence suggests that government bureaus are less proficient at guiding the market in areas of high uncertainty and risk.

Export performance and the discrepancy between domestic costs and international prices have then been used, in all three countries, to guide subsequent government policies for the chosen industries (Pack and Westphal 1986). The importance attached to export performance—or at least to the difference between domestic costs and international prices—has helped to reveal mistakes or excesses fairly quickly, and the aim of competitiveness has required correction. In general, these governments have not for long promoted industries whose value-added in world prices was negative (on grounds that the industries were necessary to supply the domestic market). Where they have tolerated negative value-added industries for several years, it was generally because they had faith in the abilities of people in those industries to get to positive returns before too long. In contrast, long-run tolerance of negative value-added industries has been a not uncommon experience in parts of Latin

America and Sub-Saharan Africa. The most recent case of this in Taiwan—the joint truck-making venture with General Motors, which granted GM unlimited protection and a product price 60 percent higher than the import price—was cancelled once it had served the government's political objectives.

More than this, the emphasis on export performance or other indicators of international competitiveness provided government officials and businesspeople with a widely known principle by which the government would adjust to or adjudicate unforeseen contingencies, and thereby helped them enter transactions which they would not undertake if the government's mode of response to unforeseen contingencies was unclear. In this sense there has been a national "export culture," including in Japan where exports to GNP have not been especially high. The importance attached to exports reflected the lack of natural resources and the sense of external vulnerability.

However, all three countries combined their "outward orientation" on the export side with an "inward orientation" on the import side. They carried through import liberalization and foreign exchange liberalization very gradually, placing the emphasis on export promotion. Export competitiveness, in other words, has not been attained by greatly liberalizing imports except for imports to be used in export production. Japan, indeed, maintained obstacles to imports of intermediate goods (as distinct from raw materials) even for export production, offsetting the antiexport bias by means of other export incentives such as tax credits and export-import links (Wade 1988b). The interesting question for comparative research is how the resources were found for both rapid export growth and production for the protected domestic market without generating strong inflation (which would have hindered the export drive). Part of the answer is that protection notwithstanding, final goods markets are intensely competitive in all three countries, even when oligopolized (hence Hadley's phrase for Japanese competition, "cut-throat oligopoly"). In any case, it is clear that these countries have no more left their trade to the free market than they have left their defense to international treaties. But they have also used protection very differently from the stereotyped Latin American, Indian, or New Zealand way.

Finally, the three countries established institutional arrangements to avoid the pitfall of government officials taking the lead role in a new industry while knowing little about it. Government officials are involved in a policy network with sources of information much closer to the operating level of particular industries. In Japan and Korea this includes the peak federations of business, the business groups, and the state-owned or state-influenced banks. In Taiwan it includes less representation of private business, but links the Ministry of Economic Affairs and CEPD with public enterprises, public research and service organizations, and public banks. And government economic officials read the business press diligently, paying attention to its free-swinging criticism of economic policies. However, we know rather little about how the information that lies with the parts of the bureaucracy in intimate contact with particular industries is flushed up to the level of strategic, governmentwide decision-making. Indeed, we know rather little about the inner workings of East Asian bureaucracies generally (Wade 1982a: chapters 5, 6, 8).

In short, what differentiates the industrial targeting efforts of these governments compared to many others is their combination of a stabilized investment climate, a consistent and coordinated attentiveness to the problems and opportunities of the designated industries, and a commitment to industrial competitiveness in world markets.

A Hard State

A second kind of government failure is the failure to carry through government policies because of the fragility or abuse of public power. The shortest answer to why this type of failure is limited in East Asia is that East Asian states are relatively hard. The position of a state in relation to its society can be thought of as varying along a continuum from decentralized and constrained by social groups, to centralized and relatively insulated from society—from ''soft'' to ''hard.'' Soft states do little more than register the demands of social groups or at most resist private demands. While they have the capacity to produce effects in the economy, they lack the capacity to control the direction of those effects in line with intentions. Hard states are able not only to resist private demands but actively to shape the economy and society. They are able to exert more control over the direction of the effects of their interventions. In these terms the United States is a soft state; Taiwan and Korea are hard states. The European social corporatist states are mixed, with societal influence being strong but channelled through centralized peak associations. Japan is between them and the other two East Asian cases.

What conditions have made for relatively hard states in East Asia? Joel Migdal (1988: chapter 8) suggests five sets of factors that generally make for hard states: (1) massive social dislocation, which weakens existing patterns of social control, occurring within the previous fifty years or so; (2) the existence of a serious military threat from outside or from other communal groups in the country, which raises the prospect of the leaders' demise if they do not assert the state's order throughout the society; (3) support from the international state system for a concentration of social control in the hands of states; (4) the existence of a social grouping with people sufficiently independent of existing bases of social control and skillful enough to execute the grand designs of state leaders; and (5) skillful leaders whose ideology favors strong state control. Let us consider East Asia in these terms.

Taiwan and Korea have both undergone wrenching social dislocations in the past half-century, which weakened social control throughout the society. The military and economic effects of World War II were followed by a yet more devastating war in Korea and on the Chinese mainland. Mass migration accompanied these upheavals. Two to three million Koreans returned to Korea from Japan and Manchuria after World War II, and three to four million, in a total population of twenty-five million, fled south and north across the new boundary during the Korean War (Cumings 1981). About two million mainlanders retreated to Taiwan between 1945 and 1949, swelling the existing population by nearly one-third.

Furthermore, the Japanese colonial administration of both countries had carefully limited the growth of organizations in native hands. Distinct from other colonialisms, the Japanese administrators did not build up dispersed strongmen as their agents of rule; and no Western entrepreneurs had independent access to the economies through which to make reinforcing deals with organizations outside the state.

Therefore, the postwar rulers had unusual scope to mobilize the population around their symbols and codes of behavior—and their agricultural and industrial policies. Concentrating control in the hands of the state did not require a risky challenge to the prerogatives of other powers in the society.

At the same time, both countries faced a continuing severe threat from outside, South Korea from a belligerent north, tiny Taiwan from a vast army 150 kilometers across the straits. This external threat posed to the rulers the prospect of their political—and physical—demise if they failed to mobilize resources and assert the state's ordering of society. Any sign of internal weakness would invite aggression from their looming enemies.

A similar argument holds for Japan. The leaders' fear of invasion, aroused by the opium wars in China and by Perry's landing in 1853, prompted agonized debate on how to strengthen political organization to deal with the outside threat. This occurred as the Tokugawa pattern of control was in any case weakening. These developments drove the strong Japanese state of the late nineteenth century. The subsequent dislocations of the Sino-Japanese War, followed by World War II, prepared the way for a renewed concentration of social control in the hands of the state.

Social disorganization and an external military threat presented both an opportunity and a need to tighten the state's ordering of society. U.S. aid and the social basis for an independent and skilled bureaucracy presented the means to do so.

Because of their geopolitical position in an area of chronic international tension between the Soviet Union, China, and the United States, they received massive amounts of U.S. assistance. The aim was to create economically viable and politically stable regimes on the West's defense perimeter. This aid helped to strengthen the state vis-à-vis nonstate organizations.

The social basis for an independent and skilled bureaucracy came from the long Confucian tradition of rule by a mandarin elite. In Japan, the early Meiji bureaucrats were drawn from the 2 to 3 percent of the population who manned the *samurai* bureaucracies in the Tokugawa period. Even after modes of entry were rationalized by examinations during the Meiji period, the bureaucracy continued to be staffed by their children, the pool widening slowly with the growth of educational opportunity. Taiwan is an especially vivid case of an independent bureaucracy in place from the early days of the state. State bureaucrats down to quite low levels were mainlander emigres, seeing themselves and seen by the native Taiwanese as an alien force. They had no choice but to identify their own interests with those of the state, their protector, making for an unusual merging of interests between state rulers and their officials.

Once in existence the hard state has been relatively easy to maintain. Facing only weak centrifugal forces, the rulers could generate enough centripetal forces to risk the growth of powerful and effective state agencies. The "needs of legitimacy" could be made more nearly congruent with the "needs of economic development" (Wade 1979, 1982a, 1982b, 1985c). By constructing corporatist political arrangements *before* interest groups began to gain or regain strength, they could channel and restrain demands placed upon the state as those demands grew. One great advantage of corporatist arrangements is that the demands emanate from relatively "encompassing" organizations, whose memberships make up a sizable portion of the whole society. They are therefore constrained in the extent to which they use their power to urge measures which benefit their members at the expense of national income and productivity (Olson 1986). This applies especially to Japan, where interest groups were more voluntary; in Taiwan and Korea, interest groups have been more directly constrained by the state itself. Also, the legislatures in all three countries are weak in terms of a "ruling" function, which limits the scope for interest groups to pressure the bureaucracy by lobbying the legislative branch.

In this kind of political regime, the bureaucracy can more easily demonstrate competence and remain "clean," because it is neither caught between and penetrated by struggling interest groups nor subverted from above by the politics of rulers' survival. The sine qua non for a hard state can be met—officials in implementing agencies across the territory pressing forward the state's agenda.

Moreover, once an elite civil service is created, competition tends to assure a continuing flow of the brightest students. For then the best way to demonstrate outstanding talent is to take the civil service examination and win. The institutions of meritocratic recruitment and life-time career paths help to support the corporate identity and internal coherence of the bureaucracy. That identity and coherence is reinforced in all three countries by dense informal networks within the bureaucracy linking officials in different bureaus and ranks. These are based mainly on membership of elite universities, especially on ties among classmates (Evans 1989). Such ties lower the transactions costs of supervision and cooperation.

Again, a continuing sense of vulnerability to the outside has helped to discipline the leaders and the bureaucracy. That continuing sense of vulnerability, even as international tensions in the region diminish, owes much to the countries' lack of natural resources and dense populations (among the densest in the world, ranging from 320 persons per square kilometer in Japan to over 500 in Taiwan in the early 1980s). They therefore face a stark choice: either to make do with low living standards or to export manufactured goods in order to pay for imports of essential foodstuffs, raw materials, and energy. They are also very small countries: Japan is smaller than Paraguay, Korea is smaller than Guatemala, Taiwan is smaller than Costa Rica (smaller even than Switzerland, one-tenth the size of California).

Add to this the homogeneity of the populations, the absence of class-conscious or culturally disparate class division. Even in Taiwan the ethnic division between mainlanders and islanders does not translate into a class division, because while islanders have been excluded from significant political power they have not been excluded from wealth, while many mainlanders arrived and remained poor.

Given this complex of factors, it is no surprise that we find:

strenuous efforts on the part of the state leadership to assert the state's rules throughout the society, partly to mobilize material resources and political support in pursuit of foreign policy.

a sense of community amongst the central powerholders, which inhibits the play of narrowly defined self-interest; all the more so because those who experienced the earlier defeats share a sense of having suffered a terrible humiliation, to which they respond with a resolve to do better than the outsiders who inflicted it.

relatively little conflict about the basic direction of economic advance amongst the policy-makers; industrialization has had a less contested priority than where, as is common in developing countries, much power and wealth rest on ownership of land or minerals, and where, consequently, the government is sympathetic mostly to the *idea* of industrialization.

national economic effectiveness (as distinct from efficiency) given a much higher level of priority than is usual in Western or communist systems. It is seen in the rapidity with which Taiwan, Korea, and Japan adjusted to the 1973–74 oil price quadrupling, by stockpiling petroleum, raising prices, diversifying suppliers, shifting industrial structure away from energy-intensive industries, and other such measures devised as a coherent strategy within the bureaucracy.

militaries oriented toward military effectiveness rather than swashbuckling, tribute-raising, and suppressing their own populations. Military notions of authority, discipline, loyalty, and vigilance are widely diffused, partly through compulsory military training in Taiwan and Korea (almost all young men do two to three years full-time, plus onerous follow-up training to the age of thirty-five).

limited civil and political rights in Taiwan and Korea, which came about halfway down a ranking of middle-income countries in the early 1970s. The external threats proved easy to exaggerate in order to justify internal repression. In a sense, Presidents Park and Kim Il Sung were each other's best allies.

respect for free markets and private property. In order to claim the United States as their natural ally and to differentiate themselves sharply from the surrounding communist states, the governments have had to insure that they are seen as committed to these institutions. They needed to be able to claim that their success derived from free market principles. As Neil Jacoby says in his study of U.S. aid to Taiwan, the political aim of U.S. aid was to demonstrate ''the superiority of free economic institutions as instruments of social progress'' (1966:137).

a broadly based ''appreciation of the national situation,'' defined not only in terms of external vulnerability but also in terms of the necessity (given few natural resources and dense populations) to transform manufacturing processes and products as wages rise so as to sustain an internationally competitive set of industries. Appreciation of the national situation extends to recognition that the stability of government rests on good economic performance, and that government stability in turn facilitates that performance.

These factors feed back to bureaucratic procedures. They help to keep bureaucratic ''prices''—the criteria for guiding and evaluating public personnel and public organizations—fairly closely related to ostensible public purposes. Organizational or private costs and benefits are included in the calculus of officials to a lesser degree than in many other countries, and the bureaucracy is better able to act in an encompassing way. Consider the differences in the responses of Korean and Turkish higher-level civil servants to two questions: ''What is the principal task of a civil servant?'' and ''What is the most important criterion for making decisions?'' To the first, 58 percent of Koreans and only 11 percent of Turks replied, ''To serve the nation as a whole.'' To the second, 59 percent of Koreans and 17 percent of Turks gave as their first criterion, ''the views of immediate superiors.'' The most popular response (34 percent) among the Turks was, ''What I think is best'' (Heper, Kim, and Pai 1980).

In short, initial social disruption, threats from other states, poor natural resource endowment, and the social basis for an independent bureaucracy all strengthened the governments' hand and helped to maintain the edge of their commitment to economic development. One is reminded of Sun Yat-sen's dictum, ''The nation without foreign foes and outside dangers will always be ruined'' (1981:24). It may be that the rise of East Asian trading states has been helped by the military discipline and forms of organization diffused throughout society as a response to national vulnerability. As one example, the principles of military alertness may have been used to help organize commercial intelligence and surveillance of economic transactions. Far from the principles of the military-political state being opposed to those of the trading state, as Richard Rosecrance argues (1986), we may have here three successful cases where the former have supported the latter.

CONCLUSIONS

The key question is what has determined the level and composition of investment in these countries. There are plenty of facts about Taiwan, Korea, and Japan which better fit the neoclassical FM and SM theories than the political economy GM theory. But it is clear both that less economic liberalization occurred in the 1960s and 1970s than neoclassical accounts suggest, and that much government intervention has gone beyond the limits of "good" neoclassical interventions. Government resources and influence have prompted investments to be undertaken which would not have been undertaken in strictly FM or SM conditions, thereby generating production and investment outcomes different from what would have happened if government had not intervened in this way.

Indeed, the central economic mechanism of the capitalist developmental state is the use of state power to raise the economy's investible surplus; insure that a high portion is invested in productive capacity within the national territory; guide investment into industries that are important for the economy's ability to sustain higher wages in the future; and expose the investment projects to international competitive pressure whether directly or indirectly. The resulting intense cycle of investment within the national territory leads to rapid rises in labor demand, and hence to increases in labor incomes and wide distribution of the material benefits of growth (even in the absence of collective labor organization).

The balance of presumption must be that economic liberalization matters less in an explanation of East Asian success than neoclassical accounts suggest, and that actual performance was better than it would have been with FM or SM policies alone. We can grant Adam Smith his point about the efficacy of eighteenth-century English government: "Though the profusion of government must, undoubtedly, have retarded the natural progress of England towards wealth and improvement, it has not been able to stop it" (1776:327). But we should reject the unargued assertion that "without MITI Japan would have grown at 15 percent per annum" instead of only 10 percent (unnamed Japanese economist quoted approvingly by Little 1979:491); or that for Korea, "success has been achieved *despite* intervention" (Lal 1983:46). It is less plausible to say that the three countries with arguably the best development performance on record would have had still better performance had their governments intervened less, than to say that interventions made with the clear intention of accelerating development and formulated by a coherent organization did indeed have the intended effect. Those who deny this are claiming extraordinary ability to forecast historically unprecedented performance. The presumption is strengthened by the weaknesses in arguments which claim that the selective industrial policies of one or other of the countries on balance had either no effect or an adverse effect. The Hong Kong case does not support the proposition that because Hong Kong did as well as the others without industrial policies, the industrial policies of the others could not have made much difference.

But the difference between what happened in East Asia and experience elsewhere does not lie in the discovery of industrial policy instruments not known elsewhere. Many other nations have at one time or another tried most of the policy tools used in East Asia. What differentiates their efforts, above all, are a consistent and coordinated attentiveness to the problems and opportunites of particular industries, in the context of a long-term perspective on the economy's evolution, and a state which is hard enough not only to produce sizable effects on the economy but also to control the direction of the effects, which is a more demanding achievement.

These efforts have been on too big a scale to be brushed aside as something which is small in relation to phenomena that are well handled by neoclassical theory. Nor can they be treated as a simple add-on to neoclassical actions, as though the governments first met some of the neoclassical growth conditions and then went a step beyond. Rather, they probably helped those conditions to be realized and sustained. The way remains open for a reasonable person to believe that governing the market is too important to ignore in even a parsimonious explanation of East Asian success. Conversely, one should not project backwards the real economic liberalization which has occurred in Taiwan and Korea over the 1980s and Japan during the 1970s and assume they reached their present affluence by an economy as guided by free market prices as today. A less-than-bracing conclusion, maybe, but a serious challenge to economic theory nonetheless.

But the very success of these arrangements in Taiwan and Korea is causing fundamental changes in the relationship of the states to the society, as it did in Japan in the early 1970s. Rising affluence and education make for large middle classes, which demand democracy. Stronger private firms are better able to resist government direction. Government industrial policies are more conditioned by negotiations with private firms and industry associations (Samuels 1986). All this has occurred in the context of a diminished external security threat, which weakens the justification for tight government controls.

The interesting question for the future is how this more democratic and social corporatist political system will handle the growing tension between the interests of the owners and managers of internationally mobile capital, on the one hand, and those who depend on domestic industry for their incomes, on the other. From the standpoint of the former, the rapid rise of labor incomes within Taiwan and Korea—a primary indicator of national economic success—constitutes a problem: it means a rise in cost, which eats into profits. Whereas in the past, when they were less internationally mobile, they saw the economic nationalism of the developmental state as supportive of their interests, they may now, as they become more mobile, see it as an impediment to their worldwide search for profits—and be better able in the new political conditions to secure changes in public policies in line with their new interests. Their internal pressure is being reinforced by external pressure from the U.S. government, which is urging them to "open their markets" to U.S. goods and services, if not to others, and to stop their "export extravaganza" (Mulford 1987). For these and other reasons many of the policy instruments of the developmental state—protection, export promotion, foreign investment controls, foreign exchange controls, and others—are being marginalized; while at the same time the huge balance-of-payments surpluses have eroded the government's ability to channel financial assets into productive investment in industry. The net result may be that it becomes harder than before for the government to take the long-term measures which would allow wages to continue to rise fast while not impairing the competitiveness of Taiwan or Korean industry. As the earlier more direct policies of industry assistance are scaled back, these long-term measures should focus on building up technological capacity within the national boundaries. But big, internationally mobile firms may become unwilling to make such long-term investments in technological capacity at home themselves, and unwilling to support government efforts to do the same. For insofar as they define their interests globally, it matters less to them what happens to development within any specific territory, including their own home base. As wages in Taiwan and Korea rise, they can simply relocate their assets to where short-term profits are higher, whether to textile factories in Thailand or to real estate in California. Most of the population, however, cannot relocate. It is a matter of vital importance to them that the government and firms take long-term investment decisions which expand technological capacity within Taiwan or Korea rather than elsewhere and keep domestic demand for labor rising. Both governments may therefore, for this among other reasons, attempt to incorporate previously excluded "labor" into the governance process, so as to build a constituency of support for long-term and nationally focused measures in order to counterbalance opposition from some owners and managers of internationally mobile capital. This would begin to shift these developmental states toward an East Asian form of social democratic capitalism.

Chapter 11

CONCLUSIONS (2): LESSONS FROM EAST ASIA

THE DEBATE about the role of the state in economic development demonstrates the power of infinite repetition as a weapon of modern scholarship. The issue is normally posed in terms of the "amount" of state intervention or the "size" of government. The neoclassical side says that more successful cases show relatively little intervention in the market, while less successful cases show a lot (Brazil and Mexico compared to East Asia; or sub-Saharan Africa at the bottom). It uses this evidence to urge governments to shrink the size of the state and remove many of its interventions in the market. The political economy side says that the neoclassicals have their facts wrong: the most success-ful cases show "heavy" or "active" intervention. It concludes from this evi-dence that governments *can*, in some circumstances, guide the market to produce better industrial performance than a free market, even in the absence of neoclassical-type market failure. But neither side has been noticeably en-thusiastic to specify just what evidence would be consistent with its position and what would not. Both have exercised a selective inattention to data that would upset their way of looking at things. So the debate about the role of the state is less a debate than a case of paradigms ("parrot-times") talking past each other.

I have shown for Taiwan—and suggested for Korea and Japan—that ample evidence is available in support of both the free market/simulated free market (FM/SM) and the governed market (GM) theories. This poses an identification problem. How important are those facts which are consistent with the FM/SM interpretation, and how important are those which are consistent with the GM approach? My argument is simply that the GM facts are too important to ignore in an explanation of Taiwan's (and Korea's and Japan's) superior perfor-mance. This challenges economics to deploy—or invent—theories which will make the non-neoclassical facts of East Asia analytically tractable. But does it also support the prescription that other middle-income countries should try to govern the market in a broadly similar way (with appropriate adjustment for national circumstances)?

That depends on the answers to three questions. First, are the conditions of the international economy as favorable to a rapid, forced, and export-depen-dent industrialization today as they were for Taiwan and Korea? Second, is there a general economic rationale for GM policies? Third, can governments significantly improve their administrative and political capacity to govern the market?

CONDITIONS OF THE WORLD ECONOMY

Both the FM/SM and the GM interpretations of East Asian success emphasize the importance of domestic factors, in particular "right" policies—though they differ on what constitutes "right." Implicitly, they assume that the trajectories of states are parallel and theoretically independent, each separately subject to the same economic tendencies. Development is a kind of marathon race, in which each runner's position is a function of his internal resources and in which all runners could in principle cross the finish line at the same time.

Yet it is clear from what has been said that a good part of the reason for East Asian success has to do with international factors. These created opportunities for relatively low-cost industrial production sites to be integrated into the world economy. In the 1960s several conditions came together to produce at one and the same time relatively favorable access to industrial country markets, dramatically increased access to international finance, and increasing relocation of production by multinational corporations to low-wage sites. These conditions created opportunities, but did not determine which countries would seize them. Which countries seized them can be explained partly in terms of domestic factors—including the existence of an industrial base resulting from prior import-substitution and the existence of a hard state pursuing GM policies. Location and geopolitical importance are also relevant. The United States "invited" Taiwan, Korea, and Japan to become economically strong because of their location on the West's defense perimeter (which made them more strategic than, say, the Philippines, Indonesia, or Brazil). Japan, the most dynamic economy of the postwar era, had special ties with Taiwan and Korea derived from proximity and colonial history. Hence, part of the success of GM policies in East Asia is due to the favorable historical and international conditions in which they were implemented (Bienefeld 1982; Brett 1985; Cumings 1984). To the extent that these factors are different at other times and places, this throws doubt on the possibilities for other countries at other times to emulate East Asian success.

A central difference between the world economy of today and that of the 1960s, when Taiwan, Korea, and Japan made big inroads into Western markets, is that it is no longer in an expansionary phase. There has also been a dramatic fall in the demand for unskilled labor and raw materials per unit of industrial production. Consequently, developing countries in the 1980s face an external environment more hostile than in any previous decade since the Second World War (IMF 1988; Stewart 1988). They are doubly squeezed on trade and on capital. Growth in world output slowed from 4.1 percent in 1970–79 to 2.6 percent in 1980–87. Terms of trade for nonfuel exports from developing countries deteriorated from a 1.1 percent per year decline in 1970–79 to a 1.7 percent per year decline in 1980–87. Protection in developed country markets has increased since the early 1970s, accelerating in the early 1980s to the point where by 1986 21 percent of manufactured goods imported into the United States and Europe were restricted by quantitative barriers (UNCTAD 1987: table IV.4). This protection is being applied with special discrimination against developing countries. Eighteen percent of manufactured imports from developed countries were covered by quantitative restrictions, and 31 percent of manufactured imports from developing countries. Yet manufactured imports from developing countries account for a mere 1.5 percent of manufactured consumption in developed countries. Meanwhile the microelectronics revolution has reduced the advantage of cheap labor sites, slowing the inflow of foreign direct investment to developing countries at large. The debt service burden for indebted developing countries increased sharply in the 1980s, while voluntary private lending to developing countries almost stopped (US$3.5 billion in 1987 compared to $73.4 billion in 1980).

On top of these trends has come a sharp increase in the volatility of the international economy, and therefore much more uncertainty facing developing country governments and producers (UNCTAD 1988a). With the internationalization and deregulation of financial markets, financial capital is ricocheting around the world in amounts thirty to forty times bigger than trade flows. The relationships between exchange rates and trade, interest rates and investment, and fiscal and monetary policies have become unhinged (Drucker 1986). Governments' ability to control as fundamental a parameter of economic activity as money supply is diminished, and long-term investment is depressed. Dealing with currency fluctuations "is like changing the handicap in golf on every hole," protested the president of Sony recently. "Wouldn't you lose interest in playing golf eventually? If money scale expands or shrinks every day in different currencies, how can we make up our minds to invest?" (*Toronto Globe and Mail*, 1 June 1987). If Sony finds long-range investment difficult in current conditions, think of the predicament of would-be exporters and investors in developing countries with free trade and capital movements. They are forced to adjust and readjust to signals from the international economy which are essentially short-term. These adjustments to price signals that turn out to be misleading guides to economic fundamentals may cause high costs. They are "distortionary" in a sense different from but as important as the conventional meaning in economics, of price misalignments which arise when an economy has not adjusted sufficiently to international price signals (Bienefeld 1988).

The implications are ominous for those developing countries that would seek to "follow the NICs." If many countries are to succeed in increasing their exports of light manufactures, world trade would have to expand fast; but all the signs are it will not. The new protectionism is directed especially at the light manufactured goods which the next tier countries are urged to make their leading export sectors. Moreover, the East Asian four are "stretching" their industrial structures as they expand into more advanced sectors, using technology to remain competitive in light manufactures and thereby only slowly vacating these sectors for others to enter. It will therefore be more difficult for the others (such as Mexico, Brazil, Thailand, Poland, and Hungary) to use industrial and trade policies "successfully."

Underlying these ominous trends are shifts in technology which imply potentially far-reaching effects on the competitive position of nations. It is difficult to forecast these effects, for the implications appear to be mixed. The increase in the capabilities of machines to perform the tasks of unskilled labor may facilitate a shift in the location of production back to the developed countries; but it may also enable some developing countries to become more competitive through better quality control and cheaper engineers. The reduced importance of unprocessed inputs worsens the export prospects of raw material producers; but the new technologies enable them to process the raw materials in-country, and free some regions from some of nature's constraints (biotechnologies can make deserts bloom).

Faced with these new dangers and opportunities, what broad lines of economic policy should developing countries follow? We can be fairly sure that policies to impart an East Asian kind of directional thrust will have a smaller effect than they did in East Asia, if for no other reason than the less favorable conditions of the international economy. On the other hand, this does not mean that FM/SM policies are the better alternative.

We have seen that the confidence with which the neoclassical school prescribes liberalization and privatization cannot be grounded in theory, for the theory which shows how liberalization and privatization generate growth is scarcely developed. We have also seen that it cannot be grounded in the experience of the East Asian NICs, for with the partial exception of Hong Kong they have pursued a mix of policies—many of which are inconsistent with neoclassical prescriptions. Hong Kong, though historically much wealthier than Taiwan and Korea, has not been doing as well in terms of income growth and industrial transformation. But what about the other 98 percent of countries? Does the experience of a broad cross-section of countries provide solid grounds for the neoclassical confidence? My review of the cross-sectional evidence in chapter 1 suggests not.

Given this, we might usefully deploy a more inductive approach to policy and policy-making. We can ask what policies the most successful countries actually adopted, and then construct a rationale for why those policies may have helped their growth. Due recognition has to be given to the Darwinian or Malinowskian fallacy in this exercise—the assumption that because something exists it must be vital to the survival of the organism or society in which it exists. Translated into East Asian terms, this leads one to argue that because these most successful countries used high protection, tightly controlled financial systems, and the like, such measures must have been vital to their success. But what could be called the Ptolemaic fallacy is more prevalent and more inhibiting of learning: the assumption that only those features of economic policy consistent with neoclassical prescriptions could have contributed to superior economic performance, so that everything else can be safely ignored. It seems useful to err for a change on the side of the former.

A distinction must be made between what is consistent with neoclassical theory and what is consistent with neoclassical prescription. There is room within the confines of neoclassical theory for practically any mix of markets and intervention. Most neoclassical economists argue the costs of government regulation and industrial targeting and the virtues of very wide choice by individual market agents on (often implicit) empirical grounds. The empirical significance of market failure has been exaggerated, they say, and government efforts to repair such failure are likely to make matters worse because government failure is empirically more acute than market failure.[1] In what follows I use ideas that are familiar in neoclassical analysis, as well as some that are unfamiliar, to reach different conclusions about the possible economic benefits of governed market policies. These conclusions have the merit of being consistent with what the governments of very successful economies—the East Asian ones—actually did. I state the argument in the form of six prescriptions for micro- and mesoeconomic interventions.[2]

The argument is most relevant to the circumstances of newly industrializing or newly industrialized countries with per capita incomes in the middle-income range (World Bank 1987a). For the most part I duck the question of its relevance to the industrialized market economies. I am unclear about how a world economy would work in which the leading economies, especially the United States, adopt the kinds of actions endorsed here. Past experience suggests it could be benign: the laissez-faire world of the 1920s had disastrous economic consequences, while the postwar era of stable but negotiable exchange rates and national controls over capital movements generated steady expansion. Keynes used his understanding of the prewar boom and bust to argue passionately in favor of import controls and central bank control of international capital movements as instruments of postwar economic management (Crotty 1983; Polanyi 1957; Bienefeld 1988). But in any case, the late-

[1] On the frontiers of economics the theoretical analysis of market failure has become a minor growth industry in the 1980s. But note what I call the "Helleiner effect." Gerry Helleiner observes: "On the frontiers of the discipline, vigorous experimentation can be found in the juggling of assumptions, the empirical testing of hypotheses, and the adaptation and improvement of both theoretical and quantitative economic models. Once in the difficult world of policy formation, however, students of economics are prone to forget all of the qualifications and assumptions, and frequently apply instead the simplest and crudest versions of the models they were taught, using, as they would put it, only 'the basic principles' " (1981a: 541).

[2] Here, as in earlier discussion, I say little about agriculture and agriculture-industry links. But in many countries the starting point for an internal demand-led strategy must be in farming. See Adelman 1984; Lipton 1977. I also say little about macropolicies, though such policies affect competitiveness both directly and indirectly.

comer industrializers, which constitute only a tiny part of world income and world markets, can use different principles from those appropriate to the older industrialized market economies. They can, as have many latecomers before them, free ride on the (more or less) liberal norms embraced by the latter out of self-interest. After all, the per capita income of the fifty-two middle-income countries is still, after four decades of self-conscious development, only 10 percent of the per capita income of the "industrialized market economies" (2 percent for the low-income countries; World Bank 1988: table 1).

My argument is also relevant mainly to noncrisis conditions, when a longer-term view can be taken. Sadly, that currently excludes many countries of sub-Saharan Africa, the Caribbean, and Latin America. Fully two-thirds of middle-income countries had negative growth of gross domestic investment in 1980–86, compared with only 2 percent in 1965–80; one-third had negative growth of GDP (World Bank 1988:table 4). Many have not been investing enough to maintain essential infrastructure. Many are unable to obtain even basic economic statistics, because so much activity has moved into grey and black markets.

I also assume benign political leaders, whose concerns go beyond using state power to support the affluence of a small group. Some rulers, it is true, are predatory, in the sense that their efforts to maximize the resource flow under their control erode the ability of the resource base to deliver future flows. In these cases enhancing the power and autonomy of the state could be disastrous. But states vary in terms of the benignness or maliciousness of their leaders,[3] and the more any particular case is toward the benign end of the spectrum the better the argument applies.

Prescription 1: Use national policies to promote industrial investment within the national boundaries, and to channel more of this investment into industries whose growth is important for the economy's future growth. We must note at the outset that the objective of such policies is not efficient allocation of resources in a Pareto-optimum sense, but growth and innovation. This means that the theorems of welfare economics about the conditions of market failure are largely irrelevant for development purposes. They judge failure in terms of the allocation of resources to the most efficient uses, rather than in terms of the generation of new resources (Kaldor 1972). Theories about market failure in a growth context are not well developed. Here I shall do no more than sketch out a plausible rationale for national industrial policies.

The first step is to consider why the government should take steps to inten-

---

[3] A vampire state at one extreme, a ruminant state at the other? The vampire extracts so much as to debilitate; the ruminant grazes the resource base while fertilizing it at the other end. "Ruminant" is John Waterbury's happy term, while "vampire" is the word used by a senior Kenyan finance official to describe his own state in the late 1980s.

sify the level of investment and reinvestment within the national boundaries. The point of interest is not the causal effect of investment on growth, for that is well established theoretically and empirically (Romer 1987). So also is the connection between high investment and growth, on the one hand, and high labor demand; and between high labor demand and high wages. The point of interest, rather, is the need for political power to focus the investment process on the national territory, which means channeling the options of both domestic capitalists and foreign capitalists by means of import restrictions, domestic content requirements, foreign exchange controls, conditions on the admission of foreign investment, export incentives, technology incentives, and the like. The reason is that as capital becomes internationally mobile, its owners and managers have less interest in making long-term investments in any specific national economy, and hence less interest in the overall development of any specific economy—including their home base. As wages rise, they may be inclined to relocate their assets abroad, or divert them into short-term speculative uses at home, or use their influence over state power to keep labor costs lower than otherwise. From the perspective of a national interest, however, they should be encouraged or cajoled to reinvest at home, and specifically to invest in technological improvements as a way of remaining internationally competitive despite higher wages. For the domestic workforce is not internationally mobile, and its rising real wages are a primary indicator of developmental success. This argument has to be qualified in several ways—by the desirability of some outward foreign investment in terms of a national interest test, and by the problems of overcoming purchasing power constraints on the investment cycle if large export markets are not available. But the qualifications do not change the basic point. Empirically, the work of Alexander Gerschenkron (1962) and Dieter Senghaas (1985), among others, supports the proposition that the more successful European latecomers used a political mechanism to channel the competitive process in the direction of higher-wage and higher-technology activities. (The United States is an exception, where the same result occurred because of the scarcity of labor in relation to land and capital. Hong Kong is also a partial exception. Wages have risen and the benefits of growth have been widely diffused even with capital operating wholly in terms of an international perspective partly because of its very small size and partly because of its role as a regional service center. And to repeat, in the past decade or so it has been less successful in transforming its industrial base than Taiwan and Korea.)

The next step is to consider why government efforts to concentrate investment in selected industries may help overall growth and productivity. One reason involves economies of scale and learning. Whereas neoclassical analysis normally assumes rising cost curves, in many manufacturing processes a doubling of production volume per unit of time gives rise to a substantial fall in unit costs, commonly on the order of 20 percent. But the size of plant or firm required to achieve these economies of scale is typically large in relation to the existing assets of firms in developing countries.[4] The risks confronting potential investors are therefore high, and the investment process will be slowed if the risks are not partially lifted. If domestic producers are given assistance to enable them to compete against foreign suppliers in the domestic market despite higher costs, they may be able to expand their production volume to the point where, thanks to economies of scale and the transactions cost of imports, they can compete without further assistance.

The Japanese-targeted industry strategy takes this logic further. With the government providing protection and socializing some of the risks of large-scale investment, firms are able to price exports at below current average costs in order to gain market share against foreign rivals. The government in effect carries the firms' negative cash flow through these various forms of subsidy. As the firms capture market share and increase production, costs eventually fall to match this "forward" price. Assistance is then removed and applied to the next set of higher-technology industries to be nurtured to international competitiveness (Magaziner and Hout 1980).

Gains in productivity come not only from static economies of scale but also from technological effort based on experience. Even without increases in volume, repetition of production can lead to productivity improvements. Decreases in real unit costs of 100 percent in less than a decade are not unusual in infant industries that have become internationally competitive (Pack and Westphal 1986:106). This gain cannot be obtained simply by buying into the technology; it requires prolonged experience of production, and generally also investment in a deliberate effort to adapt the technology—so the gain does not accrue simply by dint of repetition. (There is a difference between, say, steel and electronics. Learning in a steel plant, where once bought the basic technology will not be changed for a decade, consists of continuous incremental improvements in operating procedures and equipment. Learning in electronics consists not only in how to make existing products more efficiently but also in how to design and produce a new product every nine months—production and innovation learning, perhaps, or static and dynamic learning.)

In short, the forces that lie behind the orthodox assumption of rising cost curves are in many manufacturing processes overwhelmed by economies of scale and learning. Producers who expand production can have falling unit costs. They can therefore race down these falling cost curves and capture market share from existing producers. However, when the international productivity frontier is itself advancing rapidly (as in electronics), the time needed for an infant industry to catch up may be long and the amount of assistance large. This strengthens the case for selective rather than across-the-board assistance.

---

[4] The new flexible manufacturing techniques decrease economies of scale at product level; but tend to go with increases in scale at firm level, because of rising indirect costs (R&D, marketing).

Of course, if producers have perfect foresight and if capital and insurance markets are perfect, these potential cost gains need not warrant state assistance. When markets covering all possible future conditions are available to all and when lenders base lending decisions on expected future costs and earnings rather than on a firm's existing assets, neoclassical theory could not justify state assistance to firms facing potential economies of scale and learning. The justification comes from the unreality of these assumptions in developing country conditions. Borrowing is typically constrained by a firm's existing assets and lack of reputation. Equity and insurance markets are weak or absent. Building them up is a slow and difficult business. In the meantime government comes in as the "second-best" risk insurer and capital provider, so as to bring a private cost/benefit calculus more into line with a social cost/benefit calculus. Max Corden, impeccable neoclassical credentials notwithstanding, concludes that, "in spite of many qualifications, a valid, practically relevant infant industry argument for subsidization of new manufacturing industries resting on capital market imperfections can be made for many less-developed countries" (1974:255). Governments, in other words, can substitute for missing and difficult-to-develop capital markets (Stiglitz 1989).

A third justification, in addition to scale and learning economies and capital market imperfections, comes from that most elastic of concepts, "externalities" or "spillovers." In the general sense, external costs or benefits are those which are created by a firm or other economic agent but which do not bear on or accrue to it. Simultaneous externalities occur where a firm's potential gains from an investment are contingent upon complementary decisions by other firms. Even if all the parties know they would gain by coordinating their investments to capture the externalities, they may face inherent contradictions of interest, as in a Prisoner's Dilemma game.[5] Hence market prices may not adequately signal the interdependence that exists among these investment decisions, and uncoordinated firms may invest at suboptimal levels from a national perspective. A big push, involving simultaneous expansion of several industries, can insure the profitability of each investment, even though each on its own would be unprofitable. One important reason is that such simultaneous expansion helps to overcome the constraint of a small domestic market, when entry and participation in world trade entails significant costs.

There is also a second kind of externality, sequential rather than simultaneous. Sequential externalities occur where a large upstream plant would, if built, induce the entry of downstream firms to make use of new profit opportunities created by the upstream firm but not appropriable by it. The upstream plant brings greater social benefit, in the form of induced downstream growth, than is reflected in its private profit (Biggs and Levy 1988).

---

[5] For an introduction to the literature on Prisoner's Dilemma, see Rapoport and Chammah 1965; Lipton 1985; Wade 1988d.

To the extent that simultaneous and sequential externalities are spatially concentrated the investment process may become cumulative as more spill-overs are generated and more firms enter to secure access to them. Market size increases, helping to reduce the risk of large-scale investments. In practice, diseconomies of agglomeration (such as congestion costs) may arise and some factors will be immobile, so that competitive advantage can shift from estab-lished centers to new ones (Brett 1983). We can expect the advantages of coordinating investment to capture these externalities to be particularly large where the domestic market is small, where the input-output structure is "holey," where entrepreneurs with the resources and experience to undertake large-scale investment are few and far between,[6] and where access to world markets is limited by high transactions costs and trade restrictions. The role of government is not only to push the process by coordinating upstream indus-tries, but also to lower entry barriers at the downstream end to facilitate the induced response. Conventional notions of "efficiency" are poor guides to what the government should do, because when externalities are considered one may find that a set of microeconomically less efficient industries, consid-ered individually, produce a macroeconomically efficient result through the linkages between them; while a set of microeconomically efficient industries may produce a macroeconomically inefficient result.[7]

Another justification for governing the market has to do with the adverse effects of market instabilities on long-term investment. Any moderately com-plex economic system encounters a source of instability arising from the un-certainty inherent in the attempt to match present supply decisions with future demand decisions. One would expect that if prices and quantities are left wholly to the instabilities of the market, investment in industries or technolo-gies which require a large commitment of time or capital may not be made, and a higher than desirable proportion of the economy's investment will go into quick return projects. Individual firms on their own may be more inclined to stick within a narrow range of familiar product lines than branch out into

[6] In situations characterized by lack of efficient risk-sharing institutions such as stock markets, "the size of the entrepreneurial class . . . is smaller than would be first-best optimal" (Grossman 1984:613).

[7] A longer discussion would distinguish between pecuniary and technological externalities. Pe-cuniary externalities occur through market transactions. They make for market failure, in the neoclassical sense, only in the presence of economies of scale. Government coordination can help to reduce this source of market failure provided the structure of domestic prices is not closely fixed by the structure of international prices (perhaps because of the investment costs of getting into exporting). Technological externalities are not transmitted through market transactions. Ex-amples include labor training, when a firm invests in training workers who then join another firm, or machinery adaptation, when the firm invests in modifications to existing machines which are then easily copied by others. Technological externalities may be more important causes of neo-classical market failure than pecuniary ones, and may occur independently of capital market im-perfections. See Pack and Westphal 1986 and references therein.

new industries and products. It may well be that, within limits, price *instability* has a more adverse effect on growth than price *distortions* as conventionally defined. A context of deliberately created stability, achieved by risk-spreading mechanisms such as protection or subsidies, can facilitate industrial deepening, export expansion, and political compromises to share adjustment costs.

Again, a role for industrial targeting can be warranted by the fact of differences between industries in prospects for long-term growth in output, profits, and wages. Unassisted entrepreneurs may not have either the foresight or the access to capital to follow long-term potential. Their decisions may lock the country into specialization in industries with inferior prospects (an issue beyond the scope of comparative advantage theory). Given a world of technical change, falling cost curves, and differential rates of growth across industries, it can be rational for a government to select from within the plausible industries those which have high growth potential and to use the powers of government to supplement those of the market in marshalling resources for entry and successful participation (Scott 1985:95). This means diverting resources from currently profitable activities into ones that might be fast-growing and/or profitable in the future—which is risky. But any successful large company follows a strategy of diversifying from currently profitable activities into new ones, on the assumption that the future will probably be different from the present. Governments at the national level can aim to carry through a parallel strategy of diversification. The scarcer the supply of capital and the higher the entry barriers of the new industries, the stronger the case for selective assistance.

But can comparative advantage really be modified, made, or achieved in this way? Traditional theory takes comparative advantage as exogenous, largely determined by "factor endowments." In a gross way these considerations are still relevant: Burundi should not go in for computer production just yet. But as Bela Gold says,

> Virtually all empirical findings of comparative advantage represent no more than ex post facto rationalizations of past trade patterns, often reflecting *market interventions* rather than substantial differentials in efficiency and costs. Moreover, even the demonstrable comparative advantages prevailing in a given period have frequently been undermined and even reversed thereafter through determined efforts to advance technologies, shift input requirements, alter transport costs, and develop new markets. . . . The very identification of current comparative disadvantages often represents the first step in developing means of overcoming them.
>
> (1979:311–12, emphasis added)

William Cline reaches a similar conclusion: "Increasingly, trade in manufactures appears to reflect an exchange of goods in which one nation could be just as likely as another . . . to develop comparative advantage, and the actual outcome is in a meaningful sense arbitrary" (1982a:39–40). In place of "arbitrary'' I would say "subject to strategies of firms and governments.'' Talk of "revealed comparative advantage" (measured by the relative preponderance in a country's exports of product x compared to its preponderance in the trade of the world as a whole) is hence misleading, for the export pattern may reveal government assistance as much as factor endowments. And factor endowments, it should be remembered, can themselves be arranged on a spectrum from unalterable to alterable, with sunshine at one end and knowledgeable brains at the other. The classic case of Portuguese wine and British sheep reflects unalterable natural endowments; the modern case of British whiskey and Japanese electronics reflects human capital build-up, long-term horizons, and other acquired advantages. Government assistance can create new advantages of the acquired kind, some of which are industry-specific.

The popular belief that governments cannot "make winners" rests on remarkably little empirical research into the record of different governments in selective industrial promotion. Many governments, especially in small countries, routinely target industrial assistance at specific industries and even at specific firms, particularly where economies of scale call for a minimum level of subsidy per firm. Yet we do not have systematic data on the performance record of different governments which would allow us to distinguish those with one failure out of four from those with seven failures out of eight. (No failure is itself failure, because it means that the targeters are not taking enough risk.) Research on this question has to balance the record of government failure against the record of failure by private business; and examine, too, what happens to economies where few transformation projects are attempted because the government declines to take an initiative and private business declines to take the risk.

In short, several considerations—economies of scale and learning, capital market imperfections, externalities, market instabilities, and differential growth potential—give grounds for state assistance to industry and to some industries more than others.[8]

---

[8] The question of the degree of selectivity of protection and promotion has hardly begun to be studied empirically. Pack and Westphal say of Korea: "The set of promoted infants has changed over time, but it has generally been small at any one point in time" (1986:94). They prescribe that "selective intervention must indeed be selective," focused on "a select few extensive changes" (1986:118), those that result in distinctly new capabilities and occur through investments with large indivisibilities. On the other hand, Shinohara contrasts the general prescription for infant industries with Japanese practice. "In general, the nurturing of infant industries is limited to a certain period of time and to a certain number of industries. In Japan, however, these measures were across the board and applied to almost all industries. . . . Because of the vastly extended promotion of infant industries and across-the-board encouragement of exports, MITI's approach ran counter to the basic principles of modern international economics" (1982:49). One of the theoretical points at issue is the industry-specificity of the dynamic factors; the more they are industry-specific the smaller should be the set of promoted industries, while the more they are a function of the size of the entire industrial sector the more widely should assistance be spread.

These arguments for assistance to particular industries are especially relevant to capital goods industries and microelectronics. In medium- and large-sized countries, developing a domestic capital goods industry is a necessary condition for enhancing a country's capacity to develop embodied industrial innovations. The social costs of not doing so are not fully captured in free-market prices used to choose between domestic and imported capital goods. Such prices do not include either the costs of the chronic trade deficits of medium- and large-sized countries that do not produce capital goods or the costs of the lack of capacity to innovate or adapt technologies associated with the capital goods industries. The relative absence of a machinery industry means that an increase in investment becomes an increase in imports. Since much of the multiplier effect on aggregate demand leaks abroad while the machinery imports increase productive capacity, the profitability of investments is reduced. Moreover, the relative absence of a capacity to adapt imported technologies means that when domestic demand arises for a new product which has just appeared in developed country markets (the lag is typically short because those with discretionary purchasing power in developing countries tend to imitate the consumption patterns of developed countries), it is met by imports. These imports, being in the initial fast-growth-of-demand stage of the product cycle, tend to grow faster than manufactured exports, which tend to be in a later and slower-growing stage; and tend to grow all the faster than agricultural exports, most of which face very slow growth of demand. These elements cause a tendency toward chronic trade imbalances. The state therefore has a role in directing the sectoral allocation of investment so as to reduce imports and thereby increase the multiplier effect, check the tendency toward trade imbalances, and enhance domestic capacity to adapt imported technologies.

Furthermore, over the 1970s and 1980s the development of capital goods and microelectronics have become intertwined, many innovations taking place in the course of applying microelectronics to capital goods. National policy has to play a still bigger role to push domestic producers into the new microelectronics technology than was true of the older electromechanical technology; for entry barriers are typically much bigger (as in the case of numerically controlled machine tools compared to conventional machine tools, for example). But microelectronics constitutes more than just a radical change of technology. It constitutes a change in technoeconomic paradigm, a set of changes which not only leads to new industries and products but pervades almost every branch of the economy (Freeman and Perez 1988). The last such change of paradigm was in the 1930s and 1940s, associated with the utilization of cheap energy (especially oil). The change underway since the 1970s is associated

---

See Rodrik (1987) for a theoretical and empirical study of the implications of imperfect competition and economies of scale for trade policy.

with microelectronics. In the early stages of diffusion of this paradigm "windows of opportunity" open for countries which have already built up a certain level of infrastructure, industry, and technical knowledge but which have not made heavy physical and organizational investments in the now superseded technology system. Newcomers which meet these difficult threshold conditions can catch up with the previous leaders by early entry into the new information technologies (Perez and Soete 1988). A necessary but not sufficient condition is substantial amounts of government assistance in concentrating investment and socializing risk. Much of the assistance may have to be in a leadership rather than a followership mode, because private entrepreneurs are unwilling to take enough risk, quickly enough, to assure that the new opportunities are taken.

Of course, whether national welfare is actually enhanced by the assistance depends on the wisdom of the choice of targeted industries and on the effectiveness of implementation. And industrial policies are only one set of factors on which the competitive success of an industry, or of the country's whole industrial sector, depends. In the total pattern of causation they are much less important than the capabilities of the country's private companies. But those capabilities are themselves able to be augmented by assistance from the public sector.

We now consider several guidelines about how governments can assist industries to be more competitive. No attempt is made at completeness. The subjects chosen for discussion meet two criteria: they loom large in East Asian policies, and they involve some skewing of market processes by changes in prices or opportunities for exchange.

Prescription 2: Use protection to help create an internationally competitive set of industries. Two of the things which economists disagree least about are that protection, whether for restraining the demand for imports or for promoting domestic industries, is always second-best, and that quantitative restrictions (QRs) are always inferior to tariffs. When unrestrained demand for imports leads to balance-of-payment difficulties, the solution is devaluation plus restrictive expenditure (fiscal and monetary) policy. If for some reason it is deemed necessary to promote specific industries, credit subsidies should be used (Corden 1974).

These prescriptions are backed by an impressive body of theoretical reasoning. But once one moves beyond a concern for what is logically consistent with the theoretical system of neoclassical economics, they are not compelling guides to decision-making in the real world. As regards devaluation, the first problem is that experts often disagree by large margins as to what the "desirable" exchange rate should be, not only in developing countries but in industrialized countries as well (notably the United States). Second, even where experts agree that the exchange rate is substantially overvalued, "markets" often seem to be poor at correcting the imbalances. Third, the policy instrument is the nominal exchange rate, but there may be no close connection between changes in the nominal rate and changes in the real rate except in the very short run; and it is the real exchange rate which counts for resource allocation. Fourth, the neoclassical argument recognizes no limits on how far the exchange rate can be made to fall. But a fall in the real exchange rate means a fall in the price of noninternationally tradable goods and services relative to the price of tradables. The most important nontradable is labor, so a fall in the real exchange rate tends in practice to cause a fall in the real wage. Workers may revolt. More generally, inflexibilities of import-dependent production processes and consumption patterns may mean that the needed fall in the exchange rate is not possible without disruption of production, inflation, social unrest, and political conflict, fear of which may induce a well-meaning government to find other methods of maintaining external balance.

The argument to replace protection with credit subsidies as a means of assisting particular industries is also not compelling. First, there can be no presumption that the subsidies needed for infant industries to compete equally against foreign suppliers would match the finance available. Unless a close connection is assumed between the revenue-raising capacity of government and the amount of subsidies needed, the subsidies may exceed the capacity. Second, the advantages of subsidies cannot be presumed to outweigh the "distortionary" effects of raising revenue through the existing tax system. Third, protection through tariffs raises revenue in an administratively simple way, compared to the difficulties of raising revenue through direct taxes; and is probably no more difficult to administer effectively than a subsidy program (Luedde-Neurath 1986). Fourth, subsidies are generally a more visible means of transferring resources and may therefore generate more political conflict than protection, which transfers resources more invisibly. (Whether this is desirable depends on whether the pattern of protection makes national sense.) Finally, insofar as changes in subsidies are more contested politically than changes in protection, subsidies are unlikely to be changed enough to buffer short-term external fluctuations.

There are indeed many cases where protection has not had any noticeable innovation- or investment-enhancing effect (e.g., India). This reflects the failure to integrate protection with a wider industrial policy, or link it to export performance, or make the quid pro quo conditions credible, or to maintain macroeconomic stability. If protected producers know that in the foreseeable future protection will be much reduced or that government will pressure them to enter export markets, then protection may give them breathing space in which to undertake the necessary investment and innovation. They can use higher than normal profits in the domestic market to subsidize their entry into export markets, practicing discriminatory pricing. The same effect may be induced by awarding import licenses for targeted products only on evidence that the product could not be obtained from domestic producers within some reasonable margin of the import price. Such an "approval" mechanism or "law of similars" at least forces would-be importers to obtain full information about domestic supply capability. It also helps to stabilize demand for domestic producers of import substitutes, thereby lowering their risk and encouraging them to invest enough for economies of scale. But at the same time, the price criterion means that international competitive pressures are brought to bear on domestic producers, though in a modulated way.

There is, of course, a tension between stimulating demand for nationally made products by protection (or domestic content requirements, or government procurement) and stimulating the international competitiveness of users of those nationally made products. Supply-side measures of assistance to the domestic producers can help to reduce the conflict. But in any case, it is important that exporters be exempt from most import restrictions, the exemption being greater the bigger the price and quality differential between imports and domestic substitutes. The government can, however, use its import-restricting ability to encourage users of imported inputs to negotiate with local suppliers for upgraded production or lower prices in return for guaranteed sales. Repeated across many products, this mechanism can nudge the production structure of the country upwards.

Notice that the mechanism uses QRs rather than tariffs. QRs (and domestic content requirements) have merit when the acquisition of technological capacity and subsequent adaptive innovation depend on extensive interaction between users and suppliers (Lundvall 1988; Pack and Westphal 1986). However, QRs have the costly consequence of amplifying the volatility of price signals, because with changes in domestic prices the tariff-equivalent of any given QR also changes. But where macroeconomic stability prevails, as in East Asia, this familiar cost of QRs is much less significant. The East Asian experience supports the argument that QRs have lower costs in stable than in unstable macroeconomic conditions.

The desirable degree of import liberalization is much affected by country size. For most small countries—most of the time and in most industries—a relatively liberal trade regime is a necessity because of the lack of domestic economies of scale. Bigger countries have a wider latitude of choice. In general, the wider the latitude of choice, the more the overall degree of trade freedom should emerge as the result of calculations of the appropriateness of lowering protection to particular industries, bearing in mind that domestic competition can substitute for foreign competition, as in Japan, and that domestic competition, even between oligopolists, can be stimulated by government policies. Taiwan and Korea show how liberal trade policies in some industries can be combined with import substitution policies for other industries, resulting in different incentives to different industries. They also show how a rapidly industrializing country can soften pressures from its trading partners to open its markets or face retaliation, by a judicious combination of camouflage, statements of intent, and real liberalization.

Some developing countries, particularly in sub-Saharan Africa, are unable to earn enough foreign exchange to cover import demands at any politically viable exchange rate, because of the limited supply of internationally saleable products. Here it makes no sense to talk of protection only as a temporary measure to assist the emergence of infants able within five to ten years to compete against international competition with no protection. Protection has to be seen as a part of longer-term measures to gain experience of industry and large-scale organization. In its absence resources may remain largely unemployed or confined to very small-scale production. The trick is to use such longer-term protection in a way which does not eliminate all competitive pressures.

In short, import protection is, as neoclassical theory says, a powerful tool. Like any powerful tool it can be badly used, producing a trade regime full of inconsistencies. But that is not the end of the story. The East Asian evidence—whose challenge to mainstream trade theory has produced little more than an elliptical pirouette by way of response—suggests that protection can also be used in combination with other measures to foster the creation of internationally competitive industries.[9] Where such industries are not on the horizon, protection can at least help to begin the process of acquiring the capital needed to make new capital, the knowledge needed to absorb new knowledge, the skills needed to acquire new skills, and the level of development needed to create the infrastructure and agglomeration economies that make further development possible.

All this suggests an important analytical point, that the international trade literature is wrong in identifying some policy instruments as unambiguously better or worse than others without regard to the way those instruments are administered. QRs administered in a conditional way are not the same as unconditional QRs. Protection may be administered more easily than subsidies, and so more reliably achieve the intended effects.

Prescription 3: If the wider strategy calls for heavy reliance on trade, give high priority to export promotion policies. East Asia's fast growth and equitable distribution was undoubtedly helped by the rapid growth of exports. Ex-

---

[9] It is surprising that Jagdish Bhagwati, one of the most theoretically creative proponents of nearly free trade regimes, does not attempt to grapple with the effects of Korea's, Taiwan's, and pre-1970 Japan's protection system on their industrial growth. In writing a book called *Protectionism* (1988), or in addressing the question of "Is free trade passé after all?" (1989), he might have been expected seriously to address the empirical association between substantial and selective protection in East Asia and superior industrial performance, this being critical evidence and not just another set of cases. But his oversight does keep him consistent with his own law of economic miracles: "Economic miracles [Taiwan et al.] are a public good; each economist sees in them a vindication of his pet theories" (1988:99). For a descriptive account of the East Asian trade regimes, see Wade 1988b.

ports faced less of a demand constraint than output in general; they provided a channel for technical assistance from buyers; and they gave more scope for labor utilization than the manufacturing sector as a whole or the existing import-substituting industries in particular. However, export growth is not the only important reason for fast and equitable growth, and other countries with different natural resource endowments and larger economic size may be able to achieve "good" growth and distribution with less reliance on exports (Adelman 1984; Sen 1981). Indeed, they may not have much choice in the matter, because Western countries will probably intensify protection to avoid big (especially China-scale) increases in competing imports from developing countries.

Where, nevertheless, heavy reliance is to be placed on trade, the government must recognize that successful exporting of manufactured goods to richer countries is not just a matter of getting the exchange rate right and keeping labor cheap, even in the absence of protection.[10] This is because many kinds of manufactured exports to richer countries are only saleable as complete packages meeting all buyer specifications, including packaging, labeling, colors, raw materials, finishes, and technical specifications. Costs rule out the option of importing an incomplete or defective package and correcting the defects in a subsequent stage of manufacturing. Thus, marketing, transmission of information, and quality control turn out to be key activities for export success. Buyers can supply some of these services; but especially because of the externalities the government also has an important role. The government can arrange for information about foreign markets and about domestic suppliers to be easily and freely available; it can directly help the promotion of some products (e.g., through trade fairs); and it can help to curb the tendency of firms without brandnames to compete by producing shoddy goods, spoiling the country's reputation for other producers. Very importantly, the government can also inspire producers to seek out export markets as a normal part of their operations (Keesing 1988).

All this holds even in the absence of protection. If the economy is protected, cheap labor and a proexport exchange rate are still less likely to be sufficient. Without quick and automatic access to imported inputs at world market prices, free of customs duty, quantitative restrictions, and indirect taxes, would-be exporters will be handicapped in world markets by being forced to pay more than competitors for the same inputs or by being forced to use inferior domestic substitutes. Since manufactured exports from developing countries are normally sold in intensely competitive markets, producers in a country without a scheme for duty drawback and relaxation of quantitative restrictions are unlikely to obtain big export orders. Buyers for industrialized countries will sim-

---

[10] There is disagreement between economists on whether conventional neoclassical trade theory does or does not support export subsidies. See Bhagwati 1988:95, n.11.

ply pass them by. However, even once export sales have near-free trade conditions producers of manufactured goods may still face net incentives to sell on the protected domestic market, and exports may still be uncompetitive because the costs of nontradable inputs (especially labor) are raised by demand for those same inputs from the protected and hence larger-than-otherwise domestically oriented industries. An export subsidy scheme may be needed to make export sales as attractive as domestic market-related sales.

Combining this discussion of export promotion with the preceding discussion of import protection, we see how misleading it is to present import substitution and export promotion as mutually exclusive strategies, as in Anne Krueger's claim that "export promotion outperforms import substitution" (1981:5). They are mutually exclusive only if defined to refer to the overall balance of incentives between domestic and foreign sale. But at the individual industry level, import-substituting incentives and export-promoting incentives can be complementary. On the one hand, development of the supply side through import substitution may be a prerequisite for the demand-side growth of exports. On the other hand, export growth can be helpful for the further development of industries that are nearing the limits of import substitution. Likewise, export promotion in one industry can complement import substitution in another by providing foreign exchange, for example. At any one time export promotion and import substitution should coexist, reflecting the different development stages of different industries.

We also see how misleading is the common assumption that policy-induced neutrality (as when export incentives "counteract" the effects of import controls) is equivalent to free trade. It is not clear how the many kinds of incentives for export- and import-substituting industries can be commensurated (effective protection rates are hardly adequate). It is fairly clear that the structure of relative prices at the time when "neutrality" is achieved reflects the prior rounds of intervention, and differs from that of an economy with untrammeled prices and exchanges throughout. Therefore we cannot presume that relative prices and resource allocations would be unchanged if the entire array of incentives and protection were eliminated at a stroke.

Prescription 4: Welcome multinational companies, but direct them toward exports. Multinationals are the primary source of knowledge about technology and production and an important source of knowledge about marketing. No country is going to get far in knowledge-intensive manufacturing and services without their help. Hence the government of a newly industrializing country should establish attractive policies for foreign capital, whether as subsidiaries, joint ventures, or licensors. However, foreign firms should be under pressure to direct their sales toward exports and their input purchases toward local suppliers. For if their products dominate the domestic market the developmental consequences of the protection system may well be worse than if domestically owned firms dominate the domestic market.

First, with multinationals restricted in terms of their dominance of the domestic market, government efforts to promote the growth and restructuring of domestic production do not have to go through the multinationals, whose objectives will not wholly coincide with the development of national production capability. The government is able to use investible funds according to priorities designed to further integrate the domestic market, through having more influence over the firms that produce for the domestic market than if those firms were predominantly multinationals. (The multinationals should also be under foreign exchange controls, for if they are free to move funds in and out of the country they may start to function as de facto bankers for their domestic customers and suppliers, eroding the government's own credit policy.) Second, multinationals operating in the domestic market tend to follow marketing strategies that have little to do with average incomes or traditional consumer behavior, thereby accentuating income inequalities. By limiting their access to the domestic market the diversification of goods made available to consumers can be a gradual process geared to the population's purchasing power. In particular, the most modern of consumer goods, produced chiefly by multinationals, should be restricted to exports until basic needs in food and clothing have been met—as the Korean government did under Park (Ikonicoff 1985). Third, export requirements on multinationals not only generate foreign exchange, but also, less obviously, insure that the companies adopt an internationally competitive technology, rather than one which is viable only on the protected domestic market. However, export requirements may be eased in return for higher domestic content.

The government should attempt to tie the magnitude of direct foreign investment incentives to either export performance or local content performance.

Application of these principles has to recognize that, given the increasing "footlooseness" of much industrial production, the balance between the costs a country imposes on enterprises and the facilities it provides has to compare with other countries'. If requirements on foreign firms have to be relaxed in order to attract and keep them, it is important to compensate with discriminatory state support for competing domestically owned firms to prevent them from being backwashed out of existence.

Prescription 5: Promote a bank-based financial system under close government control. A closely regulated bank-based financial system has several advantages in industrializing country conditions.[11] First, it permits higher in-

---

[11] For a discussion of "bank-oriented" financial systems (such as Japan and Germany) and "market bank" systems (United States and Great Britain), see Mayer 1987; Zysman 1983. One of Mayer's themes is that "the separation between investment and finance, which is the basis of most existing models, is untenable" (p. iii). My discussion tries to bridge this separation by showing how a certain type of financial system may affect the "real" economy in developing country conditions.

vestment than would be possible if investment depended on the growth of firms' own profits or on the inevitably slow development of securities markets. In a capital market-based system, the decentralized preferences of the public largely determine the allocation of potential savings into productive investment, financial speculation, or consumption. In a bank-based system, in which enterprises depend heavily on banks for finance and less on a broad public of shareholders, the long-term growth preferences of government officials and/or bank executives have more weight. Investment decisions are hence more insulated from the preferences of the public. Credit can be more cheaply provided for productive investment, in the context of a long-term approach to the economy's investment activity. In a capital market-based system, on the other hand, government attempts to stimulate investment by tax cuts and deregulation may have only a modest effect on investment, as in the economic reforms of President Reagan and Prime Minister Thatcher.

Second, a bank-based system encourages more rapid sectoral mobility and permits the government to guide that mobility insofar as it can influence the banks. Even small changes in the discount rate or in concessional credit supply between sectors can have a significant effect on resource allocation (provided the use of credit is controlled enough to prevent unlimited fungibility), because the effect of such changes on firms' cash flow position is greater than where firms have smaller debt/equity ratios. Where the government is trying to foster key sectors, a bank-based financial system gives it a powerful mechanism for inducing firms to enter sectors they otherwise would not. Where, on the other hand, capital is allocated mainly in decentralized markets, the government's ability to extend a visible and vigorous hand in the functioning of the industrial economy is limited, because firms are less susceptible to state influence (Zysman 1983).

Third, a bank-based system can help to avoid the bias toward short-term company decision-making inherent in a stock market system. The creditor needs the borrowing company to do well: it is concerned about the company's market share and ability to repay loans over the long term, which depend on how well the company is developing new products, controlling costs and quality, and so on. So these become the criteria which managers are concerned with, rather than stock market quotations (Johnson 1986; Dore 1985).

The fourth advantage is more directly political. Industrial strategy requires a political base. Control over the financial system, and hence over highly leveraged firms, can be used to build up the coalitions needed to support the government's objectives—thus helping to implement the industrial strategy. Firms are dissuaded from opposing the government by the knowledge that opponents may find credit difficult to obtain. Of course, such a practice is easily abused. If it becomes common to allocate credit for "loyalty" rather than for economic performance or potential the legitimacy of the administrative discretion will be impugned. Sparing but well-publicized use may reap the political gains without the legitimacy costs.

These are four potential advantages of a bank-based, administered-price financial system. However, such a system contains certain imperatives for government action which have far-reaching implications for the government's role in the economy.

The first is that the government must help to ease the downside risk of debt-financing. Higher deposit interest rates can increase the flow of financial savings; but at the new rates the private sector may not be prepared to borrow the savings unless the government intervenes to socialize some of the prospective private losses. Even if in the short run the savings are translated into loans, the higher savings and investment made possible by the higher rates may not be sustainable in the longer run without measures to spread risk. This is because highly indebted (or leveraged) firms are vulnerable to decline in current earnings to below the levels required by debt repayment, repayments on debt being fixed (whereas payments on equity are a share of profits). With firms vulnerable in this way, so are the banks which carry the "nonperforming" loans. So where debt/equity ratios are high, there is an ever-present danger of financial instability in the economy:[12] bankruptcies, withdrawal of savings, a fall in real investment, and slower growth. To ease such dangers, firms are likely to borrow less and banks to lend less than if the government were to underwrite some of the risks to which lenders and high debt/equity producers are exposed. If the government does bear some of the risk of private losses, the supply and demand for loanable funds will be greater, so investment, technical change, and hence growth can be higher.

The need to socialize risk applies especially in the case of highly correlated risks, to which most firms in major sectors are exposed. So it applies especially to interest rate changes, or major recession, or changes in major export markets, or political risks. Therefore the impetus for government to shoulder some of the risks of investment and saving in an economy with high debt/equity ratios is especially strong in countries which are trade-dependent and/or under external threat (like Taiwan, Korea, and Japan). The impetus is reinforced in industries where both entry and exit take a long time.

This impetus then leads the government to provide a battery of ways to reduce the risks of financial instability—not only in the form of deposit insurance and lender-of-last-resort facilities, but also in the form of subsidies to banks imperiled by loan losses, product and credit subsidies to firms in financial difficulties, banks' share-holding in companies, government share-holding in banks and in lumpy projects, and even government ownership of banks.

---

[12] The implications of high debt/equity ratios also depend on profitability at the firm level. In an economy where profitability is higher and more secure the danger of overall financial instability is less. The same applies to the implications of high debt/equity ratios for the relationship between banks and firms. I am indebted to discussions with Frank Veneroso on these matters.

Government can also, of course, control interest rates and exchange rates to dampen firms' exposure to market fluctuations in these two important sources of correlated risk.

The second imperative is for the supplier of credit to become involved with company management. The supplier of credit may for this purpose be the government (Korea), or the banks (Germany), or some of both (Japan). In any case, the reason for involvement with management is that the creditor cannot simply withdraw when a company runs into difficulties by selling the securities in the secondary capital market; the secondary capital markets are too thin. Given that the "exit" option of the capital market is not available, the alternative is the "voice" option, to try to restructure company management so as to make it more competitive and to take the long-term view (Hirschman 1970).

Nevertheless the government and/or the banks must, third, develop an institutional capacity to discriminate between responsible and irresponsible borrowing, and to penalize the latter. Firms which borrow without due commercial caution and run into trouble must not expect the government or the banks to continue to bail them out (the so-called moral hazard problem). The government must also develop mechanisms of bank supervision to curb the tendency for banks faced with big loan losses to conceal them in the "performing" part of the balance sheet while making even riskier loans in the hope of getting back enough to offset the losses. This is the path that turns good bankers into bad ones, solvent banks into insolvent ones.

Once market signals are blunted by administered pricing and socialized risk, the government must, fourth, create a central guidance agency capable of supplementing market signals by its own signals as to which sectors will be most profitable—but in a way which allows plenty of scope for private pursuit of opportunities not seen by the guidance agency.

Finally, the government must maintain a cleavage between the domestic economy and the international economy with respect to financial flows. Without control of these flows, with firms free to borrow as they wish on international markets and with foreign banks free to make domestic loans according to their own criteria, the government's own control over the money supply and cost of capital to domestic borrowers is weakened, as is its ability to guide sectoral allocation. Speculative inflows seeking exchange rate gains can precipitate accelerating movements in exchange rates, with damaging consequences for the real economy. Uncontrolled outflows can leave the economy vulnerable to an investment collapse and make it difficult for government to arrange a sharing of the burden of adjustment to external shocks between the owners of capital and others; "the others" are likely to be made to take the burden, with political unrest, repression, and interrupted growth as the likely result. More generally, foreign exchange controls are needed to intensify the cycle of investment and reinvestment within the national territory, with outflows only where they can be shown to meet national economic priorities.

Otherwise domestic interest rates come to be determined in large part by U.S. interest rates, and therefore make the economy subject to the kind of macroeconomic mismanagement of the U.S. economy seen during the 1980s. Although presented here as just one in a list of several requirements, this cleavage between the domestic financial system and the international financial system is a prior condition for all the others.

If free markets for foreign exchange and other financial assets were clearly efficient one might hesitate to recommend such a controlled system. But "belief in the efficiency of the foreign exchange market is a matter of pure faith; there is not a shred of positive evidence that the market is efficient," concludes Paul Krugman. Similarly for bonds and stocks: "there is no *positive* evidence in favor of efficient markets" (1989:65). On the other hand, the disadvantages of controls can be partly offset by allowing an unregulated curb market to operate in the interstices (Biggs 1988)—and perhaps by tying a sizable portion of subsidized bank credit to export performance. Joseph Stiglitz's new work on developing country financial systems provides a cogent rationale for policies broadly in line with those recommended here. He concludes, "the LDCs should not set their sights on imitating the capital markets of the most developed countries, but rather should adapt themselves to the reality that capital markets will most likely, if not necessarily, work poorly within their country. Adopting this view suggests a major redirection of several policies which have been widely adopted within the third world" (1989:56). He emphasizes more than I do, however, the difficulties to improving the incentives on government and large public credit institutions to do a good job in selecting and monitoring loans.

Prescription 6: Carry out trade and financial liberalization gradually, in line with a certain sequence of steps. Many neoclassical analysts urge large-scale and quick liberalization, to get a whole package of reforms in place before opposition builds up. And many urge that comprehensive import liberalization should be carried out before export earnings increase, so as to flush away the inefficiencies generated by protective barriers and enable a subsequently better response to export demand (Krueger 1978; Snape 1988; Lal 1983; Michaely 1988). By contrast, the East Asian experience is consistent with a prescription for more gradual change and a different sequence. It suggests the following: (1) macroeconomic stabilization should come before trade liberalization; (2) substantial external financial assistance greatly eases the transition from stabilization to liberalization; (3) liberalization of imports of export inputs should come before deprotective competition-providing import liberalization; (4) import liberalization of the latter type is not a prior condition for successful exporting; it should follow the growth of exports; (5) successful exporting requires a large promotional role for public agencies; (6) gradual trade liberalizations can be sustained; and (7) financial liberalization should come late in the queue, after a substantial measure of import liberalization (Sachs 1987; Helleiner 1988; Edwards 1985; Wade 1988b).

With reference to financial liberalization, our knowledge of its effects in segmented and imperfect capital markets is thin. Modeling the connections between the regulated financial markets and the curb market in Korea has generated "unconventional" results from orthodox monetary and interest rate policies. Higher (regulated) interest rates and monetary restraint led to a serious slowdown in investment and growth, the effects of which exceeded any positive effects for household savings (van Wijnbergen 1983). Painful experience with rapid and far-reaching financial liberalization in the Southern Cone countries of Latin America has bred a new respect for government supervision and control of the domestic financial system, and caution about lifting external capital markets controls. These results support the gradual approach to domestic and external financial liberalization adopted in East Asia (Helleiner 1988; Mayer 1987; Krugman 1989).

More generally, the gradualness of economic liberalizations in all three countries further undermines the view that if only the government of a developing country shrinks from influencing prices or exchanges, it too can expect much improved economic performance. The East Asian liberalizations were gauged to the competitiveness of domestic industry, which was itself promoted by preceding and simultaneous industrial policies. Without them, letting prices work would have been like pushing on a piece of string.

There is also a political case for gradualism, which should be weighed against the political argument for quick and deep liberalization to preempt opposition. Liberalization typically involves changes—removal of food subsidies, for example—whose costs affect the general public widely and directly but whose benefits are more concentrated and slower to appear. If several such policies are introduced at once and entail major rather than incremental change, they can be expected to generate opposition from many interest groups, including some whose support is important for the regime's survival. They therefore carry high stakes for the incumbent political leaders, all the more so when the government is insecurely legitimated. Gradual introduction of the reforms, with some sequencing and camouflaging of who gets the costs and benefits, can provide less fuel for opposition organization and thereby make sustained implementation more likely. In the general case, this seems as plausible a scenario as that of the neoclassicals.[13]

In considering issues of liberalization we need to make a distinction between shrinkage of the public sector and reduced state capacity to manage the

[13] Indira Ghandi's post-1980 government carried out significant economic liberalization without drawing sharp political reaction partly because she made the changes look like marginal, "technical" ones. Her son and successor, by boldly proclaiming a decisive shift of development strategy to a liberal model, aroused such widespread opposition from groups on whom the Congress depended for votes as to force a drastic slowdown in the liberalization. However, in the early period Rajiv Ghandi's government did successfully introduce a number of liberalizing policies—those which "were brought about quietly, without much fanfare, as seemingly technical changes in a piecemeal fashion" (Kohli 1989:314).

market. The size of the public sector, in terms of employment, share of GDP, and other such measures, is not closely associated with state capacity to manage the market.[14] Indeed, shrinkage of the former—which would be called "liberalization" in the gross way the term is generally used—may help to expand the latter; and the latter is what counts.

The argument for economic liberalization—whether in trade, finance, or other spheres—also needs to address the question of what kinds of private sector groups will gain from the change. It cannot be assumed that they will wish to be entrepreneurial investors rather than luxury consumers. Nor can it be assumed that they will wish to place limits on the arbitrary actions of the state and discipline the state to provide effective services. Liberalization may lead to the capture of economic power by less accountable cliques around the power-holders, Marcos-style. The analytical dichotomy between "state" and "economy" can lead us to overlook the point that the same people or groups may have feet planted firmly on both sides of the divide, in which case a shrinkage of the state and expansion of the private sector may further remove economic power formerly in the hands of the state from some degree of accountability. It may further erode a "center"—a cohesive organizational structure—where collective interests can be articulated and followed.

These are six broad economic prescriptions supported by the experience of Taiwan, Korea, and Japan. But we must note another lesson to do with differences rather then similarities. While the three East Asian states all governed the market, they used somewhat different methods for doing so. Taiwan used large upstream public enterprises and selected foreign firms to provide "unbalanced" pushes in certain sectors, arms-length incentives to steer the response of myriad small downstream firms, and stable prices and real effective exchange rate. Korea used huge private business groups as the spearheads, steering them with massive credit subsidies and more direct cajoling (recently switching to more of a negotiation mode). It obtained more of its technology under license than through direct foreign investment, and sacrificed some macroeconomic stability for faster industrial transformation. Japan, which already had huge private business groups in place in the 1930s, pioneered the route that Korea was later to follow, except that consultative decision-making procedures linking government and business were in place from much earlier on. So there is more than one way to govern the market effectively.

IMPROVING STATE EFFECTIVENESS

My argument is that a necessary but not sufficient condition for more rapid industrialization is state deployment of a range of industrial promotion policies, including ones to intensify the growth of selected industries within the national territory. This is not to say that effectiveness increases with the sheer

---

[14] See chapter 1, n.12.

amount of intervention, nor that it increases the more the state imposes its will on society, ignoring other groups. State effectiveness is a function of the range of options, given by the number and force of policy instruments, and the flexibility with which those policy instruments are used. Flexibility means that the capacity to intervene, as given by the number and force of policy instruments, is used to varying degrees, more in some industries than in others at any one time, and more in one industry at some times than at others, always with an eye on the costs of interventions in political as well as economic terms. In particular, high effectiveness requires the flexibility to withdraw assistance from industries as they become internationally competitive, and the ability not to intervene in some industries at all in the interests of concentrating assistance and limiting costs. Behind these proximate determinants of effectiveness are others of a more organizational and political kind. First is the competence and coherence of the central economic bureaucracy. Second is the degree to which political authority is institutionalized. Third is the connection between the central bureaucracy and other major economic interests, especially the owners and managers of capital. We now consider four more prescriptions to do with these organizational and political determinants of state effectiveness. Again, the prescriptions are rooted in what East Asian governments actually did.

Prescription 7: Establish a "pilot agency" or "economic general staff" within the central bureaucracy whose policy heartland is the industrial and trade profile of the economy and its future growth path. For an industrial policy to be effective one or two agencies should steer the formulation and application of the policy instruments. Taiwan, Korea, and Japan have all used the "few agencies" model, in contrast to the "many agencies" model of the United States and Great Britain.

The pilot agency should have a fairly small staff (Japan's MITI had only about two thousand in the 1960s). It should be in a position to recruit from among the best and the brightest. Once a competitively selected economic bureaucracy acquires a reputation for attracting the best and brightest, the system develops a momentum of its own. It continues to attract such people (even at much lower salaries than the private sector) because selection is the stamp of outstanding talent. Its personnel need to be motivated by the belief that what they are doing promotes the national welfare. A sense of national mission, combined with a meritocratically based esprit de corps, can motivate the central bureaucracy to use its powers in line with national goals, providing a substitute for the motivational force of profits in private firms. A vigorous national press, free to criticize the economic bureaucracy (even if not the political leaders) can help to keep its actions in line with the public interest. The conflict between life-time employment and up-to-date technical and managerial knowledge can be moderated by using parabureaucratic task forces to complement in-house capabilities. The more the government intends to intervene in a leadership rather than a followership mode, the more important are the staffing, motivation, authority, and responsibilities of the pilot agency.

The pilot agency should be concerned with formulating operational goals, such as diversification of industries, diversification of markets, reduced dependence on raw material imports, and greater employment in certain industries; and with analyzing how various policies affect these goals. It should think of itself as a strategic oligopolist, scrutinizing the actions of rival governments and taking account of those actions and reactions in framing its policies for investment, trade, and technology.

It should have some power of implementation rather than devolve all concern for implementation to the ministries. It should focus on certain key industries at any one time, more or less ignoring the rest; but should situate policies for these industries within an analysis of the whole economy, bringing multiple policy instruments to bear on them. This can be done without detailed quantitative targets for investment and output for particular industries, which are only likely to distract from the more substantive business of formulating the broad vision of the appropriate directions for growth and choosing the specific industries to be promoted. Multibusiness, multinational corporations undertake a broadly similar type of strategic (rather than comprehensive) planning as a matter of course, and their techniques can, with modifications, be extended to multi-industry, multimarket countries.

In addition to the organizational factors considered above, the effectiveness of such an agency is related to the decision criteria it uses. One of the great merits of using export performance is its simplicity and clear connection to competitiveness. It can be used to make a first judgment on assistance to firms or industries; those that are doing well in export markets will be treated more favorably than those which are not, other things being equal. When a country is pursuing a domestic market-based strategy, particularly one which is led by agriculture, simple and sensible decision criteria are more difficult to find (Pack and Westphal 1986). Above all, one must deemphasize criteria that, for ease of measurement, focus on inputs, not on outputs.

The activities of such an agency are likely to be uncongenial to economists trained to believe that targeting by officials will generally fail. That is one good reason for curbing the number and influence of economists in the industrial policy-making process, as was done in Japan, Korea, and Taiwan. The other reason is that neoclassical economics has little to say about the issues raised by the present shift of technoeconomic paradigm, of how to exploit the opportunities opened by the new information technologies (Dosi, et al. 1988). Of course, in Cuba, North Korea, the Soviet Union, China, and other centrally planned economies, the more neoclassically trained economists the better.

Prescription 8: Develop effective institutions of political authority before the system is democratized. The class structure of many developing countries implies a cruel choice between faster economic development and well-defended civil and political rights. Power and wealth are often concentrated in groups engaged in socially unproductive activities (including renting out of land, money-lending, exploitation of bureaucratic or military office). Groups based on industry must grow on the margins of power, perhaps as part of a coalition of sections of the state bureaucracy and sections of the military. Often the rise of this "growth coalition" is attended by conflict as it tries to displace groups with real coercive power, capable of taking the law into their own hands. It may try to harness a popular political movement using nationalism or revolt against exploitative class relations as a rallying cry. Once it can influence state power, it has to use that influence to shape a social structure which is conducive to wealth accumulation through productive investment. Most likely this will require some curtailment of the political and civil rights of those who oppose the changes, and of the powers of democratically elected legislatures (Huntington 1968).

The argument in favor of such a state is uncomfortable to those (including myself) who cherish the civil and political freedoms of North American and Western European countries—especially when "democracy," more than any other term in political discourse, now generates such a universal hurrah. "It has been difficult for me to comprehend how free people can choose tyranny for others," declares A. M. Rosenthal, former executive editor of the *New York Times*. "There is for me only one question that really matters about any government: does it allow political freedom? Does it permit its citizens to breathe and think and talk and write as free people?" (1986:23). He goes on to say that "the apologists for tyrannies argue that economic progress has to come first, and that democracy is really too expensive a way of achieving it. This is said in all seriousness, as if there were evidence that despotism somehow is more efficient than freedom. The exact opposite seems so obviously true . . ." (p. 24). (Rosenthal includes the Park and Chun regimes of Korea as tyrannies, and would presumably so call the Nationalist government of Taiwan.)

Rosenthal's Manichean assertions notwithstanding, the balance of argument and evidence seems to me to point the other way. People who live in societies where, for a whole century or more, they have been able to see "freedom of opinion" as about whether editors get sent to jail or not, find it hard to comprehend the priorities of people in societies where freedom is also restrained by fear of the assassin's bullet and fear of being thrown off one's land by trumped-up suits and corrupt judges. In such societies the priority is to institutionalize a system of order before it is democratized—to move from a system where the press is controlled by people with wealth and private armies to one where it is controlled by the state, before reaching one where it is controlled by people with wealth but without private armies.

The executive branch needs to be stronger than the legislative branch, to "rule" while the legislature "reigns." An elected legislature is likely to be directed less by a view of the common good than by, in Adam Smith's phrase, "the clamorous importunity of partial interests" (1775:438). A state in which the legislature is strong relative to the executive will find it difficult to hold the line against unbalanced increases in consumption at the expense of investment, and difficult to direct government assistance to uses which can meet a national interest test rather than a clamorous importunity test. Conversely, where the executive is relatively strong, there is a better chance that policies will not careen from side to side because of frequent turnover in power. This makes for a more stable business environment, facilitating longer-term corporate investment. And it helps the bureaucracy to oversee the operation of the economy.

Historically, individual property rights, constitutional restraints on the state, and the rise of the bourgeoisie occurred before the advent of mass democracy (Huntington 1984). Both Taiwan and Korea now provide support for the proposition that the stability of a new democracy depends upon the development of broad-gauged political institutions prior to the expansion of political participation. As we noted, they were in the middle of a rights ranking of middle-income countries in the early 1970s; Taiwan was in the same position in the early 1980s while Korea had fallen a little lower. As of the late 1980s, they are making a transition to stable and partially democratic systems, with the prospect of more democratization to come. Japan, of course, has had much better defended rights since World War II. But Japan's primary industrial revolution took place during the late nineteenth and early twentieth centuries, at which time its political and civil rights were quite restricted, its government distinctly authoritarian and oligarchic. For the past thirty years Japanese voters have gone to the polls with slimmer expectations that the result could be a change of government than in any other industrialized democracy; and the representatives whom they elect have had less influence on the major decisions affecting the national welfare than in any other industrialized democracy.

Large cross-sectional studies of developing countries show that democratic regimes tend to grow more slowly than authoritarian ones. Robert Marsh, using a sample of ninety-eight developing countries and several development indicators for the period from 1960 to 1970, concludes that "political competition/democracy does have a significant effect on later rates of economic development; its influence is to *retard* the development rate rather than facilitate it" (1979:244). Erich Weede, using a different method and a different but also large sample of countries, concludes in part that "political democracy looks like a major barrier to economic growth in those countries where the state strongly interferes in the economy" (1983:312).[15] But there is also probably

[15] See also Adelman and Morris 1967; Huntington and Dominguez 1975. Dick (1974) finds the reverse relationship. For a useful discussion, see Kohli 1986. Interventionist governments in Weede's analysis had revenue equal to or greater than 20 percent of GDP in 1965 at all income levels. He finds thirty-four such cases (thirty-five for one regression). He uses Bollen's (1980) classification of countries as democratic or authoritarian in 1965 (excluding the centrally planned economies). The methodological difficulties of establishing a causal connection between regime

more variation in the performance of authoritarian regimes compared to democratic ones at similar per capita incomes, some having mediocre to calamitous results. Many authoritarian governments do not give high priority to economic development, being preoccupied with the task of excluding most of the population from power.[16] As per capita income approaches $4,000, the economic advantages of continued restrictions of civil and political rights—of continued consolidation of authority in the hands of the state—are probably offset by the costs of growing conflict, weak legitimacy, and overburdened state decision-making. This, at least, is a possible interpretation of the fact that over the 1980s there have been virtually no noncommunist countries at or above this income level without fairly competitive political systems. Singapore is an exception, and Taiwan would have been had it not initiated democratic reforms in 1986.

Prescription 9: Develop corporatist institutions as or before the system is democratized. State effectiveness depends on the coherence of state policies, which is difficult to maintain when important parts of the state are beholden to sectoral, ethnic, or regional interests. Effectiveness is therefore a function of the degree of insulation (or "autonomy") from the surrounding social structure. Insulation is a function of, among other things (1) officials' dependence on the state for their income, not on interest groups; (2) officials' expertise, which gives them grounds for asserting their own preferences for state action against those of interest groups; and (3) the extent to which the nation faces a threat to "national interests" from other states, in response to which nonstate groups are likely to confer substantial autonomy on state officials.

Even in a highly pluralist regime some bureaucratic insulation is conferred by these conditions. In an authoritarian regime the insulation can be much greater because the coalitional basis of the state is narrower. But insulation of central officials from pressures in the wider society also carries costs. It may erode feedback on economic conditions at the point of production and sale, and may remove a potentially strong basis for the formation of a consensus on the dominant factors influencing the course of the economy and the order of

---

type and economic growth are formidable; see Hicks and Patterson (1989) and the papers to which they are responding. The gross categories of authoritarian and democratic regimes are too crude to capture some important aspects of civil and political rights. In particular, by focusing on the freedom or lack of freedom to choose rulers they miss the greater importance in the lives of ordinary people of having power to shape the rules which govern the immediate or local aspects of their lives. Perhaps some authoritarian regimes with strong national-level executives nevertheless grant or tolerate considerable latitude in the choice of local rules.

[16] Dick (1974: table 1) provides some evidence of greater dispersion in the performance of authoritarian regimes. One might relate the dispersion not only to goals (exclusion, economic development, etc.), but also to the type of military they are associated with—the swashbuckling, tribute-raising kind or the strategic-planning, military-engineering kind. In the decade following the mid-1970s most Latin American countries have swung from authoritarian to partially democratic regimes (Gastil 1986).

socioeconomic priorities. Even in the most centralized government, the course of the economy is influenced by the decisions of many separate agencies—decisions about the exchange rate, tariffs, interest rates, availability of capital, wages, public expenditure, public borrowing, taxes, and more. Any attempt at comprehensive control from a single point would overstrain the government's information capacity and power. Without a roughly common view about decision premises, national economic policy decisions are unlikely to achieve the degree of coherence needed for their overall success. Moreover, when the thinking classes are wholly familiar with a certain range of ideas and assumptions about the longer-term future there is a base of legitimacy for government-sponsored measures with long-term payoffs. This base of legitimacy is especially important when some will be losers.

But such a consensus is always fragile, vulnerable to the whims of important interest groups because of changes in circumstances, priorities, or evaluations. A corporatist structure[17] to represent a limited set of major economic interest groups—and thereby also to channel the demands placed upon the state—can help to insure acceptance of negotiated outcomes. It can help to mediate the uneasy tension between unrestricted market forces and social peace, buffering the costs of economic adjustments to external market changes while allowing adjustments to occur (Ruggie 1982). It does so by facilitating reciprocity between big firms, government, and perhaps unions,[18] in which government help is made conditional on stipulated performance by the other parties; and by facilitating the use of state authority to steer groups away from hostile strategies that yield the worst outcomes in Prisoner's Dilemma situations. However, such arrangements are difficult to sustain where the idea of the public or national interest is used primarily as a cover for advancing private, class, or ethnic interests, where a core meaning shared by all the parties is lacking.

The only evidence I know of on the economic performance of corporatist

[17] In a corporatist structure, the state charters a limited number of major economic interest groups, granting them a near monopoly of representation. In authoritarian regimes of the common garden variety, the leaders control and appeal to the people directly, without this intermediating structure of representation. And pluralist regimes differ from both in having a geographical rather than functional basis of representation, and in having "free trade" in interest group access to the state.

[18] Inclusion of labor is obviously desirable in principle. But note that if labor exclusion is part of a set of arrangements which generate high-speed growth, workers are protected to some extent by high labor demand. Labor exclusion also gives a government more room to maneuver when austerity comes, and that latitude can be used to restore fast growth more quickly (compare Mexico and Taiwan). But the more mature an economy becomes the less likely is economic growth to be sufficiently fast to meet the normal aspirations for economic security. It is then of the first importance that the institutional arrangements made to provide security do not erode the pressure on people to work hard or convert security guarantees into obstacles to adjustment. The key is to build up labor commitment, so that effort is not based simply on an exchange of effort for pay.

regimes comes from already wealthy and democratic countries, whose corporatism is of the "social corporatist" type. Here peak associations have more of a policy-initiating role than under "state corporatism." The evidence suggests that countries with social-corporatist arrangements (such as Austria, Norway, Switzerland, and Sweden) have enjoyed above-average incomes and economic growth, with lower inflation and unemployment, than pluralist countries. In particular, those countries with arrangements for centralized bargaining, politically dominant social democratic parties, and centralized unions, tended to weather the international economic crises of the 1970s better than others. Pluralist countries like the United States and Great Britain, which tolerate raw adversarial outcomes between economic interest groups, have been less successful in adjusting to these crises.[19] But this conclusion cannot readily be extended to cover corporatism in developing country conditions, about which there is little evidence. I expect that state corporatist regimes vary more in their economic performance than pluralist ones. Salazar's Portugal and Perón's Argentina, both state corporatist, had dismal records, while Taiwan and Korea have had exceptionally good ones (also Japan in its extreme state corporatism of 1940–41). The variation may be closely connected to rulers' objectives. In East Asia a shared sense of the external vulnerability of the nation has helped to concentrate the rulers' minds on performance-enhancing measures as a means of their own survival.

The Taiwan case shows an interesting variant of state corporatist arrangements. Formal industrial associations are weak, as we saw; but there is plenty of communication between government officials and firms of an informal, often dyadic kind. Industrial Development Bureau officials often spend several days a month visiting industry associations and firms in "their" industry, for example.[20] These and other means of keeping in touch with firm-level facts are vital if the government is to intervene to promote specific industries, whether as leader or follower.

Prescription 10: Make piecemeal reforms even in soft states so as to create an institutional configuration better able to support a modest industrial policy. Suppose one agrees that governed market policies can improve on the economic results of free or simulated free market policies. Whether such gains are realized depends on the existence of certain organizational arrangements, as just indicated. When such arrangements are not already in existence, administrative and political reforms can create them. But these reforms cannot be simply willed into existence, and their effects take a long time to come

---

[19] Wilensky 1981; Schmitter 1981; Schmidt 1982; Wilson 1985:110; cf. Zeigler 1988:chapters 3–4. I have not examined the Latin American evidence. U.S. and British economic performance has improved during the 1980s in terms of many aggregate indicators, though market share in many of their high-technology industries continues to erode.

[20] For a South Korean example of little formal communication combined with abundant informal communication, see Wade 1982a:54–56, 90.

through. Given this, one might argue that—even accepting the potential gains of governed market policies—most states should move toward free market policies as fast as possible, on grounds that softer states can sustain these policies more easily than governed market ones.

Paul Krugman, for one, argues that even though recent work in trade theory provides a rationale for an activist trade strategy in certain conditions (which are, however, unlikely to apply to developing countries), the gains may not be large and the strategy is difficult to implement because of its vulnerability to hijacking by special interest groups. Hence, he says, free trade rules are best for "a world whose politics are as imperfect as its markets" (1987:143). Instead of political factors being blamed for the inability of governments to follow economically rational free trade policies, political factors are now brought in to say why free trade remains politically best even after it is shown to be not always economically best (Helleiner 1988). This is but a special case of the "practical optimality" of free markets. Even if free markets can be shown to be suboptimal according to some ideal allocation system, they are the method which produces the least inefficient resource allocation in practice, the argument runs. The alleged alternative, administrative allocation, will produce worse results because it is not subject to *anybody's* bottom-line constraint.

There *is* something to be said for this argument. The image of the high-salaried official who knocks off to play golf at 4:30 leaving a pile of files on his desk and then, when he gets to your application three weeks later, casually says no, *is* more outrageous than that of the wheeler-dealer entrepreneur who is continually creating monopolies, rigging prices, making false advertising, and so on. But proponents of this argument fail to explain why, if vested interests are strong enough to defeat sensible selective interventions, they will not also be strong enough to distort markets and defeat free trade. Free trade is not self-enforcing. Vested interests seek to maintain the structures in which their interests are vested, rent-seekers seek to preserve the conditions that create rents. Karl Polanyi reminds us that Adam Smith's "natural propensity to truck and barter" had not sufficed to produce free markets in England. "The road to the free market was opened and kept open by an enormous increase in continuous, centrally organized and controlled interventionism" (1957:140). A passionate exponent of free trade agrees that "a courageous, ruthless and perhaps undemocratic government is required to ride roughshod over . . . special interest groups" that stand in the way (Lal 1983:33). In practice, then, free trade may be no easier to sustain than sensibly managed trade. (One wonders, incidentally, what fraction of GDP the United States spends on competition policies, including not only the cost of the relevant government agencies but also the "chilling" effect of antitrust legislation in inhibiting agreements which might have been beneficial, as well as the transaction cost of the legions of lawyers involved in every move.)

Even in the context of a relatively soft state it should be possible to institute higher levels of effectiveness in limited parts of the state. It should be possible for the state's industrial policies effectively to do more than put a seal of approval on what the private sector would have done anyway. By bringing to the negotiations its own sense of the appropriate direction of the economy, and by paying for more rather than less of the costs of a new project which fits that direction, it can still impart a directional thrust. The organizational arrangement might take the form of a pilot agency which, though lacking the implementation power of MITI or Taiwan's Industrial Development Bureau, still has some statutory power which makes it necessary to the making of policy, so that it can force its long-term perspective into pluralistic bargaining. One would need to insure that appointment to the senior positions of such an agency is by merit criteria; that the incumbents cannot be rotated in and out according to the sway of factions or money; that the standard operating procedures allow the agency to stick to a purpose, so as to deal with surprises and opposition in line with enduring goals; and that it has secure funding.

Elsewhere in the economic bureaucracy effectiveness and responsiveness can be improved by several kinds of measures. There are the standard institution-building ones, including more financial resources, higher status, and bigger supervisory infrastructure. But more interesting are ones which attempt to introduce more market-like features into bureaucratic incentive systems, while remaining incremental in nature and not requiring sweeping changes in order to have some effect (Lamb 1982; Murray 1989). These include ways of changing internal incentives and options, such as decentralizing managerial accountability within bureaus or agencies, inducing competition between sections within a bureau or between agencies and parabureaucratic task forces, establishing more performance-based salary and promotion rules, creating a super cadre with better pay and more exacting performance standards than in the normal civil service, establishing public management accounting systems which record output and performance as well as costs, and developing a random-check performance auditing capability by senior managers. These changes can be complemented by ones which seek to put more market-like pressure on the bureaucracy from outside, such as publicizing performance targets and rates of achievement, organizing would-be beneficiaries into industrial associations and turning over much of the high-cost "retailing" end of industrial service delivery to industry associations or private firms. Shifting from "control by ownership" to "control by contract" can both improve work incentives and reduce the administrative burden on the state. The state retains control over a key segment of a service operation while subcontracting out the other parts. Taiwan and Korea show how some of these ideas can be operationalized (for Korea, see Wade 1982a).

These organizational requirements are no doubt difficult to meet in many states, even if focused on only a small part of the civil service. But they are not of the kind that ask elephants to fly; they should not cause us to say that outside the configuration of a hard state political reality dictates a close approximation to free market policies as the best practical way forward. We tend to assume, wrongly, that the ills of public bureaucracy are intrinsic to this generic type of organization, and therefore are inclined to embrace "the market" as the preferred alternative. In fact, many of those ills are features of one particular—though predominant—model of organization found in the corporate as well as the public sector. This "mechanical" model, characterized by elaborate specialization of tasks and standardized procedures, by extended chains of command and written communications, is now being radically reformed in the corporate sector of the West, so as to create organizations better adapted to the exigencies of the new information and production technologies (Hoffman 1989). These new forms of corporate organization can provide experience for new forms of public administration.

The current economic difficulties, and budgetary pressures in particular, are making many governments more prepared to tackle difficult institutional issues than would be the case in more normal times; they are running out of alternatives. At the same time, the current conditions in the world economy increase the potential advantages of pursuing GM policies—to modulate the volatility of the world economy on the domestic economy, to help domestic firms compete internationally in the face of increasingly fierce international competition, and to force an early entry into information technologies. Firms whose governments decline to provide assistance may relocate, or they may resort to squeezing labor costs and intensifying work practices in order to avoid losing market share, enlisting the power of the state to help them do so. This higher premium on GM policies raises the advantages of undertaking the organizational improvements needed to support them.

In any case, whether government seeks to promote particular industries or seeks only to make all markets freer, it is likely to have to make organizational changes along these lines. Even a government committed to free trade must be purposeful, must have a system of policy management that recognizes the effects of interactions among its own activities, and must be able to insure that desired responses are forthcoming from the commitment of public resources used as side-payments to those who would otherwise block market processes (Heclo 1986). Free trade policies are no means of escape from the need to improve the capabilities of governments.

The United States is a telling example. Lacking these capacities, the U.S. government uses leaky protectionist instruments as much as most other industrialized economies. But its departures from free trade are largely a case-by-case response to domestic political pressures rather than being part of a strategy for gestating or nurturing future competitive industries. With no one being required to explain or defend what is being done, its industrial policies remain ad hoc and implicit. Indeed, the philosophical repugnance against government involvement in industrial promotion is such that the government lacks both detailed knowledge of industries and analytical capacity to select appropriate actions. If an industry is in trouble, the government is meant to become involved only when trade is said to be "unfair" or when national security is involved; otherwise, whether the industry becomes more competitive, moves offshore, or goes out of existence is a matter of government indifference— because the market outcome is assumed to be best. This repugnance is translated into and then confirmed by organizational incompetence at carrying out concerted industrial policies. The personnel policies of the federal government compound the problem, for they are designed to attract (in the approving words of a former associate director of the Office of Personnel Management) "competent people, not the best and most talented people," who should be encouraged to migrate to the private sector, "the true vehicle for prosperity" (cited in Allison 1989).

In these several ways, the United States is a model of what developing countries should avoid. Yet the thinking of most of the international aid community, including USAID and the World Bank, is profoundly shaped by American conceptions of the role and competence of government. And the political meta-assumptions of neoclassical prescriptions are calibrated to those same ideas. All the more reason for developing countries to study the East Asian experience to see how government and capitalism are arranged where economic development has been a top national priority for decades. And all the more reason for economists to accept the challenge of constructing a theoretical rationale for the non-neoclassical East Asian facts. When the next *Wealth of Nations* comes to be written, it will look more favorably upon governing the market. The first Adam Smith would surely approve. It was he who warned from his study of the history of astronomy, "The learned give up the evidence of their senses to preserve the coherence of the ideas of their imagination" (in Lindgren 1967:77).

FISCAL INCENTIVES

1970

Electric Manufacturing Industry

1. Electric motors
2. Blast-proof electric motors
3. Telecommunication equipment or full-time manufacture of components and parts (limited to telephone sets, manual telephone switchboards, automatic telephone exchanges, wire and wireless telegraph receivers and transmitters)
4. Wire
5. Electric cable (including aluminum wire and steel-core aluminum cable)
6. Electric fans
7. Transformers
8. Lightning arresters
9. Switches and switchboards
10. Dry cells and instant rechargeable batteries
11. Fluorescent lamps and accessory equipment
12. Television sets (assembly excluded)
13. High-voltage input capacitors
14. Permanent magnets
15. Semiconductors and assembled circuits
16. Electronic tubes (those for lighting use excluded)
17. Electronic computers and important components
18. Fish detectors
19. Tape-recorders and video recorders (assembly excluded) and important components
20. Navigation instruments
21. Elevators and escalators
22. Electronic supplies (including transformers, coils, capacitors, resistors, electromagnetic supplies and components, micro-motors, printed circuit boards, filters, tuners, speakers, switches, relays, and delay lines)

Note: For industries handling items 1, 4, 5, 6, 10, and 11 above, a minimum of 50 percent of the output must be exported.

23. Manufacture or processing of semifinished electronic and/or electrical components and parts, including control facilities, meters, and their

semifinished components and parts. (Names of proposed products must be submitted to the Ministry of Economic Affairs for approval prior to commencement of production. If imported raw materials are to be used, the factory must be either registerd as a bonded factory or using bonded warehouses or located within an export-processing zone. To be eligible for encouragement measures, enterprises manufacturing or processing articles covered by this item must export all their output.)

Textile Industry

1. Knitted goods
2. Garments
3. Cloth
4. Yarns

Note: Products must be made of cotton, wool, hemp, silk, artificial fibers, or blends. For industries handling items 1 and 2 above, a minimum of 80 percent of the output must be exported. For industries handling items 3 and 4 above, a minimum of 50 percent of the output must be exported.

1982

Electrical Equipment
Manufacturing
Industry

1. Generators
   a. Diesel electric generators (limited to those with a generating capacity of 500kw of electricity or above)
   b. Hydroelectric generators
   c. Turboelectric generator assembly and parts and components thereof (limited to those specially designated by the Ministry of Economic Affairs)
2. Electric motors
   a. Explosion-proof electric motors
   b. DC electric motor (limited to those where such products are produced with the capacity of one-half HP or above and put together with locally made rotors and staters)
   c. Servo motor or synchronous motor
3. Power transformers and capacitors
   a. Dry transformer
   b. Power transformers (limited to those which transform voltages of 161KV or above)
   c. Pad mount transformer
4. Transmission and distribution equipment
   a. Potential transformer (limited to those which are of the 33KV class or above)

b. Current transformer (limited to those which are of the 33KV class or above)

c. Breakers (switches)

(1) Minimum oil circuit breakers (limited to those which are of the 11KV class or above)

(2) Vacuum circuit breakers (limited to those which are of the 33KV class or above)

(3) Leakage circuit breakers

(4) Other high-voltage circuit breakers (limited to those which are of the 24KV class or above)

d. High-voltage power safety fuse (limited to those which have a voltage rating of 3,000 volts or above)

e. High-voltage connector, high-voltage select switch, subconnector for power distribution use (limited to those where such products are produced with a working voltage of over 3,000 volts)

f. High-voltage lightning arresters (limited to those which are of the 24KV class or above)

g. Overload relays

h. Motor-starting relays

i. Marine electric motor distribution panel (control panel) (with a minimum local content ratio of 70 percent)

5. Air-conditioning or refrigeration equipment

a. Air-conditioning or refrigeration equipment for marine use (with a minimum local content ratio of 70 percent)

b. Refrigerant compressors (excluding those used in refrigerators)

6. Elevators

a. Automatic elevators (limited to those which manufacture control systems by themselves)

b. Automatic escalators

7. Lighting materials

a. Fluorescent mercury lamps (limited to those where such products are produced with self-made inner tubes)

b. Sodium mercury lamps (limited to those where such products are produced with self-made inner tubes)

c. High-efficiency fluorescent tubes (limited to those which have an intensity of illumination of 80 lumen or above)

8. Electric wires and cables

a. Double-coated enamelled wire

b. Corrugated cables

c. Power cables (limited to those which are of the 69KV class or above)

d. Optical fiberglass communication cables

9. High-voltage insulating tubes, tapes (limited to those where such products are produced with a working voltage of over 6,600 volts)

10. Bakelite (limited to those where such products are made of phenolic or expoxy resin)
11. Electrically operated hand tools with double insulation
12. Cells
  a. Hg cells
  b. Ni-Cd cells

Textile Industry

1. Tire cord fabrics of synthetic fiber
2. Dyeing and finishing of textiles (limited to those which after inception or expansion have a minimum annual production capacity of fifteen million meters and are equipped with pollution preventive equipment)
3. One hundred percent cotton or blended cotton sewing thread whose yarn count is 60/1 ECC or more: (1) limited to those which after inception or expansion have a minimum annual production capacity of 150 M/T; (2) whose products conform to the CNS National Standard; (3) which engage in full-time production
4. Silk fabrics (limited to those which produce silk fabrics using indigenous silk yarn and which constitutes 50 percent or more of the materials used)

Sources: "Categories of Enterprises Eligible For Encouragement by Way of Reduction or Exemption of Profit-seeking Enterprise Income Tax," Industrial Development & Investment Centre, May 1970; "Categories and Criteria of Productive Enterprises Eligible for Encouragement," Industrial Development and Investment Centre, May 1982.

Note: These lists give only the items eligible for the tax holiday (or accelerated depreciation). Other lists give the items eligible for the other fiscal incentives.

POLITICS OF THE 1958–62 ECONOMIC REFORMS

TAIWAN'S LIBERALIZING REFORMS of 1958–62 are normally presented as a rational response to the exhaustion of first-stage import substitution. More by omission than commission, the transition is portrayed as smooth and unproblematic. Only Gustav Ranis makes the qualification that the period between 1954 and 1958 was characterized by a good deal of "backing and filling and indecision" on the question of the appropriate direction ahead (1979:219). The following account, based in large part on unpublished research by Robert Silin,[1] shows what that "backing and filling was about. With little other research available on the interplay of interest groups in Taiwan's development, the argument should be interpreted as a series of propositions in need of further examination rather than a statement of settled facts. It may give too much weight to interests and too little to the trial-and-error shift of policies and to the process of institutional rationalization.

The early period of the Nationalist government on Taiwan was characterized by much greater conflict between rival groups within the bureaucracy than has been the case since the early 1960s. At first it was between officials of the incoming central government and those of the *in situ* provincial administration. After that struggle was won by the central government side, the conflict took place between two main groups within the central government competing for the president's support. This second conflict was very important for the direction of economic policy.

It may seem surprising that the central government on its arrival from the mainland should have to struggle for control of the governance of Taiwan against its own subordinate provincial administration. What happened is as follows. From 1945 until the early 1950s, the provincial administration of Taiwan province had far more autonomy than the other provinces under Nationalist party rule on the mainland. The reasons were the fifty years of separation under the Japanese, the Nationalist party's preoccupation with the civil war, and the determination of the early governors to set an independent course for their administrations, especially so as to insulate Taiwan from the raging inflation on the mainland. (Taiwan was allowed to issue its own currency after 1945.) As a corollary, the early governors centralized control over economic

[1] Untitled, undated, unfinished typescript, received from the author April 1984. I am grateful to him for sharing his work. I am also grateful for comments on the argument from Tun-jen Cheng, Stephan Haggard, and Ying-mao Kau.

activity—monetary policy, trade, and transport—at the top levels of their administrations. So when the central government retreated to Taiwan, a fairly strong provincial administration was already in place. What is more, that administration controlled the funds on which the central government, having lost the mainland, was reliant. Even after the central government arrived, its disorganization meant that control of foreign exchange and foreign trade continued to rest with the provincial government. Only gradually and against bureaucratic opposition did the central government succeed in reestablishing its control by coopting key financial institutions and sources of revenue.

In particular, the central government acted to get control of U.S. aid funds out of the hands of the provincial administration and into its own. This it did through the creation—''at the suggestion of the director of the (U.S.) Mission'' (Jacoby 1966:59)—of the Economic Stabilization Board (ESB) in 1951. ESB was made an agency of the central government, responsible directly to the cabinet, and to it were gradually transferred the major economic management functions which had previously been with the provincial government's Production Control Board. The latter was abolished in 1953, signalling the triumph of the central government's three-year struggle for ascendancy. From then on the major guiding organization was ESB, which was responsible for preparing plans, formulating monetary, fiscal, and trade policy, coordinating military and civilian expenditures, formulating the expenditure budget for the counterpart funds, screening private investment applications, and approving all large loans from domestic banks and all foreign loans of whatever size. Some 60 percent of total industrial production still came from public enterprises in 1953–54, so ESB had many direct administrative responsibilities in matters of production. The principal members of ESB included the finance minister, who was its chairman, the ministers of economic affairs, communications, and defense, the head of the Bank of Taiwan (the de facto central bank), the head of the government procurement agency, the provincial governor, and the heads of the provincial bureaus of finance, reconstruction, and communications. U.S. officials were present in the formal capacity of observers.[2]

In 1953 the ESB decided to delegate some of its work load to two newly created organizations. One was called the Foreign Exchange and Trade Control Commission.[3] The commission's job was to deal with exchange rates, allocation of foreign exchange, and other trade policy issues. Its great power came especially from the considerable undervaluation of foreign exchange, which meant its officials had the power to confer large windfall ''rents'' to those who got access to underpriced foreign exchange, because the market

---

[2] U.S. staff had much more influence than ''observer'' status suggests.

[3] In fact, the Foreign Exchange and Trade Control Commission began as a provincial government agency in 1951, when Yui was provincial governor. It became a central government agency when Yui became premier.

value of imported goods was much greater than the valuation given by the official exchange rate. ESB created the Industrial Development Commission (IDC) at about the same time. IDC was responsible for identifying industrial projects and getting them started: this is the body which, following the former National Resources Commission of the central government and the Production Control Board of the provincial government, guided and stimulated the laying down of an industrial base in Taiwan.

One of ESB's agencies, then, dealt primarily with monetary aspects of trade and aid, the other directly with issues of what industries should be created. The two agencies became the focus of the two groups which struggled for ascendancy in economic policy determination through the 1950s, up to the liberalizing reforms of 1958 and beyond.

The leaders of the two groups were Chen Cheng and O. K. Yui (Yui Hung-chun). They were both close to Chiang Kai-shek. Chen Cheng had a reputation for military prowess, and his loyalty to the president was never in doubt. O. K. Yui enjoyed the president's closer personal trust, perhaps partly because he successfully organized the transfer of a large part of the Nationalists' gold reserves to Taiwan. The two men followed each other around the top positions of government, as the president attempted to keep power in his own hands by encouraging competition between them. Chen Cheng was governor of Taiwan for a year from 1948 to 1949; then premier in the central government until 1954; then vice-president (a largely honorific post to which the president transferred him in order to curb his growing power); and premier again in 1958, a position he held until 1963. O. K. Yui, for his part, was governor of Taiwan in 1953; premier following Chen Cheng in 1954; and resigned as premier in 1958 to make way for the return of Chen Cheng.

The two men stood at the head of long faction chains with distinct locations in the government apparatus, and they pursued economic objectives consistent with building the strength of the part of the apparatus they controlled. Basically O. K. Yui's group had power in the financial agencies and Chen Cheng's had power in the industrial agencies. Yui's group had the Finance Ministry, the Bank of Taiwan, and the Foreign Exchange and Trade Control Commission (whose chairman was the finance minister). The crucial Economic Stabilization Board was also primarily under the control of Yui's group; it too was chaired by the finance minister. Chen Cheng's group had the Production Control Board, the government procurement agency, and subsequently the Industrial Development Commission. Chen Cheng's main lieutenant and chief economic advisor on industrial strategy, K.Y. Yin (Chung-yung Yin), was from 1953 to 1955 head of the Industrial Development Commission.

Yui's group stood for monetary stability, a balanced budget, no trade deficit, more consumer goods imports and fewer capital goods imports; and also, strangely in the normal Western syndrome of ideas, for more public sector control of economic activity, for a continuing predominant role for public enterprises. Yui and his associates supported multiple exchange rates as a way of limiting the inflow of imports while at the same time allowing cheap imports of necessities so as to keep prices down. Their views followed a long Chinese tradition which stressed that the key to economic prosperity lay in prudent monetary policy. But their views were also congenial to the most powerful military figures, who placed the immediate retaking of the mainland as the number one objective. Yui did not attach great importance to broad-based industrialization and, therefore, by default allowed the military to get a greater share of government revenue. Moreover, Yui's support for public enterprises (e.g., by reserving the Bank of Taiwan's loans for public enterprises) helped to maintain state dominance in the economy, which the military also wanted.

Chen Cheng supported the president's belief that retaking the mainland was the number one objective, but argued that it could only be done as a medium-term objective once Taiwan had built up a strong industrial sector and had a sufficiently prosperous economy, involving both mainlanders and native Taiwanese, to win popular support behind the government. But Chen himself did not claim to be a strategist of industrialization; he relied heavily for his economic views on a group of people, mostly American-trained engineers, headed by K. Y. Yin. Yin, an electrical engineer, had worked in the government procurement board's U.S. office during the Second World War and then in a senior capacity in the Taiwan Production Control Board before becoming chairman of the Industrial Development Commission in 1953. Yin and his associates argued that rapid and broad-based industrialization was the first and immediate priority. This was the way to (as they put it before the term came into general fashion) a more self-reliant economy, able to pay its own way in the world. They argued from the early 1950s onwards that this would require reduced government control of foreign trade and increased competition between domestic firms. This would in turn require more activity in the private sector; and specifically the government would have to give up the automatic assumption that new industrial projects should be developed by public enterprises. But Yin found that the emphasis on monetary stability, zero trade deficit, and multiple exchange rates coupled with import controls which Yui and his group gave priority to, ran contrary to this strategy—as also, obviously, did Yui's favoring of public enterprise. In particular, Yin found it difficult to find private entrepreneurs to take on the projects he wanted them to (such as the window glass factory, the man-made fiber factory, and the plastics factory) because the banking system, controlled by Yui's group, was unwilling to lend and because the exchange rate policies pursued by Yui's group meant that entrepreneurial profit was to be found in *trade* more than in production. So undervalued was foreign exchange for many items that huge profits could be obtained if a license to import could by one means or another be obtained. In this way, the issue of exchange rate policy came to be the central point of contention between the two groups.

Yin had some striking successes. In particular, his allocation of the plastics industry (initially a single factory) to the private sector was considered a triumph, because he had been under strong pressure to reserve it for public enterprise. He was helped by several overseas Chinese economists (including T. C. Liu, S. C. Tsiang, and John C. H. Fei) and U.S. advisors. The latter (including the influential Wesley Harrison) exercised power especially via their aid leverage. They were keen to promote a larger private sector as part of a wider strategy of discouraging the build-up of military preparedness for retaking the mainland and instead encouraged economic competition with the mainland. Taiwan, they argued, should be developed as an economic and political showplace for the free enterprise system in Asia (Jacoby 1966). It was important that the private sector be built up, for an economy with 60 percent of industrial production coming from state-owned enterprises might be thought to be other than a model free enterprise system.

However, predominant power in economic policy-making remained with the monetarist group. Yui was the premier during this period (1954–58), and Hsu Peh-yuan, his leading lieutenant, was minister of finance, chairman of the Economic Stabilization Board, and head of the Foreign Exchange and Trade Control Commission. The Industrial Development Commission, headed by Yin, depended on funds approved by the Economic Stabilization Board; and so the rate at which it could promote industrialization depended on the willingness of Yui's group to supply funds. Chen Cheng could help Yin a little, but since being elevated to the honorific post of vice-president he lacked the power of Yui and Hsu. Yin became minister of economic affairs in 1955, but this ministry was then less powerful than the Ministry of Finance; so this advance in Yin's position did not greatly alter the balance. In any case, Yin resigned as minister in the same year, because of allegations of involvement in a malconduct case (of which he was later acquitted).

The big change came in 1958. In that year, the president forced Yui to resign as premier and appointed Chen Cheng in his place. Chen had already been given one of the top positions in the party, and had got one of his close associates into another very senior position in the party. Chen then proceeded to install his people in all the key posts—except minister of finance, which Hsu retained. But the finance minister lost his concurrent post as head of the powerful Foreign Exchange and Trade Control Commission. That post was given to K. Y. Yin, who was also made secretary-general in the Economic Stabilization Board (whose chairman continued to be Hsu, the finance minister). This change is important, because it signals the first time that the crucial agency of monetary and exchange control had been put in the hands of a member of the industrializers' group, the first time that substantial financial and trade control had been fused with industrial policy control. At his first press conference after taking charge, Yin announced that financial policy would no longer be an end in itself but would be made subordinate to wider economic policy. Later in the same year, 1958, Chen dissolved the Economic Stabilization Board altogether, giving its responsibilities to the already existing Council on U.S. Aid (CUSA). Into the key role of CUSA vice-chairman stepped K. Y. Yin.

Shortly afterwards, the now celebrated "liberalizing" reforms were announced. They included the unification of the exchange rate; easing of import and export controls on many items; increased incentives for exporting (in the form of greater availability of export finance and of duty rebates on the import of items to be processed into exports); and more loans to private industry—all things that Yui's group had opposed.

The big question, of course, is why this change took place. The liberalization is normally presented as a move from darkness to light, from error to sense. In Taiwan's political system, the question has to be more specific: Given the extraordinarily great concentration of authority in the hands of the president, why did the president accept economic reforms at this juncture? Was it largely because he saw that reforms were a sensible response to growing economic difficulties? Silin suggests that the president's acceptance of reforms probably came as a by-product of his wish to reorganize the chief personnel in his government rather than because he had reconsidered his economic priorities.

By 1958 Yui had been premier for four years. In this time his personal integrity had been damaged; he had lost several struggles with the legislative assembly, which was taken as a sign of declining administrative effectiveness; and ironically, given that his policies favored the military, he was not seen by the mainlander group as a sufficiently martial figure. Chen's personal integrity remained untarnished, and he had a public reputation as a great military leader. That mattered, especially in 1958. That year the militaries of the People's Republic of China and the Republic of China fought air and sea battles over possession of Quemoy island in the Taiwan straits. In return for its assistance, the United States persuaded Chiang Kai-shek to agree that henceforth the Republic of China would be only defensive; it would not attempt to recapture the mainland. This agreement marked a consolidation of the view that the Nationalists had to give top priority to economic development of Taiwan. At the same time, to deter adventurism on the part of the mainland, Chiang wanted to refurbish the image of military preparedness. Chen in any case was the only obvious alternative. Chen himself may perhaps not have believed particularly strongly in the liberal reforms, but as the leading opponent of Yui, he had to be seen to be pushing a distinctly different strategy, which happened to be the liberalizing strategy as formulated by Yin. Yin of course wanted the strategy because he thought it a sensible solution to growing economic difficulties. But the president accepted the strategy mainly because he wanted to change his leading personnel for reasons not closely connected with economics, and the change in strategy came along with the new personnel.

It is important, however, not to interpret this struggle in terms of the dichotomy of market versus plan and claim the result as a victory for the free market side. In fact, the difference in the role of government wanted by both groups was not very large, and both groups were much closer together than to the prescriptions of neoclassical economics or to the actual role of government in economies of the Anglo-American type. The victory of Chen Cheng and Yin gave rise to a determined state-led establishment of heavy and chemical industries, at the same time as it ushered in the celebrated liberalization.

In those few accounts of Taiwan which make any reference at all to governmental institutions and institutional change we have to make do with explanations of the kind that Jacoby gives for the abolishment of the Economic Stabilization Board. "By the mid-1950s inflation had been restrained, and the objective of economic development had gradually come to the fore. *Hence*, the Board was dissolved in 1958, and the Council on US Aid and the Joint Commission on Rural Reconstruction took over the administration of the whole aid program" (1966:60, emphasis added). Here as elsewhere Jacoby simply omits politics and the interplay of interests. Specifically, he fails to mention that ESB had been dominated by Yui's group, which had just lost a round in the struggle against Chen's. Dissolution of the ESB was part of Chen's consolidation of victory. It would be highly desirable to have similar accounts of interest interplay for later stages in Taiwan's development.

REFERENCES

General

Academia Sinica, 1967, *The Economic Development of Taiwan*, Institute of Economics, Taipei, June 19–28.

Adelman, I., 1984, "Beyond export-led growth," *World Development* 12(9):937–49.

Adelman, I., and C. Morris, 1967, *Society, Politics, and Economic Development: A Quantitative Approach*. Baltimore: Johns Hopkins University Press.

———, 1968, "Performance criteria for evaluating economic development potential: an operational approach," *Quarterly Journal of Economics* 82(1):260–80.

Agarwala, R., 1983, "Price distortions and growth in developing countries," Staff Working Paper No. 575, Washington, D.C.: World Bank.

Aikman, D., 1986, *The Pacific Rim: Area of Change, Area of Opportunity*. Boston: Little, Brown.

Allen, G., 1981, "Industry policy and innovation in Japan," in C. Carter (ed.), *Industrial Policy and Innovation*. London: Heinemann.

Allison, G., 1989, "Biting the hand that governs," *Washington Post*, 1 Jan.

American Institute in Taiwan, various issues, *Foreign Economic Trends and Their Implications for the United States: Taiwan*. Washington, D.C.: U.S. Department of Commerce.

Amnesty International, 1980, "Taiwan (Republic of China)," Briefing Paper No. 6, London: Amnesty International Publications.

Amsden, A., 1977, "The division of labor is limited by the type of market: the case of the Taiwanese machine tool industry," *World Development* 5(3):217–34.

———, 1979, "Taiwan's economic history: a case of etatisme and a challenge to dependency theory," *Modern China* 5(3):341–80.

———, 1984a, "The state and Taiwan's economic development," mimeo, Graduate School of Business Administration, Harvard University.

———, 1984b, "Taiwan," in Exports of Technology by Newly-Industrializing Countries, *World Development* 12 (5/6).

———, 1989, *Asia's Next Giant: South Korea and Late Industrialization*. New York: Oxford University Press.

———, forthcoming, "Big business and urban congestion in Taiwan: the origins of small- and medium-size enterprise and regionally decentralized industry," mimeo.

Aoki, M., 1988, *Information, Incentives, and Bargaining in the Japanese Economy*. Cambridge: Cambridge University Press.

Appleton, S., 1976, "The social and political impact of education in Taiwan," *Asian Survey* 16(8), Aug.:703–20.

Apter, D., 1965, *The Politics of Modernization*. Chicago: University of Chicago Press.

Arndt, H., 1988, " 'Market failure' and underdevelopment," *World Development* 16(2):219–29.

Arnold, W., 1989, "Bureaucratic politics, state capacity, and Taiwan's automobile industrial policy," *Modern China* 15(2):178–214.

Arrow, K., 1974, *The Limits of Organization*. New York: Norton.

Automotive News, 1988, "Hyundai Canada guilty of predatory pricing," 22 Feb.: 1, 37.

Bae, Myung, 1987, "The Korean semiconductor industry: a brief history and perspective," *Solid State Technology* 30(10), Oct.: 141–44.

Bagchi, A. K., 1984, "The terror and the squalor of East Asian capitalism," *Economic & Political Weekly* 19(1), 7 Jan.

Balassa, B., 1971, "Industrial policies in Taiwan and Korea," *Weltwirtschaftliches Archiv* 106(1):55–77.

———, 1975, "Reforming the system of incentives in developing countries," *World Development* 3(6):365–82.

———, 1980, "The process of industrial development and alternative development strategies," *Essays in International Finance 141*, Princeton University.

———, 1981, "The process of industrial development and alternative development strategies," in *The Newly Industrializing Countries in the World Economy*. New York: Pergamon.

Balassa, B., et al., 1971, *The Structure of Protection in Developing Countries*. Baltimore: Johns Hopkins University Press.

Balassa, B., et al., 1982, *Development Strategies in Semi-industrial Economies*. Baltimore: The Johns Hopkins University Press (for World Bank).

Bannock, G., R. Baxter, and R. Rees (eds.), 1978, *Penguin Dictionary of Economics*. Harmondsworth: Penguin Books.

Barclay, G., 1954, *Colonial Development and Population in Taiwan*. Princeton: Princeton University Press.

Barret, R., and M. Whyte, 1982, "Dependency theory and Taiwan: analysis of a deviant case," *American Journal of Sociology* 87(5):1064–89.

Batchelor, R., R. Major, and A. Morgan, 1980, *Industrialization and the Basis for Trade*. Cambridge: Cambridge University Press.

Beal, T., 1981, "Japan and development in East Asia," mimeo, University of Sheffield.

Bedeski, R., 1981, *State Building in Modern China: The Kuomintang in the Prewar Period*. Berkeley: Institute of East Asian Studies, University of California.

Berger, F., 1979, "Korea's experience with export-led industrial development," in B. de Vries (ed.), *Export Promotion Policies*, Staff Working Paper No. 313, Washington, D.C.: World Bank.

Bhagwati, J., 1966, *The Economics of Underdeveloped Countries*. New York: McGraw-Hill.

———, 1978, *Anatomy and Consequences of Exchange Control Regimes*. Cambridge: Ballinger (for National Bureau of Economic Research).

———, 1982, "Directly-unproductive profit-seeking (DUP) activities," *Journal of Political Economy*, Oct.:988–1002.

———, 1986, "Rethinking trade strategy," in J. Lewis and V. Kallab (eds.). *Development Strategies Reconsidered*. Overseas Development Council, New Brunswick: Transaction Books.

———, 1988a, "Export-promoting trade strategy: issues and evidence," *World Bank Research Observer* 3(1), Jan.: 27–57.

——, 1988b, *Protectionism*. Cambridge: MIT.

——, 1989, "Is free trade passé after all?" *Weltwirtschaftliches Archiv* 125(1):16–44.

Bienefeld, M., 1980, "Dependency in the eighties," *IDS Bulletin* 12(1) Dec.

——, 1981, "The informal sector and women's oppression," *IDS Bulletin* 13 (1) Dec.

——, 1982, "The international context for national development strategies: constraints and opportunities in a changing world," in M. Bienefeld and M. Godfrey (eds.), *The Struggle for Development: National Strategies in an International Context*. Chichester: John Wiley.

——, 1988, "The significance of the newly industrializing countries for the development debate," *Studies in Political Economy* 25, Spring: 7–39.

——, 1989, "Global development trends in the eighties: a time of growing disparities," in M. Molot and B. Tomlin (eds.), *Canada among Nations 1988*. Toronto: James Lorimer.

Biggs, T., 1988, "Financing the emergence of small and medium enterprises in Taiwan," EEPA Discussion Paper 16, Harvard Institute of International Development.

Biggs, T., and B. Levy, 1988, "Strategic intervention and the political economy of industrial policy in developing countries," EEPA Discussion Paper 23, Harvard Institute of International Development.

Biggs, T., and K. Lorch, forthcoming, "Structure, dynamics and performance of Taiwan's industry," EEPA Discussion Paper, Harvard Institute of International Development.

Biggs, T., and C. H. Yoon, forthcoming, "Market structure and export performance: Korea and Taiwan in the American market," EEPA Discussion Paper, Harvard Institute of International Development.

Blau, P., 1964, *Exchange and Power in Social Life*. New York: Wiley

Blomstrom, M., I. Kravis, and R. Lipsey, 1988, "Multinational firms and manufactured exports from developing countries," mimeo, U.N. Center on Transnational Corporations, New York.

Bollen, K., 1980, "Issues in the comparative measurement of political democracy," *American Sociological Review* 45:370–90.

Boltho, A., 1975, *Japan: An Economic Survey 1953–1973*, Oxford: Oxford University Press.

——, 1981, "Italian and Japanese postwar growth: some similarities and some differences," *Rivista Internazionale di Scienze Economiche e Commerciali*, 28 July–Aug.:626–41.

——, 1984, "Was Japan's industrial policy successful?" *Cambridge Journal of Economics* 9:187–201.

Bonavia, D., 1982, *The Chinese*, Harmondsworth: Penguin Books.

Borrus, M., and J. Zysman, 1985, "Japan's industrial policy and its pattern of trade," paper presented to the subcommittee on economic goals and intergovernmental policy, joint economic committee, U.S. Congress, 9 Dec.

Bradford, C., 1984, "The NICs: confronting US 'autonomy,' " in R. Fienberg and V. Kallab (eds.), *Adjustment Crisis in the Third World*. New Brunswick: Transaction Books (for Overseas Development Council).

Bradford, C., 1986, "East Asian 'Model': myths and lessons," in J. Lewis and V. Kallab (eds.), *Development Strategies Reconsidered*. Overseas Development Council, New Brunswick: Transaction Books.

———, 1987, "Trade and structural change: NICS and next tier NICS as transitional economies," *World Development* 15(3):299–316.

Braudel, F., 1981, *The Structures of Everyday Life: The Limits of the Possible*. London: Collins.

Brett, E. A., 1983, *International Money and Capitalist Crisis: The Anatomy of Global Disintegration*. London: Heinemann.

———, 1985, *The World Economy Since the War: The Politics of Uneven Development*. London: Macmillan.

Broad, R., and J. Cavanagh, 1988, "No more NICS," *Foreign Policy* 72, Fall: 81–103.

Bruce, P., 1983, "World steel industry: the rise and rise of the Third World," *Financial Times*, 22 Nov., London.

Bryce, M., 1965, *Policies and Methods of Industrial Development*. New York: McGraw-Hill.

Buchanan, J., and G. Tullock, 1962, *The Calculus of Consent*. Ann Arbor: University of Michigan Press.

Buffie, E., 1984, "Financial repression, the new structuralists, and stabilization policy in semi-industrial economies," *Journal of Development Economics* 14(3):305–22.

Burton, J., 1983, *Picking Losers . . . ? The Political Economy of Industrial Policy*. Hobart Paper, London: Institute of Economic Affairs.

Business International Asia/Pacific Ltd., 1976, "Taiwan," in *Capital Markets in Asia's Developing Countries*. Hong Kong.

———, 1979, "Taiwan," in *World Sourcing Sites in Asia: Manufacturing Costs and Conditions in Hong Kong, Korea, Singapore, and Taiwan*. Hong Kong.

Business Week, 1987, Survey, 12 Jan.:68.

———, 1988, "Hyundai is cooling off after its hot start," 26 Dec.:63.

Caves, R., and M. Uekusa, 1976, *Industrial Organization in Japan*. Washington, D.C.: Brookings Institution.

CETDC (China External Trade Development Council, now CETRA), 1981, *CETDC in Retrospect 1970–1980*, Taipei.

Chandler, A., 1980, "Industrial revolution and institutional arrangements," *Bulletin of American Academy of Arts and Sciences* 33, May:33–50.

Chang, H., and R. Myers, 1963, "Japanese colonial development policy in Taiwan, 1895–1906," *Journal of Asian Studies* 22.

Chang, Jui-meng, 1987, *The Determinants of Trade Policies in Taiwan*, Monograph Series No. 18, Chung-hua Institution for Economic Research, Taipei.

Chang, P., 1983, "Taiwan in l982: diplomatic setback abroad and demands for reforms at home," *Asian Survey* 23(1), Jan.

Chen, E. K. Y., 1979, *Hyper-growth in Asian Economies: A Comparative Study of Hong Kong, Japan, Korea, Singapore and Taiwan*. London: Macmillan.

Chen, G., 1982, "The reform movement among intellectuals in Taiwan since l970," *Bulletin of Concerned Asian Scholars* 14(3):32–54.

Chen, T., 1982, "Industrial structure in Taiwan," *Quarterly Journal of Enterprises and Banks* 5(3):75–97 (Chinese).

————, 1984, "Industrial concentration rates of Taiwan," *Quarterly Journal of Enterprises and Banks* 8(2):35–57 (Chinese).

Chen, T. H., 1981, "The educational system," in J. Hsiung, et al. (eds.), *Contemporary Republic of China: The Taiwan Experience*. New York: Praeger and the American Association for Chinese Studies.

Chen, W., C. Tu, and W. Wang, 1987, "The principle of trade liberalization in Taiwan, ROC, and its impact on industry," mimeo, Taipei: Chung-hua Institution for Economic Research (Chinese).

Chenery, H., 1959, "The interdependence of investment decisions," in M. Abramowitz (ed.), *The Allocation of Economic Resources*. Stanford: Stanford University Press.

————, 1961, "Comparative advantage and development policy," *American Economic Review* 51(1):18–51.

Chenery, H., et al., 1974, *Redistribution with Growth*. London: Oxford University Press.

China Credit Information Service, 1972, *The 100 Largest Industrial Corporations in the Republic of China 1971*. Taipei.

————, 1981, *Top 500: The Largest Industrial Corporations in the Republic of China 1981*. Taipei.

Chiu, P. C. H., 1982, "Performance of financial institutions in Taiwan," in *Experiences and Lessons of Economic Development in Taiwan*, Institute of Economics, Academia Sinica, Taipei.

Chou, Ji, 1987, "Economic evaluation of investment incentive scheme from a macro standpoint," research report, Taipei: Chung-hua Institution for Economic Research (Chinese).

Chu, Yun-han, 1987a, "Authoritarian regimes under stress: the political economy of adjustment in the East Asian NICs," doctoral diss., Department of Political Science, University of Minnesota.

————, 1987b, "State and economic adjustment in the East Asian newly industrialized countries," mimeo, Political Science Department, Taiwan National University, Taipei.

Clifford, M., 1988, "South Korea prepares to privatize part of its steel-making giant," *Far Eastern Economic Review* 14 Apr.:58.

Cline, W., 1982a, *Reciprocity—A New Approach to World Trade Policy?* Institute for International Economics, Washington, D.C.

————, 1982b, "Can the East Asian model of development be generalized?" *World Development* 10(2): 81–90.

Clough, R., 1978, *Island China*. Cambridge: Harvard University Press.

Colander, D. (ed.), 1984, *Neoclassical Political Economics*. Cambridge: Ballinger.

Cole, A., 1967, "Political roles of Taiwanese enterprisers," *Asian Survey* 7: 645–54.

Cole, D., and P. Lyman, 1971, *Korean Development: The Interplay of Politics and Economics*. Cambridge: Harvard University Press.

Comisso, E., and L. Tyson (eds.), 1986, *Power, Purpose and Collective Choice: Economic Strategies in Socialist States*. Ithaca: Cornell University Press.

Computer Products, 1987, "Technology in Taiwan," Nov.: 376–83.

Coote, H., 1983, "Consumer electronics: employment, production and trade," ILO Employment Program, Geneva.

Corbo, V., and J. de Melo, 1987, "Lessons from the southern cone policy reforms," *World Bank Research Observer* 2(2):111–42.

Corbo, V., J. de Melo, and J. Tybout, 1986, "What went wrong with the recent reforms in the southern cone," *Economic Development and Cultural Change* 34(3): 607–40.

Corden, M., 1974, *Trade Policy and Economic Welfare*. London: Oxford University Press.

———, 1987, "Why trade is not free; is there a clash between theory and practice?," mimeo, forthcoming in *Free Trade in the World Economy*, Kiel: Institut fur Weltwirtschaft.

Crotty, J., 1983, "On Keynes and capital flight," *Journal of Economic Literature* 21 Mar.:59–65.

Crozier, B., 1976, *The Man Who Lost China*. New York: Charles Scribner.

Cumings, B., 1981, *The Origins of the Korean War*, vol. 1, *Liberation and the Emergence of Separate Regimes*. Princeton: Princeton University Press.

———, 1984, "The origins and development of the Northeast Asian political economy: industrial sector, product cycles, and political consequences," *International Organization* 38(1):1-40.

———, forthcoming, *Industrial Behemoths: The Northeast Asian Political Economy in the Twentieth Century*. Ithaca: Cornell University Press.

Dahl, R., and C. Lindblom, 1963, *Politics, Economics, and Welfare*. New York: St. Martins.

Dahlman, C., 1989, "Structural change and trade in the East Asian NIEs and emerging NIEs," in R. Purcell (ed.), *The Newly Industrializing Countries in the World Economy: Challenges for U.S. Policy*. Boulder: Lynne Rienner.

de Melo, J., 1985, "Sources of growth and structural change in the republics of Korea and Taiwan: some comparisons," in V. Corbo, A. Krueger, and F. Ossa (eds.), *Export-Oriented Development Strategies: The Success of Five Newly Industrializing Countries*. Boulder: Westview.

Department of Commerce, 1988, *Commissioner of Patents and Trademarks: Annual Report Fiscal Year 1987*, Washington, D.C.

Deyo, F., 1987, "Coalitions, institutions and linkage sequencing," in F. Deyo (ed.), *The Political Economy of the New Asian Industrialization*. Ithaca: Cornell University Press.

Diaz-Alejandro, C., 1983, "Open economy, closed polity," in D. Tussie (ed.), *Latin America in the World Economy: New Perspectives*. London: Gower.

Dick, G. W., 1974, "Authoritarian versus nonauthoritarian approaches to economic development," *Journal of Political Economy* 82(4): 817–27.

Directory of Taiwan 1983. China News, Taipei.

Djang, T. K., 1977, *Industry and Labor in Taiwan*, Monograph Series No. 10, Institute of Economics, Academia Sinica, Taipei.

Dore, R., 1977, "South Korean development in wider perspective," *Pacific Affairs* 50(2).

————, 1985, "Financial structures and the long-term view," *Policy Studies* 6(1), July.

————, 1986, *Flexible Rigidities: Industrial Policy and Structural Adjustment in the Japanese Economy 1970–80*. Stanford: Stanford University Press.

Dosi, G., et al. (eds.), 1988, *Technical Change and Economic Theory*. London: Pinter.

Drucker, P., 1986, "The changed world economy," *Foreign Affairs* 64(4):768–91.

Durdin, T., 1975, "Chiang Ching-Kuo's Taiwan," *Pacific Community* 7(1), Oct.:92–117.

ECLA (Economic Commission for Latin America), 1984, "Recent problems of Latin American industry reactivation and long-term policies," E/CEPAL/Conf. 76/B.2, 12 Apr.

The Economist, 1983, "How not to develop," 30 Apr.:89.

————, 1987, "Taiwan: too rich to stay a lonely beacon," 28 Mar.: 21–24.

————, 1988, "Taiwan Survey," 5 Mar.: 1–18.

Edwards, S., 1985, "The sequencing of economic liberalization in developing countries," Country Policy Department, World Bank.

Electronic Engineering Times, 1989, "IBM and Samsung swap," 3 Apr.

Electronics, 1988, "The timing was just right for Taiwan silicon foundry," Oct.:169.

Electronics Weekly, 1988, "Korea hot on tails of leaders in chip race," 1 June: 3.

Emmerson, D., 1982, "Pacific optimism II: explaining economic growth: how magic is the market place?," University Field Staff International Report No. 5.

Encarnation, D., and L. Wells, 1986, "Evaluating foreign investment," in T. Moran (ed.), *Investing in Development: New Roles for Private Capital?* New Brunswick: Transaction Books in cooperation with Overseas Development Council.

Enos, J., 1984, "Government intervention in the transfer of technology: the case of South Korea," *IDS Bulletin* 15(2), Apr.

Erzan, R., et al., 1988, "The profile of protection in developing countries," Discussion Paper No. 21, Geneva: UNCTAD.

Evans, D., and P. Alizadeh, 1984, "Trade, industrialization, and the visible hand," *Journal of Development Studies* 21(1), Oct.: 22–44.

Evans, P., 1979, *Dependent Development: The Alliance of Multinationals, State and Local Capital in Brazil*. Princeton: Princeton University Press.

————, 1989, "Predatory, developmental and other apparatuses: a comparative analysis of the Third World state," mimeo, sociology department, University of New Mexico.

Fajnzylber, F., 1981, "Some reflections on South-east Asian export industrialization," *CEPAL Review* 15, Dec.: 111–32.

————, forthcoming, "The United States and Japan as models of industrialization for the Latin-America and East Asian NICs," in G. Gereffi and D. Wyman (eds.), *Manufactured Miracles: Patterns of Industrialization in Latin America and East Asia*. Princeton: Princeton University Press.

Fallows, J., 1987, "Japan: playing by different rules," *Atlantic Monthly*, Sept.:22–32.

FEER (*Far Eastern Economic Review*), 1981, "The bureaucrats: sons of the samurai," 20 Mar.:34–40.

————, 1985, "Hong Kong's problems masked by prosperity," 26 Sept.: 102–3.

FEER (*Far Eastern Economic Review*), 1988, "Awash in a sea of money," 15 Sept.: 49–70.

———, 1989a, "Overseas attractions," 16 Mar.: 88–89.

———, 1989b, "Chipping In," 25 May:82.

Fei, J. C. H., 1983, "Evolution of growth policies of NICs in a historical and typological perspective," conference on patterns of growth and structural change in Asia's newly industrializing countries (NICS) and near-NICs in the context of economic interdependence, East-West Center, Honolulu, 3–8 Apr.

Fei, J., G. Ranis, and S. Kuo, 1979, *Growth with Equity: The Taiwan Case*. New York: Oxford University Press.

Felix, D., 1986, "Import substitution and late industrialization: Latin America and Asia compared," Department of Economics, Washington University, St. Louis.

———, 1987, Review of *Economic Structure and Performance: Essays in Honor of Hollis B. Chenery*, *Economic Development and Cultural Change*, 36(1): 188–94.

Financial Times, 1988, "FT Report—Asia's Pacific Rim," 30 June.

Fishlow, A., 1984, "Summary comment on Adelman, Balassa and Streeten," *World Development* 12(9).

———, 1985, "The state of Latin American economics," in *Economic and Social Progress in Latin America: Annual Report*, Inter-American Development Bank, Washington, D.C.

Fong, H. D., 1968, "Taiwan's industrialization, with special reference to policies and controls," *Journal of Nanyang University* 2:365–425.

Forbes, 1985, "The Koreans are coming," 25 Feb.:44.

Frank, I. (ed.), 1975, *The Japanese Economy in International Perspective*. Baltimore: Johns Hopkins University Press.

Fransman, M., 1986, "International competitiveness, technical change and the state: the machine tool industry in Taiwan and Japan," *World Development* 14(12):1375–96.

Freeman, C., 1987, *Technology Policy and Economic Performance: Lessons from Japan*. London: Pinter.

Freeman, C., and C. Perez, 1988, "Structural crises of adjustment: business cycles and investment behavior," in G. Dosi, et al. (eds.), *Technical Change and Economic Theory*. London: Pinter.

Friedman, M., and R. Friedman, 1980, *Free to Choose: A Personal Statement*, New York: Harcourt Brace Jovanovich.

Gadbaw, R. M., and T. Richards, 1988, *Intellectual Property Rights: Global Consensus, Global Conflict*? Boulder: Westview.

Galenson, W. (ed.), 1979, *Economic Growth and Structural Change in Taiwan: The Postwar Experience of the Republic of China*. Ithaca: Cornell University Press.

———, 1982, "How to develop successfully—the Taiwan model," *Experiences and Lessons of Economic Development in Taiwan*, Taipei: Institute of Economics, Academia Sinica.

Galli, A., 1980, *Taiwan: Economic Facts and Trends*. IFO Development Research Studies. Munchen: Weltformum Verlag.

Gastil, R., 1973, "The new criteria of freedom," *Freedom at Issue* 17, Jan.–Feb.:3–23.

————, 1984, "The comparative survey of freedom 1984," *Freedom at Issue*, 76, Jan.–Feb.:3–15.

————, 1986, *Freedom in the World: Political Rights and Civil Liberties 1985–1986*. New York: Greenwood.

Gates, H., 1979, "Dependency and the part-time proletariat in Taiwan," *Modern China* 5(3).

Gereffi, G., and D. Wyman (eds.), forthcoming, *Manufactured Miracles: Patterns of Industrialization in Latin America and East Asia*. Princeton: Princeton University Press.

Gerschenkron, A., 1962, *Economic Backwardness in Historical Perspective*. Cambridge: Harvard University Press.

Ghamen, H., and A. Rajaram, 1987, "The ineffectiveness of selective credit policies: empirical examples from Korea and Tunisia," mimeo, Country Policy Department, World Bank, Washington, D.C.

Givens, W., 1982, "The US can no longer afford free trade," *Business Week* 22 Nov.: 15.

Gold, B., 1979, *Productivity, Technology, and Capital*. Lexington: Lexington Books.

Gold, T., 1981, "Dependent development in Taiwan," doctoral diss., Department of Sociology, Harvard University.

————, 1983, "Differentiating multinational corporations: American, Japanese and overseas Chinese investors in Taiwan," *Chinese Journal of Sociology* 7, July:267–75.

————, 1986, *State and Society in the Taiwan Miracle*. Armonk: M. E. Sharpe.

Greenhalgh, S., 1982, "Demographic differentiation and the distribution of income: the Taiwan case," doctoral diss., Colombia University.

Grossman, G., 1984, "International trade, foreign investment, and the formation of the entrepreneurial class," *American Economic Review* 74(4):605–14.

Guisinger, S., 1986, "Host country policies to attract and control foreign investment," in T. Moran (ed.), *Investing in Development: New Roles for Private Capital?* New Brunswick: Transaction Books in cooperation with Overseas Development Council.

Hadley, E., 1970, *Antitrust in Japan*. Princeton: Princeton University Press.

Hager, W., 1982, "Protectionism and autonomy: how to preserve free trade in Europe," *International Affairs* 58(3):413–28.

Haggard, S., 1986, "The newly industrializing countries in the international system," *World Politics* 38:343–70.

Haggard, S., and C. Moon, 1983, "The South Korean state in the international economy: liberal, dependent, or mercantile?," in J. Ruggie (ed.), *The Antinomies of Interdependence: National Welfare and the International Division of Labor*. New York: Columbia University Press.

Hamilton, C., 1983, "Capitalist industrialization in East Asia's four little tigers," *Journal of Contemporary Asia* 13(1): 35–73.

————, 1986, *Capitalist Industrialization in South Korea*. Boulder: Westview.

Hamilton, G., M. Orru, and N. Biggart, 1987, "Enterprise groups in East Asia: an organization analysis," *Financial Economic Review* (Tokyo), 161-78-106.

Hasan, P., 1976, *Korea, Problems and Issues in a Rapidly Growing Economy*. Baltimore: Johns Hopkins University Press.

Havrylyshyn, O., and I. Aiikhani, 1982, "Is there a cause for export pessimism?" *Weltwirschaftliches Archiv* 118(4):651–63.

Heclo, H., 1986, "Industrial policy and the executive capacities of government," in C. Barfield and W. Schambra (eds.), *The Politics of Industrial Policy*, Washington, D.C.: American Enterprise Institute.

Helleiner, G., 1981, "The Refsnes seminar: economic theory and North-South negotiations," *World Development* 9(6):539–55.

———, 1981b, *Intra-firm Trade and the Developing Countries*. New York: St. Martins.

———, 1988, "Growth-oriented adjustment lending: a critical assessment of IMF/World Bank approaches," mimeo, South Commission, Geneva.

Heller, P., and A. Tait, 1984, "Government employment and pay: some international comparisons," Occasional Paper No. 24 (Mar.), International Monetary Fund, Washington, D.C.

Henderson, D., 1983, "The myth of MITI," *Fortune* 8 Aug.:113–16.

Heper, M., Chong Lim Kim, and Seong-Tong Pai, 1980, "The role of bureaucracy and regime types: a comparative study of Turkish and South Korean higher civil servants," *Administration and Society* 12(2).

Hicks, A., and W. D. Patterson, 1989, "On the robustness of the left corporatist model of economic growth," *Journal of Politics* 51(3):662–75.

Hicks, G., and S. Redding, 1982, "Industrial East Asia and the post-Confucian hypothesis: a challenge to economics," pt. 1, mimeo, University of Hong Kong.

Hindley, B., 1984, "Empty economics in the case for industrial policy," *World Economy* 7(3), Sept.:277–94.

Hinrichs, H., 1968, *A General Theory of Tax Structure Change During Economic Development*. Cambridge: Harvard Law School.

Hirschman, A., 1970, *Exit, Voice, and Loyalty*. Cambridge: Harvard University Press.

Ho, S., 1978, *Economic Development of Taiwan, 1860–1970*. New Haven: Yale University Press.

———, 1980, "Small-scale enterprises in Korea and Taiwan," Staff Working Paper No. 384 (Apr.), World Bank, Washington, D.C.

———, 1981, "South Korea and Taiwan: development prospects and problems in the 1980s," *Asian Survey* 21(12), Dec.

Hoffman, K., 1989, "Technological advance and organizational innovation in the engineering industry," Industry Series Paper No. 4, World Bank, Washington, D.C.

Hofheinz, R., and K. Calder, 1982, *The Eastasian Edge*. New York: Basic Books.

Hosomi, T., and A. Okumura, 1982, "Japanese industrial policy," in J. Pinder (ed.), *National Industrial Strategies and the World Economy*. London: Croom Helm.

Hou, Chi-ming, 1987, "Strategy for industrial development," *Industry of Free China* 68(4), Oct.: 1–18.

Hsiao, R., 1977, "Dual economic structure and factor markets in Taiwan—the role of public enterprise," Discussion Paper 114, Department of Economics, University of Colorado, Boulder.

Hsing, M.-H., 1971, *Taiwan: Industrialisation and Trade Policies*. Oxford: Oxford University Press.

Hsiung, J., et al. (eds.), 1981, *Contemporary Republic of China: The Taiwan Experience*. New York: Praeger and the American Association for Chinese Studies.

Hsu, J., 1982, "Balance-of-payments adjustment and oil shocks in an export-oriented economy: the experience of Taiwan," *Academia Economic Papers*, 10(2), Sept.

Humphrey, C., 1983, "Divestiture of state enterprises in Taiwan: a case study of an economy in transition," mimeo, USAID, Washington, D.C.

Huntington, S., 1968, *Political Order in Changing Societies*. New Haven: Yale University Press.

———, 1970, "Social and institutional dynamics of one-party systems," in S. Huntington and C. Moore (eds.), *Authoritarian Politics in Modern Society*. New York: Basic Books.

———, 1984, "Will more countries become democratic?," *Political Science Quarterly* 99(2), Summer: 193–218.

Huntington, S., and J. Dominguez, 1975, "Political development," in F. Greenstein and N. Polsby (eds.), *Handbook of Political Science* Reading, Mass.: Addison-Wesley.

Ikonicoff, M., 1985, "Making the most of multinational capital," *Manchester Guardian Weekly*, 4 Aug.:13.

International Cooperation Administration, Mutual Security Mission to China, 1956, *Economic Development on Taiwan, 1951–1955*, Taipei.

IMF (International Monetary Fund), *International Financial Statistics*, various issues, Washington, D.C.

———, 1985, *World Economic Outlook*, Washington, D.C.

———, 1988, *World Economic Outlook*, Washington, D.C.

Industry of Free China, 1976, Oct. 7–10.

Industrial and Commercial Times, 1982, "A great debate on economic issues: notes on a seminar on Taiwan's economic problems and policies," Taipei (Chinese).

Inkster, I., 1983, " 'Modelling Japan' for the Third World," in *East Asia: International Review of Economic, Political, and Social Development*, pt. 1. Frankfurt: Campus Verlag.

Ishida, T., 1968, "The development of interest groups and the patterns of political modernization in Japan," in R. Ward (ed.), *Political Development in Modern Japan*. Princeton: Princeton University Press.

Ishikawa, S., 1967, *Economic Development in Asian Perspective*. Institute of Economic Research, Hitotsubashi University, Tokyo.

Jacobs, J. B., 1976, "Taiwan's press: political communications link and research resource," *China Quarterly*, Dec.:778–88.

———, 1978, "Paradoxes in the politics of Taiwan: lessons for comparative politics," *Politics* 13(2):239–47.

———, 1979, "Taiwan 1978: Economic successes, international uncertainties," *Asian Survey* 19(1).

———, 1980, "Taiwan 1979: 'normalcy' after 'normalization,' " *Asian Survey* 20(1).

———, 1981, "Political opposition and Taiwan's political future," *Australian Journal of Chinese Affairs*, No. 6, July.

Jacobsson, W., 1984, "Industrial policy for the machine tool industries of South Korea and Taiwan," *IDS Bulletin* 15(2), Apr.

Jacoby, N., 1966, *U.S. Aid to Taiwan: A Study of Foreign Aid, Self-Help and Development*. New York: Praeger.

Jain, S., 1975, *Size Distribution of Income*. Washington, D.C.: World Bank.

JETRO (Japan External Trade Organization), 1983, *A History of Japan's Postwar Export Policy*. Tokyo.

Joekes, S., 1987, *Women in the World Economy*, New York: Oxford University Press.

Johnson, C., 1977, "MITI and Japanese international economic policy," in R. Scalopino (ed.), *The Foreign Policy of Modern Japan*. Berkeley: University of California Press.

————, 1981a, "Introduction—the Taiwan model," in J. Hsiung, et al. (eds.), *Contemporary Republic of China: The Taiwan Experience*. New York: Praeger and the American Association for Chinese Studies.

————, 1982, *MITI and the Japanese Miracle: The Growth of Industrial Policy, 1925–1975*. Stanford: Stanford University Press.

————, 1984, "The industrial policy debate re-examined," *California Management Review* 27(1), Fall:71–89.

————, 1985, "The moral equivalent of defeat," *Atlantic Monthly*, Dec.: 106–12.

————, 1986, "The challenge of Japanese capitalism," in J. Kirlin and D. Winkler (eds.), *California's Policy Choices*, vol. 3, Los Angeles: University of Southern California, School of Public Administration.

————, 1986, "East Asia," in E. Comisso and L. Tyson (eds.), *Power, Purpose, and Collective Action: Economic Strategies in Socialist States*. Ithaca: Cornell University Press.

————, 1987, "Political institutions and economic performance: a comparative analysis of the government-business relationship in Japan, South Korea, and Taiwan," in F. Deyo (ed.), *The Political Economy of the New Asian Industrialism*. Ithaca: Cornell University Press.

Jones, L., and E. Mason, 1982, "Roles of economic factors in determining the size and structure of the public-enterprise sector in less-developed countries with mixed economies," in L. Jones (ed.), *Public Enterprises in Less Developed Countries*. New York: Cambridge University Press.

Jones, L., and I. Sakong, 1980, *Government, Business and Entrepreneurship in Economic Development: The Korean Case*. Cambridge: Harvard University Press.

Jowitt, K., 1971, *Revolutionary Breakthroughs and National Development: The Case of Romania, 1944–1965*. Berkeley: University of California Press.

Jung, W., and P. Marshall, 1985, "Exports, growth and causality in developing countries," *Journal of Development Economics* 18(1):1–12.

Kaldor, N., 1972, "The irrelevance of equilibrium economics," *Economic Journal* 82 Dec.:1237–55.

Kaplan, E., 1972, *Japan—The Government-Business Relationships: A Guide for the American Businessman*. U.S. Department of Commerce.

Katzenstein, P., 1980, "State strength through market competition," paper presented to the Council of Foreign Relations, working group on industrial policy, New York, Apr.

Kavoussi, R., 1985, "International trade and economic development: the recent experience of developing countries," *Journal of Developing Areas* 19 (April): 379–92.

Kau, Ying-mao, 1988, "Political outlook for Taiwan, 1988," unpublished paper, Political Science Department, Brown University.

Keesing, D., 1988, "Institutional support for export marketing: the experience of Singapore, Hong Kong, Taiwan and Korea," mimeo, Country Economics Department, World Bank, Washington, D.C., Mar.

Kerr, G., 1965, *Formosa Betrayed*. Boston: Houghton-Mifflin.

Khan, M., and M. Knight, 1985, "Fund-supported adjustment programs and economic growth," IMF Occasional Paper No. 41, Washington, D.C.: International Monetary Fund.

Kim, K. S., and M. Roemer, 1979, *Growth and Structural Transformation. Studies in the Modernization of the Republic of Korea: 1945–75*. Cambridge: Harvard University Press.

Kim, P. S., 1985, "GNP industry sector analysis: telecommunications," U.S. Embassy, Seoul.

Kindleberger, C., 1975, "The rise of free trade in Western Europe, 1820–1875," *Journal of Economic History* 35, Mar.

King, R., 1982a, "PTA import ban," *Asia Wall Street Journal*, 27 Apr.

———, 1982b, "Stainless steel industry in Taiwan," *Asia Wall Street Journal*, 2 Mar.

———, 1982c, "Taiwan's import ban against Japanese goods," *Asia Wall Street Journal*, 15 Feb.

Kirby, W., 1986, "Technocratic organization and technological development in China: the Nationalist experience and legacy, 1928–1953," paper for conference on China's new technological revolution, Fairbank Center for East Asian Research, Harvard University, 9–11 May.

———, forthcoming, *The International Development of China: Nationalist Industrial Policy and Its Heirs*. Stanford: Stanford University Press.

Klein, L., 1986, Foreword, in L. Lau (ed.), *Models of Development: A Comparative Study of Economic Growth in South Korea and Taiwan*. San Francisco: Institute for Contemporary Studies.

Kohli, A., 1986, "Democracy and development," in J. Lewis and V. Kallab (eds.), *Development Strategies Reconsidered*. Washington, D.C.: Overseas Development Council.

Koo, S. E., 1976, "Foreign investment and industrialization in Taiwan," *Academia Economic Papers* 4(1), Mar.:125–63.

Koo, Y., 1985, "East Asian lobbies in Washington: comparative strategies," Occasional Paper 21, Wilson Center, Washington, D.C.

Korea Exchange Bank, various issues, *Monthly Review*.

Korea Industrial Research Institute, 1986, *Industrial Technology White Paper*, Seoul.

Krasner, S., 1978, *Defending the National Interest: Raw Materials Investment and U.S. Foreign Policy*. Princeton: Princeton University Press.

Krausse, M., 1978, *The New Protectionism: The Welfare State and International Trade*. New York: New York University Press.

Kreps, D., 1984, "Corporate culture and economic theory," mimeo, Graduate School of Business, Stanford University.

Krueger, A., 1974, "The political economy of the rent-seeking society," *American Economic Review*, June:291–303.

————, 1978, *Liberalization Attempts and Consequences*, vol. 10, *Foreign Trade Regimes and Economic Development*. New York: National Bureau of Economic Research.

————, 1980, "Trade policy as an input to development," *American Economic Review* 70(2):288–92.

————, 1981, "Export-led industrial growth reconsidered," in W. Hong and L. Krause (eds.), *Trade and Growth of the Advanced Developing Countries in the Pacific Basin*. Seoul: Korea Development Institute.

————, 1983, *Synthesis and Conclusions*, vol. 3 of *Trade and Employment in Developing Countries*. Chicago: University of Chicago Press.

Krugman, P., 1979, "Trade, accumulation and uneven development," Discussion Paper No. 311, Yale University.

————, 1987, "Is free trade passe?" *Journal of Economic Perspectives* 1(2).

————, (ed.), 1986, *Strategic Trade Policy and the New International Economics*. Cambridge: MIT.

————, 1989, "The case for stabilizing exchange rates," *Oxford Review of Economic Policy* 5(3):61–72.

Kubo, Y., et al., 1986, "Interdependence and industrial structure," in H. Chenery, S. Robinson, and M. Syrquin (eds.), *Industrialization and Growth: A Comparative Analysis*. New York: Oxford University Press.

Kuo, S. W. Y., 1983, *The Taiwan Economy in Transition*. Boulder: Westview.

Kuo, S., G. Ranis, and J. Fei, 1981, *The Taiwan Success Story: Rapid Growth with Improved Distribution in the Republic of China, 1952–1979*. Boulder: Westview.

Kuznets, P., 1982, "The dramatic reversal of 1979–1980: contemporary economic development in Korea," *Journal of Northeast Asian Studies* 1(3).

Kuznets, S., 1968, "Notes on Japan's economic growth," in L. Klein and K. Ohkawa (eds.), *Economic Growth: The Japanese Experience since the Meiji Era*, Homewood, Ill.: Irwin.

————, 1979, "Growth and structural shifts," in W. Galenson (ed.), *Economic Growth and Structural Change in Taiwan: The Postwar Experience of the Republic of China*. Ithaca: Cornell University Press.

Lakatos, I., 1978, *The Methodology of Scientific Research Programmes*. Cambridge: Cambridge University Press.

Lal, D., 1983, *The Poverty of Development Economics*. London, IEA, Hobart Paperback 16.

Lal, D., & S. Rajapatirana, 1987, "Foreign trade regimes and economic growth in developing countries," *World Bank Research Observer* 2(2): 189–217.

Lamb, G., 1982, "Market-surrogate approaches to institutional development," mimeo, Public Sector Management Division, World Bank.

Landau, D., 1986, "Government and economic growth in the less developed countries: an empirical study for 1960–1980," *Economic Development and Cultural Change* 35(11):35–75.

Lau, L. (ed.), 1986, *Models of Development: A Comparative Study of Economic Growth in South Korea and Taiwan*. San Francisco: Institute for Contemporary Studies.

Lawless, R., and T. Shaheen, 1987, "Airplanes and airports: the subtle skill of Japanese protectionism," *SAIS Review*, Fall:101–20.

Lee, J. M., 1975, "Political change in Taiwan 1949–1974: a study of the process of democratic and integrative change with focus on the role of government," doctoral diss., University of Tennessee.

Lee, J. S., 1980, "An empirical study of the functioning of the labor market in Taiwan," *Academia Economic Papers* 8 (1), Mar.

Lee, T. H., et al., 1975, "Structure of effective protection and subsidy in Taiwan," *Economic Essays* 6:55–175.

Lee, T. H., and K. S. Liang, 1982, "Taiwan," in B. Balassa, et al., *Development Strategies in Semi-industrial Economies*, Baltimore: Johns Hopkins University Press, chap. 10.

Lee, Y. S., 1983, "The influence of monetary policy on the industrialization of Taiwan," *Industrial Development in Taiwan*, Academia Sinica (Chinese).

Leff, N., 1985, "Optimal investment choice for developing countries: rational theory and rational decision-making," *Journal of Development Economics* 18(2/3):335–60.

Leibenstein, H., 1978, *General X-Efficiency Theory and Economic Development*. New York: Oxford University Press.

Lew, W., 1978, "Education in Taiwan: trends and problems," *Asian Affairs* 3(5):317–22.

Lewis, J., 1989, "Government and national economic development," *Daedalus* 118(1), Winter:69–83

Lewis, J., and V. Kallab (eds.), 1986, *Development Strategies Reconsidered*. Overseas Development Council, New Brunswick: Transaction Books.

Lewis, W. A., 1955, *The Theory of Economic Growth*. London: Allen and Unwin.

Li, K. T., 1976, *The Experience of Dynamic Economic Growth on Taiwan*. Taipei: Mei Ya Publications.

———, 1981, "A strategy for technological development," in J. Hsiung, et al. (eds.), *Contemporary Republic of China: The Taiwan Experience*. New York: Praeger and the American Association for Chinese Studies.

———, 1987, "Technology development and cooperation among NICs in the Western Pacific," *Industry of Free China*, Sept.

Li, K. T. and W. Yeh, 1967, "Public policy and economic development in Taiwan," *Economic Development of Taiwan*, Academia Sinica, Taipei.

Liang, C., and M. Skully, 1982, "Financial institutions and markets in Taiwan," in M. Skully (ed.), *Financial Markets and Institutions in the Far East: A Study of China, Hong Kong, Japan, South Korea and Taiwan*. London: Macmillan.

Liang, K. S., and C. H. Liang, 1980, *Trade Strategy and the Exchange Rate Policies of Taiwan*. Taipei: National Taiwan University.

Lim, L., 1983, "Singapore's success: the myth of the free market economy," *Asian Survey* 23:752–65.

Lin, C. Y., 1973, *Industrialization in Taiwan, 1946–72: Trade and Import-Substitution Policies for Developing Countries*. New York: Praeger.

Lin, C. Y., 1986, "Policy response to external shocks: Brazil versus Taiwan and South Korea," mimeo, Research Department, IMF, Washington, D.C.

Lindbeck, A., 1986, "Public finance for market-oriented developing countries," mimeo, Stockholm, Institute for International Economic Studies.

Lindblom, C., 1959, "The 'science' of muddling through," *Public Administration Review* 19, Sept.

Lindgren, J. (ed.), 1967, *The Early Writings of Adam Smith*. New York: A. M. Kelley.

Lipton, M., 1977, *Why Poor People Stay Poor: A Study of Urban Bias in World Development*. London: Temple Smith.

————, 1985, "Prisoners' dilemma and Coase's theorem: A case for democracy in less developed countries?" in R. Matthews (ed.), *Economics and Democracy*. London: Macmillan.

List, F., 1966 (1885), *The National System of Political Economy*. New York: Augustus Kelly.

Little, Arthur D., Inc., 1973, *The Outlook for the Electronics Industry in Taiwan*, Taipei: Ministry of Economic Affairs.

Little, I., 1979, "An economic reconnaissance," in W. Galenson (ed.), *Economic Growth and Structural Change in Taiwan: The Postwar Experience of the Republic of China*. Ithaca: Cornell University Press..

————, 1981, "The experience and causes of rapid labour-intensive development in Korea, Taiwan Province, Hong Kong and Singapore, and the possibilities of emulation," in E. Lee (ed.), *Export-led Industrialization and Development*. Asian Employment Programme, International Labor Organization, Geneva.

————, 1982, *Economic Development: Theory, Policy and International Relations*. New York: Basic Books.

Little, I., T. Scitovsky, and M. Scott, 1970, *Industry and Trade in Some Development Countries: A Comparative Study*. New York: Basic Books.

Liu, A. P. L., 1987, *Phoenix and the Lame Lion: Modernization in Taiwan and Mainland China 1950–1980*. Stanford: Hoover Institution Press.

Liu, C. T., and C. L. Liu, 1988, "A comparison of public and private sector incomes in Taiwan area," conference on Taiwan's labor market, Department of Economics, Taiwan National University, 16–17 Jan.

Luedde-Neurath, R., 1986, *Import Controls and Export-Oriented Development: A Reassessment of the South Korean Case*. Boulder: Westview.

————, 1988, "State intervention and export-oriented development in South Korea," in G. White (ed.), *Developmental States in East Asia*. London: Macmillan.

Lumley, F., 1981 (1976), "The educational reform," in J. Hsiung et al. (eds.), *Contemporary Republic of China: The Taiwan Experience*. New York: Praeger and the American Association for Chinese Studies.

Lundberg, E., 1979, "Fiscal and monetary policies," in W. Galenson (ed.), *Economic Growth and Structural Change in Taiwan: The Postwar Experience of the Republic of China*. Ithaca: Cornell University Press.

Lundvall, B. A., 1988, "Innovation as an interactive process: from user-producer interaction to the national system of innovation," in G. Dosi, et al. (eds.), *Technical Change and Economic Theory*. London: Pinter.

MacEwan, A., 1983, "New light on dependency and dependent development," *Monthly Review*, Jan.

McNamara, D., 1986, "Survival strategies: Korean solidarity in a hostile world," mimeo, Georgetown University, Feb.

Magaziner, I., and T. Hout, 1980, *Japanese Industrial Policy*, Monograph 585, London: Policy Studies Institute.

Maizels, A., 1963, *Industrial Growth and World Trade*. Cambridge: Cambridge University Press.

March, J., and H. Simon, 1958, *Organizations*. New York: John Wiley.

Marsh, R., 1979, "Does democracy hinder economic development in the latecomer developing nations?" *Comparative Social Research* 2:215–47.

Mason, E., 1984, "The Chenery analysis and some other considerations," in M. Syrquin, L. Taylor, and L. Westphal (eds.), *Economic Structure and Performance; Essays in Honor of Hollis B. Chenery*, New York: Academic.

Mason, E., et al., 1980, *The Economic and Social Modernization of the Republic of Korea*. Cambridge: Harvard University Press.

Matthews, R., 1959, *The Trade Cycle*. Cambridge: Cambridge University Press.

Mayer, C., 1987, "The assessment: financial systems and corporate investment," *Oxford Review of Economic Policy* 3(4):i–xvi.

Meier, G., 1984, *Leading Issues in Economic Development*. New York: Oxford University Press.

Meier, G., and R. Baldwin, 1957, *Economic Development: Theory, History, Policy*. New York: John Wiley.

Metzger, T. A., 1987, "Success and the sense of predicament: a cultural perspective on modernization in the Republic of China," paper for conference on dynamism in Asia: noneconomic elements in economic development, Institute of International Studies, University of South Carolina, 11–13 Feb.

Mezzetti, F., 1982, "North Korea and its Divine Kim II Sung," *Asian Wall Street Journal*, 8 Dec.

Michaely, M., 1977, "Exports and growth: an empirical investigation," *Journal of Development Economics* 4(1):49–53.

————, 1988, "Trade liberalization policies: lessons of experience," mimeo, World Bank, Apr.

Michell, A., 1984, "Administrative traditions and economic decision-making in South Korea," *IDS Bulletin* 15(2):32–37.

Migdal, J., 1986, *Strong Societies and Weak States: State-Society Relations and State Capabilities in the Third World*. Princeton: Princeton University Press.

Ministry of Science and Technology (Korea), 1986, "Long-term technology forecast for the year of 2000," Seoul.

Mody, A., 1987, "Information industries: the changing role of newly industrializing countries," paper presented at the conference on technology and government policy in telecommunications and computers, Brookings Institution, Washington, D.C., 4–5 June. Forthcoming in book edited by K. Flamm and R. Crandall.

————, forthcoming, "Recent evolution of microelectronics in Korea and Taiwan: an institutional approach to comparative advantage," *Cambridge Journal of Economics*.

Moore, J., 1988, "Underground shelters: Taiwan's fringe investment firms face investigation," *Far Eastern Economic Review*, 25 Feb.: 73–74.

———, 1989, "Banking: shaking the system," *Far Eastern Economic Review* 18 May: 56–57.

Moore, M., 1987, "From statism to pluralism: government and agriculture in Taiwan and South Korea," in G. White (ed.), *Developmental States in East Asia*. London: Macmillan.

Moran, T. (ed.), 1986, *Investing in Development: New Roles for Private Capital?* New Brunswick: Transaction Books in cooperation with Overseas Development Council.

Morss, E., 1987, "Reformulating the theory of international trade for policy application in developing countries," mimeo, Center for Asian Development Studies, Boston University.

Mulford, D., 1987, Remarks by the Honorable David C. Mulford, Assistant Secretary for International Affairs, U.S. Treasury, in *Treasury News*, 17 Nov., Washington, D.C.

Murray, R., 1989, "New forms of administration," mimeo, Institute of Development Studies, University of Sussex.

Murrell, P., 1979, "Planning and coordination of economic policies in market economies," *Journal of Comparative Economics* 3(2).

Myers, R., 1983, "The contest between two Chinese states," *Asian Survey* 23(4), Apr.

———, 1986, "The economic development of the Republic of China on Taiwan, 1965–1981," in L. Lau (ed.), *Models of Development: A Comparative Study of Economic Growth in South Korea and Taiwan*. San Francisco: Institute for Contemporary Studies.

Myers, R., and A. Ching, 1964, "Agricultural development in Taiwan under Japanese colonial rule," *Journal of Asian Studies* 23(4), Aug.

Myint, H., 1982, "Comparative analysis of Taiwan's economic development with other countries," *Experience and Lessons of Economic Development in Taiwan*, Institute of Economics, Academia Sinica, Taipei.

Myrdal, G., 1957, *Economic Theory and Underdeveloped Regions*. London: Duckworth.

———, 1960, *Beyond the Welfare State*. New Haven: Yale University Press.

———, 1968, *Asian Drama II*. New York: Pantheon.

Nathan, A., 1976, *Peking Politics 1918–1923: Factionalism and the Failure of Constitutionalism*. Berkeley: University of California Press.

Noble, G., 1987, "Contending forces in Taiwan's economic policymaking: the case of Hua Tung heavy trucks," *Asian Survey* 27(6):683–704.

———, 1988, "Between competition and cooperation: collective action in the industrial policy of Japan and Taiwan," doctoral diss., Harvard University.

North-South, A Programme for Survival, 1980, Report of the Independent Commission on International Development Issues, London.

Nove, A., 1983, *The Economics of Feasible Socialism*. London: Allen and Unwin.

Nunnenkamp, P., 1981, "The efficiency of state-owned enterprises in the manufacturing industry of Taiwan," *Academia Economic Papers* 9(2):87–124.

Nurkse, R., 1953, *Problems of Capital Formation in Underdeveloped Countries*. Oxford: Blackwell.

O'Donnel, G., 1973, *Modernization and Bureaucratic-Authoritarianism: Studies in South American Politics*. Berkeley: Institute of International Studies, University of California.

OECD (Organization for Economic Cooperative Development), 1972, *The Industrial Policy of Japan*. Paris.

OECD *Observer*, 1986, "Change and continuity in OECD trade in manufactures with developing countries," Mar.:3–9.

Office of the U.S. Trade Representative, *Foreign Trade Barriers*, various issues, Washington, D.C.: U.S. Government Printing Office.

Olson, M., 1982, *The Rise and Decline of Nations*. New Haven: Yale University Press.

———, 1986, "A theory of the incentives facing political organizations: neo-corporation and the hegemonic state," *International Political Science Review*, 7(2):165–89.

Oshima, H., 1982, "Comment on 'How to develop successfully: the Taiwan model,'" *Experiences and Lessons of Economic Development in Taiwan*, Institute of Economics, Academia Sinica, Taipei.

———, 1986, "The transition from an agricultural to an industrial economy in East Asia," *Economic Development and Cultural Change* 34(4):783–809.

Ouchi, T., 1967, "Agricultural depression and Japanese villages," *Developing Economies* 5(4):597–627.

Ozawa, T., 1980, "Government control over technology acquisition and firms' entry into new sectors: the experience of Japan's synthetic fibre industry," *Cambridge Journal of Economics 4* (1): 133–46.

Pack, H., forthcoming, "Industrialization and trade," in H. Chenery and T. Srinivasan (eds.), *Handbook of Development Economics*.

Pack, H., and L. Westphal, 1986, "Industrial strategy and technological change: theory versus reality," *Journal of Development Economics* 22:8–128.

Page, S., 1979, "The management of international trade," Discussion Paper 29, National Institute of Economic and Social Research, London.

———, 1987, "The rise in protection since 1974," *Oxford Review of Economic Policy* 3(1): 37–51.

Pang, Chien-kou, 1988, "The state and economic transformation: the Taiwan case," doctoral diss. Department of Sociology, Brown University.

Park, Yong-chan, 1987, "The national system of innovation in Korea, with an introduction to the semiconductor industry," MSc diss., Science Policy Research Unit, University of Sussex, Great Britain.

Parry, T., 1988, "The role of foreign capital in East Asian industrialization, growth and development," in H. Hughes (ed.), *Achieving Industrialization in East Asia*. Cambridge: Cambridge University Press.

Pathirane, L., and D. Blades, 1982, "Defining and measuring the public sector: some international comparisons," *Review of Income and Wealth* 28(3), Sept.

Patrick, H., 1977, "The future of the Japanese economy: output and labor productivity," *Journal of Japanese Studies* 3(2), Summer.

———, 1983, "Japanese industrial policy and its relevance for United States industrial policy," statement before the Joint Economic Committee, U.S. Congress, 13 July.

Pempel, T., 1978, "Japanese foreign economic policy: the domestic bases for international behavior," in P. Katzenstein (ed.), *Between Power and Plenty*. Madison: University of Wisconsin Press.

——, 1987, "The unbundling of Japan, Inc.: the changing dynamics of Japanese policy formation," *Journal of Japanese Studies* 13(2):271–306.

Pepper, T., M. Janow, and J. Wheeler, 1985, *The Competition: Dealing with Japan*. New York: Praeger.

Perez, C., and L. Soete, 1988, "Catching up in technology: entry barriers and windows of opportunity," in G. Dosi, et al. (eds.) *Technical Change and Economic Theory*. London: Pinter.

Petit Larousse Illustre, 1975, Paris: Librairie Larousse.

Pinder, J. (ed.), 1982, *National Industrial Strategies and the World Economy*. London: Croom Helm.

Pluta, J., 1979, "Wagner's law, public sector patterns and growth of public enterprises in Taiwan," *Public Finance Quarterly* 7(1):25–46.

Polanyi, K., 1957, *The Great Transformation*. Boston: Beacon.

Pye, L., and M. Pye, 1985, *Asian Power and Politics: The Cultural Dimensions of Authority*. Cambridge: Belknap Press of Harvard University Press.

Ram, R., 1986, "Government size and economic growth: a new framework and some evidence from cross-section and time-series data," *American Economic Review* 76(1):191–203.

Ranis, G., 1979, "Industrial development," in W. Galenson (ed.), *Economic Growth and Structural Change in Taiwan: The Postwar Experience of the Republic of China*. Ithaca: Cornell University Press..

——, 1983, "The NICs, the near-NICs and the world economy," paper presented at the conference on patterns of growth and structural change in Asia's newly industrializing countries and near-NICs in the context of economic interdependence, East-West Center, Honolulu, 3–8 Apr.

Ranis, G., and Chi Schive, 1985, "Direct foreign investment in Taiwan's development," in W. Galenson (ed.), *Foreign Trade and Investment*, Madison: University of Wisconsin Press.

Rapoport, A., and A. Chammah, 1965, *Prisoner's Dilemma*. Ann Arbor: University of Michigan Press.

Reich, R., 1982, "Why the U.S. needs an industrial policy," *Harvard Business Review*, Jan.–Feb.

Reynolds, A., 1987, "Public investment, not a binge," *Wall Street Journal*, 27 July.

Reynolds, L., 1983, "The spread of industrialization to the Third World: 1850–1980," *Journal of Economic Literature* 21(3), Sept.

Rhee, Y. W., 1984, "A framework for export policy and administration: lessons from the East Asian experience," Industry and Finance Series 10, World Bank, Washington, D.C.

Riedel, J., 1984, "Trade as the engine of growth in developing countries revisited," *Economic Journal*, 94 Mar.:56–73.

Riegg, N., 1978, "The role of fiscal and monetary policies in Taiwan's economic development," doctoral diss., University of Connecticut.

Rivlin, A., 1987, "Economics and the political process," *American Economic Review* 77(l): 1–9.

Rodrik, D., 1987, "Imperfect competition, scale economies, and trade policy in developing countries," Discussion Paper, Kennedy School of Government, Harvard University.

———, 1988a, "Industrial organization and product quality: evidence from South Korean and Taiwanese exports," mimeo, Kennedy School of Government, Harvard University, June.

———, 1988b, "Closing the technology gap: does trade liberalization really help?" 170D, Discussion Paper, Kennedy School of Government, Harvard University.

Romer, P., 1987, "Crazy explanations for the productivity slowdown," *Macroeconomics Annual* 2:163–202.

Rosecrance, R., 1986, *The Rise of the Trading State: Commerce and Conquest in the Modern World.* New York: Basic Books.

Rosenstein-Rodan, P. 1943, "Problems of industrialisation of Eastern and South-eastern Europe," *Economic Journal,* June–Sept.

Rosenthal, A., 1986, "Journey among tyrants," *New York Times,* 23 Mar.

Rosovsky, H., 1972, "What are the lessons of Japanese economic development?" in A. Youngson (ed.), *Economic Development in the Long-Run.* London: Allen and Unwin.

Rostow, Walt, 1960, *The Stages of Economic Growth, A Non-communist Manifesto.* New York: Cambridge University Press.

Rudolph, L., and S. Rudolph, 1986, "Regime types and economic performance," in D. Basu and R. Sisson (eds.), *Social and Economic Development in India: A Reassessment.* New Delhi: Sage.

Ruggie, J. G., 1982, "International regimes, transitions and change: embedded liberalism in the postwar economic order," *International Organization,* Spring 36(2):379–416.

Sachs, J., 1987, "Trade and exchange rate policies in growth-oriented adjustment programs," symposium on growth-oriented adjustment programs, World Bank and IMF, 25–27 Feb.

Samsung Semiconductor and Telecommunication Corporation, 1987, *Retrospect for Last Ten Years of Samsung Semiconductor and Telecommunication* (Korean).

Samuels, R., 1987, *The Business of the Japanese State: Energy Markets in Comparative and Historical Perspective.* Ithaca: Cornell University Press.

Sandeman, H., 1982a, "South Korea survey: Asia's most ambitious nation," *Economist,* 14 Aug.:1–18.

———, 1982b, "Taiwan—an island on its own," *Economist,* 31 July.

Saxonhouse, G., 1983a, "The micro and macroeconomics of foreign sales to Japan," in W. Cline (ed.), *Trade Policy in the 1980's.* Washington: Institute for International Relations.

———, 1983b, "What is all this about 'industrial targetting' in Japan?" *World Economy* 6(3):253–73.

———, 1985, "What's wrong with Japanese trade structure," Discussion Paper 166, Department of Economics, University of Michigan.

Scalapino, R., 1968, "Elections in pre-war Japan," in Ward (ed.), *Political Development in Modern Japan*. Princeton: Princeton University Press.

Schak, D., 1987, "The effects of economic development on the poor in Taiwan," mimeo, Modern Asian Studies, Griffith University.

Schelling, T., 1960, *The Strategy of Conflict*. Cambridge: Harvard University Press.

Schive, Chi, forthcoming, "The next stage of industrialization in Taiwan and Korea," in G. Gereffi and D. Wyman (eds.), *Manufactured Miracles: Patterns of Industrialization in Latin America and East Asia*. Princeton: Princeton University Press.

Schive, C., and B. Majumdar, 1981, "Direct foreign investment and linkage effects: the experience of Taiwan," paper presented at the American Economic Association meeting, Washington, D.C.

Schive, Chi, and K. T. Hsueh, 1987, "The experiences and prospects of high-tech industrial development in Taiwan, ROC: the case of the information industry," Conference Series No. 6, Chung-hua Institution for Economic Research, Taipei, Feb.

Schmidt, M., 1982, "The role of parties in shaping macroeconomic policy," in F. Castes (ed.), *The Impact of Political Parties*. London.

Schmitter, P., 1974, "Still the century of corporation?" *Review of Politics* 85 (Jan.):85–131.

Schmitter, P., 1981, "Interest intermediation and regime governability in contemporary Western Europe and North America," in S. Berger (ed.), *Organizing Interests in Western Europe: Pluralism, Corporatism and the Transformation of Politics*. Cambridge: Cambridge University Press.

Schreiber, J., 1970, *U.S. Corporate Investment in Taiwan*. New York: Dunellen.

Schultze, C., 1983, "Industrial policy: a dissent," *Brookings Review*, Fall.

Scitovsky, T., 1963, "Two concepts of external economies," in A. Agarwal and S. Singh (eds.), *The Economics of Underdevelopment*. New York: Oxford University Press.

———, 1986, "Economic development in Taiwan and South Korea, 1965–1981," in L. Lau (ed.), *Models of Development: A Comparative Study of Economic Growth in South Korea and Taiwan*. San Francisco: Institute for Contemporary Studies.

Scott, B., 1985, "National strategies: key to international competition," in B. Scott and G. Lodge (eds.), *U.S. Competitiveness in the World Economy*. Cambridge: Harvard Business School Press.

Scott, M., 1979, "Foreign trade," in W. Galenson (ed.), *Economic Growth and Structural Change in Taiwan: The Postwar Experience of the Republic of China*. Ithaca: Cornell University Press.

Scott, W. D. (Australian Management Consulting Firm), 1984, *Review of Indonesia Enterprises Mobilization for Export Development, Overseas Studies No. 3, The Republic of China-Taiwan*, a limited circulation study for Department Perdagangan, Jakarta, Sept.

Sease, D., 1987, "Taiwan's export boom to U.S. owes much to American firms," *Wall Street Journal*, 27 May.

Sen, A., 1981, "Public action and the quality of life in developing countries," *Oxford Bulletin of Economies and Statistics*, 43(4):287–319.

———, 1983, "Development: which way now?" *Economic Journal* 93, Dec.: 745–92.

Senghaas, D., 1985, *The European Experience*. Dover, N.H.: Berg.

Shea, J. D., 1983a, "A review of the financial market in Taiwan," paper presented at the conference on current economic problems in Taiwan, Chinese Economic Association and Academia Sinica, Taipei, Apr. (Chinese).

———, 1983b, "Financial dualism and industrial development in Taiwan," paper presented at the conference on current economic problems in Taiwan, Chinese Economic Association and Academia Sinica, Taipei, Apr. (Chinese).

Shiao, M., 1983, "Taiwan: CPAs under fire," *Asia Wall Street Journal*, 27 June.

Shinohara, M., 1982, *Industrial Growth, Trade and Dynamic Patterns in the Japanese Economy*. Tokyo: University of Tokyo Press.

Shonfield, A., 1965, *Modern Capitalism: The Changing Balance of Public and Private Power*. Oxford: Oxford University Press.

———, 1982, *The Use of Public Power*. Oxford: Oxford University Press.

Short, R., 1983, "The role of public enterprises: an international statistical comparison," Department Memorandum Series 83/84, International Monetary Fund, Washington, D.C.

Silin, R., 1976, *Leadership and Values: The Organization of Large-Scale Taiwanese Enterprises*. Cambridge: Harvard University Press.

Simon, D., 1988a, "Implications of Taiwan's success for the PRC," in *Agents of Change: Chinese Enterprises and Foreign Technology in Comparative Perspective*, Washington, D.C.: Wilson Center.

——— 1988b, "Technology transfer and technology policies on Taiwan," in E. Winkler and S. Greenhalgh (eds.), *Contending Approaches to the Political Economy of Taiwan*. Armonk: M. E. Sharpe.

Singer, H., 1949, "Economic progress in underdeveloped countries," *Social Research* 16(1):1–11.

———, 1950, "The distribution of gains between investing and borrowing countries," *American Economic Review* 40(2):473–85.

———, 1988, "The *World Development Report 1987* on the blessings of 'outward orientation': a necessary correction," *Journal of Development Studies* 24(2):232–36.

Singer, H., and P. Gray, 1988, "Trade policy and growth of developing countries: some new data," *World Development* 16(3):395–403.

Singh, A., 1981, "Third world industrialisation and the structure of the world economy," in D. Currie, D. Peel, and W. Peters (eds.), *Micro-Economics and Economic Development*. London: Croom Helm.

———, 1983, "Third world industrialisation: industrial strategies and policies in the 1980s and 1990s," mimeo, Faculty of Economics, University of Cambridge.

Smith, Adam, 1776 (1937), *An Enquiry into the Nature and Causes of the Wealth of Nations*, E. Cannan (ed.), Modern Library, New York: Random House.

Snape, R., 1988, "East Asia: The trade reform experience in Korea and Singapore," mimeo, World Bank.

Specter, M., and A. Tanzer, 1983, Feature on Taiwan, *Far Eastern Economic Review*, Dec. 8:65–72.

Spencer, B., and J. Brander, 1983, "International R & D rivalry and industrial strategy," *Review of Economic Studies* 50:707–22.

Sricharatchanya, P., 1982, "Investment—hospitality can hurt," *Far Eastern Economic Review*, 12 May.

Stepan, A., 1978, *The State and Society: Peru in Comparative Perspective*. Princeton: Princeton University Press.

Stewart, F., 1988, "Proposals for a review of Article XVIII of GATT: an assessment," mimeo, Queen Elizabeth House, Oxford.

Stigler, G., 1965, "The economist and the state," *Amerian Economic Review* 55(1): 1–18.

Stiglitz, J., 1989, "Financial markets and development," *Oxford Review of Economic Policy*, 5(4):55–68.

Streeten, P., 1964, *Economic Integration*. 2d ed., Leyden: A. W. Sythoff.

Summers, R., and A. Heston, 1984, "Improved comparisons of real product and its composition, 1950–80," *Review of Income and Wealth*. 30:207–62.

Sun, C., 1981, "Inflation, trade and economic growth," *Industry of Free China*, May.

Sun, C. and M-Y Liang, 1982, "Savings in Taiwan, 1953–80," in *Experiences and Lessons of Economic Development in Taiwan*, Institute of Economics, Academia Sinica, Taipei.

Sun, Y. S., 1981, *The Three Principles of the People*. Taipei: China Publishing.

Sung, Y. K., 1986, "The economic development of the Republic of Korea, 1965–1981," in L. Lau (ed.), *Models of Development: A Comparative Study of Economic Growth in South Korea and Taiwan*. San Francisco: Institute for Contemporary Studies.

Tai, H. C., 1970, "The Kuomintang and modernization in Taiwan," in S. Huntington and C. Moore (eds.), *Authoritarian Politics in Modern Society, the Dynamics of Established One-Party Systems*. New York: Basic Books.

Taizo, Y., 1984, "Government in spiral dilemma: dynamic policy interventions vis-a-vis Japanese auto firms, c. 1900–1960," in Aoki Masahiko (ed.), *An Economic Analysis of Japanese Firms*. Amsterdam: North Holland.

Takeuchi, K., 1988, "Does Japan import less than it should?" Working Paper Series 63, World Bank, Washington, D.C.

Tanzer, A., 1981, "A naphta crack-up," *Far Eastern Economic Review*, 3 Apr.:30–132.

———, 1982, "Charge of the bright brigade," *Far Eastern Economic Review*, 17 May.

Tedstrom, J., 1986, "Trade policy formation in Taiwan," Discussion Paper, 12 Mar., Hudson Institute, Indianapolis.

Thorbecke, E., 1979, "Agricultural development," in W. Galenson (ed.), *Economic Growth and Structural Change in Taiwan: The Postwar Experience of the Republic of China*. Ithaca: Cornell University Press.

Thurow, L., 1985, "The case for industrial policies in America," in T. Shoshido and R. Sato (eds.), *Economic Policy and Development: New Perspectives*, Dover, Mass.: Auburn House.

Ting, W. L., and C. Schive, 1981, "Direct investment and technology transfer for Taiwan," in K. Krishna and M. McLeod (eds.), *Multinationals from Developing Countries*. Lexington, Mass.: D.C. Heath.

Todaro, M., 1981, *Economic Development in the Third World*. New York: Longman.

Trezise, P., 1983, "Industrial policy is not the major reason for Japan's success," *Brookings Review 1*, Spring:13–18.

Tsiang, S. C., 1980, "Exchange rate, interest rate, and economic development," in L. Klein, M. Nerlove, and S. Tsiang (eds.), *Quantitative Economics and Development*. New York: Academic.

———, 1982, "Monetary policy of Taiwan," *Experiences and Lessons of Economic Development in Taiwan*, Institute of Economics, Academia Sinica, Taipei.

Tsiang, S. C., and Wen Land Chen, 1984, "Developments towards trade liberalization in Taiwan," paper presented at the joint conference on the industrial policies of the ROC and the ROK, Chung-hua Institution for Economic Research, Taipei, 28 Dec.

Tsiang, S. C., W. Chen, and A. Hsieh, 1985, "Developments towards trade liberalization in Taiwan, ROC," in proceedings of the conference on U.S.-Taiwan Economic Relations, Chung-hua Institution for Economic Research, Taipei.

Tu, C. H., and W. T. Wang, 1988, "Trade liberalization in the Republic of China on Taiwan, and the economic effects of tariff reductions," paper presented at the joint conference on the industrial policies of the ROC and the ROK, Korea Development Institute, Jan.

Turner, L., 1982, "Western Europe and the NICs," in L. Turner, et al. (eds.), *The Newly Industrializing Countries: Trade and Adjustment*. London: Allen and Unwin (for Royal Institute of International Affairs).

Tyler, W., 1974, "Employment generation and the promotion of manufactured exports in less developed countries: some suggestive evidence," in H. Giersh (ed.), *The International Division of Labour: Problems and Perspectives*. Tübingen: Mohr.

Tyson, L., and J. Zysman, 1983, "American industry in international competition," in J. Zysman and L. Tyson, *American Industry and International Competition: Government Policies and Corporate Strategies*. Ithaca: Cornell University Press.

Ueno, H., 1980, "The conception and evaluation of Japanese industrial policy," in K. Sato (ed.), *Industry and Business in Japan*. White Plains: M. E. Sharpe White Plains.

UNCTAD (United Nations Conference on Trade and Development), various years, *Yearbook of Trade and Development Statistics*, Geneva.

———, 1983, *Handbook of International Trade and Development Statistics*, New York: United Nations.

———, 1987, *Revitalizing Development, Growth and International Trade*. Report to UNCTAD VII. Geneva: UNCTAD.

———, 1988a, *Trade and Development Report 1988*, Geneva.

———, 1988b, "Fighting protectionism," *UNCTAD Bulletin* No. 241, Mar.

UNIDO (United Nations Industrial Development Organization), 1979, *World Industry Since 1960: Progress and Prospects*, United Nations, New York.

United Nations, 1979, *The 1973 World Programme of International Statistics. Summary of Data from Selected Countries*. New York.

UN Statistical Office, 1986, *Monthly Bulletin of Statistics*, New York: United Nations.

U.S. Bureau of the Census, 1976, *The Statistical History of the United States from Colonial Times to Present*. New York: Basic Books.

U.S. International Trade Commission, 1985, *Foreign Industrial Targetting and Its Ef-*

fects on U.S. Industries: Phase III: Brazil, Canada, The Republic of Korea, Mexico, and Taiwan, USITC Publication 1632, Washington, D.C.

Vaitsos, C., 1974, *Intercountry Income Distribution and Transnational Enterprises*, Oxford: Clarendon.

van Agtmael, A., 1984, *Emerging Securities Markets*. London: Euromoney Publications.

van Wijnbergen, S., 1983, "Interest rate management in developing countries: theory and simulation results for Korea," Staff Working Paper 593, May, World Bank.

van Wolferen, K., 1986–87, "The Japan problem," *Foreign Affairs* 65:288–303.

Wade, R., 1979, "Fast growth and slow development in South Italy," in D. Seers, B. Schaffer, and M. Kiljunen (eds.), *Underdeveloped Europe: Studies in Core-Periphery Relations*. Brighton: Harvester.

————, 1982a, *Irrigation and Agricultural Politics in South Korea*. Boulder: Westview.

————, 1982b, "Regional policy in a severe international environment: politics and markets in South Italy," *Pacific Viewpoint* 23(2), Oct.: 99–126.

————, 1982c, "The system of administrative and political corruption: canal irrigation in South India," *Journal of Development Studies* 18(3):287–328.

————, 1983, "South Korea's agricultural development: the myth of the passive state," *Pacific Viewpoint* 24(1), May:11-28.

————, 1984a, "The economics and politics of India's state accumulation policy: review of J. Toye, *Public Expenditure and India's Development Policy 1960–1970*," *Economic Development and Cultural Change* 32(2):437–44.

————, 1984b, "Dirigisme Taiwan-style," *IDS Bulletin* 15(2), Apr.:65–70.

————, 1985a, "East Asian financial systems as a challenge to economics: lessons from Taiwan," *California Management Review* 27(4), Summer:106–27.

————, 1985b, "Taiwan," in *Some Pacific Economies*, ESRC Newsletter 54, Economic and Social Research Council (UK).

————, 1985c, "The market for public office: why the Indian state is not better at development," *World Development* 13(4):467–97.

————, 1988a, "State intervention in outward-looking development: neoclassical theory & Taiwanese practice," in G. White (ed.), *Developmental States in East Asia*. London: Macmillan.

————, 1988b, "The rise of East Asian trading states—how they managed their trade," mimeo, Trade Policy Division, World Bank, Washington, D.C.

————, 1988c, "How to organize a duty drawback scheme—a successful non-Korean example," mimeo, Trade Policy Division, World Bank, Washington, D.C.

————, 1988d, *Village Republics: Economic Conditions for Collective Action in South India*. Cambridge: Cambridge University Press.

Wang, Y. C., 1966, *Chinese Intellectuals and the West 1872–1949*. Chapel Hill: University of North Carolina Press.

Ward, R. (ed.), 1968, *Political Development in Modern Japan*. Princeton: Princeton University Press.

Watanade, T., 1985, "Economic development in Korea: lessons and challenges," in T. Shishido and R. Sato (eds.), *Economic Policy and Development: New Perspectives*. Dover, Mass.: Auburn House.

Weede, E., 1983, "The impact of democracy on economic growth: some evidence from cross-national analysis," *Kyklos* 36.

Wei, Yung, 1987, "Planning for growth, equality and democracy: the non-economic factors in the ROC's development process," in *Conference on Economic Development in the Republic of China*, Conference Series 7, Chung-hua Institution for Economic Research, Taipei.

Weiss, J., 1986, "Japan's post-war protection policy: some implications for less developed countries," *Journal of Development Studies*, Apr.: 385–406.

Westphal, L., 1978, "Industrial incentives in the Republic of China (Taiwan)," mimeo, World Bank, Washington, D.C.

———, 1982, "Fostering technological mastery by means of selective infant-industry protection," in M. Syrquin and S. Teitel (eds.), *Trade, Stability, Technology, and Equity in Latin America*. New York: Academic.

Westphal, L., and K. Kim, 1982, "Korea," in B. Balassa, et al. (eds.), *Development Strategies in Semi-industrial Economies*. Baltimore: Johns Hopkins University Press (for World Bank).

Westphal, L., L. Kim, and C. Dahlman, 1984, "Reflections on Korea's acquisition of technological capability," Development Research Department, World Bank.

Wheeler, J., and P. Wood, 1987, *Beyond Recrimination: Perspectives on US-Taiwan Trade Tensions*. Indianapolis: Hudson Institute.

White, G.(ed.), 1988, *Developmental States in East Asia*. London: Macmillan.

White, L., 1980, "The political effects of resource allocations in Taiwan and mainland China," *Journal of Developing Areas* 15:43–66.

Wildavsky, A., 1973, "If planning is everything, maybe it's nothing," *Policy Sciences* 4, June: 127–53.

Wilensky, H., 1981, "Democratic corporatism, consensus and social policy: reflections on changing values and the 'crisis' of the welfare state," in *The Welfare State in Crisis: An Account of the Conference on Social Policies in the 1980's*, Paris: OECD.

Wiles, P., 1977, *Economic Institutions Compared*. Oxford: Blackwell.

Williamson, J., 1985, "Comment on Jeffrey Sach's 'External debt and macroeconomic performance in Latin America and East Asia,' " *Brookings Papers on Economic Activity* 2: 565–70.

Williamson, P., 1985, *Varieties of Corporatism: A Conceptual Discussion*. Cambridge: Cambridge University Press.

Wilson, G., 1985, *Business and Politics: A Comparative Introduction*, Chatham, N.J.: Chatham House.

Winckler, E., 1981, "National, regional, and local politics," in E. Ahern and H. Gates (eds.), *The Anthropology of Taiwanese Society*. Stanford: Stanford University Press.

———, 1984, "Institutionalization and participation on Taiwan: from hard to soft authoritarianism?" *China Quarterly* 99, Sept.: 481–99.

Winn, J., 1986, "Decriminalizing bad checks should help to rationalize Taiwan's financial system," East Asia Executive Reports, 8(8) Aug.

———, 1987, "The Cathay scandal and financial regulation in the Republic of China," paper submitted to Harvard Law School in connection with J. D. degree.

Wolf, C., 1979, "A theory of nonmarket failure: framework for implementation analysis," *Journal of Law and Economics* 22(1):107–39.

———, 1981, "Economic success, stability, and the 'old' international order," *International Security* 6(1): 75–92.

Womack, J., and D. Roos, 1988, *Case Study: The Automotive Industry*, ITE Program, Office of Technology Assessment, Washington, D.C.

Woo, Jennie Hay, 1988, "Education and industrial growth in Taiwan: a use of planning," EEPA Discussion Paper 18, Harvard Institute of International Development.

World Almanac and Book of Facts 1984, 1984, Newspaper Enterprise Association, New York.

World Bank, 1981a, *World Development Report 1981*, World Bank, Washington, D.C.

———, 1981b, *Accelerated Development in Sub-Saharan Africa: An Agenda for Action*, World Bank, Washington, D.C.

———, 1983a, *World Development Report 1983*, World Bank, Washington, D.C.

———, 1983b, *World Development Report*. New York: Oxford University Press.

———, 1984, *Korea's Development in a Global Context*. Washington, D.C.

———, 1987a, *World Development Report 1987*. World Bank, Washington, D.C.

———, 1987b, *Korea: Managing the Industrial Transition*, vols. 1 and 2, World Bank, Washington D.C.

———, 1988, *World Development Report 1988*, New York: Oxford University Press.

Wu, Wen-Tien (ed.), 1975, *Essays on Taiwan's Industrial Development*. Taipei: Lien-ching Publishers (Chinese).

Yen, G. L., and T. L. Chang, 1985, "The management of public enterprises: a case study of SMEs," paper for joint conference on the industrial policies of the republic of Korea and the republic of China, Korea Development Institute, 12–22 Nov.

Yin, K. Y., 1960, *Economic Development in Taiwan 1950–1960: Record and Prospects*. Taipei: Council for United States.

Yoffie, E., 1981, "The newly industrializing countries and the political economy of protectionism," *International Studies Quarterly* 25(4): 569–99.

Yoon, C. H., 1988, "International competition and market penetration: a model of the growth strategy of the Korean semiconductor industry," mimeo, Korea University.

Yosaburo, T., 1978 (1907), George Braithwaite (trans.), *Japanese Rule in Formosa*. London: Longman, Green. Reprinted in 1978 by Southern Materials Centre, Inc., P.O. Box 36–22, Taipei.

Young, Soogil, 1984, "Trade policy reform in Korea: background and prospect," paper for joint conference on industrial policies of ROC and ROK, Seoul: Korea Development Institute.

Yu, T. S., 1981, "Foreign trade and export instability," *Academia Economic Papers* 9(1), Sept.:69–86.

Yu, T. S., and T. A. Chen, 1982, "Fiscal reforms and economic development," in *Experiences and Lessons of Economic Development in Taiwan*, Institute of Economics, Academia Sinica, Taipei.

Yusuf, S., and R. K. Peters, 1984, "Is capital accumulation the key to economic growth? Neoclassical models and development economics on Korea's investment policies," mimeo, World Bank, Washington, D.C.

Zeigler, H., 1988, *Pluralism, Corporation, and Confucianism: Political Association and Conflict Regulation in the United States, Europe and Taiwan*, Philadelphia: Temple University Press.

Zymelman, M., 1980, *Occupational Structure of Industries*. World Bank, Washington, D.C.

Zysman, J., 1978, "The French state in the international economy," in P. Katzenstein (ed.), *Between Power and Plenty: Foreign Economic Policies of Advanced Industrial States*. Madison: University of Wisconsin.

―――, 1983, *Governments, Markets and Growth: Financial Systems and the Politics of Industrial Change*, Ithaca: Cornell University Press.

Zysman, J., and S. Cohen, 1982, "Double or nothing: open trade and competitive industry," *Foreign Affairs*, 61(5), Summer.

GOVERNMENT OF TAIWAN

Bank of Communications, 1974, *Annual Report 1973*, Taipei.

BCIQ (Bureau of Commodity Inspection and Quarantine), 1981 and 1984, "A brief introduction to the Bureau of Commodity Inspection and Quarantine," Ministry of Economic Affairs, Republic of China, Taipei.

―――, *List of Quality Controlled and Graded Plants*. Annual.

Central Bank of China, various issues, *Financial Statistics Monthly*. Taiwan District, Republic of China, Taipei.

―――, Economic Research Department, various issues, *Survey of Financial Conditions of Public and Private Enterprises in Taiwan, ROC*, Taipei.

―――, 1983, *Balance of Payments, Taiwan District, Republic of China 1958–82*, Taipei.

CEPD (Council for Economic Planning and Development), 1983, "The ROC's four-year plan (1982–1985): industrial sector," in *Industry of Free China*, Mar.:9–29.

―――, various years, *Taiwan Statistical Data Book*. Taipei.

CETRA (China External Trade Development Council; formerly CETDC), 1980, *CETDC in Retrospect 1970–1980*. Taipei: CETDC.

China Productivity Center, *Taiwan Buyer's Guide*. Annual.

CIECD (Council for International Economic Cooperation and Development), 1965, *Fourth Four-Year Plan for Economic Development 1965–68*. Taipei.

DGBAS (Directorate General of Budget, Accounting and Statistics), various years, *National Income of the Republic of China*, Taipei.

―――, 1983, *Monthly Bulletin of Labor Statistics, Republic of China*, May, Taipei.

―――, 1981, *Report on the Survey of Personal Income Distribution in the Taiwan Area, Republic of China*, Taipei.

―――, 1981, 1986, *Statistical Yearbook of the Republic of China*, Taipei.

Economic Planning Council, 1965, "Exchange of notes between the Republic of China and the United States of America concerning the establishment of the Sino-American Fund for Economic and Social Development," Executive Yuan, Taipei, Aug.

ERSO, 1987, "ROC and ROK comparative development of the information industry," May (Chinese).

Executive Yuan, 1957, *Highlights of the Second Four-Year Plan for the Economic Development in Taiwan*, Taipei.

Executive Yuan, 1968, *Report of the Commission on Tax Reform*, Taipei, June.

————, 1986, *Central Government Total Budget*, Taipei

IDB (Industrial Development Bureau), 1987, "The country paper for promoting center-satellite factory system in the Republic of China," mimeo, 11 Nov.

————, 1982, *Development of Industries in Taiwan*. Ministry of Economic Affairs, Republic of China, Taipei.

Inspectorate General of Customs, 1982, *The Trade of China*, Taipei.

————, 1987, *Briefing on the Chinese Customs Service*, Taipei.

————, 1987, *Information Management of R. O. C. Customs Service*, Republic of China, Taipei.

Ministry of Education, 1979, *Education in the Republic of China*, Taipei.

Ministry of Education, 1981, 1987, *Educational Statistics of the Republic of China*, Taipei.

Ministry of Finance, 1982, 'Briefing on the Development Fund', April, Taipei.

Ministry of Economic Affairs, 1961, *Taiwan's Third Four-Year Economic Development Plan*, Taipei.

————, 1985, *Manufacturers and Traders of the ROC with Good Export Records*, Taipei.

————, Investment Commission, 1982, *An Analysis of the Operation and Economic Effects of Foreign Enterprises in Taiwan*.

National Science Council, 1988, *Science and Technology Data Book*, Taipei.

National Youth Commission, 1983, "Current problems and policies of college and university graduate manpower" (Chinese).

National Youth Commission, 1987, "Report on the Employment of University and College Graduates, 1984 and 1985" (Chinese).

Research, Development and Evaluation Commission of the Executive Yuan, n.d. (1981). *Annual Review of Government Administration, ROC, 1979–80*, Taipei.

Small and Medium Business Credit Guarantee Fund, n.d. (1984), *Report*, Ministry of Finance, Taipei.

Taiwan Statistical Data Book (TSDB), various years, Council for Economic Planning and Development, Taipei.

INDEX

Italic page numbers indicate material in tables or figures.